WELDON J. TAYLOR

Professor of Marketing
College of Business
Brigham Young University

ROY T. SHAW, JR.

Professor of Marketing
University of Utah

marketing

AN INTEGRATED ANALYTICAL APPROACH

THIRD EDITION

D1307490

Published by

S72 **SOUTH-WESTERN PUBLISHING CO.**

CINCINNATI   WEST CHICAGO, ILL.   DALLAS   PELHAM MANOR, N.Y.
PALO ALTO, CALIF.   BRIGHTON, ENGLAND

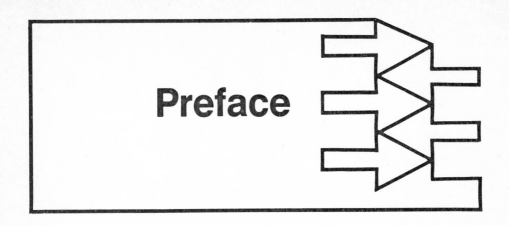

Preface

Two basic reasons for studying marketing are (1) to achieve business competence and (2) to better understand the strategic function of marketing in increasing productivity in an environment of individual freedom.

Basic to competence in business is an awareness of the relationship of all business functions to the satisfaction of the consumer. This awareness is described as the marketing concept—a concept which is composed of supporting concepts that relate the firms, the market functions they perform, the products or services they sell, and the decisions they make to consumer satisfaction. The knowledge of which such supporting concepts is composed is constantly changing. The specifics are never the same. There is, however, an enduring and common core of concepts which are based on this knowledge. A mature understanding of this important area will increase the effectiveness of marketing management. It is impossible to separate these concepts from the analytical and creative skills required for business competence, for these ingredients interact as one in marketing management.

There are additional and more stringent environmental restraints affecting consumers and the firms that serve them than there were when the paragraphs above were written for the preface to the second edition of this book. Nevertheless, the experience of colleagues in business and in schools of business convinces us that the concepts and techniques of marketing still apply. The basic principles that underlie marketing concepts as contributors to the more effective use of resources are applicable when there are critically short supplies of important resources.

In this edition there is continued and increased emphasis on the importance of an integration of skills and ingredients within the firm. Also, the importance of understanding and responding properly to the environment within which the firm operates is stressed.

An integrated social-psychological human behavior is introduced which emphasizes the interactions and influences of the whole ecology affecting the use and exchange of resources.

To those many persons named in the prefaces to the first two editions, to our colleagues who have generously shared their ideas and criticisms, and to our students we continue to be grateful. Albert A. Pool, Vice-president, Marketing, First American National Bank of St. Cloud, Minnesota, revised several of the chapters and was a careful critic of much of the rest of this revised edition. His generous help can not be repaid by these words, but they are a gesture of appreciation.

W.J.T.
R.T.S.

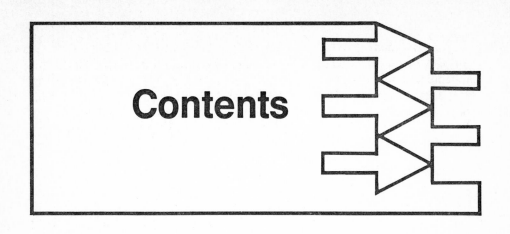

Contents

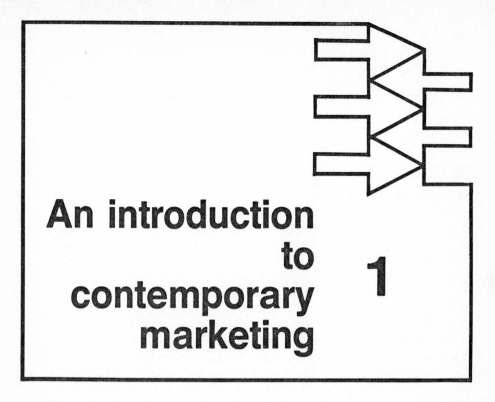

An introduction to contemporary marketing

1

Everyone of you knows something about marketing. From the time when you first made a choice of what to do with a nickel you earned—or that someone gave you—you have been exposed to consumer choice.

You enjoy or are repulsed by a particular advertisement; you are satisfied with a price bargain or unhappy about a high price; you are pleased or displeased with the performance of a product; it is easy or difficult to find just exactly the item you want. These are some of your responses to marketing efforts. What is behind it all? What has to happen in order to fill stores with the many thousands of items you can see in a one-hour visit to Main Street or a shopping center? Why does one business prosper and another fail?

You have a huge laboratory to work in for your study of marketing. During the next few weeks observe what happens in stores, on the highways, on railroads and airlines, and at the shipping docks of factories. Relate what you see to what you read in this book and you should finish the course with a good idea of what constitutes an effective, efficient, and even socially acceptable marketing effort. You will observe that there are marketing *institutions*—retail, wholesale, advertising, design establishments; marketing *functions*—the economic activities needed to accomplish the task; and *concepts*—the underlying ideas and philosophies that are the bases of company policies.

WHAT MAKES OUR ECONOMY COMPLEX

The history of man shows that when he focused his skill on the creation of one product, he became a specialist. It followed, however, that to obtain a

1

complement of goods for living he had to use some of his time to trade his surpluses for products created by other specialists. The time and energy thus devoted to trading were the first evidences we have of marketing costs. Trade, though it cost time and energy, made specialization and greater productivity possible, grew more common, and became a specialization in its own right. The dividing and simplifying implied in such specialization invited the use of the machine and technology. The growth of this integrated process of specialization, technological development, and exchange is responsible for our present complex economy. Today approximately as much time, energy, and skill are used in marketing as in the making of products. This distribution task has grown more strategic during the last few decades. As technology has increased the degree of specialization, marketing, which includes the functions of trade and exchange, has played an increasingly important part in the economy.

Expressed in 1958 dollars, the personal consumption per capita in the United States grew from $1,520 in 1950 to $2,512 in 1972, an increase of 65 percent.[1] In addition to being able to buy more products, the consumer has available to him today products which yield a more exciting kind of satisfaction than those of the past. Solomon, with his millions, could not have entertained Sheba by whisking her down a freeway from Jerusalem to Jericho in a T-Bird or Lincoln Continental. Nor could he, at any price, have watched the Olympic games by Telstar on color TV. These great advances in the volume and quality of satisfying goods and experiences are not wholly due to marketing activities. It is the entire industrial process that is responsible. Yet marketing is the strategic ingredient of this process. It finds the demand for new products and channels them into expanding market areas for exchange. Thus, if the marketing processes can be improved, the whole economic or industrial system can make more rapid progress and yield significantly greater satisfaction. It is to this goal that our study of marketing is dedicated.

MARKETING DEFINED

The Committee on Definitions of the American Marketing Association defines marketing as "the performance of business activities that direct the flow of goods and services from producer to consumer or user." [2] The existence of the flow of goods is assumed. Although the consumer is mentioned, emphasis is given to the business of directing the goods to the consumer or user.

Mazur-McNair Definition

As if in response to a desire for a definition that describes marketing in a more consumer-oriented and dynamic manner, Paul W. Mazur, a New York investment banker and authority in retailing, suggested that marketing is the

---

[1] U.S. Department of Commerce, Bureau of the Census, *Statistical Abstract of the United States: 1973* (94th ed.; Washington: U.S. Government Printing Office, 1973), p. 322, #521.
[2] Committee on Definitions, *Marketing Definitions* (Chicago: American Marketing Association, 1961).

delivery of a standard of living. Malcolm McNair, formerly Lincoln Filene Professor of Retailing at Harvard Business School, suggested that marketing is the creation and delivery of a standard of living. While such a definition provides a conceptual scope and correctly emphasizes creativity, it still leaves us with no clear concept as to where marketing fits into the business process.

Marketing as a Part of the Business Process

In recent years marketing the growing volume and rapidly changing flow of products has required increasing attention from the corporate chief executive officer. Charles G. Mortimer, former President and Chairman of the Board of General Foods, took a broad view of the entire business process; and he describes marketing in a setting which enables us to see it as a part of the whole process. Mortimer cites the fact that marketing begins long before the flow of goods starts from the factory to the consumer. Seed peas, for example, are developed especially for certain brands of frozen peas long before the freezing process begins. Likewise, before production lines are set up for a new model car, plans are perfected on the drawing board as prompted by guidelines from the market. To give the entire business process an all-inclusive perspective, Mortimer quotes from A. W. Shaw who stated: "Isolate any phase of business, strike into it anywhere, and the invariable essential element will be found to be the application of motion to materials." [3] He suggested that, as part of the business process, there are three types of motions applied to materials.

The first type includes the motions applied to raw materials to change their shape into usable form. This class of business activity he calls production. Secondly, another series of motions is applied to goods to move them from the point of production to the point of consumption. This process Mortimer describes as distribution. Third, interwoven with production and distribution is a series of motions embracing those activities which are responsible for making goods move. Mortimer points out that when goods stop moving, storage costs mount and spoilage and obsolescence costs increase; therefore, it is important that they move. This series of motions which makes goods move includes ". . . forceful advertising and persuasive salesmanship, implemented with all ingenious inducements and techniques that resourceful marketing people can bring to bear." [4] Certainly these activities would include market research, product innovation, and demand creation. This third series of motions Mortimer describes as marketing. From the standpoint of the entire business process, the first series of motions applied to materials could be classed as production, and the second and third series include what would be described as marketing.

Each management decision to apply these motions to materials as they move as products toward their ultimate consumption is designed to change the

---

[3] A. W. Shaw, *An Approach to Business Problems* (Cambridge: Harvard University Press. 1916).

[4] Quoted from a speech sponsored by the National Industrial Conference Board by Charles G. Mortimer, President of General Foods Corporation. The speech was published under the title *"Two Keys to Modern Marketing,"* by the Updegraff Press, Ltd., Scarsdale, New York.

nature of the product or to channel its direction. Changing products and channeling their direction is for the purpose of making the product acceptable to a certain segment of the market.

This discussion, then, suggests another definition for marketing: *Marketing* consists of the motions applied to materials designed for consumption that would not be necessary if the goods were consumed by their producers. These motions are marketing activities that are an integral part of business operations.

The above definition has the virtue of enabling us to see the marketing process in relief apart from other functions, but it would be desirable to define marketing positively rather than by exclusion. The marketing staff at Ohio State University, sensing this need, submitted the definition that—"Marketing is the process in a society by which the demand structure for economic goods and services is anticipated or enlarged and satisfied through the conception, promotion, exchange, and physical distribution of such goods and services."[5] Now add the phrase, "in a socially responsible manner" and we have the definition to be used in this text.

Distinction Between Marketing and Production

Production, for our purposes, refers to the meaning given to the term by Charles Mortimer, "those . . . motions concerned with changing the shape of raw materials." It is closely related to agricultural production or manufacturing. Since this process combines with marketing in one continuous flow of goods and services to the ultimate consumer, what is the justification for a separation of marketing and production?

Production includes the change in the form of materials and the coordination and control of all processes that result in the flow of goods through the plant. Effecting the most efficient layout of plants and setting up production lines are some of the special tasks of production men. Such operations suggest an engineering approach.

Marketing, on the other hand, includes the activities that are related to the consumer. A sequence of these activities known as functions includes determining what the customer wants and in what amounts, the means of reaching the customer with the product, and how to convince the customer to buy the product.

In other words, although production and marketing may be considered a continuous process, the "center of gravity" in the study of marketing is the consumer. The vice-president in charge of production of X Corporation would probably have a background in engineering, production control, or chemical research. The vice-president in charge of marketing would have to be keenly aware of consumer psychology. The management staff of a concern must understand both processes as interrelated, but keener skills and judgments can be achieved by some degree of specialization. By singling out for study those

---

[5] Marketing Staff of Ohio State University, "A Statement of Marketing Philosophy," *Journal of Marketing,"* Vol. 29, No. 1 (January, 1965), pp. 43-44.

areas which are more closely related to marketing or that have a focus in the consumer rather than in the plant, a better judgment of this phase of the process can be achieved. In the case of production, greater efficiency can be achieved by a study in which the center of gravity rests in the plant.

Table 1-1 illustrates how production and marketing costs are interwoven in the manufacture and sale of Ritz crackers. The first two columns of the table show all the elements of cost necessary to manufacture and sell the crackers. Columns 3 and 4 present the marketing costs and percentages of the total. Columns 5 and 6 show the production costs and percentages.[6] The example separates, insofar as it is possible, elements of cost applying to each process. Raw materials, manufacturing labor, and manufacturing overhead are clearly production costs. Packaging materials, shipping and distribution expense, sales, branch selling, delivery expense, and advertising are activities that would not be necessary if the producer of the goods also had consumed them; these, then, are marketing costs.

Table 1-1

ANALYSIS OF COST PRODUCING AND SELLING RITZ CRACKERS—ONE-POUND PACKAGE

Elements of Cost	Total Costs		Marketing Costs		Production Costs	
	(1) Cents	(2) % of Total	(3) Cents	(4) % of Total	(5) Cents	(6) % of Total
Raw Materials	17.10	26.31			17.10	26.31
Manufacturing Labor	5.17	7.95			5.17	7.95
Manufacturing Overhead	3.30	5.08			3.30	5.08
Packaging Materials	5.10	7.84	5.10	7.84		
Shipping and Distribution Expense	2.96	4.56	2.96	4.56		
Sales, Branch Selling, and Delivery Expense	12.04	18.52	12.04	18.52		
Advertising	2.50	3.85	2.50	3.85		
Income Taxes *	2.96	4.56	1.35	2.08	1.61	2.48
Manufacturing Profits *	3.20	4.92	1.46	2.24	1.74	2.68
Summary of Manufacturer's Costs	54.33		25.41		28.92	
Retailer's Expenses	9.87	15.18	9.87	15.18		
Retailer's Profit	.80	1.23	.80	1.23		
TOTAL	65.00	100.00	36.08	55.50	28.92	44.50

* Profit and income taxes divided on the basis of costs in each category up to this point.

---

[6] National Biscuit Company supplied the data dealing with manufacturer's costs. The company controller states that these figures may never have existed exactly as they appear, but are comparatively accurate. The price, 65 cents, was selected from various selling prices observed at retail stores.

The total manufacturer's cost of a one-pound package of crackers of this type was 54.33 cents. Of this amount 25.41 cents constituted the marketing costs. In other words, even before the retailer's expenses were included, 46.7 percent of the manufacturer's cost was for marketing (25.41 ÷ 54.33). By adding the 10.67 cents that the retailer received for his services, total costs were 65 cents. Of this cost 36.08 cents was for marketing. Thus, 55.5 percent of the total cost resulted from the performance of marketing activities.

MARKETING INSTITUTIONS

In this course since we are concerned with how marketing institutions and the marketing functions they perform contribute to marketing strategy it is appropriate to define them at this point.

Marketing institutions are of two general types. The first type includes the primary industries, such as farming, mining, fishing, forestry, and manufacturing. Firms in this group are distinguished by the fact that their principal interest is in the production of goods, that is, the creation of form utility. We shall observe, however, that they also perform significant marketing functions.

The second type of marketing institution includes middlemen—those firms that are usually located in the channel through which goods flow from the producer to the ultimate consumer. They perform significant operations in moving the goods to the point of their consumption. These firms are concerned solely with distribution, that is, the creation of time, place, and ownership utility.

Primary Producers and Manufacturers

Primary producers and manufacturers are first concerned with bringing a product into being. Why, then, do we consider such firms as marketing institutions? In spite of their principal function as producers, the success of these firms depends upon their ability to sell their products at prices that exceed their cost. One of the basic problems of the farmer is marketing. Marketing is also a basic problem for manufacturing firms. As compared with other types of businesses, manufacturing firms have the largest advertising budgets and the largest and most highly paid sales forces. Considerable amounts of money are also expended by manufacturing firms to develop new products. Before manufacturing a new product, however, the firm must attempt to determine such things as the market reception for the product, the costs to market the product, and the most desirable price for the product. Thus, a significant part of the work of a manufacturing firm deals specifically with marketing.

Middlemen

As the name implies, middlemen are the firms that are between the producer and the consumer. Since their sole function is to buy from one source and sell to another, directly or indirectly, these firms may be termed *pure market institutions.* The primary producer and the manufacturer, on the other hand, may be termed *hybrid marketing institutions* because their interests are divided between producing and marketing. Middlemen have entered the marketing scene in great numbers since the Industrial Revolution.

It requires a chain of transactions to get a bushel of apples from the grower in Washington to the consumer in New York. The aid of a farmers' cooperative, a broker, an auction wholesaler, and a retailer may be necessary for the consumer in New York to enjoy an apple grown in Yakima, Washington, at the price and with the facility which is now possible. Essential though these firms are in bringing the producer and the consumer together, they do not change the form of the product. They perform all the transactions between the producer and the consumer and are therefore properly called middlemen.

Two general classes of institutions perform this interconnecting function, and there are specialists within each of the general classifications. One class is designated merchant middlemen, and another type is called agent middlemen. *Merchant middlemen* are distinguished from agents in that the former actually buy or take title to the products in which they deal. On the other hand, *agent middlemen*, though performing many of the functions necessary to distribution, do not take title to the goods. They facilitate buying and selling and may perform other necessary services. Their compensation comes as a commission or a fee for performing the services.

Merchant Middlemen. There are two main types of merchant middlemen—wholesalers and retailers. The *wholesaler* seeks out and purchases from manufacturers, other wholesalers, or primary producers a supply of goods which he in turn sells to his customers who purchase for resale or for furthering production. He is able to buy in large lots. This operation reduces the number of calls the manufacturer or the producer must make to dispose of his product and reduces his credit and carrying costs. It allows the manufacturer or the producer to give greater attention to his specialty of production. The contribution of the wholesaler is treated in greater detail in Chapter 8.

Of all marketing institutions the retailer is best known to the public. A retail transaction is one in which a purchase is made for personal or household use. It is from *retailers* that ultimate consumers buy. Retail institutions constitute the front that the marketing process presents to the public. Most retail stores, therefore, are designed to attract customers, and are conveniently located for the greatest number of consumers. A retail sale is the culmination of a process which may have had a beginning in distant lands involving goods that have passed through many hands. It is the retailer who joins the ultimate consumer in performing the final transaction in the marketing flow. He provides the facilities by which thousands of commodities are made available under one roof to all consumers who may desire them. For example, a variety store in a comparatively small city may offer customers a choice of 10,000 or more items. The management of this product offering is a task which requires the attention of firms that specialize in its performance. Retailing is discussed in Chapters 5 and 6.

Agent Middlemen. Agents buy and sell for the accounts of institutions that take or hold title to goods. Agents occasionally serve as intermediaries between manufacturers and retailers. Their principal function, however, is to serve as intermediaries between manufacturers or between manufacturers and wholesalers. They will be studied in greater detail in the chapter devoted to wholesaling. Since our purpose in this chapter is to provide a structural view of the marketing system, it is well to understand that distribution of a substantial portion of the nation's goods is facilitated by the use of agent middlemen who specialize in certain goods and/or specific markets. The principal types of agent middlemen are brokers, manufacturer's agents, selling agents, and commission merchants.

Facilitating Agencies

In addition to the above institutions, nearly every business and government organization provides some assistance to the marketing process. Warehouses provide storage, banks provide capital funds in addition to operating and consumer credit, and there are a growing number of transportation institutions available to facilitate the movement of goods. In some instances the government establishes and administers standards and supplies valuable market information.

MARKETING FUNCTIONS

Early scholars attempted to discover why goods costing $1.00 to produce were often priced at $2.00 or more retail. Since no tangible change in the product was evident as a result of marketing, it was difficult to account for this increase in price. But careful study revealed that there were certain activities in business operations that related distinctly to marketing. Scholars described these activities that were peculiar to marketing as functions.

A *marketing function* is defined by the American Marketing Association's Committee on Definitions as "a major specialized activity or group of related activities performed in marketing."[7] These activities require the time of people, some of whom are very high-salaried. Also, even though no change in the form of the product is effected by the marketing function, costly equipment often is required to perform marketing tasks. Thus, people and equipment costs in performing functions provide the base for the high cost of marketing.

The functions which have been considered major by most marketing students include the following:

Functions of Exchange
1. Buying and merchandising
2. Selling
Functions of Physical Supply
3. Transportation
4. Storage

---

[7] Committee on Definitions, *op. cit.*, p. 16.

Facilitating and Other Functions
5. Financing
6. Risk
7. Pricing
8. Standardization
9. Market information

A discussion and analysis of these market functions is presented in Parts IV and V.

PRODUCTS

Another basic area of marketing concern is the product. In modern marketing we view the product as more than a physical object. Actually each product is a complex bundle of satisfactions which are related to the manner in which the product is perceived by the prospective buyer. Throughout our treatment considerable emphasis will be given to the problems of supplying the desired product at the opportune time and place. However, at this point we will present only the basic classifications used in marketing literature.

Business and Industrial Goods

Approximately one half of the manufactured goods are consumed by business firms in the course of trade or business. These goods are called industrial or business goods. They are defined as goods which are destined to be sold primarily for use in producing other goods as contrasted with goods destined to be sold primarily to the ultimate consumer. Industrial goods may be divided into five groups: (1) raw materials, (2) fabricated parts, (3) operating supplies, (4) installations, and (5) accessory equipment. A comprehensive description of these products and the problems in marketing them is given in Chapter 9.

Consumer Goods

Consumer goods reach the ultimate or the household consumer. They are defined by the Committee on Definitions of the American Marketing Association as follows: "Goods destined for use by ultimate consumers or households and in such form that they can be used without commercial processing."[8] They are not classified in the manner of industrial goods but are sometimes divided into three groups as determined by the attitude of the buyer at the time of purchase. These classes are shopping goods, convenience goods, and specialty goods.

As suggested by their name, *shopping goods* are those consumer goods which the customer in the process of selection and purchase characteristically compares on such bases as suitability, quality, price and style. *Convenience*

---

[8] Committee on Definitions, *op. cit.*, p. 14. The definitions of the groups of consumer goods quoted in this text are from the same source.

goods, on the other hand, are those consumer goods which the customer usually purchases frequently, immediately, and with the minimum of effort in comparison and buying. The product differences are slight in the case of convenience goods, and the unit of purchase is small. Thus, there is little motivation to shop extensively for convenience goods. *Specialty goods* are those consumer goods with unique characteristics and/or brand identifications for which a significant group of buyers are habitually willing to make a special purchasing effort. With a certain clientele they have established preferential consideration. Examine advertisements for convenience goods, and you will notice that much of the advertising is an attempt to develop a buyer preference for a particular brand—i.e., contrive *specialty* attitudes for the brand. Each manufacturer would like to establish such a preferential position for his product, and a few actually do.

It is impossible to draw sharp lines between goods in these classifications. Some people shop meticulously for all food items; others buy food as a convenience good. Some men examine the alternatives thoroughly when they buy a suit of clothes; others have a special place to buy and a special brand they prefer. However, the fact that classifications cannot always mean the same thing nor apply to all people does not make them of no value in analysis. There is considerable uniformity in the population regarding these motives and attitudes. A knowledge of classifications and their relationships to people and products is helpful in marketing analysis.

Services

During the past few years services have taken an increasing share of the consumer's dollar. Services are defined as the "activities, benefits, or satisfactions which are offered for sale, or are provided in connection with the sale of goods."[9] This growing body of activities includes the service of professional men, banking, cleaning and dyeing, and many others. Since they take a significant share of the consumer's dollar, they compete directly with products. The problems peculiar to the marketing of services are discussed in Chapter 12.

VALUE ADDED BY MARKETING

The value added concept has been used by marketing scholars as a means of illustrating what actually takes place in marketing and why costs accrue. By *value* we mean the personal appraisal of the good or service. Value influences the price which people are willing to pay for the product.

The method used to show the value added is to follow a product step by step from its point of production to the point of consumption. In this manner we can see the functions performed as the product proceeds through the market channels. In each instance we can see why costs accrue and specifically what

---

[9] Committee on Definitions, *op. cit.,* p. 21.

they are. The total of such costs equals the value added to the product by marketing.[10]

Notice in the Ritz Crackers cost analysis, Table 1-1, that the costs identified can be categorized under four headings. In older economics books there was usually a discussion of economic utilities. These were form utility, place utility, and time utility, which were the economic activities that made up the value of a product. To this last was sometimes added possession utility—the economic activity of facilitating exchange and ownership. In the Ritz Crackers cost analysis those utilities are present. The product has value because it is in a form (manufacturing from raw materials) that is acceptable; stored and shipped to have the product available where and when desired; packaged, advertised, and displayed in retail outlets to facilitate possession.

The Ritz Crackers example which shows something over one-half the retail price being accounted for by marketing services is reasonably typical for processed and packaged consumer goods.

For the entire economy it has been calculated that 46 percent of the sales price of goods is made up of marketing costs. Methods of calculating marketing costs vary, but all estimates from respected sources fall between 45 percent and slightly over 50 percent of total sales prices as the share of marketing in the market value of goods in the United States. Is that too much? That question will be discussed in subsequent chapters. For now consider the choices available to consumers; the desire by businessmen to achieve competitive advantage in the market place (and price is one of the strongest factors of competition); and the alternative means available to satisfy consumer desires. Also consider that any cost is too high when improved efficiency can lower that cost.

DECISION MAKING IN MARKETING

Statistical theory describes four conditions under which decisions are made, and an awareness of these conditions can increase the probabilities that successful decisions will be made.[11] Decision making takes place under conditions of (1) certainty, (2) conflict—the subject matter of game theory, (3) risk—where knowledge of the probabilities of successful performance is possible, and (4) complete ignorance. In the latter instance the decision maker

---

[10]One of the explanations of value added which has become almost classic in its logic and acceptability is described in "Value Added by Distribution," a report completed under the sponsorship of the Domestic Distribution and Business Statistics Committees of the Chamber of Commerce of the United States. It was prepared under the supervision of Dr. Theodore N. Beckman, Professor of Business Organization at Ohio State University, who had previously employed the concept in his business consulting work and in testimony before Congressional committees. Research for the report was conducted by Robert D. Buzzell of the Ohio State University staff and by David D. Monieson, formerly of the Ohio State staff and now a member of the Faculty of the Graduate College of the University of Toronto, Canada. The Chamber of Commerce of the United States, "Value Added by Distribution," as reprinted in S. George Walters, Morris L. Sweet, and Max D. Snider (eds.), *Marketing Management Viewpoints: Commentary and Readings* (2d ed.; Cincinnati: South-Western Publishing Company, 1970), pp. 447-465.

[11] Samuel B. Richmond, *Statistical Analysis* (2d ed.; New York: The Ronald Press Company, 1964), pp. 257-260.

may resort to philosophy or psychology in a search for guiding elements of predictability.

Three of the above categories are involved in the making of marketing decisions. First, practically all marketing decisions must consider conflict with competitors where game theory subject matter is relevant; second, certain marketing decisions are made under conditions of lesser or greater risk where to some extent probabilities of overall results may be projected; and finally, in some instances where no quantitative knowledge is available, psychological and philosophical insights are needed as guides to decision making. It should be noted that a blend of these three conditions often faces the decision maker and that changing conditions as the game progresses necessitate modifications in the decisions made.

Marketing is Dynamic

One of the basic attributes of marketing is its dynamic quality. In spite of many scientific advances which improve predictability, there are always large areas in marketing where decisions must be made under conditions of risk. The shifting competitive strategy of sellers, the scientific breakthroughs resulting in new products, and the possibility of success of new product ideas require an almost continuous flow of decisions. Both men and firms in their respective orbits are constantly revising their approach in response to their competitor's actions the day before. There is always the chance of winning, losing, or enjoying different and unpredictable degrees of success.

The Challenge of Change

Changes in marketing strategy are inevitable with the changes in attitudes of recent years. In place of acceptance of "bigger is better—more is desirable" philosophies, there is now concern with balancing quality of life and technological developments. The marketer must understand and make proper response to those changes.

Specific Opportunities or What Do Marketers Do?

Marketing is not simply an assembling of distinct activities or functions. It is a coordinated and integrated system of related activities. The student who aspires to a marketing management position will, however, start in one identifiable activity and then get a variety of experiences as he moves towards a broader management position. Among the positions related to careers in marketing that recent graduates have obtained are those in the list below.

advertising
credit management
customer relations
dealer relations
inventory control
marketing logistics

marketing research
packaging
pricing
product planning and development
product scheduling
brand or product manager
product service
public relations
quality control
retailing—buyer, promotion
sales
sales control
sales forecasting
sales promotion
sales recruiting
sales training
warehousing

Importance of marketing in major companies is illustrated in Table 1-2. Note that there are several routes to key positions, with the increasing recognition that companies must be customer oriented. There is evidence that persons with marketing backgrounds hold more key positions, especially in consumer goods companies, than do those with other business backgrounds.

Table 1-2

BUSINESS BACKGROUNDS OF KEY INDIVIDUALS AND GROUPS—ALL COMPANIES
(N = 640)

| Key Positions | *Business Background* | | | | | | |
	Engineering	Finance	Legal	Manufacturing	Marketing	Research and Development	General
Board Chairman	15%	25%	5%	16%	26%	4%	9%
Vice Board Chairman	12	22	4	22	23	1	16
Internal Board of Directors	8	16	3	16	24	1	32
Outside Board of Directors	5	37	19	7	4	1	27
President	15	16	5	22	31	2	9
Chairman of the Executive Committee	14	23	5	19	30	3	6
Executive Committee	6	19	3	15	23	1	33
Group Executive	13	3	1	30	34	2	17
Operating Executive	14	5	0	37	30	1	13
Product or Brand Manager	14	1	0	7	71	2	5

Source: Reprinted from Carlton P. McNamara's "The Present Status of the Marketing Concept," *Journal of Marketing*, Vol. 36 (American Marketing Association, January, 1972), p. 54.

MARKETING AND THE AMERICAN ECONOMY

How does the marketing process as we view it influence the level of living? Are the resources and income of the nation allocated among the population on a fair and equitable basis? Does the economy of the nation have the vitality to grow and adapt to changing conditions?

Under the free market system, market forces emanate from the likes and dislikes of people. The demand is relatively greater for those products for which the likes are intense. Supply is relatively smaller for those goods produced at great cost or disutility. Price is the factor which equates the supply with the demand. The price that people pay at the marketplace is a measure of what those who have supplied the goods receive. When a thousand people decide to buy a product at a certain price, however, they choose on the basis of their desire for the product. They give little thought to the fact that their choice is a reward to the various parties who have had a part in supplying the product. If a better product becomes available at a comparable price, they shift their allegiance immediately. Such market shifts take place constantly.

Sellers are rewarded in proportion to their ability to discern the desires of the consumers and to supply products that satisfy them. Consumers refused to reward Ford for the Edsel automobile. Yet in 1965 they responded by the hundreds of thousands to the Mustang. The company was penalized in the former case and rewarded in the latter according to the impersonal judgments of the market.

The significant factor, however, is that both the buyer and the seller are free agents. The consumer is free to choose any product he can afford; the producer is free to decide what he will produce. The producer who can supply the product of the greatest significance to consumers gains the largest share of the total market. The market is the device that determines values, which are expressed in prices. A vigorously defended characteristic of the free market system is that it is just. Theoretically it rewards every individual in proportion to how much he produces. The individual who feels that he will be rewarded for greater effort, for creative imagination, or for an enterprising spirit, will be more likely to respond positively. With a population made up of enterprising people who possess creative imagination and who work vigorously, a nation employing the free market system should be much more productive.

A second and frequently overlooked advantage is the facility which the free market has to accomplish an infinite number of market calculations. Almost without conscious effort, millions of market calculations are made daily, each representing the individual preferences of the people. This process can better be appreciated if we visualize the operation of an average-sized supermarket. A fairly typical annual sales volume for a supermarket is $1 million; a single day's operation approximates $3,333. At an average unit price of 33 cents in a food store, 10,000 individual value calculations are made at one store in one day. Each of the selections is the free choice of some person. Each transaction becomes a part of the calculations that are responsible for the changing consumption and production patterns of our economy. The marketing system, then, serves in its stock control and merchandising activities as an immense value-calculating and communicative system. An infinite number of choices are reflected back to wholesalers, to manufacturers, and even to the farms and primary industries.

The free market system is not without its faults. Until recently the economy has experienced waves of depression and prosperity. Large numbers of people have been unemployed because some firms could not sell their products even though there was a surplus available to sell. Early in the history of the system, some firms became so powerful that they threatened smaller companies with extinction because of unfair competition. Advertising and selling, in some instances, have been unfair and deceptive. The free market system without support from other agencies leaves many problems of national economics unsolved. It does not guarantee a protection of our natural resources; it contributes to urban disintegration and air pollution. There is nothing inherent in a free market system unsupported by government that will get at the roots of civil strife.

Hence, present policies in the United States arise from belief that the best solution to the problem of resource allocation appears to be a combination of both government allocation and the free market. In the United States, for example, we have pure food and drug laws, laws to prevent deceptive advertising, and laws to prevent monopoly and promote fair competition. The government also gives authority to railroads and public utilities under regulation. It builds dams, sells irrigation water, and generates and sells electric power. Government at various levels supplies the major part of our education.

As the economy has grown larger and more complex, the government has assumed an increasing share of the economic responsibility. Because there are many who fear this trend, it has been the basis for considerable controversy. On the other hand, some leaders in the business community have affirmed that business must take a more progressive attitude toward government. They believe that cooperation with the government would be a mature solution to present antagonisms and would be mutually beneficial.

There is also a healthy trend expressed by many leaders that the business firms themselves might be helpful in solving some of the problems heretofore considered the domain of the government. Such cooperation would seem desirable. It would appear, however, that in all thinking about change, the domain of free choice as a basis for resource allocations and as a motivating force, and its corollary, voluntary, and automatic market calculations, should be encouraged in as many areas as feasible.

AN INTEGRATED, ANALYTICAL APPROACH TO MARKETING

One purpose of this textbook is to present a background from which you can learn how to assist in the provision of more efficient distribution of goods and services. As the varied activities, processes, and ideas required for that task are introduced, you will see how interrelated they are. Also, however, you see that emphasizing one activity will often make difficulties for, and even reduce efficiency of another activity. Hence, for the study of marketing we suggest an integrated, analytical approach. That phrase appears to contradict itself, but it is a good way to make sense of this complex and interesting topic.

Integrate means "to bring together, incorporate into a whole"[12] while analysis is "the separating of any material or abstract entity into its constituent elements . . . (the analytical) process as a method of studying the nature of something or of determining its essential features and their relations."

To make sense of the whole—to develop a *concept* of marketing—you first need to understand the constituent parts and their relationships—especially as they affect and are affected by consumers. For example, you may determine that the least cost method of gaining broad physical distribution of your product is through a wholesaler, but it may be found that the wholesaler cannot assist in promotion nor assure that your product will be well displayed in retail outlets. In another case you may learn that store rent in the most desired location is prohibitive, but the nature of demand for your product is such that a carefully planned promotion will enable you to achieve satisfactory results in a lower rent location. The point of these examples is that for a proper marketing program one must analyze what each marketing institution or function can do for you, then integrate the activities of those most desirable institutions into an efficient operation. You will see that there are some trade-offs. Some of the trade-offs are illustrated in the discussion of the marketing mix, which is in the next chapter.

To design and execute an optimum marketing program the marketer must understand the operation, advantages, and limitations of the various institutions. The role of each function must also be clearly understood. If one determines that some considerable amount of education of consumers is required about some new product, what specific marketing institutions are best for that? What kind of message should be in the advertising, and where should that advertising message be placed? Is there a *real* differential advantage in a new product? To answer those and other questions one must analyze the market, the product, and the marketing institutions, and then integrate the required activities-functions into a "best" marketing program. Hence the approach we recommend for your study of marketing.

QUESTIONS AND ANALYTICAL PROBLEMS

1. Define and clearly distinguish in the context of the discussion in the text: (a) marketing, (b) production, (c) marketing function, (d) industrial goods, (e) consumer goods and the three classes of consumer goods which are: (1) convenience goods, (2) shopping goods, (3) specialty goods, (f) merchant middleman, (g) agent middleman.

2. Is marketing productive in the sense, for example, that a potter who produces a useful container from a lump of clay is productive? Make a list of statements that support the idea that marketing is productive and a list of contrary arguments.

3. If it is true as held by some authorities that production and marketing proceed in one continuous flow

---

[12] *The Random House Dictionary of the English Language* (New York: Random House, Inc., 1967).

of service to the consumer, how can the two fields be separated for purpose of study? Assuming that a separation can be made, why might it be desirable to conduct some classes in production processes and others in marketing?

4. Choose the household object in your home that, in your opinion, has the highest portion of marketing costs in its retail price. Do the same for the one that you believe has the lowest portion of marketing costs. How do you account for the difference?

5. It has been estimated that the cost of marketing products is equal to 46 percent of the retail price. Do you think this cost has increased or decreased over the decades? What do you predict for the future?

6. Examine the Ritz Cracker cost analysis on page 5. Explain why there is such a spread between production costs and retail selling price.

7. What are the main types of merchant middlemen? of agent middlemen?

8. A steel executive stated that it was easier to build a plant than a market. Can a market for goods be purchased? By what specific methods can a market be acquired?

9. A young mechanic has developed a safety device for home workshop power tools. He is certain that the product will have wide acceptance. He estimates that it can be manufactured on a small scale of about $3. He has about $200 in his savings account but no other financial resources. How can he introduce his product to potential buyers?

10. "If it works, it's obsolete." This statement is frequently heard in the product-development division of industrial organizations. What are the implications of such a statement, and how does it affect the marketing problems of firms?

11. What is dynamic about marketing?

Case 1 ● MRS. SAMANTHA WEISS

In order to support herself after the death of her husband Mrs. Samantha Weiss began a small catering business for various community groups in the vicinity of Buena Park, California. She was kept reasonably busy until two years later when a new restaurant built nearby began capturing much of her business. As an alternative Mrs. Weiss thought that she might profitably package and market an orange conserve of exceptional quality which she had served as a specialty at her catered dinners. She therefore purchased a supply of two-ounce glass containers, made up small quantities of conserve, and began selling her product to souvenir and gift shops around her area.

With her selling price of 40 cents a jar, she was able to clear 12 cents a jar over her cost. As a result of her early success, Mrs. Weiss earned $1,500 the first year and $3,500 the next year. By 1969 she had improved her conserve, added new flavors, and had begun offering the jars in gift-wrapped redwood boxes of three. By this time, due to the successful acceptance of her product and a substantial mail-order business which she had built up, she was considering how she might expand the market for her product. She was unable to find a partner to supply needed funds for expansion, so she decided to try to build a larger market by herself. She could not, however, determine the best way to approach the market.

● What factors would favor and what factors would discourage Mrs. Weiss from taking such action? List the marketing institutions which would normally participate in selling Mrs. Weiss' conserve to an ultimate consumer in another state. Suggest how such an arrangement might affect the cost of the product.

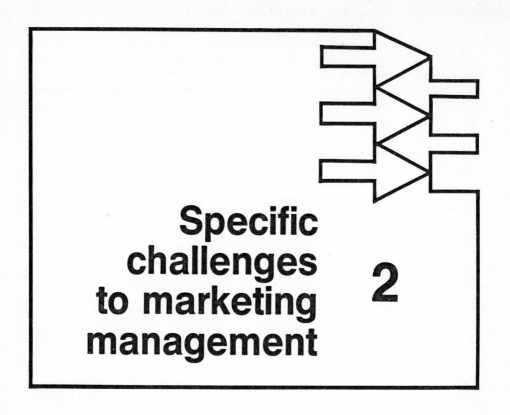

Specific challenges to marketing management

2

Marketing management consists of the acquisition, organization, and directing the use of economic resources to the end that the excess of product or service sales income over and above costs, or outgo, is maximized. In plain business language, marketing management organizes and directs its assets to the end that sales exceed costs and yield maximum profit.

The dominant challenge in management is change. Because of the accelerating rate of innovations in products and services, the marketing manager finds himself under constant pressure to adapt to the competitive demands of the marketplace. The specific challenges which face the marketing manager considered in this chapter are: (1) balancing cost with satisfaction in order to achieve maximum favor with consumers; (2) administrating the "marketing mix" in order to build satisfactory volume; (3) understanding the nature of the market and some of the mechanics involved in marketing processes; and (4) examining changes that have taken place in marketing management during the past two decades.

BALANCING COST AND SATISFACTION

Underlying all marketing strategy is the execution of the most desirable balance between satisfaction and cost. To understand and manage the forces that influence choice, based on these two factors, is marketing in its simplest yet most profound sense. Every decision to buy, whether by an industrial purchaser or by a household consumer, is the result of weighing satisfaction against costs and making a choice. A marketing manager must make decisions based on his judgment of consumer response to the satisfaction-cost aspects of his company's products or services and his evaluation of his ability to educate or otherwise influence that consumer response.

In every successful sales presentation and advertisement, emphasis is given to satisfaction and cost. Either explicitly or implicitly, the idea of high comparative satisfaction for low cost is communicated. The advertisements shown in Exhibit 2-1 are illustrative (the first is for an industrial product which appeared in a magazine for executives).

To understand the true nature of satisfaction and cost as they relate to marketing, let us examine and define each concept individually.

Exhibit 2-1

DOWTHERM

Lower costs, increased safety . . . Dowtherm not only provided the pin-point heat control that direct fire couldn't, but it *lowered fuel costs* and reduced safety hazards as well.

❋ ❋ ❋ ❋ ❋ ❋ ❋ ❋ ❋ ❋

ELECTRIC TIMEX

Just because a watch is electric, *its price doesn't have to be a shocker.*

▐▊▐▊▐▊▐▊▐▊▐▊▐▊▐▊▐▊▐▊▐▊▐▊▐▊

GREYHOUND

The best things in life *don't have to be expensive.*

━● ━● ━● ━● ━● ━●

CHEVROLET

This is luxury . . . spacious Body by Fisher surrounding you with yards of elegant vinyl and deep-twist carpeting, a firm Full Coil suspension smoothing your way below. And as if this weren't enough to give you a lift, *wait till you see the down-to-earth Chevrolet price!*

KODAK

Specially timed for you to save your summer fun in movies, Kodak dealers are now featuring this special offer: A quality movie camera and roll of fast color film for lifelike movies of exceptional quality at *amazing low cost.*

● ● ● ● ● ● ● ● ● ● ● ● ● ● ● ● ●

CLORETS

Clorets cost a little more . . . But Clorets do so much more.

✳ ✳ ✳ ✳ ✳ ✳ ✳ ✳ ✳ ✳

BELL SYSTEM

Talk about a bargain! *A second phone costs only a fraction more a month than the first . . .* but gives you twice as much telephone convenience, and saves you many steps and minutes every day. To order an extension phone for bedroom, kitchen, or any location—in your choice of color and style—just call the Business Office or ask your telephone man.

Cost and Satisfaction Defined

Cost is used here to mean any negative or resistance factor which is involved when choices are being made. Negative factors include costs of money, time, or inconvenience. Also, such factors as less favorable alternatives and the subtle influence of unattractive surroundings or poor service are costs.

Satisfaction means any positive quality that influences a market transaction. Satisfaction relates directly to cost since any money spent on development, production, promotion, or distribution, if successful, will build into the product, package, or means of distribution some quality that will add strength to its bid for consumer choice and, hence, result in greater satisfaction.

A brief look at the development of a new product will serve to illustrate the preceding definitions. The Timex, for several years promoted as an inexpensive, almost disposable watch, now has an electric companion also carrying the name Timex. The electric wrist watch was introduced at $39.95. This price had to be sufficient to cover costs of development, manufacturing, promotion, and distribution. In addition, it had to cover implicit costs and risks.

In marketing the electric Timex, some of the negative factors (costs) for consumers were: the much higher price as compared with nonelectric Timex watches; the low-quality connotation of the product name; the unproven quality of the watch; and the low-quality image of some stores which sell Timex watches. The list of negative influences could be extended; those mentioned above illustrate what were considered to be costs by some potential purchasers. It must be noted, though, that a considerable number of consumers think of some cost factors as being positive or satisfaction-giving qualities. For example, to be among the first owners of a new kind of watch and to pay more than is usual are sources of satisfaction to some people. The test of whether a feature is a cost, is a satisfaction, or is neutral is the influence it has on the choice of any one consumer.

A company will attempt to overcome all possible resistance to a new product and to convince as many consumers as possible that satisfaction will outweigh cost. Efforts to overcome resistance to the electric Timex included making the watch attractive and dignified looking, communicating to consumers the fact that through "steady electric energy" high standards of accurate time-keeping are possible; selecting wholesale and retail outlets consistent with quality and good taste; and conducting an advertising campaign which complemented the qualities built into the watch. Satisfaction with this watch, or any consumer product, may be based just as much on the feelings and beliefs aroused by the advertising message or the retail outlet which sells it as on the tangible quality of the product.

Equating Cost and Satisfaction

The point where each person's cost and satisfaction evaluation finds a working equilibrium triggers a market transaction. This point is a measure of that one person's feeling toward that particular purchase opportunity. Very likely no two people would feel exactly the same regarding a prospective purchase. Since the seller who moves products *en masse* cannot discover by bargaining or by approximation each person's specific point of purchase equilibrium, he aims for central clusters and sets a price. He may, of course, price his product low or high on the demand scale in the interest of having more buyers at low prices or fewer buyers at high prices.

With most buyers the point of working equilibrium between cost and satisfaction represents a range of prices. A majority of buyers will purchase a product at a price below the maximum they would have been willing to pay. Such buyers enjoy what is called a *buyer's surplus* of satisfaction. In some instances product differences are so small that they do not encourage a careful weighing of alternatives. No purchase is ever made, however, without the purchaser discovering a workable equilibrium between the cost of a product and the satisfaction it will yield. Unsatisfied desires and limited incomes work as constant and opposing forces. They strive persistently, but unsuccessfully, to come together at a point of complete satiation.

Two Special Cases

Although the balancing of cost with satisfaction explains forces that lie behind all marketing transactions, two special cases should be noted—the high income family and the inefficient consumer.

The High Income Family. A few people may be immune to the necessity of watching costs carefully because they possess an abundance of wealth. So many attractive products are available today, however, that many families with high incomes find it difficult to satisfy their wants. In spite of careful planning and borrowing, these people have to leave some of their wants unsatisfied. In the majority of cases, even those few high income families who do satisfy most of their wants give careful attention to getting their money's worth of satisfaction. In fact, many families have acquired their high incomes as a result of skillful and judicious buying, for this provides them with additional money for profit-making investments.

The Inefficient Consumer. Some consumers apparently do not weigh carefully the satisfactions they obtain from the expenditures of funds. Furthermore, individuals may vary from time to time in the amount of attention they give to getting the most for their money. One explanation for this attitude is economic laziness, carelessness, or ignorance. Such people are not aware of the satisfaction that might be obtained from a wise balancing of their incomes with their desires for goods. Another explanation of the apparent failure to weigh values may be that the spender wishes to create the impression that he enjoys a status of comparative wealth. But even in such instances, the spender simply obtains satisfaction of a sort that involves his vanity.

Competitive Advantage Through an Understanding of Cost-Satisfaction

Competitive advantage for a manufacturer or retailer may be gained by emphasizing elements of the cost-satisfaction formula. The following examples illustrate four possibilities in changing the relative weight given to various elements of transactions to gain greater net customer satisfaction over cost.

Example 1. Marked Quality Increase—Moderate Price Increase. A company manufactured a lawn mower that could retail at $22.95. It had four cutting blades on a reel mounted in a simple friction bearing, a wooden handle, and steel wheels. This company later produced a new mower with five steel cutting blades on a 16-inch reel that was mounted in ball bearings. It had a lightweight tubular steel handle, rubber tires, and a heavier, higher-quality blade. This, through careful design and production economies, was manufactured to retail at $37.95. Sales were gratifyingly high. The price increased, but quality, including extra features, increased much more. Hence, satisfaction to the purchaser was greater.

Example 2. Quality Decrease—Sharper Price Decrease. Cotton carpeting may be used as an example of a product having costs that decrease more than the resulting decrease in satisfaction. Certain firms, for example, can offer cotton carpeting for $7 a square yard while comparable designs in wool would cost the consumer $14 a square yard. The wearing qualities of the cotton may be doubtful, and the pride of ownership may not be so great. Yet the decrease in these two satisfactions does not prevent the seller of cotton carpets from gaining a large following in a certain segment of the market. The sellers have reduced the cost of the carpeting and also the satisfaction. But they have not decreased the satisfaction to a considerable number of buyers as much as they have decreased the cost. In addition, we must bear in mind that wool carpeting may be out of the price range of some low-income families.

Example 3. Quality of Service Increase (Decrease)—Nominal Price Increase (Decrease). If for product quality we substitute some other element such as store environment (service, decor, and location), the same sort of relationships between cost and satisfaction can be observed. Proper advertising, use by respected persons, and other non-product ingredients can have similar effects.

A store that provides less service, less ornate surroundings, and a less desirable location provides less satisfaction for the customer. As a rule, it is forced to sell its products for a lower price. For example, some food stores are selling food items for cost plus 10 percent. This margin is measurably lower than that of the average food store. On the other hand, the store that invests in a prestige building, gives more service, and has a convenient location provides additional satisfaction. Such a store can exact a higher price for similar products. A difference of this kind is reflected in expenses and sales as measured and expressed in dollars and cents.

Example 4. Self-Service—Moderate Price Decrease. The change to self-service in retail stores provides a striking illustration of reduction in cost and increase in satisfaction that result from an innovation in service methods. Consumers approve of this innovation because it reduces the cost of the products they purchase and because an increase in satisfaction results from the change. When shopping for food, housewives enjoy the freedom of browsing through the store and picking up merchandise at their pleasure. Another satisfaction factor that is not entirely measurable, yet undoubtedly is instrumental in increasing sales, is the power of suggestion resulting from an effective display of all products to the consumer. As a result of this innovation, food distribution costs decrease and food sales increase.

In summary, any innovation that serves the needs and desires of consumers better than products, services, or methods presently available will provide greater satisfaction and will give a competitive advantage to the innovator. In order to have its executives aware of the importance of innovation, one company even defines marketing as the management of change.

Innovation is used here to mean any better way of providing goods or services to consumers. Thus, achievements such as the following are innovations: better products at the same or slightly increased prices; new uses for old products; new marketing techniques; better material-handling methods and physical distribution practices; improved management practices; and increased consumer services. Innovations must take place at all market levels in order that a better cost-satisfaction balance may be achieved. Whether the buyers be manufacturers, wholesalers, retailers, or consumers, they appraise the cost of the products and services on the one hand and the satisfaction on the other and make their choices according to alternative and optimum opportunities.

Costs Equal Sales

Since the price at which the consumer purchases a product involves his evaluation of the satisfaction it will yield, it can be said that the total sales of a firm represent the sum of the satisfactions, as measured in dollars and cents, which it has delivered to its customers. In providing products to consumers, costs are, of course, incurred by a company. If profits are considered as an essential cost of providing the enterpreneurial skill and the risk-bearing functions, profits would be added to the other costs of producing the products; thus, total costs would equal total sales. Since making a profit is a basic goal of a company, management attempts to maximize the satisfactions inherent in its product and to minimize costs other than profit.

Future Effects of Current Purchases

Even though a marketing cycle is complete with a purchase, equating cost and satisfaction at a money price does not include all marketing aspects of the transaction. Often there are repercussions of a psychological nature that are vital elements affecting the future success of marketing programs. Some purchasers may have gained what we defined above as a ''buyer's surplus''—they paid less for the product than their evaluation of the satisfaction it contained. Others may obtain more satisfaction from the use of the product than they perceived they would receive at the time they made the purchase. The sellers of such products are in a stronger position because of the surplus satisfaction they have given these buyers. However, the constant reinforcement of such a satisfied clientele is a requirement for survival in a competitive system.

On the other hand, there are many buyers who do not receive the satisfactions from a product which they anticipated they would receive. They experience what is termed a *buyer's deficit*. When the purchase of a product results in a buyer's deficit, the chances for future sales of the product are diminished. Thus, balancing cost and satisfaction is a process that continues to affect buyers' behavior even beyond the time of purchase. In Chapter 4 this cost-satisfaction equation is the foundation of a buyer's model that illustrates in more detail the many facets of the marketplace which influence the buyer.

THE MARKETING MIX

Recognition that money cost to the consumer, or price, was only one of the many bases of consumer decisions prompted James Culliton, in 1948 (then a professor at Harvard Business School), to describe the business executive as a "decider," an "artist," a "mixer of ingredients." Professor Neil H. Borden responded to this idea and began using the term "marketing mix."[1]

The challenge and creative nature of marketing today consist of blending the ingredients of the marketing mix, which can be catalogued under four headings: (1) the product and its marketability; (2) the price as a balance between the seller's interest and the buyer's value judgments; (3) promotion, or the company's selling and advertising program; and (4) the marketing channels and outlets used for distribution of the product. It is necessary to integrate these elements into a unified marketing plan. An executive who sees and feels the impact of this basic idea becomes aware of marketing as a process that is constantly evolving and never static. He must examine, and continue to reexamine, his line of products and the market he wants to reach in order to build a marketing program best suited to attracting the buyers of that market. As will be shown, this may mean price adjustments: but it may also mean better product design, increasing (or decreasing) promotional efforts, changes in the retail outlets, or various combinations of all these. Picture the total marketing effort of a firm as a pie chart. A firm's strategy consists of allocating different portions of that effort to one or another of the ingredients of the mix.

Marketing strategy—that is, how the marketing manager adjusts and uses the ingredients of the marketing mix—is influenced by forces outside the

---

[1] The first written discussion of this subject is included in the report by Neil H. Borden, "Note on Concept of the Marketing Mix," No. 2M4R, Adv. 720R (Soldiers Field, Mass.: Harvard Business School, Intercollegiate Case Clearing House). The story of the development of the concept is presented in an article by Neil H. Borden, "The Concept of the Marketing Mix." *Journal of Advertising Research*, Vol. IV, No. 2 (June, 1964), pp. 2-7.

control of the marketer. As a minimum the manager must be aware of the influence of the following:

cultural-social patterns
economic conditions
geographic-climatic influences
legal restrictions
technological developments

Hence, consumer response to each of these influences to which the manager must respond but cannot control, as well as to the four basic elements of the marketing mix under his control, is examined in appropriate sections throughout the remainder of the book.

Every large city in the United States provides a common example of marketing strategies based on the distinctive use of several components of the marketing mix. That example is food retailing. Despite competition from supermarkets, every city has a few highly profitable small food stores that maintain their strong position based largely on the excellent products they sell. For example, a few blocks from the office in which this is written is a small store that stocks and sells a wide variety of carefully selected cheeses, specialty bread products, and some imported delicacies. A recent check on the customers of this store identified women from all parts of this metropolitan market. The reader will know of similar stores which do almost no promotion, maintain rather high prices, and are not conveniently located; they prosper by emphasizing an assortment of special products.

Also, in food marketing one will find low-price stores with sales well over $1 million annually; their basic strategy revolves around price. Others, of similar size, may not meet all low prices but advertise heavily to maintain their volume. These stores emphasize promotion. Every part of the country has a regional chain that retains its position by being quite competitive in price, although it may not have the lowest prices. Such regional chains do some advertising and provide their clientele with the cleanest store, the most attractive displays, and a considerable amount of service. The reader will be able to identify similar examples of a variety of marketing ingredients emphasized in other kinds of retailing and by various manufacturers.

THE MARKET

The business activities of balancing costs with satisfactions by the skillful administration of the marketing mix come to a focus in the marketplace. It is at the market that the consumer makes the controlling decisions as to which product, service, or marketing institution is gaining or losing.

The market is a remarkable device by which consumers maximize their satisfaction by matching their desires against available alternatives. For example, a consumer may wish to buy a dress for about $25. She has only a general idea what she wants, but is eager to examine the alternatives. She does not have the time nor the energy to consider individually the thousands of alternatives available. However, she knows from experience and hearsay about a number of ready-to-wear retailers, and she knows the style and quality of dresses they offer for sale. Therefore, she is able to make a decision as to which stores will most likely carry the dress she seeks. Thus, the marketing system has performed the task of preselecting and sorting. This process of sorting and collecting goods and bringing them to a location which is convenient for consumers takes place with all classes of industrial and consumer goods. Sorting may take place at many marketing levels before the product reaches the point of ultimate sale.

The producer or the seller must be aware of the many levels and classes of markets, for he cannot effectively sell his product in all segments of the market. Rather, he must channel his products into selected segments of the market and direct his promotional efforts to support his products in these segments.

The Forces of Supply and Demand

Supply forces originate with the seller, and the forces of demand are represented by the buyer. Successful sellers must communicate to the buyer the want-satisfying qualities of the products offered for sale. The buyer who purchases the products must pay a price that, in the long run, is at least high enough to cover the costs that the seller has incurred in bringing the product to market. If the buyer performs his function successfully, he will examine all the offerings of those who sell the products he seeks. He will select that offering which enables him to acquire the greatest amount of satisfaction for the money expended. Usually the seller takes the initiative in establishing marketplace business firms, such as retailers, manufacturers, wholesale establishments, and sales branches. Some markets, such as the Chicago Board of Trade, are established by those who buy and sell. Grain elevators and some other agencies are established primarily to buy products.

The forces of supply and demand are independent forces which operate whenever there are people who wish to buy and sell. The New York Stock Exchange for securities, the Chicago Board of Trade for grains, and stores such as R. H. Macy and Company or Marshall Field and Company for consumer goods are great marketing centers; but a marketplace exists whenever the forces of supply communicate with the forces of demand to set a price. For example, a marketplace exists if one student attempts to sell his car to another, for communication is taking place in the interest of setting a price.

Firms appraise the forces of supply and demand carefully in advance of the sale of the products. They then set prices based on their judgments. Manufacturers, in some instances, suggest the price at which their products may sell at retail on the market. In other instances they allow wholesalers and retailers to establish prices. Whether it is the manufacturer, the wholesaler, or the retailer that establishes the price, the seller surveys carefully the forces of supply and demand operating on the market. He next sets a price or establishes a price policy in accordance with such forces.

The price may be printed in catalogs and on packages and be difficult to change. For example, a popular cosmetic specialty package sold for 98 cents.

This price, which was fixed by the manufacturer for the retailer, fitted logically into the price structure of other products of the manufacturer and was affixed to the package. The package and the idea were copied by a competitor who offered the product for 68 cents. The price of 98 cents was so structured that considerable time was required to adjust it to meet competition. Lags in price communication and lethargy of management to respond to new conditions also tend to prevent a prompt and accurate response of price to demand and supply stimuli. Prevailing demand and supply forces operating through a period of time tend, however, to adjust price structures. This subject will be considered further in the discussion of price policy.

Market Communication Not Perfect

The market does not perform its function in a perfect manner. In many instances the market fails to provide individuals with the maximum satisfaction available for the expenditure of their funds. Such failures may occur because communication between all possible buyers and all possible sellers at all market levels is imperfect. Therefore, the best possible choice is not always made. For example, assume that a suit of clothes pleases you and you make a purchase. At a subsequent date you might visit another store and discover several suits that would have given you more satisfaction for the same price. This failure was due in part to your failure to shop more and to seek more information, and it was due in part to the failure of the second merchant to promote his better values to the extent that you were made more aware of them before your purchase. In order for one to make the best possible choice, he would need to keep perfectly informed on all offerings. Since changes are constantly taking place in the products offered and since many institutions are involved, it is impossible to keep completely up to date on every purchase. Perfection in getting the best value offered on the market is a goal that can only be approached.

In other instances information given to buyers by sellers may convey the wrong impression. In such cases choices are sometimes made that would not have been made if complete and accurate information had been communicated. For every person to get all the information about desired products would require a great deal of shopping. To reach every possible prospect with accurate promotional information about his product would be equally difficult for the seller. The extent to which each fails to achieve perfection in this unattainable objective measures the extent to which imperfection of market dealings may occur. Nevertheless, buyers and sellers gain their objectives in proportion to the extent to which they do successfully communicate. Marketplace communication is improving, for more buyers are seeking more information in order to improve the quality of their product choices. As a result sellers must be more alert to the forces of the market in setting their prices.

Change in the Type of Competition

The description of the market would not be complete without an explanation of the dynamic nature of competition. A seller must be constantly alert to assure the sale of its products in profitable volume. Competitive firms are constantly making overtures to customers in attempts to win their patronage. Before the recent emphasis on innovation, this competition between sellers tended to center more around costs and prices. One firm would attempt to win patronage by offering to sell its product at a price lower than that for similar products. This practice is called *price competition*. Today technology has made it possible to offer infinite variations in product qualities. Consequently, rather than reduce a price to win patronage, a firm now is more likely to differentiate its product and advertise the difference as an improvement; or, it may increase the amount of promotion in an effort to change consumer attitudes with respect to the product.

Some firms compete in convenience by offering their products for sale at various places. All the ingredients in the marketing mix are areas in which a company may improve its competitive position. *Nonprice competition* is the term used to refer to the overtures which are made to the customer in product differentiation, promotion, or convenience of time and place. Although price is still an important factor in influencing consumer choice, the competitive battle has broadened to include other features in the marketing mix.

Marketing—A Flow of Costs into Satisfactions

Adequate management of the marketing process requires an awareness of the many forces that influence the movement of a product from idea-conception to consumption. In developing such an awareness, it is helpful if the marketing process is viewed as the forward flow of costs into satisfactions. Such a view enables one to develop skill in identifying each of the costs (explicit or implicit) and the corresponding satisfactions that result at the point of purchase.

Buyers do not seek pounds of steak, yards of cloth, or tons of steel as the end products of marketing effort—they seek customer satisfaction. All goods that yield satisfaction originate from natural resources, human energy, and tools. All cost payments are made to people for supplying these factors. In turn, the people who supply these factors convert the funds that they receive into goods which yield satisfaction. Costs are applied to manufacturing and marketing in the ratio that we have discussed. Both production and marketing costs are applied to the creation of some type of utility or satisfaction. The desires of the consumer attract resources into those productive areas which are judged to be more significant as a result of consumer willingness to pay relatively higher prices.

The skillful administration of the marketing mix, to achieve the optimum cost-satisfaction balance, is the foundation of marketing success. This process constitutes the basic challenge to marketing management.

RECENT CHANGES IN MARKETING

The accelerating rate of improvements in technology and in management procedures plus the changing patterns of consumer behavior have had a striking impact on marketing. Static methods are soon outdated and are replaced by new and improved practices. In the academic area a description of marketing rules and procedures is no longer adequate. The need for radically new perspectives was pointed out as long ago as 1948 by the late Lyndon Brown when he stated:

> Progress in marketing management and research can come only from leadership which will bring radically broader perspective to bear on our progress as a profession. To pass from an occupation based primarily on description to a profession founded on systematic analytics, we will not be pushed, we cannot crawl, we must literally leap in our thinking.[2]

As if in answer to Brown's plea, a new and sounder way of looking at marketing was evident in the following statement made by the General Electric Company in its 1952 annual report:

> The concept introduces the marketing man at the beginning rather than at the end of the production cycle and integrates marketing into each phase of the business. Thus marketing, through its studies and research, will establish for the engineer, the design and manufacturing man, what the customer wants in a given product, what price he is willing to pay, and where and when it will be wanted. Marketing will have authority in product planning, production scheduling, and inventory control, as well as in sales distribution and servicing of the product.[3]

This statement, and others in a similar vein, heralded the entrance of a more practical and realistic approach to marketing. "What the customer wants" became the guiding rule. It was apparent to the General Electric management that the performance of every division in the firm had some influence on the customer's acceptance of its product. Therefore, every division was in some manner related to marketing. Management's task under this new concept was to coordinate the activities in all departments so that each would have a maximum and positive impact on the consumer. Planning (the first step in the process of managing) under this new approach would start with the consumer rather than with the product.

The Marketing Concept

There are two basic reasons as to why traditional discussions of marketing are inadequate. First, technological, managerial, and social changes cause rapid innovation in marketing institutions and practices; thus, descriptive materials soon become obsolete. Second, management methods which accomplish the marketing task vary greatly with different firms; therefore, a description of the management methods used by some firms is incomplete and inadequate. Academicians and managers have come to agree that marketing needs to be viewed as an integrated body of conceptual knowledge. When so viewed, marketing institutions, functions, and practices are described as concepts. These concepts are all interconnected with a root or basic concept.

---

[2] Lyndon O. Brown, "Toward a Profession of Marketing," *Journal of Marketing,* Vol. XIII (July, 1948), p. 28.

[3] From a survey conducted by Robert F. Vizza, Dean of the School of Business, Manhattan College, entitled "Marketing Concept: Is it Working?"

As has already been stated, the basic concept is that all marketing activity begins and ends with the customer.

The term "marketing concept" has been widely used since the early 1950's. Each person, however, sees the concept in terms of his own experience and background, and there is a need for a consensus as to the term's precise meaning. Currently, most scholars and marketing managers agree that it is an awareness of the central importance of customer acceptance of a company's product or service. The following is the authors' definition of the *marketing concept*: An awareness which enables one to assess the relationships of the interdependent forces as they influence directly or indirectly each step in the path of a product through the various phases of idea-conception, production, and distribution, with the focus always on maximizing the consumer's satisfaction with his purchase of the product at a price which is profitable to him and to the company.[4] One who has achieved an understanding of the marketing concept visualizes the administrative activities which are influential in every phase of the product flow, and is able to relate these activities to his own performance. Such an individual can, therefore, properly direct his performance so that it is complementary to the whole.

Market-Oriented Firms

In some companies the developing awareness of the central importance of the consumer has permeated all divisions of the company so that each division examines its activities in terms of its ultimate effect on the volume of sales. With such an orientation, production managers assume some of the responsibility for sales volume by improving products and systems so that the customer gets what he wants at a price he is willing to pay. Similarly, finance managers develop an interest in how decisions, with respect to budgeting, controlling, and allocating funds, can influence sales. Likewise, managers of personnel, purchasing, product development, and other divisions observe means of improving their programs in order to increase the company's overall effectiveness in the marketplace.

Some organizational changes are needed if all divisions of a company are to become market-oriented. The most needed organizational change is the establishment of a top management position for marketing. The title given to such a position is usually vice-president for marketing. As a member of top management, a vice-president for marketing is able to participate effectively in determining how the entire business can best coordinate its efforts to achieve a greater impact on consumer satisfactions. He is able to coordinate the marketing division's activities with those of the other divisions of the firm, and he is in a position to build an intercompany communication system which will keep all divisions aware of market problems. In companies not market-oriented, the top corporate officer in marketing is at a lower level on the

---

[4] The reader's own thinking about the meaning of the marketing concept will be enriched by reading Edward Whitehead's views on a "Blueprint for Marketing," *Journal of Marketing,* Vol. 29 (July, 1965), pp. 7-8.

executive ladder and is usually called the vice-president for sales. The vice-president for sales is only responsible for the conduct of the sales division, and he spends his time and talents on such things as sales gimmicks, territory analysis, and the motivation of sales personnel. In his position he does not have the authority to exercise the leadership which is essential if a market orientation is to permeate all divisions of the business.

Robert Vizza, Dean of the School of Business at Manhattan College, has conducted a survey among 500 companies on the progress that has been made in changing the structure of organizations to comply with the marketing concept. He reports that there is much progress yet to be made. Only 2 percent have made what he considers to be a complete integration of the concept into their organizations, 7 percent have made no changes at all as a result of the concept, and the remainder are in the process of a changeover to a market orientation. The companies which have implemented the concept have enjoyed impressive and dramatic success.[5]

QUESTIONS AND ANALYTICAL PROBLEMS

1. Define, as used in the text, the following: (a) cost, (b) satisfaction, (c) marketing mix, (d) marketing concept.

2. Prices of men's ready-made suits cover a wide range. List all possible reasons why a man might purchase a suit for $45. Make a similar list of reasons why a man might purchase a suit priced at $100. On the basis of the lists, prepare a diagram that illustrates the possible relationships between cost and satisfaction, and compare the individual costs with the corresponding satisfactions.

3. It is suggested by some that price is not important to many people when they are contemplating a purchase. Today, in this age of high incomes, buyers are influenced more by quality, their relationship with the seller, and other characteristics. To what extent does such a condition exist? Does this mean that price is no longer important in regulating what is bought and sold in the economy?

4. In what ways might a marketer gain a competitive advantage by manipulating the cost-satisfaction ratio? For example, it may be possible to increase sales by furnishing a better product at the same price. Name or diagram at least three other possibilities.

5. Which of the elements of the marketing mix would you stress if you were introducing a new kind of toothpaste? State the approximate portions of total marketing effort that you would allocate to each of the elements and explain why.

6. How much control does the marketer of a particular product have over each of the elements of a marketing mix? Discuss each separately.

7. Find an example outside your text of a firm that clearly emphasizes one of the elements of the marketing mix over all the others.

8. Why do market forces of supply and demand not always result in the best prices and greatest possible satisfactions for consumers?

9. What distinguishes a market-oriented firm from a product-oriented firm?

10. Why is coordination among functional departments that results in an

---

[5] Vizza, *op. cit.*

integrated unit essential for a market-oriented firm?

11. What are the factors which mitigate against price reflecting only the forces of demand and supply?

12. Explain precisely what is meant by the phrase "marketing—a flow of

costs into satisfactions."

13. What changes in management philosophy are implicit in a change from a production-oriented concept to the marketing concept? What organizational changes should follow?

Case 2 ● THE HOLBRITE AND MAXIM COMPANY

Mr. Holbrite, of Holbrite and Maxim Company, a large department store dealing primarily in medium-priced merchandise, was considering the idea of having each department stock a few high-priced articles. His thought was that such a pricing policy would result in a storewide increase in sales of medium- and medium-high-priced merchandise and that greater profits would be realized. He explained the reasoning behind his idea as follows:

> When a man comes to our store wishing to buy a handbag as a gift for his wife, he usually comes with some idea of how much he wants to spend, for example, $15. After seeing the handbags in the display case priced around $125 to $200, a $15 handbag appears so cheap by comparison that he probably will purchase a $20 or $25 bag instead. Even though we may be forced to dispose of our expensive merchandise at a heavy loss, our store stands to make a greater profit because many customers will be induced to purchase higher-priced articles than they had originally intended.

● Was Mr. Holbrite's idea sound? Discuss. How does the problem raised in the Holbrite and Maxim Company case relate to the cost and satisfaction and marketing mix concepts discussed in this chapter?

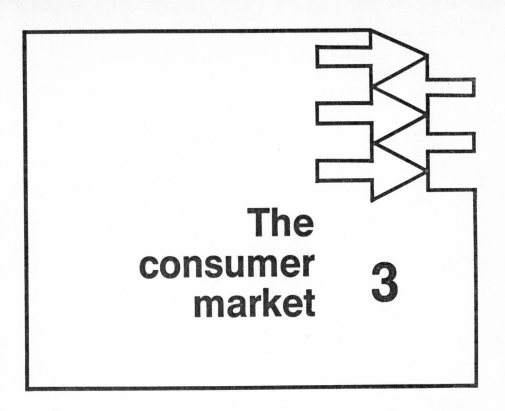

The consumer market 3

A consumer market is people with money to spend—true, but not sufficiently precise for purposes of planning marketing policy. A market is also said to be the place or time where forces of demand meet forces of supply to establish a price—in other words, places or times where trading is done, such as an oriental bazaar or a suburban shopping center. Or a market may be a region within which a particular product finds favor; for example, a particular group of people who suffer from some malady and are, therefore, the market for a special medicine. Also, it may mean a certain time of the year, such as the spring fashion goods market. Finally, it may be a combination of all these meanings.

CHANGING PATTERNS OF THE CONSUMER MARKET

The meaning and extent of the consumer market are modified with the changing of the times. To illustrate, it has been calculated that if men still lived by hunting alone, the population of the world could not be more than approximately 7 million persons, because about 7 square miles per person are required to support human life in a hunter's economy, and the earth's total is only 50 million square miles. Ponder a moment the implications of the increasing productivity of agriculture in the United States. When Cyrus McCormick developed the first practical reaper in 1831, a full-time farmer could produce enough to feed 3½ persons, including himself. Now each farmer in the

33

United States can grow an amount sufficient to feed himself and about 30 others. Production advances have been made on all fronts in the United States during the past 100 years. Increased production means that more goods can be sold or marketed.

The American people have realized a gain in real income during this same period of 5 times per capita, and yet they work 40 percent fewer hours. The tempo of this change seems to be increasing. Even in the decade 1960-1970 there was an increase in real purchasing power per capita, despite inflation. In 1973, however, inflation was of such magnitude that there was a decrease in real income. Purchasing power data must be examined frequently and in local areas for proper planning. Executives of several basic industries estimate that 25 percent or more of their sales volume in the next decade will come from products now unknown to the general public. Today in a typical supermarket there are 7,000 different brands and varieties, of which 1,500 are new each year.

Changes in people's habits also influence marketing methods. It is estimated that about 25 percent of consumer food purchases are now made in public eating places. Also, food prepared and consumed in the home each day is subject to changing patterns. Increased leisure time, including longer vacations with more meals on the road, an increase in the number of factories and offices serving lunches to employees, and the increased number of women working outside the home influence marketing trends. The effect of these changes on methods of packaging and selling by food manufacturers cannot be ignored.

Marketing is dynamic. Patterns of consumption change. Producers and the institutions who market their goods must remain aware of changes. They must constantly evaluate the impact of such changes upon trade in various commodities and upon the methods of supplying consumer wants.

While it is practically impossible to know the needs and tastes of every family, it is possible to learn much about groups and, hence, produce goods that will satisfy specific needs or desires. Mistakes have been made by manufacturers who presume to sell their products to everyone. A nationwide mass market is actually a conglomeration of many small local markets. Within each are families with differences in income, heritage, intelligence, education, number of children, ages, social class, and other characteristics; consequently, they have different needs and desires.[1] *Market segmentation,* or the process of grouping identifiable consumers who possess similar needs and desires, is one approach towards improving marketing strategies.

As a beginning four broad bases may be used for identifying market segments. Those bases are geographic, demographic, income, and psychosociological (including cultural).

---

[1] One can follow consumer expenditures by examining the survey conducted by the Bureau of Labor Statistics in connection with the revision of the Consumer Price Index, frequent studies by the National Industrial Conference Board, New York; also, the Annual Buying Power Index prepared by *Sales Management* magazine, and the annual *Guide to Marketing* published by Printers' Ink magazine.

GEOGRAPHIC SEGMENTATION OF MARKETS

Commonly used geographical divisions of markets are international, national, regional, wholesale trading area, metropolitan market area, and local or neighborhood markets within a metropolitan area.

International markets, which are discussed more fully in Chapter 20, are those that entail trade across national boundaries. Facility of trade between nations varies widely because of the diversity of incomes, of goods available, and of government policies. Many corporations in the United States describe themselves as covering the national market. In fact, very few have distribution in every state, and those who do must usually alter their practices between areas to meet varying local conditions. Sears, Roebuck and Company, as an illustration, publishes a separate catalog for each of its eleven mail-order houses. Much of the merchandise, such as basic clothing and some household supplies, will be found in every catalog; but a fairly large number of items will appear in only one or two because they satisfy certain local requirements. Exhibit 3-1 shows how sales of some nationally distributed appliances and packaged food products differ in penetration of market areas.

Even though a company may require careful analysis of the many local markets in a nation to obtain maximum efficiency of distribution, it is still reasonable to speak of large-scale national markets. This is possible in the United States because of the ease and freedom with which goods flow among the states.

Regional markets are those developed within loosely described geographic areas that do not necessarily coincide with political boundaries. For example, some firms may sell their products only in New England, or the corn belt, or the Pacific Coast states. There are no sharp and sacred boundaries for such trading. Manufacturers that become established in one of these areas may find that contacts are made easily, and channels of communication and transportation may be economical and convenient. It is also possible that the population may cluster in the area, and strong competition may be established in other areas. For such reasons, a company may choose to sell its product in a regional area.

Wholesale trading areas are sometimes defined two ways. One definition is that such an area includes the territory that covers points commonly reached by wholesale firms in a major city. Since, however, certain kinds of wholesalers can economically operate groceries and drug houses in a restricted area, while others serve appliance stores over large numbers of miles the term is sometimes used to describe the territory covered by one type of wholesaler. Nevertheless, in the broader sense there are several quite well-defined wholesale trading areas. Advertising agencies, chambers of commerce, news media, and wholesale firms make it a point to collect and furnish market data on such trading centers.

A *metropolitan market*, also called a standard metropolitan statistical area by the U.S. Bureau of the Census, is an area in and around a comparatively large city (50,000 population or more). The city dominates the retail business in the area, although there may be smaller cities and clusters of shopping centers in the region that are socially and economically integrated with the central city. There are 222 such districts in the United States as designated by the U.S. Bureau of the Census.

Exhibit 3-1

PROPORTION OF SELECTED ITEMS SOLD
IN MAJOR MARKET AREAS

A Home Appliance

The home appliance field is strongly influenced by distributor relations and by distribution problems and opportunities. For example, although the Northeast accounts for only 29% of total volume for this product, Brand C gets 40% of its volume there. In the South, on the other hand, Brand C's volume drops sharply to 5%. Brand E faces the same problem in the West.

	North East	North Central	South	West
Total Volume	*29%*	*29%*	*23%*	*19%*
Brand A	32	25	31	12
Brand B	28	26	21	25
Brand C	40	29	5	26
Brand D	33	24	31	12
Brand E	30	43	24	3
Brand F	25	25	24	26
All Others	27	29	26	18

A Packaged Food Product

Perhaps the most extreme cases of regional marketing problems are found in food products. For not only is the diversity of tastes in food products especially marked; so is the competition of local and private brands (usually at lower prices). As the table shows, for example, although metropolitan New York accounts for 19% of the total volume of this packaged food product, Brand A places 34% of its volume there, while Brand D places only 6%. Yet Brand D places 28% of its volume in the Central region, which accounts for only 15% of total volume, while Brand A places 13% there.

	New York	East	Chicago	Central	South	Los Angeles	West
Total Volume	*19%*	*26%*	*6%*	*15%*	*16%*	*8%*	*10%*
Brand A	34	22	7	13	12	6	6
Brand B	24	20	8	11	12	16	9
Brand C	15	31	6	15	15	8	10
Brand D	6	13	5	28	26	10	12

Source: "Myth of the National Market," *Dun's Review and Modern Industry* (May, 1964), p. 43. By permission.

Most large cities are losing population within the city proper, but suburbs and satellite cities continue to grow. Hence, data from an area that trades in a city has more significance for market planners than does population data restricted by city limits. Not only do such centers have an effect on sales of the city, but also, as its influence widens, there is a marked effect upon small towns that were formerly free of city competition on frequently used items.

Local or neighborhood markets vary from an area served by the old crossroads country store to modern shopping centers. Data on such markets are difficult to obtain from secondary sources because government-generated studies usually are undertaken for political units, i.e., cities, counties, and states. Exhibit 3-2 relates how one merchant solved a problem of store location within neighborhood markets.

The market potential of a retail store area can be calculated quite accurately by collecting and analyzing pertinent facts and figures. Exhibit 3-2 shows an example of such a computation. The left set of concentric circles surrounds an area where an established store (store A) is operating. This store had sales of $1 million. The addresses of the store's customers during a sample period were collected, and it was discovered that the store obtained a certain

Exhibit 3-2

ESTIMATING MARKET POTENTIAL OF A PROPOSED RETAIL STORE

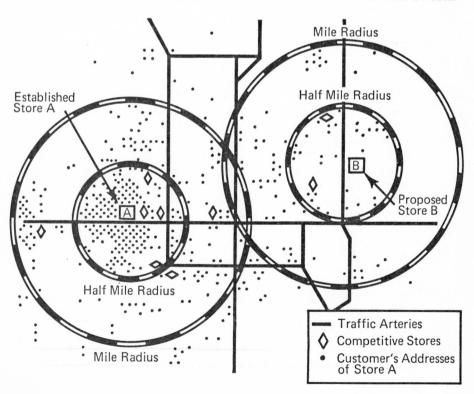

percentage of the business out of the first half mile, a decreasing percentage out of the area between the half mile and mile, and so on. The share was calculated by obtaining from the city planning office the total number of homes in each area, and computing the percentage that traded in the store under investigation. The merchant then made similar charts for the two competing stores in Circle B. It was noted that population density was as great in the area included in Circle B as in the area included in Circle A. Since the competing stores would be at the edge of a circle swung one-half mile around the proposed location, and since it was demonstrated that most of his trade in the existing store was generated within one-half mile, it can be concluded that the proposed location should be successful. Of course, traffic patterns, income levels and other factors must be considered; but this does illustrate a good initial step in estimating local or neighborhood market potential.

DEMOGRAPHIC FEATURES OF CONSUMER MARKETS

The information that follows is concerned primarily with the United States, but the type of analysis that is suggested can be applied to any country or region.

In 1972 there were 208.5 million people in the United States. In brief, the important characteristics of that population can be catalogued as follows:

1. TOTAL POPULATION has increased and is still increasing, despite a declining birthrate.
2. FAMILY SIZE has changed during the past one hundred years. The birthrate declined steadily for many years until it was less than sufficient to replace itself, then it increased during World War II. This rate is declining slightly again. In 1960 the average family was 3.61 persons, and in 1971 it was 3.52 persons.
3. AGE GROUPINGS of the population are shifting. Average age of the population increased until about 1960 when 54.4 percent of the population population was under 35 years of age. In 1970 the figure was 58.4 percent. If the declining birthrate continues, that figure will change again during the next decade.
4. GEOGRAPHICAL DISTRIBUTION of the population is undergoing change. Increasing movements to the West and South are evident, along with decreasing numbers on farms and increasing movement to suburban areas.
5. The nature of cities is changing. The historical movement of more well-to-do families to outlying areas is accelerating, and there is an increasing proportion of low-income families in the central core areas.

Total Population

The following data are total magnitude for the United States. Similar information can be determined for individual census tracts and for postal zip code districts. A *census tract* is an area of approximately 4,000 persons with similarity of population and income characteristics. Hence, it is possible to identify areas that have characteristics which indicate possible acceptance of a product or, conversely, to evaluate probable acceptance of a product in a specified area. The United States has a decennial census of population (every

10 years since 1790). In intervening years estimates are made. Publications of the Bureau of the Census, of business and economic research bureaus at major universities, and in such reports as the annual Buying Power Index reports by *Sales Management* magazine in its May issue each year are sources for demographic characteristics and trends.

A marketing manager must determine which population characteristics will affect acceptance of his product. Some broad analyses are illustrated in the following paragraphs.

Where They Came From

The population of a nation may be increased by any one of the following factors: a higher birth rate, a lower mortality rate, more immigration, or less emigration. In the United States and in most other parts of the world, recent population growth has been due primarily to the first factor—an increase in the number of live births.

Since 1900 the birth rate per 1,000 persons has declined in the United States from over 30 per 1,000 to 17.3 per 1,000. Throughout the greater part of the century the rate has been below 20 per 1,000. However, even though the birth rate is lower than in earlier years, more people added each year means an actual increase in the number of families. Furthermore, the death rate is also decreasing in the United States; there were 17 deaths per 1,000 persons in 1900 and only 9.3 in 1971—which is about one half of the 1900 rate. With respect to immigrants into the United States, a total of close to 23 million have been admitted since 1900, with an average of about 300,000 each year from 1961 to 1970.[2] These data balance out to an increase in the United States of over 250 persons per hour.

Number of Households [3]

Most consumer marketing is for family units. It is, therefore, important that marketing men be aware of family formations, family size, and number of households. The number of households is of more importance in determining the sales of a number of products than is the number of people. As prosperity increases, more persons are enabled to establish separate dwelling units, and there is also an increased rate of marriages, establishing new families.

The present marriage rate of 10.6 per 1,000 population compares with 10.3 per 1,000 in 1910. The highest rate for the United States of over 12 per 1,000 was during World War II and the immediate postwar years. The lowest rate in this century was 8.5 per 1,000 in the early 1960's. This was due to low birth rates of the depression years (1930's) and deferred families of early World War II years.

---

[2] U.S. Department of Commerce, Bureau of the Census, *Statistical Abstract of the United States: 1973* (94th ed.; Washington; U.S. Printing Office, 1973), p. 96, #145.

[3] Household, according to Census Bureau usage, "comprises all persons who occupy a 'housing unit.' That is, a house, apartment, group of rooms, or a room that constitutes separate living quarters."

The implications of such trends on sale of furnishings, dwelling spaces, food preparation practices, and other consumer expenditures are significant in making market plans and budgeting sales figures.

Family Size

The old expression that the rich get richer and the poor have children cannot be used for marketing planning. The upper-middle income class had the greatest "baby boom" in the 1950's. Now that group forms the chief constituency of the zero population growth movement. In other words, one must check the trends annually.

Age of Population

Even though the growing numbers of young persons annually add to the percentage of people under 35 years of age, total numbers of older persons in the country increase year by year; and even the proportion increases because greater numbers live beyond the age of 65 years. In 1800 the median age of all persons in the United States was only 16 years. Now it is 28 years. One hundred years ago only 2½ percent of the population were over 65 years old; now 10 percent are past this age. Ten percent of approximately 200 million provides a considerable market if they have purchasing power. Since 1936 social security and pension programs have greatly increased this purchasing power. In 1970 over 85 percent of all married couples over 65 years reported some retirement benefits.

One must also note the ever-growing proportion of our population under 14 years. We shall leave it to the student to calculate the market implications of these trends. A beginning may be made by charting the probable sales of infants' and children's wear and the leisure-time needs of the older people. One should also note, with interest, the large number of magazine articles about the importance of the teen-age market. Not only are there large numbers in that age group, but also they seem to have money.

Geographic Distribution of Population

During the years that a decennial census has been taken in the United States, the center of population has moved westward 686 miles. This is, of course, not surprising since the country was settled largely along the Atlantic coast at the time of the first counting. What interests us here is the recent westward movement. During the decade of 1940-1950, the center point moved 42 miles west—the greatest change since 1880-1890. There is some very slight variation in birth and death rates between the states, but it is not sufficient to account for any appreciable population movement. Variation in growth rates of the states is caused almost entirely by migrations.

There have been movements of people in the United States as long as such statistics have been gathered. Even the 1910 census showed that one third of the population was born outside the state in which it was then residing.

Presently, within each year, about 20 percent of the people move to a different house, and over 6 percent of all families move to a different county.

As a result of this movement, population growth has not been uniform in all sections. While population in the Pacific Coast area increased 25 percent from 1960-1970, that in the West North Central section grew only 6 percent. Such analyses only bear out what casual observation indicates. To the marketing man, more precise studies of specific areas are of importance. Thus, while the West South Central area, for example, showed a gain of 14 percent, this area includes several cities that grew to three or four times their original size.

Urban And Rural Distribution of Population

Manufacturers and merchants will gain a clearer market perspective by understanding what the movement to urban areas means. The growth of urban areas has been largely in fringes around large cities and in towns of 5,000 to 10,000 population. The older, large cities have grown only one fifth as rapidly as have the smaller places and the areas adjacent to cities. This kind of urban growth means that different kinds of living equipment and different types of stores and distribution channels will be utilized than if the growth had been in central parts of established large cities.

A further result of this kind of changing pattern of abode is that the cultural difference between the city and country dwellers is decreasing. There is no longer a clear-cut occupational distinction between urban or suburban residents and residents of the open country or small villages. The evidence indicates that in some parts of the northeastern region two thirds to three quarters or even more of the open-country residents make their living at nonfarm work. Nor does the increasing move to urban areas mean the end of small-town business.

Suburbs

The standard dictionary definition of a *suburb* is a smaller place adjacent to a city. By that definition, roughly half of the United States population is suburban. More meaningful to marketing men is the definition adopted by the editors of *Fortune* magazine for their studies of the "Changing American Market." Their count of suburbia includes only communities "whose residents (1) earn their income primarily in the city, (2) are, culturally speaking, city folks, (3) are willing to go to some expense to journey to and from the city because they have better-than-average income." The suburb is also almost a state of mind. The demand for goods contributing to comfortable outdoor living develops largely in suburban furnishings, clothing, and recreational equipment.

Working Women

In the United States many women work outside the home. While women have long been accepted in business, there has been an upturn in the percentage of jobs held by women and in the percentage of women who are working. In 1890 only 4 percent of the married women in the United States held jobs, but by 1971 over 40 percent of the married women were working. That is, over 20 million married women in the United States held salary-paying jobs. In addition to the married women, there are slightly more than 10 million other women working at jobs in office and industry. That means that approximately 38 percent of those in civilian employment are women.

Two effects immediately come to mind. One is the effect on family income, and the other is the effect on types of goods that are demanded when the housewife spends a large part of the day away from home. Regarding income, one authoritative estimate is that roughly two fifths of family incomes in the middle range would fall into low-income categories if supplementary incomes of working wives were eliminated.

The second effect—the influence upon consumption patterns when the housewife works—is of significance to consumer goods producers. The demand for convenience foods would be considerably less were all women to stay in the kitchen. Many of the convenience items find a market, or a larger market, because of the demands of families that must prepare meals and keep house after office hours. It has had an effect also upon retail patterns of store hours. Shopping centers that are open from 12 noon to 8 or 9 in the evening result, in large part, from the needs of working families.

INCOME AND THE CONSUMER MARKET

Since each consumer weighs the satisfaction he will gain from a purchase against the cost of the transaction, it is not possible to forecast precisely how any one person will respond in the marketplace under specified conditions of income. Furthermore, knowledge of the total income of a nation helps little in estimating what specific products and services will be consumed by families. It is often helpful, however, to generalize upon the basis of past experience as to how consumers, as a group, may be expected to allocate their incomes. Most of the following discussion is devoted to an examination of the effects of income distribution upon levels of living and more general expenditure patterns. Some recent data bearing upon the outlook for family incomes in the United States are also presented.[4]

Distribution of income [5]

What is happening to the distribution of incomes in the United States is presented in Table 3-1. The significance of the changes indicated in the table can be appreciated more if we understand just what an income of $2,000

---

[4] Inasmuch as most students of a course in marketing will have completed courses in basic economics, it is presumed that they understand the meaning of "income." Those persons interested in knowing how income figures are derived and reported are referred to the *Federal Reserve Bulletin* or any recent standard textbook on economics principles.

[5] The Office of Business Economics introduced a new series which will have value for evaluating markets. It is "Personal Income in Metropolitan Areas." Presented are estimates of personal income in 97 standard metropolitan statistical areas (SMSA's) for selected years. See Robert E. Graham, Jr. and Edwin J. Coleman, "Personal Income in Metropolitan Areas: A New Series," *Survey of Current Business*, Vol. 47, No. 5 (May, 1967), p. 18, and for following years.

Table 3-1

DISTRIBUTION OF INCOME
PERCENT OF ALL HOUSEHOLDS IN
EACH INCOME GROUP IN CURRENT
DOLLARS—1970 = 100

	1970
Under $4,000	14.0%
$4,000 to $6,000	12.1
$7,000 to $9,999	19.9
$10,000 to $14,999	26.8
$15,000 and over	22.3

Source: U.S. Department of Commerce, Bureau
of the Census, *Current Population Reports:* 1971,
No. 80, p. 60.

represents, as against an income of $7,500, for instance. Sociologists once found it convenient to measure levels of living in order to compare the welfare of groups of people. It is now recognized that comparisons between nations or between time periods within a nation are not valid on the basis of levels of living—products and patterns of consumption change. Nevertheless, for purpose of illustration, categorization of levels of living is made here with the caution to the reader that only broad generalizations are to be drawn.

1. BARE SUBSISTENCE. Only the most inexpensive food, largely cereals, practically no meat; little clothing; no money for recreation; only charity medical and dental care.
2. MINIMUM HEALTH AND DECENCY. Occasional cheap cuts of meat, some fruit; some small recreational expenditures; decent, minimum clothing allowance; adequate shelter but no luxuries in housing or furnishings.
3. COMFORT. Complete, adequate diet; occasional vacation and amusement expenditures; some books; comfortable housing; small amount of "frivolous" spending for clothing and household furnishings.

There is, of course, no fixed standard for the categories above, but it is reasonable to assume that to enjoy "comfort" a family income close to the present median household income of $9,800 is required in the United States today. An annual family income of less than $4,000 would put the family on the bare subsistence category (the 1970 "poverty" level family income was $3,600).

Through the years there has been a quite remarkable improvement in family and household incomes. In 1930 about 55% of those units had incomes low enough to place them in the poverty level. Now there are 14 percent of households in that category. (It is beyond the scope of this book to argue whether that figure is closer to 20 percent, as is recently claimed.) However, when one seventh of the population of a developed nation is below a subsistence level, some considerable concern is indicated. Even if one were to ignore the misery and social problems inherent in this situation (which we certainly cannot do) and look only at the effect on the economy, it is clear that an improvement in buying power of that lowest one seventh is worth pursuing. Greatly increased sales of better food, houses, appliances, and other items purchased only after basic needs are met explain the importance to the economy of larger numbers of families in income categories above $4,000. It is the discretionary income—that left after necessities of food, rent, basic clothing and transportation to work—that one is concerned with in estimating markets for most products and services. In other words, a large national income widely distributed means larger markets for more goods and services than does a similar income that is narrowly held.

How Incomes Are Spent [6]

The significance of income distribution can be further illustrated by consumer purchases at various income levels. Table 3-2 is based on shares of total annual expenditures according to annual household incomes.

Note that certain patterns can be discerned and that the percentage of total spending allocated to each of the major items changes from one income group to another. Frequently it has been reasoned that, if such changes could be charted and found to be consistent, then a valuable forecasting tool would be developed for planning marketing of consumer goods. In fact, for approximately one hundred years, certain patterns have been observed and used to illustrate the value of income distribution studies. Over 100 years ago a German statistician, Ernst Engel, studied the budgets of working men in Saxony, and from his data economists deduced the following generalizations.[7] As family income increases:

1. The percentage of the total that is spent for food will decrease.
2. The portion of total spending for clothing will remain approximately the same.
3. The portion of total spending for housing, fuel, and light will remain the same.
4. The portion of total, expenditures for "sundries" such as education, medical care, religion, recreation, and travel will increase.

For many years such studies of family budgets as were made seemed to confirm "Engel's Laws." In general, they still hold sufficiently true to be utilized in marketing. Careful students of market patterns learn, however, that generalizations can be misleading when applied to specific problems and particular markets. Further, buying habits can be changed by properly planned

---

[6] For detailed analysis refer to two monumental studies on consumption patterns: University of Pennsylvania, Wharton School of Finance and Commerce, *Study of Consumer Expenditures, Incomes, and Savings–Urban U.S.–1950.* This work consists of 18 volumes, largely statistical tables. For more recent, but less detailed, data see Fabian Linden (ed.), *Expenditure Patterns of the American Family* (New York: National Industrial Conference Board, 1965), p. 18, and periodic studies by the U.S Bureau of Labor Statistics, of which Table 3-2, p. 45, is an example.

[7] Benjamin S. Loeb discusses Engel's Laws as a means of predicting sales in "The Use of Engel's Laws as a Basis for Predicting Consumers' Expenditures," *Journal of Marketing,* Vol. XX (July, 1955), pp. 20-27. Richard D. Millican tests the validity of Engel's Laws in economic affluence in his article, "A Re-examination of Engel's Laws Using BLS Data (1960-1961)," *Journal of Marketing,* Vol. XXXI, No. 4 (October, 1967), p. 18.

Table 3-2

ANNUAL BUDGETS FOR A 4-PERSON FAMILY/1970
IN STANDARD METROPOLITAN STATISTICAL AREAS

Item	Lower Budget		Intermediate Budget		Higher Budget	
	$ Amount	% of Total Budget	$ Amount	% of Total Budget	$ Amount	% of Total Budget
Food	$1,933	27.4%	$ 2,491	22.8%	$ 3,162	19.8%
Housing	1,453	20.6	2,579	23.6	3,915	24.5
Transportation	481	6.8	916	8.4	1,204	7.5
Clothing and Personal Care	820	11.6	1,153	10.5	1,676	10.5
Subtotal of the 4 Items	4,687		7,139		9,957	
Total Budget	7,061		10,933		15,971	
Balance for Discretionary Spending	2,374		3,795		6,269	

Note: Based on spring prices. Assumes 4-person family of 38-year-old, employed husband, wife not employed outside the home, 8-year-old daughter, and 15-year-old son.

Source: U.S. Bureau of Labor Statistics, *Three Budgets for an Urban Family of Four Persons,* 1967-1970, Bulletin 1570-5.

and executed selling. To test these observations, we can examine the United States market. Since food, clothing, and shelter are common needs, present-day expenditures for each of these major items deserve further analysis.

Expenditures for Food. Table 3-2 shows that the percentage of expenditures for food does apparently decline as income increases. In any event, higher income groups allocate a smaller portion of expenditures for food than do lower income groups. Inasmuch as this has been demonstrated in many countries, it was assumed by many persons that a fair general gauge of the economic development of any nation was the percentage of national income expended for food—the lower the percentage for food, the higher the state of economic development. Because the United States is enjoying a much higher per capita income than in former times, it could be expected that while more dollars will be spent for food, those dollars will be a small portion of total expenditures.

Are some major changes taking place that outmode all previous expenditure patterns? The sociological and economic changes in the United States, resulting in large measure from increasing real incomes, rural to urban migrations, higher degrees of specialization, and increasing leisure time make it important that the marketing executive learn to interpret and synthesize all apparent trends. The share of expenditures going to food can probably be explained by the combination of a number of factors. There was, of course, inflation in food prices, but there were other changes also. Movement from rural to urban areas increases food costs because of increased transportation, storage, and refrigeration requirements. Smaller family units, partly due to "undoubling" as housing increased, as well as to new family formation (marriages), called for smaller packages and decreased the economies of large-unit food preparation.

Perhaps the most important factors accounting for increased food expenditures have been upgrading of the diet—fewer starchy foods; more meat, fruit, vegetables—and the spectacular rise of convenience features in foods. Prepackaged, precooked, frozen, premixed, concentrated products of various kinds are the rule in America's kitchens. The spectactular growth of demand for soft drinks, the frozen fruit juices, and the creamy whip varieties of ice cream are modern foods marketed for counter, corner, and home consumption that, like the drive-in movie or hamburger stand, did not exist or extend the daily eating habits a generation ago. The costs of additional processing added to the costs of more services, lumped together as convenience or service, constitute another important reason for the increased portion of consumer spending allocated to food purchases. Stated another way, this increased allocation of income for food shows that the American public can be sold a higher standard of living when the economy permits.

Clothing. In Table 3-2 the percentages of expenditures for clothing are quite close to the experience stated in "Engel's Laws" but with a slight difference. A slowly increasing portion of expenditures is spent for clothing as incomes increase. This is in conformance with long-time experience. The tendency for Americans to purchase more special-use clothing and the extra demands for special clothing as they travel or engage in sports probably account for the slightly higher percentage expended for clothing among the higher income groups. On the other hand, increased leisure and casual living have sharply reduced the demand for "dressy" apparel. Clothing manufacturers present new styles and aggressively promote their products to keep their share of the American consumer market.

Housing. As indicated in Table 3-2 the average portion of expenditures that goes to housing changes little from one income group to another after the lowest income group (below $3,000). The pattern displayed is very like that shown in various consumption studies. There is a steady decline in the percentage of expenditures from the lowest income groups to a point between $3,000 and $5,000, at which point it levels off and remains a fairly constant percentage of total expenditures.

THE USE OF MARKET SEGMENTATION INFORMATION

From the general information provided by various government and private sources, can a marketing manager predict sales of his product? It is fair to say that such data, if properly used, can at least help one make a good educated guess.[8]

Given the same income, will a family in a large city develop the same spending patterns as a similar-sized family in a small town? Analysis of the consumption pattern studies mentioned in this chapter indicates that city dwellers tend to spend greater amounts and percentages of income for food, shelter, education, and recreation but less for automobile expense than small-town families. This suggests other factors for examination. Among those commonly examined in consumer studies are: education, age of head of the household, number of children in family, regional location, and metropolitan or nonmetropolitan location. Regarding education, there is a tendency for households with college-graduate parents to spend relatively less on food, clothing, and medical care but relatively more on home and automobile expenses.

In the comprehensive study of American consumption patterns completed by the Bureau of Labor Statistics, it was demonstrated that manual laborers as a group do not conform to spending patterns of the entire population in the major spending classifications. For example, manual laborers, on the average, spent only 75 percent as much for housing as did self-employed or white-collar workers with the same income.

Segmenting factors affect each part of the marketing mix. Stephen Dietz of Kenyon and Eckhardt, Inc., a well known advertising agency, said that results of one of their studies show:

> . . . startling differences in people's reactions to advertising . . . as a result of the amount of education they have had . . . for instance we found that the familiar old advertising claim of a certain famous national advertiser is almost totally disbelieved by the upper 30 percent of his audience . . . even though it continues to work with lower educated groups. In another case, the manufacturer of a mass market grocery product is using copy which is far over the heads . . . even incomprehensible to women whose education stopped midway in high school. . . . We have seen examples of certain kinds of advertising tricks—diagrams, tests, and demonstrations—which seem to penalize, not add to believability, the higher up you get on the education scale.[9]

Hence, it can be illustrated that by segmenting the population a marketing manager can more nearly identify his potential customers. Also, it is now clear that more than just the number of people, their location, and income distribution is needed in order to understand any market. For this reason psychological and sociological factors that affect consumption or spending are discussed in the following chapter.

---

[8] The dynamics of the consumer market as it applies to the amount spent, the kinds of goods purchased, and the volume of the consumers is portrayed with relevant facts and logic in Robert Ferber, "Our Changing Consumer Market," *Business Horizons*, Vol. I, No. 2 (Spring, 1958), pp. 49-66.

[9] From a speech to the Philadelphia Chapter, American Marketing Association, November, 1965.

QUESTIONS AND ANALYTICAL PROBLEMS

1. Define "market" as used in this chapter. How does this concept differ or agree with the definition you derived from Chapter 1?
2. Why is it more valuable to use data from standard metropolitan statistical areas than data on a city basis?
3. List and explain the pertinent facts about population that would be helpful in analyzing a particular market.
4. Why has the classification "Rural Nonfarm" been added to the population census?
5. What are the most significant geographic trends in the United States markets as they affect the metropolitan area? the entire nation?
6. What is a suburb?
7. What portion of the United States labor force are women?
8. What direct effects upon marketing can be attributed to working wives?
9. What facts should a marketing man know about income in an area?
10. Show, graphically, the trends in amount and distribution of income in the United States. Name at least five products whose sales will be directly affected by the trends depicted.

11. What are "Engel's Laws"?

12. How do the patterns of consumption stated in Engel's Laws compare with present-day consumption patterns in the United States?

13. A manufacturer of furniture began, last year, to emphasize two lines of furniture for "young moderns with taste." One line he calls "Modern with a Future" and the other line follows modified traditional patterns. His furniture enjoyed moderate success last year—indeed, sales exceeded his expectations since his new brand was unknown. In planning for the next year, the manager is considering a reduction in the price of his entire line. To do so he must reduce quality. Two other manufacturers have introduced lines similar to his, and he desires a larger share of the market than he now has. On the basis of information in this chapter regarding spending and income patterns, would you advise him to reduce prices? Explain.

Case 3 • THE WHEELER CONSTRUCTION COMPANY

In 1956 the Wheeler Construction Company was one of the largest construction firms in the Long Beach, California, area. Al Cobden, a vigorous college graduate and company sales manager, was struck with the idea of building a certain kind of dwelling complex exclusively for senior citizens (people over 65 years old). His idea included a well-defined area bordered by a golf course on two sides, a private beach on a third side, a wall-enclosed fourth side and an entrance bordered by fountains and shrubbery. Within the area would be a few small stores and service shops for convenience, a recreation center providing all facilities, and private dwellings built on quiet, winding streets. The arrangement would be condominium in nature, with maintenance services provided by the management and included in the price of the lease contract. Mr. Cobden presented his idea to Mr. Wheeler, the owner of the firm, and received enthusiastic approval, with the condition added that Cobden investigate the demand for such a "senior citizens' haven" before proceeding with plans.

Mr. Cobden learned that some 9 percent of the total U.S. population is over 65 years old and that approximately 8 percent of the nation's population resides in California. He was also informed that about half of all families in the U.S. had annual incomes above $5,000 and that the Far West accounted for nearly 30 percent of the national personal income. The data also showed that over 80 percent of all couples over 65 receive some retirement benefits in addition to social security. Therefore, Mr. Cobden felt that his company's required investment of approximately $1,000,000 in the project could net a profitable return due to the existence of a large market in the surrounding area.

• What other important factors should Mr. Wheeler consider before going ahead with this project.

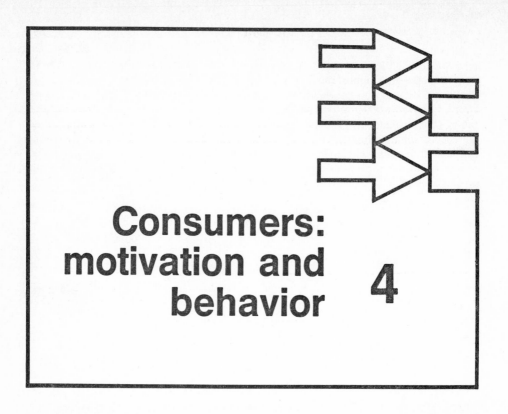

Consumers: motivation and behavior 4

Marshall Field, the great Chicago merchant, stressed two slogans in talking with associates and employees. The first, which became a classic in marketing, was "The customer is always right." The second emphasized the customer's importance with even more directness—"Give the lady what she wants." When Marshall Field gave this counsel, the importance of the customer in the marketing scene was not generally recognized. However, his vision of the future has been vindicated by the contemporary emphasis on the marketing concept. This emphasis places the satisfaction of the consumer at the very heart of the marketing universe.

This chapter deals with some of the means by which the market manager may become more effective in reaching prospective customers with the story of his product or service. First, some of the problems that arise as the result of aggressive or misdirected promotional activities are discussed. Second, the evolving background out of which market choices arise is examined. Third, the class society is discussed in terms of its potential for the development of a more effective market strategy. And fourth, the nature of influence groups is analyzed with the objective of using it as a guide to a more efficient means of communicating with potential customers.

CONSUMER ECONOMY vs. CONSUMPTION ECONOMY

Many of the most vigorous and successful managements today are challenged by the necessity of finding the narrow line which divides a healthy and energetic selling program from one which is considered to be manipulative, deceptive, and high-pressured. There are organized forces in society which are dedicated to the protection and welfare of the consumer, and these forces draw sharp distinctions between what they term a "consumer economy" and a "consumption economy." They favor a *consumer economy*—an economy in which the satisfaction of the consumer is the dominant motivation; and they look with skepticism on a *consumption economy*–an economy in which the seller attempts to maximize his profits by gaining high sales volume through undue pressure and deceptive practices.

Ralph Nader has become famous for his part in the consumer movement. He was influential in the passage of six consumer protection laws: The National Traffic and Motor Vehicle Safety Act of 1966; The Wholesale Meat Act of 1967; The National Gas and Pipeline Safety Act of 1968; The Radiation Control for Health and Safety Act of 1968; The Wholesale Poultry Products Act of 1968; and The Federal Coal Mine Health and Safety Act of 1969.[1] This legislation illustrates the reality of the fact that the marketing concept has not worked sufficiently well to forestall this consumer movement.

THE CONSUMER'S RESPONSIBILITY

A significant factor in the attitude of those who vigorously defend the interests of consumers is their inability to see competition as a means of control. They imply that profit is selfishly motivated and cannot be adequately sublimated to conform to the consumer's best interest. And, in tones of abject resignation many consumers have shared at one time or another, Marya Mannes laments:

> As a housewife I buy what is sold to me. It is packaged. I buy it on faith. This is why these days the word consumer is spelled "sucker."[2]

The consumer has taken a much more active position in determining what is produced and consumed. The hope of a partnership between business (with its attitude toward the marketing concept) and the consumer has faltered to the "consumerist movement."

Even more redirection which gives more attention to consumer interests appears inevitable because (1) of the consumerist movement; (2) progressive and competitive business is being forced to be more effective in providing increasing satisfaction to the consumer; (3) the President's office is giving significant emphasis to consumer interests and is getting considerable support from private and public agencies; and (4) many consumers now have the leisure and affluence to give increasing attention to their role as consumers.

---

[1] "The U.S.'s Toughest Consumer," *Readers Digest,* Vol. 96, No. 575 (March, 1970), pp. 76-80.

[2] James R. Withron, Jr., "The Inadequacies of Consumer Protection," *Consumerism Viewpoint: From Business, Government, and the Public Interest,* edited by Ralph M. Gaedeke and Warren W. Etcheson, (San Francisco: Canfield Press, 1972), p. 193.

THE EVOLVING ENVIRONMENT OF CHOICE

It is in the best interest of businesses to move their products through sales channels with a minimum of resistance. Product acceptance is achieved as a result of choices made by individual consumers; thus, a focal point of interest for progressive management is the choice made by the individual consumer. Advertising and selling strategies that properly assess the fundamental nature of these individual choices are much more likely to achieve the acceptance of products by consumers. Furthermore, much of the criticism of business practices discussed above is the result of an inaccurate appraisal of the forces that lie behind the marketplace choices made by individuals.

Culture—Its Influence on Choice

Although choices are expressed individually, the individual is a product of the culture in which he lives. While the consumer's responses or purchases may have an individual character, they are strongly influenced by the many forces which surround him. Therefore, the marketing plan or strategy should be consistent with the language and the goals of the culture from which the consumer gets his buying cues. Scholars in marketing have recognized this relatedness of marketing to culture and have recommended that those who aspire to' the goal of making marketing a science should include psychology, sociology, and even anthropology in their studies. The logic for such recommendations is that the present behavior of the individual is an outgrowth of the past; thus, one can understand better the contemporary buying psychology if he understands how it came to be.

Choice, then, is a moving target—it moves with the culture out of which it spawns. Other things being equal, the market manager will achieve a more effective strategy if he senses the evolving nature of the culture and some of the patterns which characterize changes that are taking place.

Early Cultural Patterns Affecting Choice

In a primitive society tradition provided the cue for practically all choices. The range of means for satisfying individual differences in desires was at best limited. Having enough was the goal rather than the satisfaction of a unique personal desire. The traditions established by parents were adequate guides for the choices made by their offspring.

Riesman notes that the beginning of a break with tradition as a guide for choices came when the motivations which attended the accumulation of capital introduced some new values into the social pattern.[3] Men began to see the possibility for accumulating wealth as a result of savings. This was the period when the Protestant ethic, which supplied motivation for the "American dream" of the poor boy becoming rich and famous, became one of the guides which influenced consumer choices. During this period rules for success, such as "A penny saved is a penny earned," were substituted for the traditions of

---

[3] David Riesman, *The Lonely Crowd* (New Haven: Yale University Press, 1962).

the past. Saving and thrift during this era meant more than mere accumulation; it meant a multiplication of productive resources through capital formation. As a result of the increasing productivity of capital, many of the aggressive and enterprising were able to accumulate large fortunes. Getting ahead in the world became one of the principal motivations for the individual, and he demonstrated his success by his purchases. Thus, products such as fashion goods were developed, for obtaining them was not only a way of expressing taste, but also a means of obtaining status.

Trends Which Are Affecting Choice

There are still societies in some parts of the world that get their market guides from tradition. And, certainly, the pattern of thrift, saving, and conspicuous consumption is much in evidence today. It is quite possible that a majority of individuals retain as their principal goal the amassing of wealth and the products it will buy. There is a trend, however, toward wanting to get along with others rather than trying to impress them—a development which Riesman refers to as an "other-directed society."[4] According to Riesman, "The other-directed person . . . is kept within his consumption limits not by goal-directed but by other-directed guidance, kept from splurging too much by others' envy and from consuming too little by his own envy of others."[5] For the other-directed individual, for example, the large ornamental house has given way to the comfortable home which is unique, but which evidences no display of vanity. This change has developed as a result of the disappearance of the anxiety which attended scarcity. For a generation that has not been haunted by the spectre of famine or poverty, there is less urge to demonstrate an undue accumulation of wealth—to be a pleasant and an agreeable companion seems more appealing.

Another current trend is the movement toward greater consumer autonomy—that is, greater initiative and independence on the part of the consumer. Developments among consumers themselves are favorable to greater consumer autonomy. Consumers today are more affluent and, thus, have more money with which to experiment. They can afford items which have individual characteristics and which are not a part of the mass market. Many consumers also have more leisure time with which to cultivate individual tastes and personal consumption characteristics. The consumer's tendency to show more independence in pleasing his own personal tastes is in harmony with the objectives of the President's Consumer Advisory Council. Business firms will have more to gain from cooperating with the trend toward greater consumer autonomy than they will by resisting it. Cooperating with the trend means that the business firm will have to develop a closer selling and market-research relationship with the consumer. In addition, improved feedback must be developed by means such as the establishment of consumer panels that take an active part in the selection of the development of new products. The larger market shares will

---

[4] *Ibid.*, p. 21.
[5] *Ibid.*, p. 79.

go to firms that develop the largest percentage of new and improved products, and those firms that have a closer liaison with customers would seem more likely to excel in this area. Many experts believe that this desire for creative expression on the part of customers will become the base for an added drive for new products by the modern corporation.

The problem of a people in transition presents a challenge to the marketing strategist. Current trends would seem to indicate that the marketing manager must increasingly give attention to specific market segments, far as is pointed out by Ernest Dichter:

> One can safely predict that the mass market per se will die out, and it will become increasingly difficult to capture more than a small percentage of a particular market. Instead, it will become necessary for producers to develop merchandise which is keyed toward specific segments of the market! Therefore, displays of the future will be arranged not on the basis of technological classifications, but more along psychological lines. . . . Modern advertisers will do well to build into their messages an image of the functional, the beautiful, the individualistic, and aristocratic—to agree with the emotional climate of today's consumers—as long as the product gratifies the inner man. Present-day consumer tastes dramatically emphasize this theory.[6]

MARKETING STRATEGY AND THE CLASS SOCIETY

The intensity of competition and the growing diversity of products are encouraging the marketing manager to seek a more effectively planned strategy. A marketing plan that defines the geographic areas with their known population and estimated average incomes is most essential, but not adequate. It may always have appeared reasonable that purchases of products would not correspond in perfect proportion to income and age patterns. Yet, it has been only recently that marketing scholars and practitioners have developed a more satisfactory approach. Certainly, it is not yet possible to reach each person with an individually tailored marketing message. But research has been able to identify certain classes that have common characteristics in terms of the kinds of products and services they prefer, even though their incomes may differ.

The identification of these classes, then, adds an entirely new dimension to the marketing plan. Population, income, age, and other demographic data are important in forecasting volume and guiding promotional expenditures. The basic strategy of the marketing plan, however, is determined by qualities that will influence the subjective choice of individuals. What are their basic interests and goals? With whom do they associate? What kind of recreation do they prefer? Where do they build their homes? And what are their tastes in decorating? It has been found that these and other subjective characteristics tend to cluster. Such being the case, these clusters, or social classes supply a new basis for guiding marketing promotion plans.

---

[6] Ernest Dichter, "Discovering the 'Inner Jones'," *Harvard Business Review* (May-June, 1965), pp. 6-10, 157.

The Warnerian Social Classes

A *class* is defined as people who are more or less equal in prestige and community status; they regularly interact among themselves, both formally and informally. They form a class to the extent that they share the same goals and ways of looking at life.

The pioneer in identifying social classes, whose descriptions are still the basis for the social-class concept, was W. Lloyd Warner. Warner studied social patterns in a group of comparable cities and made generalizations. The concepts relevant to marketing became obvious immediately, and other scholars have written extensively on the subject. To facilitate an understanding of the meaningfulness of these classes for marketing, a tabled description of this class system is given in Table 4-1.

The marketing manager, then, cannot hope to assume categorically that his line of products will always have an appeal to one of the social classes. He will have to research his hypotheses constantly and verify assumptions as to changes that are occurring within the social pattern.

Table 4-1

THE WARNERIAN CLASS SYSTEM

Class	Employment	Percent of Total	Education
1. Upper	professionals, executives, corporate owners	1 to 2%	ivy league, fashionable schools
2. Upper Middle	senior managers, professionals, independent businessmen	10%	state university
3. Lower Middle	white collar, governmental or corporate bureaucrats, small businessmen, "grey-collar" service technicians	33%	trade or technical degrees or junior college
4. Working Class	unionized blue collar workers	40%	high school
5. Lower Class	no steady job, skill, or trade	15%	less than high school

Source: Adapted in part from Richard P. Coleman and Bernice L. Neugarten, *Social Status in the City,* (San Francisco: Jossey-Bass, Inc., 1971), pp. 262-263.

Social Class as a Guide to Marketing Strategy [7]

The identification of products with each of the respective classes is not easily accomplished. At best the social class will furnish the marketer with a rough guide to assist him in his strategy. The following hypothetical examples, though, illustrate some of the differences that might occur because of different class affiliations.

Three families with annual incomes of $18,000 each may be classified into separate social classes. A family consisting of a young lawyer and his wife belongs to the upper-middle class. Their house is in a prestigious neighborhood, and their furniture was purchased from a high-class store. The second family, which is headed by a grocery store operator, is in the lower-middle class. Their home is nicer and they have more furniture than the upper-middle class family, but the neighborhood in which they are located and the store from which the furniture was purchased are not as prestigious. The second family's clothes are more expensive, and they have much more money in a savings account. The third family earning $18,000 a year is headed by a cross-country truck driver and is an upper-lower class family. Their house is less ornate and the neighborhood is not as high class as either of the first two families. However, the family has a larger, later model car; more expensive appliances; and a bigger TV set. This third family spends less on clothing and furniture and more on food. The man of the house spends more on hunting, bowling, and tickets for athletic contests. Although the above examples are brief, they indicate consumption patterns which provide clues as to other goods and services which would attract each of the three families.

The group whose income is lower than the average of its class is considered the underprivileged group. For the $18,000 a year lawyer to maintain an environment in the upper-middle class means, for example, that he will have to do some scrimping on items that do not, to him at least, seem as important as others. On the other hand, the $18,000 a year truck driver does not find it difficult to maintain his status level and still have money left over to splurge on certain items; and he is considered to belong to an overprivileged group that has an income above the average of its class. This income distribution within classes creates market situations between classes. A case in point is the automobile market. The $18,000 a year lawyer in the upper-middle or lower-upper class furnishes his home with the appropriate furniture, but he buys a compact car or an economical foreign car. To him the car is not a status symbol. On the other hand, the overprivileged in the lower-middle and upper-lower classes are the main support for the big car market. They buy the Pontiacs, Buicks, Oldsmobiles, Chryslers, and even Cadillacs. The upper-upper class does not consider an automobile to be a class symbol. Even the overprivileged individual in the upper-middle class would normally invest

---

[7] The late Pierre Martineau has done much to popularize the social class theory. One of his most popular contributions is "Social Class and Spending Behavior," *Journal of Marketing,* Vol. 23, No. 2 (October, 1958), pp. 121-130.

his funds in travel or something which he feels would give him more cultural refinement. Individuals in the upper-lower class, however, are still interested in "things," and to them the big car has status meanings.

In meeting competition an effective marketing manager will be aware of the interests of prevailing classes or groups within classes and will direct his strategy accordingly. The published studies on class structure have popularized a vocabulary of terms and have defined class status as of a certain time. It should not be presumed, however, that the classes as Warner described them can be used as permanent guides. Marketing institutes, universities, and business firms must continue research activities which can serve as guides in the development of marketing strategies.

INFLUENCE GROUPS IN MARKETING

The social class concept deals with external factors, such as residential location and occupation. These factors are guides which are helpful in devising a market strategy, but they do not reflect interpersonal relationships. Information with respect to interpersonal relationships supplies an added dimension which aids in achieving a successful marketing plan. Individuals in the process of interacting with others acquire ideas and information, and the interactions which an individual has with other individuals in the groups with which he identifies himself influence his marketplace choices.

The Reference Group [8]

The *reference group* consists of several people who have a fairly well-established system of interpersonal communications. The interactions among individuals may be formal, such as may exist in a Rotary Club or a ladies' literary club; or they may be informal, as in the case of a car pool which is used by the same people with sufficient frequency that informal interpersonal relationships are developed.[9] It is not necessary, though, that all who are influenced by a group be members or even have face-to-face contact with individuals in the group. For example, the American Marketing Association is a group that influences the thinking of many who are not members and who do not attend the meetings.

With respect to their influence on the choices made by buyers, reference groups can be classified into two types. The first most important group for marketing purposes is a group to which an individual belongs. Such a group serves as a point of reference for the marketplace decisions of the individual—he observes other people in the group to establish his norms, and these norms become the guide to his purchasing activity. The second type of

---

[8] Gerald Zaltman provides a comprehensive analysis of group influence in marketing in *Marketing: Contributions from the Behavioral Sciences* (New York: Harcourt, Brace & World, Inc., 1965), pp. 75-102.

[9] Tamotsu Shibutani provides a very thorough examination of the reference group as a means of communication in "Reference Groups as Perspectives," *American Journal of Sociology* (May, 1955), pp. 562-569.

reference group is a group to which the individual would like to belong; thus, he tends to imitate the tastes of the group even though he is not a member.

Most groups would fit into one of these two categories. Note, however, that the classification into which these groups fall is determined by the attitudes and status of the individual in question. Thus, a reference group such as high school seniors would, depending on the individual involved, be a group which would represent each of the two types of groups discussed above. As a member of the group, a senior's marketplace choices are influenced by other members of the group. To advance their status, many juniors and some sophomores would like to associate with seniors, and their purchases are influenced by their efforts to play the role of seniors.

Role, Status, and Norms

The choice that an individual makes is determined by what his goals are. He may wish to establish himself more securely in his present role, or he may aspire to a higher role. *Role* consists of the expectations other group members have regarding the behavior of a person within the group. If the individual wishes to alter his role in a group, he will have to change his behavior sufficiently to influence the manner in which he is viewed by other members of the group. For example, the aspiring member may wish to command more respect from his associates and, hence, have more influence with them. He will then attempt to change his role to achieve more status. His role as related to other members of his group, or the deference in which he is held by other group members, is termed *status*.

The attempts to change roles and status provide the group with a dynamic quality. New attitudes are spawned that are within the range of the group's tolerable behavior—which is determined by the group norms. A *norm* is a group standard of behavior to which members are expected to conform. Norms are expressed as concepts or generalizations. Formal groups have explicit rules which may describe their norms. Informal groups have implicit rules which distinguish them from other groups. Whether the group is formal or informal, it has an informal organization based on role and status. An election of officers by the formal group may affect the informal role of a member and also his status. The relationships between the individual, his role, the individual's status, and group norms are depicted in Exhibit 4-1.

The Flow of Influence Within a Group

The greater number of reference groups are informal. The organization within such groups is an influence pattern, with each person enjoying a status and a role determined by group interaction. These individual interrelationships within the group are seldom formalized or discussed within the group in any explicit manner. Nonetheless, they exist and are as clearly set forth as though they were described in formal bylaws and rules. Students of the subject have found certain similarities in groups with respect to leadership, procedures, and channels of communication.

Exhibit 4-1

RELATIONSHIPS OF THE INDIVIDUAL

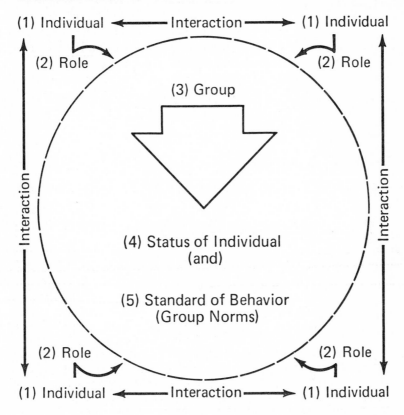

The *gatekeeper* of a group keeps the communication channels open. For example, the gatekeeper sets the agenda for discussions, opens doors to new ideas, and controls the flow of discussions. *Opinion leaders* are people who, in a given situation, are able to exert personal influence on a group because they are generally more courageous and innovative than others in the group. If a seller knows who the gatekeepers and opinion leaders of groups are and how to make efficient use of their strategic positions, he may be able to reduce the cost of a promotion program and to speed up the process of securing acceptance for his products.

INNOVATION

Innovation, as it is viewed in marketing, relates to changes in the product offering. The products may be completely new or they may be used to replace others already in use. The change may range from a slight alteration in a product that enjoys a steady market to a product idea that must create an entirely new demand. A Chevrolet, for example, is always a Chevrolet. Yet, each year some innovations make it in many aspects a different product. Even the brands of laundry detergent, which do not stimulate enough interest to be a topic for reference-group discussion, undergo slight changes from year to year. "In drug and grocery channels alone, there are now some 6000 new products a year—more than twice the figure of 10 years ago."[10]

For the three major types of companies, the median failure rates for new products were:

- Industrial product manufacturers—20%
- Consumer product manufacturers—40%
- Service industries—15 to 20%[11]

The stream of new products and product changes is constant, and it is as necessary for the firm to gain consumer acceptance of a product change as it is to develop the product itself. Innovation, as a part of the marketing process, includes gaining consumer acceptance for product change or addition, and this is the aspect of innovation that is emphasized in this chapter.

Innovation as a Learning Process

When a buyer of Brand A switches to Brand B, what actually takes place? Or, what happens when the buyer discards the old product for the new? What powers do the advertiser and the salesman have in influencing this process? If the marketing manager has some concept of exactly what is taking place, his strategy can be more effective. Research in the behavioral sciences indicates that in making a decision to purchase a product, the buyer participates in a learning process.

In the process of making a buying decision, an individual takes some action which adds to his total experience. His motive for making the decision was the result in part of some external stimuli. John A. Howard defines learning as a "systematic change in behavior."[12] In this context the buyer becomes aware of the product, learns to like it, and accepts, to some degree, the habit of using it. In the process of learning, the buyer's mind moves through a series of stages. Each product, because of its unique characteristic, has a different pattern for gaining acceptance and continued use. However, there is a sequence of stages through which all products pass to gain adoption, and considerable insight can be gained from an understanding of these stages.

---

[10] "New Products: The Push is on Marketing," *Business Week*, No. 2218 (March 4, 1972), pp. 72-77.

[11] David S. Hopkins and Earl L. Bailey, "New Product Pressures," *The Conference Board Record*, Vol. VII, No. 6 (June, 1971), p. 20.

[12] John A. Howard, *Marketing Management: Analysis and Planning* (Homewood, Illinois: Richard D. Irwin, Inc., 1963), p. 35.

Stages in the Innovative Process

A successful innovation is represented by an adoption, which is a more permanent commitment than a one-time purchase of a product. There may be several buying experiences before an adoption is accomplished. For the purpose of this discussion, an *adoption* is the process whereby the individual comes to accept an item as the best choice available at the time. Should all circumstances remain equal, when the same need or choice occurs again, the same item will be purchased.

The most widely accepted classification of the stages in the innovative process, and the one used below, appears in *Communication of Innovations* by Everett M. Rogers and F. Floyd Shoemaker.[13]

The *knowledge function* begins when the individual is exposed to the innovation's existence and gains some knowledge of how it functions. When one's "wants" outruns one's "gets," a state of frustration exists. Being affected by social system norms (social and personality characteristics), one can generally be classified as either an early or late knower of an innovation. Most of the time the early knowers possess the same attributes as the actual innovators or purchasers of products.

In the *persuasion function* the potential consumer learns of the relative advantages of the product; its compatibility with his norms, attitudes, and values; and the complexity of the product. He might try the product for a brief period. Throughout this stage he is seeking information from specific sources, interpreting these messages, and developing his own attitude about change in general and about the specific product. The development of a favorable attitude does not always lead to adoption of the product. Many times *innovation dissonance* can develop, which is a conflict between a favorable attitude toward a product and reluctance to adopt the product. However, in most cases a favorable attitude toward a product leads to purchase.

In the *decision function* the consumer actually makes the choice between adoption and rejection. Small-scale trial can be an important influence to adopt when the product has any degree of relative advantage for the consumer. Rejection can come either at this stage or after a decision to adopt (then it is called discontinuance).

Dissonance can occur during the *confirmation function.* When an individual finds his knowledge out of balance or in disequilibrium with his actions, he seeks to remedy the imbalance. Awareness of a new idea, new information about a problem, or the knowledge of a felt need may cause this unrest. The information function of a marketing program must assume this additional responsibility for providing supporting messages about the product to the consumers who have adopted it to avoid discontinuance of use of the product.

---

[13] Everett M. Rogers and F. Floyd Shoemaker, *Communication of Innovations* (New York: The Free Press, 1971), p. 102.

The buying process varies with different products. The marketing manager, therefore, would do well to analyze his product innovation status with answers to questions such as:

(1) What proportion of potential consumers occupy each stage?
(2) How can the potential consumers be moved from the knowledge stage to the confirmation stage?
(3) What are the costs for moving the potential consumers through the stages?
(4) How long will it take to move potential consumers from one stage to another?

CLASSES OF INNOVATING CUSTOMERS

Some prospective customers require a greater length of time than others to pass through the learning stages which precede innovation. Research by behavioral scientists conducted over a number of years has discovered these differences and has described some of the characteristics of each group. Advertisers and sales managers would find it desirable to know how to distinguish among these groups. They then would be able to design a promotion program that would reach the members of each group with a message appropriate to their attitude toward innovation. The lines which divide these groups are not sharp; the groups shade into each other. The following descriptions identify the major characteristics of each group, as shown in Exhibit 4-2.

The *innovators* are venturesome. They compose approximately 2.5 percent of total adopters. The communications channels are often wide open among this venturesome, rash, and daring group.

The *early adopters*, who comprise 13.5 percent of the adopters, like being asked for information and advice about an innovation. They are many times typed as the model of their social system, highly respected by their peers. They seek above all to maintain this esteem to retain their social status.

The *early majority*, who make up 34 percent of the adopters, are seldom the first or the last to adopt a product. Being deliberate and cautious (important keys in the adoption process), the early majority interact frequently with peers and seldom occupy leadership positions in formal or informal groups.

The skeptical *late majority*, who also comprise 34 percent of the adopters, are cautious in all of their decisions. It should be noted that this group seldom moves before the tide of social pressure (norms) has swung toward the product.

Exhibit 4-2

PERCENT OF CONSUMERS IN EACH ADOPTER CATEGORIZATION ON THE BASIS OF INNOVATIVENESS

Innovators	Early Adopters	Early Majority	Late Majority	Laggards
2.5	13.5	34	34	16

The traditional *laggards* are 16 percent of the adopters. These people seldom exercise opinion leadership, are conversative to the point of being isolates, hold points of reference in the past, and adopt products many times when they are already obsolete. They are suspicious of innovations and fear knowledge of the future.

The firm should analyze its promotional efforts around a segmenting model which describes the role their potential consumers play. Knowing the socioeconomic, personality, and communication behavioral traits of consumers helps the firm to gain valuable insights into the character of the buyers of their products. Such guides enable the marketing manager to reach the right person, at the opportune time, with the most persuasive message possible.

PRODUCT CHARACTERISTICS AND INNOVATION

Resistance to the adoption of new or improved products can be greatly reduced by the recognition of some basic research findings dealing with product characteristics. Not only do these findings influence the product itself, but also they provide guides for advertising and selling the product to its appropriate market. Five of the most fundamental of these product concepts are discussed below.[14]

Advantages

Basic to the successful introduction of a new product are two factors: (1) that the product has a quality which will make it desirable to the buyer, and (2) that this quality is clearly perceived. In the case of industrial goods, the advantages may consist of the means of increasing sales or decreasing costs in the interest of profitability. In the case of consumer goods, the advantages may be satisfaction that relates to stimulating experiences, to convenience, to pleasantness of application, or to other qualities. Whether it is a completely new innovation, such as the Polaroid Land Camera, or a product improvement, such as a higher-speed film, the advantages must be made objectively clear in communications with the customer. In getting the product accepted, the effectiveness with which the advantages are communicated is as important as the advantages themselves.

Compatibility

Consumers are not disposed to venture too far from their conventional practices. A product or an idea that has little compatibility with some already established behavior pattern will not be as readily adopted as a product that is relatively familiar. Such compatibility insures a degree of emotional security for the prospective adopter. While the new qualities of a product may stimulate desire, the purchase must be built upon patterns, practices, and preferences that already exist. Too sharp and too wide a break from past practices is

---

[14] Everett M. Rogers lists and provides brief backgrounds for eight experiments in *Diffusion of Innovations* (New York: The Free Press, 1963), pp. 127-129.

avoided by consumers.[15] Compatibility with the past, therefore, reduces customer resistance.

Complexity

An innovation must represent a change or it will not appeal to the customer. On the other hand, if the change is too great, the risk involved will discourage the customer. There must be sufficient difference to reach and exceed the *differential threshold*. "The differential threshold refers to the minimum difference that can be perceived between two stimuli."[16] When an item departs from this threshold to a point of great complexity, resistances prevent adoption, and devising means for reducing the resistance is a critical problem for the marketing manager. Often, though, such products offer new and exciting experiences which can become the basis for effective sales approaches which decrease resistance and create desire.

Divisibility

When a product has the quality of *divisibility*, it is possible for a customer to purchase the product in small increments. Some advantages accrue to the seller if he makes it possible for the customer to buy without making an excessive monetary commitment. This quality is especially desirable to innovating buyers and early adopters who take the risk of purchasing the untried and stand to lose if their purchases prove disappointing.

Communicability

Certainly one of the most important characteristics of a product which influences its acceptability is the degree to which its qualities can be communicated to customers. The attempt to market a new weed-killer spray is illustrative of a product with qualities which are difficult to communicate to customers. The spray was to be applied to the soil before the weeds came up. Since it was not possible to demonstrate the product by showing dead weeds as evidence of what the product would do, the rate of adoption was very slow. Obviously, if visible evidence of satisfaction can be related to the product, the process of product acceptance can be hastened.

To summarize, each one of these five product qualities relates directly to the point at which the customer may feel some resistance to positive choice. If their meaning is properly understood and their market implications are integrated with the appropriate strategy, resistance to the innovation of new or improved products can be reduced greatly.

---

[15] Raymond A. Bauer indicates that some of these buying experiences can be traumatic in "Consumer Behavior as Risk Taking," *Proceedings of the 43rd National Conference of the American Marketing Association*, edited by Robert S. Hancock (June 15-16, 1960).

[16] Gerald Zaltman, *Marketing: Contributions from the Behavioral Sciences* (New York: Harcourt, Brace, & World, Inc., 1965), p. 140.

QUESTIONS AND ANALYTICAL PROBLEMS

1. Distinguish between the consumer economy and the consumption economy.
2. What are the consumers' responsibilities if competition is to be an effective means of serving their best interests?
3. What are the principal elements of a culture that influence choices of consumers?
4. Define "consumer autonomy." If such consumer influence has developed or is developing, what does this mean for alert marketing managers?
5. (a) Find examples, outside your text, of the influence of social class on market behavior. (b) Find examples that seem to contradict the idea that social class influences consumer behavior.
6. Define and explain the relationship to marketing strategy of the following: (a) reference group, (b) norm, (c) opinion leader.
7. Define innovation.
8. Name and explain the stages of the innovative process.
9. What should a marketing manager know about the innovative stages for one of his products?
10. What classification can we make of customers according to their readiness to accept innovations?

Case 4-1 • DRAIN-EASE MANUFACTURING COMPANY

The high cost of plumbers' services and drain chemicals caused Mr. Horace Palmer, a retired businessman, to attempt the development of a method to clean out drains and fixtures which would save many dollars a year for the average homeowner. After experimenting with numerous devices and chemicals, he developed a product which used a device to apply a special chemical and did the job very satisfactorily, utilizing the water pressure readily at hand in all sinks, tubs, and drains. After improving his product, he manufactured 2,300 of them in his garage and sold some 850 to various stores in his area for $1.50 apiece. The remainder of the lot he sold door-to-door for $2.50 each. He patented his invention under the name "Drain-Ease."

Shortly thereafter Mr. Palmer presented his product to a friend who operated a successful restaurant. The friend, Mr. Charles Hall, was so enthusiastic about the way in which Mr. Palmer's invention filled a need for his enterprise that he offered to join forces with Palmer to develop it. After they incorporated, the men set aside $12,000 for development and began considering ways of entering the market. If they produced the item themselves in Palmer's garage, the cost per unit would be around 55¢, including overhead. A St. Louis firm offered to produce the item and deliver it to a warehouse in the same city for 41¢ in minimum lots of 1,000. Distribution by consignment to wholesalers in the local area had not stimulated sales; therefore, such dealers were reluctant to stock the item on a normal purchase basis. After considerable discussion of alternatives, the two men decided to come to you for advice regarding how the product should be priced and what kind of distribution system could successfully convey the message of the product's merit to consumers.

• How would the above item be regarded by reference groups? How could knowledge of the product best reach the customers most likely to buy? What procedures should this company follow in getting the product accepted?

Case 4-2 • THE GLADSTONE GLASS CORPORATION

Gladstone Glass Corporation produces several products made of glass fibres, including thermal insulation for buildings, yarns, cords, "wool" products, porous glass sheets, etc. One of the products manufactured by the company from Gladstone "wool" is acoustical tile. The "wool" is pressed into panels and cut into blocks 12 inches square and ⅝ of an inch thick. These blocks are then painted in a variety of colors by a special process. Acoustical tile has excellent qualities for sound control and will not burn, thereby creating a large potential market for its use for ceilings in all types of buildings.

The Gladstone Glass Corporation was considering the modification of its acoustical tile because of disappointing sales results. Even though tests showed conclusively that Gladstone's tile was superior to similar products of competitors, sales were so unsatisfactory that a market investigation was undertaken to determine the reason. During the investigation consumers expressed the opinion that unless holes were punched into each block of acoustical tile, it would not be effective in quieting sound; they also preferred a white tile. Fifteen years of advertising by other manufacturers who used inferior materials had conditioned consumers to be reluctant in purchasing Gladstone's new product. The company experimented with punching the same number of holes (884) in each piece of tile as did its competitors and found that the holes decreased considerably the acoustical effectiveness of the tile.

• What procedure should the company follow in getting its product accepted? To which buyer behavior theory can the company refer?

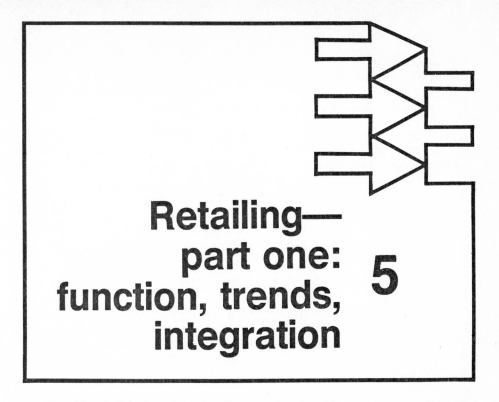

Retailing— part one: function, trends, integration

5

Retailing is "the last three feet" separating the ultimate consumer from the producer. Whether "the last three feet" is the distance between the salesclerk and the customer or the space separating the customer from the self-service display, it is the strategic segment of the marketing flow. In order to move the goods at this vital point, the retailer endeavors to provide an environment that encourages people to buy. It is at the retail level that the marketing system presents a glamorous front for the consumer. Colorful windows, plush carpets, soft music, expensively decorated displays, rest lounges, and artistically packaged merchandise are provided in order to enhance the customer's pleasure in buying. This is the portion of the marketing system with which consumers are well acquainted. It is the retailer who directly courts our favor at the scene of the purchase. To the general public, the retailer *is* the marketing system.

CONTRIBUTIONS OF THE RETAILER

In one form or another, the retailer is the manufacturer's representative to the public. The manufacturer entrusts the retailer with the responsibility of seeing his product across the strategic three feet. The manufacturer can obtain the support of the retailer in one or a combination of methods: he can pull customers into the store by national advertising; he can offer the retailer substantial margins; he can advertise and sell directly to the retailer; or he can cultivate his friendship and goodwill. Unless the manufacturer enjoys unusual public favor, in no case can he ignore the retailer, for the goodwill of the retailer and his salesmen is essential to providing an environment conducive to the final sale of the product.

Functions Performed by the Retailer

In concentrating and dispersing goods the retailer performs most of the market functions. By bringing goods to a point where they are readily available to the public, placing them in an attractive display, advertising their satisfaction-giving qualities, and virtually creating a demand for them, the retailer performs the significant function of selling. The demands of the public are anticipated by the retailer in his purchasing. He often has been described as the purchasing agent for the public. He preselects the goods that are made available to the public, and in so doing, he performs the buying function.

The retailer also performs the storage function. We often underestimate the importance of this contribution. Usually retail stores are located in the high-rent districts where space is at a premium and where the stores must be attractively furnished; yet the average department store must be spacious enough to store at one time one fourth of the store's annual sales.

Finance is another important service or function that retailers perform. A department store with sales of $20 million a year that does 60 percent credit business will have credit sales of $12 million. If the average outstanding account is 60 days old, the financing of this function will require $2 million, in addition to the approximately $3 million that is necessary for the purchase of the inventory itself. Many stores now pass part of this financing function to specialists by accepting various credit cards. The retailer also is charged with the task of taking risks in price and style changes. He must keep his market information current. In many instances the retail store provides transportation by the delivery of the merchandise and arranges for its shipment to his place of business. In some instances the retailer even undertakes the function of standardization and grading, such as when eggs or fruits and vegetables are purchased in an ungraded form directly from the farm or from a roadside market.

Significance of Retailing in Our Economy

The relative significance that retail stores play in the American's way of life is revealed by the method by which he spends his income. Since 1929, the earliest year for which we have adequate records, over half of the personal income of the American consumer has been spent for goods at retail—in 1971 retail sales were 51.2% of total personal income (retail sales = $408.9 billion). In that year, retail sales volume employed 11,395,000 persons, which is approximately 15 percent of employed civilians.

GROWTH PATTERNS OF RETAIL TRADING CENTERS

A trading center is in large part made up of a cluster of retail stores in an urban area in order to make it convenient for consumers to shop. Consequently, urban development usually has been guided by convenience and the desires of the people rather than according to a preconceived plan. The clustering tendency evident in the locating of stores has resulted because consumers wished to do their shopping from store to store without traveling over a long distance.

For the convenience of the customers, retail institutions tended to choose locations at natural transportation terminals, at crossroads, or at harbors. They located, also, where other shops had created shopping areas and had already attracted prospects. As a result, New York, Philadelphia, Boston, San Francisco, Los Angeles, and Seattle were established at harbor points; Chicago located on traffic routes convenient to both land and lakes; and St. Louis and Cincinnati were founded on important rivers. In the proximity of productive industrial, agricultural, or mining areas, such cities as Des Moines, Omaha, Denver, and Butte developed.

People must find a means of livelihood, and where resources are abundant, cities are most populous. Primary resources, such as industry, agriculture, and trade routes, have a cumulative effect on populations because those engaged in services and retailing must also buy from retail stores. The demand for goods by retailers, in addition to that by workers in the primary industries, creates opportunities for even more tradesmen, and thus we have a city.

The Spreading-Out Process

After trading centers develop at a central point, they grow up and out. The best example of this development is Manhattan. Space on the island, where trading opportunities were convenient, grew more expensive as the traffic increased in its intensity. This development made it desirable to build upward, and the skyscrapers of today are the result. Since such building was more expensive, the expansion moved farther up the island. Because building space was at a premium under such conditions, residences were much too expensive, except for the favored few. Apartment and tenement houses became the rule. Living in such quarters was often crowded and undesirable. Many people, therefore, left Manhattan and moved to Connecticut, New Jersey, and Long Island, and we have the genesis of the suburban movement.

Such a pattern of development is common to practically all metropolitan areas, although most other cities have had more space and have not built structures so high as Manhattan. Significant from the standpoint of the student of retailing is the fact that convenience-goods retail establishments tended to follow the people closely. Consequently, we have a repetition of the process that gave rise to the city in the first place—a group of people find it desirable to move out of the city, and they are sufficiently numerous to justify the opening of a food store, a drugstore, a service station, and possibly some specialty stores.

As such a movement progresses, the stores grow larger and more numerous until there develops another small city, and farther out another similar development may be spawned. In many instances these developments become trading centers in their own right. Observe Long Beach, Hollywood, and Pasadena, which surround Los Angeles. In such instances a completed pattern develops, consisting of a main shopping center of large department stores, high-volume specialty stores, and small stores. From these centers still more "clusters" of retail stores develop. Farther out, where the population becomes less congested, the retail store clusters become smaller and are more dominantly of the convenience type.

Shopping Centers. Shopping centers appeared in significant numbers in the early 1950's. A *shopping center* is a group of stores contiguously located and developed under a single master plan. Its success is based on convenience and the provision of a sort of county fair or circus atmosphere. The shopping center is the result of a promotion which has as its objective, the housing of a variety of retail stores together. It usually includes at least one, and usually two or more, large and prestigious department stores. These institutions are described as power units since they have the power to attract the customer by their established prestige, broad lines of merchandise, and effective advertising programs. Smaller specialty lines, financial institutions, and service units are located strategically on lines of traffic between the power units and along the egress and ingress routes. Thus, within the shopping center itself, there is nearly every good or service that one would find in the city.

The latest innovation in shopping centers is the covered mall. Typically this is a closed-in structure with a complementary and competitive cluster of stores. The stores are arranged according to the master plan of a skilled architect. The entire area is completely air-conditioned, both in the stores and in the spacious mall area, where customers can stroll in a pleasant and leisurely manner from store to store. In some cases this area is decorated with fountains and art work. This covered mall type of retail structure began to appear in America in the late fifties and early sixties. It has reached such popularity that some of the expanding department organizations indicate that they will build no new branches except as a part of a covered mall structure.

Downtown vs. Suburbia. During the period of rapid suburban growth from 1930 to 1960, the population living in outlying areas increased from 17 to 55 million—an increase of over three times. During this period the cities themselves increased in population from 37 to 58 million, or less than double. Retail trade followed the population from inside the cities out to the suburbs. In the decade 1960-1970 the central city population fairly well stabilized, but incomes increased somewhat more in the suburbs. Hence, downtown business districts throughout the country continued to lose retail trade relative to sales in the suburbs. The most recently published data shows that the 129 major metropolitan markets' central city business districts had a 4 percent increase in retail sales in the Census of Retail Trade for the period 1963-67. In the same period retail trade in suburbs of those metropolitan markets gained 34 percent. That 4 percent gain, small though it was, marked a reversal of declines for central city retailing that began in the 1940's.

Reaction of the Central Cities

In most instances the movement of the population to the suburbs is only one of the causes of lost business by the downtown stores. Many of the older and established downtown merchants often do not encourage business with up-to-date merchandising methods. Some of them have assumed that they could hold volume without adapting to the many innovations and overtures to the customer made by the progressive retailers in the newer shopping centers.

In some instances downtown rehabilitation consists of a shopping mall in the heart of the city, thus applying the same ideas that have proved so successful in the outlying shopping centers. Presently in Los Angeles, Chicago, Salt Lake City, and a few other cities, multimillion dollar "centers" constructed to house specialty shops, theatres, restaurants, and usually one dominant department store are being built. (Visitors to Berlin have seen such a center called Europa Center.) These centers incorporate the best features of excellent shopping centers.

The slight nationwide increase in retail business of downtown areas has resulted from quite large increases in a few cities. Among them were Buffalo, New York, which enjoyed a 13 percent increase in retail sales in its central business district; New Haven, Connecticut, 32 percent gain; and Washington D.C., 14 percent. In each case there was some significant action taken, such as improvement of public transportation, traffic-free malls, remodeling, or changes in merchandise offerings.

Much of the retail gain in central business districts is resulting from changes involving shifts to specialty shops geared to pedestrians, public transit riders, and those persons who can shop during lunch breaks or in the evening when they visit downtown for cultural and entertainment events.

There may be, however, a return of regular shoppers to downtown. Increasing awareness of costly land, costly and finite limits on energy, smaller families, and desirability of fashionable and convenient in-town living will probably accentuate such developments. Edmund Faltermeyer, an editor of *Fortune*, reporting on a study tour by American real-estate developers, city planners, and architects of Paris, Stuttgart, and Munich, emphasizes the livability and pleasure that can be enjoyed by inhabitants of cities. When easy access by convenient, comfortable mass transportation is provided to superb shopping malls, such as that surrounding the neo-Gothic city hall on Munich's Marienplatz, shopping downtown gains favor.[1] The planned communities in the United States and elsewhere and the success of the best suburban shopping centers result from a recognition by alert retailers that many households "now want shopping to be part of an experience involving interesting crowds, food, and entertainment—not just buying and loading up the car."[2]

---

[1] Edmund Faltermeyer, "We're Building a New Kind of Togetherness," *Fortune* (October, 1973), p. 130, and "For a Glimpse of the Future, Look at the Old World," *Fortune* (October, 1973), p. 134.

[2] "Fortune's Wheel," *Fortune* (October, 1973), p. 2.

The preceding discussion provides an illustration of the forces which make marketing dynamic. Retail trade areas respond to consumer custom and convenience just as products do. Even the comparatively new shopping center is undergoing change. Those that are being built today, with their covered malls and convenience features, are as different from those originally constructed as the 1975 Chevrolet is from the 1950 model. There is only one thing that is certain about tomorrow's shopping areas—they will be more convenient and will offer the consumer a more pleasant and exciting shopping experience.

RETAIL INSTITUTIONS

Almost all retailing in the United States takes place at retail stores—that is, in fixed identifiable establishments, which in total, make 97.5 percent of all retail sales. Other forms of retailing are door-to-door sales (1 percent of total retail sales volume), vending machines (.5 percent), and mail order sales (1 percent).

One way to analyze retailing is to examine retail institutions according to the types of goods they handle. Hence, the U.S. Bureau of the Census prepares a *Monthly Trade Report* and publishes monthly data each year in the April issue of *Survey of Current Business*. From that information we can see retail sales by line of business, as in Exhibit 5-1. The largest change in the period shown was in general merchandise. The census of business includes department stores, most discount stores, and variety stores in that category. The larger discount operations were selling most items needed for housekeeping and recreation.

The census of business has begun to publish a "merchandise series line of reports" which makes it possible to trace distribution of several types of merchandise. As an illustration of the analysis possible, note the data in Table 5-1 on the product line: "major appliances, radio, TV, and musical instruments."

Figures do not total to 100 percent because only a few kinds of businesses were shown to illustrate the possibility of tracing sales of the merchandise lines in this particular report. Dollar sales volume is not shown because it is not necessary for this illustration. The figures in the third column are changes in dollar sales volume from 1963 to 1967 and are not percent changes in share of market, as in the first columns. The largest volume increase is by radio and TV stores (96.8 percent), and they also increased their share of the market (12.4 percent in 1963 to 16.4 percent in 1967).

The largest percent change from 1963 to 1967 was by drug stores (151.3 percent), but this brought them to only one percent share of the total market —of course, one percent of a $10 billion market (total sales for the line in 1967 was $10.1 billion) provides a desirable merchandising activity. By analysis of the merchandise series line, one may also determine what portion of sales volume of a particular kind of business is accounted for by a certain line of merchandise.

Exhibit 5-1
RETAIL SALES BY LINE OF BUSINESS
EACH LINE AS A PERCENT OF TOTAL RETAIL SALES
1963 AND 1973

		10	20	30	40	50
Food	1963	———————— 23.4%				
	1973	—————— 21.0				
Automotive	1963	—————— 18.6%				
	1973	——————— 20.0				
General	1963	———— 12.3%				
Merchandise	1973	————— 16.5				
Eating and	1963	—— 7.5%				
Drinking Places	1973	—— 7.5				
Service	1963	—— 7.3%				
Stations	1973	— 6.8				
Lumber,	1963	— 6.0%				
Building	1973	— 4.5				
Apparel	1963	— 5.7%				
	1973	— 4.8				
Furniture and	1963	— 4.5%				
Appliance	1973	— 4.8				
Drug and	1963	— 3.5%				
Proprietary	1973	— 3.1				

1963 data: U.S. Department of Commerce, Bureau of the Census, *Census of Business: 1963* (Retail Trade), Vol. 1.

1973 data: U.S. Bureau of Economic Analysis, *Survey of Current Business* (March, 1974), Table S-12.

Other ways to examine retailing are by size of retail establishments, by type of ownership (single unit or multi unit), by the kind and amount of integration (vertical and horizontal), and by type of operation (such as supermarket, discount store, department store). Keep in mind that these are not mutually exclusive categories.

Retailing by Size of Store

On the average retail establishments are growing larger while the number of establishments is growing smaller. In 1940 there were 1,770,000 retail stores

Table 5-1

MAJOR APPLIANCE, RADIO, TV, MUSICAL INSTRUMENTS SALES BY KIND OF BUSINESS HANDLING THE PRODUCTS

Kind of Business	Percent of Total Sales by Kind of Business (Share of Market)		Percent Change in Dollar Sales Volume 1963 to 1967
	1963	1967	
Household appliance stores	24.7	22.1	33.4
Radio and TV stores	12.4	16.4	96.8
Musical instrument stores and record shops	9.3	8.6	37.5
Department stores	22.5	26.0	72.6
Drug stores	0.6	1.0	151.3
Mail order houses	3.7	3.7	49.9

Source: Derived from *Census of Business: Retail Trade: 1967,* Vol. 1, p. xxx. *Merchandise Line Sales Reports* (Series BC67-MLS) are available for major merchandise line shifts, 1963-67. Similar reports are due soon for shifts 1967-71 (Series BC71-MLS).

and by 1970 the number declined to approximately 1,760,000. Remember that the U.S.A. population was 132 million in 1940 and almost 205 million in 1970. That means that for every 100 persons there were 1.3 stores in 1940 but only 0.8 in 1970.

There is no official data on store size by type of business. We can, however, infer from data about independent (single-unit) operations, compared with chain (multiunit) operations, something about lines of business that are dominated by small stores and by large chain operations. Exhibit 5-2 shows the portion of retail sales accomplished by single-unit stores and chain stores.

Competitive Position of Small Independents. Unquestionably, small retailers in the aggregate have suffered from large-scale competition. One should not draw a trend line based on the data in that table and predict the near-future demise of small-scale retailing, however. It is evident from census information that there has been very little change in the amount of total retail trade enjoyed by single-unit firms in the past 25 years. Not all single-unit firms are small, but most are. It is reasonable to infer that there are certain strengths of the smaller operations that account for their continued existence, just as there are certain advantages in some kinds of retailing for very large firms.

Since there is tremendous variation between capabilities of independent merchants, a quantitative study of small businesses to determine factors affecting successful operation would be almost meaningless. We can examine certain areas that aid our understanding of why small-scale retailers may succeed in some fields better than in others, however, and this helps us understand some trends in retailing. The discussion includes several areas of

Exhibit 5-2

SINGLE UNITS AND MULTIUNITS RETAIL TRADE PERCENT DISTRIBUTION OF SALES BY SIZE OF FIRM FOR SELECTED KINDS OF BUSINESS: 1973

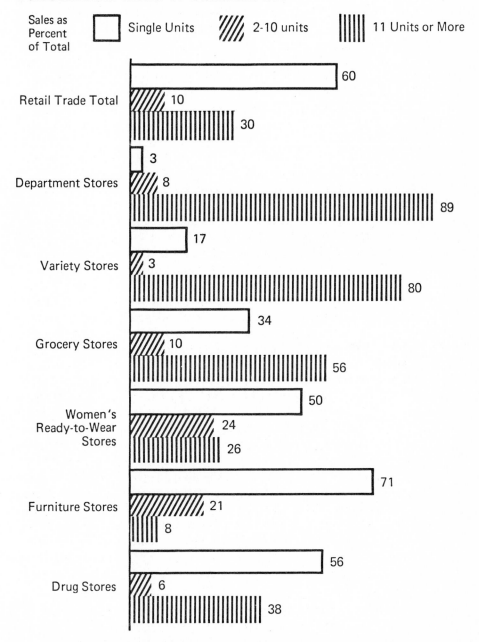

SOURCE: Derived and adjusted from the U.S. Department of Commerce, Bureau of the Census, *Census of Business,1967,* and *Current Business Reports: Monthly Retail Trade, January, 1974.*

store operations, namely, retail management, buying, operation expenses, promotional activities, and financing.

Retail Management. A one-store, small-sales-volume merchant cannot hire experts and specialists in management. He is of necessity his own merchandising manager, chief accountant, advertising and display manager, and chief policy-making officer. Consequently, many merchandise and sales promotion activities suffer in comparison to those of his large-scale competitors. Further, many small merchants are so engrossed in details that they have no time (even if they have the inclination) for basic management planning. Because of lack of merchandise budgets and other planning devices, they are often induced to overstock merchandise. Again, due to lack of planning, they often do not readily take markdowns to facilitate the disposal of slow-selling merchandise, with the far too common result that operating capital is tied up in unsalable inventory. Poor management is not, however, a necessary corollary to small-scale retailing.

If the independent merchant is somewhat lax in customer services and modern merchandising methods, there is no supervisory staff to improve his operations. On the other hand, he has flexibility and freedom of action precisely because he is not responsible to any higher management authority. If he is alert to customer needs and local conditions, he can take action immediately. Supervision, then, is necessary in large organizations to assure that all members of the organization conform to company policy. This is a cost that the small independent merchant can escape. Although large-scale research and expert advice are not so readily available to the independent as to the unit manager of a chain, for example, the alert small merchant finds an increasing number of sources of managerial aids available to him.

Trade organizations and federal government agencies provide information designed to assist nonspecialized operations. An excellent example of materials available through trade organizations includes those provided by the Independent Retail Hardware Association. IRHA, as it is commonly known, provides store layout help, merchandising aids, promotion kits, accounting advice, and other services that an independent hardware merchant might need. The United States Department of Commerce has available published materials of varying degrees of excellence on practically all management problems. The Small Business Administration has been formed to provide help structured specifically to small business of all kinds. Also, the National Council for Small Business Management Development can offer training programs of value to managers of small businesses. Very likely there will be a member of the council in the nearest university college of business and in large cities in the public school system.

Buying. The small merchant, generally, is at a comparative disadvantage in buying. He has a buying disadvantage when compared with department stores and chains since he seldom buys in quantities large enough or regularly enough to gain preferred treatment, which might include first choice of materials and favorable discounts and terms. Consequently, cost of goods sold will be relatively large in the small store. Whereas a department store or chain may have an initial markup of 42 to 45 percent on a man's suit, for example, the independent may well have an initial markup of only 30 to 35 percent. Yet the suit will carry the same retail price in both stores because of the higher cost to the independent.

Chain and department store buying advantages are not confined to discounts and favorable treatment due to large quantity purchases. They often have access to research organizations that help them buy according to their customer demands. While such stores often do not have so wide a variety of goods available to customers as do independent merchants in the same field, customers often believe that the chain store and the department store provide them a wider selection because their research facilities have helped them decide what the larger portion of their customers want. Also, many manufacturers give preferential treatment to well-known department stores because they want their goods to benefit from the prestige of those stores.

On the other hand, a well-managed small independent, even with a limited merchandise budget, can buy selectively for his customers. With careful records and knowledge of the market, a small merchant of fashion goods, for example, can build customer loyalty because of attention to individual demands that is seldom accorded by any large organization. As a matter of fact, the flexibility of the small merchant, contrasted with his larger competitors, can be one of his strongest weapons. Selective buying and highly personalized selections from the market have built solid places in the retail community for many smaller retailers.

Operating Expenses. At this time there has been no study that shows precisely how chain stores and independent stores compare in their operating expenses. Department stores, we know, tend to have relatively high operating expenses. Both chains and department stores effect much of their buying economy through performance of some of the wholesaling functions. Consequently, if we see only retail operating statements without evidence of how much transportation, storage, packaging, and other usual wholesale expenses are included, we do not have a valid comparison.

In general, it is safe to say that many small merchants survive because their out-of-pocket expenses are low. The owner-manager may not allocate any salaries, for example. He operates the store, his wife watches it while he eats lunch, his high school boy helps after school, and the entire household lives from whatever profit the store can make. Strict accounting might show not only a high cost of goods sold but also a relatively high operating expense if a reasonable salary is allotted to the small store proprieter and if overtime, car expense and depreciation (when a car is used for deliveries), and similar assessments are made for all operating costs.

Sales Promotion. In serving a small geographic area and a limited clientele, the little retailer could, for instance, not take full advantage of sales promotion devices. The small store cannot use newspaper advertising as effectively as can the retail establishments with a large trading area, since the neighborhood grocery store, for example, draws its customers from an area of only a few blocks. It is not economical for such a merchant to advertise in the newspaper or radio where he is charged for reaching all the potential customers in a large retailing area. Further, the small store is at a disadvantage in making innovations that may attract new customers. He can seldom experiment with new marketing methods. A large department store or a unit of a chain, on the other hand, may limit experiments to a small segment of its business; and if the new idea should prove ineffective, the entire company will not fail, since the bulk of its business goes on as formerly.

While it is true that the small establishments do not have full advantage from well-trained advertising and display personnel, they have a strong promotional device in their ability to establish pleasant personal relations with their customers. There are numerous examples of independents who have created a unique style or form of direct mail or handbill advertising that helps them establish loyal followings. A women's and misses' shop in California started direct-mail advertising on old wallpaper samples, since that was the only paper they could afford at the outset. Even after the business prospered, they continued the theme to keep a home-town, neighborly approach.

Financing. Department stores and chain organizations enjoy financial advantages over small stores. There are many individual exceptions, of course. Large retail enterprises receive more credit from manufacturers because they are large-quantity customers and also because they usually have financial resources adequate to their merchandise requirements. It is also easier for large-scale retailers to borrow from commercial banks or other lending institutions—often at more favorable interest rates than those required of small operators. They can more readily acquire the financial resources for credit selling. These advantages place them in a position to get better deals in buying, which in turn adds to their financial edge.

The growth and economic development of the nation favored larger establishments in certain respects. Better roads, easier transportation, and good postal and telephone systems minimized the advantage of convenient location enjoyed by such retailers as the cross-roads general stores and the neighborhood grocery stores.

Small Retailers Can Compete. An examination of the various business censuses since 1929 will reveal that multi-unit firms have not made any significant inroads into certain retailing lines but have become dominant in others.

Exhibit 5-3 is a list of selected lines of business in which single-unit firms account for over 75 percent of total annual sales volume. The dominance of single-unit operations can be explained by the brief analysis that follows. Further, identification of the areas of strength of smaller firms should suggest that effort be applied in those areas to provide competitive advantage to the single-unit firm.

In earlier paragraphs it was pointed out that personalized services are a strong, competitive weapon for small stores. Does this hold true for all small

Exhibit 5-3

KINDS OF BUSINESS DOMINATED BY SINGLE-UNIT FIRMS

Passenger Car Dealers Drinking Places Florists Gift, Novelty, Souvenir Stores	Single-unit firms account for 90-97 percent of total annual retail sales.
Sporting Goods Gasoline Service Stations Meat and Seafood Markets Camera, Photographic Supply Stores Eating Places Book, Stationery Stores Hardware Stores	Single-unit firms account for 75-89 percent of total annual retail sales.

stores? Consider those stores in which the selection of merchandise to fit particular tastes or requirements cannot be made in a routine manner. For example, slightly over 80 percent of hardware store sales are made by single-unit firms; whereas, over 80 percent of variety store sales are made by multi-unit firms. Much of the merchandise handled by variety stores is hardware. Can we postulate, then, that the particular reason for the strength of single-unit operations in hardware lines is the need for personalized services in much hardware purchasing? If the reader will observe purchases of hardware items in variety stores, and also in hardware stores, he will notice that a high proportion of the transactions in hardware stores involves consultation—i.e., the customer goes in with a problem and depends on the store people to help solve it.[3] In variety store transactions, frequently not one word is exchanged.

It has been suggested that the central reason for the growth of chain stores in a certain field is that decision making can be routinized.[4] When the decisions of what to buy, of promotion and display, and of credit and pricing can be made routine, centralized management of several outlets is feasible. Holton suggests that mass distribution can be a means of reducing the cost of decision making per dollar of sales.[5] This thought can be extended to postulate that for certain kinds of businesses there will generally be a high cost of decision making per dollar of sales volume. Personalized service is necessary because the transactions cannot be made routine. Hence, in order to assess the probable strength of independent, single-unit firms in a given line or with a given group of customers, one could consider the extent to which all of the transactions can be made routine.

---

[3] Until recently the hardware store held a place of prominence among retail institutions, but it is gradually losing its position. Clarence E. Vincent examines some relevant statistical data in an attempt to explain this situation in "The Retail Hardware Decline," *Journal of Marketing*, Vol. 28 (January, 1964), pp. 26-29.

[4] Richard H. Holton, "Dynamic Marketing for a Changing World," *Proceedings of the 43rd National Conference of the American Marketing Association*, edited by Robert S. Hancock (June, 1960).

[5] *Ibid.*

In Exhibit 5-2 note that even in the fields dominated by multi-unit firms, there still exist sizeable sales volumes enjoyed by single-unit firms. There will always be a portion of the market that demands, or at least desires, personalized service. Further, there exist sizeable numbers of customers who do not respond to price or even to nonprice competition in a way that the majority does. For a number of customers for any kind of merchandise, personal service at the point of sale is critical, and the price elasticity of demand is small. Where there are sufficient numbers of these people, an independent small store can thrive. This group of customers becomes larger as personal disposable income increases. Hence, it should not surprise us that small stores are increasing their share of the market in some sections of cities, as well as in suburban centers.

Economic and sociological changes in the United States have favored concentration of retailing in many instances, and large-scale retailers have financial and promotional advantages over small merchants. Small-scale retailing is, nevertheless, certainly not doomed. Independent merchants who have reassessed their positions have found competitive weapons with which to strengthen their standing. Primarily, the competitive position of independent retailers rests upon the cost-versus-satisfaction formula.

While his buying position may give him a high cost of merchandise sold, with the consequence that he cannot compete pricewise in the market, the independent retailer may capture a worthwhile market through providing other satisfactions. He should examine the following sources of satisfaction and determine which he can promote: quality of the product itself; atmosphere and surroundings for shopping; attitude of the public toward the product (prestige or satisfaction from possessing well-known product from well-accepted outlet.)

Integration in Retailing

A phrase that is coming into common use as a means of describing some operations in retailing is *integrated retailing*. Integration in retailing can be *horizontal* or *vertical,* with the possibility that some retail organizations are integrated both horizontally and vertically.

Horizontal Integration. Horizontal integration means some measure of control either by ownership or contractual agreement of retail operations on one plane. A *corporate chain* is a type of horizontal integration. A corporate chain consists of several retailing units (individual stores) handling essentially the same lines of goods which are centrally owned, that is, owned by the corporation. In Exhibit 5-2, note that there are lines where retail chains account for over 50 percent of total retail sales. Familiar examples of corporate chains in those lines are Macy's and May Company in department stores; Woolworth and Kresge in variety stores; Safeway and A & P in grocery stores. Large corporate chains are discussed further in Chapter 6.

Mixed merchandising is another kind of horizontal integration. This refers to selling a variety of merchandise lines by one retail outlet. Clothing, household furnishings, auto supplies, sporting goods, personal care items, and pharmaceutical goods are frequently observed combinations.

Retailing groups, such as I.G.A. (Independent Grocers Alliance), AG (Associated Grocers), and Rexall can be classified as horizontally integrated because of their cooperative efforts in purchasing and promotion. Inasmuch as there is usually some arrangement for wholesaling, they can also be categorized as examples of vertical integration. To avoid repetition, they are distinguished from corporate chains because the retail outlets are individually owned, whereas in corporate chains there is central ownership of all the units in the chain.

Vertical Integration. Vertical integration takes different forms. Corporate vertical integration means that a manufacturer has some, or complete, ownership position in distribution outlets, or that a retailer has equity in wholesaling or manufacturing facilities. Manufacturers, such as Sherwin-Williams, Hallmark, and Hart, Schaffner and Marx, own and operate retail outlets. Sears owns some equity in many of the manufacturers supplying that chain.

Contractual vertical integration can be a franchise operation. A *franchisor* is one who develops a type of institution, a method or system of merchandising, a trade name or insignia, or a distinct kind of service, and grants rights for the use of what he has developed (or some part of it) to another party for a contractual consideration. A franchise arrangement might exist under two sets of circumstances. In the first instance, a manufacturer, or the promoter of a formula on a specific method of specialized selling, grants other parties the right to sell his product or provide service under his name in a specified area. Examples are Dairy Queen, McDonald's Hamburgers, Esther Williams' Swimming Pools, Arthur Murray Dance Studios, and Ben Franklin Stores.

A second and popular usage of the term franchise applies where either a wholesale group or retailer-owned group of stores joins an organization which provides them the advantages of joint advertising, buying, services, and the privilege of operating under a successfully established trade name. Examples of this kind of franchise are the Associated Grocers and the I.G.A. (Independent Grocers Alliance).

Sometimes the term franchise is used to describe what is called *administrative integration.* For example, Florsheim Shoes, Schwinn bicycles, and Head skis are said to have franchises in particular markets. That means that firms who have developed a strong consumer appeal "own" some part of a specific segment of a market. Procter and Gamble, by reason of a wide product line and aggressive, effective promotion, have built a place in the market that makes it nearly impossible for a retailer to refuse to handle that company's products. There is, hence, *administrative* integration, as contrasted to a contractual agreement.

Note that there is frequently a combination of horizontal and vertical integration. Sears, for example, is horizontally integrated because the corporation owns many retail outlets, and it is vertically integrated by owning some portion of the stock in many manufacturers who supply goods to the Sears corporation. The retailer-owned cooperative groups own their wholesaling facilities and are also joined by policy agreements regarding purchasing and promotion among the several retailers who own the distribution outlets.

A principal strength of well conceived and properly managed franchises is their provision of management guides and assistance to franchisees. It has been estimated that the failure rate among small business franchisees is only about one-tenth the failure rate of unaffiliated small businesses when there is an equitable and fair contract between franchisor and franchisee when such contracts provide for viable management training and assistance. The high rate of failure generally cited for franchises arises from the several franchisors who have exploited inexperienced persons.[6]

Cooperative and Voluntary Groups.[7] Group action has attracted retailers in certain lines, notably food, hardware, automotive supply, and dry goods. In fairly large numbers, merchants have banded into organizations to gain competitive strength. Two types of associations have developed. The first one was the so-called retailers' cooperative—more formally named retailer-owned cooperative groups; and the second, the so-called voluntary groups, that are distinctively named wholesaler-retailer voluntary groups. Note the use of the term "group." Some writers call these voluntary and cooperative chains. Since merchants who belong to them retain their identity and individual ownership, and because they do not like to be linked with regular corporate chains, members of these two types of organizations much prefer the name "group."

Retailer-Owned Cooperatives. The retailer-owned cooperatives almost always had their beginning in a desire to buy merchandise favorably, in the belief that the principal advantage enjoyed by large-scale retailers was that of great purchasing power. As the name suggests, retailer-owned cooperatives were organized at the initiative of individual retailers who financed the beginnings of the cooperative by purchasing shares of stock. Many of them started as quite informal groups; a few merchants pooled the purchase of a carload of flour, for example, or other basic commodities and often learned that they could do so to their advantage. In many communities, either after a modest beginning in a small buying group, or after an organizational drive on the part of merchant leaders, warehouses have been purchased or built; and regular cooperatives, complete with warehouses and managerial organization, have been established. The AG stores (Associated Grocers of Utah, AG of West Texas), the FROG (Florida-Retailer-Owned Grocers), or those in other regions are good examples of retailer-owned cooperatives.

---

[6] See the statement by Robert M. Dias, president of National Association of Businessmen in the *Congressional Record, Vol. 116* (January 19, 1970). Also, there is an unpublished study by the authors of business failures in Rocky Mountain states. This is an ongoing study based on work in a Small Business Management Development program derived from reports on approximately 280 small businesses.

[7] The authors appreciate the use of materials collected by Carlton Gillespie who wrote an excellent master's thesis on such groups in the food field in the department of one of the authors at Florida State University.

Until recently it was common for retailer-owned cooperatives to wholesale only fast turnover, staple goods. In the case of grocers, this meant that for meat and produce, as well as slower-moving dry groceries, the member dealt with regular wholesalers of those items. Quite often, although by no means universally, retailer-owned cooperatives operated the warehouse as a cash-and-carry wholesaler. No salesmen were employed, no credit was granted, each buyer hauled his purchase to his own store, and advertising to the members quite usually consisted simply of a mimeographed list of available merchandise and prevailing prices. With such economies, the wholesale end of these cooperatives operated at a figure that was roughly one-half the margin required for full-service wholesalers in the same line. During the years following World War II, many retailer-owned cooperatives remodeled or built new warehouses and developed distribution systems that allowed them to operate at a low cost and still provide delivery service.

Even though retailer-owned cooperatives antedate wholesaler-sponsored voluntary groups, the cooperatives have fewer members and sell less merchandise than do the voluntary groups. Several factors account for the lesser success of retailer-owned cooperatives. First, it is not only the buying advantage of corporate chain stores that enables them to draw business from smaller independents. The complete range of store management—including planning, location, housekeeping, display, promotion, and service—has been neglected by many of the small merchants who suffered from large-scale competition. In other words, money-saving purchases of basic staples will not, in itself, save a merchant who is not a good manager.

A second factor has been the difficulty of getting all members of the cooperative to cooperate. The organization is composed of independents, and they naturally tend to carry their independence into decisions affecting operations of the association. It is not uncommon for arguments over apparently petty matters to cause dissension. One retailer-owned cooperative, in a southern state, almost completely disintegrated because of disagreements over "Saturday specials." It was the practice there, as elsewhere, for association members to meet periodically to determine promotions, as well as group purchases. Some of the members disagreed with sales and advertising methods, and even with the choice of items to be advertised. They, thereupon, refused to cooperate in the Saturday-special advertisements. When all member stores are identified by a uniform store front and uniform sign, the customers of each tend to think only of that store when they read an advertisement of the association. If a particular store does not participate in a promotional deal, customers who go to the store expecting a bargain purchase are told that the advertisement does not apply in that store and goodwill is lost.

The chief limiting factor to success of retailer-owned cooperatives is the same fault that is found in weak cooperatives of any type, namely, poor management. Too often the members hesitate to hire competent managerial personnel because it does not seem right that some "smart young fellow" should make as much or even more money than individual members, who have struggled to initiate and keep their businesses. Consequently, all too often a warehouse and wholesale manager is chosen because he is cheap and available rather than talented.

Wholesaler-Retailer Voluntary Groups. The companion organization of the retailer-owned cooperative group is the wholesaler-retailer voluntary group (or wholesaler-sponsored voluntary group). The wholesaler who organizes a "voluntary" contacts the retailers in an effort to induce them to "tie in" with him. Thus, a retailer contracts to purchase a specified amount of goods over a set period of time from the wholesaler in return for lower prices. This is in contrast to the cooperative group in which the individual retail member grocers take the initiative.

The wholesaler-retailer voluntary group, as defined by the Federal Trade Commission, is "a group of independent retailers affiliated with a wholesaler for buying, advertising, or other merchandising activities."[8]

In effect, a voluntary group is organized primarily to secure a stabilized outlet for the wholesaler's goods as well as to insure him a continuing profit. The fact that he secures a fixed outlet for his merchandise enables him to buy with more confidence in quantity lots, thus securing this merchandise at lower prices, part of which saving is passed on to the retail stores affiliated with him.

IGA (Independent Grocers Alliance) and Red and White Stores are outstanding examples of voluntary groups in grocery merchandising. Ben Franklin Stores (independents affiliated with Butler Bros. wholesalers) and the associate outlets of Western Auto are examples in variety, dry goods, and general merchandise lines.

Distinguishing Features. One distinguishing feature of the two kinds of associations has been cited—in the cooperative group the initiative for organizing lies with the retailers, and in the voluntary group, with the wholesaler. A further distinguishing feature of the two groups is the amount and degree of control exercised by the retailer members. In a cooperative group, the control of the cooperative is vested in the members themselves. Each member has one vote in the operation and management of the organization; each has a chance to express himself freely and to defend his statements openly. Control over the operation of each store is retained by the member-owner of that store. As a rule, each member operates his store to his own liking. He does have the benefit of skilled supervisory services and merchandising aids from the cooperative if he indicates a desire for them. In general, the attributes of individual initiative and ownership are not sacrificed materially by members of a cooperative group.

Retailer members of voluntary groups have no direct voice in the formulation of group policies. This prerogative is exercised by the sponsoring wholesaler. Members of the voluntary groups sacrifice, to some extent, a part of their authority and initiative for planned supervision and control of each store exercised by headquarters. The headquarters office is charged with the responsibility of determining retail prices, checking competition, following business trends, preparing advertisements, and supplying merchandise

---

[8] U.S. Federal Trade Commission, *Cooperative Grocery Chains,* pp. xv-xvi.

assistance and aids. Recommendations made by the supervisory personnel are supposed to be carried out with the employee-like faith evident in chain store personnel. Each merchant retains independent ownership, and the voluntary cannot fire him if he chooses not to follow every suggestion from the sponsoring wholesaler.

QUESTIONS AND ANALYTICAL PROBLEMS

1. What is meant by the statement that the retailer is the manufacturer's representative to the public?

2. In what manner is retailing productive? Give specific examples.

3. List and give examples of the functions performed by retailers.

4. Define "shopping center." Why do shopping centers develop? Compare the present relationship between central city shopping districts and shopping centers.

5. What relationships exist between the growth of suburban developments and the retailing structure? Consider volume of sales, method of operation, products handled, and locations of retail structures.

6. How does downtown retail sales volume compare with suburban area retail sales? What causes the trends? What actions are possible to increase downtown retail sales? Cite specific examples.

7. There is considerable expert opinion that we will be faced with high prices for and some long term limitations of gasoline. If the predictions are correct, what effects on downtown and on suburban retail sales do you foresee as a result? Evaluate carefully.

8. What use can a manufacturer make of a "merchandise series line of reports"?

9. Explain in detail why certain lines in Exhibit 5-2 are dominated by single-unit operations, while others are dominated by multiunit operations.

10. Compare the competitive position of small retailers with that of large retailers for each of the following: (a) retail management, (b) buying, (c) operating expenses, (d) promotion, (e) financing.

11. What is vertically integrated retailing?

12. What is meant by horizontal integration in retailing?

13. What reasons can you give to explain a lower failure rate among small-scale franchises than small-scale retailers in general?

14. What sources of assistance are available to small merchants?

15. Get examples of the materials available from sources named in the answer to question 14. Why is there no widespread use of such materials?

16. In what lines have retailer-owned cooperative groups been most successful? Why in those particular lines? Why not in furniture stores, for example?

Case 5 • THE KIDDIE MART

The Kiddie Mart, a small department store for children, was opened in early 1959. It maintained a small toy department which was stocked with only one make of toys—the nationally advertised Mattel brand. Mr. Krebbs, the store owner, knew that much of the success he had enjoyed since opening the Kiddie Mart was due to his ability to stock national brand merchandise. He had decided to handle Mattel toys for the following reasons: (1) good potential volume, (2) competitive prices, (3) quality backed up by a sound guarantee, (4) innovative and attractive appeal, and (5) protection against competition (Kiddie Mart could get an exclusive right to Mattel toys in its trading area). Mr. Krebbs also made it a policy to limit his merchandise in all the other departments to only one brand as well. He carried more than one brand only when a particular brand could not offer ample style selection or was limited to a few special types of products.

For some time, however, Mr. Krebbs had been receiving many requests from his customers for a less expensive line of toys. After extensive checking, he found only one manufacturer who produced a line of lower-price toys of the quality he was willing to sell. This manufacturer did not advertise its toys but sold them primarily to large purchasers who, in turn, sold these toys under their own private labels.

If Mr. Krebbs decided to sell the cheaper line of toys, he would be changing his basic merchandising policies. Futhermore, he felt that he would be competing directly with larger department and chain stores by adding this new line of toys and that his regular customers might substitute the cheaper toys for Mattel products. However, he also realized that he was losing a number of customers every day because he did not have less expensive toys to offer.

• What alternatives were open to Mr. Krebbs and how might they be made effective? Should he change his present policy? If so, how?

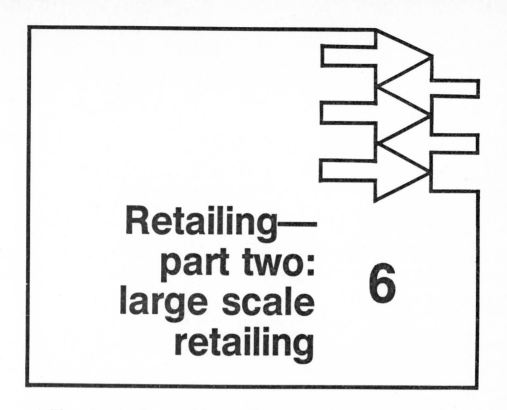

Retailing—part two: large scale retailing

6

The categories for examining retailing are not mutually exclusive. In this chapter is an overview of chain store beginnings and operations, followed by discussions of several types of retailing: department stores, mail-order houses, supermarkets, and discount stores. The types of merchandise handled and kinds of integration discussed in Chapter 5 can apply to the retail operations in this chapter. The division used in the two retailing chapters is a convenience rather than a precise, taxonomic treatment.

INDEPENDENT CHAINS

A retail chain is defined as a centrally owned group of stores, each of which handles essentially the same types of merchandise. The relative sales volumes of single-unit independents and multiunit chains is shown in Table 6-1.

Since chains became well established in the United States, they have gradually increased their share of retail business. Even though single units have declined from 70 percent of retail sales in 1948, they are still dominant, with 60 percent of sales. In Exhibit 6-1 you can see that chains do dominate certain types of business. If our statement that chains can succeed to the extent that they can make a large number of decisions routinely and centrally is true, we can expect even greater portions of retail sales going to chains. Improvements in communication, as in data handling, facilitate such decision making.

Chains have existed for centuries. In the ashes of Vesuvius in Pompeii are found chain stores, and they are also described in the oldest histories of China. The present development dates from the 19th century.

Table 6-1

COMPARISON OF SINGLE-UNIT AND MULTIUNIT OPERATIONS PERCENT OF TOTAL RETAIL ESTABLISHMENTS AND PERCENT OF TOTAL RETAIL SALES

| | 1954 | | 1964 | | 1974 | |
	Establish-ments	Sales	Establish-ments	Sales	Establish-ments	Sales
Single-unit	90	70	87	63	87	60
Multiunit	10	30	13	37	13	40

Source: Derived and interpolated from the U.S. Department of Commerce, Bureau of the Census, *Census of Business;* and the U.S. Department of Commerce, Bureau of the Census, *Current Business Reports: 1954-1974.*

The Chain Store Movement

The Great Atlantic and Pacific Tea Company was founded in 1859, and F. W. Woolworth opened his first successful store in 1879. By 1910 there were 3,000 chain-store systems in the United States operating 13,500 stores. The most significant growth from the standpoint of retailing was in the areas of groceries, variety stores, and drugstores.

The principal appeal of the chain store was economy, which seemed obvious in the theory of integration. The number of middlemen necessary to move the goods was decreased, the management overhead costs were spread over many stores. Specialization, both of task and of function, could be integrated into one operation. These were the arguments advanced in favor of chain operation, although there were negative arguments, such as inflexibility of large-scale operations, overstandardization, lack of employee motivation, and failure to win community support.

Typical Beginnings

All early chain-store organizations had small beginnings. They grew slowly over a period of time. The story of their growth will do much to reveal the forces that are responsible for their development. Hence, histories of a few of the prominent chains are presented.

The Great Atlantic and Pacific Tea Company. The Great A & P was started as a result of the spread between the importer's price of tea and the price at which it was sold to the consumer. In 1859 George Gilman and George Huntington Hartford chose to import tea from China and to offer it at a price considerably lower than that charged by contemporary merchants. They did business in a small shop on Vessey Street in New York. Although the store carried no groceries, their business proved most profitable. After their first opening, they added stores until in six years, or by 1865, the company operated 25 stores, an average of four new stores a year. By this time they were prepared to embark on a program of carrying a full line of groceries. They reasoned that if they could sell tea below competitive prices, they could also sell other items at lower prices in the same manner.

Exhibit 6-1

**SINGLE UNITS AND MULTIUNITS RETAIL TRADE
CHANGE IN PROPORTION OF SALES:
1948 TO 1967**

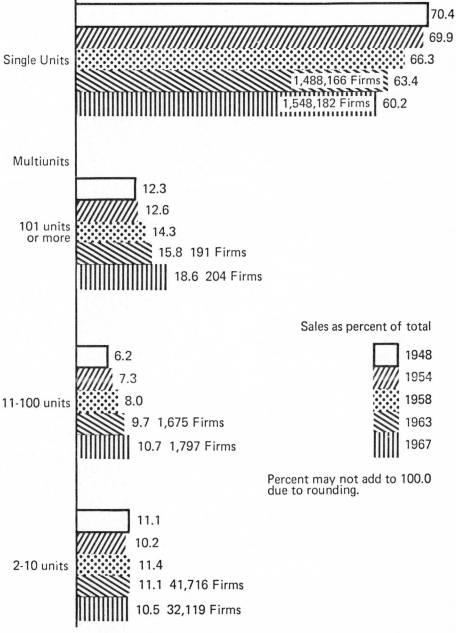

SOURCE: U.S. Department of Commerce, Bureau of the Census,
Census of Business, 1967.

Impressed with the success that they enjoyed in getting volume sales by selling for low prices, the founders decided to experiment further in this area. They established small stores that did not provide delivery service nor grant credit, and they called these stores Economy Stores. Indeed, this was the beginning of the cash-and-carry idea of this chain. To Hartford it was an experiment with a merchandising idea. In addition to cash and carry, the stores were small, low-rent, one-man affairs with modest fixtures. Every policy adopted was in the interest of gaining volume. Even expected profit rates were low to increase volume by the use of low prices.

The Economy Stores proved so successful that the company chose to expand rapidly, opening stores wherever they could expect a reasonable degree of success. The real expansion of the cash-and-carry economy merchandising concept began in 1912. Early in 1913 the company opened its 500th store. Before the year was over, the company was operating 585 stores. During the next two years 1,600 more stores were opened, and by 1919 the company was operating over 4,200 stores. The peak of the expansion was reached in 1930 when the company operated 15,700 units. Although the number of stores declined rapidly thereafter, the company continued to enjoy a tremendous increase in sales.

Two factors accounted for the dollar sales increase. First, much of the increase from $1 billion in 1930 to over $5 billion in 1960 was due to an inflationary doubling of food prices. The other factor was that stores were getting larger in terms of size and sales per store. Today the A & P operates approximately 4,000 stores. Rather than small stores, however, most of them are supermarkets that are exceeding sales of $1 million a year. Thus, we have a story of how an idea based on price spreads stimulated two men and resulted in a multibillion-dollar operation.

F. W. Woolworth Company. F. W. Woolworth Company was the original variety store—an entirely new type of store. As in the case of the famous cash-and-carry idea, the "five and dime" was the result of an idea and an experiment.

While a clerk in a Watertown, New York dry goods store, young Frank W. Woolworth had a unique experience. A table of miscellaneous small wares, over which he had placed a sign, "Anything on this table for five cents," was almost cleared on the first day. The possibility of an entire store based on this principle excited Woolworth, and he could not rest until he had tried it. He obtained merchandise worth $300 from his former employer on credit, and, with some savings of his own, he opened a store in Utica, New York. In this store he did well, but only for a short time; then he went out of business. The faith of young Woolworth, however, was undaunted and he tried again in Lancaster, Pennsylvania, in 1879. His merchandise consisted of that which remained in his Utica store and more stock from his former employer.

This store vindicated his faith. In a letter to his father, on the day following his opening, he reported that his first day's sales amounted to $127.65, "the most I have ever sold in one day." His opening stock had cost him only $410.

Thus, his enthusiasm seemed to be well justified. Indeed, in the same letter he stated, "I think some of starting a branch store in Harrisburg, Pennsylvania, and putting Sum in it." (He referred to his brother, Charles Sumner Woolworth.) He attempted the store in Harrisburg and another in York, Pennsylvania. Both failed. He opened a fifth store in Scranton, Pennsylvania, however, and succeeded. This experience made the score three failures and two successes. Woolworth decided, at this time, that the idea was basically sound, provided the stores were opened in the right locations. Another fundamental concept growing out of his experience was that a large number of stores would be required to make the venture successful. Only with the great volume afforded by many stores could mass buying economy be possible. By the turn of the century there were 59 Woolworth stores with a combined sales of $5 million.

Woolworth's idea invited competition. John G. McCrory opened a similar store in Scottdale, Pennsylvania, in 1881, which became the nucleus of a chain totaling over 200 stores. S. H. Kress and Company opened a similar store in Memphis, Tennessee, in 1896; S.S. Kresge Company acquired its first variety store in 1899. The chain variety store idea caught on in many sectors.

Piggly Wiggly. Clarence Saunders, the inventor of self-service stores, began his first Piggly Wiggly store in 1916. Customers passed through a turnstile into a store layout fashioned to guide them past all the merchandise which was on shelves very similar to the gondola center aisle shelving in present day supermarkets. His idea was successful, and he developed another innovation; that was to sell franchises incorporating his ideas. Safeway, Kroger, National Tea, Colonial, and other chains operated Piggly Wiggly stores for several years. Godfrey M. Lebhar, in *Chain Stores in America: 1859-1950*, credits Mr. Saunders with laying the foundation for supermarkets.

Walgreen's. In 1909 Charles Walgreen operated in Chicago a single drugstore that he had bought from his employer in 1901. He was just breaking even when he was confronted with an opportunity to purchase another store. "Chicago has too many drugstores now," his friends warned. "Why buck the tide?" His reply was a confident, "Chicago may have too many drugstores, but not enough Walgreen stores."[1] This venture was the beginning of what is now the largest drug chain in the country. No special merchandising idea or plan marked the growth of this chain. It was purely a livelier imagination and a greater ambition.

A Summary View. The purpose of relating these stores of growth is not only to provide historical facts, but also to show that in every instance the beginning was small. Usually these beginnings grew out of an idea, a happenstance opportunity. We also note the presence in every instance of a man with courage and an enterprising spirit. It is significant, too, that most of these firms grew on their own reinvested earnings. They could not expect help

---

[1] Godfrey M. Lebhar, *Chain Stores in America: 1859-1950* (New York: Chain Store Publishing Corporation, 1952), p. 16.

from the money markets until they had demonstrated their ability to earn a sustained profit. Investors would not loan money unless there was a record of successful earnings. Woolworth, who began his operations in 1879, did not go to the public for money until 1912. J. C. Penney Company financed itself until it had 197 stores and annual sales of $21 million.

It is likely that such a process of a germination of ideas into an institution of major significance is taking place almost constantly in some form. For example, in 1933 J. Willard Marriott, at the age of 39, sold his A & W Root Beer franchise on Florida Avenue in Washington, D. C. He took his equity and started the Hot Shoppe on Connecticut Avenue. In 1967 he had 125 restaurants in 60 cities and 6 major motels. To extend our historical sketches to include other examples would not add to the essential elements of this picture. The stories of J. C. Penney, Montgomery Ward, People's Drugs, S. H. Kress, or Safeway Stores would demonstrate forces similar to those we have observed.

Forces Making for Chain-Store Growth

During the period from 1918 to the beginning of the great depression, the chain stores experienced their greatest growth in terms of numbers. What were the specific reasons for the rapid growth of the chains during this period? There were several. First, the population during the period from 1918 to 1929 increased from 106 million to 123 million, an increase of 16 percent. Also, more people were able to buy more goods because increased productivity resulted in higher incomes.

Second, as the volume of sales possible to merchants increased, competition between firms in obtaining increased business encouraged the adoption of economy measures and innovations. In this quickened environment, the character of much merchandising was changed by self-service.

The variety of goods available to the consumer resulting from improved 'transportation facilities was also a factor. Improved highways made it desirable and pleasurable for customers to shop around. This same development made it possible for merchants to warehouse goods at convenient points and to establish retail outlets at locations desirable to shoppers. Then, too, the process of urbanization was moving at a rapid pace during this period. People were moving to the city, thus creating new business opportunities that were inviting to chains.

Fourth, the high prices of World War I and the depression that followed made people more conscious of price than they otherwise would have been. The chain stores, for the reasons we have pointed out, featured economy and low prices. They continued to popularize the cash-and-carry concept introduced by the Great A & P. They practiced mass buying, mass movement, mass warehousing, and mass selling of goods, capitalizing on the savings of volume operations in all of these functions.

Fifth, lethargy on the part of independent stores in adopting innovations to give better service and lower prices was also a significant factor in encouraging chain-store growth. Poor layouts and methods that required clerks to help shoppers with each item tended to shift people away from old, established stores to those with improved services.

Comparative Efficiency of the Chains

In speaking of efficiency of marketing, we have a problem of lack of conclusive data. Chapter 12 describes how marketing efficiency in an institution is determined by measuring sales (output) against the cost (input). As is the case in all social sciences, such concepts cannot be reduced to absolutes; but it may be possible to develop opinions having some validity by comparing the costs of the chain stores with those of independent stores in similar lines.

Specialization. The chain operations are large enough so that specialization is possible. For example, the work of the buyers can be restricted to certain products in which they can become expert. Also a manager who is free to examine and analyze operations, follow up with research, and formulate policy may achieve a skill in management greater than one who is constantly preoccupied with broad areas of responsibility and detailed operations.

Operating Economies. Operating economies may be achieved by standardizing equipment and supplies. Advertising cost per store and per unit of sales may be decreased because one advertisement covering a city may serve a number of stores, thus spreading the cost on a per store basis. The chain system eliminates one purchase and one sale as a result of integrating the function of the wholesaler into the retail function. It is possible that some saving may result from the elimination of this step. Indeed, the mass buying advantage often claimed by chain stores is not really significant unless there are economies resulting, in part, from this integration.

While the chain has great buying power because of volume sales, the wholesaler from which the independent merchant buys also has sufficient volume to purchase in trainload lots, if necessary. It is possible, however, that the chain buyer, acting directly for his own firm in a specialized area, may be more effective than if he were buying for an institution which had to resell the product to another institution.

The economy achieved by integration is often debatable. Results are too difficult to discern in order to generalize conclusively. In general, we would assume that there would be economies, but there are instances of small independents operating profitably and still underselling competitive large chains. From this observation we see that there is some danger in being too quickly satisfied with generalizations. Especially is the use of overall average misleading when comparing chains with independent units. In 1963 there were only 162,000 units with 4 or more stores under one ownership out of 1,708,000 total stores. The latter stores included small stores, old stores, and marginal operations, many not in the same competitive plane with the chains. If one were to select the 162,000 independent stores that were competing directly with the chain stores, the advantages in efficiency and price favoring the chain method of operation might not be so marked as some statistics seem to indicate.

Price Advantage. Probably the nearest to an ultimate measure of efficiency for the chain versus the independent is the comparative price that the two types charge the public for comparable merchandise. A number of studies have been made on this subject. The Federal Trade Commission conducted studies in the late twenties and early thirties that gave some evidence of a chain-store advantage. In the food field the study revealed that on national brands the chains undersold the independents by approximately 10 percent. In a similar study of nationally branded drug items, the survey revealed that independents charged over 20 percent higher than chains on a selected list of well-known drug items.[2]

There are two elements in this survey, however, that we might examine more closely in the light of contemporary developments. First, this period was one of chain supremacy. The independent store fought back at the time by going to the government for legislation against the chain store. Subsequently, however, the independents recognized the necessity of improving their merchandising practices. In many instances they met the chain competition on their own ground of cash, carry, joint advertising, and self-service operations. Later studies show that the difference in price is not so marked. In a study of 40 nationally advertised brands conducted in the Milwaukee area in 1948, prices averaged 4 percent lower in regular chains than in independent stores.[3]

We are confronted again, however, with the problem of averages. These surveys base their comparisons on typical averages. Let us view an instance in which results are based on competition in terms of size and class of store. A price-level comparison survey conducted in 1952 covered a sample of 140 stores in 28 cities. Stores selected were of the supermarket type having sales of $500,000 or more per year. They were divided among national chains, local chains, and independents. Seventy-eight food items were selected, divided among general dry grocery items, meat items, and produce items (including frozen foods) according to the average sales of food stores. This distribution resulted in the inclusion of 51 grocery items, 15 meat items, and 12 produce items. The findings indicate that the national chain sells at slightly lower prices than do the independents. The difference in price, however, is not significant.

No recent reliable price comparison studies have been made. On the basis of historical data, however, if the chain stores are compared with independent stores in a similar size and competitive class bracket, the results do not show marked superiority of chains over independents.

By Type of Operation. At one time general stores were common. They were mainly food stores with a limited selection of hardware, cloth and clothing, tools, and other items needed by rural families. General stores are now so scarce that they have not been rated in the Census of Business since 1948. As population centers grew, there was sufficient market size to support

---

[2] C. F. Phillips, "The Federal Trade Commission's Chain-Store Investigation: A Note," *Journal of Marketing,* Vol. II, No. 3 (1938), p. 191.

[3] Ralph H. Oakes, "Price Differences for Identical Items in Chain, Voluntary Group, and Independent Grocery Stores," *Journal of Marketing* (October, 1949), pp. 434-436.

more specialized establishments, which provided a wider selection within part of some broad line. Hence, stores for shoes, ladies' wear, appliances, luggage, and so on developed. These stores, called specialty stores, are the most numerous. Their relative advantages and disadvantages are those of small businesses which were discussed earlier.

Four types of large-scale retailing establishments not nearly as numerous as the smaller specialty stores are highly visible. A brief discussion of each type provides more information on trends in retailing. Those are department stores, mail order houses, supermarkets, and discount stores.

THE DEPARTMENT STORE

The rise of the department store provides additional evidence of the forces that give rise to the chain store. First, growing incomes and population increased the potential for sales volumes of marketing institutions. Second, the urbanization of population tended to concentrate purchasing power and buying in the shopping areas of cities. Third, the growth in the manufacturing and industrial structure was geared to turn out an increasing flow of manufactured goods. Fourth, the progress of scientific management pointed up the importance of getting maximum volume under one set of overhead costs and under one group of skilled managers. Fifth, the integration of the buying function made it possible for the store to bypass the wholesaler and to buy directly from the manufacturer.

Advantages and Limitations of the Department Store

The department store enjoys certain inherent advantages. By virtue of the large volume of business, the department store can create an impact on the buyer's attitude that small stores cannot achieve. The department store is characterized by its wide offering of merchandise with separate classifications, divided into departments, each with a separate set of records. On the average its sales exceed those of other stores in the vicinity of its operation, and its clientele is made up of mostly women. Department stores usually offer a considerable number of free services.

An aspect of the department store which appeared as a threat to competition was that theoretically it could undersell because it was able to bring a large number of lines of merchandise under one set of overhead costs. It also could advertise extensively and build a prestigious image which was not possible for the smaller specialty stores. These smaller operators became anxious about their ability to hold their business in the face of such ominous competition. One authority reports that, "Attempts were made to get state legislation to pass laws taxing department stores out of existence, and Missouri did pass a law taxing department stores."[4] Such appeals to get the protection of laws have characterized the retail revolution down to the present day.

---

[4] J.A. Hill, "Taxes on Department Stores," *Quarterly Journal of Economics*, Vol. XV, p. 299.

The fears of the small operator were not completely justified. The department-store type of operation had its limitations. It was difficult for the large store to convey the atmosphere of warmth and personality achieved in the smaller shops. Men buyers were especially reluctant to patronize the department store. Many preferred the close relationship with a clerk of his acquaintance to help make a selection, and this service was more likely to be available in a specialty store. Further, management of the department store was not so simple as it appeared. Active management was far removed from the point of sale. The organization of management influence that would reach to the floor of the store and get the clerk to respond with the same enthusiasm and interest as was found in the specialty shop was difficult to achieve. This is the weak link in the marketing flow. Department stores have often employed low-paid, part-time clerks who have not been properly trained to give desirable service. More than any other institution, the department store is affected by this problem.

Another factor is that the department store has a high expense rate. Although such stores achieve a high volume of sales, approximately 50 percent of their employees and 40 percent of their floor space are devoted to nonselling activities and functions. Thus, the average expense ratio for department stores ranges from approximately 35 percent to 40 percent. While such figures may be slightly lower than those of specialty stores handling similar merchandise, no distinguishable or marked savings are consistently evident.

Status of the Department Store

Even though they constitute only about 0.2 percent of all the retail outlets in the country, the 5,700 stores classified as department stores are spectaculars on the marketing scene. They account for slightly over 10 percent of total retail sales—in 1973 it was 10.4 percent. For many years department store sales were about 8 percent of total retail sales; they slowly declined in importance to about 6 percent of the total in 1954, but since then have been increasing their share.

The move toward branch stores in shopping centers probably accounts for this trend back to the department store. These figures, however, are not indicative of the importance of the department store in the area in which it operates most effectively. In many high-volume lines the department store does not compete in a significant manner. For example, few department stores sell food, liquor, or automobiles. Yet, a significant part of total retail sales are made in these areas. On the other hand, department stores sell more than half of boys' wear, infants' clothes, and women's dresses, and 72 percent of all piece goods and linens. In many of those areas in which department stores operate, they probably account for sales of more than half of the goods sold.

Organization of the Department Store

One of the reasons for the development of the department store is specialized management. In this type of store the various responsibilities are magnified to a degree that each activity becomes a separate division. Most department stores follow a pattern of dividing responsibilities among four major functional areas—merchandising, operating, controlling, and publicity.

Merchandising. First, and probably the most significant functional area, is merchandising, already defined as "the planning involved in marketing the right merchandise or service at the right place, at the right time, in the right quantities, and at the right price."[5] This function is administered by a merchandise manager who is one of the four top executives of the store under the general manager. In this capacity he directs the activities of all who are engaged in buying.

Store Operation. Another significant area of organizational responsibility is the maintenance of store plant and personnel. Competition requires that the selling floor be attractive and presentable to the public. Constant innovations in arrangement of layout are necessary. A nonselling staff numbering over one half of the total employees must be maintained and supervised. Service departments, such as receiving and marking merchandise and maintenance of parking areas, are significant operations in their own right in the large store.

The coordination of these operations is the function of the store operation manager. Some stores divide this function into two areas: one dealing with store operation proper and the other with personnel.

The Controller. Another significant function in a department store is that of the controller. Like all firms, the store is successful only if it shows a financial profit. Accounting and control of the funds constitute a most significant area of management. The statements prepared by the controller's department provide information enabling management to analyze the operation of each segment of the business. The expenses and profits of each department are available in a separate statement.

The department store uses accounting data for achieving management goals more effectively than most other types of business organizations. Similar problems and standard accounting procedures make it possible to compare ratios and operating data among many stores. Such comparisons are useful because the success of merchandising methods and innovations can be tested by some stores, and reports of successes and failures can be shared with a group of stores.

Publicity and Advertising. One of the great challenges of the department store is the establishment of institutional prestige. Furthermore, it must communicate its merchandise values to the public in an effective manner. Arrangements of display windows, for example, are significant in enhancing the satisfaction of the customers of the store. So important is this selling and communicative function that one of the four divisions of the department store management devotes itself entirely to its performance. Newspaper spreads,

---

[5] Ralph S. Alexander and the Committee on Definitions, *Marketing Definitions* (Chicago: American Marketing Association, 1963), p. 17.

television and radio programs, and direct-mail services are the advertising media used. Window displays and women's programs are used to establish the prestige of the department store. The publicity division works very closely with the merchandise division since it must advertise the merchandise that this latter division offers for sale.

Typical Beginning

Department stores began in Europe. By the mid-1850's they were established in the United States. Wanamaker's in Philadelphia, ZCMI in Salt Lake City, and Macy's in New York are among the earliest.

One of the most famous department stores, as well as one of the earliest, is Macy's of New York. Indeed, Macy's famous statement, "6 percent under," and Gimbel's retort, "Nobody—but nobody—undersells Gimbel's," give color to one of the classic retailing competitive battles. Rowland Hussey Macy abandoned a seafaring life and opened a dry goods store in Boston in 1837. He established this store primarily because of his faith in the soundness of low prices for cash as an effective appeal for volume sales. The store failed despite the fact that he used thousands of flamboyant signs to advertise his policy of selling merchandise "for cash for less." Macy failed a second time in San Francisco and a third in Haverhill, Massachusetts. Refusing to be discouraged by these three failures, in 1858 he set up the original Macy's at 14th Street and Sixth Avenue in New York City. The store occupied the street floor of an unpretentious brick building with counters running the entire length of the store on both sides. With fifteen employees, the store sold $90,000 the first year in ribbons, laces, artificial flowers, feathers, handkerchiefs, furnishings, hosiery, and gloves.

Macy died 19 years later leaving a merchandising mart consisting of several departments with drugs, toilet goods, silver, house furnishings, sporting goods, luggage, toys, musical instruments, and books. In 1902 the store moved to its present 34th Street location, where it occupies an entire city block. Just previous to moving, L. Straus and Son, successful glassware merchants, acquired a partnership share in the firm, and subsequently, complete ownership. However, the store continued to operate under the old R. H. Macy and Company name.

Growth of Chain Department Stores [6]

Macy's could well be classed as a chain since it has over fifty retail outlets. There has been a different kind of chain movement, however, among department stores. We refer specifically to such chain movements as Allied and Federated stores, sometimes called ownership groups. Although the stores are

---

[6] In assessing the more recent forces that are influencing the thinking of large-scale retailing, John McDonald goes behind the scenes to discover what has wrought the changes that have revolutionized the J. C. Penney operation from a firm that emphasized cash-and-carry theory limited line department stores to a regional merchandising strategy which features a retail store complex that includes the lines of a complete shopping center within the store. See "How They Minted the New Penney," *Fortune* (July, 1967), pp. 110-113, 158.

owned by the same organization, the operating policies of the individual stores may be quite different and distinct. The individual stores do not carry the name of the chain but retain their original names or take a distinct name if they are new. When they are purchased by the chain, as is frequently the case, the personnel and many of their operating policies remain unchanged. The degree to which these practices obtain success depends upon the policies of the respective operators of such chains. Allied Stores and Federated Stores are the two well-established department store chains.

Earl Puckett, who was the power behind the growth of Allied Stores, began his life on a Midwest farm. Like many of his contemporaries, the farm presented no challenge or future to him. He studied accounting by correspondence and became an accountant for Loeser's Department Store in Brooklyn in 1928, revamping the entire accounting system. When the crash came on Wall Street in 1929, he helped the store remain in the black. For his efforts the store paid him $50,000 a year as its president in 1931.

In 1934 Puckett was in charge of the nationwide Hahn Department Store chain of 27 units. He reorganized the corporation and gave it the new name of Allied Stores. He put new life into the local managers by sharply reducing the authority of the central office. Not only were the men on the operating level of the individual stores encouraged by more freedom and responsibility, but he was always ready to help those who were in trouble. The central office cooperated in buying certain lines of goods for stores in Allied—sheets, men's clothing, and appliances.

Puckett believed that to be effective in winning a place of prestige and goodwill in a community, a store must be recognized as part of the community. The Jordan Marsh store, therefore, remained Boston's Jordan Marsh; Bon Marche of Seattle retained its original name. Even Joske's new store in Houston was not known by the public as a link in a prosperous chain but was advertised as a store with many distinct innovations as "Joske's of Texas."

There are certain advantages which the chain department store enjoys. It can acquire high-level and specialized management men to serve a large number of stores. It can spread its supervisory costs over many operations, thus decreasing the cost per unit. It can acquire professional promotional services and establish a prestigious image. It is a challenge, however, for a management to establish centralized controls and still provide desirable freedom and inititative to local management. Also, there is always the chance of a chain department store being identified as outsiders by the populace of the local communities.

Trends in the Development of Chain Department Stores

Although the chain movement in the department store field may continue, the form that such expansion may take cannot be predicted. Department stores are becoming greatly concerned over the competition from the supermarkets. To discover methods by which this threat may be met is one of the great challenges of department store management. One method is the establishment of a unit or branch in a suburban area. Such establishments bring the dignity and prestige of the department store into the vicinity of the suburbanite, enabling the department store to compete more on a convenience and location basis with the supermarket. This tendency to establish branches is quite similar to the development of food chains. Many of these innovators prefer that their extensions be referred to as branches rather than chains. If two or more institutions under one ownership are doing business in the same line of merchandise at separate locations, however, they are similar to a chain in all significant respects.

There is also a chain movement in the direction of building main stores. We have mentioned Macy's six main stores. The May Company also operates 12 main outlets with 34 branches. Broadway in Los Angeles has nine stores, not necessarily referred to as branches. Other large operations that have succeeded in their own respective locations are viewing opportunities in other locations as ' prospective areas for expansion. As populations increase in new centers, we can expect the established department store to move in and absorb some of the business.

Establishment of Branch Stores

Certain advantages should result from the establishment of branch stores. First, the increase in satisfaction to the consumer by having a store conveniently located would be a factor. Second, the increased sales volume should tend to reduce overhead costs as a percentage of sales and, thus, increase the profit ratio. The recent development of shopping centers and shopping malls is accentuating the trend toward branch stores. In several instances the branches in suburbs have greater sales volume than does the main store downtown.

As to the savings that accrue from distributing overhead costs over a number of units, it appears that savings result only if the store does over 30 percent of its business in its branches. Figures from the National Retail Merchants report on retail branches show stores with no branches that averaged expenses of 31.2 percent of sales; stores with less than 30 percent of their business in branches averaged expenses of 31.4 percent of sales.[7] Savings appeared, however, in those stores that did over 30 percent of their business in branches; their expenses averaged 29.8 percent. In the stores with less than 30 percent branch sales, the higher expenses appeared in payroll costs. Gross margins in these stores varied only slightly in 1965. Those without branches achieved a 34.4 percent gross margin; those with less than 30 percent of their business in branches, 34.6 percent; and those with more than 30 percent in branches, 34.9 percent.

The above figures are significantly different from those contained in an earlier study by Malcolm McNair in 1955. His study showed that gross margins of stores without branches averaged 35.4 percent. Those with branches selling less than 20 had an average gross margin of 36.4 percent, while stores with over

---

"Financial and Operating Results of Department and Specialty Stores of 1966," published by the Controllers Congress, National Retail Merchants Association. Copyright NRMA.

20 percent of their business in branches enjoyed an average gross margin of 36.8 percent.[8]

THE MAIL-ORDER HOUSE

Before the turn of the century, it was more convenient for consumers to sit in their parlors with a catalog than to travel the distances that might have been necessary to make the purchases which would give them comparable satisfaction. This convenience was responsible, in part, for the growth of the mail-order house. The catalog of Sears, Roebuck and Company, for example, brought into the home an accurate and comparatively complete description of items, including price, shipping weight, and all the data necessary to order. The mail-order business is based on this fundamental convenience satisfaction and also on certain elements of cost. Contrary to a popular conviction that mail-order business is decreasing, mail-order business is holding its own, with about one percent of total retail sales.

In terms of the number of establishments, we can observe the rapid growth that has taken place in the mail-order business. In terms of total retail sales, the mail-order method has also shown significant growth. When we measure the share of the market, however, this method of selling has barely kept pace with direct sales through retail stores since 1939.

According to available information, the first mail-order catalog was issued by E. C. Allen of Augusta, Maine, a retail store.[9] Sales by mail were made by many stores well before the Civil War. Of the presently operating retail mail-order firms, the two best known and largest were founded after the Civil War. Montgomery Ward and Company began operations in 1872, and Sears, Roebuck and Company was organized in 1893. While there are no records of the sales of all mail-order houses before 1929, it is doubtful if the total share of the business ever exceeded 1.5 percent of the total retail sales of the nation.

Sears, Roebuck and Company

The manner of growth of the largest of the mail-order chains is typical of the history of many such firms. It also illustrates the manner in which the firms diversified their services to include direct retail store sales.

Richard W. Sears, station agent at North Redwood, Minnesota, obtained permission from a shipper to dispose of a box of watches that the consignee refused to accept. He undertook to sell these watches to his friends by mail at a low markup, and this experience convinced him that selling by mail at low prices was possible on a larger scale at a profit. He began his business in 1886 in Minneapolis and later moved to Chicago, taking Alvah C. Roebuck as a partner

---

[8] Murray Sawits, with the aid of computer technology, has developed a means of determining the answer to a crucial problem in retail dynamics—how much of a new branch store's volume represents new business to the company? His treatment of this problem provides clues that might be useful in a number of other places. See, "Model for Branch Store Planning," *Harvard Business Review* (July-August, 1967), pp. 140-143.

[9] F. Preslerey, *History and Development of Advertising* (New York: Doubleday and Company, Inc., 1929), pp. 284-286.

soon after he moved to that city. Mr. Roebuck had skill as a watch repairman that young Sears felt would be useful to the business. In 1893 the young firm took the name Sears, Roebuck, and that year's sales totaled $388,000. Julius Rosenwald joined the firm in 1895 when sales approached $800,000. Rosenwald, a clothing merchant, formulated some principles that became known as the "Rosenwald Creed." Stated briefly, the creed is this:

1. Sell for less by buying for less. Buy for less through the instrumentality of mass buying and cash buying. *But maintain the quality.*
2. Sell for less by cutting the cost of sales. Reduce to the absolute practical minimum the expense of moving goods from producer to consumer. *But maintain the quality.*
3. Make less profit on each individual item and increase your aggregate profit by selling more items. *But maintain the quality.*[10]

Today these appear to be simple maxims, but their power as fundamentals for merchandising success was not so clearly understood at the end of the nineteenth century. All of them emphasize different aspects of the cost-satisfaction concepts that were introduced in the early chapters.

Sears opened its first retail store at Evansville, Indiana, in 1925. Before the year was over the company had eight such stores in operation. In the six years from the beginning of this movement in 1925, the company sold more through its retail outlets than it did through its mail-order outlets. This six-year progress compares with almost forty years of mail-order experience. The company has achieved a position now in which its retail business far exceeds its mail-order sales. Although Sears began as a mail-order store, today it is also a chain department-store operation. Thus, in Sears' history three kinds of forces encouraging large-scale operation were operative—those relating to the mail-order house, the retail chain, and the department store.

Advantages of the Mail-Order House

It has been stated that convenience was the main motivation for the founding of the mail-order business. To convenience must be added additional satisfactions and, in certain instances, reduced costs. Mail-order houses, especially Sears, Roebuck and Company and Montgomery Ward, established themselves as trustworthy merchants who would provide an accurate description of the merchandise offered and stand by their product with a money-back guarantee. This reputation for integrity was an essential for mail-order business, both in description and guarantee, since it overcame the fear that the ordinary customer might have of sending cash for merchandise which had never been examined or seen. Indeed, even though only a small share of the total retail sales has been transacted by mail-order houses, the goodwill that the successful firms acquired as a result of standing behind their merchandise strengthened their position in retail store competition.

---

[10] Godfrey M. Lebhar, *Chain Stores in America*, 1859-1950 (New York: Chain Store Publishing Corporation, 1952), p. 110.

Another advantage that the mail-order houses enjoyed over local specialty stores was the great variety of merchandise they were able to carry. Just as was the case in other large retail institutions, mail-order firms were able to purchase in large volume and with favorable credit terms, passing these savings in buying on to the patrons. The strongholds of the mail-order firms were in the rural areas, where merchandise facilities were not adequate to provide the customers with the variety of the low prices that could be found in the catalogs. Also, the development of the mail-order system was timed with, and made possible by, improved postal service. Mail-order firms still enjoy these advantages.

Just as have retail stores, these firms have nad to improve both their products and their services to keep competitive. Among the innovations they have adopted are telephone service from retail stores to merchandise warehouses and catalog booths in the cities. Such services provide satisfaction in making it possible to deliver merchandise to the buyers in less time; they also make it unnecessary for the customers to make out and mail orders. Then, too, most mail-order firms have improved the quality of their catalogs by including certain sections in color. In order to keep abreast of the increased interest in fashion and innovation, many of the mail-order firms have been issuing catalogs seasonally, rather than annually, as was the practice at one time. As have other stores, mail-order houses have traded up. Although they still use bargain and low-price appeal, they carry higher quality merchandise than originally.

Problems and Disadvantages of Mail-Order Houses

One of the problems which mail-order firms have had in keeping abreast of competition is that they have lost the advantage of the isolated rural market which they at one time enjoyed. Improved highways and the increased number of cars have made it not only possible but also pleasurable for the farmer to visit the metropolitan centers on shopping tours. Also, competition of stores such as Penney's and Grant's has made it necessary for the mail-order firms to provide better service than they did at one time. Another great disadvantage of the mail-order firm, which they have overcome only in part by the telephone service, is the time lag necessary in obtaining the merchandise from the mail-order firm. Many people dislike waiting for a product once they have made up their mind to buy it.

An additional problem of the mail-order firm is the publishing of the catalog and keeping it up to date. We have noted the emphasis given to fashion and innovation. Once a catalog is issued, it is most expensive to change it, but such a change is necessary if merchandise and prices are changed. An average mail-order catalog costs approximately $2.50. To achieve a selling cost of 8 percent, which might be an average for personal selling in a department store, each catalog must be responsible for selling over $30 worth of merchandise. What is more, catalogs are only part of the selling cost. When catalog costs are added to the other costs of the mail-order house, they enjoy only a small economy differential over the average retail store.

THE SUPERMARKET

The Supermarket Institute defines this store as follows: "A complete departmentalized food store with a minimum sales volume of one million dollars a year and at least the grocery department fully self-service." [11]

The real contribution of the supermarket is in the importance that it gives to large volume, self-service, and parking space. Another significant contribution is in the added element of competition that has been successful in lowering cost margins and prices of products to the public. In a sense, the chain stores that preceded the supermarket had contributed innovations in most of these areas. The supermarket also expands merchandise lines that it carries in an effort to achieve volume. [12]

> Like the trading post of old, the supermarket draws no lines in possible wares. It features anything from radios to canned peas. Its aisles may be lined with hardware, soft wares, toothpaste, produce, even wearing apparel. But the very diversity of the products, as with the village counters of old, provides allure. And when these heaping counters also appeal to customers' saving instincts because of their good values, the combination is irresistible. [13]

This quotation may be biased in an attempt to sell the idea of the supermarket. Let us look at the environment in which it spawned and the forces that gave it the power to evolve in the brief span of time since it was introduced.

Evolution of the Supermarket

The circumstances were right for the development of the supermarket. Indeed, as we shall observe, great and unknown market pressures were gathering force and waiting to be tapped by the right merchandising innovation. These forces had their roots in somewhat the same factors that gave rise to the chain and the department store. Rapid increases in industrial production and a growing population and income increased the possibilities for volume savings. Not only was the population concentrating in urban areas, but more and more people moved on wheels and could move in the direction of the spectacular, especially when it possessed an economy appeal. [14] The supermarket offered elements both of the spectacular and of economy. [15]

---

[11] *The Supermarket Industry Speaks*, 1965, Seventeenth Annual Report by the members of Supermarket Institute (Chicago: Supermarket Institute, Inc., 1965), p. 9.

[12] An example of one firm that realized sales of $400,000 with a margin of 25 percent is cited by Maurice Warsaw, "Toys, A Boon to the Super Market," *Super Market Merchandising* (August, 1953), pp. 2-8.

[13] M. M. Zimmerman, *The Super Market* (New York: McGraw-Hill Book Company, Inc., 1955), p. 19.

[14] William Applebaum reports on the problem of "Measuring Retail Market Penetration for a Discount Food Supermarket with a Case Study," *Journal of Retailing* (Summer, 1965), p. 1.

[15] The means of dramatizing the store's offering in a manner that will keep the customer's loyalty are legion. Indeed, the selection and execution of a promotional problem becomes a very complex challenge which is discussed by Stanley J. Shapiro and Robert J. Colonna in "Store Loyalty as a Measure of Promotional Effectiveness of Supermarkets," *Business Horizons* (Fall, 1964), pp. 97-104.

Specific Beginnings

In terms of idea, and even of practice, the supermarket was quite common in certain localities before it burst into the national marketing picture with a blaze of spectacular profits. Southern California was the area in which many such institutions developed as grocery coliseums. Ralph's Grocery Company, a pioneer in the food business since 1873, developed supermarkets that were operating successfully in 1930. Other operators in this area, and in Texas, Colorado, and Michigan, had stores that were in every respect supermarkets. Two developments were so spectacularly advertised that the whole system of distribution in the nation caught fire with the idea.

Michael Cullen. One of the major characters in this dramatic spectacle was Michael Cullen. A most interesting part of supermarket history is that portion describing the manner in which Cullen worked out the complete blueprint of his idea. He included every possible expense as a part of his calculation. He illustrated how he could make 2½ percent on a $10,000-a-week grocery business and 3 percent on a $2,500-a-week meat business. Such a business would have brought net sales of $650,000 and net profit of nearly $17,000 in a year. He was working for the Kroger chain stores at the time and tried every possible device to get his story before top management in the Kroger chain, but he was unsuccessful.

He then went to Long Island, New York, obtained financial aid from a partner, and opened his first store in Jamaica in 1930. It was the first unit of the "King Kullen" chain, still a thriving organization. His success was phenomenal. People responded in hordes to his offering and his advertising. A typical headline was "King Kullen, the world's greatest price wrecker. How does he do it?" He would then proceed to tell his public the story of volume and low costs. By 1932 he was operating 8 markets in which the grocery departments alone were selling an annual average of $750,000 each. By 1935 he had 15 units. He was thinking of a national franchise and expansion when he died in 1936, at the age of fifty-two.

The Big Bear Markets. In 1932 Robert M. Otis and Roy O. Dawson began their experiment in the supermarket field. They persuaded a Hoboken wholesaler to join them in leasing the vacant Durant Automobile Plant at Elizabeth, New Jersey, and in converting the plant into a circus-like emporium with the food department as a hub. This department was surrounded by eleven others; auto accessories, paints, radios, hardware, drugs, soda fountains, and lunch counters were among the departments featured. Only 30 percent of the space was devoted to food. Full-page ads with huge streamers announced the opening with such captions as "Big Bear, the World's Champion Price Fighter." The first ads featured Lifebuoy soap at 4 cents, Quaker Oats at 3 cents, Maxwell House coffee at 22 cents, and pork chops at 10 cents a pound.

In the first three days, the customers paid over $30,000 to the cashiers. The second week the store sales exceeded $75,000. Many of the customers drove over 50 miles. At the close of one year's operation, Big Bear had collected $3,873,280. With a modest investment of a little more than $10,000, of which, according to Mr. Otis, only $1,000 in cash was actually paid at the beginning, Big Bear earned as net profits to its promoters over $166,000 in its first year of operation.

Those who predicted that the new type of store was only a novelty were disappointed. The idea of the supermarket was sound. The King Kullen and Big Bear examples have been repeated in many areas throughout the country. Satisfactions have been increased and costs reduced as a result of ventures into this type of promotion.

As with other spectacular innovations, the supermarket movement met resistance. The local press took up the battle against Big Bear. Chain store papers published adverse editorials. Newspapers carried stories under such captions as "Municipal Suicide," "Big Bear Raids," "Chains and Anti-Chains Take Time Out to Wage War Against Supermarkets," "Grocery Manufacturers Take Time Out to Wage War Against Price Wrecker Supermarkets," "Another Challenge to Nationally Advertised Brands." In some form these statements had their counterpart in every community. The final arbiter in such situations, however, is the housewife, and she decided that the supermarket should stay.

THE DISCOUNT STORE

Reduced prices have been widely used as a competitive weapon and, consequently, there have always been merchants who attempt to "discount" prices on some items. The name "discount house," however, is attached to the type of operation that began right after World War II. The usual beginning was to advertise and sell brand name appliances at discounts as much as 40 percent lower than the usual price in other stores. The discounters gradually added to their lines and finally offered about everything found in department stores. The discount house entered the mass market with a low status image, and its margins and prices are also low.

There is no specific classification for the discount house in the census reports or other published organs. Official figures, therefore, are not available. The trade paper, *Discount Store News,* however, defines the *discount* store as "(1) Over 10,000 square feet; (2) Both hard and soft goods: (3) Cost structure below that of a traditional store." [16] This definition does not permit us to draw a sharp line of demarcation between a department store and a discount house. The offices of the F. W. Woolworth Company, for example, would rather have their Woolco stores considered as department stores, yet the *Discount Store News* lists Woolco as a discount store.

In the late forties and early fifties the discount house entered the marketplace quietly by passing out membership cards to selected clientele. It featured hard goods of respected brands and sold them below the fair trade prices. At this time the discount house was not a low-status store. It was a mark of distinction for a man to hold a discount store card and buy at prices which were significantly lower than was legal under the resale price maintenance law. However, this period was short-lived. The idea spread throughout the nation—first in the large cities, then the smaller ones.

---

[16] *Discount Store News,* Vol. V, No. 7 (August 22, 1966), p. 1.

The rapid growth of the discount house provides evidence of the difficulty of maintaining a price structure based on law when it is contrary to the laws of supply and demand as expressed in the marketplace. For example, a 40 percent markup on refrigerators was not uncommon under the resale price maintenance law, and such a markup presumed a certain number of services. Such a margin, however, would make it possible for retailers to buy a refrigerator for $210.00 and sell it for $350.00. The discount house, if it could acquire sufficient volume, could sell the refrigerator for $262.50—a difference of $87.50. Other products were marked proportionately low. Such a savings was of sufficient magnitude to offset the services provided by the conventional store.

This explanation should not be understood to mean that discount houses sell all of their merchandise significantly below competing department stores. Like most other marketing institutions, discount houses have their price leaders and also products where margins are comparable with department stores in the same city.

As is commonly true with innovations in retailing, there was a great expansion in discount stores. The expansion was followed by considerable numbers of failures. At least eight large discount chains sharply retracted operations or filed for bankruptcy in 1973. Those that are successful keep stores physically attractive, carefully follow consumer preferences, stress known brands, have credit facilities, provide for exchange or return of items, and staff the stores with people who can provide assistance and information.

Retail consultants point out that the discount chains that fail or are in trouble have not traded up in quality and fashion to meet needs of consumers who are better educated and have more disposable income than did the customers attracted to discount stores two decades ago.

Despite present difficulties of some of the discount chains, there are approximately 3,600 discount stores in the United States, according to the Massachusetts Merchandise Institute—the trade association of discount stores. Their sales volume in the aggregate is approximately eight percent of total United States retail dollar sales. That is about the same as sales of all department stores.

The conflict between the department store and the discount house is typical of the battle between high and low margins. This conflict has characterized retailing from the days of the general store to the present time. Professor Malcolm McNair of the Harvard Business School describes the process as "the wheel of retailing."[17] He points to a cycle that begins when a store enters the market with low status, low prices, and few services. At this point in the cycle, the prices of other institutions are high, and such stores gain a substantial following and become numerous. As these stores begin to compete with each other, they offer more service, better location, higher status, and improved surroundings. Although such additions to motivate the consumers are nonprice-competition factors, the price of their products must increase to cover the costs.

---

[17] Stanley C. Hollander presents McNair's case and analyzes it in "The Wheel of Retailing," *Journal of Marketing* (July, 1960), pp. 37-42.

This cycle is best illustrated by the supermarket itself. It began with a mere shell as a cover for merchandise and a cost margin of less than 10 percent. At the present time average gross margins of supermarkets are above 20 percent of sales, and they provide decorative surroundings and a number of services. Likewise, the first department stores were able to realize encouraging profits with a 25 percent markup. They had a larger starting markup than supermarkets because their merchandise turned over less frequently. Today their margins approximate from 35 to 40 percent, depending on the clientele they seek and their policy for service and quality of merchandise.[18] A period of increasing volume, such as the period following World War II, makes possible lower gross margins. Prices based on conventional and old margins created a vacuum which actually invited the entrance of the discount house.

In spite of the competition and rapid growth of discount houses, the average margins of department stores are still increasing. These well-established institutions have been unwilling to compromise their prestige and quality image. In spite of their higher prices, they have been able to increase their sales significantly (if not their share of the market). There has been a significant increase in per capita income, and many customers have sought satisfaction in quality with as much zeal as others have followed low prices. This trend has favored the department store. There will most likely be more innovations that enter the market with a price appeal and, in the process, there will probably be stores completing a price-quality spectrum from the high-class, exclusive department store to the lowest priced, no-service discount house.

QUESTIONS AND ANALYTICAL PROBLEMS

1. What portion of total dollar volume retailing in the United States is accounted for by multiunit (chain) establishments?

2. What factors did the A & P, Woolworth, and J. C. Penney organizations have in common?

3. Are chain stores more efficient retailing operators than single-unit operators? Discuss fully.

4. Do chain stores sell at lower prices than single-unit, independent stores? Discuss fully.

5. What advantages, if any, do mail-order organizations have over more ordinary retailing methods? What limitations must mail-order operators overcome if they are to succeed?

6. What advantages, if any, do department stores have over other retailing operators? Are there any advantages that are peculiar to department store operations?

7. What is a branch store? What is the effect of branch-store operation on total organization sales and expense? Discuss fully.

8. Define supermarket.

9. Why did supermarkets develop in the food field rather than in hardware, for example?

10. Define discount store.

11. What are the principal causes for failure of discount store chains? What do the successful discount stores have in common? In your answers emphasize management practices.

---

[18] Herman Rodolf, consulting editor for *Retailer*, reports the average cumulative margins of department stores in 1964 as 40.1 percent as compared to 39.51 percent in 1963 and 38.60 percent in 1962, in *Journal of Retailing* (Winter, 1965), p. 50.

Case 6 • MORGAN'S INCORPORATED

Located in a large metropolitan area, Morgan's, Incorporated, a fast-growing department store, had built for itself a substantial reputation for quality merchandise and reliable service. The president of the company was considering eliminating the patio and lawn department and leasing the space to a beauty salon because of the steadily decreasing trend in the former's contribution to the store's profit. Total contribution by all the departments averaged 14 percent.

The patio and lawn departmental operating statement for last year was:

Net sales	$196,000	100.0%
Total gross margin..........	66,640	34.0%
Direct expenses:		
Advertising	11,760	6.0%
Selling payroll	8,820	4.5%
Delivery.................	11,760	6.0%
Other	29,400	15.0%
TOTAL	$ 61,740	31.5%
Departmental contribution....	$ 4,900	2.5%

The company president estimated that the proposed beauty salon must make a contribution of about $10,000 in order to make its share of the contribution to overhead. If the salon occupied 2,200 square feet of floor space, on the basis of a typical average of $50 of sales per square foot, the salon should attain a sales volume of $110,000 annually. The president proposed that Morgan's, Incorporated, should receive 15 percent of the sales volume from the leaseholder for underwriting the cost of installing the salon. This proposal would result in a contribution of $16,500.

• What considerations, other than profit, should Morgan's, Incorporated, weigh in making the decision to adopt the proposed change? What would be your recommendation and why?

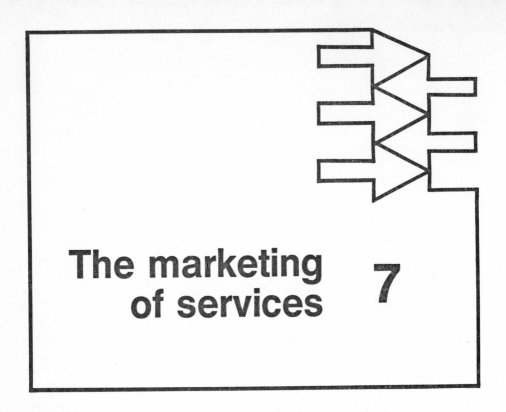

The marketing of services 7

Major emphasis on the marketing of services is new. This is not because the marketing of services is new, neither is it because the value of services purchased has been increasing so rapidly, although such increase is a factor. Rather, more attention is being given to the sales of services because the tempo of growth and innovation has affected services, just as it has other goods.

Within the single field of transporting goods, the railroads used to enjoy a monopoly. Now trucks, air freight, improved waterways, and pipelines compete with them. Banks today must compete with an increasing number of small loan companies, savings and loan firms, and institutional credit unions. Gas is competing with electricity for heating and cooking. These and other services compete not only within their respective fields but also with other services and products for a share of the consumer dollar. Innovations growing out of the competitive race are as frequent in services as in products. Walkie-talkies and telephones in automobiles are increasingly being used where they can increase satisfaction and, in some instances, reduce the costs of communicating.

The seller of services has the same advertising and selling problem in demand creation as the seller of products in that he must introduce new features to the customer and urge the purchase of his service rather than that of his competition. As is the case with the seller of products, the customer is the center of the service seller's universe. The only essential difference in the marketing problem is that the seller of service has no storage problem and is not concerned with a change of title.

The service industries are increasing their total market share of consumer expenditures. In the twenty years between 1953 and 1973 their market share increased from 23 percent to 41 percent. Whether it is the result of more effective marketing services, innovation, or the natural growth of the economy, services are winning a greater proportion of the sales dollar on the competitive market. To gain a clearer concept of the marketing of services, we will first define services and examine their relationship to products and the consumer. Second, we will examine the growth of services and their importance in the economy. Third, we will discuss the marketing procedure and the problems of different service institutions and compare them with the marketing of goods.

DEFINITIONS OF SERVICES

In our discussion of services, it is important to have a clear concept of what services are as distinguished from goods. The Committee on Definitions of the American Marketing Association defines services as follows: "Activities, benefits, or satisfactions which are offered for sale or are provided in connection with the sale of goods."[1] This definition represents a consensus of marketing authorities and does define the general area of services. It does not, however, suit the purpose of our discussion because we consider the services rendered in connection with the sale of goods as a part of the goods. For our purposes *services* are defined as activities, benefits, or satisfactions that are offered for sale where there is no exchange of tangible goods involving a transfer of title. This definition includes the sale of such services as amusements, hotel, electric services, barber and beauty shops, repair and maintenance firms, financial institutions, and professional services of doctors, lawyers, and teachers.

There are three reasons why our definition serves the purpose of this discussion better than the more comprehensive definition. First, we have already discussed services in connection with retailing and will discuss the sale of goods by other institutions in additional chapters. Second, it would be difficult to separate the value of service from the value of the product for purposes of accounting and analysis in many institutions. Third, we are able to see marketing forces as they apply to services in clearer relief if we observe them when no product or transfer of title is involved.

THE IMPORTANCE OF SERVICES IN THE ECONOMY

From a study of the growing volume of services, it appears that as people grow more affluent they have a greater need or desire for services. Indices indicate that since World War II the rate of growth in the service industries has been greater than in the market for goods. To observe the degree to which this growth exists and also to become aware of the volume of services sold in comparison with goods, we will examine the gross national product and

---

[1] Committee on Definitions of the American Marketing Association, *Marketing Definitions* (Chicago: American Marketing Association, 1963), p. 21.

determine what proportion of it originates with services. We will also examine the national income and employment figures to see the relative importance of services as they relate to the change and growth of the economy.

Importance as Measured by Gross National Product and National Income

A clear view of the relationship of services to other sectors in the economy and of the direction of their change can be determined by examining the contribution of the service industries to the total national product. Such a presentation is published by the Department of Commerce in the *Statistical Abstract of the United States: 1973.* Four categories—durable goods, nondurable goods, services, and other—are listed which permit direct comparison in year-to-year figures. Table 7-1 shows that the percentage spent on services has decreased from 36 percent in 1930 to a steady 26 to 27 percent during the years 1960 to 1971.

Table 7-1
SERVICES AS A PART OF THE GROSS NATIONAL PRODUCT
(BILLIONS OF DOLLARS)
(CURRENT DOLLARS)

	1930	% of Total	1960	% of Total	1965	% of Total	1970	% of Total	1971	% of Total
Gross National Product	164.5	100.0	503.7	100.0	684.9	100.0	976.4	100.0	1050.4	100.0
Durable Goods	20.5	12.5	45.3	9.0	66.3	10.0	90.5	9.3	103.5	9.8
Nondurable Goods	63.0	38.2	151.3	30.0	191.1	28.0	264.7	27.1	278.1	26.5
Services	59.3	36.0	128.7	26.0	175.5	26.0	261.8	26.8	283.3	27.0

Source: U.S. Department of Commerce, Bureau of the Census, *Statistical Abstract of the United States: 1973* (94th ed.; Washington: U.S. Government Printing Office, 1973), p. 320, #517.

Another measure of service magnitude and change is the data presented by the U.S. Department of Commerce in the *Survey of Current Business* that shows the amount of national income which originates with services. Table 7-2 shows a breakdown of services by various classifications taken from national income accounts and indicates the relative changes in income derived from each.

During the period 1950 to 1971, the overall increase in all services was 409.63 percent. Some of the services that showed a sizable increase were: miscellaneous business services, which climbed from $1,168 to $14,241 (million)—an increase of over 745 percent, and miscellaneous professional services—which rose over 710 percent in the same time period.

Table 7-2

INCOME CHANGES IN SERVICES, 1959-1971

Classification	%Increase
Hotels & Lodging Places	147.30
Personal Services·	745.67
Private Households	352.89
Misc. Business Services	236.24
Misc. Repair Services	80.60
Motion Pictures	346.07
Amusement & Recreation	659.07
Medical Services	451.41
Legal Services	625.79
Misc. Professional Services	402.66
Educational Services	710.38
Nonprofit Membership Org.	98.81

Source: Derived from the U.S. Bureau of Economic Analysis, *Survey of Current Business: July, 1972.*

Importance as Measured by Employment Figures

An even more realistic magnitude than that which is reflected in the gross national product or the income figures is the change in the proportion of workers employed in the service industries. Table 7-3 reveals a steady increase in the proportion of employees in the service industries. The increase between 1950 and 1972, from 58 percent to 68 percent of the total, or an increase of 10 percent, is most noteworthy. This classification covers the broad view of services, including government and retail and wholesale trade.

Table 7-3

**EMPLOYMENT IN GOODS AND SERVICE INDUSTRIES
(IN THOUSANDS)**

	1950		1972	
	Number	Percentage	Number	Percentage
Construction, Manufacturing, and Mining	18,189	42	23,061	32
Services, Trade, Government, Finance, Insurance, Real Estate, and Transportation	25,337	58	49,704	68

Source: Derived from the U.S. Department of Commerce, Bureau of the Census, *Statistical Abstract of the United States: 1960* (81st ed.; Washington: U.S. Government Printing Office, 1960), pp. 209-211, #271, and the U.S. Department of Commerce, Bureau of the Census, *Statistical Abstract of the United States: 1973* (94th ed.; Washington:U.S. Government Printing Office, 1973), pp. 230-232, #370.

CHANGES IN THE SERVICES SECTOR

In addition to the rapid growth of the services sector, other changes have occurred that are relevant to the development of a complete understanding of its characteristics. Knowledge of the productivity of service workers, of the rise of prices in the service industries, and of the basic reasons for faster growth is essential for an analytical frame of reference with which to analyze the trends and forces in the service industries.

Changes in Productivity

Productivity can be defined for our discussion as the value of the goods or services delivered to the consumer by one man-hour of work. According to the Federal Reserve Bank of St. Louis, during the period from 1968 through 1972 the output per man-hour in the economy rose 2.6 percent.[2]

During this same period, productivity in finance, insurance, and real estate services lagged to 1.9 percent while business and professional services lagged to 1.2 percent.[3] An effect of this productivity lag has been the inflationary push caused by rising prices in the service sector.

There are two specific reasons why the productivity in the service industries might have lagged behind the product areas. First, services cannot be mechanized. For example, one cannot style a lady's hair on an assembly line or use the latest automatic devices. Second, there is evidence that large numbers of service workers are drawn from workers not previously employed, such as women, the young, the old, and the less educated groups.

Price Changes in Services

Through the period from 1955 to 1971, service prices included in the consumer price index rose annually without interruption at a rate almost triple that of commodity prices. In the period from 1970 through 1971, service prices increased 8.1 percent as compared to only 4.7 percent for commodity prices.

It is evident that much, if not all, of the increase in the consumer price index was the result of the increase in the price of the services included in the consumer price index. Significant in this consideration of indexes is the fact that the consumer price index in 1956 was changed to reflect 41 percent of the consumer dollar going to services instead of the previous 35 percent.[4] If such had been the case during the previous decade, the consumer price index would have gone up even more. Table 7-4 shows selected price indexes from 1955 to 1972. With the exception of housing, the increase of prices in service industries is above average, while that of all categories of goods is less than average.

The price of medical care has been the principal culprit in increasing the service price index to higher levels. The increase in this category, 68 percent,

---

[2] Federal Reserve Bank of St. Louis, *National Economic Trends* (May 24, 1973), p. 12.

[3] "Services Grow While the Quality Shrinks," *Business Week* (October 30, 1971), p. 51.

[4] U.S. Department of Commerce, Bureau of the Census, *Statistical Abstract of the United States: 1972* (93d ed.; Washington: U.S. Government Printing Office, 1972), p. 342.

Table 7-4
CONSUMER PRICE INDEXES (1967 = 100)

	1955	1960	1965	1970	1971	1972
All items	80.2	88.7	94.5	116.3	121.3	125.3
Medical Care	—	79.1	89.5	120.6	128.4	132.5
Food	81.6	88.0	94.4	114.9	118.4	123.5
Apparel	84.1	89.6	93.7	116.1	119.8	122.3
Housing	82.3	90.2	94.9	118.9	124.3	129.2
Transportation	77.4	89.6	95.9	112.7	118.6	119.9
Personal Care	—	90.1	95.2	113.2	116.8	119.8
Reading & Recreation	—	87.3	95.9	113.4	119.3	122.8
Other Goods & Services	—	87.8	94.2	116.0	120.9	125.5

Source: U.S. Department of Commerce, Bureau of the Census, *Statistical Abstract of the United States: 1973* (94th ed.; Washington: U.S. Government Printing Office, 1973), p. 354, #577.

between 1960 and 1972, was primarily due to rising costs of hospital care rather than of doctors' fees. During the same period transportation costs increased by 32 percent and rent, 38 percent.

The implications for the future in this change may be significant. Evidence seems to indicate that with increasing incomes there will be an increase in the proportion of the consumer dollar spent for services. In an economy of near full employment, the service industry may find it difficult to secure the employment of men who are highly skilled. It is likely, therefore, that productivity in services will continue to increase at a lower rate than products, and service prices will increase faster (see Table 7-5).

Table 7-5
CHANGE IN U.S. EMPLOYMENT—1965-1972

Occupational Group	Employment (in millions)		Net Change (Percent)
	1965	1972	
Professional & Technical	8.8	11.5	31
Proprietors & Managers	7.5	8.0	7
Sectrl. & Clercl. Workers	11.0	14.2	29
Sales Workers	4.6	5.4	18
Skilled Workers & Foremen	9.2	10.8	17
Semi-Skilled Workers	13.0	13.5	4
Service Workers	9.5	11.0	16
Unskilled Workers	3.6	4.2	17
Farmers & Farm Workers	4.3	3.1	−28
TOTAL	71.5	81.7	14

Source: "Current Labor Statistics," *Monthly Labor Review*, Vol. 96, No. 5 (May, 1973), p. 81.

According to well-publicized Bureau of Labor Statistics estimates, the shift from goods-producing to service industries could lower the rate of productivity growth by about 0.2 percent a year during the 1970's. The slowdown in the shift away from the farm will reduce it by an additional 0.2 percent. On the other hand, the Bureau of Labor Statistics is currently projecting an *increase* in productivity gains in many industries, e.g., construction and trade. These increases will affect about half of the loss from occupational shifts, leaving a net potential decline of about 0.2 percent. And it is true that any such long-term decline—from, say, a 3 percent to a 2.8 percent rate of gain in productivity—could lower the potential output of the economy by a total of $120 billion during the 1970's.[5]

Difficulties in Classifying and Analyzing Service Data

The separation of services from product categories is a complex and sometimes confusing task. We have defined services to include transactions where satisfaction was sold unaccompanied by tangible goods and transfer of titles. Transportation clearly falls within this category. Yet transportation costs become a part of the cost of the good that is sold and are counted as a good in computing the gross national product. When computed as a part of the national income, transportation is a separate category that can be listed with services where it rightfully belongs, because it is an intangible service where no title changes hands in the completion of the transaction.

In view of the recent emphasis on services, today there are many publications discussing services and almost an infinite number of statistical studies. Some of these studies are specific in delineating what is covered and what is excluded. Others are less precise and merely refer to services, implying that the reader will know whether the figures include retailing, wholesaling, transportation, government services, and other services where no clear line of division has been agreed upon. In the three classifications we have presented, insofar as figures are available, we have adjusted them to conform to our definition. For example, transportation was included in the total services according to its contribution to the national income, and wholesaling and retailing were not. In the number of employees engaged in services, we departed from our definition to include wholesaling and retailing employees, since this study did not show a separate classification. The term "services" can have completely different meanings according to the context in which it appears.

There are two basic reasons for the present chaotic state of statistical data applying to services. First, statistical studies, which include nearly all business and economic data, are comparatively new. Most series, at best, date back to 1929. Service institutions were not a significant part of these tabulations and, therefore, did not receive adequate attention. The second reason is corollary to

---

[5] Sanford Rose, "The News About Productivity is Better Than You Think," *Fortune*, Vol. 85, No. 2 (February, 1972), p. 184.

the first. Service industries are so diverse that it is extremely difficult to separate them into neat and clear-cut compartments. Services have been described as:

> . . . not a group of industries at all but a potpourri of businessmen and professionals with nothing in common except that none has goods to sell. They sell only labor, wisdom, or the use of goods. From psychiatrists and charwomen in Manhattan skyscrapers to tree surgeons and chair-rental firms in Seattle, the many-splendored galaxy of services is something that only an economics statistician can comprehend with a single glance.[6]

Even such diversity, however, is certainly within the scope of classification and approximate tabulation with today's modern data processing and recording capacity. Indeed, it is unlikely that a clear concept of the true significance of services, which can become a basis for clear thinking and public policy decision, will emerge until services are more adequately defined and described.

Reasons for the Growth of the Service Industries

Basic to an adequate understanding of the forces responsible for the growth of the service industries is an understanding of why such increases have taken place since 1950. Two principal reasons account for this increase. First, rising incomes have permitted people not only to increase their overall consumption of goods and services but also to shift some of the tasks they formerly performed themselves to those who sell such services in the marketplace. Second, increased demand for services has pressed the supply to such an extent that the high price of services has been accompanied by an increase in the volume of services sold. It is likely that this situation will continue to prevail and may result in even more rapid growth of the service industries.

MARKETING OF SERVICES COMPARED WITH MARKETING OF GOODS

The sustained performance of services, even though they do not possess material substance nor involve a transfer of title, depends upon the application of marketing skills. Service institutions and individuals, just as those concerned with the marketing of goods, must make a profit to remain in business. As is the case with products, the choice of a specific company's service is the result of many influences apart from the service itself. Such preferences arise because of the effects of advertising, selling, a favorable price, and the availability of the service at a convenient time and place. Furthermore, service institutions must also constantly innovate and improve to increase and hold their market share. For example, the dentist today has a less painful method of filling teeth and has an assistant to provide constant comfort to the patient. Gas and electric utilities

---

[6] "The Do-It-For-Me-Boom," *Newsweek* (April 8, 1957), p. 89.

have men that visit the user's home to analyze problems and make minor repairs.

The marketing functions that do not relate to service sellers are stock control, inventory investments, product spoilage and obsolescence, and transportation. The product seller also must arrange for transfer of title although in most cases this task requires no more effort or skill than the consummation of service transactions.

FINANCIAL SERVICES

One of the major services that are bought and sold at the marketplace is financial service. This service includes making money and credit available, protecting it, and in some instances selecting investment opportunities that provide a major occupation and income to many. The money flow managed by financial institutions contributes a significant facility to the functioning and growth of the economy and provides satisfactions to many that would otherwise be impossible. There are many types of financial institutions, but most of them are included in these general classifications—banks, insurance companies, and investment houses. The relationship to marketing of each of these types of financial institutions is discussed in the following paragraphs.

Banks

Only in recent years have banks departed from traditional patterns and entered the competitive race with vigor. Since the base from which a commercial bank operates is its deposits, a bank aggressively seeks the patronage of depositors. Such aggressive seeking of deposits is economically desirable because banks can render improved services in varying degrees of excellence and achieve different levels of efficiency. They can dignify or abuse their customers, the depositors. It is, therefore, important that banks be stimulated to higher levels of performance by competition just as are other marketing institutions.

Competition in banking services has some of the characteristics of product competition. A bank uses depositors' funds as a base for making money available to other parties; thus, the main marketing efforts of banks move in two directions. First, a bank attempts to sell people on the practice of depositing money with its institutions. In most instances the bank pays a price determined by the interest rate for this money set by the Federal Reserve Board. Second, the bank loans money to others for which it collects interest. Both the interest that is paid the depositor and the rate that is charged on loans are prices that are determined by marketplace forces. The management of a bank, though, still has a certain amount of leeway for charging higher or lower interest rates, depending upon its specific strategy. The interest that the bank pays the depositor, as compared to the rate charged the borrower, is somewhat similar to the wholesale price paid by the retailer and the retail price charged the ultimate consumer, although one should be cautious in pushing this comparison too far. In the last five years, most states have passed legislation limiting the ceiling that banks can charge in the form of interest rates.

A commercial banker does more than buy the money from depositors at one price and sell the same money to borrowers at a higher price. The commercial banker can multiply the volume of loans to exceed the base provided by the deposits, as limited by the amount of deposits required. Furthermore, skill in dealing with money is quite different from skill in retailing.

The fact that banks must compete on a price basis, both in terms of loans and deposits, is particularly significant to marketing students. Customers for loans are secured by innovations in the interest-rate price and in contract provisions designed to make it convenient for the individual to repay the loan. Innovations in the interest-rate price and in the frequency with which the interest is computed to obtain a multiplying effect are means by which depositors are secured. To achieve a degree of stability in deposits, banks employ the merchandising inducement of paying a higher rate of interest on a certificate of deposit than is paid for the ordinary time deposit.

Banks also engage in nonprice competition by selecting convenient locations and providing for night depositories, drive-in service, an adequate number of tellers to avoid lines and waiting, cheerful service, a friendly atmosphere, and cash dispensing machines, which give 24-hour banking to the consumer. While these areas, both in the price and nonprice fields, are subject to different policies, means of performance, and innovations, they are all designed to win the support of bank customers, be they depositors or borrowers.

Bank Credit Cards. An innovation in the banking field that has an almost revolutionary potential is the credit card. Large banking firms are offering credit cards that are honored in most kinds of businesses in all parts of the nation. Holders of the card can use it for all kinds of purchases or payments in all parts of the nation and pay all their bills with one check to the bank issuing the card. The cost of the card to the bank is paid by charging a certain percentage of sales to the firms where the credit purchases are made. There were 47 million credit card holders in January of 1971.[7]

The bank credit card is only one step away from another more startling innovation that might be described as the checkless society. This plan will handle clearing of balances by an interconnection of depositors with all points where payments are made. Recognition or identification of the purchaser will be made, social security number provided, and, by wire service, the appropriate account will be charged with the amount of the purchase or the payment.

An Illustrative Example. The Meadow Brook National Bank on Long Island, New York, is an example of what a bank can do if it uses the marketing tools available to it. This bank had assets of less than $50 million and two offices in 1959; by early 1965 it had 66 offices and $850 million in assets. The bank had hired six young and aggressive salesmen from industrial companies. These men surveyed the respective areas to which they were assigned to discover the best prospects for expanding business. They then studied the

---

[7] U.S. Department of the Commerce, Bureau of the Census, *Statistical Abstract of the United States: 1973* (94th ed.; Washington: U.S. Government Printing Office, 1973), p. 455, #724.

business opportunities of individual businesses before calling on them. With a clear concept of each firm's opportunities in mind, they called on these businesses and sold them on the idea of using bank loans and services to improve their business. The rapid growth of the bank attests to the success of this marketing program.

Insurance Companies

Only a short time ago, all the insurance salesman had to know was the provisions of three main kinds of policies: term insurance, twenty-pay life, and the twenty-year endowment policies. Today even the small companies have almost as many kinds of policies as General Motors has automobile models. The productive insurance salesman now studies the entire financial condition of the prospect and sets up an insurance program tailored to the specific needs of the individual. It is common for insurance programs to be designed to begin repayment when the children start to college, to provide retirement at a specified income, and to build up an emergency fund as preparation for unexpected crises. Today even small insurance companies employ actuarial experts to assist them in fashioning policies that will differentiate their offerings from their competitor's.

Some insurance companies are now innovating to meet a need brought about by a change in the nature of the economy. Inflation to most people has been accepted as a permanent characteristic of the economy. Insurance or annuities with fixed dollar values are less likely to appreciate in value as much as common stocks. To adapt to this change, insurance companies are merging with mutual funds and selling both insurance and mutual funds with insurance and appreciating income provisions in one package. Others have adopted a means of disbursing gains of portfolio appreciation in their dividend program. Still others have tied the cash value of the customer's claims to stock price levels and advertise and sell variable annuities. Thus, it appears that the success of the insurance company is tied closely to marketing skills. The effectiveness of the selling and advertising program of insurance companies is strategic and an absolute necessity. The constant adaptation and improvement of the kinds of policies and contracts closely resemble an industrial firm's program of product research and development. The other source of income for the insurance company is from investments. Excellence in this area also requires expertise in the area of analyzing markets.

Demand Creation. Just as insurance companies have made effective use of the innovation concept, they have also pioneered in the field of demand creation. Not nearly as many people would be aware of the circumstances that might result from accident or death were it not for the effective advertising and selling of insurance companies. They also dramatize effectively the positive effects that can result from a well-managed insurance and annuity plan. Whichever motive or selling appeal is used, demand for the product is created in true marketing fashion.

Abuses. As is the case with products, purchases of life insurance are not always the best buys available nor even wise purchases. Insurance and annuity contracts are complex, and the buyer is often dependent upon the judgment and skill of the insurance salesman. As a result, unfortunately, there have been abuses. The percentage of policy cancellations is very high, and in most instances such cancellations represent losses to the purchasers. Insurance companies, in sensing this danger of abuse, have responded by the adoption of professional standards of procedure embodied in the Certified Life Underwriter Certificate, which includes provisions that tend to guarantee the competence of the underwriter as well as ethical standards.

Some abuse has also developed in the automobile accident insurance field. Rates have skyrocketed to such proportions that insurance cost today has become a major factor in deciding whether or not to purchase an automobile. For example, the average annual premium for a standard liability policy in 1968 was $80, and this cost did not include property damage or collision and upset. In 1969 total claims paid for automobile accident insurance came to $8 billion as compared to only $3.5 billion in 1958.[8] Although it is true that there are valid reasons for the rapid increase in the cost of automobile insurance (rising costs of parts and of labor for repair and the fact that the bodies of modern cars are constructed in such a way that it is now more expensive to repair them than was the case with earlier models), it is also true that certain abuses are being committed in this area. For example, many garages have an agreement with competitors that they will submit courtesy bids on repair jobs; that is, they will not underbid their friends. Further, there are some auto repair shops that favor their patrons by repairing damages which were incurred on occasions other than the accident which was covered by a particular claim. The extent to which these practices influence insurance rates may be minimal, but government investigations are now looking into the costs of automobile insurance.

Economic and Social Contributions. The economic and social contributions of insurance companies, aside from spreading risks and absorbing shock, are significant. Insurance companies contribute significantly to economic progress by providing the expertise necessary to invest the billions of dollars paid in by policyholders in areas that tend to yield the largest income. Many insurance companies loan money to builders who contribute to community development by building high-standard apartment houses and shopping centers. An example of another worthwhile social contribution is the research conducted by the Metropolitan Life Insurance Company to discover means of increasing the longevity of policyholders. After researching ways of improving health and of increasing the life span, the company advertised its findings in national campaigns. This program not only contributed to the general welfare but also benefited the company, for any increase in the length of life would increase the length of time that each policyholder paid premiums.

---

[8] U.S. Department of Commerce, Bureau of the Census, *Statistical Abstract of the United States: 1972* (93d ed.; Washington: U.S. Government Printing Office, 1972), p. 549.

Investment Companies

The growing affluence of the population has created opportunities for an increasing proliferation of different kinds of firms that sell investment securities. Now even small cities with 50,000 people have access to direct wire services to Wall Street and have several investment agencies competing for business from which they realize a commission on the sales they make. In the large centers security firms tend to specialize in certain kinds of stocks and bonds, for large populations and income make specialization possible, as is the case in the marketing of goods.

Another financial service organization that has grown significantly is the mutual investment fund. This organization is composed of security specialists who invest the money of the company's clients in securities as defined by the company's policy. Many of these companies offer their clients a choice of investment programs or a combination of plans. Some programs emphasize safety with a low but certain income such as can be obtained by the purchase of bonds. Other programs are designed for the individual who prefers slightly less security and more income. Still a third possibility is one that places less emphasis on income and more on growth and appreciation of capital values. The organizers of mutual funds profit by charging loading fees to cover the cost of their selling campaign and their expertise in the selection of securities. Thus, their income is for the service rendered and not from the income of the securities. Their success depends upon their ability to combine securities into contracts that are attractive to customers and to sell them. Like the product sellers, they are concerned with effective marketing of their services at minimum costs.

TRANSPORTATION SERVICES

Transportation of people is a service of both private and public concern, and, unfortunately, the services available at present are very unsatisfactory. Metropolitan highways are jammed to the point of frustration, a difficulty which is being compounded by population and automobile-sales increases. Although subsidized, commuter agencies in many metropolitan areas are losing money and are providing substandard service. It is evident that at many points the demand for people transportation is outrunning the supply. Neither the genius of free enterprise nor the assistance of government has provided the answer, as has been typically done in other fields. Nevertheless, there are some hopeful signs on the horizon. The city of San Francisco, for example, is leading out with a system of interurban high-speed trains, known as the Bay Area Rapid Transit System, or Bart, that moves a greater volume of traffic at higher speeds than any known system has heretofore accomplished. Another reassuring sign is that Congress has authorized the construction of a railroad from Boston to Washington, D.C., on which trains will travel at over 125 miles per hour. This means that the trains will be able to make the trip of about 400 miles in three hours.

The significant factor in the above developments is that corrective action is being initiated by the government. It is indeed commendable that action is being taken and that partnership arrangements with private companies appear compatible. However, would it not have been economically healthier if private enterprise had adapted to provide the needed services without government subsidy or assistance?

In conclusion, we can say that nonproduct enterprises are strongly committed to marketing programs. They utilize market studies to determine their competitive weaknesses and to discover opportunities for greater and better service. They conduct sales and advertising programs with growing insight. Finally, they are acquiring a growing awareness of their customers' needs and characteristics and are involving themselves in both research and promotion to satisfy those needs.

PERSONAL SERVICES

In personal and miscellaneous services, there is an almost infinite diversity of levels of marketing skills. A knowledge of the marketing concept and the need for market orientation could be useful to these services, but awareness of such needs is nil. The repairman, the barber, and the beautician would prosper by being more intelligently articulate about their services and reasonably aggressive in selling and explaining them. Such an approach could be almost as important as the quality of their work.

The legal and medical services have ethical codes that prevent aggressive advertising and selling. Since these services are highly professionalized, it is assumed that a man or firm should be judged by performance and not by selling skill. Obviously, demand creation has no place in either profession. Other areas that absorb the service dollar, such as education and government, are major fields of study in their own right. Marketing knowledge is helpful to them, though hardly in the same sense that it is when applied to the business segment.

RECREATIONAL SERVICES

The marketing of recreational services is somewhat different from that of financial services or utilities. Recreational services are more heterogeneous in nature. It is difficult to think of the New York Mets or the Los Angeles Rams as being in the same kind of business as the Bank of America. Nonetheless, these athletic teams must either make a profit or be financed by some form of philanthropy. Moreover, the owners of such athletic organizations share the same entrepreneurial drives as do other marketing organizations. For example, the Baltimore Orioles moved from St. Louis, where they shared the baseball crowd with the Cardinals, to Baltimore because of a promise of greater financial return. Since 1950 Americans have spent 251 percent more for recreation, as is shown in Table 7-4.

With respect to services, it should be noted that there are five significant points which aid the development of an accurate concept regarding the progress which has been made in the marketing of services. First, the service industries have been growing faster than the product industries—they have been taking a larger share of the consumer's dollar and are the source of a growing share of the national income. Second, as incomes increase and the population becomes more affluent, this trend will probably continue. Third, productivity in the service area has not advanced as fast as productivity in the goods area primarily because of the heterogeneous nature of services. Fourth, service prices are increasing faster than the prices of goods. Fifth, competitive innovation and promotion are becoming a very significant part of the marketing of services.

QUESTIONS AND ANALYTICAL PROBLEMS

1. Define services and distinguish them from products.

2. Compare the rate of growth (sales volume) in service industries with the rate of growth in the market for products. Compare employment in service industries with employment in other major sectors of the economy. Evaluate and explain what the comparisons indicate.

3. Compare trends in production per man-hour of persons engaged in production of goods and in service industries. Explain the differences.

4. What is the trend in consumer spending for services as compared to products? How can you explain this trend? What are the implications?

5. Compare the duties and functions of the marketing department of a service firm with those of a product firm. What similarities and what differences occur?

6. What would you stress in a marketing program for a financial institution, such as a bank?

7. Choose any personal service and explain how you would promote it.

Case 7 • THE MERCHANTS AND FARMERS BANK

The president and the vice-president of the Merchants and Farmers Bank were not in agreement on a proposal to improve and modernize the drive-in depository and teller service of the bank. The vice-president favored an investment of $100,000 to purchase real estate and build a small unit apart from but connected with the bank building. The president of the bank was not convinced that such an investment was merited.

The Merchants and Farmers Bank, with total resources of $10,000,000, was located on a prominent corner of a city with a population of 45,000 and a trading area of 110,000 people. This location was three blocks west of the intersection of the two main commercial arteries which was considered to be the center of the business district. There were three other banks in the city. One was organized only five years ago and is located in the center of the city. It has total resources of $1,500,000. The second bank—one of the oldest in the city and part of the regional chain—is located one block north of the intersection at the center of the city. This bank has total resources of $12,000,000. The third bank is located across the street and south of the regional chain, away from the main intersection. This bank recently merged with a progressive bank in a small city only six miles away and is engaged in a vigorous promotion program. It has total resources of $6,000,000.

The Merchants and Farmers Bank presently has drive-in arrangements at a window of the main bank building. The entrance to the window is the same as the entrance to the bank's parking lot. There is room for only two lines of traffic. Often a single car would pull into the driveway at such an angle that it would block the entrance to the parking lot. Such incidents would frustrate traffic to the extent that during busy periods the automobiles would often line up until the street itself was blocked. The vice-president proposed to purchase additional real estate and build a small building just opposite the present window. This small building would have depository windows on both sides of the new addition. Thus, during the busy periods of the day, the bank could use the present facilities along with the new and serve three lines of traffic. The additional purchase of real estate would enable adequate room for ingress and egress from both the depository service and the parking lot.

In spite of the fact that two of the competing banks already had more adequate depository service than the Merchants and Farmers Bank, the president was not convinced that three windows were necessary. He felt that, if a boy could be employed to direct traffic during busy periods so that the parking lot lane would not be blocked, the depository patrons would not mind waiting. In supporting his position the president contends that: (1) drive-in banking will not increase, (2) patronage of a bank is not determined so much by convenience as by the integrity, the financial skill, and the respect which the public has for an institution, (3) an increasing amount of banking will be done by mail, and (4) electronic data processing equipment will make it possible to clear balances by automatic communication thereby making visits to the bank less necessary.

- Whose views do you support, and why?

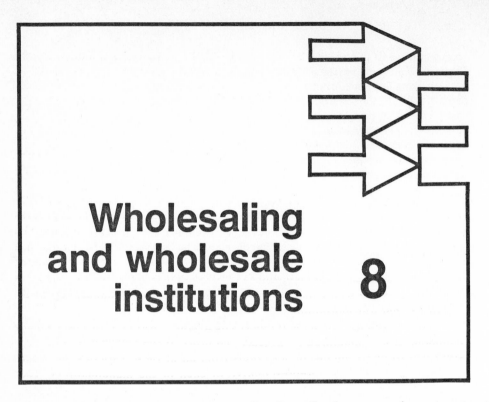

Wholesaling and wholesale institutions 8

Wholesaling, in its broadest sense, involves all sales transactions except those made to individuals or families for their personal consumption. Thus, it includes all sales of raw materials, of industrial goods from one producer to another or to an intermediary who resells to another producer, of all imports and exports, and of all sales to retailers.

Wholesaling evolved, and continues in existence, because of certain characteristics of production and use. Goods are seldom consumed in the place and at the rate they are produced; certain geographic areas have a comparative advantage in product, but they are not always the areas of high consumption of their product; and industrial users do not always have local access to the variety of goods they want or need. Also, the most efficient rate of production seldom coordinates with the most desirable rate of purchase and consumption. Hence, provision must be made to have the required assortment of products at the place and the time they are needed or desired. The wholesaler serves both manufacturers and retailers or industrial consumers in the performance of this function. In the following brief discussions of some of the economic tasks performed by wholesalers, the explanation of the role of wholesaling will be restricted largely to consumer goods; but the principles will apply in some measure to the marketing of industrial goods as well.

ADVANTAGES OF WHOLESALERS

Because of the conditions stated in the introductory paragraph above, there are certain economies inherent in wholesaling. In the following seven sections are summaries of each of the economic activities that allow efficient wholesalers to maximize their advantages.

Economies of the Re-sorting Function

Probably the most significant contribution of the wholesaler is in economizing the time and energy required in the movement of goods and in the number of transactions that control them. The goods of a single manufacturer are sold by many retailers, and the goods sold by an average retailer are produced by many manufacturers. When a manufacturer concentrates his sales on a few wholesale accounts instead of selling directly to the many retailers who sell his product, the number of orders that the manufacturer must process and the number of accounts which he must service are greatly reduced. To illustrate, if a producer of breakfast food wishes to serve 2,000 stores in a wholesale region, he probably would be able to achieve a complete coverage of these stores by dealing with ten wholesalers. Instead of 2,000 transactions there would be only ten with consequent savings in sales calls, bookkeeping, credit expenses, and transportation.

Savings also accrue to the retailer. The average grocery store carries 6,000 commodities manufactured by at least 200 firms. If the manager of a grocery store had to make intelligent selections from all of these varieties, he would have to allow time for a representative of each of the manufacturers. That would leave little time for other management functions. Furthermore, the retail buyer is not specialized in the purchase of the different commodities as are wholesalers who have specialized buyers of the several lines they handle.

Savings in Transportation Costs

The sum of transportation costs for a given supply of goods depends on the number of shipments made by the buyer and the seller and the rate charged on the product being shipped. The rate tends to decrease as the size of the order increases. A manufacturer may ship enough of his entire line to a wholesaler to serve several hundred retailers. The wholesaler will then re-sort this merchandise into the goods demanded by each retailer, and he may deliver a full load of merchandise to the retailer which represents the products of many manufacturers. By this operation a large-volume shipment of merchandise moves in both instances, and the number of shipments also is reduced.

To illustrate the economies possible in re-sorting and transportation, let us assume that ten retailers carry the products of ten manufacturers. If there is no intermediate wholesaler, each manufacturer must make a shipment to each of the retailers, a total of 100 shipments. Each manufacturer must keep an account and enter transactions for each retailer, which means keeping 100 accounts receivable. At the same time, each of the retailers must receive ten salesmen and keep ten accounts payable. This represents a total of 100 salesmen's contacts and 100 accounts payable.

Now assume the presence of the wholesaler. Each of these manufacturers needs to make only one call and one delivery and carry one accounts receivable account, a total of 10 rather than 100 of each of these costly operations.

Similarly, the retailer receives only one salesman and keeps one accounts payable account, reducing the total accounts payable to 10 instead of 100. The wholesaler makes 20 contacts, one each with the retailers and the manufacturers.

To recapitulate, without the wholesaler there were 200 contacts; with the wholesaler there were 40 contacts. Without the wholesaler 100 shipments were necessary to make contacts; with the wholesaler only 20 shipments were necessary, and these shipments were made in volume at lower rates. Thus, the savings in time, bookkeeping, wages, carrying costs of inventory, and transportation costs are what make wholesalers economically feasible.

Better Sales Coverage

For a number of reasons, the wholesaler has a distinct advantage in performing the selling function. First, the permanence of the relationship that exists between the wholesaler and the retailer provides a reliable contact; second, the maximum degree of coverage of all types and sizes of retailers to which the wholesaler sells cannot be achieved easily by the manufacturer; third, the wholesalers and retailers have a common tie, especially since the prosperity and the existence of both have been challenged by the growth and development of integrated distribution systems. In some instances this competitive pressure has forced the wholesaler into legal partnerships with voluntary and cooperative groups. Such a common challenge makes the wholesaler welcome in a store in which it would be difficult for the manufacturer's salesman to develop a trustful relationship.

In the matter of coverage, the wholesaler enjoys an advantage. When the wholesaler's salesman visits the small store, he usually receives some kind of an order because of the trusted relationship and also because of the wide variety of products that he carries. The order will probably be quite large. On the other hand, the manufacturer's salesman may not get an order because his line is narrow. If he does, the order is likely to be small by comparison. This fact makes it profitable for wholesale salesmen to call on stores that would not purchase enough from the manufacturer's salesman to make a call pay for itself. These small stores individually may not handle a significant percentage of the total merchandise that a manufacturer sells, but as W. C. Dorr says regarding such stores:

> (1) . . . for many manufacturers it is not small potatoes. In the aggregate, it runs as high as 50 percent of the total retail business of the country; (2) it's often the extra value that gets the sales department over the break-even point, where the headache stops and the profits begin; (3) it has been pretty well established that the wider the distribution in the secondary and third line stores, the greater are the sales in the major outlets. On many items people buy what territory-wide displays make them remember.[1]

---

[1] W. C. Dorr, "Direct vs. Jobber Distribution; An Appraisal of the Pros and Cons," *Sales Management* (February 1, 1949), pp. 37-39; (February 15, 1949), pp. 56-62; (March 1, 1949), pp. 92-98.

Facility of the Merchandising Function

Being out of stock is evidence of failure in merchandising. Retailers are out of stock because they do not order enough of the right stock at sufficiently frequent intervals. With the wholesaler's cooperation, the retailer can purchase smaller amounts because the wholesaler makes it possible for the retailer to reorder and accept delivery at shorter intervals.

In addition to this assistance, the wholesaler, by being a specialist in each classification of goods and by being in contact not only with many sources of supply but also with a wide field of retailers, is able to advise the retailer on lines that are selling fast and products that are new and that have shown promise. This is especially valuable for a small retailer whose own staff cannot specialize.

Time and Place Utility

Manufacturing economies are frequently achieved if the manufacturer can produce goods at an even rate; but sales, especially of consumer items, usually vary throughout the year. Some manufacturers sell an entire year's output for a special season. A combination of storage by manufacturers and by wholesalers in anticipation of peak sales periods relieves producers of the entire burden of carrying inventories.

On the other hand, the wholesaler adds one additional stop for a product en route to the consumer. If the product is of a nature that requires consumption as soon as possible after it is produced, the delay caused by this extra stop may be serious. To avoid this delay may be of sufficient importance to merit the additional expense entailed in direct sale. Perishable food and fashion items must reach the point of sale in the shortest time possible. If the wholesalers cannot streamline his operation, the advantage that he gains by providing time utility will be diminished; and the producer may go directly to the retailer.

Economy of Storage Services

By keeping a supply of goods available in the vicinity of the retailer, the wholesaler reduces the inventory that the retailer must carry to maintain an adequate assortment. The wholesale warehouse is a stock reservoir upon which the retailer may call in case of need. If all the goods that are held as wholesale warehouse stock were to be stocked in retail stores, carrying costs would soar, since retail stores are located in high-rent districts; and such costs would be passed on to the consumer. The manufacturer can also warehouse his goods in the vicinity of the retailer. Because of the large volume resulting from carrying many lines of merchandise, however, the wholesaler can perform this function with less cost. There are exceptions that we shall discuss later.

Time utility is closely related to storage. Stock held in the vicinity of retailer demand would not be necessary if customers were willing to wait until the goods could be ordered and shipped a distance. It is also important to note that during the period of time when stock is in transit and in storage, it is the property of the wholesaler. In this respect the wholesaler assumes risks. If the products are damaged or the price drops, the wholesaler bears the loss.

Facility of Credit

On many occasions the wholesaler makes a merchandise advance to a new business to enable it to get started. The wholesaler also carries the running account credit of most firms. It would be most difficult for the manufacturer to perform this credit function as efficiently as does the wholesaler. A firm that is on the scene of the retailer's activity and has a personal acquaintance with the management can act with greater wisdom and skill in the administration of credit. Often, because of factors that the distant manufacturer could not know, the wholesaler extends credit when not to do so would mean the failure of a firm which otherwise could become successful. On the other hand, investments have been saved as a result of the same wisdom in withholding credit or in collecting an account—decisions that might have been difficult if handled from a greater distance.

DISADVANTAGES OF WHOLESALERS

Even with these advantages, in many instances there are difficulties which render the wholesaler less effective in achieving the kind of selling effort that is desirable. In the areas of business where the wholesalers are strongest, they usually carry several lines that are in direct competition with one another. Under these circumstances it is difficult for the salesman to emphasize one line of goods because (1) in a single interview the salesman can aggresively sell but few products since sales efforts must be divided over many lines and (2) he cannot, in justice to all his suppliers, afford to push one line above the others.

It is a great advantage for some products to receive direct, continuous, and active promotion from the time they leave the manufacturer until they reach the consumer. Hence, some manufacturers find it desirable to control their products and to sell vigorously at every point along the channel. The decision of whether to sell through a wholesaler or directly to the retailer is primarily one for each manufacturer to make. This consideration is of sufficient importance to merit a special treatment in Chapter 10.

WHOLESALERS VERSUS MANUFACTURERS

The conflict of interest between the manufacturer and the wholesaler is of significance. The wholesaler has been the brunt of a popular appeal to cut distribution costs. Our purpose in setting forth the case for the wholesaler so carefully at the beginning of the chapter was to make clear some obvious facts that may have been forgotten in this attempt to recognize the wholesaler as one of the "too many middlemen."[2]

---

[2] The wholesaler as a dynamic force in our business and cultural progress has been defended by Herman C. Nolen in his talk, "The Modern Wholesaler and His Adjustment to the Changing Economy," given before the American Marketing Association Conference, Harvard University School of Business, June 25, 1958. Even though delivered several years ago, this talk well explains the wholesaler's shift from passive order-taker to a dynamic force in economic progress.

During the decade of the 1930's, the eyes of the public were focused on distribution. It was easy to conclude that marketing cost too much because there were too many middlemen. One factor which gave the argument significant force was that in many cases it was true. It was also true that the impact of the competition which the chain store introduced into the retail field was not completely understood by the wholesalers. However, a change had to come. Chain stores began using their own warehouses. The development of highways and trucks revolutionized transportation; the means of communication via telephone and telegraph improved. With the barriers of travel and communication decreased, new routes to market became less costly and more convenient both in terms of time and trouble. These developments, which had accumulated over the years, converged on the wholesaler in the decade of the 1930's.

The Manufacturer's Case Against the Wholesaler

One of the problems that the wholesaler had to meet during this period of challenge was a growing lack of enthusiasm on the part of the manufacturer for his services. Manufacturers began to seek a more effective route to the retailer. Some of the specific reasons for the manufacturer's attitude follow:

1. Failure to sell aggressively. Every manufacturer is strongly motivated to get his product to the marketplace first. Frustration results from the failure of the manufacturer to get the wholesaler to share his enthusiasm for his product. We have noted that the promotion of individual products is difficult for the wholesaler.
2. The fact that some expenses may be eliminated by going directly to the marketplace. This statement has seemed obviously true. Many firms have found from costly experience, however, that the reverse has been true. We have noted that when all other things are considered equal, cost reductions favor the wholesaler because of re-sorting, transaction, and transportation savings. In some situations size of unit sales, volume of business, or location of outlets favor direct or branch sales.
3. The wholesaler promotes his own private brands in competition with the manufacturer's brands. Usually the wholesaler's brands bring retailers better margins and, when all else is equal, the wholesaler will sell his own brands. Such competition within the same company puts the manufacturer at a disadvantage in his promotional program.
4. Failure of the wholesaler to assume merchandising and risk responsibilities.

Wholesalers have a small gross margin to cover all operating expenses and profit. They must then buy carefully, since they cannot afford to carry obsolete or slow-moving stock but, as noted earlier, the market life of many products is short, which increases risk of obsolescence. The wholesaler attempts to achieve maximum sales with an inventory investment as low as possible, and this in turn means that much of the burden of carrying adequate stocks still rests in large part with the manufacturer. All these factors have motivated the manufacturers to seek further the practicability of setting up their own system of distribution. Other conditions, such as failure to service the product and to provide more rapid distribution to retailers, would be possible but most difficult for the wholesaler to overcome. Still, other factors inherent in the very nature of wholesaling and manufacturing render the services of the wholesaler inadequate for some manufacturers and retailers. These factors will be discussed in the chapter dealing with the selection of marketing channels.

The Wholesaler's Answer

The wholesaler has an answer to many of the charges made by the manufacturer and some accusations that he himself can make against the manufacturer. Like any other businessman, the wholesaler requires a volume operation if he is to be successful. He claims that he cannot sell a product with vigor when a manufacturer deals directly with the large accounts and leaves the small ones for the wholesaler. Such a line may be carried if there is any popular demand for it, but the promotional effort will be given to the firm whose products are sold by the wholesaler to large and small outlets alike. Volume is important to the wholesaler's profit, and it is difficult to achieve if the large accounts are serviced by the manufacturer.

The wholesaler also maintains that the manufacturer must take a long-time view in his relationship with the wholesaler. Such a relationship would be disturbed by the manufacturer's developing a new product and package for a certain line of products and then unloading the surplus of the old products before announcing the new one. The manufacturer who wins the support of the wholesaler must show a common interest with him. He should be taken into confidence on the development of new products even before they are announced to the public. In line with his general program, one of the drug manufacturers discovered a method of manufacturing penicillin at a greatly reduced cost. When the price reduction was announced to the trade, the company absorbed the losses that accrued on stocks held by the wholesalers. Such a relationship results in sound wholesaler-manufacturer relationships and is the only type that will endure to the advantage of both.

Other conditions, such as failure to service the product and to provide more rapid distribution to retailers, would be possible but most difficult for the wholesaler to overcome. Still other factors inherent in the very nature of wholesaling and manufacturing render the services of the wholesaler inadequate for some manufacturers and retailers. These factors will be discussed in the chapter dealing with the selection of marketing channels.

Economy Innovations

Following the lead of the retail field, wholesalers have sought means of economizing by the use of modern techniques and by streamlining their operations. A certain food wholesaling firm was not making money because it did not have sufficient volume. The company had reduced its expenses from 10 percent of sales to 7 percent, but it continued to suffer a loss of volume. The consulting team which studied this situation discovered that two of the company's strong competitors, operating at margins of approximately 4 percent of sales, were winning the big accounts with their reduced prices. Significant, too, was the fact that the losing wholesaler was unaware of this price differential. Single-story operation, pallet and truck movement of merchandise, and machine accounting and control of stock and accounts receivable had been adopted by his competitors. These are but a few of the economies that the wholesalers have made in order to meet competition.

Increased Aid to Retailers

One hardware wholesaler has stated that he could increase the sales of practically every store he served by 33 percent, and some of them as high as 50 percent, by teaching them merchandising techniques and layout fundamentals. This wholesaler had a model retail store set up in the showrooms of his establishment that he used as an instructional device for retailers. The same practice has been adopted by voluntary chains in the food field. Throughout the wholesale business, wholesalers have found it desirable to give aid to the retail accounts that they serve.

Increased Specialization

In some instances wholesalers have become specialists. In those areas where aggressive selling and promotion are important factors in the distribution of a line of merchandise, some wholesalers have taken exclusive distribution responsibility for this line and have sold the product aggressively. Look in the yellow pages under radio, stereo, TV, or kitchen appliances, and note that certain wholesalers have exclusive distribution for certain brands. These instances indicate that where it is necessary and where the volume possibilities are adequate, a wholesale firm can distribute products in the same manner as a manufacturer's branch.

Improved Inventory Control

Increasing use by wholesalers of electronic data processing has improved stock control. Better inventory balance, anticipation of demand, and fewer stock-outs have resulted.

These examples of adjustments suggest that there are many other methods by which the wholesaler can improve his operation. He will always have three fundamental factors in his favor: first, the economies that arise from the re-sorting process; second, close acquaintance with the retailer and his problems through constant contact in a service capacity that is significant to the retailer; and third, the complete coverage of retail firms, large and small.

Magnitude of Wholesaling

The wholesale firm is not fronted with brilliant lights, nor does it dazzle with frequent double-page spreads in the daily newspaper or in the national magazines; seldom do we see wholesalers advertise on our television sets. Yet if we contemplate the institutions that make up the vast area of the city, we become much more aware of the significance of this type of business. In 1967 a total of 311,464 wholesale establishments did $460 billion worth of business, compared with $310 billion for 1,577,000 retailers during the same period.[3]

WHOLESALING INSTITUTIONS

Wholesaling institutions include "establishments or places of business primarily engaged in selling merchandise directly to retailers; to industrial, commercial, institutional, or professional users; or to other wholesalers; or acting as agents in buying merchandise for, or selling merchandise to, such persons or companies."[4] Establishments of varying size, function, manner of business, and type of service are included within the scope of this definition.

The wholesale establishment did not spring into existence fullblown. Each type has evolved to meet specific needs of the period in which new opportunities become evident. Those which have been able to move goods through market channels more efficiently than manufacturers and retailers could have prospered without the services of wholesalers. In their constant adjustments to meet requirements of a dynamic economy, many mutations and combinations have taken place, and still others are in process. Hence, it is difficult to phrase precise definitions of various types of wholesalers and to place each in a well-defined, clearly labeled category. Nearly always some areas overlap. A manufacturer's agent, for example, may be difficult to distinguish from a broker because many of their operations are similar. Further, it must be remembered that census classifications are based on the principal business of an establishment. Hence, if 51 percent of a firm's volume derives from brokerage operations, it would be counted as a broker event though part of its effort was in another type of operation. Therefore, almost every description of a middleman that follows must either include or imply such qualifying words as "generally" or "usually."

Table 8-1 is a listing of the principal types of wholesale institutions now counted by the Bureau of the Census. Note that merchant middlemen are by far the most numerous, totaling 87½ percent of all wholesale establishments. They also account for approximately 87 percent of total wholesale sales. Refer to Exhibit 8-1 for a comparison of total sales of each of the major classifications of wholesalers in the census years of 1963 and 1967. The exhibit also includes the percentage of total wholesale sales and percentage of wholesale establishments by class of wholesaler.

Exhibit 8-2, from the most recent Census of Business, portrays the principal customers of each of the broad classes of wholesalers. Note that retailers continue to be the principal customers of merchant wholesalers, while for all other wholesalers, industrial and commercial establishments are the main sources of revenue.

A brief description of each of the major types of wholesalers will assist in an understanding of the role and importance of wholesaling. Only

---

[3] U.S. Department of Commerce, Bureau of the Census, *Statistical Abstract of the United States: 1973* (94th ed.; Washington: U. S. Government Printing Office, 1973), p. 75, #1253, and p. 740, #1241.

[4] U.S. Department of Commerce, Bureau of the Census, *Census of Business: 1967.*

Table 8-1

**UNITED STATES WHOLESALE TRADE
BY TYPE OF OPERATION**

Type of Operation	Percent of Total Wholesale Establishments	Percent of Total Wholesale Sales
Wholesale Trade Total	100.0%	100.0%
Merchant Wholesalers, Total	68.4	44.8
Wholesale Merchants	6.6	39.6
Importers	1.7	2.3
Exporters	0.7	2.1
Terminal Grain Elevators	0.2	0.9
Manufacturers' Sales Branches, Total	9.8	34.2
Mfrs' Sales Branches—with stock	5.4	14.6
Mfrs' Sales Branches—without stock	4.5	19.5
Petroleum Bulk Stations	9.7	5.4
* Merchandise Agents, Brokers, Total	8.5	13.4
Auction Companies	0.5	1.0
Merchandise Brokers	1.4	3.1
Commission Merchants	1.7	3.1
Import Agents	0.1	0.4
Export Agents	0.2	0.7
Manufacturers' Agents	3.9	3.3
Selling Agents	0.6	1.4
Purchasing Agents, Resident Buyers	0.1	0.2
Assemblers of Farm Products	3.6	2.2

* Note: These are agent middlemen—all others are classified as merchant middlemen.

Source: Derived from preliminary reports, U.S. Department of Commerce, Bureau of the Census, *Census of Business: 1971*, and "Current Business Reports," *Monthly Wholesale Trade: 1974*.

categorization and description by type of operation is undertaken here. That is, merchant wholesalers, manufacturer's sales branches, petroleum bulk plants, merchandise agents and brokers, and farm products assemblers will be covered. One may refer to the Census of Business for classification by line of business, location, and ownership.

Merchant Wholesalers

Earlier reference was made to merchant middlemen and agent middlemen. The principal categories of each type are noted in Table 8-1. The first category, merchant wholesalers, includes those who are referred to as "service" or "full-service" wholesalers and others who are called "limited-function" wholesalers.

Exhibit 8-1

**UNITED STATES WHOLESALE TRADE: 1963 AND 1967
SALES IN MILLIONS OF DOLLARS AND PERCENT OF TOTAL
WHOLESALE TRADE**

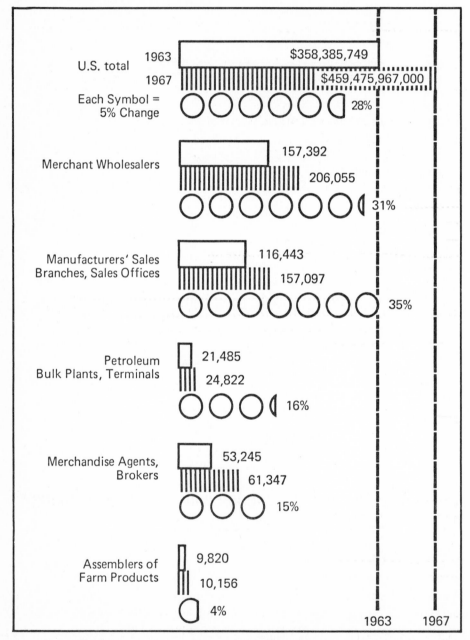

SOURCE: U.S. Department of Commerce, Bureau of the Census, *Census of
Business, 1967* (Wholesale Trade—Sales by Class of Customer). Vol. 1ll, p.1-4

Exhibit 8-2

PERCENTAGE DISTRIBUTION OF SALES BY TYPE OF OPERATION AND CLASS OF CUSTOMER: 1967

☐ Retailers   ▨ Wholesale Organizations   ▨ Export

||||| Industrial, Commercial, Etc., Users   ▨ Consumers and Farmers   ≡ Federal Government

MERCHANT WHOLESALERS

- 39.4 (Retailers)
- 37.0 (Industrial, Commercial, Etc., Users)
- 14.5 (Wholesale Organizations)
- 1.6 (Consumers and Farmers)
- 5.9 (Export)
- 1.5 (Federal Government)

MERCHANDISE AGENTS AND BROKERS

- 17.6 (Retailers)
- 40.3 (Industrial, Commercial, Etc., Users)
- 32.0 (Wholesale Organizations)
- 1.8 (Consumers and Farmers)
- 6.5 (Export)
- 1.8 (Federal Government)

ASSEMBLERS OF FARM PRODUCTS

- 10.6 (Retailers)
- 46.7 (Industrial, Commercial, Etc., Users)
- 26.9 (Wholesale Organizations)
- 12.4 (Consumers and Farmers)
- 2.6 (Export)
- 0.7 (Federal Government)

SOURCE: U.S. Department of Commerce, Bureau of the Census, *Census of Business, 1967* (Wholesale Trade—Sales by Class of Customer)

Usually wholesale merchants are full-service wholesalers. They provide storage, salesmen, delivery, order desks, credit, and usually, where required, repair services. They can provide wide coverage of retail outlets and the full range of services because they can spread the cost of each sales and delivery call over a wide range of products.

A particular type of full-service wholesale merchant is the industrial distributor. The Census Bureau has defined an *industrial distributor* as an establishment that "handles a general line of industrial goods and sells largely to industrial users . . . establishments dealing in a more or less complete line of materials and/or supplies for mines, factories, oil wells, public utilities, and similar industries. Establishments engaged primarily in selling machinery are not included." For general purposes it is usually convenient and accurate to include organizations that buy and sell such equipment as machine tools and special screening and filtering equipment, even though such establishments would not maintain large general warehouse stocks and otherwise specifically meet the census definition.

As is the case with other full-service wholesalers, the industrial distributor usually can be classified as either (1) a *general house*, which carries a wide line of supplies and tools used by many types of businesses; (2) a *product specialty house,* which carries a rather complete assortment of each of a limited number of lines; or (3) a *trade specialty house,* which serves the needs of a particular type of customer and carries a full line of goods required by such customers—hotel and restaurant supplies, oil field supplies, and similar items. The range of services, if reflected in their operating costs, average 14 percent (see Table 8-2). One must remember that those costs are average. Food wholesalers' costs are frequently as low as 3 to 4 percent.

Importers and Exporters. Merchants who largely confine their operations to buying primarily from foreign sources are classified separately from wholesale operations even though in other ways they may be similar to other purchasing merchants. They are described in census publications simply as importers. Merchant wholesale establishments that are primarily engaged in selling to foreign markets are likewise separated in wholesale trade statistics and are classified as exporters.

Limited-Function Wholesalers.[5] Among the limited-function wholesalers are truck distributors, rack jobbers, drop shippers, retail-cooperative warehouses, and wholesaler establishments operated by and for consumer cooperatives.

Merchant wholesale establishments distinguished by the fact that they combine sales and delivery functions and that they normally carry a limited assortment of fast-moving items of a perishable or semiperishable nature are commonly called *truck distributors*.

---

[5] Limited function here means wholesalers who do not provide all the services commonly associated with large merchant wholesalers—services such as salesmen, delivery, granting of credit, an order desk in the warehouse, large stocks in a warehouse, and repair facilities.

Table 8-2

SELECTED MIDDLEMEN OPERATING EXPENSES

Type of Operation	Operating Expenses as Percent of Sales
Merchant Wholesalers	
Service Wholesalers:	
Wholesale merchants, distributors	14.4
Terminal grain elevators	4.5
Importers	10.3
Exporters	4.1
Limited-Function Wholesalers:	
Cash-carry wholesalers	8.8 est.
Truck, wagon distributors	14.2 est.
Manufacturers' sales branches with stocks	11.3
Manufacturers' sales branches without stocks	4.1
Merchandise Agents, Brokers *	
Auction companies	2.9
Brokers	3.2
Commission merchants	3.4
Export agents	1.9
Import agents.................................	2.2
Manufacturers' agents	6.4
Selling agents................................	4.2
Purchasing agents, resident buyers	3.6
Assemblers of Farm Products	8.6

* For all types of merchandise agents and brokers, the data represent the amount of brokerage or commission received rather than total expenses incurred.

Source: U.S. Department of Commerce, Bureau of the Census, *Census of Business: 1967*, Vol. III, Table 2, pp. 1-9, with estimates from preliminary reports from U.S. Department of Commerce, Bureau of the Census, *Census of Business: 1971*.

These establishments commonly carry relatively small stocks in storage; indeed, in some cases, they buy only enough for one day's operation. The driver of the truck is also the salesman, making his sales call and delivery at the same time. Such operations are among the most costly for the various types of wholesaling because a truck is an expensive warehouse and because representatives make relatively small sales per call, usually buy in small quantities, and provide frequent delivery service. (See Table 8-2 for comparative cost of operation data.)

Tidbit items, fresh coffee, salad dressings, some dairy products, and other goods that sell best when they are fresh and frequently restocked are the main stock in trade for truck distributors. Grocery stores, restaurants, and taverns are the chief customers of this type of wholesaler.

Not all trucks that deliver small quantities to such stores are truck jobbers. The classification is reserved for merchant wholesalers who buy for their own account and attempt to sell at a profit. Quite commonly such institutions are small business enterprises, with the owner handling one truck and two or three other driver-salesmen working for him in trucks that he owns.

A recently developed class of wholesale establishment is the *rack jobber*, actually an extension of the truck distributor. Rack jobbers are merchant middlemen who sell mainly through grocery stores of the self-service type. The rack jobber arranges with the store owner for display space, which the rack jobber then supplies with various items. As a rule, rack jobbers specialize to some extent and generally confine their sales to one brand in a line such as drug items, household and kitchenware, or inexpensive clothing—socks, children's underwear, ladies' hose, and the like.

The rack jobber keeps stocked and in order the display rack on which his merchandise is arrayed. He prices, displays, and sets up whatever point-of-sale material is appropriate. On his periodic visits to the outlet, he restocks and bills the store for the amount replaced, thus, in essence, dealing with goods on consignment. Because of the services performed by the rack jobber, such as stocking, arranging displays, and pricing, retailers are generally willing to sell items that normally carry a markup of 30 percent, for example, for a markup of 20 percent when they are put in the stores by rack jobbers.

A *drop shipper* is a wholesaler who buys and sells goods but does not store them. Rather, he arranges for the shipment of goods directly from the producer to the buyer. Drop shippers deal in goods that are bulky—bulky in the economic sense that they are inexpensive per pound. Generally these goods are easily graded and are sold by grade; they usually are sold in large quantities and are most often available from several sources. From a sales volume measurement, coal and lumber are probably the most important items. An example of drop-shipper operations is found when a building contractor desires lumber of certain specifications. It is much easier and, in the long run, more economical for him to buy from a drop shipper than it is for him to make all arrangements on his own. The drop shipper takes the order, finds lumber to meet the required specifications, buys it, arranges for its handling and shipment, and sees that the contractor receives the right goods at the time and place desired. The drop shipper may not actually see the goods, but he bears all enterpreneurial risks involved in buying and selling goods. He owns the goods from the time he purchases them until they are delivered and sold to his customers.

The nature of the goods in which this type of wholesaler deals makes such storage and handling prohibitively expensive. Because the drop shipper has no storage expense and very little handling expense, he operates on a close margin—a much smaller gross than does the typical regular full-service wholesaler.

Other limited-function wholesalers, such as retail-cooperative warehouses and wholesale establishments of consumer cooperatives, are discussed with their retail counterparts; hence, no further explanation of them will be made here.

Merchant Wholesaler Trends

Noticeable trends in merchant wholesaler statistics illustrate how marketing institutions respond to changes in the economy. The census of 1939 showed that retailers were the customers for 59 percent of merchant wholesaler sales. In 1967 that figure was 39 percent. This is understandable since, as retail institutions become larger, they tend to do more buying direct from producers and manufacturers or through resident buyers.

Another development is that there are more smaller, specialty wholesalers in this group than in 1939 and previous years. As more people move to urban centers and as average incomes increase, markets for specialized products grow sufficiently large to support specialty stores and specialty departments. Hence, wholesalers specialize to provide better information and more depth in certain types of merchandise. Large, general-line wholesalers who provided a wide range of products have almost disappeared.

Manufacturers' Sales Branches

A succinct description of activities of manufacturers' sales branches is that found in the Census of Business definition:

> Manufacturers' sales branches are establishments owned by manufacturers or mining companies and maintained apart from producing plants primarily for selling or marketing their companies' products at wholesale. (Branch stores selling to household consumers and individual users are classified in retail trade.) Sales branches or sales offices located at plants or administrative offices are included when separate records were available.

It should be noted that in the *Census of Business* manufacturers' branch houses which sell appliances to retailers and builders are counted as merchant wholesalers.

Petroleum Bulk Plants

This is a category that does not differ greatly in type of operation but is counted separately because of the special and restricted nature of products handled. Inventories are usually restricted to gasoline, kerosene, fuel oils, lubricating oils, and other bulk petroleum products. The principal customers of bulk plants and terminals are retail outlets, service stations, industrial accounts, and other wholesalers.

Merchandise Agents and Brokers (Agent Middlemen)

The diversity and overlap of the services rendered and methods of operation employed by agent middlemen render accurate, distinct classification an impossibility. Hence, data on these establishments are often approximations, and those who measure them occasionally must use arbitrary definitions to determine where sales and establishments are to be counted. Within those limitations the following descriptions of operations are presented.

Merchandise Brokers. Merchandise brokers negotiate transactions—that is, bring about a "meeting of minds" rather than consummate sales as do regular wholesalers' salesmen. In a strict definition sense, brokers never take possession of goods, assume title, or take the risk of price fluctuations. Normally brokers do not handle invoices nor finance either principal or customer. Producers who make use of brokers generally limit brokers' powers as to prices and terms and require confirmation by the principals to make a bona fide transaction. Brokers are paid a commission based, in most cases, upon the value of merchandise moved, but, in some lines, the commission or fee is based upon the physical quantity of goods.

Brokers deal principally in food, farm products, and related trades, although they are found in some industrial lines. Since brokers assume none of the risks of price fluctuation or physical damage to goods, their fees are, of course, relatively low. Some high-volume brokers handle their business from home or hotel rooms without maintaining a regular office. This is possible because the brokers' most valuable product is their knowledge of market conditions, sources of supply, and other general market information. This may be pointed up by examining the brokers' cost of doing business shown in Table 8-2. The average brokerage fee is 3.2 percent of sales.

Commission Merchants. The commission merchant is not a merchant middleman because he does not take title to goods. In an earlier discussion we called this type of wholesaler a "commission man"—the terms "commission merchant" and "commission man" are used interchangeably and will be so used here. *Commission merchants* are distinguished from other agent middlemen in that commission merchants regularly take possession of the goods they handle, even though they do not take title to them. The type of commission man most familiar to readers will probably be that one commonly found in large city produce markets. The commission merchant accepts goods on consignment and undertakes to sell them at the most favorable price and terms he can get.

Commission merchants have declined in volume of sales relative to other wholesalers of produce and basic commodities. Formerly, when farm goods were distantly removed from consumer markets in terms of time and information, there was so much risk attendant upon handling produce that wholesalers were not generally anxious to purchase for their own accounts. The risks of price fluctuation and physical deterioration that followed when goods were a long time reaching the market and when market information was not readily available were too great. Farmers also found it difficult to follow price trends in central markets and, hence, had to rely on someone else to dispose of their produce. Commission merchant establishments developed to fill the needs created by these conditions. Today produce is sent to them on consignment; they receive and display it to the best of their ability. A commission, agreed upon as a percentage of the sales price received, is deducted by the commission merchant from the cash receipts, and the balance is sent to the producer.

Commission merchants handle a limited amount of merchandise other than agricultural commodities, but they are not major outlets for any such goods. Under the generally accepted definition, *factors* who specialize in such raw farm products as cotton are commission merchants and are counted as such by the Census of Business.[6] Even though commission merchants appear to provide a fairly wide range of services, the fees and commissions they charge are, on the whole, roughly equivalent to those received by brokers. This indicates that receiving and holding goods costs about the same as the seeking out that brokers do.

Manufacturers' Agents.[7] According to the Census of Business definition of *manufacturers' agents,* they are "Establishments selling, on an agency basis, a part of the output of manufacturers, usually two or more, whose goods are noncompeting. Their principal duty is selling, although some of them warehouse goods for their principals." Manufacturers' agents are found principally in industrial and durable goods lines, but they also handle a relatively small volume of such lines as housewares, commonly found in grocery and limited-price variety stores.

The value and use of manufacturers' agents can perhaps best be explained by a hypothetical example. Let us suppose that the Agnew Company manufactures a high-quality industrial pump. For several years Agnew enjoys considerable success in markets close to the plant by selling direct, with one or two company salesmen. A decision is made to expand operations into West Coast, Southwest, and Southeast markets. The company is not financially able to set up company outlets in centers of each of those markets; and even if it were, it is doubtful that its specialized product would achieve a sales volume sufficient to support an entire sales office in any of the areas. Manufacturers' agents, one in each of the market areas to be covered, who handle lines of goods that go to potential users of Agnew pumps, can be utilized. By spreading costs over several other lines in one or two industries with which he is intimately acquainted, the manufacturers' agent can give good coverage for the Agnew product.

Characteristics of manufacturers' agents make them reasonable outlets for such cases. These agents restrict their activities to a specified geographical area, handle part of the output of two or more noncompeting, but complementary lines, and are usually somewhat restricted by their principals as

---

[6] Factor—(1) A specialized financial institution engaged in factoring accounts receivable and lending on the security of inventory. (2) A type of commission house which often advances funds to the consignor, identified chiefly with the raw cotton and naval stores trades. Committee on Definitions, *Marketing Definitions* (Chicago: American Marketing Association, 1960), p. 13.

[7] The manufacturers' agent is a much more important party in the distribution function than the layman gives him credit for being. In the presentation of some empirical data and in a narration describing functions and relationships, Stuart W. McFarland provides some basic and interesting insight regarding his contribution in "Manufacturers' Agents," *Atlanta Economic Review*, Vol. 11, No. 12 (December, 1961), p. 15.

to sales and price policies. These agents generally have thorough knowledge of one or two industries that use the type of products in which they specialize.

It must be remembered in all these descriptions that the ideal is described. There is wide variance in capabilities of manufacturers' agents as in all other types of middlemen. Indeed, one may easily find among agent middlemen as a class a fairly large number of incompetent agents who are attracted by the lure of potentially large earnings and who enter the field without the knowledge and abilities that would make them valuable representatives to their principals' products.

A particular type of manufacturer's agent, not classified separately in the wholesale census, but always considered as a distinct group in the trade, is the *food broker*. These agent middlemen, as described by their title, deal almost exclusively in grocery store and food products. Many of the most familiar products on the shelves of grocery stores are sold over the nation through food brokers. Generally speaking, food broker establishments are relatively small, usually consisting only of the food broker himself and, at the most, one or two assistants, although a small number of them have fairly large staffs.

Quite commonly, the food broker handles from 6 to 12 or 14 noncompeting items for that many principals. He covers a clearly defined territory that is of a size sufficiently small to enable him to give intensive coverage. He (we are assuming, of course, the efficient operator) knows his territory intimately and by spreading his costs over several items is able to cover it thoroughly. His main job is to sell the principals' products by the best means available, such as store display, samplings in stores, assisting retailers with promotions that help to move the goods off the retailers' shelves, and intensive coverage of wholesale and chain-store buying offices. He is not expected to store, deliver, or otherwise handle goods but often maintains a small stock of each of his items from which he may make emergency delivery if a retailer runs short before a regular order arrives.

Selling Agents. Selling agents, like manufacturers' agents, have as a primary duty selling goods for a principal on a commission basis. Selling agents often are confused with manufacturers' agents, but they do differ, chiefly in scope of authority. Whereas the manufacturers' agent is limited geographically and policywise, the selling agent arranges to assume full responsibility for selling the entire output of one or more products, but not necessarily the full line of his principals' plants; and he usually receives authority commensurate with that responsibility. Typically, a selling agent handles the output of two or more manufacturers. He uses his best judgment, based on wide experience, to choose the most desirable markets and selling methods. In some lines it frequently is found that selling agents perform such services as credit and collections, product design, and even production scheduling for the principals.

Extent and type of services rendered by selling agents and other middlemen are reflected in their cost of doing business. In Table 8-2, on page 139, one will note that selling agents as a group receive commissions of only 4.2 percent of sales. One must remember that the figure given is an average and that it may include commissions ranging from around 2 percent to as high as 8 or 9 percent. This is true of most of the operating expense figures stated for agent middlemen.

Selling agents are well suited to handle the output of a factory operated by skilled production men who have not become experienced in marketing techniques. Factory men frequently are more efficient if they direct their skills exclusively to production and leave marketing problems to a sales specialist. As a result, selling agents often are found in an industry that is characterized by many relatively small producing units which turn out products suitable for sale through many kinds of outlets and to a large number of users. Cotton textile mills in the middle and deep South are often served by selling agents. Manufacture of quality cotton fabrics requires a great deal of specialized training and attention to detail and is of a type that may well be conducted by relatively small mills. Customers of fabric mills are often also small-scale operators who are demanding in quality and design requirements. Hence, production men in that field generally find it profitable to attend to manufacturing and to have a selling agent seek out and satisfy the buyers.

Auction Companies. Auction companies are found most commonly in the marketing of leaf tobacco, livestock, fruit, and vegetables. These establishments usually provide places where the merchandise may be inspected prior to the auction sale, and then they either sell from that floor or provide an adjacent room where buyers and auctioneers meet.

Almost all cigarette tobacco is sold from auction barns by auction companies or single auctioneers that travel with the harvest. In large terminal markets, such as Chicago or New York, a major portion of produce and fruit is sold through auction companies; and in many rural areas livestock auctions account for an important portion of total livestock marketing.

Fruit and produce auctions in terminal markets illustrate the essential features of this kind of marketing. Typically the goods are moved from rail cars or trucks throughout the night and early morning onto the floor, where "lots" of fruit and vegetables are on display. Around 5 or 6 a.m. a catalog is available for buyers. Buyers inspect the goods until sale time, commonly about 7 a.m. At sale time the buyers move to their places in the auction room, which is simply a large hall with seats for buyers and a platform for the auctioneer and the shippers' representatives. Individual sales proceed rapidly, but it still takes a buyer most of the morning to obtain a full line of produce.

Auction companies are among the oldest types of wholesaling establishments and are found in all parts of the Western World, as well as in lesser numbers throughout the Middle East where they first may have developed. Auction companies furnish the selling staff and, in some though not all instances, the physical facilities wherein the sale can take place.

An auction is an excellent place to observe free interplay of price-making forces at work. Quality of goods on display, expert judgment on the part of buyers competing for the goods, and amounts of stocks on hand all have their part in establishing the price.

Auctions are rather cumbersome marketing agencies in that the buyers must physically inspect the goods and be on hand during the entire selling period. It is much less expensive to pick up a telephone and order a given quantity of a specific grade of an item. Nevertheless, auctions remain fairly important in sales volume since many goods do not lend themselves readily to simple classification.

Auction companies usually are paid a commission on the goods sold, although in a few markets a flat fee is charged. In Table 8-2 on page 139 it may be noted that auction companies have operating expenses of 2.9 percent of sales. Thus, it can be readily observed that they do not have great investments in facilities and services. Compare that operating expense ratio with a typical department store operating ratio of about 36 to 38 percent of sales.

Purchasing Agents. Purchasing agents, resident buyers, and syndicate buyers who are in business for themselves and who purchase for clients on a commission basis are included in the category of purchasing agents. Actually, these agent middlemen differ from buying brokers only in name and in the fact that they confine their operations to the dry goods, apparel, and general merchandise fields, while the group known as buying brokers are commonly found in industrial goods fields.

One classification of this group, the resident buyers, is clearly distinctive in manner of operation and in clients served. Resident buyers are found in the apparel and dry goods manufacturing and trading centers, where they maintain offices to serve retail store buyers. Resident buyers, or resident buying offices, become specialists in certain lines. A number of the larger offices have quite large staffs organized somewhat along typical department store lines, with each person concentrating in the merchandise his retail counterparts will buy. When the retail buyer goes to market, he gets product and price information bulletins from his resident buyer. Through such cooperation and service, the resident buyer learns the needs of his clients; and when it is not practicable for the store buyer to make a market trip, often the resident buyer is able to buy needed fill-in merchandise particularly suited to any given store client.

Farm Products Assemblers

Assemblers of farm products exist because there is frequent need to gather quantities of products from several producers to provide for efficient performance of marketing functions, such as having optimum shipping lots. They are "establishments primarily engaged in purchasing from farmers and assembling and marketing farm products in local producing markets and in cities of producing regions."[8]

RECAPITULATION

Choice of proper outlets and channels of distribution for a product is one of the most important decisions to be made by the producer of a good. There is no formula by which the choice may be made. Since quality of performance by various firms within a given category of middlemen varies widely, and because

---

[8] U.S. Department of Commerce, Bureau of the Census, *Census of Business: 1963.*

one can never know for certain whether or not his product would move better through another channel, it is difficult to determine which is the best type of outlet to use. The brief description of middlemen given above does indicate the kind of service that may be expected from each of the more important wholesale institutions and does show that in large measure one gets what he pays for—this is, a broker provides less service and advice than a selling agent. Hence, the broker's fees, on the average, are less than selling agent fees. Nevertheless, it must be stressed that differences in abilities of men and firms within categories of wholesalers are great. A producer should exercise great care in selecting the institution through which he wants to sell his goods. He should learn how similar goods go to market, the reputation and abilities of various kinds of middlemen, and the type and quality of services available to him.

Remember that a middleman cannot do anything for producers or retailers that they could not do for themselves. The value of middlemen lies in their ability to do better and more economically the jobs required for effective distribution.

QUESTIONS AND ANALYTICAL PROBLEMS

1. If you called on a manufacturer of a low-priced, widely used consumer good in the United States, Europe, the Far East, or any other place, he would almost certainly remark, "We use general wholesalers because _____. However, we don't like to use them entirely because _____." Fill in the blanks with what you think the manufacturer will say.

2. List the advantages of wholesalers as given in your text. For each of the stated advantages, explain why wholesalers can perform the economic activity more efficiently than can retailers or manufacturers.

3. (a) What inherent disadvantages do wholesalers have? (b) What disadvantages, not inherent, often appear when a manufacturer chooses to use wholesalers rather than his own sales force?

4. How can you justify the existence of wholesalers in the grocery field, using cost as the only basis?

5. List the criticisms that manufacturers often level against wholesalers. Opposite each, state the wholesaler's answer to the criticism. Evaluate both the criticisms and the answers.

6. How have wholesalers, as a class of institution, met the problem of increasing operating costs over the past two or three decades?

7. Why is there a seeming trend toward specialized types of wholesaling?

8. What will a manufacturer's sales force do better than a wholesaler?

9. Check the wholesale section of the most recent Census of Distribution and list the principal lines handled and the sales volume of each. What conclusion can you draw from the table thus prepared?

10. In a large Western city the oldest general line wholesaler has been selling parts of the business during the past few years. First, the firm sold its grocery business. Next, the drug department was sold, and recently the company sold its hardware department. A speaker at a business lunch referred to those sales and to examples of purchases direct from the factory in his own business. His conclusion was that wholesale institutions

were doomed since better transportation and communication facilities had rendered them no longer necessary. Do you agree? What can you learn from the wholesale portion of the Census of Distribution about the increasing or decreasing importance of wholesalers? Is the trend for various types of wholesalers the same as the trend for all wholesale business?

11. Why are service wholesalers more important in the distribution of consumer goods than they are in industrial goods?

12. Why have rack jobbers been a development of recent years? Why were they not prominent wholesalers ever since 1900, for example?

13. Draw a chart on which you show the distinguishing characteristics of each type of agent middleman. List the various agent middlemen down the left side. Make headings across the top that describe characteristics. For example, length of contract, extent of authority, etc., could be headings.

14. A cannery that is one of the three or four largest volume processors of various fruits and vegetables in the United States is reviewing its sales methods. The company packs under its own label as well as under chain store brands. There is reason to believe that the present company sales force is too expensive. What middlemen should the company consider? Which one would you choose? Analyze the alternatives and give detailed reasons for your choice.

15. Explain the statement that there is nothing a wholesaler does that a manufacturer or a retailer could not do for himself.

Case 8 • THE SEA FRESH COMPANY

The Sea Fresh Company is a medium-sized Northwestern fish packer and canner that deals mainly in shellfish, Alaskan halibut, and salmon. The company currently maintains a sales force of 20 men who call on wholesalers and chain stores in 15 principal cities. It also maintains a warehouse stock in each of these cities.

Due to increasing expenses, company executives are considering a change in the present distribution policy. As an alternative Sea Fresh is considering the use of food brokers in each of the areas now covered by a salesman, thinking that better area coverage as well as decreased costs would result. In the larger cities more than one broker could be used.

Brokers normally receive commissions of 3 to 5 percent of sales. The wholesalers to whom the brokers sell receive a margin of 12 percent, and retailers take a markup of 25 percent. The total marketing expense ratio of Sea Fresh Company currently stands at 20 percent of net sales, of which $350,000 is spent on national magazine advertising. Last year's sales were just over $4,000,000.

• What losses in effective marketing would be incurred if the change being considered were adopted? Would there be any gains? Estimate the savings in cost that might result from the adoption of the change.

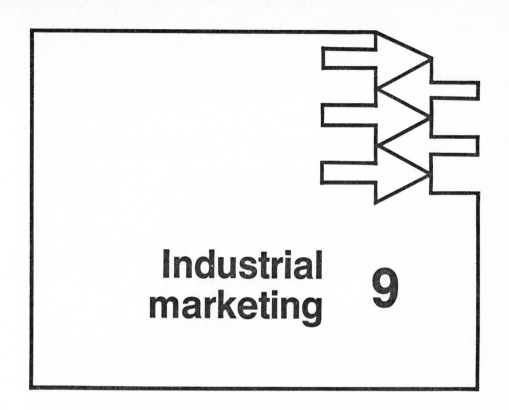

Industrial marketing 9

The same basic functions are performed in the industrial market as in the consumer market. Differences between marketing of industrial goods and consumer goods occur mainly because of characteristics and needs of customers. A few distinctive characteristics of industrial marketing also occur, however, because of the sources of types of goods.

In order to emphasize the conditions, problems, and opportunities that are peculiar to the industrial market, this chapter presents, first, a definition of industrial marketing; second, the characteristics of demand in industrial markets; third, the characteristics of supply; and fourth, the characteristics of transactions in this segment of the market.

DEFINITION OF INDUSTRIAL MARKETING

Industrial marketing is the marketing of goods and services destined for use in providing other goods or services. This is a workable but somewhat sterile definition. Some features of the industrial market must be understood to make the definition viable.

Since the goal of all production is consumption, it is obvious that the demand for goods used to produce other goods depends ultimately upon individual and family purchases of consumer goods. Hence, the demand for industrial goods is a derived demand and tends to result in fluctuating demand. Further, the development of industrial processes and products is marked by increasing complexity. These three features of the industrial market—derived demand, fluctuating demand, and increasing complexity—lie behind the definition of industrial marketing and influence the methods and institutions that move industrial goods. Each is briefly discussed below.

Derived Demand

The demand for machine tools depends upon demand for the items produced by the machine tools which are, let us say, steel brackets. In turn, the demand for the brackets will depend upon the demand for the kitchen shelves and other building items that they support. The same is true for material used in production. The demand for copper depends upon the demand for radios, kitchenware, costume jewelry, and other consumer goods.

Hence, the only reason for extracting or producing a good for the industrial market is that consumers will purchase an item in which the industrial good has played a productive part or an item which is included in the consumer good.

Fluctuating Demand

Heavy commitments of capital are necessary to expand plant capacity or replace obsolescent equipment. During periods of low and falling business activity, it is often convenient, and sometimes wise, for the manufacturer of both capital and consumer goods to delay expansion or replacement until the markets are more promising. On the other hand, regardless of the economic conditions, consumers do not find it convenient to postpone or delay their consuming practices. Consequently, there are greater fluctuations in the industrial market than in the consumer market.

Increasing Complexity

It is told that the Wright brothers purchased all the parts for their first airplane from the shelves of small shops in Dayton, Ohio, but it is doubtful that one could build the simplest sort of craft today from parts available in his neighborhood. Available products are increasingly complex. Special metal alloys are developed; intricate and complex outputs of screw machines guided by taped programs become parts of objects we handle and enjoy daily. Enterprising persons even seek out witch-doctor remedies along the tributaries of the Amazon to determine whether such remedies, if useful, can be produced synthetically.

CHARACTERISTICS OF DEMAND

Demand in the industrial market is influenced by characteristics of customers which can be grouped into three broad classes. Industrial markets are also characterized by concentrations of customers and supplies. The concentration is both by geographical region and by size of establishment. Finally, industrial customers have purchasing motives related to efficiency and economy.

Classes of Customers

Three broad classes of customers can be identified in the industrial market. They are:

1. *Industrial users* who purchase finished products for use in the business. The goods are not to be changed or incorporated in other products. Machine tools, typewriters, trucks, and supplies are examples of this part of the industrial market. This customer class will include marketing institutions as well as manufacturing establishments.
2. *Assemblers, or manufacturer customers,* are those who purchase goods to incorporate them in products they sell, such as raw materials, automobile wheels and frames, or other component parts.
3. *Wholesaler customers* are distributors who purchase products and resell them in the same form to manufacturers, users, or perhaps to other distributors.

It is not feasible to make precise distinctions between products that are offered to each customer class. All will be customers for some products but may buy for different uses. Small electric motors, for example may be sold to some firms to become a part of the equipment they manufacture, but the same type of motors may be used to power small grinders used in the same plant. Hence, each supplier should make his own classification of customers based on uses of his products and on the portion of the market that they comprise.

Concentration of Industrial Markets

As shown by the tables and exhibits in this section, there are geographical concentrations of manufacturing. Further, each census of manufacturing reveals greater concentrations of manufacturing into large firms.

Geographic Concentrations. Exhibit 9-1 depicts regional concentration. Notice the preponderance of manufacturing in the northeast section of the United States. There is a continual growth in the South and West, but the bulk of our manufacturing still remains east of the Mississippi River and north of the Mason-Dixon line, whether measurement is made by value added or by manufacturing payroll.[1]

The several states are ranked by amount of manufacturing in Exhibit 9-2. Note that a few states outside the northeast region (for example, California, Texas, North Carolina, Tennessee, and Georgia) are high on the scale even though only California (8.9 percent) is among the states accounting for a sizeable percentage of total United States manufacturing. Other major-producing states are New York (10.2 percent), Illinois (7.6 percent), Pennsylvania (7.3 percent), and Michigan (6.8 percent).

Concentration by Size of Company. Of all value added by manufacturing in the United States, one fifth (20 percent) is accomplished by firms having fewer

---

[1] Value added = value of shipments, minus total cost of materials. (In these computations materials = supplies, fuel, electric energy, cost of resales, and miscellaneous receipts.)

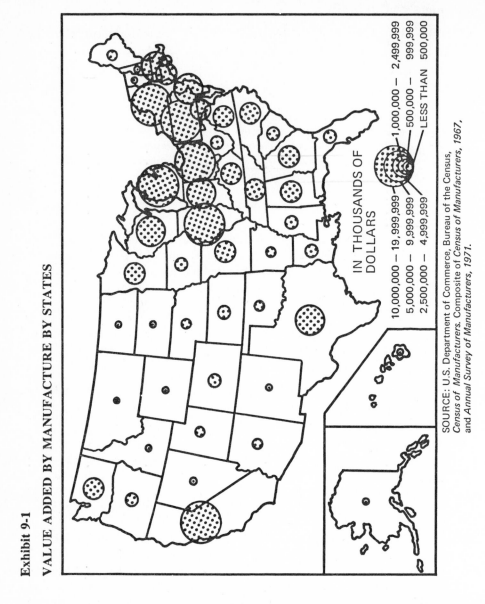

Exhibit 9-1

VALUE ADDED BY MANUFACTURE BY STATES

IN THOUSANDS OF DOLLARS

10,000,000 — 19,999,999
5,000,000 — 9,999,999
2,500,000 — 4,999,999
1,000,000 — 2,499,999
500,000 — 999,999
LESS THAN 500,000

SOURCE: U.S. Department of Commerce, Bureau of the Census, Census of Manufacturers. Composite of Census of Manufacturers, 1967, and Annual Survey of Manufacturers, 1971.

than 100 employees. Interestingly, approximately another one fifth is done by firms who have 2,500 or more employees. In Table 9-1 one can see that the concentration by size of company is even more marked than the above information would indicate. Only 0.3 percent of manufacturing establishments in the United States have over 2,500 employees, but that small number of firms have an output slightly greater than that of the 89 percent of the firms who hire less than 100 employees.

The concentration is not uniform for all industries. A large portion of the output in certain lines is accomplished by small firms. In Table 9-2 the 20 largest

Exhibit 9-2

STATES RANKED BY VALUE ADDED BY MANUFACTURER: 1971 (BILLIONS OF DOLLARS)

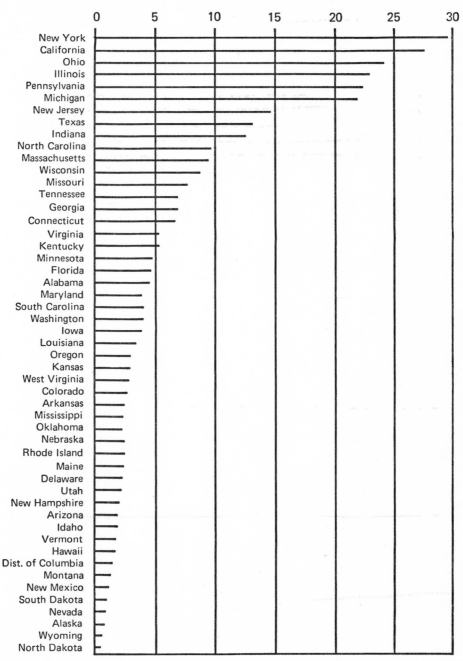

SOURCE: Derived from the U.S. Department of Commerce, Bureau of the Census, *Survey of Manufacturers, 1971.*

Table 9-1
MANUFACTURING CONCENTRATION—1967
CUMULATIVE PERCENTAGE OF MANUFACTURING ESTABLISHMENTS
AND VALUE ADDED BY MANUFACTURING BY SIZE CLASS

Size Class All Establishments Average Number of Employees	Cumulative Percent of Establishments (100.0)	Cumulative Value Added by Manufacturer (100.0)	
1-4	38.4	1.1	89% of firms
1-9	51.3	2.3	have under
1-19	64.9	5.1	100 employees. They account
1-49	80.9	12.1	for 20% of value added.
1-99	89.0	20.0	
1-249	95.5	34.9	0.3% of firms have 2,500
1-499	98.0	48.7	employees or more.
1-999	99.2	62.0	
1-2.499	99.7	77.0	
2,500 & over	100.0	100.0	They account for about 23% of value added.

Source: U.S. Department of Commerce, Bureau of the Census, *Census of Business: 1967* (Manufacturers), Vol. 1, p. 5, Table E.

Table 9-2
PERCENT OF SALES MADE BY LARGEST COMPANIES
IN SELECTED INDUSTRIES

	4 Largest	20 Largest
Motor Vehicles	92%	99+%
Aircraft	69	99
Sawmills and Planing Mills	11	22
Radios and Related Products	49	85
Paperboard Boxes	27	67
Structural and Ornamental Work	13	26
Tires and Inner Tubes	70	97
Footwear	27	46
Plastic Products	8	21
Paints and Varnishes	22	48
Dresses	7	14
Farm Machinery (except tractors)	44	68
Gray-iron Foundries	27	50

Source: U.S. Bureau of the Census, Annual Survey of Manufacturers, *Concentration Ratios: 1971.*

dress manufacturers accounted for only 14 percent of sales; similarly, for the sawmills and planing mills, structural and ornamental work, plastic products, and furniture, the 20 largest firms do not dominate production and sales as they do in the prepared cereal, major appliance, and other concentrated industries.

Among the reasons why small firms account for most of the production in some product lines are: requirements for close attention to frequent changes in customer needs (as in dress manufacture and structural steel); skill (planing mills and radios); and small lot manufacturing (as in foundries).[2]

Buying Decisions in the Industrial Market

It once was considered correct to say that the industrial buyer was dominantly rational, while consumer choices resulted more from emotional promptings. This same contrast may still largely prevail, but motivations are examined more carefully today. To classify some motives as emotional and others as rational merely begs the question. Every decision or choice on the consumer market contains some elements of rationality. On the other hand, most decisions in the industrial market must recognize the emotional nature of man; consequently, they may be considered emotional.

Bases of Buying Decisions. Much of the industrial market consists of firms that have been developed by persons with technical skills for whom careful measurement and calculation are part of their routine. Also, the calculations for profitable operations of manufacturing establishments result in objectification and assignment of numerical measures to expense and income magnitudes. Hence, rational, objective, numerical calculations are to be expected in industrial purchasing decisions. Nevertheless, the industrial consumer must consider the emotional responses of the people who are directly and indirectly included in the purchase and use of the product.

This was illustrated when one of the large pipe manufacturing companies of the Midwest constructed a new office building off the highway several miles from the nearest city. Since the company sells to industrial concerns and municipalities throughout the United States, it is unlikely that a great many customers will be impressed by the structure. Yet the firm hired the most expensive landscape artist and building architect to design both grounds and building. The president's spacious office is furnished throughout with expensive furniture and deep, thick carpeting, as is the directors' conference room. There is also a relaxation room for the employees, which is so placed that it commands a scenic view of the lakes and hills. Extending clear across the front wall of this room is a large picture window. This room is also furnished with expensive furniture and carpets. Industrial firms are also becoming art- and design-conscious in the construction and layout of their plants and offices.

These qualities of plant and office structure may be justified specifically on the basis of beauty and comfort only. Motives springing from the desire for

---

[2] Arnold C. Cooper's research indicates that it is possible for the smaller companies to be successful in the innovation role in "Small Companies Can Pioneer New Products," *Harvard Business Review* (September-October, 1966), pp. 162-179.

these qualities have ordinarily been considered emotional. There is no direct reason why a luxuriously furnished relaxation room or a beautiful plant will increase the profit of a manufacturing plant that sells on a market far removed from its operations.

Industrial purchases result from a complex mixture of motives. There are, of course, more attempts to support purchases with the aid of objective data than in the case of consumer goods buying. Even in the presence of ample measuring devices and quantitative data, however, an ability to view and properly appraise subjective forces and emotional motives is important. For convenience such factors may be grouped into the following categories: (1) characteristics of product or service that affect the efficiency of the purchaser, (2) effects of technology and productivity, and (3) effects of innovations.

Characteristics of Product or Service That Affect the Efficiency of the Purchaser. The value of an industrial good to a customer is dependent upon its ability to assure efficiency and profitability in his operations. The highest-priced material may be the least costly if it saves time, for example. Even the quantity discount on large purchases may be foregone when small regular shipments reduce storage requirements and provide the materials required in more manageable lot sizes. Demand characteristics usually include those discussed below.

Efficiency of Product Supplied. This can be based on such qualities as speed of new tools, wearing and lasting qualities of abrasives or bearings, and ease of use or installation. For example, a product might be furnished with features that make possible economies growing out of the use of only semiskilled workers.

Certainty of Supply. A supplier may entice the buyer with low prices but may not have the competence to meet requirements or guarantee a dependable, long-term supply.

Dependability in Meeting Schedules. Industrial customers must meet schedules in their sales and, hence, must assure themselves of supplies in the quantities, with the specifications, and on the dates promised.

Technical Assistance. This includes information on qualities and use of products or processes as well as advice on maximizing the customer's efficiency in their use. Problems of installing and incorporating equipment into existing productive methods are also important to the customer.

Product Motives and Patronage Motives. In dealing with the industrial consumer, it is desirable to bear in mind that industrial businesses base their decisions on both the product and the institution that sells the product. To clarify some of the areas of significance in these two classes of motives, the following discussions and listings will be helpful.[3] Some typical product motives are:

---

[3] Werner Z. Hirsch traces the method by which industrial decisions are made from "intuitive judgment" to "considered opinion" to "scientific decisions." Werner Z. Hirsch, "Decision Making in Industrial Marketing," *Journal of Marketing*, Vol. XXIV (January, 1960), pp. 21-27.

Efficiency	Protection from loss
Economy	Dependability or reliability
Quality	Accuracy
Speed	Uniformity and stability
Strength	Low maintenance cost
Durability or endurance	Simplicity

There is some overlapping in these motives. This is especially true in the case of efficiency. Excellence in each of these areas would improve the efficiency of the buying firm. Each item on the list, however, suggests "appeal" areas, wherein the industrial consumer would respond to a sales approach.

The trigger action that determines choice in the industrial market is often the buyer's image of the selling institution. This is especially important when deciding about goods which are so nearly alike that they provide no basis for a decision. Some of the characteristics that influence market choices are:

Completeness of line	Monopoly position
Completeness of stock	Financial or managerial
Offer of free service	connection
Reputation in trade	Friendship
Reciprocal patronage	Past services
Price and discount policies	Research and pioneering

Quite clearly, the attitude and policy of a firm with respect to increases of new products and the innovation of complex processes have an effect on building a following among its patrons. The discussions on technology and productivity and innovations provide some additional insight into developments in these areas.

Technology and Productivity. The industrial consumer usually chooses to buy a product because it will yield results or profits at a greater rate than its cost. Thus, industrial purchases and sales are closely related to their effect on productivity. The tempo of technological innovations in modern business is such that much of the industrial equipment is less likely to wear out than to become obsolete. Obsolesence results from conditions wherein a new machine or process is more efficient or productive than the one in use. It becomes profitable, therefore, for the producer to discard the old machine and to purchase the new one.

A long-time and a short-time view of productive evolution in industry will be helpful in revealing such trends. For example, in the eighteenth century the average American farmer possessed $15 worth of tools. Today, including the thousands of small part-time farmers, the average farmer owns $2,600 worth of tools or 173 times as many as his great-grandfather. During the early period, 90 percent of the population was required to produce agricultural products. Today, with America consuming an unprecedented amount of food, both in terms of total volume and per capita, less than 8 percent of our population is engaged in agriculture.

In the nineteenth century, chips were cut from metal at the rate of 4 ounces per minute. Today, with more scientifically hardened metal and improved mechanical arrangements, machine tools trim off 20 pounds per minute. The modern tool is 10 times more accurate and 80 times faster than that of the nineteenth century. Modern machine tools are also multipurpose tools. Some can measure 32 different points simultaneously, and a multiple spindle drill can bore 98 holes at the same time.

Innovations. In the industrial market, change requires the constant purchase and sale of new, different industrial products. This process of industrial evolution includes not only the marketing of installations but also of repairs, fuel, lubrication services, and even the buildings in which production machinery is housed. Constant innovation and the replacing of the less efficient with the more efficient in this market prevent the task of the buyer and the seller of industrial goods from becoming routine to the point where marketing skills are not necessary. While it is true that many industrial goods can be standardized and purchased from specifications, a large part of goods going to the industrial market is being improved constantly. Even a common product such as paint is tested with competitive products for durability before it is purchased by General Motors, and new formulas are announced almost daily.

CHARACTERISTICS OF SUPPLY

For convenience industrial suppliers are classified in this section according to the use of their goods or services. The categories are raw materials, fabricated parts, operating supplies, accessory equipment, and installations.

Raw Materials

The sources of raw materials are the primary industries of agriculture, mining, forestry, and fisheries. Except in some instances of forestry and mining, most of the operations here are comparatively small. The seller has limited choice as to where his business is located. Raw materials must be taken at the point where nature provides them. Here we have a problem of collecting the materials, a problem made greater by the number of firms and the distances involved. Usually this process is carried out by a market institution that assumes the responsibility of collecting and dispersing. That is, wholesale or cooperative firms collect the products from the numerous small producers, store them for a necessary period, and then sell them to processors. Thus, in the case of both cotton and wool, middlemen collect the crops from the growers. They may then process them to the extent of ginning the cotton or combining the wool and then sell them to the manufacturer.

In the case of mining, lumbering, and production of petroleum, however, direct sale to the first processor is the most common method of sale. Frequently, in these instances the processor owns the primary source. As examples, U. S. Steel owns its iron mines and Weyerhauser Lumber Company in the Northwest owns its forests. In some industries such integration has been common for several years. For example, many of the large petroleum companies own their own oil fields or they may achieve control through subsidiary companies. Likewise, the steel, copper, and aluminum fabricating companies own their own source of raw materials.

Fabricated Parts

The buying and selling of fabricated parts exist where the industrial consumer, in effect, delegates the manufacture of parts of his product to another manufacturer. These parts are often custom-made according to specification, although, in some instances, a fabricated part may have a general market appeal and be sold to many buyers.

Probably the best example of the purchase and sale of fabricated parts is the automobile (see Exhibit 9-3). Practically no automobile manufacturer produces its own carburetor. Stromberg and Carter are specialists in this field. Automobile manufacturers generally agree that they cannot duplicate the quality of these products for a comparable cost. The degree of emphasis that the fabricated-part buyer gives to these purchases depends to some extent upon their significance in the economy and the quality appeal of the final product to the consumer. For example, shirt manufacturers make a special point of the fact that their products are made of easily laundered cloth that does not require ironing. In such instances the fabricated part is of significance. In the case of parts with less influence on consumer appeals, the fabricated part may not receive so much of the buyer's attention.

In most instances manufacturers of fabricated parts cluster in the area of the large assemblers and manufacturers, although there are some exceptions where raw materials and labor resources make other areas more desirable. Usually the sale of fabricated parts is made by the manufacturers' salesmen making direct contact with the buyer. Naturally, the seller wishes to maintain a permanent relationship and have the buyer use his product exclusively.

Operating Supplies

Operating supplies seldom take up a great deal of the time of top policy makers. Usually much of the responsibility of buying is left to the purchasing agent. However, such supplies as coal and lubrication oil, which are necessary for the sustained and smooth operation of the plant, must be purchased with care. On occasions where such items are used in large amounts, contracts run through several years. In some instances flexible provisions are made as to price. The coal must maintain a certain B.T.U. rating, and oil must measure up in standard tests as to viscosity at changing temperatures and have a minimum flash point rating. Supplies are necessary for the operation of all industrial and commercial institutions. Although supply costs per unit of output might be small, overall constant use makes their purchase a significant factor in maintaining efficient operations and cutting costs.

In many cases purchases are made directly from the producer. This relationship prevails when the consumer uses a considerable volume of the items. For example, the Twenty-Mule Team Borax Company salesmen contact both industrial and distributional firms that have large volume possibilities. Agreements are made to ship specific amounts at stated intervals, or orders are taken to replenish supplies. In addition to such direct selling, industrial supply houses and wholesalers serve as middlemen between industrial producers and consumers.

Exhibit 9-3

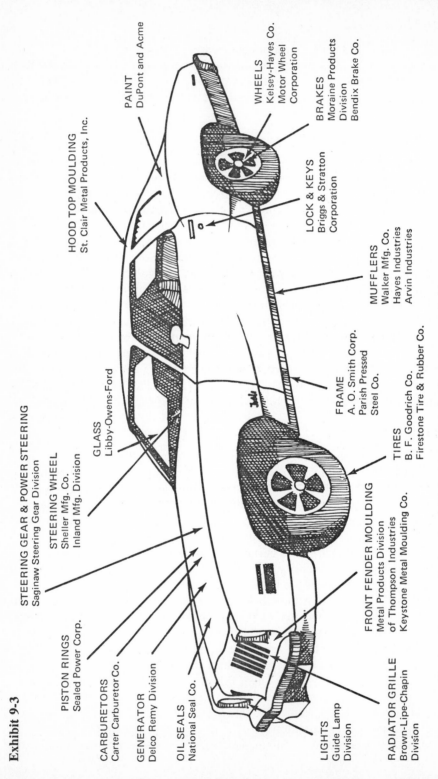

STEERING GEAR & POWER STEERING
Saginaw Steering Gear Division

STEERING WHEEL
Sheller Mfg. Co.
Inland Mfg. Division

PISTON RINGS
Sealed Power Corp.

CARBURETORS
Carter Carburetor Co.

GENERATOR
Delco Remy Division

OIL SEALS
National Seal Co.

GLASS
Libby-Owens-Ford

LIGHTS
Guide Lamp
Division

RADIATOR GRILLE
Brown-Lipe-Chapin
Division

FRONT FENDER MOULDING
Metal Products Division
of Thompson Industries
Keystone Metal Moulding Co.

TIRES
B. F. Goodrich Co.
Firestone Tire & Rubber Co.

FRAME
A. O. Smith Corp.
Parish Pressed
Steel Co.

HOOD TOP MOULDING
St. Clair Metal Products, Inc.

PAINT
DuPont and Acme

WHEELS
Kelsey-Hayes Co.
Motor Wheel
Corporation

BRAKES
Moraine Products
Division
Bendix Brake Co.

LOCK & KEYS
Briggs & Stratton
Corporation

MUFFLERS
Walker Mfg. Co.
Hayes Industries
Arvin Industries

The above illustrates only a few of over 400 firms from which the Pontiac Division of General Motors purchased materials and parts to complete one of its models. Printed with the permission of Pontiac Motor Division of General Motors.

Accessory Equipment

The unit of sale in the case of accessory equipment is small when compared with installations. Its sale and purchase does not, therefore, merit as much attention as do installations. The purchasing agent, however, frequently requires the aid of engineers to make a proper selection. For example, the motor of the telescope at Lick Observatory at Mount Hamilton, California, is 1/500 of a horsepower. The purpose of this motor is to keep the 14-ton, 36-inch telescope moving slowly enough to hold a star in view. The purchase of this motor required painstaking calculations. Although this may not be a purchase of a typical accessory, fractional horsepower motors fall in this class, and tolerance judgments frequently are very fine. The accuracy with which such motors fit the task and the economy with which they are operated are important items requiring careful computation.

It is also claimed, by reliable sources, that the electric typewriter speeds up production and operates with less fatigue to the operator. Thus, a decision to buy or not to buy such equipment, just as in the case of installations, may be made subject to minute calculations. Similar application may be made of objective or scientific analysis in most instances where accessory equipment is involved.

Accessory equipment on the industrial market is sold both directly from maker to user and through regional or area distributors. The relationship between the maker and the user is not so close as is that in the case of the installation. Yet large manufacturers of accessory equipment usually have salesmen who maintain company contacts with large users. Manufacturers' agents, selling agents, and industrial supply houses serve as middlemen for the sale of the proportion of the goods that are not sold directly to users.

Installations

Probably more than any other classification, installations typify the true meaning of industrial goods. No decisions on any other type of product merit as painstaking, careful consideration as do those relating to major installations. The number of buyers is comparatively small. The cost of installations is great. Negotiations often run over long periods. Usually sales of installations are made directly from manufacturer to ultimate user. Decisions on installations depend on cost reductions, increased production, reliability of machines, financial arrangements, and relationships with the seller company. The major portion of our discussion aptly applies to installations.

Product Evolution

The problem of adjusting the immediate supply to the immediate demand has been considered as a problem of the merchant. It is also a challenge to the manufacturer, who must answer the questions: What in my line is the consumer going to want next year? What new products that I have been testing will be acceptable? How many will be marketable at prices that will cover costs? In other words, the merchandising problem is the same for the manufacturer of industrial products as it is for the middleman selling consumer goods. The difference is that the middleman has the problem of buying goods to suit the consumer demand, while the manufacturer has the problem of making the right product at the right time, at the right price, for the right industrial users. He also has the problem of coordinating his production facilities and raw materials so as to meet the demands of his market. A close relationship with sellers of industrial products will assist him in keeping up with changes and will provide the means of making positive adjustments.

Quality Control

In the sale and purchase of industrial goods, quality is a strategic element. Although quality is important in the consumer good, the emphasis is on the subjective valuation. In the case of industrial goods, on the other hand, emphasis more frequently is on precision and measurable conformance to standards. Quality control must begin when the product has an identity and must continue until it is finished and is in successful use. Thus, steel companies make a chemical analysis of the coal, ore, and other materials that enter the process of steelmaking. Such analysis influences their purchases and also serves as a quality guide in the productive process. Dairies, in their purchase of raw milk, must exercise control precautions that would have been considered ridiculous in 1930. Wheat is purchased according to the protein and moisture content. It is not uncommon in installations to control tolerances in bearings to the thousandth of an inch.

Quality control is probably more closely related to manufacturing than to marketing; yet if the production processes protecting quality fail, the market reflects the impact of the failure. Quality that is superior is a strong selling point. Inferior or irregular quality dissipates prestige and market goodwill and strains relations between buyers and sellers.

Distribution Facilities

The supplier is usually responsible for delivery. Many producers have built a competitive advantage by working with transportation companies to deliver products faster and in more usable condition and form. Fabricated parts for automobiles are shipped to assembly plants in specially designed railroad cars, sugar is transported as a liquid in tankers to bakeries and candy makers, and flower growers in the San Francisco Bay area send flowers by air to Chicago and New York markets so that they are available for sale to retailers only six or seven hours after cutting. Revere Copper Company and other metal fabricators have located warehouses where most of their customers can receive service within a day or less.

This subject is part of an entire chapter on logistics. It is inserted here to point out the importance of a supplier recognizing that an industrial customer determines his purchases on more than the specifications of a product. Value may, and usually will, include availability as well as inherent features.

CHARACTERISTICS OF MARKET TRANSACTIONS

Some features of the industrial market cannot be identified as belonging exclusively to either the demand or the supply side. In this final section some of these features are pointed out: (1) the interdependence of buyer and seller, (2) the decision whether to make or to buy, (3) leasing of installations, (4) reciprocity, (5) who makes the buying decision, and (6) planning.

Interdependence of Buyer and Seller

Frequently close relationships develop between suppliers and customers in design and manufacturing of products or techniques. For example, salesmen of firms that sell data processing equipment must learn enough about a customer's firm to develop and install complete systems for accounting and management control. Business machine companies have specialists in supermarket organization, store layout, and stock control who work with store supervisors of the customer firm. Other examples of this kind of creative selling and engineering that overcome vested industrial inertia will illustrate the value of recognizing the interdependence of buyer and seller.

Creative Engineering and Selling. It is just as important to sell a customer on the progressive steps leading to technical efficiency as it is to discover the step or to invent a better process or machine. An example significant in illustrating the inertia of methods in use is a study of a large wholesaling firm that was losing money. The study indicated that this company was located in a five-story building, and merchandise was stacked by hand. The expense ratio of this company was 7 percent of its sales. The two firms with which this house competed had modern one-story warehouses, and all merchandise was handled by a pallet and trucks. Outgoing orders were loaded from the merchandise stacked in the same sequence as it was listed on the order forms. This arrangement made it possible to load an order on a truck that was attached to a power line which was moving constantly through the warehouse. This operation, along with other similar modifications, enabled these two firms to operate on an expense margin of 4 percent of sales.

The policy decisions that would have kept the losing firm up to date in the installation of cost-reducing innovations could have been influenced by reliable data skillfully organized and effectively presented. This is the domain of the industrial salesman. Viewed in a social perspective, he performs the service of keeping at a minimum the lag between the technology of the laboratory and that of the industrial plant.

Close Relationship of Buyer and Seller.[4] The product that the industrial consumer chooses to buy must be reliable and productive. The reliability and

---

[4] For an appraisal of the importance and problems of buyer-seller relationships, see T. F. Dillion, "How Purchasing Handles New Product Evaluation," *Purchasing*, Vol. 63 (July 13, 1967), p. 77; A. P. Beckloff and P. V. Farrell, "Critical Evaluation of Purchasing," *Purchasing*, Vol. 62 (June 29, 1967), p. 44; and George W. Aljian (ed.), *Purchasing Handbook* (2d ed.; New York: McGraw-Hill Book Company, 1966).

productivity of major industrial sales in many instances are subject to test and calculations. This situation requires a close relationship between the firms of the buyer and the seller in transactions of major significance. Frequently negotiations reach a point where the engineering departments of the buyer and the seller confer at length on the needs of the buyer to determine how well the seller's product meets the buyer's needs.

John Callan, late professor of industrial management at the Harvard Business School, related a significant experience that illustrates this point. Professor Callan at one time was employed by General Electric. Since he had over a hundred significant mechanical patents registered in his name, he was employed in the product development division. Some of the company's products in the western silver mines were not giving satisfaction, and Callan was sent out to work on the problem. After going over the situation, not only did he correct the installations that were giving trouble, but also, out of his interest in aiding the mine operators, he installed thousands of dollars worth of equipment for a few comparatively small mining companies.

The significance of this incident is in the large sales figure that resulted from the technical know-how of the seller being applied to the operations of a buyer. Visualize the industrial consumer as being in a comparable situation with the ultimate consumer. The latter depends on a large group of firms to apply their specialized talents to provide him with consumption satisfactions from the area of their respective specialties. So, in the case of the industrial consumer, many selling firms are specialists in the different phases of an industrial consumer's operations.

Reliability Plus Confidence. To be successful in selling the industrial market, firms must first obtain the confidence of their prospect. Buyers must be convinced that the selling company knows its business and will support its claims. Second, industrial selling entails the proper conveyance of the technical information which will convince the buyer that the seller's product will maximize his productivity more than other possiblities. It should not be presumed that the latter function is sufficient to the exclusion of the first requirement. Calculations are more applicable in determining acceptability of industrial goods than of consumer goods, even though exact calculation cannot anticipate all the possible problems of operations or measure with perfect accuracy the comparative value of complex technical machines. Realizing this fact, the buying firm is influenced by the confidence it has in the seller's past history and its reputation for standing behind its product. For this reason, on important installations the staff of the seller, from the president to the production engineer, may be brought into contact with the staff of the buyer.

To Make or To Buy

One of the significant decisions all industrial concerns must make with respect to the fabricated parts entering into their products is whether to make the parts themselves or to buy them from other manufacturers. We have noted how automobile manufacturers buy a large percentage of their parts. How far should they go in this practice? Henry Ford became famous for building an industrial empire wherein he purchased virtually nothing. He even made his own glass, rubber, and steel. He built his own railroad and provided much of his own transportation. He found such complete independence from specialized fabricators unprofitable, however, and discontinued this policy. The amount of preprocessed food purchased by restaurants, even many of the most famous, further illustrates the willingness of some managers to hand over problems to specialists.

The scientific enterpriser will decide whether to make or to buy a part on the basis of the cost and satisfaction involved. It is possible that the prospective supplier who specializes in a particular type of part can routinize his production in the area of his specialty and achieve economies not possible to the larger assembling firm in question. It is also conceivable that his quality reputation may enhance the salability of the assembled product.

The reliability of the supply of the parts and the willingness of the selling firm to meet certain quality specifications important in the final product are other considerations. It is also apparent that when suppliers with parts of acceptable quality are available, the management problem is not so great as it is in the case of making the part. Manufacturing of parts involves finance, material, labor, and engineering problems that expand the scope of management responsibility.

Leasing of Installations

In some instances agreements are made by the seller of installations to lease the equipment to the user instead of selling it outright.[5] Leasing is common with such products as ships, trucks, railway cars, derricks, machinery, steel machinery, and office machines. Several factors favor this practice. In the first place, the high cost of most installations creates a problem of financing. Since the leasehold method permits payments to be made as the machine is used, the net amount of working capital required is reduced. Second some machines are complex and require special servicing. If the purchasing firm does not secure skilled, competent service, the work may be poorly done. Improper repairs will result in inefficient operations, which will reflect on the quality of installations and on the manufacturing firm that made them. The lease arrangements include provision for service by the lessor.

Third, manufacturing firms are hesitant to make large financial commitments for new installations when equipment in current use is operating in a satisfactory manner. With a lease arrangement, however, the manufacturer can introduce the machinery or any of its parts with little extra cost to the user. What might have been a major capital expenditure is changed to a relatively small operating cost. The user is less reluctant to adopt a new method, and sales resistance is overcome. Fourth, property taxes are not charged against

[5] R. Hlavacek and R. V. Ranestack, "Leases Mobile LIN Freezer for Five Weeks Maximizes IQF Cherry Quality and Profit," *Food Processing–Marketing*, Vol. 28 (December, 1967), p. 24; and "Industrial Leasing, Does It Work in Europe?" *Business Abroad*, Vol. 92 (October 16, 1967), p. 11.

installations that are leased. Thus, there is a tax advantage in leasing. To determine net savings one must calculate whether the property tax advantage offsets the depreciation that could be charged against owned equipment.[6]

The seller benefits from the steady income from lease payments. This arrangement enables the manufacturer of installations to escape in part the impact of cyclical declines, which are usually quite severe in the area of capital goods. He also enjoys a captive market for supplies and parts that may comprise a substantial portion of his profit business. The seller of such equipment can also charge each customer on the basis of the amount of use to which he puts the machine. If an outright sale were made, the Robinson-Patman Act would prevent him from charging different prices to buyers regardless of the amount of use intended.

On the other hand, the seller must arrange for the financing of the equipment that he owns and, in addition, must bear the cost of obsolescence and tax. At present, the favorable factors both in the case of the buyer and of the seller seem to indicate the soundness of this method of marketing certain installations. The practice is viewed with increasing favor.

Reciprocity

There is no way to measure accurately the amount of business that comes to the industrial seller because he does business with his prospective customers. Many business deals are the result of friendships, and friendships are the result of doing business. This circle of buying and selling could be described as spontaneous, arising from mutual friendship and confidence. In their eagerness to build sales, however, some firms have pressed the accounts from whom they have purchased goods to buy their own goods in return.

This type of dealing becomes somewhat more popular with the downturn phase of the business cycle. When sales drop down near break-even-point levels, and every dollar of sales counts, many firms consider the list of firms from whom they buy as sales prospects. The proposal is made on an "I'm scratching your back, now you scratch mine" basis. Sometimes the proposal may go so far as a threat to change suppliers unless reciprocity is practiced. On occasions the following three company situations develop: Company *A* buys heavily from Company *B*, who buys heavily from Company *C*. Company *A* will put pressure on Company *B* to get Company *C* to buy *A's* product.

During periods of prosperity less use is made of this method of acquiring sales. Theoretically, such a policy is sound only if the extra costs to the seller are less than the income from extra sales. All other factors being equal, the firm should buy its industrial products from the supplier that gives the most value for the money. Reciprocity influence that tends to deter a buyer from this procedure cannot be justified on the basis of efficient management.

Who Makes the Buying Decision?

It is unusual for only one person to influence the purchase of industrial goods. A purchasing agent will likely process the order, but he may rely on the

---

[6] D. F. Rock, "Equipment Leasing and the Investment Credit," *Taxes*, Vol. 46 (January, 1968), p. 4.

men who use the equipment for advice as to what to buy. Hence, it is common to find within companies that buying influence is found at all levels of executive and productive ranks.

In the newer industries an electronic component manufacturing specification may go out from the research laboratory, the production developing department, or the production facility. Conversely, it is difficult to determine who is responsible for the sale of new technical products. The research people often claim credit for the sale, as do engineers in development engineering departments and, naturally, the marketing division. The understanding and acceptance of the marketing concept enables these divisions to see this seeming diversity of views as a unified, cooperative effort.

In any event the industrial salesman must learn enough about each customer's processes and problems to identify the level at which purchase decisions are made. In general it is reasonable to assume that for new products or techniques top management will be involved. As a product enters the routine productive phase, either engineering development or production executives make buying decisions. The selection of possible suppliers and negotiations for price and terms, based on specifications, are most commonly handled by the office of the purchasing agent.

Planning

Planning for growth assumes greater importance each year. Many existing industrial markets are shrinking or, at best, are not growing as rapidly as the economy.

Effort must be balanced between selling existing products and finding new or improved products and techniques. Provision must be made for planning to take advantage of change in social patterns. Increased leisure time, recreational opportunities, and demand for housing influences the dynamics of the industrial market. Progress in technology, resulting both in and from increasing research, military demands, new fuels, and space exploration, requires an alertness to opportunity which distinguishes the contemporary industrial market from that of former years.

Note that this section does not include a cataloging of the kinds of market institutions and channels required to distribute industrial goods effectively and efficiently. Chapter 8, on wholesaling and wholesaling institutions (which by definition includes industrial marketing), and Chapter 10, on the selection of marketing channels, explain the types of institutions and proper linkage required to meet the needs of the industrial market.

QUESTIONS AND ANALYTICAL PROBLEMS

1. Define: (a) industrial goods, (b) industrial marketing.
2. Explain each of the following statements:
   (a) The demand for industrial goods in a derived demand.
   (b) There tend to be greater fluctuations in the industrial market than the consumer goods market.
3. What are the characteristics of each of the three broad classes of customers in the industrial market?

4. What geographic concentration of industrial marketing is evident in the United States?

5. What concentration by size of manufacturing firms is evident in the United States?

6. What marketing policies will be affected by the concentrations noted in questions 4 and 5?

7. What will be the effect on the choice of types of middlemen to be used in areas of high industrial concentration?

8. Examine Table 9-2 on page 154. Find the five lines in which small manufacturing firms are most important. Explain why manufacturing in those lines should be dominated by small firms.

9. What are the most important demand characteristics for purchasers of industrial goods? Are these the same as for consumer goods?

10. Can industrial goods be sold? Is it more nearly correct to say that industrial goods are purchased because of a recognized need and that they cannot be sold in the sense that a second television set is sold to a householder?

11. Write a list of motives likely to influence a 50-year-old business executive when he purchases an automobile for his personal use. Write a separate list of motives likely to influence the same man as he purchases automobiles for the use of his salesmen. Explain any differences.

12. Find five advertisements in trade magazines—preferably those used by production men—that make some use of emotional appeals. Discuss their probable effectiveness. Do rational appeals or emotional appeals predominate in the advertisements of such journals? Why?

13. Why might a manufacturer decide to lease certain equipment rather than purchase it?

14. Why might a manufacturer of equipment desire to distribute it through leasing arrangements rather than by outright sales?

15. Which would be the more difficult job—to be a purchasing agent responsible for buying equipment for a manufacturer of electronic products or to be the merchandise manager responsible for buying for a store selling fashion goods?

Case 9 • COLORADO MANUFACTURING COMPANY

The management of the Colorado Manufacturing Company (CMC), a firm which makes mining machinery, was confronted with choosing the best method of distribution for a newly developed line of paving breakers for road construction work. The firm's present line of equipment is sold direct to mining companies by a 12-man sales force. By contrast, some competitors sell through mine supply firms, companies that stock a wide range of equipment and replacement parts.

In order to sell its new product, CMC must break into a market which is new to the company—a market of national scope and tremendous size. Construction contractors ordinarily purchase their equipment from supply firms and equipment dealers. These equipment dealers often represent several manufacturers and sometimes carry competing lines. A few companies manufacturing heavy construction equipment use salesmen to sell direct to contractors. Although such an approach would require enlargement of their present sales force, CMC executives are considering this type of distribution program.

• Weigh the costs and benefits of a direct contact with the road construction industry against the services obtained from the equipment dealers and recommend a decision. Are there any conditions that you would specify in your recommendation or are there other alternatives?

Building and managing the distribution channel

10

Only in rare cases does a company that manufactures a product sell it direct to its ultimate consumer. It would be a tremendous and probably unwise undertaking for General Mills, for instance, to sell and deliver each of its brands of breakfast foods directly to the more than 80 million consumer units that are its potential customers. However some manufacturers do reach their ultimate consumers through their own retail stores, while others hire door-to-door salesmen. Still, it is likely that the cases in which a product moves in only one step from producer to consumer amount to less than 4 percent.[1] This means that over 96 percent of all goods sold are resold one or more times by sellers other than the original producer. Such being the case, it is clear that the success of the producer or manufacturer is dependent on how effective these resellers do their job. These resellers are composed of a linkage of the different kinds of agents, wholesalers, and retailers. The manufacturer usually takes the initiative in putting together a chain of such institutions that will bridge the gap between the factory and the ultimate consumer. This linkage is referred to as a channel.

In this chapter we shall first define the concept of channels; second, we shall discuss the conventional channel routes through which products flow to reach the market; third, we shall examine some of the alternative policies which manufacturers use in selecting the institutions that will resell their product to the consumers; fourth, we shall introduce the basic factors to consider in selecting institutions with which to build a channel; fifth, we shall explore the dynamic

---

[1] U.S. Department of Commerce, Bureau of the Census, *Census of Business: 1967.*

forces which bring about change in the channel flow; and sixth, we shall present an overall view of the effective use of distribution channels.

DEFINITION OF A MARKETING CHANNEL

According to the Committee on Definitions of the American Marketing Association, *a market channel* is "the structure of intracompany organization units and extracompany agents and dealers, wholesale and retail, through which a commodity, product, or service is marketed."[2] A market channel might also be defined as the sequence of institutions listed in the order of their participation as buyers, sellers, or holders of the physical products or services in providing the facility to move these products or services from producer to consumer.

As an example Exhibit 10-1 shows the channel involved in the movement of apples from Yakima, Washington, to upstate New York. Note that the broker did not take title or possession of the product. The auction assumed the responsibility of physical possession but did not take title. Yet both of these institutions were in the channel.

CONVENTIONAL CHANNELS

Of the conventional routes that manufactured goods take to reach the consumer, the most common are as follows (see Exhibit 10-2):

1. Manufacturer direct to consumer.
2. Manufacturer to retailer to consumer.
3. Manufacturer to wholesaler to retailer to consumer.
4. Manufacturer to agent middleman to wholesaler to retailer to consumer.

The problem of selecting a channel would be simple if all one had to do was to select one of these routes according to the type of merchandise each one handled. Regardless of the classification of the institutions, however, each one differs in the amount, kind, and quality of the service it provides. If a company

Exhibit 10-1

**THE CHANNEL FLOW OF A BUSHEL OF APPLES
FROM WASHINGTON TO NEW YORK**

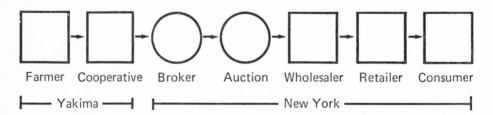

Farmer   Cooperative   Broker   Auction   Wholesaler   Retailer   Consumer

|—— Yakima ——| |———————— New York ————————|

---

[2] Ralph S. Alexander and the Committee on Definitions, *Marketing Definitions* (Chicago: American Marketing Association, 1963), p. 10.

Exhibit 10-2

CONVENTIONAL CHANNELS OF DISTRIBUTION

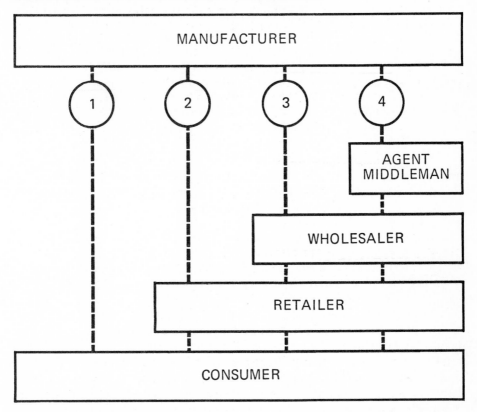

were forced to choose a designated wholesaler as a route to market, it might be wise to sell direct and not use the wholesaler. Yet because of the kind and quality of services given by another unusually aggressive wholesaler, the company might find it more efficient to sell through this wholesaler. There are strengths and weaknesses in each of the conventional methods, and it is difficult to make broad generalizations about them. In selecting a channel, the specific institution and its management should be considered along with the classification of service rendered.

Manufacturer Direct to the Consumer

The manufacturer can reach the consumer directly by the use of one or more of the following routes: door-to-door sales, sales through the manufacturer's own retail stores, direct selling (through an advertising medium such as television), and sales by mail order. None of these methods account for a very high percentage of total retail sales. Door-to-door methods account for approximately one percent; mail-order sales, one percent; sales through manufacturer's retail stores, less than one percent, and direct sales, one percent.

When a manufacturer decides to go directly to the consumer, he assumes the responsibility of performing or directing the performance of all the marketing functions necessary to complete the flow of the good. Since he will be applying these functions to only one product (or line of products) and must extend the services to a large number of accounts, we can see why this particular channel is reputed to have the highest marketing costs. The following conditions specifically contribute to increased costs:

1. Building and maintaining a large, well-supervised sales staff.
2. Building and maintaining extensive systems of warehouses and inventories in order to make prompt deliveries to many different customers.
3. Providing adequate financing of the additional functions.
4. Assuming the risk of credit extension.

The offsetting advantages that should lead to increased sales volume by direct selling are:

1. More aggressive, concentrated, controlled selling.
2. A closer contact with the consumer, which makes it easier to determine his needs.
3. The elimination of the profits that would ordinarily accrue to middlemen.
4. The opportunity to provide technical knowledge in selling.
5. More rapid physical movement of goods than if they had to travel through several middlemen, which is especially important in the case of perishables.

Door-to-Door Sales. Under this method the manufacturer has complete control of the product and can provide for the right amount of sales push at the point of sale. This method provides a means of introducing a product that retailers may be reluctant to stock and which requires considerable and complicated communication to sell. The feedback from a well-managed, door-to-door sales force should be excellent since the salespeople are controlled directly from the home office. The entire sales force should be very flexible and sensitive to the control of management. This method does place a significant hindrance on management, however, in the maintenance of an adequate sales force. While a great deal of capital is not necessary to carry on this type of operation, unit selling costs are usually higher than for other types of selling.

Selling Through Manufacturer's Own Stores. Manufacturers achieve two significant advantages by selling through their own retail stores. First, they exercise greater control and influence over their product; and, second, they get a direct feedback from the consumer. With such information they can provide the control and sales push that is required to move the product completely through the channel. The problems of perishability and service to the company's product can be managed in a manner that will enhance the company's prestige. A considerable capital outlay is necessary to set up and operate such stores, however, and the company must have a product that sells in sufficient volume to absorb the overhead of operating a retail store.

As one alternative to high-volume sales of its own products, the company may stock complementary lines of other manufacturers. Once a company adopts this policy, however, it finds itself in the retail business with additional management problems. Unless the company does have adequate lines in the stores, physical movement and control of stock and overhead render the method expensive. In instances where it is practiced, it is presumed that the advantages of feedback, control of product, promotion, and service outweigh costs in the judgement of management.

Mail-Order Selling by the Manufacturer. The mail-order channel from the producer to the consumer has survived against great odds. The convenience it offered, which was the main reason for its growth, is not so great a factor today. Suburban shopping centers, supermarkets, and the greater mobility of the consumer have removed the barriers to shopping which once encouraged the user of the mail-order channel. Manufacturers who have an unusual product or who can offer bargains are still finding some success in this type of sales, in spite of spiraling postal costs.

Direct Sales. Developing in the late 1960's, direct selling differs from mail-order sales basically in the method of delivery of the appeal to the consumer. Direct sales manufacturers market products through radio and television media to mass target markets. Consumers respond directly to the manufacturer by either mail or telephone. Subsequently, the manufacturer either delivers the product or sends it through the mail. Automobile accessories, kitchen appliances, and records were early favorites in direct sales. Even though accounting for only one percent of manufacturer to consumer sales, direct selling is the fastest growing method in this marketing channel today.

Manufacturer to Retailer to Consumer

Some manufacturers find it desirable to make direct contact with the retailer rather than to use agents or wholesalers. This channel, though not as effective as the manufacturer-owned store, is especially desirable when the company wishes to enjoy direct control of its products. This need for close control might occur if the product is perishable or highly fashionable, thereby making time an important factor. A manufacturing company may also prefer a direct contact with the retailer for strategic or competitive reasons. With products of high unit value, such as pianos, jewelry, silver, and agricultural machinery, the price of each unit is large enough to cover easily the overhead costs of selling direct to the retailer. Other circumstances that tend to encourage direct selling are: (1) when the products of a single firm constitute a substantial part of the retailer's stock and savings can be made on bulk shipments, (2) when products command a large enough market that their consumers are fairly numerous in relation to the territory that must be covered, and (3) when the product requires installation and replacement parts.

By relying upon his own salesmen rather than by using a wholesaler to represent him, the manufacturer knows that he will receive the concentrated effort of his salesmen. He will not have to compete with other products in a wholesaler's line including, perhaps, private brands of the wholesaler. Having his salesmen make regular visits to a store allows the manufacturer the opportunity to build goodwill with the retailer's sales personnel by passing on to them important sales information and helping them with point of sales displays.

This channel allows cooperative advertising and promotional campaigns between the manufacturer and the retailer without a wholesaler's intervening. It provides a means to resolve difficulties and to promote better cooperation.

Just as with direct selling to consumers, the obvious disadvantages of the program are:

1. The high cost of selling and processing sales to a large number of accounts.
2. Bearing the risk of credit extension.
3. The physical movement of goods in small lots to widespread places.
4. Maintaining adequate storage facilities and inventories.
5. The small volume and distances from some warehouses. These conditions make it impractical to sell to some retailers. Yet, when a company sells the large accounts direct, it is difficult to maintain desirable relations with wholesalers on whom the company depends to sell the small accounts.

Manufacturer to Wholesaler to Retailer to Consumer

Best known of all channels of distribution is the one that utilizes the wholesaler. In fact, it is commonly known as the traditional or customary channel. In spite of its popularity, it is seldom used exclusively. Most manufacturers reserve the right to sell to chains or large retailers, to associations of small retailers, and sometimes even directly to small retailers besides selling to the wholesaler. The functions that a wholesaler performs—buying, storing, selling, making deliveries, and extending credit—and the advantages of using his service have been discussed in Chapter 8.

Manufacturer to Agent Middleman to Wholesaler to Retailer to Consumer

The last major channel of distribution that we shall consider is one which utilizes the services of the various types of agents and brokers. Their prime function is selling (or buying if they represent wholesalers or large retailers). In Chapter 8 we have discussed the contribution of the broker, the manufacturers' agent, the selling agent, and the commission merchant. Agents and brokers have found their greatest popularity among manufacturers who either are not large enough to profitably establish their own sales organizations or who wish to concentrate their efforts on production and transfer to others the major responsibility of marketing their goods.

SELECTIVITY OF DISTRIBUTION

The forces that encourage the flows and the barriers that cause resistances inherent in each channel alternative must be appraised carefully. A significant decision that each manufacturer must make is how many retailers and wholesalers to include in the channel to achieve the greatest promotional push with the least resistance. At first glance it may appear that the company would benefit by having its products in as many outlets as will agree to handle them. The question then arises, would such a policy provide the company's product as much promotional push as would a more selective policy? Consumer attitude and prestige must also be considered. In the formation of such policy, three broad courses are open to the manufacturer: first, extensive or widespread distribution; second, careful selection of the outlets through which he sells; or third, the use of exclusive outlets.

Extensive Distribution

For many goods, especially those classified as convenience goods, a maximum exposure to the public is desirable to capture a significant share of the market. Wrigley's chewing gum, Gillette Trac II blades, Coca-Cola, Scotch tape, and Kleenex tissues are examples of goods that are found everywhere—in drugstores, grocery stores, variety stores, supermarkets, and department stores, not to mention vending machines, magazine stands, and candy counters. Because such goods could easily be replaced with another brand, the manufacturer must either arrange his channels to provide a widespread availability or must be content to service only his most profitable accounts. To obtain complete coverage will generally require that he utilize more than one type of channel. He may wish to sell directly to his largest accounts and to use a wholesaler to reach his widely scattered outlets.

Selective Selling

When a manufacturer wishes to build an image for his product with a certain class, he will select those outlets which identify with this class. He can expect better service if he cultivates a few resellers who have the same objectives he has in reaching preferred customers. His costs will probably be less since his contacts will be limited and his individual shipments fewer and larger.

Selective selling requires a well-planned system of evaluating outlets of selecting only the most desirable. Working on the assumption that no representation is better than poor representation, manufacturers have been able to reduce their selling costs and increase their sales by distributing only through institutions that will work closely with them in pushing their particular product. The manufacturer gains the advantage of having a smaller number of the most preferred institutions to serve him in the promotion of his product.

Exclusive Agencies

The exclusive agency extends the advantages of the selective selling policy. There are also risks inherent in the adoption of exclusive agency contracts. By careful selection of qualified dealers, the manufacturer can expect close cooperation and enthusiastic promotion of his product. He can select firms that will provide a maximum of prestige for the product and which will be most likely to sell to the clientele the manufacturer has designed his product to reach. He runs the risks, however, of not having the product widely enough distributed to achieve the maximum selling impact. He may also gain the ill will of other prominent sellers by refusing them the privilege of handling his product. He must use care in drawing up the contract in order that agreements are clearly understood and that they meet the requirements of the law.

These three methods are described merely to indicate a range of choices open to the manufacturer. Actually a company may adopt a policy that is a combination of the ingredients of all three. It is impossible to get complete market coverage and to enlist the promotional loyalty and full cooperation of outlets. A company must examine the possible outlets for its product and tailor a program to include as many of the desirable qualities while avoiding as many disadvantages as possible.

VITAL CONSIDERATIONS IN CHANNEL SELECTION [3]

The foregoing discussion has provided an outline of the conventional structure and basic distribution policies of manufacturing firms in building their market channels. It is impossible to list and discuss the pluses and minuses of the great number of relationships that might exist between a manufacturer and the institutions which he selects as his marketing channels. There are, however, certain universal objectives which he will attempt to realize in order to get the best results. The five following considerations describe the qualities which the channel should possess in order to provide management with a maximum of excellence in building an effective linkage to the consumer.

1. It should provide for the physical movement of goods to the point of consumption and for the consummation of necessary market transactions in the most economical and satisfactory manner and in a minimum of time.
2. It should provide the optimum amount and quality of promotion and communication to assure the rapid sale of the product to all buyers in the channel, especially the ultimate consumer.
3. It should provide an adequate feedback of information that will enable the company to modify its product or procedures to meet market demands.
4. It should possess sufficient flexibility in its institutional patterns to adapt itself creatively to changing market conditions.
5. It should coincide with the company's capacity and function as a unit that is completely sensitive to company objectives and complementary to the cooperating institutions in the channel.

Movement of the Physical Products

Costs in terms of money and time are basic elements to consider in evaluating any method of moving goods from the producer to the consumer. For example, a city with a population of 50,000 people may have 20 stores that may handle the company's product. It probably would be much more costly for the company to make 20 calls in this city and others under similar circumstances

---

[3] See Louis P. Bucklin, "Theory of Channel Control," *Journal of Marketing*, Vol. 37 (January, 1973), pp. 39-47. Also, Bert Rosenbloom, "Conflict and Channel Efficiency: Some Conceputal Models for the Decision Maker," *Journal of Marketing*, Vol. 37 (July, 1973), pp. 26-30. These present some simple models which illustrate possible relationships of conflict in channels.

than it would be to sell to one wholesaler and let him make the contacts. Indeed, the extra cost likely would be so great as to offset other advantages that might accrue from personal contact, such as servicing the product or more intense selling effort.

On the other hand, if the city had a population of 400,000 and the company's business was done through 20 outlets, it is conceivable that the volume of sales to each store might be sufficient to make direct contacts profitable. Especially would this be true if there were advantages that might accrue from more effective selling as a result of a direct contact.

Here the question of the economies of re-sorting and reducing the number of transactions, the transportation costs, and the volume of business included in each transaction are controlling factors. These economies were discussed in Chapter 8. If the volume of a company's line of products directed to a specific area is sufficient to justify the establishment of its own warehousing and delivery system, such an arrangement may be desirable.

The National Biscuit Company uses a direct contact for its most competitive and perishable products. Nabisco wishes to have its own salesmen visit the retail store in order to sell the company's line and to see that only fresh products remain on retail shelves. On the other hand, Procter and Gamble, also selling to many outlets in specific communities, meets the problem of dispersing a large volume through many small units by selling through the wholesaler. In this instance, the wholesaler performs the warehousing, delivery, finance, and selling functions. The principal reason for the difference in the channel policies of these companies is that Procter and Gamble products are not perishable, while certain Nabisco lines provide more satisfaction when they are fresh.

If a comparatively large volume of a company's product is sold through a few outlets, a direct manufacturer-to-retailer contact may be desirable. This may be true in spite of higher costs of dispersing the physical product. A direct contact with the customer and better control of the product may offset the greater costs of transportation and the making of numerous contacts. A method of distribution is especially desirable when the element of perishability or fashion is a factor. Thus, the progressive and high-volume ready-to-wear stores buy directly from manufacturers. Furniture manufacturers usually enjoy direct contact with retail outlets. In these instances the volume of sales, as well as the unit of sale to the individual store, is large enough to absorb the costs of additional transactions and possibly additional transportation costs.

In some instances, it may be desirable for one company to use two channels. A large food company might sell to the high-volume stores by direct shipments; and where the volume does not justify the overhead expense, the company may sell through wholesalers. There is a risk that such a policy may incur the hearty displeasure of the wholesalers. They would resent the company's selling the large accounts and leaving the units with small profit possibilities to the wholesalers. All these alternatives are closely related to the economy of re-sorting in time, number of transactions, and transportation costs. This economy is always an important consideration, yet the other factors to be discussed must also be considered in a final selection of institutions making up the channel.

Promotion and Communication Qualities

The movement of most products requires a promotional push; they do not always move as a result of low prices or the pure force of gravity. In certain circumstances, however, the flow seems almost automatic, and little or no promotion is necessary. During World War II, when there was a scarcity of goods, few promotional efforts were required. The unsatisfied desires of customers resulted in a suction that pulled products through the channels. Under such conditions the economy of movement of physical goods to the point of consumption and the number of transactions were the dominant factors to consider in choosing a channel.

Even during normal times different goods require varying amounts of promotion. Raw materials change but little over a period of time and require less promotion than consumer goods. They are pulled through the market by the sale of products of which they are a part. Steel is in demand not because a desire has been created for it, but because it is a component of the automobile. Copper has a conventional market flow, where selling by the institutions in the channel is less important than the goods for which there may be an array of alternative choices. Even under these circumstances copper and steel companies must do some selling and advertising. On the other hand, the ultimate consumer of manufactured goods is almost constantly confronted with a multiplicity of choices. Since the ultimate consumer has so many alternatives from which to choose, the movement of each product must be aided with a positive selling story.

What is true at the consumer purchasing level is also true at the retail and wholesale purchasing levels. Wholesalers and retailers who are alert to market opportunities are sensitive to consumer desire. They stock what is asked for most frequently. They build their business by selecting from the many alternatives available those goods that are most likely to satisfy the consumer's request.

The Pull of Advertising. If the manufacturer is in a position to advertise extensively, he may create a "suction force" for his product. This desire which he creates may be so strong at the consumer level that retailers and wholesalers will almost be forced to have the stock available. Some popular TV programs carry such a demand-creating impact with little support from other advertising. The soap companies with their tremendous national advertising campaigns create such a suction force at the consumer level that a retailer is embarrassed not to have the product in stock and on display.

The Push of the Salesman. The pull of advertising may need to be supplemented with the push of salesmen. The nature of this need determines, more than any other factor, whether a manufacturer will send out his own salesmen, set up his own branches, or entrust the selling to wholesale institutions. The full-line wholesaler carries too many brands to make it possible for him to provide any selling-promotion push for a single brand. The most he can offer is the economy of a positive contact and some possible savings in physical distribution. The specialty wholesaler is better equipped. A limited line with a promotional focus on one brand in a certain shop enables him to give both selling and service attention to a product. Here, again, the manufacturer must answer the question of cost and satisfaction. Are the selling and service provided by the specialty wholesaler sufficient to pay for the extra margin of cost that he exacts for his services? Or, for a similar margin, can the manufacturer send out his own salespeople who are especially trained to tell the company's story? By using his own sales force, the seller can maintain greater control of his product, organize his own selling program, and get a complete feedback from the market. Again there is the question of adequate volume to absorb the costs of an extensive program of this kind.

The Cooperation of the Reseller. Almost as strategic as the push or pull of advertising and selling is the building of goodwill with the reseller. These resellers may be brokers, wholesalers, or retailers, who have the discretion and skill to provide the product with constant availability. Often they choose the site of the product display and the amount of shelf space. The maintenance of amiable relations with all institutions in the channel flow is imperative even when the demand pull is strong. Well-advertised products will experience a decrease in sales if stock is not available, exposed, and presented in a positive manner at all selling points.

The goodwill of the food retailer was so important to one of the major manufacturers that it undertook a costly program to develop positive relationships. First, the company did a great deal of research to collect cost figures for different retail operations. Then, it made an extensive study of the effectiveness of shelf space and determined how profits could be increased by placing high-margin items at strategic selling points. The chief executive officer of the firm then contacted the presidents of larger food chains, which did a high percentage of the food business, and made a personal presentation of the research findings. He succeeded in building excellent relations with these firms which his salesmen have taken special pains to maintain.

There are infinite combinations of institutions and programs that provide for the promotional needs of a particular company. To obtain an optimum combination of the above described promotional ingredients, considered in the light of costs and potential results, is the challenge which confronts marketing management.

Feedback Information

The tempo of new product introduction and improving distribution patterns is constantly accelerating. Unless prompt and carefully designed action is taken to keep a company abreast of these changes, the newer and better products and services of competitors will steal its market. Furthermore, the growing tendency to segment markets according to the desires of individual customers, reference groups, or classes of customers accentuates the need for accurate feedback. The demands for consumer satisfaction, encouraged by the Consumer Council sponsored by the federal government, provides an additional reason for securing accurate feedback from different segments of the market.

Companies such as Singer Sewing Machine, Eastman Kodak, and Avon have direct contact with customers and, therefore, are in a position to secure the feedback information they need. But when a company entrusts its products to resellers, how can it be sure that the feedback it obtains is adequate and accurate? To be helpful to a company, feedback information from institutions which sell the product should cover at least four areas: (1) the product characteristics as compared with competition; (2) inventory conditions of the channel institutions; (3) appraisal of the service provided by the company; and (4) changes in market conditions.

A manufacturer would do well to recognize two basic conditions that affect the feedback available to him. One is the number of resellers he uses to reach the market. The shorter the channel, the more likely it is that the manufacturer will get quick and accurate feedback. The other condition is the degree to which the cooperation of the channel institutions is secured. Often the manufacturer can win their support by performing some useful service to them.

Institutional Flexibility

The institutions selected to sell the company's product should be both progressive and flexible. Once a channel has been established, it is not easy to change it; however, it should be able to adapt itself to the inevitable market shift. Progressive improvements in channel services are made necessary by the evolving nature of the product, the market, and the strategy of competing institutions. The history of marketing is a record of changing routes to the ultimate consumer. The general store gave way to the specialty store. Department stores developed and grew in importance. Then the chain store, especially in the food field; made a spectacular growth during the 1920 decade and effected a shift in the prevailing trade channels. Since World War II, the discount house in its various forms has become a competitive threat to different kinds of businesses. The supermarket, with its scrambled merchandising policy, has also been a factor.

The food wholesaler provides an excellent example of change. Chain stores, with their own warehouses and their low margins, became a serious threat to the food wholesalers. Existing grocery wholesalers had to adapt themselves to changes or go out of business. Many food wholesalers were sufficiently flexible to adapt, but many others failed. Some of those that succeeded changed their patterns of operation and reduced their expense margins from 12 percent in 1930 to 4 percent in 1969 and have increased their services to retailers. They achieved this goal by several methods.

First, as a result of a common interest with the food retailer, food wholesalers were able to encourage him to purchase a greater volume with a smaller selling cost to themselves. Weekly order blanks were prepared that simplified ordering without the aid of a salesman. Second, single story warehousing was adopted that reduced the time and the energy necessary to unload and load the food products. In this connection considerable savings were effected as a result of the use of conveyors, pallets, and trucks. Third, machine accounting and better management of credit and delivery operations reduced costs. Fourth, the food wholesalers were able to hold their volume by adopting various methods of increasing the sales of their customers. They organized voluntary chain store associations, such as the Independent Grocers Alliance, by which means they guaranteed themselves a certain percentage of the retailer business. In return for this guaranteed percentage of the retailer's sales and a small fee, the wholesalers disseminated specialized price and merchandising data and prepared a cooperative advertising campaign. In some instances independent grocers effected a close-knit organization and set up their own wholesalers who performed all the above functions. Most of these economies were passed on to the retailer which made it possible for him to compete with the chains.

Complementary Unity

Few manufacturers have sufficient volume to bear the expense of a complete distributional system. How then can those who do not have a distributional system of their own approach the advantages of having one by using existing institutions? Can a simple arrangement of institutions be set up that will give a company's product the right selling push, reach all possible sales prospects, provide the protection and service required by the product at a minimum cost, and keep all engaged institutions in a positive cooperative attitude?

For example, a small firm had enjoyed spectacular success with stagelight dimmers. It found its most promising market in high school buildings but experienced difficulty in setting up one channel that would cover its entire market. It had contracts with 27 manufacturers' agents, providing excellent coverage of the new school building outlets. These agents, however, did not contact the established high school market, and they objected to the firm's engaging others in the territory. The company was reluctant to press this issue since the agents were so well suited to the new school market and were doing an exceptionally fine selling job and since the market was making a profit from this volume. At the present time, however, the company is considering the possibility of sending its own representatives into a test area to contact both the new and the existing school market. Such a representative will be able to aid in the promotion of specialty items that the company contemplates producing.

This case illustrates an instance in which one channel does an excellent job in one segment of the market but fails in another. It does not give the service that the company would desire if it had its own sales force. For this reason, the company is giving thought to the establishment of its own sales force.

An excellent example of the functioning of a completely integrated, unified program can be observed in the manner in which Procter and Gamble Company uses its chosen channels. One of the advantages which this company enjoys is that its volume allows the company to supply its wholesale customers with added services. Procter and Gamble's sales organization and activities may be described under four headings:

1. (a) The company sells the masses of independent dealers entirely through the wholesalers who feature the respective product lines and, as a result,

Procter and Gamble enjoys the following advantages: economical warehousing, delivery, credit and collections, and complete coverage of the independent retail outlets through which the company's products are sold.

(b) The company reaches large retailers who agree to buy as a part of a pool by classifying them as special dealers and shipping to the pool members in carload lots. In these instances the orders are billed through the wholesalers.

(c) Sales are made directly to large chains that do their own warehousing.

2. The company introduces most of its new products with samples and premiums to individual homes. In those cases in which samples are not given, other effective promotional methods are used. This practice guarantees the company an almost immediate volume for new products.

3. The company sends salesmen to retail outlets to encourage the sales of its products by obtaining favored floor positions and adequate facings. Such activity aids the wholesaler in getting volume sales and supplements his selling efforts.

4. The company spends millions of dollars every year in advertising to the consumer to create a suction that pulls the product through both the retail and the wholesale outlets.

The company uses the wholesalers in the channel to the extent of their capacity, but it supports that program with its own sales force and advertising. Thus, the distributional system, including the wholesaler, operates as an integrated unity.

THE DYNAMIC FORCES INFLUENCING CHANGE

Technology, competitive strategy, changing habits of customers, and living conditions of the people are factors responsible for change in all marketing practices. Especially is this true with respect to market channels. A change in a channel does not always refer to a different combination of institutions, although such changes are often made. Rather, constant adaptations are being made in the type of services that are given by the institutions in the channel. One expert states:

> Some of the most fundamental channels of trade in the United States seem to have been in a constant state of evolution for decades.[4]

The fact that retail sales are approximating $450 billion today, compared to only $40 billion in 1929, accounts for many changes in the institutional flow. Increasing volumes in the flow create opportunities for new firms and force the firms already in the channel to alter their practices.

Forces affecting marketing methods are almost infinite in number, being as complex as the forces that are responsible for social evolution. A discussion of four areas, however, will reveal many of the important forces for channel

---

[3] Wroe Alderson, "Factors Governing the Development of Marketing Channels," *Marketing Channels*, edited by Richard M. Clewett (Homewood, Ill.: Richard D. Irwin, Inc., 1954), p. 21.

change. First, the innovation of new products prompts an examination of new routes to market. Second, institutions adapting to new levels upset market equilibrium and encourage further change. Third, changes in buying habits of the customers create opportunities for institutional evolution. Fourth, the growth of research encourages firms to seek better methods of reaching the market with their product. It is likely that most changes in the channel are some combination of these forces. Seldom is a case so simple that it may be solved by the analysis of just one cause-and-effect relationship. Nevertheless, an integrated view of the whole will be improved by a look at each of the areas separately.

Product Innovation

A significant change in a product or in its rate of sale, or a new product entering the market frequently alters the type of service required of a market channel. The frozen-food industry made it necessary for food wholesalers to expand their operations to handle frozen products. Equipment was expensive; its use increased both capital requirements and fixed operating costs. Moreover, increases in fixed costs require greater volume and higher break-even points. Those institutions that cannot adapt to such changes are forced out of the market, and those which remain obtain the increased volume.

On the retail side of food marketing, the increasingly higher capital investment required because of frozen foods, prepackaged meats, and other innovations restricted entry into the field in recent years. The fact that there now are fewer and larger food retailers changes the channel strategy with respect to the number and type of wholesalers necessary to reach those retailers. With larger volume outlets, direct sale to the retailer by the manufacturer is more profitable. Wholesalers are forced to adapt their costs and services to such changes or lose their volume. The entry of the frozen-food industry into the market is only one of the contributing reasons why there has been a reduction in the wholesale and retail outlets in the food trade; but it has been a typical innovation that illustrates one force influencing changes in channel flows.

Another excellent example of product innovation and of the adaptation of channels is the rapid increase in the number of home appliances sold during the last 30 years. A backlog of demand accumulated during the war. Technological advances brought new appliances and improved models of established appliances on the market. How could the manufacturer keep abreast of competition in handling this increased volume? Since the unit of sale was large and the number of appliance stores was limited, direct sales from manufacturers to retailers was the prevailing method of sale. Following the war, however, the greater volume of sales and the spectacular increase in the number of outlets created new opportunities. Even though the volume increased, many manufacturers chose to sell their appliances through wholesale distributors and to concentrate on production. The volume of sales was sufficiently large to justify the entrance of many wholesalers into this field. Once established, many of them expanded to include other lines of hardware and equipment. When the backlog of demand was spent, some of these firms expanded their lines or went out of business. Yet the permanence of the home appliance business had an impact on the routes that many appliances take to reach the consumer.

Another interesting, but normal, aspect of this situation is that different companies still do not agree on the most efficient methods. Westinghouse and General Electric decided that a distributor on the scene with warehouse, sales, and service facilities would to the job better. Philco-Bendix and RCA Whirlpool, however, sell their products through independent wholesalers. Such variations are common in many fields where similar products are offered. Availability of capital funds, adequate management talent, and breadth of the line offered for sale may influence companies to sell directly to the retailer. On the other hand, the lack of such resources, narrowness of line, and limited management skills may prompt another company to allow wholesale distributors to sell and service their products. In any event, the examples cited illustrate that change in types of products sold or the velocity of their flow has an impact on the services performed by the outlets making up the channel and, in some instances, invites the entry of new institutions.

Institutional Innovation

Several impelling forces encourage changes in the institutions making up the channel. First, the tendency to modify the distributional machinery to correspond to the changes brought by the entrance of mass production techniques in industry is growing; second, the distributors have grown to be such an important factor in the economy that they seek to become independent from the producers; and third, evolutionary changes result from a combination of progress in technology, social evolution, and competitive strategy.

The increased flow in goods from 1929 to the business census year of 1971 was due primarily to improved technology in production and to increased efficiency in distribution. During this period of time, retail stores increased from 1.5 million to 1.8 million, an increase of over 20 percent in the number of stores; while the sales in constant dollars increased 170 percent. The average sales per store in 1971-1972 dollars increased from $55,000 to $228,000. This more than quadrupling of sales per store represents more than the sale of the same kinds of goods. It means the acquisition of more lines of merchandise. Seldom, today, do we see a food store that does not carry meats and vegetables. Not too many decades ago the "combination" food stores—those which sold meat as well as groceries—were quite uncommon. The drugstore also has spread its line to include sundry items not carried in the drugstore several years ago. The discount house, also a new kind of dealer, accounts for a considerable volume of sales in certain fields.

In order to meet the competition from other institutions, as well as meeting the threat of direct sale by manufacturers to retailers, wholesalers are forced to spread their line to include additional items. Food wholesalers now sell meats, vegetables, and frozen foods. The hardware wholesaler has expanded his line to include furniture, appliances, and other sundry items that were not a part of his line in the 1930's. Some of these wholesalers have even spread so broadly that they have included drug items under the same operation.

The food wholesaler has spread his activity to the extent that he performs many of the functions formerly performed by the retailer. To survive in competition with chain stores and with other wholesalers, the food wholesaler, in many instances, furnishes the capital to finance a retail store, supplies credit for merchandise inventory, prepares promotion and advertising, and provides information on merchandising and layout fundamentals. The wholesaler must innovate or discontinue business. Such innovation creates still new opportunities for the flow of goods and stimulates reappraisals of channels by sellers. Thus, channels are in a constant state of innovation and flux.

For example, one comparatively large food chain has departed from the traditional chain store policy of doing its own warehousing. This chain buys in large volume from established wholesalers in the location in which it operates. Its large volume account is sought by the wholesalers. But to satisfy the demands of this chain and others in the same category, competing wholesalers have had to reduce their margins of cost and to increase their volume. They have also been forced to expand their offerings in order to match the lines sold by the supermarket chains. In one locality, competition to obtain the business of these stores has motivated two wholesalers to add meats and other products of their offerings.

At present, this chain of supermarkets is offering specials in boy's wear. The wholesalers now are debating as to whether or not they should add a line of dry goods and drugs. The issues at stake are: Will the volume of such additions be sufficient to compensate for added costs of supervision, overhead, selling, and other expenses? What facilities will they require that they do not now possess? To what extent can their present excess capacity in plant and facilities be absorbed by such addition? Will the adoption of these lines provoke retaliation by drug and dry goods wholesalers? Is it possible that the other institutions may increase competition by invading the food lines? Is it likely that the wholesalers will attempt to spread their offerings to include products to supply the outlets they serve, provided the demand is sufficient to justify such innovation? This is only one area of institutional change; similar forces are at work on practically all marketing fronts.

Changing Buying Habits of Consumers

The final test in the dynamics of change rests with the decisions of the consumer. If the consumer chooses to buy drugs and dry goods in volume from the supermarket, the wholesaler will stock these goods and seek the business. This movement creates a new focus of competition among the food wholesaler, the rack jobber, and the established wholesalers in dry goods and drugs. It is true that many changes in the manner of consumer response result from the overtures of the seller to win consumer favor. Yet changes arise independently of the seller's efforts. The automobile is largely responsible for shopping centers and one-stop shopping. This change is also the result, in part, of the increasing number of wives who work now and share shopping responsibilities with their husbands. Suburban living has given rise to new customs, new habits, and an entire array of new products and types of selling. Increasing the amount of discretionary spending money has changed the proportions in which goods are sold. Travel, both domestic and abroad, has influenced business and consumer preferences.

These are but a few of the factors that have altered patterns of consumption, and with each change in the pattern of consumption come new opportunities in retailing. Changes in retailing are reflected to wholesaling and agency firms. Indeed, they influence the entire channel policy of manufacturers.

Influence of Research

Effective channel strategy emerges as an integrated process evolved from a plan that recognizes all the forces that influence change. It is usually impossible to determine exactly what changes ought to be made and when they should be effected. Yet if the business executive postpones action too long, it may be too late.

Specific questions which puzzle the typical business executive are: What channel changes should be made, and when? These are also the questions he must act upon. He cannot postpone decisions until the "best" method of arriving at answers is devised. Consequently, he does act. By methods which he himself admits are not perfect, he arrives at decisions which, even when they prove to be workable, he cannot be sure are good. He wishes that he knew more about how to make the decision and how to appraise the results.

Today's business executive can take a less fatalistic view of this problem than could his counterpart two decades ago. Business research tools have been developed to remove some of the guesswork. For example, one of the large food manufacturers added a line of cereals to its offerings. The company did not have sufficient facts to determine what marketing channel it should use. It had a distribution system of branch warehouses for its present line, but it would have had to expand those facilities considerably to sell the new line of cereals. According to the findings of a consulting firm hired to analyze the problem, distribution costs through established wholesale channels would be 16 percent of the retail price. If the company sold the products through its own branch houses, it would cost 21 percent. Hence, the company chose to channel the new product through wholesalers. This cost differential raised the question as to whether or not the company was wise in retaining its branch distribution system for its main line of products. The system already was established and functioning efficiently, the company's product was a delicacy that was perishable, and competition was keen. In order to exercise greater control over the product and to provide the necessary promotion push all the way through to the consumer, the company chose to retain its branch warehouses and to increase its staff of salespeople.

Another analytical pattern that is much too frequently neglected is the analysis of customers to determine whether or not all are being reached by the most effective, as well as the most economical, channel. In one case an analysis showed that 95 percent of all customers sold in one area were unprofitable. By applying this test to the overall company market, two-thirds of the customers were estimated to be unprofitable accounts. These accounts were transferred from the direct sale list to those that it could serve through its dealer organization. The company was encouraged by the results. The inventory, break-even points, and overhead costs were lowered. There was a 15 to 30 percent decrease in expenses and a 20 percent increase in net profits.

Another means of determining the relative efficiency of different channels is to experiment. Representative test divisions of the market may be selected using prospective channels to reach each division. Costs and advantages in each area can then be compared. Careful control must be kept to see that adjustments are made so that the different divisions are comparable.

Research and analysis assist in clarifying issues and point the way for action. As the skills and machinery for analysis improve, solutions will become more reliable and available. With the multiplicity of forces operative in the marketplace, however, "best" and "sure" solutions are goals that may only be approached.

AN OVERALL VIEW

The problem of channel selection must be a part of the overall planning of the company. It cannot be separate and apart from production, pricing, transportation, or promotion. As an example let us examine the case of the Polaroid Land Camera, a product that came on the market in the early 1950's and has been unusually successful because the company's marketing program has been innovative and alert to the problem of channels.

In spite of the customary method of selling cameras through distributors, Polaroid chose to employ a sales force adequate to sell through retailers. Why was this method chosen? In terms of the cost of moving the physical volume of goods, this method was consistent. The camera was not bulky; the unit value was comparatively high. At the outset the company chose to sell through only 5,000 selected outlets. This number could be called on and serviced without excessive outlay in making contacts and completing transactions. If the product had been of lower unit cost, of greater bulk, and sold to 50,000 retailers, direct sale to retailers might not have been the answer.

The strategy of selling directly to retailers was also consistent with the promotional potential of the product. The company, in the early stages, faced a market wherein the photographic trade was both hostile and doubtful. Photographic equipment dealers were fearful that if the product were too successful, it might hurt their film-developing business. On the other hand, they were doubtful if the process would be as successful as the company claimed. Both of these factors tended to create resistance at the retail level, resistance of a nature that required the explanation and selling of a person with adequate training. Such a person must also have as his sole purpose the selling of the camera and the demonstrating of its operation. Distributors could not be trusted to provide the promotional zeal for the product to achieve this goal. On the other hand, the company had faith that its product would become a mild sensation at the consumer level. The strategy, then, was to adopt a promotional program at the consumer level that would provide a suction to draw the product through the channel to the consumer.

If the company's assumptions were correct and the product did become a mild sensation, it would have an added advantage. Retailers who handled the product would buy from the company with little selling and servicing. In view of the small bulk and high unit value, minimum warehousing would be necessary and the company could distribute directly to the retailer at little cost. Because of the great popularity of the product with the public, the company could exact a high price. It could also expect the retailer to sell at a comparatively low margin, since much of the selling cost of the retailer could be the result of national advertising and the nature of the product. The company provided encouragement to its dealers by offering them selective contracts and agreeing not to sell to any who would not sell at a price that would provide the retailer with a satisfactory margin.

The company's projected plans were realized. Once the camera was on the market, the selling and advertising campaign brought it enthusiastic consumer response. Dealers who were doubtful and hostile at the outset eventually stocked the product, first because consumers demanded it and second because the camera and the film brought them profit. The manufacturing company's profits and stock have risen steadily.

This example illustrates many of the forces that must be considered in selecting a channel. The wholesalers and agent middlemen who may have played a part in the distribution of cameras and camera equipment were not used because of special circumstances in the nature of the product. We also note the interrelationship of product, price, promotion, and place as factors that enter into channel consideration.

Effective Utilization of Distribution Channels

The selection of the distribution program that the manufacturer prefers to use does not bring to an end his distribution problems. On the contrary, it places him in the position where he can turn his factually supported suppositions into real profits by the execution of his well-laid plans. The thoroughness and care that have gone into his planning must continue in the execution of his plan. Efficient handling of his channels will be more of a determinant of his volume than the market potential inherent in any particular marketing channel. Just as wise and effective selling helps to answer his sales volume problems, so will such selling help to activate the channel institutions he has chosen. No organization can, in and of itself, accomplish anything. Accomplishment comes from live men within the organization. The manufacturer's problem now becomes one of establishing better-than-favorable relations with the individuals who comprise the institutions in his channel and of supplying the "oil that will make the machinery run smoothly." Adequate profit margins, of course, will inspire the basic movement, but beyond profit there must be a recognition of long-term goals and conditions rather than a concentration on the immediate; there must be the integrity that inspires confidence; there must be the regard for the well-being of others that assures their satisfaction.

Constant Review

With the execution of his program, the manufacturer still finds his job unfinished. Just as he will constantly review his production processes and analyze them in the light of technological improvement, so must he constantly consider the changes that occur in the dynamic area of marketing. Besides bringing new and progressive methods, the movement of time also brings altered conditions in markets, in consumer's habits, and in the availability of resources. Each requires a review of the existing institutions and an evaluation of the distribution program as a whole.

Such an evaluation program was initiated by General Electric Company in 1954.[5] At that time sales of appliances were very uneven throughout the year. This condition made it necessary to follow a widely fluctuating production schedule. Since such "jerky" production was expensive in terms of overtime, delays, lost sales, and high shipment charges, the company conducted a major survey and took a new look at the consumer. The survey revealed that the fluctuations were not the fault of the consumer but resulted from a weakness in the company's linkage with its distributors. So, the company conducted a two-year program to educate top and middle management on improving relations with their distributors. As a result of this program, General Electric achieved a leveling of its production schedule as well as a much closer communicating relationship with all the institutions in the distribution channel so that the distributors would respond effectively to the introduction of new products. For example, the company succeeded in marketing the electric toothbrush and the electric carving knife. In connection with new products, General Electric's marketing management found that its distribution system could handle about five new products a year. The company learned that if more products were introduced, the distributors would tend to neglect already established products which were maintaining a strong profit potential.

QUESTIONS AND ANALYTICAL PROBLEMS

1. Define channel of distribution.
2. Why does the door-to-door sales method almost always cost more than the method of selling products through the channel of manufacturer-wholesaler-retailer-consumer?
3. How does direct sales differ from door-to-door? From direct-mail selling?
4. Under what conditions might a manufacturer successfully and economically sell his output through the channel of manufacturer's sales force-retailer-consumer?

5. Well under 10 percent of manufactured consumer goods go directly from manufacturers to ultimate consumers, while probably as much as 70 percent of manufactured industrial goods go from manufacturer directly to industrial consumers. Explain why the difference exists.
6. Define and clearly distinguish between (a) extensive distribution, (b) selective selling, and (c) exclusive agencies.
7. What are the most important considerations in selecting a marketing

---

[5] "GE Seeks the Answer in Its Distribution System," *Business Week* (October 2, 1954), pp. 68-75.

channel? What effect does each of these considerations have on the structure of a marketing channel for (a) a widely used, low-priced consumer good and (b) a technical, complex, high-priced industrial product?

8. What marketing channel changes take place when consumers show that they will purchase kitchen items in large quantities from grocery stores? The goods formerly were sold only by hardware and department stores.

9. Why might a supermarket operation that owns five food stores, each selling approximately $1.5 million annually, decide to use regular wholesalers? Why not set up their own warehouse operation?

10. Give two examples of products that lend themselves to successful extensive distribution. Explain clearly

why you would choose to market these products in the widespread manner suggested by extensive distribution.

(a) Do the same for selective selling.
(b) Do the same for exclusive agency.

11. A young man invented a product that had ready acceptance at service stations in his city. The product can be manufactured for 85 cents each with his present facilities. He has been selling the product for $2.10 which pays his present sales costs and returns him a net profit of 27 cents each. Assume that his manufacturing and sales costs are properly calculated. How do you suggest that he sell the product in an area covering the Rocky Mountain and Pacific Coast states?

Case 10 • GRADE MANUFACTURING COMPANY

The Grade Manufacturing Company sells its line of hay mowers, rakes, and bailers, as well as replacement parts, to about 20 wholesalers, many of whom also distribute the farm equipment of other larger firms. In 1965 executives of the company decided to evaluate the company's distribution policy to determine whether or not it would be more profitable to sell direct to retail outlets. This move was prompted by the fact that company sales, which had remained stable for the past five years, were expected to be less for the current fiscal year than the previous year. Grade products are not as competitive on the market as the equipment of most larger companies (International Harvester, Case, Deere, etc.) because Grade equipment is of extremely high quality and is consequently higher priced. Therefore, company officials felt that, since Grade products are slower moving items, the distributors were devoting their principal efforts to selling the products of larger manufacturers and were not giving proper emphasis to Grade products.

The sales division of Grade Manufacturing Company consisted of the sales manager, Mr. Bohn, and four salesmen. All five men tried to spend most of their time working with the wholesalers. However, since they were often called to do missionary work with the retail dealers (of which there were 250 in 10 states) and with farmers, very little time was left for them to do an adequate selling job. Mr. Bohn therefore recommended that the company establish five strategically located warehouses to service their retailers. He stated that even though such a move would require an immediate financial outlay, the company would receive benefits from it very shortly. He pointed out that the 20 percent allowance which Grade was giving to its current distributors would be adequate to cover the expenses of a large company sales force and several company distribution outlets.

• Do you agree with Mr. Bohn in recommending a more direct contact with the users of Grade products? If you were the general manager, what additional information would you ask Mr. Bohn to supply in support of his recommendation?

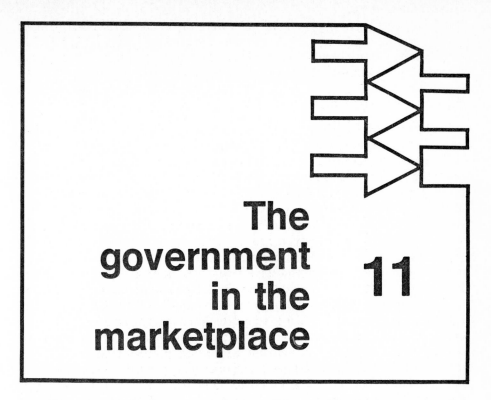

The government in the marketplace

11

There are two basic reasons why we might consider the government in a classification with marketing institutions. The first reason is that the three levels of government—local, state, and federal—are the largest buyers and sellers of goods and services in the nation. In 1973 the local, state, and federal governments collected taxes in excess of 20 percent of the gross national product. The more important reason, however, is the government's influence as a lawmaker and a referee for the competing market institutions. As was pointed out in Chapter 1, a partnership arrangement between government and business is desirable to provide an environment of equality and fairness in competition and to achieve certain social objectives.

One of the challenging questions of the day is to what extent and by what administrative methods can the government perform its function of lawmaker and referee and still preserve the freedom and creative initiative which provide vitality to the marketing process. In the chapter we will discuss specific points where the government exerts direct influence on the marketplace.[1]

GOVERNMENT AND TAXATION

The government can have a profound influence on the amount and kind of marketing that is done by the use of its power to tax. In some cases its purpose may be economic stability and, in other instances, the raising of revenue. In any

---

[1] The Commerce Department's National Marketing Advisory Committee gives marketing leaders a bigger role in government decision making. See "Marketing's New Voice in Washington," *Sales Management* (June 1, 1967), p. 33.

case its policies must be adopted with the realization that when it collects money for taxes, some changes in economic activities will result.

Effects of Taxes on Demand

The tax policy of the government is a factor in the rate of growth and the expansion of markets. The graduated income tax, for example, can be used not only as a means of raising revenue but as an economic tool to speed up or slow down the economy. When rising prices are threatening because money tends to be more plentiful than goods, the government views our income tax as a means of absorbing increased purchasing power and taking the pressure off the demand for goods. On the other hand, when the economy is dragging and there is a surplus of production capacity, the government would decrease the tax so that a greater share of the personal income would be spent for goods on the market. An increase in the rate of growth and employment was the explicit purpose of the tax reduction in 1964. From the evidence available, the move appeared successful.

The government adopted another tax innovation in 1962 which was designed to influence the market. In order to stimulate the economy by means of industrial expansion, a 7 percent investment credit was allowed on certain equipment which was considered strategic for expansion purposes. When inflation threatened in 1966, the government temporarily suspended the tax. Obviously the government intends to use this device to influence the market according to the needs of the economy.

Taxes on Commodities

Governments traditionally finance their operations from taxes of various kinds. In the early history of the United States, the major portion of the revenue required to carry on the functions of the federal government came from an excise tax. Although all taxes have some indirect influence on the market, the excise tax has special meaning in terms of marketing because it is a tax imposed on some items selected by the government. In making such selections, the government tends to influence the choices of people by placing a higher price on some items than would be the case without the tax. For example, liquor and tobacco have been two items on which heavier taxes have been placed. In these instances the government has made a judgment which in a completely free market would be left to the individual.

During recent years this tax has been more widely applied to include fur coats, jewelry, cosmetics, theater tickets, and many other so-called luxury items. Since many of these items have some demand elasticity, the tax definitely influences the volume purchased. In granting the government these powers, we allow it to say to some extent which products are necessities and which are luxuries. This is a choice that we might be more reluctant to give the government with the passing of time.

Certainly the collection of taxes and the manner in which they are levied have an influence on the flow of goods, both quantitatively and qualitatively. If the government attempted to collect equal amounts from each individual, the low-income group would pay more taxes and the high-income group, correspondingly less. Consequently, the low-income group would spend a smaller percentage of their income on the market than they spend at present and the high-income group, a larger share. But the total amount of goods sold would likely be reduced because there are so many more individuals in the low-income group that would be affected, and they would normally spend a greater share of their income. Qualitatively, the market choices would be different since the expenditures by the higher income group would tend to be in the luxury class, while the low-income group would buy products more closely related to necessities.

Tariff

In one sense, the tariff has an effect similar to the excise tax. There is a difference, however, in that the *tariff* is a tax levied on goods that are imported. Although the excise tax is usually placed on luxuries, it is never intended actually to discourage their purchase. The fundamental motive always has been revenue. In the case of the tariff, however, it is often placed on products that will compete with our domestic products. This tariff is designed to increase the price of the imported products in order to give domestically produced products a competitive advantage. Such a tariff is known as the protective tariff because it is designed to protect and encourage local producers.

There are two elements in this practice that are significant to marketing. First, the prices of such products are higher to the public than they would be without the tariff; and when the demand is elastic, the amount consumed is less. Thus, the market pattern is altered, and certain choices are directed by this device to the purchase of domestic commodities.

The second factor to be considered is that we customarily accept as one of the functions of the government the creation of the proper environment for sound competition. In the instances of such protective tariffs, we tend to limit competition, or, as a defender of such tariffs might say, "We attempt to equalize competition." In other instances, local industry may need protection because of defense needs or because of the need to safeguard the economic well-being of significant communities. This concept is more applicable to the developing countries than it is to the United States today. The point we wish to illustrate, however, is the fact that the government enters the marketplace and changes the pattern of market choices. In the instance of the tariff, we see activity on the part of the government that parallels on a smaller scale many of our subsidy and price floor difficulties today. It is not our purpose to defend or to criticize either of these activities. Rather, our intent is to describe an area in which the government entered the marketplace at an early date in our history and influenced market decisions by its activity.

GOVERNMENT AND COMPETITION

In a condition of pure competition, we would have so many sellers of a given product that the effect of one seller's addition or withdrawal of his product from the market would have no influence on the price of the product or the behavior of the other sellers. In the same manner the buyers would be so numerous and comparatively so small that no single buyer would be able to influence the market. Another quality that must exist under hypothetically pure competition is that the product being offered by all sellers be exactly the same.

In actual practice the concept of pure competition is quite unrealistic for two basic reasons. First, in the case of a large share of the products sold on the market today, there are comparatively few producer-sellers. It is easy and natural for each of these producers to watch each other and be influenced by each other's action. How much competition is optimum? For example, if there were forty automobile manufacturers in the United States instead of four major companies, the price of automobiles would probably be increased because the savings resulting from size and mass production are most significant in the production of such products. But what if there were twenty?

In the second place, the growth in the number and variety of products on the contemporary market scene represents an attempt to escape pure competition. Billions are spent for research to discover positive differences in products. In terms of competition for the benefit of social welfare, innovative competition represents a desirable trend. The public is interested in better product qualities made possible by technology. As a matter of fact, this new type of competition may make competition even more effective, though less pure. This brings up the important question as to what type of competition is desired.[2] In view of the responsibility of the government in providing a favorable climate for business as a means for promoting the general welfare, just what should be its goal?[3]

Three important results injurious to the social welfare might accrue if a program which was destructive to competition ran its complete course. First, out of desire for gain and for more economic power, the seller with a monopoly would increase the price of his products. Second, such increase in price would likely decrease the amount sold and the amount consumed by the public. Third, and even more serious, such a power would continue to destroy its competition and the benefits that derive from competition.

It has also been observed that when persons or firms are secure in what normally may be a competitive field, they become sluggish and slothful. The improvements that have characterized our period of competitive innovations are less likely to come; and when and if they do, they are slower and are offered at higher prices partly because costs have not been studiously reduced to meet competition and, also, because more profit may be made when there is no competition.

The business expansion which followed the Civil War provided evidence that market power would likely become too concentrated. A few sellers in strategic fields might gain abusive power unless some steps were taken to preserve an equality of competition. Indeed, there was a rapid increase in the

---

[2] What kind of competition? How is it changing? What do these changes imply for contemporary marketing? These problems are all raised and discussed by George W. Stocking and Willard F. Mueller in the context of "The Cellophane Case and the New Competition." *The American Economic Review*. Vol. XLV. No. 1 (March, 1955), pp. 29-63.

[3] Richard Austin Smith reports on the key role played by the Washington representative of a company's management in "The Company Man in Washington," *Fortune* (April, 1966), pp. 132-135, 186.

number of mergers from 1887 to 1904.[4] This was also a period when some firms would deposit their stock in trust to be voted by larger strategic firms or individuals in the interest of gaining some economic power on the market. Many individuals and smaller businesses were injured by such aggressive action and appealed to the courts to redress their injury. The common law which did favor the preservation of competition by virtue of its adherence to the laissez-faire doctrine was not adequate. To preserve competition and to reduce the number of business failures, Congress saw fit in 1890 to pass the Sherman Antitrust Act.

Sherman Antitrust Act

This act made it illegal for a company to use its market power to gain a position of monopoly. It declared that contracts, combinations, or conspiracies in restraint of trade were unlawful. The act also made illegal actual monopolies or attempts to monopolize any part of trade or commerce. Numerous convictions were obtained in this era.

Standard Oil Company, 1911.[5] The management of the Standard Oil Company sought to establish itself in the oil industry so strongly that it would have no need to fear competition. A very common device to achieve this goal was to have the company establish a business in the vicinity of the competition and sell products at a price so low that the competitor could not meet it. The only alternative for the competitor was to liquidate or to sell to the only available buyer, the Standard Oil Company.

American Tobacco Company. In 1911 a decision was made concerning the American Tobacco Company which stated as follows:

> The existence from the beginning of a purpose to acquire dominion and control of the tobacco trade, not by the mere exertion of the ordinary right to contract and to trade, buy by methods devised in order to monopolize the trade by driving competitors out of business, which were ruthlessly carried out upon the assumption that to work upon the fears or play upon the cupidity of competitors would make success possible (221 U.S. 181).

The Rule of Reason. In the above cases and in other cases tried up to this time, the courts found it difficult to determine what specific direction they should take. In one instance in 1895, the Supreme Court refused to accept manufacturing as trade when it refused to break up the sugar trade in the Knight case.[6] It reversed this reasoning in 1904 in the Northern Securities case when it declared that a holding company formed for the purpose of controlling certain business enterprises was in violation of the law.[7]

But the real problem which the legislation and the courts finally had to grapple with was the interrelationship between size, monopoly, and desirable

---

[4] George Fisk, *Marketing Systems, An Introductory Analysis* (New York: Harper & Row, 1967), p. 655.

[5] Not all rules against mergers apply to large companies. For example, see "How a 'Little' Merger Is Ruled Illegal," *U. S. News and World Report* (June 13, 1966), p. 58.

[6] *United States* v. *E. C. Knight*, 156 U. S. 1 (1895).

[7] *Northern Securities* v. *United States*, 193 U. S. 197 (1904).

competition. During President Theodore Roosevelt's period of trust-busting, this problem came into focus many times. The rule of reason expressed in the Standard Oil Case and reaffirmed in the United States Steel Case became a guide that was accepted by the courts. The court stated in the first case:

> The Statute (Sherman Act) . . . evidenced that intent not to restrain the right to make and enforce contracts, whether resulting from combination or otherwise, which did not unduly restrain interstate or foreign commerce, but to protect that commerce from being restrained by methods, old and new, which would constitute an interference that is an undue restraint.[8]

Here we have the high court contenancing as legal a certain amount of restraint of trade but frowning on "undue restraint" of trade. In the latter case the court further affirms: "The law does not make mere size an offense or the existence of unexerted power an offense."[9] Thus was introduced the "rule of reason" which suggested that the courts must determine whether the defendant's act constituted such an unreasonable restraint of trade as to be illegal. The need for some more explicit statement in the control of monopoly remained. Neither the courts nor the firms that are large and powerful have a dependable guide as to what is undue restraint of trade. In other words, the rules for the game of competition were not definite and specific. They left a great deal of discretion to the referee. Consequently, there was a general feeling that a more clearly defined area of abuse was necessary.

Clayton Act

Congress recognized the existence of a great deal of confusion and frustration in the antitrust proceedings. This undesirable condition was due in part to the vagaries of the rule of reason and in part to the delays incident to normal court procedures. In 1914, it passed the Clayton Act and the Federal Trade Commission Act, both designed to define more clearly the meaning of "undue restraint" and "unfair competition."

The Clayton Act was specific in pointing to certain forbidden practices. This act stated that it was illegal to discriminate in price between purchasers of similar grades, qualities, and quantities of the same product. It denied firms the right to make "tie-in contracts" that would force buyers to purchase less desirable goods in order to obtain the goods that were more desirable but harder to obtain. It warned against interlocking directorates in directly competing corporations, except banks and common carriers of more than $1 million capital. It also forbade the purchase by one corporation of the stock in a competing corporation, except in limited amounts.

Thus, we have special areas pointed out where the courts should look for abuse. Even with these specific guides, the philosophy of the rule of reason was included in the qualifying clause: "Where the effect will be substantially to lessen competition or tend to create monopoly."

---

[8] *Standard Oil Co.* v. *United States*, 221 U. S. 1.
[9] *United States* v. *U. S. Steel Co. et al.*, 251 U. S. 417.

Federal Trade Commission Act

The Federal Trade Commission Act included provisions outlawing unfair methods of competition and unfair, deceptive acts in commerce, although it did not specify particular practices. The operative part of the statute states simply, "Unfair methods of competition in commerce, and unfair or deceptive acts or practices in commerce are hereby declared unlawful."[10]

Both in the Clayton Act and in the Federal Trade Commission Act, this body was given enforcement authority. Its administrative officers can investigate abuses and sue violators of the provisions of these two acts. The Commission can issue cease-and-desist orders. While such orders are intended to bring about a voluntary compliance, final enforcement is vested in the courts. Thus, the acts provided more specific definitions and also quicker action by giving the Federal Trade Commission enforcement authority.

In 1938, the Wheeler-Lea Amendment to the Federal Trade Commission Act was passed. This amendment extended the powers of the act beyond cases in which there was an injury to competition to those cases where there might be some injury to the public. The Commission could originate a case on its own initiative when it felt that business practices were unfair to the public. For example, a consent decree, obtained in 1957, prevented Libby-Owens-Ford from selling automobile safety glass to General Motors at prices lower than those charged to competing customers.

Probably the best-known and most frequently applied order of the Wheeler-Lea Amendment is that provision which is designed to prevent dishonest advertisements on the air and the examining of printed advertisements. Those which materially misrepresent products are forbidden. An example was another consent decree in 1957, obtained when a company advertised that is was offering its product for sale at greatly reduced prices. Investigation by the Commission revealed that the advertised price from which the product was reduced was not a real, but rather a fictitiously high price. The device was deceptive in that it led the customers to believe that they were being offered a savings based on the regular selling price.

Size—Efficiency and Competition

As we have indicated, the question of size of the business has been basic to the question of preserving fair competition since its inception. The courts have always found it difficult to discern clearly where to draw the line between what was an undesirable or a desirable degree of monopoly or competition and what size and power were necessary for the greatest efficiency. In the early development of this concept, sheer bigness was almost enough evidence for a conviction. In many instances, however, it became evident that bigness was necessary for economy and stability. Great savings result from specialization, which is related in the mechanical sense to technology. Advanced technology, or

---

[10] This may be a strong point of the Act. See Warren G. Magnuson and Jean Carper, *The Dark Side of the Marketplace: The Plight of the American Consumer* (Englewood Cliffs, N.J.: Prentice-Hall, 1968), p. 64.

machine operation, is possible only when the volume of sales is high enough to pay the large fixed costs of technological production without placing an undue burden on unit costs. For example, when Hudson merged with Nash to form American Motors, competition in the automobile business improved.

There are those who believe that the restrictive legislation dating back to 1890 and 1914 express an outdated philosophy. For example, Walton Hamilton states:

> In antitrust we are meeting the great economy with a weapon of control designed for petty trade. . . . The direction of industrial activity to public ends is a constructive, not a punitive task. . . . The larger questions of holding the regulated industry to its function of improving its capacity to serve the public, of looking to the hazards ahead and of making of it (federal regulatory agency) a more effective instrument of the general welfare are neglected.[11]

John Galbraith sees the present antitrust legislation as a senseless harassment of large firms that have invested heavily in research and development programs responsible for progressive innovation.[12] Sylvester Petro goes so far as to assert that if antitrust principles had been applied as vigorously in the earlier periods as they are now, our economy would have been frozen into a primitive cast. We would not have reached our present state of technological progress nor would we have enjoyed our present standard of living.[13]

Certainly there is some logic in the views of these men. Yet on the other hand, there still appears to be a need for some restraining influence. The following two cases are cited to illustrate the complications of more recent enforcement problems.

The A & P Case

One of the dramatic conflicts involving competition between marketing institutions was the battle between the chains and the independent stores. The heat of controversy was especially great in the food store business. In the A & P case, among the practices examined were the locating of chain stores in strategic areas and the lowering of prices in these stores to eliminate competition. While a specific store was selling at a lower price, stores of the chain in other areas of a less competitive nature were charging higher than average prices. A & P was found in violation in a criminal action before the Circuit Court of Appeals in 1949.[14] In 1954 an attempt was made to get injunctive relief from this company which was again engaging in the same practices. The company signed a consent decree thereafter. In spite of its conviction, the company felt that it was abused by the vagueness of the law.

---

[11] Walton Hamilton, *The Politics of Industry* (New York: Knopf, 1957), p. 78.

[12] George Fisk, *Marketing Systems, An Introductory Analysis* (New York: Harper & Row, 1967), p. 656.

[13] Sylvester Petro, "The Growing Threat of Anti-Trust," *Fortune* (November, 1962), p. 128.

[14] *United States* v. *The New York Great Atlantic & Pacific Tea Co., Inc., et al.,* 67 F. Supp. 626 (1946), 173 F. 2d 79 (7th Cir., 1949).

The Electrical Equipment Case

As a result of a lead from the purchasing agent of the Tennessee Valley Authority, the Department of Justice found identical bids submitted by major electrical equipment manufacturers. An investigation uncovered an active program of secret meetings held regularly for the purpose of arranging the bidding and of rationing out the business among the participants. Thirty-seven participants in this process were sentenced to prison. Eight sentences were served and twenty-nine were suspended, although the firms were successful in the courts in establishing the innocence of their top executives.

This case became a sensational national scandal. There were two aftereffects, however, that were positive in nature. First, though the problems which it raised are far from solved, both the public and business are now much more aware of the need for integrity in business and are more sensitive to violations. The second aftereffect of the case was that it pointed out the need for a better statement of the law and a more consistent enforcement. Certainly there was no doubt of guilt in the electrical equipment case. Secret meetings and prearranged biddings were clearly illegal. Yet at the same time, agreements of this kind of a less formal nature were not at all uncommon. Price agreements which were clearly not legal were implicit in many negotiations.

Exemptions from Governmental Control of Monopoly

In order to encourage enterprise and to prevent serious market frustrations, the government has chosen to exempt some products and business activities from the antitrust laws. Especially in the field of agriculture has this been the case.

Agricultural Marketing Agreement Act. An act that has some relevance in illustrating the government's attempt to improve the economic environment of certain business firms by permitting some industry controls to exist in marketing is the Agricultural Marketing Agreement Act, which was enacted in 1937. This arrangement permits an agricultural group to set up a marketing agreement with the Secretary of Agriculture. This permission is extended to milk, certain fruits, tobacco, asparagus for canning, soybeans, hops, honeybees, and others. Such agreements, when signed by the Secretary of Agriculture, exempt the participants from the antitrust acts.

For example, the agreement may classify milk into different categories according to the purpose for which it is used and provide a means of fixing a minimum price for each classification. All handlers are bound by these prices and must make payment at a time specified in the agreement. The prices to all handlers must be uniform and can be made flexible according to production and market differentials among different classifications and to different points of delivery. The agreement is effective only if three fourths of the producers on the basis of volume are in agreement. The agreement also permits the cooperators to share in the privilege of sale in a certain milk shed according to the amount produced during a certain base period. Adjustments in the base can be made from time to time. Thus, these provisions permit price fixing, adjustment of production, terms of payment, and determination of the area wherein production for certain consumption may take place.

Webb-Pomerene Act. Another area which is exempt from the provisions of the antitrust legislation is that comprised by organizations or firms which find it desirable to combine their resources in order to compete in foreign trade. Trade cartels have been common in Europe. In order to deal with these cartels, both cooperatively and competitively, the government legalized monopolies for the purpose of trading in foreign goods. These monopolies, however, are not permitted to operate within the confines of the United States. The act enabling such combinations was the Webb-Pomerene Act, passed in 1918.

Patent Laws. The government has encouraged invention and innovation by permitting individuals or firms who invent products to control their production and sale for a period of 17 years. There is much evidence of abuse in this area. Many feel that the abuses of powerful interests who secure control of the patents and then exploit them to their own advantage and to the disadvantage of the public outweigh the good that comes from encouraging inventions, but nothing has been done to change the practice of the past. There is, in the 1975 legislature, a controversial bill relating to reform of the basic patent law.

GOVERNMENT AND PRICE DISCRIMINATION

The decade of the 1930's was one of numerous business failures. It also followed the period of rapid chain store growth, and independent merchants were agitating for relief from this new intense competition. A number of states had passed antichain store taxes in response to this outcry, and others were in the process of doing so. In this period of economic anxiety, a demand was made upon Congress to provide relief from unfair price competition. In most instances the unfair competition was attributed to the large chain. Although Section 2 of the Clayton Act prohibited unfair competition, it failed to define specifically what was meant by this term in sufficient detail to meet the needs of this era.

Two practices that resulted in lower prices to some buyers than to others were especially attacked. One was the so-called dummy brokerage allowance. A retailer would claim that in situations where he purchased directly from the manufacturer he was performing services of the wholesaler. Hence, he would insist on payment from the supplier equivalent to some portion of wholesaler markups to a dummy brokerage office operated by employees of the retailer.

Another ploy was to provide services or equipment to certain buyers only, for example, actual dollar payments to one retailer to compensate that retailer for advertising the producers' product; employees paid by the producer to work as demonstrators or sales people in a retailer's establishment—in a jewelry department or cosmetic department, for example—to push the manufacturer's product; supplying storage and display equipment such as for ice cream, soft drinks, or dress patterns to large sales outlets while smaller customers had to purchase such items. There were many instances in which such practices did create significant price differentials, and there was sufficient agitation on this subject to win from Congress the passage of the Robinson-Patman Act.

Robinson-Patman Act

The Robinson-Patman Act, an amendment to Section 2 of the Clayton Act, was passed in 1936. This act was more specific in pointing out certain types of unfair trade practices that were forbidden. Specifically, advertising and brokerage allowances were declared illegal unless actual services were rendered and such allowances were made available to all purchasers on proportionately equal terms. Under this act those who received benefits from the practice of these unfair practices through buying were as guilty as those who profited through selling. Thus, the big buyers (corporate and voluntary chains), were as guilty as the sellers if they insisted on costs that would give them preferred prices. There was a specific provision in the act, however, that justified price differentials to different buyers if cost differences in the amount of the price difference could be adequately demonstrated. Thus, if a firm could show lower costs for selling higher volume to individual buyers, prices could be lowered legally in the amount of the difference in costs. This act applied mostly to the trade structure of business. It did not apply in the case of sales to the consumer. The retailers were free to price their merchandise to the consumer as they had always priced it.

Resale Price Maintenance

Small retailers and the wholesalers who served them desired even more protection against price competition of chain stores and the so-called cut-rate retailers. Some merchants were selling well-known brands at less than the manufacturer's suggested prices. As an example, Pepsodent was the leading toothpaste on the market. In 1930 it had announced some dramatic innovations; but more important, the Pepsodent Company sponsored a radio program with ''Amos and Andy'' that was breaking all records in listener ratings. Even the movie theaters of this period changed the opening time of their shows because they found that they could not pull people away from this popular radio show. Pepsodent became a product with which all were acquainted, both in terms of quality and of price. Because of this popular hold on the mind of the consumer, it became an excellent prospect as a loss leader. Those stores that sold it for a low price tended to be judged by the public as low-price stores. On the other hand, those stores that charged enough to obtain a normal markup were considered comparatively high-price stores. That is loss-leader strategy. Cut the price on a product whose quality is accepted and whose usual price is well-known.

To satisfy demands for protection against that kind of competition, the California Legislature passed a bill in 1931 which allowed manufacturers or wholesalers to enter agreements with retailers to establish the minimum price of any branded item. In 1933 a nonsigner clause was added to the bill which made the agreed upon prices binding on all retailers in the state even if only one retailer signed a resale price agreement with the supplier. The law became known as the

California Fair-Trade Law. Merchants in other states pressed for and received similar legislation.

There was naturally a question about whether such price fixing allowed in a state law was a violation of federal antitrust legislation. In 1937 the Miller-Tydings Act allowed manufacturers in interstate commerce to enter resale price maintenance agreements with dealers in any state which had such laws. In December, 1937, California's law was upheld by the United States Supreme Court. Soon 45 of the 48 states had similar laws.

In the Schwegmann Brothers case (341 U.S. 384 (1951)), the Supreme Court ruled that the Miller-Tydings Act could not be operative if the state fair-trade law had a clause making agreed on prices binding on nonsigners. Early in 1952 the McGuire Act was passed which provided that the nonsigner clause was legal. Fair-trade prices were common for drugs and cosmetics, books, electrical appliances, liquor, pens, phonograph records, and cameras. Those were items carrying markups attractive to supermarkets and discount stores and, as the items moved in ever larger volumes through nondrug outlets, the manufacturers were increasingly reluctant to police fair-trade pricing. Several states repealed fair-trade laws, and national advertising of minimum resale prices was largely discontinued. It appeared that the issue was dead even though lobbyists representing drug stores routinely introduced such legislation in the states where fair-trade laws had been repealed. Then the Quality Stabilization Bill (1962) was passed, allowing manufacturers of trademarked, branded items to set minimum resale prices in any state whether or not that state has a fair-trade law. This explains some of the policing of channels, outlets, and prices you will have seen with certain well-known sporting goods and small appliance items.

In addition to resale price maintenance legislation, commonly called fair-trade laws, 26 states offer protection against loss leaders by another kind of legislation, commonly called unfair practice acts, which establishes a floor, usually varying from about 6 to 12 percent above cost, below which it is illegal to sell most products. In order to see both sides of the problem, it is well to review the arguments for and against such legislation. We shall view this in the context of the period in which it was passed.

The Independent Merchant. From the point of view of the independent merchants, protection or lack of protection appeared to be directly related to their success or failure. They held that the loss-leader practice actually was deceptive and resulted in higher costs to the public. For example, a certain store might advertise a number of well-known items as loss leaders and dramatize the offering vigorously. In this manner the public would get the impression that the store, as an institution, offered all of its merchandise at low prices. Actually, however, according to the claims of the independent stores, the chain stores would increase the price on other less known items. These higher margin items, they argued, would constitute the major volume of the store. As a result, in total purchases the customer would pay a greater sum than he would where the so-called loss leader was not used.

The Manufacturer. Another view is that of the manufacturer. The firm that has a valuable brand name has an interest in getting a high price for its product and in protecting its brand franchise. Fair-trade legislation achieves both goals. The resale price provision enables the manufacturer to establish a price that is high enough to maintain a satisfactory operating margin. The product cannot legally become the subject of a price war, which often results in demands to the manufacturer for lower prices and consequent depreciation of quality. High relative price has a tendency to impute high value to a product in the eyes of the customer. Such a high product-value concept, supported by advertising and a comparatively high price, and given the backing of the law, makes a most attractive arrangement for the manufacturer.

There are three dangers, however, all of which may be serious. In the first place, the product may have an elastic demand and may be priced at a level that does not permit the firm to operate at an optimum volume. Secondly, the high price of the product may invite a competitor to enter his product in the competitive field at a lower price and absorb some of the volume of the first product. Thirdly, a high margin to the retailer encourages discount houses and cut-rate sellers who disregard the law. Such a decision often places the responsibility for enforcement on the manufacturer and demoralizes his law-abiding dealers.[15]

The Economists' Views. From the point of view of the economist, additional factors influence this area of trade. In the first place, objective research into the practice of loss leaders did not indicate that other prices were increased sufficiently to increase the cost to the consumer, as held by proponents of regulatory legislation. Even though the loss leaders might tend to deceive, the stores that used them did not show a price level which on the average was higher than those that did not use such leaders. Indeed, the reverse tended to be the case. In the second place, to force a firm to sell at a price established by the manufacturer rules out the effectiveness of the legitimate forces of competition. Normal competitive practice permits the efficient operator to pass the result of his efficiency on to the consumer in lower prices. Also, it is competitive pressure that motivates innovations resulting in better service and lower prices.

Protection of the Consumer [16]

Some degree of regulation of goods and services sold to consumers started in 1848 with the Edwards Law which prohibited importation of adulterated drugs. A report by Harvey W. Wiley, chief chemist of the United States Department of Agriculture, exposed sales of dangerous drugs and adulterated foods in the early 1900's. That report and Upton Sinclair's novel, *The Jungle,* which described unsanitary meat packing practices, aroused sufficient public indignation that Congress passed two important consumer protection acts. The

---

[15] *Printers' Ink* cites the relevant factors in Sunbeam's frustrations with fair trade and lays bare some of the problems. See "How Sunbeam Sells Without Fair Trade," *Printers' Ink* (August 8, 1958), p. 48.

[16] The authors are indebted to Dr. Roger H. Nelson, College of Business, University of Utah, for help in listing all of the legislation affecting marketing since 1952, from which selections were made for this section. See his book, *Personal Money Management* (Reading, Mass.: Addison-Wesley Publishing Co., 1973), Chapters 5, 6, and 7, for a chronological list and description of all legislation affecting consumers.

Meat Inspection Act (1906) established sanitary regulations in meat packing and provided for federal inspection of all establishments selling meat in interstate commerce.

The Federal Food and Drug Act, also passed in 1906, made the manufacture, sale, or transport of adulterated or fraudulently labeled foods or drugs illegal in interstate commerce. The Bureau of Chemistry of the Department of Agriculture was empowered to make tests and recommend legal action against violators.

In the 1930's the Wheeler Amendment to the Federal Trade Commission Act prohibiting "unfair or deceptive practices or acts" provided some means of consumer protection.

President John F. Kennedy, in a special message to Congress, March, 1962, stated that, ". . . the federal government—by nature the highest spokesman for *all* the people—has a special obligation to be alert to the consumers' needs and to advance the consumers' interest." The President listed four basic rights of consumers:

1. *The right to safety*—protection against goods or services hazardous to health or life.
2. *The right to be informed*—protection against fraudulent, deceitful, or grossly misleading information from advertising, labeling, or other means of communication.
3. *The right to choose*—access to a variety of goods and services at fair, competitive prices.
4. *The right to be heard*—provision for fair consideration of consumer interest in government policy and legislation affecting commerce and opportunity for complaints to be heard.

Thus was launched the "decade of the consumer."

Actions by Presidents Kennedy, Johnson, and Nixon have made specific provision for protecting the four consumer rights noted above. Rationale for government intervention in dealings between buyers and sellers is in a special message by President Lyndon B. Johnson in 1963:

A hundred years ago, consumer protection was largely unnecessary . . . most products were locally produced, and there was a personal relationship between the seller and the buyer. If the buyer had a complaint, he went straight to the miller, the blacksmith, the tailor, the corner grocer. Products were less complicated. It was easy to tell the excellent from the inferior. Today . . . a manufacturer may be thousands of miles from his customers—and even further removed by distributors, wholesalers, and retailers. His products may be so complicated that only an expert can pass judgment of their quality.

We are able to sustain the vast and impersonal system of commerce because of the ingenuity of our technology and the honesty of our businessmen.

But this same vast network of commerce, this same complexity, also presents opportunities for the unscrupulous and the negligent.

It is the government's role to protect the consumer—and the honest businessman alike—against fraud and indifference. Our goal must be to assure every American consumer a fair and honest exchange for his hard-earned dollar.

That message was the introduction to the establishment of the President's Committee on Consumer Interests. That committee was absorbed into the Office of Consumer Affairs which was created in 1971.

Appointment of the committee, whose first director was Mrs. Esther Peterson, Special Assistant to the President for Consumer Affairs, reflected increasing interest by members of Congress and their constituents in further strengthening the federal government's role in consumer protection.

In the brief discussion of consumer legislation that follows, you will note that much of the legislation designed to protect consumers and honest businessmen from sharp practices of some sellers antedated the establishment of the committee. During the period following the President's 1963 message, however, there has been an increased interest in interpretation and enforcement of those older laws, along with the introduction of new consumer protective legislation.

Important acts included in the "Consumerism Movement" are mentioned below.

Truth in Lending. This is the popular term for the Consumer Credit Protection Act of 1968. It was aimed at (1) lack of understanding by many consumers of provisions of credit contracts, and (2) failure of adequate disclosure of all provisions of the contract. The Act requires written disclosure of true costs and all substantive facts in any credit contract, prohibits misleading advertising of credit arrangements, limits garnishments of wages, and makes it a federal offense to engage in loan-sharking.

Truth in Labeling. The Fair Packaging and Labeling Act and the Federal Hazardous Substances Labeling Act provide that labels must include names and addresses of producers, descriptions of products, exact quantities of contents (rather than such description as *King Size* and *Giant Size*), safety warnings on all potentially hazardous products, and first aid on poisonous substances.

Kefauver-Harris Drug Amendments Act, 1962. This act strengthens new drug clearance procedures to assure more safety, effectiveness, and reliability in prescription drugs.

Truth in Advertising. This is a function of several agencies and laws. The Wheeler-Lea Amendment to the Trade Commission Act specifically provides for monitoring and prosecution of fraudulent or misleading advertising. The Food and Drug Administration can issue injunctions and seize foods, drugs, cosmetics, and therapeutic devices if there are misleading false claims or misrepresentation.

Much policing of advertising claims is accomplished at the state level. All but six states have adopted the *Printer's Ink Model Statute* or a modification of that statute.[17] *Printer's Ink,* an advertising trade journal, proposed and sponsored the bill in 1911 (it was revised in 1945) and urged state legislatures to adopt it because it was believed that action would be obtained more readily in state courts than in federal courts. That bill makes it a misdemeanor to present to

---

[17] Alaska, Arkansas, Delaware, Georgia, Mississippi and New Mexico.

the public any advertising which contains "any assertion, representation or statement of facts which is untrue, deceptive, or misleading."[18]

Arguments against further federal legislation are that the advertising industry works hard to police advertising and that self-policing works quite well as evidenced by results of the FTC monitoring of advertising. In recent years the FTC has averaged about 1,200 formal investigations and 100 formal complaints annually.

Popular titles and principal provisions of other significant laws during the 1960's are the Wholesome Meat Act (1967), which extended inspection and enforcement of sanitary standards to meat processed and sold in intrastate commerce; Product Safety (1967), to study and act on potentially hazardous household appliances and home-care products; Flammable Fabrics, which establishes standards of flammability of clothing, carpets, blankets, and other fabrics in the home and public places; and Automobile Safety (effective 1968), which specified safety standards for automobiles and tires. In addition to the federal actions, over 40 states have enacted some consumer protection measures.

The thrust throughout the decade has been to make consumers aware of corrective actions available to them and to specify fraudulent or harmful practices. Studies of repairs and guarantees, automobile insurance, land sales, securities, and mutual funds, have resulted.

It is interesting to contemplate whether if all businessmen understood and practiced the marketing concept, need for study and legislation regarding consumer protection would have arisen.

CONCLUSION

We might conclude our discussion by generalizing about the function of government in business. The preamble to the Constitution of the United States charges the government with the responsibility of promoting the general welfare. Under a market economy the promotion of the general welfare presumes a business environment which will maximize the positive virtues of competition. We have already posed the question, what is the nature of the competition we desire? The competition we desire is the kind that motivates men to greater productive efforts and sharpens their skills. This competition will also provide a basis for allocating resources and the returns from productive effort on a fair and equitable basis. This environment can exist only where vital elements of freedom prevail.

We have learned in our national history that maintaining freedom based on justice is not a passive preoccupation. In business it requires the government to take positive action in restraining certain groups and in encouraging the activities of others. Such action is necessary in order to maintain the quality of competition we have described. The government also must decide in which areas and to what extent competition should be allowed and in what instances it should not, as in the case of legal monopolies exemplified by the utilities.

---

[18] A copy of the statute may be obtained from the Secretary of State or Attorney General of any of the adopting states.

It is not a simple task to determine where the government should enter the market and where it should not. The competitive battle is too dynamic for a static generalization. In the 1930 decade the passage of fair-trade laws may have been essential to the perpetuation of a free system. Today they may not be necessary. With improved communication by television, radio, and magazine advertising, and an awakened public sense of justice, there may be a better chance for freer competition than we had in 1890 when the Sherman Antitrust Act was passed. Each of the answers to the problems that arise will have to grow out of the circumstances which attend it. We can only conclude that the problem merits constant study, both in fact and in principle, with maximum freedom and the protection of the common welfare as its goals.

QUESTIONS AND ANALYTICAL PROBLEMS

1. Define: (a) excise tax, (b) tariff, (c) pure competition, (d) trust (referring to combination of organizations), (e) price discrimination.
2. List the federal and state laws mentioned in this chapter. State the principal provision of each.
3. For each of the laws listed below write three statements reflecting your reaction to the law if you were (1) an independent merchant, (2) an independent manufacturer, and (3) a spokesman for a consumer group.
   (a) Federal Trade Commission Act.
   (b) Wheeler-Lea Amendment to the FTC Act.
   (c) Robinson-Patman Act.
   (d) State Fair-Trade Law.
4. How can an income tax affect markets for consumer goods?
5. What is the basic underlying philosophy of all the laws discussed in this chapter; that is, can you find one characteristic that all the laws have in common?
6. What is the significant finding in each of the following cases:
   (a) Standard Oil Case.
   (b) American Tobacco Company Case.
   (c) The A & P Case.
   (d) The Electrical Equipment Case.
7. In what ways have certain trade associations restricted competition? In what ways have trade associations enhanced competition?
8. What, according to President Johnson's statement, is the rationale for the consumer protective laws and regulations of the federal government?
9. Truth in Lending: What is the correct name of the act? What are the principal provisions of the act?
10. What acts and agencies are included in "Truth in Advertising"?
11. Make a list of all the points you can find at which some form of government influence touches the marketing structure of the nation.

Case 11-1 • JOHN HAMMOND

John Hammond was facing a difficult decision. As chief executive officer of American Appliance, Inc., he had been approached by the Broadcast Equipment Manufacturing Company with a merger proposal. Plans were under way when the *Wall Street Journal* ran a story about the merger. Hammond learned that some of the key Justice Department personnel had reacted negatively.

John Hammond was born in a small Louisiana town in 1908. He remained in the New Orleans area until he had completed his B. S. degree and began his career with American Appliance, Inc. He started as a salesman and moved up through the sales division to his present post as chief executive officer. He had been an active member of the Methodist Church and attempted to support a Christian code of ethics. Indeed, this commitment to ethics and a positive attitude toward people had earned him a position of esteem among his associates. For two consecutive years he was elected president of the trade association which represented the appliance manufacturers to the public and to the government. One of the publishers of a popular advertising trade magazine described him as a leader of a progressive management philosophy that was gaining ground in New York City. Hammond believed that business had to become more ethical and public spirited, and the place to start was at the top.

Hammond became president of American Appliance, Inc., in 1960; and sales had increased from $400 million in 1960 to over $750 million in 1968. The company's first product was washing machines, but now it has a complete line of appliances. Some of its products have been acquired through purchasing the stock of their original manufacturers. In some of its basic lines, the company has a market share of approximately 50 percent of the national market.

Broadcast Equipment Manufacturing Company's management was reaching retirement age. The company's distribution channels overlapped with American Appliance. Their broadcasting equipment, of which television sets were the largest seller, had earned a franchise with the public that gave them high status and a quality image. Hammond envisioned that greater economy in distribution and a stronger market position would result from this merger. He wanted to complete it before he retired in about five years. However, because of his commitment to ethics and fair play, he did not want to get into trouble with the courts.

Hammond had just read that Pepsi Co., which was the result of a merger of Frito Lays and Pepsi Cola, was ordered by the Federal Trade Commission to sell ten of its plants. There was some similarity between Pepsi Co.'s position and American Appliance, Inc.'s prospective status if the merger was achieved. The *Wall Street Journal* carried another story, several days after the first, quoting Hammond as saying that there were no plans for a merger. Hammond told a friend confidentially that the merger had been placed on a back burner for the time being.

• What alternatives are open to John Hammond, and what would you recommend? What position should the Department of Justice take?

Case 11-2 • SCHRAFFT'S [19]

The W. F. Schrafft & Sons Corporation is faced with the problem of getting selling impact at the retail level which will enable the company to maintain or increase its volume, especially in its more profitable gift box line. Other top brand dealers who formerly sold only through their own retail outlets are now entering the gift box market in drugstores, department stores, and other retail outlets. The salesmen of these firms, in the majority of cases, make direct contact with the dealers or retailers. Schrafft's has acquired a loyal group of distributors who make contact with the retailers and has been effective in keeping the company one of the two largest distributors in the gift box line. Schrafft's problem is

---

[19] This case was prepared by Professor Weldon J. Taylor of Brigham Young University as a basis for class discussion. Cases are not designed to present illustrations of either correct or incorrect handling of administrative problems. This case was prepared several years ago. A recent review of the industry indicates that the principles and problems involved are still valid.

further complicated by the fact that much of the effectiveness of the company's program at both the retail and wholesale level has been due to the goodwill associated with the name of Schrafft's. The dealers handling the product in the past have maintained a price consistent with the quality of the candy. However, at the present time the company is concerned that the discount houses will obtain the candy and advertise it at discounted prices. Such action may tend to destroy the quality image which is imputed by price. A further complication which may result from selling to discount houses would be the loss of goodwill and patronage from the retailers on whom the company depends for its present volume.

The Candy Industry

Contrary to the opinion of many that candy may be a victim of the "battle of the bulge," per capita sales have been increasing. Per capita consumption in the United States increased from 16.9 pounds in 1960 to 17.2 pounds in 1961. Candy bar consumption increased by 20 percent. Production for 1961 was equal to 3,109,000,000 pounds, valued at $1,232,000,000 at wholesale prices. Of the total poundage, packaged goods accounted for 36.4 percent; bars, 33.4 percent; bulk goods, 15.2 percent; 5¢ and 10¢ specialties, 8.8 percent; and penny goods, 6.2 percent. The confectionery industry, in terms of value added by manufacture, is the eighth largest in the food and kindred products group. In terms of employment it ranked sixth, averaging 79,800 employees in 1961.[20] The spokesman for the candy industry predicted significantly greater production in 1962.

History of the Schrafft Company

In 1861 William F. Schrafft took over the confectionery business of his employer who was convinced that the Civil War meant the end of everything. The money to effect this purchase was borrowed from Mrs. Schrafft's brother who operated a boarding house which was a favorite stopping place for sailors with the Great New Bedford Whaling fleet. The first candy made by the company was gum drops. These candies became a favorite of the soldiers who received them as gifts during the Civil War. Many of them sought out the candy store on their return to Boston after the war. This success encouraged Mr. Schrafft to add to his line peppermint candy sticks, cinnamon balls, and other hard candies popular at the time. In 1895 the company became a partnership with the father, William F. Schrafft, and the sons, George F. and William E., as partners.

In 1897 Frank G. Shattuck, already a successful confectionery salesman, joined the company and was assigned the territory in New York City. Mr. Shattuck was so successful that he and his associates sold enough candy in only a few months to keep the plant producing the entire year. In the spare time which resulted, he started a candy store in New York City. In a few years lunches were served. With this idea and experience as a genesis, the first Schrafft's restaurant was opened in Syracuse, New York, in the year 1906. This restaurant was the first of the now well-known chain of Schrafft's restaurants. Mr. Shattuck was joined and supported in this venture by the Schrafft family. In 1925 the Frank G. Shattuck Company became a publicly owned corporation, and its stock was listed on the New York Stock Exchange. In 1929 the two companies joined; and since the Frank G. Shattuck Company was already listed on the exchange, it became the parent company. The company publishes its statements on a consolidated basis. A financial summary of the consolidated company's operation is shown in Exhibit 1.

---

[20] From a report prepared by the U. S. Department of Commerce for the National Confectioners Association.

Exhibit 1
FRANK G. SHATTUCK COMPANY
FINANCIAL HIGHLIGHTS FOR 1961

	1961	1960	1959	1958	1957
Consolidated net sales	$70,276,887	$66,896,769	$61,650,076	$56,484,248	$54,990,339
Earnings before federal income taxes	1,948,064	2,182,567	2,203,969	1,582,024	1,329,037
Federal income taxes	1,062,950	1,130,000	1,175,000	805,000	692,000
Net earnings	885,113	1,052,567	1,028,969	777,024	637,037
Net earnings per share	80¢	95¢	93¢	70¢	57¢
Cash dividends declared	55,081	550,000	550,000	550,000	550,000
Dividends per share	50¢	50¢*	50¢	50¢	50¢
Working capital	12,274,091	8,271,558	9,053,668	8,788,274	912,262
Retained earnings	8,555,114	8,225,082	7,942,450	7,463,481	6,971,384
Stockholders' equity per share	20.12	19.82	19.39	18.96	18.52

* Plus 1% stock dividend.

Source: From the company's 1961 annual report.

Basic Policies

Since the company's beginning, Schrafft's has depended upon a strong quality appeal as its major marketing strategy. The original William F. Schrafft told his two partner sons that ". . . quality begins with the basic ingredient. If it is not put in at the very beginning, it won't be there in the finished product." He laid down the law that: "Here we use only the best ingredients. We treat them as quality should be treated. The candy we make must be the kind we serve in our own home. We will not compromise; we will make only the best." The company built its reputation for quality on its gift box line. Although it sells in competition with makers of bulk bags, novelty, and smaller packages, over 50 percent of its volume is in the gift package line. The best known of this line is Schrafft's Gold Chest Luxuro Chocolates. The company wishes to retain the goodwill associated with its gift package since it is the conviction of the company's management that it is the gift package that gives the name Schrafft's its quality image. Mr. W. A. Silverman, Executive Vice-President of W. F. Schrafft & Sons, states that it is this quality image and the goodwill which accompanies it that enables the company to succeed in moving its product through all levels of its trade channels from wholesaler to ultimate consumer.

The company spends approximately $1 million a year on advertising. Thirty-five percent of this sum is for point-of-sales exhibits, racks, and all other media which reach the ultimate consumer. Trade advertising, which includes direct mail to distributors and dealers, trade promotions, advertising of features days, special campaigns, and the attendance of its representatives at trade conventions, consumes 50 percent of the budget. Ten percent is spent for cooperative advertising with distributors and dealers. Five percent is for art and package development and donations to various causes which the management deems worthy.

The company's price policy is consistent with its quality goods. Especially in its gift packages it seeks to avoid the vigorous price competition that is the rule in other lines of candy. For a listing of representative products offered by Schrafft's, see Exhibit 2.

Distribution Policies

Ever since the company started offering its product for sale at retail stores, it has sold through wholesale distributors. The management recognizes that if its own salesmen visit the retail stores directly, they would push the company's product more vigorously, product quality could be maintained, stale merchandise could be more effectively handled, institutional prestige could be improved, and the impact of displays might be stepped up. If the company chose to follow such a course, it already has warehouses at Boston, Chicago, Cleveland, Dallas, Jacksonville, and San Francisco.

The cost of maintaining a sales staff and selling direct to the dealer, however, is much greater than selling to a distributor. Arthur P. Chamian, Director of Marketing and a recent graduate of the Harvard Business School, supports the policy of selling through distributors. He points out that, although the company has warehouses in six cities in the nation, refrigeration must be supplied by the distributor. Over 600 distributors are served by the company, and they are not accepted unless they have adequate cooling facilities. Each of the 600 distributors employs between 6 and 15 salesmen. Thus, there are over 7,000 salesmen representing the Schrafft candy line to approximately 40,000 retail outlets. The distributors are given exclusive distribution for Schrafft's products. They are comprised of approximately 90 percent tobacco and confectionery distributors, with food and general wholesalers making up the balance. The company keeps in personal contact with the distributors by sending 35 sales representatives into specified territories throughout the nation. In addition to contacting the distributors, the salesmen report on the

Exhibit 2
FRANK G. SHATTUCK COMPANY
TENTATIVE 1962 FALL PRICE LIST

	Price		Price
Fancy Packages:			
Gold Chest ....$ 2.00		*Assorted Creams*	.98
	4.00		
	10.00	*Cherries in Cream*	
(Banquet Size) ...	.25	(½ lb. Special)	.60
All Fruit & Nut	2.00	Pick-A-Packs	.29
	4.00		
		Bars	.05-.10
Miniature	1.75		
	3.50	Patties	.05
	8.75		
		Patties in Trays	.39
American Collection	1.75		
		Window Box Line	.39
Exotic	1.60		
	3.20	Tub Pops	.29
	8.00		
		Fruit Slices—Tray	.39
Trinket Chest	1.60		
	3.20	Twist Wrapped Bag Line	.29
Classique	1.50	Imported Bag Line	.29
	3.00		
		Bag Line	.29
All Soft Centers	1.50		
	3.00	Bag Line	.10
Schrafft's			
Chocolates	1.40	Peppermint	.02
Rose	1.35	Buttercream	.02
	2.70		
		Hard Candy Tins	.98
Fair Lady	1.35		
	2.70	Hard Candy Jar Line	.39-.59
Home	.98	Lollipops (Singly and in Bag) 01-.59	

company's relationship with the retail trade and make scheduled visits in a missionary capacity on the large chain accounts. The distributors are allowed 20 percent margin on the wholesale price on merchandise sold to independent dealers and small chains. On volume purchases sold to large chains and supermarkets, this margin is reduced to 10 percent. The company also conducts promotions which in some instances are equal to 5 percent of the distributors' purchases.

In the interests of maintaining dealer and distributor relations and, at the same time, guaranteeing fresh and up-to-date merchandise, the distributor picks up stale candy and returns to the dealer the total amount of its original cost. Schrafft's, in turn, compensates the distributor to the extent of 50 percent of the latter's cost.

The company will ship a minimum of 300 pounds to the distributor. The distributor, on the other hand, sells to the retailer in orders as small as 10 or 15 pounds. Mr. Chamian cites this situation as a strong argument for the company not selling direct to the retailer.

Mr. Chamian reports that distributors are selected on the basis of their potential to push a product vigorously, their financial stability, and their general respectability with the trade. He reports that the company has little difficulty getting distributors to sell the company's product because of the image of quality which the products enjoy. He reports that the margins allowed wholesalers on Schrafft's products are considerably higher than they receive on the other noncandy products they sell.

The company's decision to sell through distributors is consistent with the prevailing practices in the trade. The United States Department of Commerce figures for 1961 show manufacturer sales of candy as follows: wholesalers, 46.8 percent; chains, 31 percent; independent retailers, 10.1 percent; department stores, 2 percent; vending machine operators, 3.7 percent; government, 2.9 percent; direct to consumer, 0.7 percent; and other outlets (including exports), 2.8 percent.[21]

Direction of Salesmen

Mr. Chamian directs the activities of the 35 salesmen in the field and supervises a program of communication that keeps them informed on the progress of the distributors in their respective territories. The salesmen are given quotas and are paid a salary and incentive pay for reaching and exceeding volume goals. In the case of high profit items, such as the 2-cent mints which are used to make change at restaurants, extra incentives are offered. Each salesman's yearly quota is equal to the sum assigned to each of the distributors in his area. Salesmen are provided by airmail with copies of invoices covering merchandise sent to their accounts. They are sent a monthly report for each of their accounts showing gross sales, credits, and net sales. The salesman receives a monthly report on each distributor and on how far up and how far down the account is in each product category. He receives a similar report on his own quota. He also receives a report of orders booked for the current month by category. Promotions are conducted each fall—the salesmen receive a record of their performance for the previous year by category for each dealer, and goals are established for the current year. The same procedure is followed with respect to "featured" days—Valentine's Day, Easter, and Mother's Day.

Mr. Silverman reports that the company has been well satisfied with its choice to sell through distributors, although the contemporary scene is somewhat different from that which has characterized the company's business during the past century. First, the character of the institutions, both at the wholesale level and retail level, are changing in the lines they carry, the patrons they serve, and the methods they use in selling. Distributors have had to alter their policies to keep abreast with the revolution that has taken place in retailing as a result of the growth of the supermarket and the discount house. Food wholesalers, for example, formerly carried a line of goods that was normally carried by retail food stores. To preserve their business when the chain store and the supermarket came on the scene, they increased their line to include most of the merchandise carried by the supermarket. They also streamlined their warehousing, ordering methods, and sales promotion programs, and reduced their margins from 12 percent to less than 4 percent. Much of this cost reduction was due to increased volume. Similar adjustments have been made by wholesalers in the dry goods and hardware lines.

Also, in the case of candy packaging and products, there has been a recent wave of innovations with which manufacturers have tempted the trade and the consumer. In both

---

[21] From a report prepared by the U. S. Department of Commerce for the National Confectioners Association.

the fields of bulk good lines and packages, the competition has been intense. Manufacturers have used liberal promotional allowances, exclusive franchise agreements, and other means to gain volume sales. In the face of this impassioned quest for volume, Mr. Silverman is eager to motivate his distributors to apply equal vigor to the company's line. The competitor poses a problem, especially when it comes to the company's principal product, the gift box package. Whitman Company, Schrafft's principal national competitor in the gift box line, sends its salesmen direct to the dealer. Loft, Barton, and Fanny Farmers formerly sold through their own retail store outlets. Now these stores are also franchising other retail outlets such as drug, variety, and others to set up special displays and sell their products. These companies also service and sell these outlets with their own salesmen. Although they gain trade patronage by exclusive agreements, they are prone to alter their policy in cases where opportunities for volume sales are promising.

Mr. Silverman firmly believes that the distributors have the potential to meet the competition of the firms with which the company is competing. While these companies are gaining in number of outlets and sales, he doubts that their exclusive franchise agreements can continue to be attractive in view of their practice of granting them so freely. He is eager to discover some new method, which characterizes the activity of the companies who sell direct, by which he can get the distributors of his products to push Schrafft products. One distributor who employed ten salesmen and was a good producer reported that all his sales were made by three of the salesmen. One retailer reported that he had dropped Schrafft's line because the salesman would not redeem spoiled merchandise, and he shifted to a distributor who would make a refund on stale products. This instance is an example of a wholesaler's salesman that did not take enough interest in the company's products to carry out its policy. Another retailer carried Schrafft's line but featured a less well-known brand in his display. He reported that the latter was delivered to him in a refrigerated truck by the company salesman while Schrafft's was delivered by a tobacco wholesaler in an ordinary truck and, therefore, was not as fresh as the competitor's brand. Mr. Silverman was aware of these problems and was working on their solution. He was confident of the quality of his company's product and was certain that volume could be maintained and would grow if the company could get the salesmen of the distributor to give adequate emphasis to sales and service policies.

The Discount House

The company also was concerned with the problem of how to handle the discount house market. On one hand, discount houses could be viewed as an excellent means of achieving volume goals. Indeed, one of Schrafft's gift box competitors sent a letter to its distributors announcing the fact that it was sending its representatives to contact discount houses to obtain their patronage, after which the account would be turned over to the distributor to service. It is apparent that the discount house will eventually sell a significant portion of the retail goods. The *Discount News* reports that discounters intend before long to sell 40 percent of all TV sets sold. Large and respected firms are seeking their patronage. For example, DuPont is now selling its Zerex brand of antifreeze directly to discounters.

The giant chains are going into the discount business. These include such firms as Woolworth, J.C. Penney, and Kresge's. In 1960 discounters sold $2.7 billion, or 21 percent as much merchandise as department stores. In 1962 it is estimated that they sold $5.2 billion, or 34 percent as much as department stores. The economy appeal of discounters with an average markup of 21 percent is bound to win even more sales from stores with average markups of 36 percent.

Discounters are now reaching the stage of development where they want to shed the image of austerity and bare floors and acquire a more dignified role in the eyes of the consumer. High-class candy displays will contribute to the atmosphere and decorative tone which they seek.

There are, however, two basic reasons why the Schrafft company is cautious. First, its product has gained a position of quality and enjoys brand preference in the market which it may not be able to retain if it becomes a "price football." Discount houses delight in taking brands that have established respectability at quality prices and selling them at strikingly low markups as loss leaders. The second problem is closely related to the first. Retail outlets selling the company's product now constitute a reservoir of goodwill and support for Schrafft's products. They are threatened by the entrance of the discounters on the scene. In courting or even serving the discount house, the company may be jeopardizing not only its quality image but the goodwill and support of the retail outlets on which it now depends. Neither does the company have an immediate solution to the problem of serving the discounters through its distributors.

• Make recommendations which you consider to be necessary if the company is to maintain or increase its sales volume, especially in the more profitable gift box line. Could the quality image which the company has successfully used to win and retain patronage with distributors, dealers, and ultimate consumers be preserved if it sold at reduced prices through discount houses as compared to margins on sales to the independent retailers and chains now served?

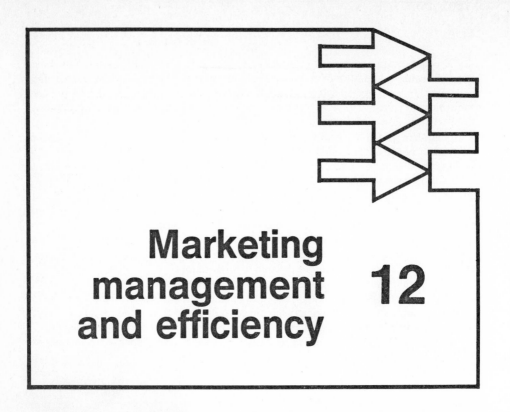

Marketing management and efficiency 12

The skill of management is strategic to successful marketing. At one time a market position or the possession of a market share had considerable durability. For example, the possession of a patent served to protect a company against the loss of its market. Today, even with patent protection, a market advantage is extremely perishable. The quality that gives a firm durability today is a management that can administer a marketing strategy that is constantly responding to the new challenges of competition. Management sensitivities must be attuned to the desires of the consumers, and management must possess the insight and administrative skill to discover or create a demand for its products and hold a market share of sufficient volume to realize profits.

In the dynamics of the marketplace today, this kind of response involves the entire company. Successful managers are those who are aware of the marketing concept and have oriented their company in all of its decisions to the marketplace. Such companies coordinate product development and production with sales to respond to the constant challenges and opportunities created by the dynamics of market changes. In this sense the entire company operates as an integrated unity with all its parts oriented to and sensitive to the consumer. In this frame of reference, a market success is a management success. Since marketing and management are so closely integrated into a single process, an enlightened marketing view must include basic management concepts.

THE MEANING OF MANAGEMENT

A clearly defined and widely accepted definition of management has not been formulated to this day. One common statement that describes management is "getting things done with people." There are many others that tend to have similar meanings. All of them involve people, and all of them involve power to achieve administrative objectives. However, for the purpose of our discussion, we will provide a framework around which we can develop a concept of the meaning of management as it applies to marketing. Such meaning should relate at every major point to the marketing process. The specific tasks of management that serve the purposes of this book and bring into focus the above qualities of management are leading, planning, and controlling.[1] In this chapter we will discuss leading and planning and will introduce some measures of efficiency in marketing.

Leading

Leading might be defined as that aspect of management where man relates to man, or as the interpersonal human relationships by which a manager communicates with his subordinate as a human being. The business manager in his function as a leader has two basic objectives that are often in conflict. The first objective is to stimulate his subordinates to follow company policy in keeping income high and holding costs down in order that profits might be maximized. The second objective is to be aware of the feelings of his subordinates and to understand the problems they face in achieving the order, timing, and discipline necessary in reaching the first objective. The normal tendency is for management, on the one hand, to want high productivity and low costs (including wages and salaries) while, on the other hand, employees want high wages, shorter working periods, and other benefits.

The personality and human relations skill of the one who leads is a basic factor in establishing a tone which makes the organization effective. Lines of communication which are formally established by the organization chart might, for example, be completely ineffective if the personnel have negative attitudes. On the other hand, positive attitudes and cooperative feelings foster ideas and effective communications to a degree beyond that which is implied in formal organizational assignments. The competitive success of the leader is significantly dependent upon the kind of attitudes he is able to generate among his associates.

The development of a dynamic attitude which responds to a positive challenge is more essential in marketing than it is in most other divisions of a company. One reason for this is that the activities in the marketing division cannot be routinized to the extent possible in some other divisions. Successful performance in marketing depends upon initiative, creative imagination, and the ability to respond with appropriate answers to new problems that are constantly evolving out of the changing market picture. Such attributes, combined with company loyalty and an enthusiastic game spirit, are tremendous assets in any marketing program. The stimulation and implementation of these qualities represent the leadership challenge to marketing management.

---

[1] The basic aspects of management are effectively dealt with and given adequate coverage by William H. Newman and Charles E. Summer, Jr., in *The Process of Management* (Englewood Cliffs, New Jersey: Prentice-Hall, 1963).

Planning

Planning is a dynamic and continuous process that influences the daily flow of administrative decisions. The term "planning" seems to imply that it precedes action. Yet while it is a prelude to performance, it also grows out of action. Plans for tomorrow must be based on how the plans of yesterday worked out today. Feedback systems provide constant information for revision and guides for execution of plans.

The following story illustrates the deep involvement that planning has with daily operations. An American corporate president was in Europe seeking to instruct in company policy some foreign firms his company had purchased. He received a cable from the vice-president for marketing who reported that the last market share analysis indicated that the company's highest volume product had dropped in its share of the domestic market from 45 percent to 35 percent. The president returned home to several planning meetings. The officers had to discover the reason for the loss in sales and make plans to revamp the market strategy. The changes involved a return to an original package, a new promotion, a change in production formulas, and certain face-saving gestures for the company's image. This is an example of plans that are in the making each day. Adjustments must be made daily that require the flow of new ideas into the reality of operations.

Certainly all planning is not in response to crises or even daily changes. It is not uncommon for a company to project a sales figure ten years in advance and then to estimate the number of successful new products it will have to add to obtain that figure. Such plans must include methods of testing products to determine which methods will succeed. The company may also plan that a certain portion of its growth will come by the acquisition of already existing companies. How to select such companies and to arrange for the financing becomes a part of the plan.

An Illustration of the Structural Process. Exhibit 12-1 helps us understand the continuous nature of planning. We see "basic objectives" at the beginning of the chart and "achieved performance" at the end. In between these two poles we observe "strategy" and "long range" and "short range" plans. The significant factor here is that these goals are in the sequence of a continuous process and are connected with feedback from all points of action. For example, if achieved performance seems to be falling short, feedback goes both to the plans and to strategy so that corrective action can be accomplished.

It will make the planning aspect of marketing much more meaningful if we use an actual case to illustrate how it applies in a real situation. We will, therefore, use the early history of General Motors to illustrate each of these planning functions. The General Motors case is almost classic since this company was one of the first to define successfully a management program in sufficient depth to illustrate planning as we conceive of it in modern marketing.[2]

---

[2] Alfred P. Sloan, Jr., *My Years with General Motors* (Garden City, New York: Doubleday and Company, 1964). Mr. Sloan's memoir has been widely read and acclaimed since it reveals the genesis of many management policies and practices that are now reaching maturity.

Exhibit 12-1

THE STRUCTURE OF PLANNING

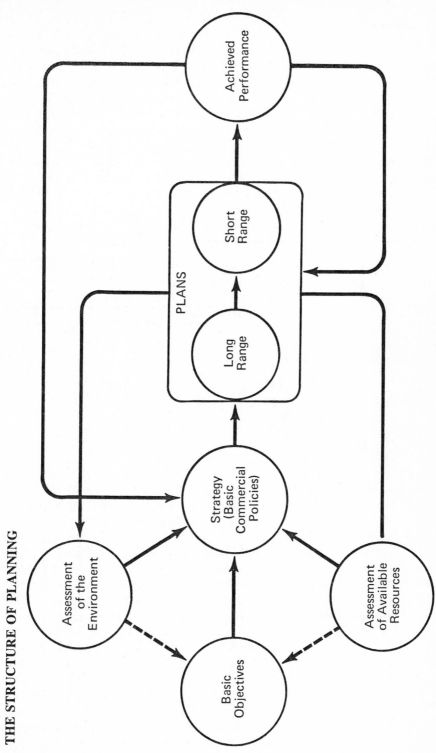

Basic Objectives. The long-term objectives of General Motors, like many other private corporations, were expressed as long-run profits for its stockholders with much of the capital growth coming from profits. In addition, the company expressed its intent to be a good citizen of the local and national community and to follow courses of action that would guarantee its long-run existence. While such objectives might be common with most companies, well-managed companies state them explicitly; and these objectives become foundations and guides to basic strategy. Other objectives of General Motors that were peculiar to its specific goals were: (1) to commit itself to rapid growth by constantly working for an increasing market share and (2) to acquire other companies if it became necessary to add to its product line. Such objectives were basic in the formulation of courses of action in all other phases of the company's activities.

Strategy–Basic Commercial Policies. Commercial policies, or strategy, differ from basic objectives in that they describe the more immediate and specific means of attaining objectives. Although basic strategy may remain the same over a period of time, often it is subject to frequent adjustments in order to meet competition. Two overall strategies guided General Motors in its marketing policies. One was succinctly capsuled in the phrase "a car for every purse and purpose." With this as a guiding strategy, General Motors has attempted to achieve complete coverage of the market—luxury, economy, and commercial vehicles of every class and size became a part of the company's line.

The second strategy was "to build quality products sold at fair prices." Today this statement might sound like a slogan to be used by any public relations department, but early General Motors' management adopted it as a basic rule to follow in its production and marketing programs. The fact that such a policy was not a simple statement to be used as a facade in building company goodwill was evident in Mr. Sloan's description of the difficulty in getting departments and dealers to represent the company with fair prices in their dealings. From his report it was apparent that Mr. Sloan used this statement of policy as a commitment, and enforcing it was one of his major challenges as a manager.

Mr. Sloan had an early insight into the important of policies as guides to action and as a means of setting standards. The significance of stating explicitly policies that were to serve as guides to action is evident in his statement, "You start on a course with a policy, and things not foreseen fall into place." Thus, a policy in this context can be defined as a guide to control activity that falls within the area defined by the policy.

The first policy stated above was a guide, and all members of the staff knew that General Motors was to offer an automotive product at every market level and for every purpose. The second policy indicates an honest and conservative program of quality and price. The articulation of and common agreement on these policies saved hours of discussion and debate and supplied direction and unity of purpose. Without the policy statements, diversity and differing opinions would have had a frustrating effect. Management frustrations are minimized where policies are explicitly stated. Coordination in some instances becomes automatic, and communication is more efficient because established and explicit policies provide a common background and become guides for discussion. We will discuss a more immediate strategy when we describe the marketing plan.

Assessment of the Environment. When the management of General Motors started on a course of planning in 1921, four trends in the automobile business were evident. First, installment buying was becoming popular. Second, the closed body model, or the sedan, was being considered and discussed as a new style in automobile circles. Third, competitive innovation in the field of automobile accessories and body styles was in the making, and the possibility of an annual model was being discussed. Fourth, the used-car market was becoming a vital factor in the success of dealers. If General Motors was to achieve its basic objectives in growth and market share, consideration would have to be given to these environmental developments in its planning.

Assessment of Available Resources. Before specific plans are made and commercial policies established, the adequacy of available resources must be examined, for inadequate resources would place limitations on the achievement of basic goals. In the case of General Motors, programs were adopted to acquire or develop resources according to the demands of environmental developments. For example, while the company already had a line of popular cars, most of which had established themselves in the market, it had only the beginnings of a successful dealer organization. One of the greatest resources that the company had developed was an up-to-date management plan. Under this plan General Motors could allow individual divisions, such as Chevrolet and Buick, to enjoy the freedom of individual companies and, at the same time, have support from a central organization. A centralized management was in a better position to supply needs, such as dealer influence for installment buying, than would an individual company with limited resources.

Long-Range Plans. It was evident that General Motors did not in 1921 have all the resources it needed to keep pace with the developing environment. However, since the company was organized to accomplish a diversity of tasks with a centralized management, it adopted long-range plans which would eventually provide the necessary resources for each task. For example, to meet the demand for installment finance, the company organized the General Motors Acceptance Corporation as one of its subsidiaries. To meet the demand for the closed car and changing body styles, General Motors acquired a major interest in the Fisher Body Company. It also began to build its relationship with its dealers by giving them support and guidance in problems concerning finance, used-car sales, and annual model changes. Such long-term plans were subject to constant review and change as market conditions warranted.

Short-Range Plans. The basic objectives, commercial policies, and long-range plans tended to move in the order named from the idea to the action stage; and the implementation of long-range plans necessitated the formulation of short-range plans.

During the period from 1921 to 1924, while the plans were in the making, the market picture change but little. The following relationships existed between Ford and General Motors car prices and market share:

Make	Price	Price Differential Between Makes	Market Share
Cadillac	$2,985		
Buick 6	1,295	$1,690	
Buick 4	965	330	20%
Oakland	945	20	
Oldsmobile	750	195	
Chevrolet	510	240	
Ford	290	220	50%

In analyzing the price differentials, General Motors observed several areas that other companies would move into if it did not. The company called these areas danger zones, and for each such zone the company planned a strategy. The strategies were to be described explicitly as to products, price, and promotion; and they were to be blended into a single integrated plan.

The first danger zone was the price gap between Ford and Chevrolet, for 50 percent of all cars sold were selling at less than $300. Chevrolet had a quality image that Ford, known then as the "Tin Lizzie," did not enjoy. However, the spread in price between these two cars was great enough to give Ford a definite advantage in acquiring volume sales. General Motors believed that it could obtain more of this high-volume market if it could preserve the quality image of Chevrolet and gradually lower its price. Advertising and promotion would be used to support these price and product-quality goals.

Two other danger zones were the price gaps between Buick and Cadillac and between Chevrolet and Oldsmobile (a gap that would be widened when Chevrolet lowered prices in an effort to take the market from Ford).

Another area which required short-term plans was the appearance on the scene of the sedan or the glass-enclosed car. This innovation required some alteration in specific price relationships but did not change the basic strategy of the company. The change made the long-range plans of General Motors in acquiring Fisher Body pay off. Without the services of a specialized body division, Ford retained the same Model T chassis and marketed a car that was clearly inferior in appearance to Chevrolet.

Execution of the Strategy. During the period from 1925 to 1927, Ford reduced its price of Ford Tudor sedans from $580 to $565, and later to $495. To implement its announced strategy of "moving down" on Ford, during the same period Chevrolet reduced it prices from $735 to $695 to $595. This reduced the spread between the two competitors from the $220 on open cars in 1924, when the strategy was adopted, to $155, $130, and $100. Since Chevrolet was able to retain its quality image because of its better body, Ford was forced to retool in 1927. But even though Ford regained its number one position in 1929, 1930, and 1935, from then on General Motors took the lead.

Sloan's hunch that a competitive model between Chevrolet and Oldsmobile would eventually appear on the market proved to be correct. Hudson Motor converted its Essex to a closed car and made a powerful bid for the mass market. The Essex coach sedan was introduced in 1921 at $1,495, or $300 above the price of the touring car. In 1923 this price was reduced to $1,145. In 1924 the Essex 4 became the Essex 6, a gesture to quality, and the price was set at $975. By 1925 the sedan coach sold for $895, which was $5 below the price of the open touring car of the same make. Hudson's move was consistent with the changing direction of the market, for the market share of the closed car increased from 40 percent to 75 percent in 1924 and to 80 percent in 1925.

To counter Hudson's move, General Motors introduced the new Pontiac (all models were closed cars) at a price of $825. This price was $75 less than that of the Essex and about halfway between the prices of Chevrolet ($645) and Oldsmobile ($950). With this move, the gap between the latter two cars was closed. Likewise, the other gap between Buick and Cadillac was closed with the entry of another General Motors car—the LaSalle—which was priced at about $2,000 and was manufactured by Cadillac. Later on, however, the LaSalle was discontinued from the line.

All progressive companies which are selling on the competitive market are engaged in activities like those discussed in this case history of General Motors. Such companies establish their objectives and define their policies. Then, on the basis of their judgments as to the availability of resources and the nature of the competitive environment, they devise a strategy which defines a niche for their products in the market. Finally, they construct and execute a plan for building a profitable volume of sales.

The Marketing Plan. In implementing their marketing strategies, progressive companies prepare a specific marketing plan for each product. This plan is presented in sufficient detail so that each man and each division knows what is expected of them. The plan consists of a statement of objectives which indicates the volume of the product that the company plans to sell in each territory and in each time interval. If there is a planned increase in sales, the plan may specify in which geographic regions the increases will take place and how much in each region. Often it specifies how much of the increase will be taken from each of several competing products.

The plan includes the direct costs for advertising, selling, and manufacturing as well as an equitable absorption of overhead or burden costs by each product. Since sales are influenced significantly by advertising and selling costs, considerable attention is given to the allocation of advertising to various territories and to the media that are to be used in each area. With this projection of data on costs and income from sales, profit on each product in the line can be estimated. The sum of the profit on all products equals the total profit. The plan is usually projected from four to five years in advance. This extension of time is especially significant in cases where a product is new and growth in volume and reduction in fixed costs are likely.

Product Strategy. A most significant part of the marketing plan is a statement of product strategy. This statement defines the place in the market where the product is supposed to fit, and it specifies the appeal that is to be used in getting the product accepted for that purpose. General Motors' strategy in 1924 was to lower the price of the Chevrolet without lowering its quality. Jello's strategy is to provide a beautiful and tasty dessert that is nonfattening. Armour's strategy with Dial soap was to win the already well-established deodorant soap market and create many new users by providing a soap possessing deodorizing qualities with a more pleasing fragrance than soap already on the market. The strategy of Macleans toothpaste is to make teeth whiter.

Each product strategy should be so carefully defined that it can be capsuled into a concise statement that can become the point of departure for discussing sales promotion as well as the central theme for advertising presentations and copy. Such a statement is very important since it tends to give unity, purpose, and common understanding to those engaged in the execution of the marketing plan.

Product Management. Many companies assign a qualified individual as a manager to administer the plan for a particular product or brand. As defined by company policy, this individual has the authority to draw on all the staff resources in the company to make the plan work. The product manager's position has considerable status, for he is the man who determines the marketing mix. Young and adventurous men crave this action-oriented post because it is often the quickest route to becoming division heads or junior executives. The marketing plan the product manager supervises becomes his bible, although it may be amended periodically when goals appear impossible to achieve or when brighter prospects loom on the horizon.

MEASURES OF EFFICIENCY IN MARKETING

Satisfaction in a product or service is measured in sales dollars. Costs are also measured in dollars. The organization and presentation of the feedback of the sales and cost data from operational areas are closely related to accounting and constitute a significant portion of the control function. This aspect of control dealing with dollar-and-cent measures of sales and cost will be the major focus of discussion in the rest of this chapter.

Up to this point emphasis on cost and satisfactions has referred to the negative and positive subjective forces influencing choice. Attitudes, feelings, and human judgments result in choices that constitute the foundations upon which successful marketing programs are based. Even though an understanding and awareness of these subjective forces are fundamental to marketing success, they are only the beginning. The goal of management is profits, and profits are measured in dollars and cents. It is, therefore, imperative that the results of these subjective forces be converted to quantity concepts and be expressed in dollars and cents.

Consumers express their preferences for products by the dollars they pay. In this sense the market becomes a device that converts subjective attitudes or feelings regarding products into objective values. If one needs a coat, he may shop for it in a store that offers a wide selection. He singles out two that please him most and examines their comparative qualities and his own reactions carefully. Up to this point he is clearly aware of values in the coats, but they are subjective. He finally makes his choice, however, and pays for the coat with a check. The money is rung up on the cash register as a credit to sales for the firm, and he deducts that amount from his bank balance. His preference now has a measurable magnitude that can be expressed objectively in terms of dollars and cents.

Mack Truck Company purchases various materials and parts and uses a vast supply of tools in a plant that is directed and operated by people to turn out the Mack truck. Whether or not the dollar costs necessary to acquire and fashion these materials into trucks can be obtained depends in large degree on the number of Mack trucks that are sold. The sales volume depends on the satisfaction yielded by the trucks according to the judgment of truck users. From the viewpoint of the consumer of trucks, the elements of satisfaction are power, durability, maneuverability, and economy as well as other more subjective qualities. All these factors influence the choice of consumers and thus provide satisfaction.

When we view this operation in terms of dollars and cents for the firm, it is easier for us to develop an efficiency concept. The profit figure is usually an index of efficiency. The management of the firm attempts to use the resources that it buys to produce a maximum of satisfaction. The degree to which it is successful in keeping costs down and sales up measures the amount of profit realized. This explanation does not mean that where competition is effective and profit margins are narrow, the firms are not efficient. In terms of their net contributions to the social welfare, they may deliver more satisfaction per unit of resource than a firm that exacts a high price and profits because of monopoly privileges. In its own plane of competition, however, all other factors being equal, the firm that makes the highest profit tends to be the most efficient. This section shows how marketing efficiency can be measured to determine from day to day how well the marketing program is succeeding.

Efficiency Formula for Marketing

Before we state a formula for efficiency in marketing, let us understand exactly what we mean by efficiency. Webster defines efficiency as "the ratio of the energy or work that is obtained from a machine . . . to the energy put in." Efficiency, in brief, is measured by the ratio of output to input. Since marketing's relationship to science is through the social sciences, we cannot expect our measures to be so exact as in physics or chemistry. Yet there is a very close similarity of cost to the energy input and of satisfaction as measured by sales to the output.

For the purpose of this discussion, our measure of efficiency will apply to the firm. If we accept the fact that input is cost and output is sales, we have all the elements necessary for the formula. When the enterpriser applies a given amount of resource cost to his operation during a period, the enterpriser should recover more than he puts in. In other words, his sales should be greater than his costs. The difference between these two elements equals the profit. So our formula may read, *the efficiency of a firm is the ratio of sales output to the cost input.* The ratio would be greater than one to one in the case of a successful company enjoying a profit. Therefore, that firm is most efficient which, with a given amount of resources, converts those resources into a form which yields satisfactions (when measured by dollars and cents) that exceed the costs by a greater degree than do similar business firms in the same plane of competition.

The value of this formula is that it helps us to see the relationship between the psychological concepts of cost and satisfaction and the accounting magnitudes of cost input and sales output. The qualitative or the subjective is linked to the quantitative or the objective. The efficiency formula may be used as a practical tool in comparing the efficiency of marketing institutions. If such a comparison is made, it would be relevant only when comparing firms that are selling a similar product in a similar market.

Marketing Efficiency Measured in Dollars and Cents

Our task of measuring the costs in marketing would be simplified if we could reduce them to specific physical units. In the case of human energy, man-hours might be the unit; in the case of resources, pounds or cubic feet of materials or acres of land could be used. Capital also might be reduced in units of measurable quantities. Indeed, there are many areas in the marketing process in which such a means of measurement can be effectively used. For example, a supermarket measures the cost of storing and moving merchandise by the ton. It is also conceivable that routine tasks which are similar in different areas can be measured and compared in terms of the man-hours required to perform specific tasks. Analysis of methods may then be devised to discover practices that made use of a smaller number of hours to achieve the same goals. Indeed, many such measures could be adopted in specific instances that are comparable and which would contribute to greater efficiency.

In comparing overall efficiency, however, such measures would not suffice. Man-hours applied to marketing operations are of infinite variety. How can one compare in terms of man-hour value a department store salesman of carpeting who may earn up to $30,000 a year with the girl in notions who gets $100 a week or the shipping clerk of a manufacturing organization who receives $8,000 a year with the vice-president for sales who earns $75,000 a year. The value of these hours is vastly different and not equally significant in gaining a profit for the firm. Even if we confined our measures of man-hours to similar types of merchandising warehouses and wished to measure the efficiency of one unit against another, there would be problems. It is likely that one such warehouse would use a different ratio of machine-hours as compared with man-hours. Capital installations in some of the units being measured would likely be different. Under such circumstances there would be no point in comparing man-hours required to do one task with man-hours needed to do another in which part of the work was done by machine. Man-hour productivity would not be comparable.

Since money is the common denominator of economic values or the measure by which the values of goods are compared with each other, it is the only unit of measure with which we can presently measure economic efficiency. The carpeting salesman and the vice-president for sales are more significant in earning a profit for the firm than are the sales girls in notions and the shipping clerk. One of the hours of the vice-president for sales may be responsible for earning or saving the company thousands of dollars, and one would find great difficulty in obtaining a replacement. On the other hand, the shipping clerk's work is routine. It can be reduced by machine installations, and there are many who can take his place. It would, therefore, serve no purpose to measure a clerk's hour against an executive's hour. But if we say the clerk costs the firm $8,000 and the vice-president costs $75,000, the magnitudes are measurable. So also are ratios of value that are expressed in prices determined by the market forces. It is logical then that our basis of measure be the money unit.

SALES—THE OUTPUT MEASURE OF EFFICIENCY

The marketing efficiency index, with satisfaction as its goal, presumes the existence of discriminating skill in the area of subjective judgments. Actually different satisfactions may be represented by quantitative magnitudes that are similar because some people obtain greater satisfactions than others through the expenditure of the same amount of money by more expert buying. Likewise, one store may be more efficiently managed than another, even though the efficiency ratios of the two are the same, because they operate under different conditions. Nevertheless, if marketing management is to improve, marketing phenomena must be expressed in specific quantitative magnitudes. It must be possible to measure them and to use them in computations. To achieve these goals, it is necessary to view satisfaction objectively measured in the sales figure. Indeed, in the objective financial sense they are one and the same, even though subjectively or psychologically there may be variations. In brief, the sales figure should be analyzed objectively and in terms of its relationship to the economy and the firm.

There are two important views of sales that will aid us in visualizing their significance in the economy and in the firm:

1. Total sales is a measure of the flow of goods in the economy. Thus, it is an index of general business conditions and prosperity.
2. The sales figure is an objective measure of the satisfaction provided by the firm and its corresponding money income.

A Measure of the Flow of Goods in the Economy

The sales figure is used extensively as a measure of the increase or decrease in the prosperity of the economy. For example, department stores sales in typical large cities are published monthly as an index of business trends. Not only are these figures used as an index to reveal general economic trends in the nation, but also differences in districts and even cities are cited to show relative changes in business activity on a geographical basis. This data provides material for purposes of analyzing economic conditions in different business areas that may be responsible for the ups and downs of business.

There are, however, two definite limitations to using the sales figure to compare changes in the flow of satisfaction over a period of time. For example, in 1950 sales were $12 billion, while in 1972 retail sales exceeded $37 billion. It would be incorrect to assume that the satisfaction flowing through the trade channels of the nation in 1970 was three times as great as it was in 1950. Prices in 1972 had doubled since 1950. (See Exhibit 12-2). The second limitation to the use of sales as an absolute measure of satisfaction is illustrated by the case of the television set. A television which sold for $280 in 1951 sold for $130 in 1958 and for $118 in 1972. The 1972 set was the same size as the 1951 set, yet technological improvements made the 1972 set more desirable, easier to operate, and generally a better piece of equipment. This phenomenon appears to contradict our statement that the sales figure is a measure of satisfaction. We can explain this conflict by noting that the satisfaction which man has received from his income has constantly increased. Technology has supplied the

Exhibit 12-2

ACTUAL DOLLAR RETAIL TRADE SALES FOR 1950-1972 AND THE CONSUMER PRICE INDEX (1967 = 100)

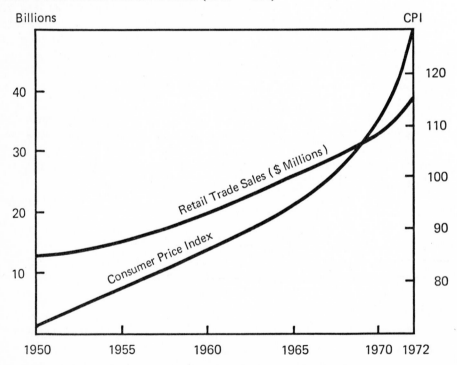

SOURCE: Department of Labor, Bureau of Labor Statistics. Department of Commerce (Bureau of Economic Analysis and Bureau of the Census).

leverage that has given him more for less. Our grandfather, in working fourteen hours a day and six days a week, did not produce the satisfactions we get from working an eight-hour day and five-day week. The increase in satisfaction results from the constant improvement in the efficiency of the processes of our economy. Such increases are not measured by the sales figure.

In the absence of other means for measurement, however, we still find sales and a useful overall measure of the economic progress of the economy. Especially is the sales figure valuable in showing relative changes when it is adjusted with an index number. Thus, we conclude that even though there is a factor of increase resulting from technological progress that cannot be objectively measured, we can measure increases or decreases in dollar sales in a manner that offers a useful guide in comprehending the progress of the economy.

A Measure of the Satisfaction Provided by the Firm

Within the scope of limitations already noted, sales of the individual firm measure the contribution of the firm to the satisfaction of the economy. The sum of the contributions of each firm to the flow of goods is equal to the total sales in a given period. In the majority of cases, the main problem area of management is increasing or maintaining its sales volume.

If sales figures are analyzed in terms of products, territories, or salespersons, they indicate areas of operating strength or weakness. Managerial attention is thus guided to areas where it can be applied strategically. The overall sales volume of a firm on a percentage basis may be decreasing or not increasing as fast as is competition. This is an indication of danger calling for study and action. The company must find where it is failing to provide satisfaction that is competitively adequate. On the other hand, sales may be increasing percentagewise at a more rapid rate than sales of competitors. Management must then appraise the reasons and safeguard the lead. Thus, for the firm as well as the nation the sales figure is a valuable guide.

The total sales figure is a component of all the payments made by the firm to different individuals. Even if we view the individual product, the selling price of the product—unless it is sold at a loss, which is an exception—includes all the payments necessary to make the sale possible. Thus, it is natural that sales be the base of all measurements in the analysis of the marketing operation and that this base be expressed as 100 percent. Very often this relationship is illustrated by showing the sales dollar divided into components indicating how each portion of the dollar is used (see Exhibit 12-3).

COST AND MARGINS

Success in gaining sales will be meaningless if there is no margin for profit. Such a margin, assuming adequate sales, depends upon successful buying. Successful buying requires first of all an ability to make the appropriate selection of products to satisfy the need. For a manufacturer the need is for raw

Exhibit 12-3

MANUFACTURER'S SALES DOLLAR DIVIDED INTO ITS COMPONENTS*

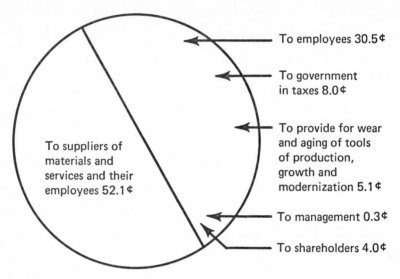

*Composite of 305,680 manufacturing establishments.

SOURCE: U.S. Department of Commerce, Bureau of the Census, *Annual Survey of Manufacturers: 1971* (Washington: U.S. Government Printing Office, 1973) , p. 265.

materials, supplies, or sundry equipment; and in the case of the wholesaler and retailer the need is for a line of goods that will appeal to the ultimate consumer. In either case the selective process can be a significant factor in building sales volume and in avoiding losses. Successful buying also requires, of course, buying at a price that will allow a margin of profit after the sale is made.

Gross Margin

As we analyze the components that contribute to the efficiency of the marketing institution, one of the most important points of reference is the gross margin. The gross margin is a composite measure of the market institution's skill in the processes of buying and selling. In simple terms, the gross margin for a pure marketing institution represents the spread between the price that is paid by the firm for the product which it buys for resale during a given period and the price at which this product is sold. In the case of hybrid marketing firms, which add value through manufacture as well as by marketing, the cost of the value added by production is included in the total cost before the gross margin is computed. In either case, insofar as accounting techniques make its measurement possible, the *gross margin* is equal to the cost of the goods to the company (plus the cost of the form utility added, if any) subtracted from the price at which the goods are sold. On the operating statement the gross margin is determined by subtracting the cost of the merchandise sold from the sales. In computing the cost of such goods, the transportation costs are added to the purchase price. Naturally, it is the aim of every firm to buy the products in which it deals at the lowest price possible for the quality or satisfaction they give. Complementing the skill in buying is the skill in selling the products for the highest price possible. Both of these skills are strategic and important to the success of the enterprise. In this sense buying and selling are the heart of marketing.

Expenses

A firm may achieve great skill in buying and selling and still fail to make a profit. The people who buy and sell must be compensated. There must be a building in which these functions take place. Customers demand service of one type or another, possibly delivery or credit. Many other elements appear as expenses that must be paid if the business is properly housed and administered. Here again management must make decisions involving cost and satisfaction. In every avenue of the store's operation, decisions and policies must be made that aim at providing maximum satisfaction without increasing expenses unduly. Assuming equal skill in the buying and selling function, management which applies its expenses most effectively in achieving the above objective excels in efficiency and profit.[3]

Profit

That portion of the gross margin that remains after expenses are paid accrues to the enterpriser. This difference is designated as profit. Profit is the motivation for enterprises, whether the enterprises be manufacturing, wholesaling, or retailing.

If profit were expressed as a formula, it could be said that a profit is the result of the enterpriser organizing human energy, resources, and tools and directing their operation so that the resulting satisfaction will have a money value when measured at the marketplace which is greater than the money cost of the resources. When viewed in this sense, if we agree that the choices of the people are sovereign, as we do in a democracy, the operation of such a firm has met the test of social desirability. On the other hand, if the firm has used an amount of human energy, resources, and tools in the manufacture of a product that fails to please the public at the marketplace enough to pay for the money value of the above named factors, then the resources have not been properly used. The final test is the response of the consumer and the management skill of the enterpriser in satisfying the customer's desires. The great virtue of our free society is this

---

[3] Raymond LeKashman and John F. Stolle state that the more management focuses the company's efforts on cutting distribution costs, the less successful it is likely to be in reducing the real costs of distribution. In this process management often waters down such costs or washes out the saving by increasing costs at other points. They recommend "The Total Cost Approach to Distribution," *Business Horizons* (Winter, 1965), pp. 33-46.

market device which places profit at the mercy of the free individual's choice. There are abuses, it is true, but generally speaking profit is a measure of the excess satisfaction that a company has supplied its patrons over its costs.

Review of Accumulating Costs

The manufacturer pays certain marketing costs for materials, purchasing, and popularizing the image of his brand through advertising and selling. All the costs of the distributor and the retailer are marketing costs. The selling price of the manufacturer becomes the product cost of the distributor. To this cost the distributor adds his gross margin, which includes payments by him for the performance of market functions. This accumulation process is repeated by the retailer. In brief, then, the selling price of one firm becomes the merchandise cost to the next firm in the channel; and the next firm adds its gross margin, which includes the costs of the marketing functions it performs.

THE OPERATING STATEMENT

The operating statement is the point where the subjective forces influencing marketing decisions and market efficiency are quantified and brought into focus. Sales, gross margins, expense ratios, and profit ratios are well-known and much used concepts for measuring efficiency. Management decisions and policies are not the result of viewing any one of these concepts alone. Rather, successful management policies result from a clear understanding of the relationship of each in the whole operation and its effect on profits. Exhibit 12-4 is an illustration of the operating statement with explanations opposite each of the concepts we have discussed.

Sales is the index of how the business offering is received by the patrons of the business as well as being the source of revenue. The cost of goods sold is viewed as the price which has been paid for the goods that are sold, and the difference between cost and realized price is the gross margin. Here we see the interaction of buying and selling. The buying and selling are consummated by people with the use of a certain amount of equipment and building space. Thus, we observe the expenses paid to maintain an effective buying and selling force and a place of business.

The performance of market functions is costly. In Exhibit 12-4 the market functions are listed opposite the payments that certain retail stores pay to cover their costs. The expenses listed under the three kinds of retail firms are typical accounting expense classifications for these kinds of businesses.

Activities such as credit, delivery, and advertising also are performed to encourage sales. These activities require the expenditure of funds. If a firm controls its expenses, is comparatively competent in selecting salable merchandise, and maintains an effective and efficient selling organization, it will be able to sell a sufficient volume at a price that will leave a residue of profits; and it will be considered an efficient firm.

Exhibit 12-4

THE OPERATING STATEMENT

The measure of public response to the offerings of the firm. A measure of the firm's efficiency in terms of output.	SALES
	less
The price which the firm has had to pay for the goods which it sells.	COST OF GOODS SOLD
	equals
The difference between the sales figure and the cost of goods sold. The margin of funds remaining after the goods sold are paid for or charged off.	GROSS MARGIN
	less
The payment made by the market institution to the suppliers of human energy, resources, and equipment. The effectiveness with which such resources are combined and applied to the performance of marketing functions affects the sales and the profit margin. The sum of these expenses when added to purchases equals the cost in the efficiency equation.	EXPENSES
	equals
The difference between the gross margin and the expenses. This is the reward to the owner of the business. It is the result of maximizing sales and satisfaction and minimizing costs. It is the ultimate measure of efficiency from the standpoint of the enterpriser.	PROFIT

EXPENSE DETAIL

MARKET FUNCTIONS	TYPICAL ACCOUNTS FOR RECORDING PAYMENT FOR PERFORMANCE OF FUNCTIONS AS RECORDED IN BOOK OF ACCOUNTS		
	FOOD STORE	DRUG STORE	DEPARTMENT AND SPECIALTY STORE
BUYING	Controllable Expense	Manager's Salary	Total Payroll
	Outside Labor	Employee's Wages	Real Estate Costs
SELLING	Operating Supplies	Rent	Advertising
	Gross Wages	Heat	Taxes
STORING	Repairs and	Lights and Power	Interest
	Maintenance	Taxes and Licenses	Supplies
RISKING	Advertising	Insurance	Service Purchased
	Car and Delivery	Interest Paid	Losses—Bad Debts
PRICING	Bad Debts	Repairs	Other Unclassified
	Administrative	Delivery	Traveling
STANDARDIZING	Legal Expense	Advertising	Communication
	Miscellaneous	Miscellaneous	Repairs
FINANCING	Fixed Expenses	Bad Debts	Insurance
	Rent	Depreciation	Depreciation
TRANSPORTING	Utilities	Telephone	Professional Services
	Insurance		
MARKET INFORMATION	Taxes and Licenses		
	Interest		
	Depreciation		

The conceptual scheme of the operating statement should assist us in visualizing the process of applying resources or costs to the performance of market functions. The actual payments, insofar as retail stores are concerned, are recorded in the accounts listed in the operating statements. Thus, the logic of the conventional recording process is shown in simple form. The costs and satisfaction expressed in terms of dollars and cents that are used in measuring the efficiency of the market institution are subjected to objective analysis.

MARKUP

Although prices are determined by the forces of supply and demand operating in a market area, the price of each piece of merchandise is not automatically or impersonally determined. Forces operating in the marketplace function with the aid of human judgment and are made effective by business decisions, but such forces of the market are usually difficult to discern. It is impossible to tell precisely how the masses of people will respond each day to prices on specific products. The enterpriser may not have a perfect knowledge of the forces of supply as they may be evidenced by competition in the field of his offerings, but judgments must be made and prices must be set. The manufacturer who sets the first price on a product begins the pricing process. Compared with the retailer or the wholesaler, however, he has but few products to price. Since we shall discuss the whole subject of pricing in subsequent chapters, attention here is confined to conventional techniques that are commonly used among retail and wholesale market institutions. These firms usually purchase goods in large variety and are forced to apply pricing techniques that differ in some respects from those of the manufacturer.

In the phraseology of marketing, the pricing operation of the retailer or wholesaler is termed the "markup." It involves buying products at one price and marking them up to a higher price. The problem is in determining the spread between what is paid for the article in question and the price at which it may be sold. This amount represents the value added by the institution. If we consider all the products purchased and sold during a period which the operating statement covers, the sum of the markups on all such products is equal to the gross margin for that period.

In retail or wholesale businesses, the markup procedure is often consummated by the application of specific markup goals to different classes of merchandise. The wide varieties and numerous lines of merchandise may require that a distinct markup percentage be applied to each class of merchandise. If we consider a food store as an example, canned milk, sugar, and shortening are staple items that remain somewhat uniform in quality. These products become very competitive because they are frequently purchased and their price can be remembered and easily compared. Since they are competitive, the spread between their cost to the retailer and the price at which he sells them is small—so small that a merchant does well if he breaks even on canned milk and sugar.

On the other hand, there may be a fancy fruit cocktail mix that is new and unusual. In addition to the quality of innovation, the product is not a staple. It lends itself well to advertising appeals and can be easily associated with high and unusual quality. This product might sell for a price that is 30 to 40 percent above its cost, while the staples mentioned earlier might sell for only 6 to 8 percent above their cost or even less. These two classes serve to illustrate the fact that differences in products influence the amount that can be added to their cost price to make them salable on the market. Men engaged in merchandising get so accustomed to marking merchandise of this kind that they frequently do not have to resort to formulas or computations. They play the pricing game by ear, so to speak. But large stores that establish profit goals must keep a closer watch on their markup policies. They cannot use uncontrolled and rule-of-thumb judgments. The careful manager who makes plans and establishes goals uses methods of markup that are the result of planned computations.

Several methods have been used by firms to apply the markup. However, only two are important enough to merit our attention: (1) a markup percentage based on cost, and (2) a markup percentage based on planned selling price.

Markup Percentage Based on Cost

The cost-base method of marking up merchandise can be illustrated by the application of this method to sugar, which may have a markup of 6 percent, and fruit cocktail, which may be marked up 30 percent. Assume that a 100-pound bag of sugar costs $6. Then we merely multiply the $6 by the 6 percent, and we get 36 cents. Add markup to cost, and the resulting sales price of the sugar is $6.36 per hundredweight.

In the instance of fruit cocktail, a case of 24 cans may cost the merchant $6. If he takes a 30 percent markup, his margin above cost will be $1.80 ($6 multiplied by 30 percent). Thus, his selling price will be $7.80, or 32.5 cents a can. This amount represents a markup of 7.5 cents above the 25 cents a can that the merchandise cost the merchant. The merchant may consider the effect that a higher or lower price might have on this volume or on profits. After a careful consideration of these factors, he will decide whether to mark this merchandise 32 or 33 cents.

MARKUP BASED ON COST

Step 1

30% Markup × $6.00 Cost = $1.80 Markup

Step 2

$1.80 Markup + $6.00 Cost = $7.80 Selling Price

Markup Percentage Based on Selling Price

Markup based on selling price differs from the cost-base method in that it bases the calculation on the projected selling price of the article. True, the selling price itself may not be known until after the calculation. However, the markup percentage desired will be determined, and the cost is known. Using the above example, if we divide the cost by the complement of the markup percentage, the selling price is obtained.

MARKUP BASED ON SELLING PRICE

Step 1

100% − 30% Markup Percentage = 70% Complement

Step 2

Cost ÷ Complement = $6.00 ÷ 70% = Selling Price $8.57

Refer again to the examples of the fruit cocktail and the sugar. Assume the same $6 cost for the fruit cocktail but substitute a 25 percent markup based on retail. If $6 (cost) is divided by .75 (complement of 25 percent markup), a price of $8 a case or $.33 a can is determined. Note that these figures are higher than the $7.80 a case or 32.5 cents a can obtained by the first method even though the markup on the previous computation was 30 percent of cost as compared to 25 percent on the planned retail price.

Comparison of Cost and Selling Price Methods

Until a few years ago, the cost basis of computation was the most popular as a means of marking merchandise. There are several reasons why this was so. The computation was simple. It was merely a matter of multiplying the cost, a known quantity, by a predetermined percentage. When it appeared that profits could be improved or when competition was such that the prices could be increased, a higher percentage figure was applied.

Of late years, however, business firms of the same class have been exchanging data. This practice enables one firm to observe the strength or weakness of business practices as they become evident in the operations of other firms. Such data also enable firms to determine wherein they differ from the norm. This data not only includes markup and gross margin figures, but also all the expenses and the net profit figures are given in terms of ratio to net sales. In presenting these ratios (Table 12-1) it is evident that ratios based on sales lend themselves more readily to analysis than those based on the cost price.

Table 12-1

**COMPARISON OF COST AND SELLING PRICE METHOD
OF RATIO MARGINAL ANALYSIS**

	COST METHOD		SELLING PRICE METHOD	
Sales	$1,000	167%	$1,000	100.0%
Cost of Merchandise Sold	600	100%	600	60.0%
Gross Margin	400	67%	400	40.0%
Expenses:				
Fixed	150	25%	150	15.0%
Variable	150	25%	150	15.0%
Total	300	50%	300	30.0%
Net Profit	$ 100	17%	$ 100	10.0%

When cost is the basis of the analysis, the sales percentage must be above the 100 percent figure, and the gross margin percentage is based on the cost of sales rather than on the sales figure. This comparison of gross margin as a percentage of merchandise cost is not a significant comparison. Even though the margin was 67 percent of the merchandise cost, such a reference does injustice to the accepted usage of the gross margin term, which in marketing establishments is expressed as a percentage of realized sales. The relationship between cost and sales is clearer when the sales figure is the base of 100 percent. Merchandise cost as a percentage of sales is subtracted to determine the percentage that is available to cover expenses and profits. Furthermore, when expenses are analyzed in terms of the cost dollar, the meaning is not so significant as it is when measured as a part of the sales dollar, since expenses are paid out of the sales dollar.

On the other hand, when the ratio analysis is based on selling price, observe how the presentation lends itself to clear understanding. In the first place, sales is the highest figure in the schedule; and it can be viewed as 100 percent, not exceeded by other significant figures. Second, all the income that accrues to the company through its merchandising practices comes via sales. All payments made by the company, as well as all its savings, come from sales dollars. Thus, it is not only more convenient but also more realistic that the sales dollar, rather than cost, be the basis for calculation.

RELATIONSHIP OF VOLUME TO EFFICIENCY

A prominent merchant, speaking before a group of marketing students, stated, "Volume is the cure for all merchandising ills." There is much truth in this statement. It is unusual for a merchant or a manufacturer who achieves a comparatively high volume of sales to have serious financial difficulties. A general statement of this kind indicates that there is some relationship between volume and efficiency. It is conceivable, however, that business may fail in spite of a high volume of sales. Furthermore, what do we mean by high volume? The corner grocery store is unable to handle a half-million-dollar volume, while the supermarket would fail if its volume were only one-half million. General Motors would lose millions if its sales were at American Motor's all-time high. In other words, volume is a relative factor. There are no definite studies that show optimum sales levels for various sizes and types of establishments. While there is some indication that certain firms can increase efficiency by reducing sales volume, the assumption that most firms now in business could operate more efficiently if they could achieve higher sales volume appears sound.

An Illustration

Table 12-2 is an illustration of a hypothetical firm operating at five different levels. In the first instance we observe the firm losing money at a volume of $700,000 per annum. The fixed expenses at this level equal 21.4 percent of the sales. Expressing the same fact in another manner, for every dollar in sales, 21.4 cents are required to pay fixed expenses. As tne volume of sales increases, the proportion of fixed expenses to sales decreases. At a break-even point of $833,333 in sales, only 18 cents of the sales dollar is needed to pay the fixed expenses. If the sales increase to $2,000,000, the amount required to pay these

Table 12-2

PROFIT FIGURES AT DIFFERENT VOLUME LEVELS

SALES 100%	$700,000	$833,333	$1,000,000	$1,500,000	$2,000,000
COST OF GOODS SOLD 67%	469,000	558,333	670,000	1,005,000	1,340,000
GROSS MARGIN 33%	231,000	275,000	330,000	495,000	660,000
FIXED EXPENSES →	$150,000 21.4%	$150,000 18%	$150,000 15%	$150,000 10%	$150,000 7.5%
VARIABLE EXPENSES 15%	105,000	125,000	150,000	225,000	300,000
TOTAL EXPENSES →	255,000	275,000	300,000	375,000	450,000
PROFIT →	($24,000) (3.4%) Loss	$ 0 Break Even	$ 30,000 3%	$ 120,000 8%	$ 210,000 10.5%

expenses is only 7.5 cents for every sales dollar. Observe in this progression that the portion saved by the reduction of fixed expenses goes directly into profit.

The increase in dollar profits is the true goal of the firm rather than percentage increases. In Table 12-2, when sales are $1,000,000, profits are 3 percent of sales, or $30,000. If sales are increased to $1,500,000, however, dollar profits are $120,000, or a figure 300 percent greater than the previous level, but the increase in profit on sales is only 5 percent.

Increased profit from greater volume is possible when the firm can increase its volume without proportionately increasing its fixed costs. It is well also to remember that fixed costs are not always completely fixed and that variable costs do not always vary in exact proportion to volume. Yet the fundamental philosophy of volume savings is vital to progressive management. Most firms operate at levels where increased profits result from greater volume. Sales more frequently than not increase at a greater rate than do costs. Thus, this area becomes a very important one in analysis for greater profits.

The Break-Even Point

Management finds it helpful to keep in view the level of sales at which the firm will just break even. This level is illustrated in Table 12-2 at $833,333. In this instance the decrease in the sale base from $1,000,000 to $833,333 caused the ratio of fixed expenses to sales to increase from 15 percent to 18 percent. This increase in costs was just enough to absorb the 3 percent profit that had existed at the former operating level. Consequently, the firm broke even.

Calculation of the Break-Even Point. The level of volume at which the firm breaks even can be determined by several methods. The first one is more conveniently applied to a retail or a wholesale establishment. There are five simple operations in this first method:

1. Separate expenses into fixed and variable.
2. Determine the percentage which variable expenses are of total sales.
3. Compute the gross margin percentage.
4. Subtract the variable expense percentage from the gross margin percentage.
5. Divide the fixed expenses by the difference between the gross margin percentage and the variable expense percentage.

Sales in our previous example were $1,000,000, and fixed and variable expenses were each $150,000. Gross margin was $330,000, or 33 percent. Assume that the gross margin will remain the same percentage of sales at all levels of operation and that the variable expense ratio will remain constant as related to sales. Then, with a gross margin of 33 percent and a variable cost ratio of 15 percent, 18 percent remains to apply to fixed costs if the firm is to break even. By dividing our present fixed costs of $150,000 by 18 percent, we obtain the break-even sales of $833,333.

Such an explanation would hardly apply in the case of a manufacturing concern since the cost-of-sales figure may not be completely variable as in the case where merchandise is purchased for resale by a wholesaler or a retailer. However, if we considered raw material purchases as a variable expense, and divided the entire payments made by such a concern into variable and fixed expenses, the same formula would apply. In our previous example, if we consider merchandise costs as variable, these costs would be 67 percent plus 15 percent, or 82 percent. This computation leaves 18 percent for fixed expenses.

An Alternative Method. Another method of computing a break-even level is illustrated in Exhibit 12-5. Plot the possible sales volume along the horizontal axis and the expenses along the vertical axis. Draw a straight line dividing equally the angle formed by the two axes. Then draw another line from a point on the vertical axis that is equal to the fixed expenses ($150,000) through a point which is equal to the sum of the fixed and variable expenses, which would in this instance include merchandise costs ($970,000), at the volume of present operations ($1,000,000). The point at which the two lines intersect is the break-even point.[4]

This method of computation has a significant advantage in that it is possible to determine what the profit or loss will be at any volume that is included on the chart. A firm can then determine what the profits might be under a greater volume of sales that, for example, might be expected if a new policy or program were put into effect. On the other hand, such a charting would show how serious a loss might be incurred if sales were to fall.

It is difficult to draw a sharp line dividing fixed and variable costs. We have already indicated that rentals may vary with the volume of sales. Also, heat, light, and power are often considered fixed costs since in most instances the amount of such costs is independent of volume. There are some instances, however, where these expenses vary with the volume sold. We must recognize therefore that such figures, even though they are close approximations of fixed and variable expense at one level of operation, may change from fixed to variable, or vice versa, as the volume increases or decreases. Yet even though such figures are but approximations, they enable us to make closer approaches to reality than could be made without them. They contribute to understanding and greatly improve the clarity with which decisions are made.

STOCKTURN RATE

Another significant index of market efficiency is the rate of stockturn. *Stockturn rate* is usually expressed as an annual rate representing the number

---

[4] Note: The break-even point of a firm can also be determined algebraically. One formula is as follows: $S = F + VS$

$$S = \text{Break-even Point}$$
$$F = \text{Fixed Expenses}$$
$$V = \text{Variable Costs} \div \text{Sales}$$

Example: Using the same data as in Exhibit 12-5.

$$S = 150,000 + (820,000/1,000,000)\ S$$
$$S = 150,000 + .82\ S$$
$$S - .82\ S = 150,000$$
$$.18\ S = 150,000$$
$$S = 833.333$$

Exhibit 12-5

BREAK-EVEN CHART

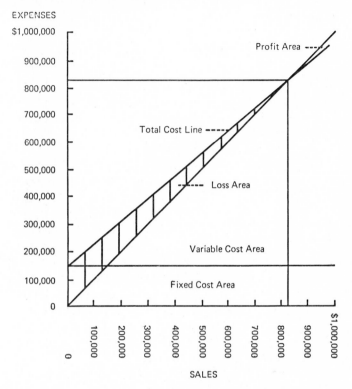

of times during a year (or other given period) that the average inventory of an establishment is sold and replaced. It relates to the volume of sales that can be achieved with a given amount of investment in stock. Investment, whether it is in a merchandise inventory, fixed plant, or equipment, represents cost. To maximize sales while keeping investment cost low is consistent with the goal of efficiency.

Stockturn rate is computed by two basic methods. For all practical purposes both methods yield the same result. The first method is to divide the cost of sales for a period by average inventory at cost price for the period. In the second method the net sales figure is divided by average inventory at its selling price.[5]

To illustrate how stockturn rate is calculated, figures relating to the hypothetical firm in Table 12-2 will be used. When sales were $1,000,000, the merchandise cost was $670,000. If the first method of computing the rate of stockturn is used, and the cost of average stock on hand is $100,000, the stockturn rate would be 6.7 (670,000 ÷ 100,000). If the second method is used

---

[5] Sterling D. Sessions prepares a method of markdown to maintain an optimum stock sales ratio by computerized simulation method in "Sales/Stock Ratios: Key to Markdown Timing," *New Research In Marketing* (Berkeley: Institute of Business and Economic Research, University of California, 1963).

and the retail value of the inventories is $150,000, the stockturn rate would be 6.67 (1,000,000 ÷ 150,000). Because most retail stores today keep their inventory records at retail, the second method of figuring the rate of stockturn is the more commonly used method.

Higher Returns on Investment

A high stockturn rate represents a greater sales volume with a given merchandise investment than a lower one. Furthermore, a higher stockturn rate makes it possible to use the fixed plant which is necessary to house inventory more effectively. In the example above, using inventories at cost of $100,000 and $200,000 for purposes of comparison, twice the physical plant investment would be necessary to store or house the larger inventory.

Assume that with a merchandise inventory of $150,000 at the selling price a firm can achieve an annual sales volume of $1,000,000. Also assume profit on sales of 3 percent. Profits in this example would be $30,000 after all expenses were paid. The value of inventory, which is $100,000 at cost, represents the merchandise investment. Thus, we would have earned $30,000 on our stock investment of $100,000, which is 30 percent. On the other hand, if our merchandise had been $200,000 at the same level of earnings, the rate of return on the merchandise investment would have been only 15 percent. Both of these figures represent a very high return on invested money.[6] Such a return is the result of a high sales volume and a most wise and effective application of funds to expenses by management. It alone is not the result of investing in merchandise stock. The high rate of income, nevertheless, does illustrate the returns from merchandising, where invested money is used as many times annually as the stockturn average. This phenomenon explains why Sears Roebuck, J. C. Penney, and other firms rent or lease their real estate and buildings. These firms find it more profitable to invest in merchandise that can be sold several times during the year than to have the same amount of capital invested in real estate.

In the example, there might not be a 3 percent profit if the annual stockturn rate were 3.35 instead of 6.7. A larger building would be required to house the larger inventory. This operation might require more rent, or depreciation, as the case may be. Insurance and taxes on the building and the stock as expenses that bear a direct relationship to the size of the stock would have to be considered. Thus, it can be concluded that one of the main advantages of a rapid stockturn rate is the fact that sales and profits are maximized with a minimum of investment and other expense.

Reduced Markdowns and Increased Sales

In our present age of dynamic change, a relatively rapid stockturn rate is important in order to prevent stock from becoming obsolete. There is also danger of stock becoming shopworn if it remains in the store too long. A firm whose merchandise moves slowly faces losses from markdowns on such stock.

---

[6] This return applies only to the money invested in merchandise.

On the other hand, a rapid turnover actually may be the cause of an increase in sales. A rapid movement of stock through a merchandising establishment tends to insure the presence of a stock on hand that represents the current demand. Furthermore, when the stockturn rate is rapid, the stocks are likely to be new and not shabby from handling and exposure.

Some Qualifications

It would be a mistake to imply that the goal of a high stockturn rate is always justified. On the contrary, it is entirely possible to achieve a high stockturn rate and cause the profits to decrease rather than to increase. If the store were able to maintain a sales volume of $1,000,000 on an inventory of $50,000 at cost rather than $100,000, such an achievement would be commendable in terms of returns on invested money and the plant assets necessary to handle the merchandise. There are, however, two additional aspects that should receive attention. In the first place, it would be difficult to keep each item of stock that might be in demand available in adequate supply. To reduce the overall stock allowance by half would mean a comparable reduction in each of the items offered for sale. To avoid loss of sales that result from being out of stock would require careful watching and skillful buying.

In the second place, when a firm greatly increases stockturn rate over a normal rate, there are dangers of great increases in the expenses. To keep adequate stocks on hand with a smaller inventory would require not only closer supervision, but also the firm would have to approximately double the number of times orders were submitted in each category. In addition to the time of the buyer in submitting orders, there would be the clerical work necessary to process the orders going out and invoices coming in. There would be almost double the number of packages to handle in receiving departments, even though they might not be so large. It is also possible that in buying in smaller amounts the freight and transportation charges might be higher. Sometimes the stockturn rate may be increased by the use of additional sales promotion aids, but such expenditures for promotion may be greater than any profit realized from the higher rate of stockturn.

A stock analysis for a large pipe manufacturing concern revealed that 25 percent of the stock had not turned over once in four years and that the company had on hand over $100,000 worth of stock that was considered obsolete. Most of this stock had to be written off as scrap. The loss could have been reduced or prevented had this company watched its stockturn rate and adopted some method of keeping stocks in balance.

THE MARKET SHARE

The market share is another measurement that has become popular as a guide for marketing management. As the name implies, it is a stated percentage of the total sales of a firm or of a product in the market under consideration; and it is used by some retail stores to determine their competitive position. For example, the Broadway Hale chain of department stores uses the market-share figure for department store sales in Los Angeles to determine its progress in meeting competition. To obtain its market-share position, Broadway Hale stores secure data on total department store sales in Los Angeles from census reports and Department of Commerce weekly reports. They then divide their stores' collective sales for the period by these totals.

With the aid of census reports or *Sales Management's Survey of Buying Power,* almost every retail store in an area can compute its market share. Determining market share is especially popular in the automobile field. General Motors, for example, enjoys a market share which is currently around 50 percent. Likewise, each car in the line can determine its share by dividing its sales by the total sales of automobiles.

A Guide to Market Strategy

The market-share concept adds a new dimension of control to the sales figure. It has already been pointed out that the sales figure, in addition to being income, measures the response of the market to the offerings of the company. Product sales, however, may be increasing even though the product may be losing favor when compared to competing products. Such would be the case if total sales of the product class in the company's market increased by 10 percent, while the company's product increased only 5 percent.

The market share, in revealing the relative position of a product compared to its competition, is an important factor in implementing strategy. An athletic team responds with greater skill if it knows the score. Likewise, a firm is in a better position to seek a means for corrective action if it knows its position as compared to its competitors.

Some Limitations of the Market-Share Index

The market-share figure does not reveal specific trouble nor the reasons for losses or gains in the share; rather, it provides a signal. Once a company knows which way a sales trend is changing, reasons for the change must be discovered either by managerial insight or by an independent survey.

If the market-share index refers to individual products and is known for specific areas, it is more reliable as a control device. Under such circumstances it is much easier to pinpoint the problem area or determine the reasons for success. In some instances firms have found a striking correlation between changes in product quality and sales figures. As an example, when a more expensive filler in one popular food product was increased by 25 percent for one sales area, the sales increased 125 percent; and the market share in this area increased proportionately.

It cannot be assumed, however, that it is always the product quality that influences market share. Changes might result from such things as price increases or reductions, effectiveness of the sales force, administration of advertising expenditures, choice of distributors, incentives or lack of incentives for salesmen, and quality of sales training.

QUESTIONS AND ANALYTICAL PROBLEMS

1. What are the specific tasks of management? State in one sentence the specific application of each of the first three tasks mentioned to marketing management.

2. It is suggested that "leading" may be more significant in the marketing function than in most other activities of a firm. Why?

3. Find an example, other than the one in the textbook, of a company that has either succeeded or not succeeded in planning well. Relate its experience to each of the planning steps illustrated in Exhibit 12-1 on page 219.

4. Define strategy. Find two recent examples of well-defined marketing strategy.

5. Read the article in the "companies" department of a recent copy of *Business Week*. Does the firm described have long-range marketing plans congruent with its short-range plans? Explain.

6. What are the duties of a brand or product manager?

7. Write a formula that measures marketing efficiency. How does this formula differ from a formula to measure production efficiency?

8. What items can you see in Exhibit 12-4 on page 233 which explain why each of the three types of stores have different gross margins? Which will have the largest gross margin? Which the smallest?

9. Compute the following:
   (a) A merchant buys a necktie for $1 and sells it for $1.50. What is the markup percentage based on cost? What is the markup percentage based on selling price?
   (b) A merchant plans for an average markup of 25 percent (based on selling price) in a certain department. If he pays $10 for an item, what should be the selling price if he gets 25 percent markup on selling price?
   (c) An item sells for $50. How much can a merchant pay for the item if he needs a 30 percent (based on selling price) markup?

10. In a southwestern city of approximately 150,000 people, a low-price chain store unit is enjoying sales of about $3.5 million annually. A short distance away is a departmentalized specialty store that sells goods of relatively high price and it, too, has an annual sales volume of around $3.5 million. The chain store's average gross margin is 29 percent of net sales, and the higher-price store operates on an average gross margin of 37 percent. The chain store last year showed a net profit of 11 percent of net sales, and the high-price specialty store finished the year with a net profit of 4 percent. This experience has been repeated for several years. Explain the different gross margins and net profit figures.

11. Which method of computing markups—cost or selling price—shows the higher gross margin percentage? Why?

12. Given a sales volume of $100,000, fixed expenses of $20,000, variable expenses (at the given sales volume) of $35,000, plot the break-even point.

13. Evaluate annual stockturn rate as a measure of efficiency.

14. What are the various means by which a stockturn rate can be increased by one firm?

15. Define market share. How can it be computed? What specific factors must be considered in determining whether or not a given market-share index is satisfactory?

Case 12 • THE ICE BOX

The Ice Box, which is located in a small southern college community, has the reputation among college students as having the best ice cream in town. As a favorite after-date hangout, the Ice Box usually sells about $150 worth of ice cream nightly.

In order to expand their daytime business, the management is considering selling sandwiches. Being able to provide students with a "quick meal" would enable the Ice Box to compete with local diners. Since the present freezing unit is much too cold for storing sandwich ingredients, a new refrigerator would have to be bought for $400. An analysis of the costs involved revealed the following:

Additional monthly wages for part-time sandwich maker $150.00
Monthly depreciation on the new refrigerator 3.33
Bread (per sandwich) 05
Sandwich ingredients (per sandwich) 20
Other (per sandwich) 10

Sandwiches were to sell for 65 cents each. Management was uncertain about how many sandwiches they would sell but estimated the number to be 500 monthly. They felt confident, however, that carrying the sandwiches would increase the ice cream sales by 10 percent. Management wanted to know not only whether they should carry the new line but also exactly how many sandwiches they needed to sell monthly in order to break even.

• What would you recommend? Present a statement of the costs and income that would accrue from this proposal. Suggest an alternative at a different volume. Graphically plot the break-even point.

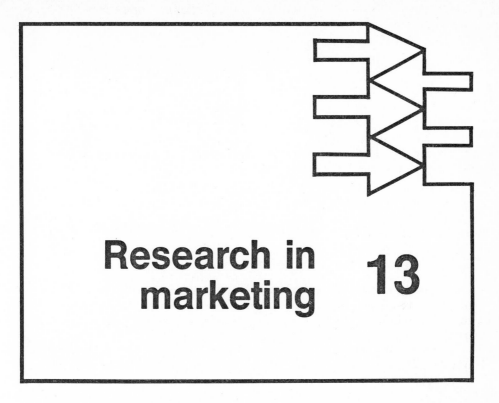

Research in marketing 13

It takes research and administrative skill combined with conditioned judgment to invest marketing money where the market is. Where and with whom is the best market for a specific product? What is the best strategy to use in exploiting the market?

An example demonstrating the basic need for information to guide a management is General Foods' campaign to sell Sanka, the company's substitute for coffee. By conducting marketing research, the company discovered that 50 percent of the total population in the United States has negative feelings about the caffeine in coffee. Yet 60 percent of the people making up this 50 percent drink coffee. They report that they do not like the flavor of Sanka, but market research also shows that when given both regular coffee and Sanka people cannot distinguish the difference. The strategy which resulted from this market information was to demonstrate that Sanka "tastes as good as coffee, with no drugs." The company implemented this strategy by TV shots dramatizing, in simulated life situations, the excellence of Sanka flavor.

The above example is relevant because it is typical. All companies could improve the effectiveness of their marketing programs by obtaining more appropriate information as an aid to market judgment.

MARKET INFORMATION AND CONTROL

While the concept of control is often related closely to the accounting function, it encompasses a broader area. Control as used here requires the use of information as a guide to policy information or as a guide to action. The search for information is based upon the presumption that there is a better product or a means of reducing costs in some manner. Information may also be needed to determine the strength of competition in the market. Information may be obtained by observation, by receiving facts or opinions from customers (usually through salesmen), and by formal, organized investigation. Organized investigation is used more and more frequently because the search for business intelligence cannot wait upon the normal and often casual flow of information. As we shall observe in future discussions, even with careful research there are limitations on how dependable such information and projections can be. Yet if the knowledge obtained bears some degree of relevance, is accurate, and is applied with skill, it will facilitate the control function and improve the degree of marketing success.

Classification of Market Information

In discussing the concept of market information in Chapter 12, the problem of making sense out of the mountains of market information was posed. One of the first steps in attempting to make marketing sense out of facts is the development of some method of classifying information flows. Now that marketing facts are being organized into systems, it is particularly important that information flows be recognized. The executive should know what facts and figures are needed at different points and should set up the administrative machinery to obtain such information.

Information flows can be divided into two major categories—external and internal. An *external information flow* is the flow of information out into the market as well as the flow of information from the market into the business firm. This flow relates to product offerings and promotions, including advertising and public relations; and it also includes information about the market. The *internal information flow* consists of information that flows within the divisions of the business. The flow of operational policy, statement of company objectives, and reports of achievements should flow from the top down. Indication of personnel attitudes, evidence of trouble spots, and reaction to executive overtures should flow upward toward the higher echelons of management. These communication flows are significant to the vitality of the business, and they are important in terms of the company's performance in the marketplace. Our concern at this point is primarily with information flows which involve accounting, and marketing research.

Information Flows

Accounting deals with the flow of financial data. Although mostly internal in character, accounting information includes data as to the sales response to the company's product; and, also, annual reports are sent outside the firm to the public. The recent managerial emphasis on accounting has expanded techniques so that more useful facts from both inside and outside the company can be obtained to guide management decisions.

The pattern of collecting, recording, and reporting accounting information is somewhat formal, and this formality tends to restrict coverage to an extent which makes it necessary to obtain needed information by other means. Nevertheless, the great advantage of accounting information is that the unit of increase or decrease is expressed in dollars and cents, and such information is essential for the determination of operational efficiency.

The marketing research information flow follows no fixed patterns such as are found in accounting. Although most marketing research information comes from outside the company, operations within the company are also analyzed for cost-reduction or product-improvement purposes. The opportunities for the use of marketing information are almost infinite in number; and a research design can be constructed to measure almost any conceivable influence related to marketing, whether it be an existing situation, a prevailing attitude, or the projected results of alternate courses of action. The selection of information to be researched is determined by weighing the potential of the information to implement company strategy against the cost of getting the information.

MARKETING RESEARCH

The American Marketing Association Committee on Definitions defines *marketing research* as follows:

> The systematic gathering, recording, and analyzing of data about problems relating to the marketing of goods and services. Such research may be undertaken by impartial agencies or by business firms or their agents for the solution of their marketing problems.[1]

The widespread adoption of marketing research during the last decade has been phenomenal. The pressures of competing market strategies have made it expedient for management to know more about the market they seek and the competition they will encounter. The principal areas of search for information relate first to the market area: second, to the characteristics of the product or the service being sold, especially as they relate to consumer preferences; third, to the effectiveness of the communication from the company to the market area; and fourth, to the prevailing attitude of the people in the market area toward the product or the company.

The Measure of Market Areas [2]

The clearer a company's concept is regarding the area that it serves, the more effective its strategies can be. Some of this information, such as population distribution, number of competitors, and comparative influence of

---

[1] Ralph S. Alexander, *Marketing Definitions* (Chicago: Committee on Definitions of the American Marketing Association, 1963), pp. 16-17.

[2] For a precise and somewhat mathematical method of determining the bounds of a trading area, see David L. Huff, "Defining and Estimating a Trading Area," *Journal of Marketing*, Vol. 28 (July, 1964), pp. 34-38.

competitors in the market, is quantitative.[3] Other information, involving such things as attitudes, class structure, and educational backgrounds, is qualitative.

Location of Retail Stores and Shopping Centers. Today the location of retail stores and shopping centers is demanding a maximum amount of effort and market data. Companies such as Woolworth and J. C. Penney carefully study market potential in the various areas of the nation in search of optimum sites for their stores. Data with respect to population, income, and the market characteristics of consumers and the already established retail facilities of the area is utilized to determine existing potentialities.

One department store chain adopted a strategy of dominating the department store business in a specific region. It divided regions into areas where the growth would eventually justify a shopping center, and it employed professional retail location consultants with a national reputation to keep current data on the growth of these areas. As soon as the areas reached a level where the population potential was 100,000 people, the store promoted a shopping center and moved in. The management reasoned that at this point it could expect break-even sales of $4 million, or $40 per capita. Every retail expansion can be effectively guided by accurate data on area potential.

Plant Location. The location of plants for marketing institutions of all kinds is dependent upon the potential stability and resources of the market area.[4] Population, income, availability of the right kind of labor, raw materials, and transportation resources and rates are indexes used to determine the quality of a location site. Educational facilities to train technical workers, the availability of desirable markets, and the business climate are also factors.

Cities, counties, states, and regions are engaging in a growing amount of promotion of their respective areas. They covet the increasing income and appreciating land values that result from economic growth. In the process of their promotions, useful data is made available to assist the researcher in identifying optimum potential. Such data must be assembled, organized, and analyzed by the individual firm or some firm employed to perform the task. Such data, however, is only a supplement to the extensive market information that is needed for judicious decision as to where to locate company plants.

Establishment and Management of Sales Territories. An important use of market area information is that it provides a guide for establishing sales territories. Establishing practical and meaningful goals and quotas for salesmen requires a refined knowledge of market potential for sales districts. Such data permits management to isolate successful salesmen and sales methods. It provides a measure of a salesman's production against his potential and becomes the basis of a motivating reward for excellence. Equally important, it points up weak performance and becomes a guide for corrective action.

---

[3] One of the most popular and respected sources of area market information is *Sales Management's* annual "Survey of Buying Power."

[4] A useful tool for building sales potential budgets in every marketing area, including retail stores, financial institutions, and services, is the Bureau of Census publication *County Business Patterns,* First Quarter issue of each year.

Directing Advertising Expenditures. Market area data is also needed to achieve a proper deployment of advertising resources. The decision as to the amount of advertising to direct to each territory must be based on the potential in that territory. Keeping abreast of the changing market potential is vital to the most efficient expenditure of the advertising budget.

Guide for Selecting Test Market Areas. Another important need for data about the market area relates to the selection of a test market. The test market must, of course, be as representative as possible of the actual market where the product will ultimately be sold. Thus, a complete knowledge of the basic characteristics of a test market is essential, for without such knowledge an expensive market test can give the wrong impression regarding the true potential of a product in the total marketplace. Methods and conceptual schemes for selecting test markets have been developed which minimize the time and the effort required to collect and organize data in a manner which facilitates accurate judgments.

Need for Refined Data

Much of the data regarding market areas may be collected from published reports or studies and be presented in quantity magnitudes. Yet the availability of such data does not render the market-area problem simple nor guarantee a perfect predictability of territory potential. The data in such studies is not specifically suited to many businesses. In the first place, even a business census (the most common source) may not include a classification which provides the data desired. In the second place, data in the business census and similar reports often is not sufficiently current, for today's society is mobile, and changes are taking place daily in market-area quantity and quality characteristics. Greater refinement of data is usually needed, and much information of a qualitative nature may be necessary to adequately describe the area either as a site for a plant or a store or a market for a product.

Importance of Qualitative Data

The new emphasis on class markets, reference groups, and consumers of special kinds of products is beginning to place more importance on the subjective characteristics of the population. The demographic characteristics of the population, while important, must be balanced with the dimensions of human behavior relating to cultural background, attitudes, and value systems. Such an assessment places an additional burden on the time and cost of market research. Yet the present tendency to segmentize markets by subjective characteristics is a sound and growing practice. For example, the value of sporting and athletic goods manufactured to appeal to that segment of the market concerned with sports activities reached the figure of $1.2 billion in 1972.

The increasing capacity to communicate, store, and analyze data about subjective factors that identify specific groups will cause market segments to grow more important as competition increases in intensity. In view of the progress in the development of these trends, it is likely that the science of describing the subjective or qualitative characteristics of the market area in the interest of achieving an enlightened and currently effective strategy is yet in its infancy.

PRODUCT RESEARCH

Stuart C. Waterhouse, a visitor from England almost three decades ago, gave an accurate portrayal of product testing in America when he stated:

> Perhaps the most thorough campaign of product testing that I have come across was carried through by a leading soap manufacturer which I visited. Before introducing a new brand of soap, this firm spent two years in finding out the exact size and shape of cake, the style of wrapper, and the potency of the odor that women would prefer. Some 40 different perfumes were tested in the field, the final choice resting not with the manufacturer, but with the consumer. By the time the surveys were finished, there was no doubt of the public acceptance of the soap, the public had literally created it.[5]

The basic goals of product testing are still the same as when Waterhouse described his experience. Product research, however, is not confined to new products. It is also used as a means of getting feedback on the reception of older products. Product research is used to seek reasons why a product is succeeding or failing. Such information provides guides and controls for future innovations of products, packages, or selling methods. The acceptability of packages and their influence on sales are also significant and related areas of testing.

Literally thousands of new ideas are generated daily. Yet all such ideas cannot be adopted and yield sufficient volume of sales to make them profitable. The means of reducing these ideas to a practical level involves realistic research. The scientific method of evolving the idea, testing it deductively, and then putting it to a practical test is the process that must be used. Many of these ideas are eliminated by deductive reasoning, and undoubtedly some ideas for products which have great potential are rejected. Yet because the testing of all products is a much too voluminous task, elimination by deductive thinking is necessary. In some instances a company may choose not to test a product that it feels sure will succeed in gaining widespread market acceptance because the test might give other firms the idea and a definite time advantage in getting a competitive product on the market.

The Concept Test

One of the means of eliminating products that are least likely to succeed is the concept test. President C. W. Cook of General Foods, where concept testing is used extensively, states that concept testing

> . . . is based on the notion, proven a pretty sound one, that consumers buy ideas rather than physical products. Each homemaker, for example, does not

---

[5] Stuart C. Waterhouse, "An Englishman Looks at American Marketing and Distribution Policies," *Journal of Marketing,* Vol. XII (January, 1948), p. 305.

simply buy a box of cereal. She is buying what she anticipates a box of cereal will do for her; how it fits in with her goal as a mother and her desire to provide the best possible nourishment for her family. . . .[6]

A concept test contains a complete and graphic description of a product and provides means for obtaining reactions to the product from a panel that is representative of prospective consumers. The methods for conducting the tests are unlimited; the method selected depends on the type of product and the genius of the researcher. One method of concept testing is to prepare an advertisement of the proposed product which includes the art work and a description of what the product will do in a real-life setting. The responses of a selected panel to this ad would then be obtained and analyzed. Getting the customer to respond to the proposed product in an unbiased and uninhibited manner is the objective of concept testing. Ideas gleaned from the responses are then analyzed, and the potential of each product is determined. Often, too, the product undergoes some changes as a result of the feedback from concept tests.

An example of a very successful use of concept testing is the testing done by Ford prior to the introduction of the Mustang. The testing method included in-depth interviews over a long period of time. During these interviews the researchers sketched a car that people said they wanted. Some people wanted a sporty car with room for the family; others wanted a car which was powerful, economical, compact, and comfortable. Engineering, styling, and marketing cooperated in designing a car that combined some of their own thinking with information gleaned from the marketplace. The car sold 419,000 units in its first year on the market.

After the first test, concepts can be refined and retested in different market segments in order to be sure that a product is selected that will be most acceptable to the consumer. However, the method is not foolproof; for concept testing can only simulate reality, and many of the forces and influences of the marketplace cannot be communicated in a concept description. Thus, even though the techniques are adequate, to get a reliable pattern of consumer views, it should not be presumed that concept testing is the final answer. One must recognize, for example, that a powerful advertising and selling campaign can add much to product acceptability.

In product tests, whether at the concept level or in later research, care should also be used to see that the product acceptability is increased where the decision to consume it will actually be made. For example, tests on Pet Glo pet food were all very favorable, but the product sales were disappointing. The trouble was that even though the persons who usually bought the dog food were impressed, the dog did not enjoy the food as well as competing brands.

The Bench Test

When the less promising ideas have been eliminated either by deductive thinking or a concept test, the next step is to test the product itself. In the case

---

[6] Kenneth Ford, "Management Guide—Test Marketing," *Printers' Ink* (August 27, 1965), p. 26.

of most products, there is a need for further evidence, even after a concept test, that the product will succeed in market competition before it is offered for sale. Therefore, a bench model is often made that is exactly like the final planned product. This model is then given a sample exposure at various points in the marketplace, and the reactions of potential buyers are observed as a basis of making certain projections. First, an estimate may be made of what the volume possibilities may be if the product is made and sold in a mass market; and second, some information may be gained on improvements that might be made in the product before it is placed on the market. This process may be repeated until an acceptable product is developed. With such information the company is in a much better position to make serious mass-market commitments.

This stage of research or testing can be performed in various manners. The automobile companies would find it difficult to bench manufacture a fancy car. However, these companies have tooled up for a limited number of models and put them out to test. When the models catch on in the marketplace, they increase their production and move them into mass production. These experiments not only have served to get a feedback from the market, but also they have had an impact on trends. The market has been guided by such experiments into new tastes and new style and performance patterns. Examples of these activities are Ford's Thunderbird and Pontiac's Grand Prix. Such activities go beyond the bench-testing stage into the actual production-introduction stage, but at no point until the mass market has developed does the company commit itself to mass production.

The Test Market

The test-market procedure consists of going into a representative market and supporting the product with the entire marketing mix. Utilizing a test market will give a better indication of the product's chances for success than will bench testing. The volume that might be expected can be more accurately estimated, and better indications can be secured as to how the product itself or other ingredients of the marketing mix might be improved.

As competition becomes keener and as an increasing flow of new products reaches the marketplace, the sophistication of test markets must improve. Even though favorable results are obtained during testing periods, many products fail because of imperfections in the tests or changes in the market after the tests. A firm must also realize that placing a product in a test market alerts the competition and that the competition may take action which will diminish the advantages of the product in the marketplace.

Using a test market as a predictor of product success has several other limitations. One problem is the fact that each region in the national market has market characteristics which distinguish it from national norms, a fact which is substantiated in a study by Foote, Cone, and Belding. This study indicates that deviation from marketshare prediction is reduced significantly as the number of test markets are increased.[7] When only one test market was used, actual

---

[7] *Ibid.*

marketshare standard deviation was 32.8 percent from the test-market share. When two test markets were used, the standard deviation dropped to 21.7 percent; and for three, there was a 15.8 percent deviation. The results suggest that the national market is a mosaic made up of hundreds of local markets each of which is different from the others and that increasing the number of markets tested increases the accuracy of the predictions based on the tests.

Further evidence of the fact that market testing is but an aid to judgment is contained in a study by Booz, Allen, and Hamilton, which found that 60 percent of the products test marketed by well-managed companies were not successful.[8] Analysis of the test-market problem reveals several reasons as to why their predictability scores are low. A basic problem is that test-market products receive special attention even though attempts are made to conduct the tests using normal marketing procedures. With a test-market product it is common to find that (1) the salesmen work harder to make the product succeed, (2) the trade is alerted and gives the product more support, (3) special introductory offers are often made, and (4) competitors change their promotion programs in the test-market area. As a result of these unnatural marketing conditions, test-market results cannot accurately reflect the potential success of the product.

Efforts are being made to improve the reliability of information secured from test markets. In this connection some companies are turning the test marketing over to their market research departments. As contrasted to emphasizing the sales potential of one specific product, the goal of the market research department is to obtain useful information as to the influence of market factors on various products. That is, the department would attempt to discover under controlled market conditions how Products A, B, and C would compare in sales with different shelf spacings, pricing, and other market factors. The comparative information provided by this approach aids in the development of effective marketing strategies.

Because of the limitations of test marketing, some firms are doing a more careful job of concept and bench testing. After completing these tests, the most promising products are picked and placed on the national market. If the products do not reach a reasonable pay-out level, they are discontinued. In such a procedure the national market is being used as the test market.

Before concluding this discussion about testing the market acceptability of products, certain things should be noted. First, many market researchers believe that the concept and bench tests serve the purpose of product success better than the test market, and, in addition, they are less expensive. The prevailing view, however, is that all these tests are complementary. Second, the sequence of idea, concept test, bench test, and test market is in no sense sacred. Not every product would have to go through an exhaustive test at each step. It would appear desirable, though, that each product test be different, for an experimental design is needed which suits the specific characteristics of each product and the various markets it is to serve. Finally, one should not assume that the techniques for testing the market acceptability of products are only

---

[8] *Ibid.*, p. 34.

used for new products. Innovations in promotion, in distribution methods, and in old products can be effected by the application of these techniques.

MEASURES OF COMMUNICATION

One of the major means of getting a product accepted in a market area is marketing communication. Marketing men are becoming increasingly aware of the complexities of getting their message understood so that demand for the product is created. The most important element in demand creation is the impact of the selling message, whether this message appears in an advertisement or is conveyed by the salesman.

The Use of Quantitative Data

Measuring the impact of the selling message comprises a significant portion of the market research dollar. Quantitative knowledge is available regarding the number of listeners to radio and viewers of TV. With the aid of audiometers, professional research firms such as A. C. Nielsen collect and organize such data and make it available to clients. In some instances data on comparative program ratings are published in trade journals and the daily press. Indeed, the stage of development in this area is such that when a radio program goes on the air the number of listeners can be predicted with a minimum tolerance for errors. Similar predictions can be made for magazine and newspaper readership. The Audit Bureau of Circulation is organized for the express purpose of providing reliable information on newspaper and magazine circulation.

It is not necessary to discuss all of the many devices used by businesses to provide quantitative guides to the advertiser, but attention to a few examples of such devices is warranted. One firm reports that it now has fed into the computer information on the circulation of the various competing printed media, their measured readership magnitude, the costs for space, and other factors influencing their value to the company. With all such figures recorded, the computer is instructed to find the combination of media that will result in the highest coverage with the least cost. The year before this exhaustive study was made, the company achieved 18 percent market coverage. After the new recommendations based on the additional data were adopted, the company was able to achieve a 38 percent coverage of the market, or an increase of 111 percent, with only a 10 percent increase in cost.

The marketing executive of the same company also had a bank of figures to show that when he ran 5 commercials a month on national TV, 32 percent of the market could be reached. Ten commercials a month would reach 39 percent; 15 would reach 42 percent; and 20 would reach 43 percent. By giving an estimated value to the impact of the commercial on customers, the executive judged that the optimum point was 15 commercials a month.

There are two areas where the executive should be cautioned to examine his procedure carefully. First, even though the audience tests of TV programs, as reported by researchers, have gained a reputation for being reasonably accurate, there have been some occasions for serious doubts as to the correctness of their claims. Sampling methods and the manner in which each survey is conducted should be examined carefully. The second area of concern is the determination of the value which is received from viewership or listenership. In the above illustration for example, five TV commercials reached 32 percent of the market; and the coverage increased 7 percent by doubling the number of commercials. Determining the value of this 7 percent requires the executive to make a subjective judgment as to how many additional purchases would result by contacting the additional viewers. Thus, he must make a value judgment as to the worth (number of products purchased) of each viewer and then compare the cost of reaching this viewer with the cost of reaching him through other media. Also, he will have to consider the relative value of having the sales message communicated by television as compared to communicating it by newspapers, magazines, radio, or other media. From this discussion it should be noted that data gathered by scientific processes are used as a basis for decision making, but the final decision also includes the making of subjective judgments. Typically, in the decision-making process the quality of the subjective judgments and the skill of executing the plans are as essential to success as the research data itself.

Another example involving television illustrates the use of concept testing for television programs. A company joined with several other national advertising firms in the interest of pretesting ideas for television programs. These companies had each of 48 programs that the advertising staff had selected as good prospects described accurately in a 100-word narrative. They then presented these narratives to a selected panel of television viewers. By choosing for production only those scripts that the panel ranked as being in the best 25 percent, these companies were able to increase the number of programs which attracted audiences for two successive years from 3.5 percent to 7.3 percent. Other methods that have been used to test the effectiveness of TV programs are: (1) to have a panel of selected consumers come into the company offices or the TV studio and preview programs and (2) to have the product manager and his staff examine one or two presentations of a program before it is run.

For newspaper advertising split-run tests are often made of advertisements in certain cities to determine which ones are the most effective, and the best are chosen to run on a national scale. For example. each of two selected ads with coupons attached will be run in one half of the total circulation of a New York newspaper, and the advertisement that draws the greatest coupon response is chosen for a national campaign. Readership studies conducted by surveryors who visit subscribers to determine advertisements recalled and the detail with which they are recalled also provide an indication of the advertisements which are most impressive.

Research in Discerning Marketing Attitudes

One of the growing areas in marketing research relates to the discernment of the subjective feelings and attitudes of potential patrons. In marketing, feelings and attitudes are the basic factors that lead to the ultimate reality of sales. People, however, often find it difficult to identify and express their true feelings. Even when they can, they frequently respond the way they think they ought to respond or to please their vanity rather than according to their true feelings or their own opinions. For example, a company made two kinds of beer. To examine the natural preferences of a certain segment of the market, the company first determined the respondents that used the company brand, and they were asked this question: "Do you drink *Light or Regular?*" (These were the trade names of the two company brands.) During the survey of the carefully selected sample, respondents stated a preference for *Light* over *Regular* more than three to one. During this time, however, *Regular* outsold *Light* nine to one. It was apparent that the respondents wanted to appear to the interviewer to be classed with the connotation favoring the term "light" rather than be placed with a commonplace group that favored "regular."

The Projective Test.[9] Market research techniques have been developed which, if carefully planned and executed, enable the researcher to discern true feelings and attitudes. Such techniques have long been used by clinical psychologists to get behind the facades that are used by patients to protect the images they do not wish to reveal. The so-called projective technique projects the respondent into situations where he indicates what someone else would have said in this situation, yet in reality the views that he expresses are probably his own. Such tests tell a great deal about the respondent and the convictions that are responsible for the way he answers.

Example of the Projective Technique. It required several years for instant coffee to gain popularity. Here was a product that was equal, if not superior, to other coffee. Why were people unwilling to adopt it?

The researchers in this area asked hundreds of women why they didn't like instant coffee. They replied they didn't like the taste. Because the researcher felt that this was not the real reason, he attempted further research. He submitted two lists of products to 100 women. All products on each list except the fifth item were the same. The reader will note that on one list we have included Nescafe Instant Coffee and on the other, Maxwell House Coffee, Drip Grind.

List A	*List B*
1 ½lb. hamburger	1 ½lb. hamburger
2 loaves, Wonder Bread	2 loaves, Wonder Bread
1 bunch of carrots	1 bunch of carrots
1 can Rumford's baking powder	1 can Rumford's baking powder
Nescafe instant coffee	Maxwell House coffee, drip grind
2 cans Del Monte peaches	2 cans Del Monte peaches
5 lb. potatoes	5 lb. potatoes

---

[9] Much of this discussion on projective techniques was obtained from Mason Haire's article, "Projective Techniques in Marketing Research," *Readings in Marketing,* edited by Philip R. Cateora and Lee Richardson (New York: Appleton-Century-Crofts, 1967), pp. 149-159.

The respondents were asked to give a word picture of a woman who might go to the store with such a list. On the list that included the instant coffee, 48 percent of the answers described a lazy woman and one who does not plan her purchases well; 12 percent stated that she was a spendthrift or a bad wife. Such qualities were not mentioned in connection with the other list at all. With this information the company was in a better position to advertise its product.

From the example given, it is evident that the respondents were not answering for themselves but were describing the kind of person they thought would use instant coffee. Research such as this provides a means for getting closer to the customer's true feelings, and the research results can serve as a guide for strategies which will increase sales.

CONDUCTING THE SURVEY

Research is a means of improving the manager's awareness of reality. He does not have, nor can he be expected to have, all the facts relevant to decisions, policies, and the execution of his plans. The marketing research survey measures additional dimensions that should make strategy more effective. The diversity and heterogeneity of the marketing universe is such that the survey procedure cannot be stereotyped and made to conform to a rigid or generalized pattern. For example, a market research executive illustrated the fact that each survey is different by pointing out that if one measured his desk top for a glass fitting, one would require an entirely different parameter than if he measured the same desk for varnishing, although the basic area would be the dimension needed for both purposes. To evaluate these differences and to select the sample, the questionnaire, and the interview to fill the specific needs of each situation is a professional undertaking. The judgment it requires can be introduced and matured to some degree in the classroom, but professional skill is the result of seasoning and sharpening by practical experience.

The Sample

Most market research is based in some way on a sample. A *sample* consists of a small collection from some larger aggregate about which information is desired. The selection of the sample to be used in market research is a critical step in the effort to secure accurate data. The researcher attempts to select individuals in the population so that the results of the sample will be representative of all the individuals in the population.

The basic sampling concept which tends to achieve this result is the *simple random sample*, which provides that each unit in the population under study has an equal chance of being selected. However, it is not easy to plan and administer a survey so that perfect randomness is achieved at a reasonable cost. Frequently some members of the population are less accessible than others. For example, a list of households that constitutes the population is prepared and a means is devised to select a random sample from the list. Often it proves to be difficult to get the desired information from the homes selected—addresses of residents do change from time to time, and some of the residents may be out when the researcher calls, which makes expensive callbacks necessary. Perfect randomness is not often achieved in marketing research where people are involved, and researchers report that reaching 80 to 85 percent of those selected is a good average. It should be noted, however, that the results of the sample cannot be extended to the population from which it came unless random selection is used at some point in the selection of the sample.

Where we wish to evaluate the accuracy of our findings in research, a *probability sample* may be drawn. In such a sample the probability of each unit being selected is known and is positive for every element in the population. Where there is any element of personal judgment used in selecting sampling units, the sample would not be a probability sample.

In most market research projects the standards of perfection described above are not reached, but are only approached. There are an infinite number of situations, however, where effective results can be obtained, even though that portion of a total population that is relevant to the solution of a marketing problem is singled out and sampled with less than perfect randomness. A concept test, for example, may use the services of some consumers who are selected as a result of the personal judgment of the researcher. They may live in the general vicinity of a central city, even though the population to be served is the whole United States. However, this simple sampling technique may bring many decisions into a range of predictability at very little cost.

A significant factor in determining the size of the sample is the judgment as to whether or not a small difference in accuracy would influence a decision. A company that wishes to change a package might interview selected persons at locations where the product is sold. A package is something that can be talked about in a group—its preferences can be socialized. On the other hand, if Procter and Gamble wish to change the flavor of Crest toothpaste, a large and carefully chosen sample would appear to be desirable. Since flavor is purely an individual matter and cannot be socialized and since every segment of the population uses toothpaste, a slight change in the flavor might jeopardize a very profitable market. Thus, the size and care with which the sample is selected ranges from the information that the executive already has in mind to a sample that includes the whole population and is, to the extent possible, based on a random selection.

Objectivity and Involvement

A survey is usually, though not always, the result of a questionnaire or an interview. Both take different forms to suit the occasion. The questionnaire must be objective; and the questions must mean the same thing to all respondents for poor communication at this point can distort results. It is important that the men conducting the research have good channels for communicating with management. This requirement is desirable (1) so that the questions will be of maximum relevance to management's strategy, and (2) so that the questions and analysis will be expressed in a management context. Of significance, too, is the fact that when researchers are closely involved with management, even participating to some extent in management, they are able to see many more areas that can be researched effectively.

QUESTIONS AND ANALYTICAL PROBLEMS

1. Define marketing research.

2. State what you believe to be the best method for determining each of the following: (a) market area; (b) consumer preference among several brands of a similar product; (c) effectiveness of a company's advertising; and (d) attitude of consumers in your market area to one of your products; to your company.

3. What factors must be considered in determining a store location?

4. What is qualitative data?

5. Define clearly and find an example of a concept test for a proposed new product.

6. What is a test market? What should be the features of a test market for a given product?

7. What are some of the limitations on test market results as an accurate predictor of success for a new product?

8. For what kinds of measurements in marketing could you use "projective techniques"?

9. Define probability sampling. What are some of the uses of probability sampling in marketing research?

Case 13-1 • SPERRY'S STORE

Professor Done was confronted with a problem that was fraught with genuine interest and challenge. Frank Sperry, from Sperry's downtown store, was deeply concerned because during the last three months his sales dropped from $12,000 weekly to $6,000. The latter figure was significantly below his break-even point and, unless some solutions were discovered soon, he would be forced to close his store. He was unable to determine the reason for the rapid decrease in sales.

Mr. Sperry opened his store on the eastern periphery of the business district of the city with a population of approximately 40,000. His store was located between the public library and a popular bakery. It was a small store with only about 8,000 square feet of selling space. He featured fine meats which were reasonably priced. In order to attract trade that came from the various residential areas of the city, he carried some specialty items which were not carried by outlying supermarkets. His was one of the few stores that carried S & H Green stamps. He had ample parking space; and with sales of $650,000 a year for several years, he felt that his trade was well established. Though he was unable to account for the decline in his business, the possible reasons he gave were as follows.

Two new stores had opened in the city during the last year. One was a part of a small shopping center, although the store itself was designed to do a volume between $1.5 and $2 million. The other store was a smaller store about the size of his own, located adjacent to many of the school dormitories of a local university. Although he expected to lose some business to these stores, he did not feel that it would have such a great effect. His clientele had never included many students.

Another possibility was the fact that he had stopped carrying S & H trading stamps and had reduced his prices. During the last year, nearly all the food stores in the city had adopted a locally-promoted stamp called Gold Strike. His patrons then showed less interest in stamps. Often they complained at the nuisance of saving them, and many of them did not bother to pick them up. He even made a careful survey of his patrons, and nearly all of them indicated that they would prefer lower prices to stamps. He was beside himself with anxiety and asked Professor Done to assist him.

● What steps should Professor Done take to find the trouble? What specific information might be helpful, and how would it be obtained?

Case 13-2 ● MERCER FOOD PRODUCTS LIMITED [10]

Mercer Food Products Limited, a small family-owned firm, carried on business in three related areas: importing raw nuts and reselling them to processors and retailers, processing peanuts into peanut butter, and roasting and packaging a wide range of raw nuts for sale in grocery, candy, and confectionery outlets. Mr. Philip Mercer, the company's president, and Mr. Arnold Sayre, the marketing director, were looking for further ways to increase the profit contribution from their packaged nut lines.

The Company

Mercer Food Products Limited had been in business since 1926 when David Mercer began importing and selling raw nuts in Canada. From the time of its founding until 1955 when David Mercer died, the major source of profits for the firm had been the importing activity he conducted. A limited amount of processing, such as peanut roasting, was also carried on; and the firm had a small peanut butter business from its "Bamby" brand, which it manufactured and sold through brokers to the grocery trade in the Toronto-Hamilton area. In 1934 the company began to manufacture peanut butter for a Toronto food chain under the chain's private brand name.

Philip L. Mercer, who succeeded his father as President and General Manager in 1955, stated that, "Dad had the instinct of a trader, and the wide oscillations in prices in nutmeat markets provided him with an opportunity to use his skills to great advantage. When he saw an opportunity to buy at a good price, he would do so; and when he felt commodity prices were too high, he would stay out of the market."

Under Philip Mercer's direction, the company gradually reduced its trading operations and slowly began to place more emphasis on its manufacturing-based business. Mr. Mercer explained this change by saying, "I just didn't have the temperament to continue as my father had done. I tried, but I couldn't do it. You've got to have a 'feel' for that kind of thing. I wanted to build up a consumer franchise and have a business with more continuity to it. The transition has been painfully slow, however, and I know we did better then than we're doing now."

Mercer's production facilities, warehouse, and offices were all located in a new single story building in Scarborough, a suburb of Toronto. These facilities had been occupied since Mercer became the first tenant in a new industrial park.

Products

Approximately 50 percent of company sales were derived from peanut butter, with two thirds of this being lower-margin, private-label business. Mercer's "Bamby" brand had doubled its sales volume in the previous three years, while their sales of private brand peanut butter had more than tripled in the same time.

The company's nut business came from four lines: "Bamby" (a complete line of nuts in the intermediate price range); "Chieftain" (a less complete line which was lower

---

[10] Copyright, 1962, University of Western Ontario. The information contained herein has been collected for the sole purpose of providing material for classroom discussion at the School of Business Administration. Any use or duplication of material in the case is prohibited except with the written consent of the School.

in price than comparable "Bamby" items); "Eldorado" (a line of gourmet nuts which were more costly to manufacture and were retailed only through gourmet food stores and gourmet food departments of supermarkets); and "Par-tee" (a line of packaged salted nuts sold on counter racks in small grocery and confectionery stores). The nut line had contributed about one fifth of the company's sales for the last five years.

The balance of company sales, which had declined from 45 percent to 25 percent of Mercer's volume over the past three years, came from its trading activities.

Exhibits 1 and 2 show income and balance sheet figures for Mercer Food Products Limited.

The president estimated that peanut butter sales and nut sales each contributed about the same dollar operating profit to the firm; and he said that since 1973 the dollar contribution from nut sales had risen, and the contribution from peanut butter had fallen. Importing operations provided the balance of profit and losses.

Because of his desire to bring more continuity into the company's operations, Philip Mercer had given great emphasis to increasing peanut butter sales since he assumed the presidency. He had been further encouraged after Robert Steiner, who was in charge of research and engineering, had developed a process for manufacturing peanut butter in which the oil would not separate and rise to the top. Mercer's rivals had been selling such a product for some time, but Steiner's work enabled Mercer to compete with a product which company executives considered to be as good as any then available on the market.

After they had heavily advertised "Bamby" peanut butter in southern Ontario without much apparent success, Mr. Mercer and Mr. Sayre decided that they could not profitably challenge the major brands and that instead the company should be more aggressive in its private label peanut butter business; much of their time had since been spent on pursuing this objective.

Mr. Mercer stated that the nut business had in common with peanut butter only its raw material sources; in other ways he felt the two were quite different. Because there were only one or two well-known brand names of nuts, there was less well-entrenched competition to fight; however, Mr. Mercer stated that his absence of well-known brands also meant to him that his firm could not develop any extensive private-label business in nuts. He said, "There is no Canada Packers or Procter and Gamble in the nut business to hold up a nice umbrella under which private brands can find a place. This also means, of course, that you don't have quite as many trips to the woodshed with the chain grocer where he hauls out not a rubber hose but a lead pipe and seeks lower prices on what you're making for him when he gets into a competitive squeeze."

A further point of difference between nuts and peanut butter as Mr. Mercer saw it was in their distribution patterns. "As far as I know," he said, "peanut butter has never been successfully sold outside a food store." In contrast with this he felt that a wider range of retail outlets were appropriate places to sell nuts.

Most of Mercer's sales were handled by food brokers who worked on a commission of from 1 percent to 10 percent, although some of the larger buyers of private-label peanut butter were sold directly by either Mr. Mercer or Mr. Sayre. Typically, a broker would get 5 percent for a new account for private-label peanut butter; and after sales to the new customer had reached $15,000, his commission would be reduced to 1 percent on all sales thereafter. All nuts with the exception of the "Eldorado" line earned brokers a 5 percent commission; brokers who handled "Eldorado" were given 10 percent commissions.

Mercer's brokers were, with two exceptions, located in southern Ontario and Quebec; outside this region there was a candy and tobacco broker in Vancouver and a food broker who dealt with a large food chain in Winnipeg. Foley's Limited, a Toronto

Exhibit 1
PROFIT AND LOSS FOR YEAR ENDING DECEMBER 31

	Three years ago	Two years ago	Last year
Sales	$1,451,800	$1,430,100	$1,705,900
Gross profit	240,100	226,000	203,000
Selling expenses	$ 137,200	$ 105,000	$ 116,900
Administrative expenses............	68,600	82,600	105,000
Operating income ..	$ 34,300	$ 38,400	$ (18,900)

Exhibit 2
BALANCE SHEET AS OF DECEMBER 31

	Three years ago	Two years ago	Last year
Current assets			
Cash.......................	$ 15,400	$ 1,400	$ 2,100
Accounts receivable	85,400	82,600	146,300
Inventories	469,600	331,100*	315,000
Total	$570,400	$451,100	$463,400
Fixed assets	122,500	128,100	287,700**
Other assets	9,100	63,000	14,000
	$702,000	$606,200	$765,100
Current liabilities			
Accounts payable	$ 58,100	$100,800	$140,700
Notes payable	174,500	70,000	157,500
Accrued taxes and wages	10,500	21,700	16,100
Total	$243,100	$192,500	$314,300
Long-term debt			
Notes payable	$ 58,500	—	$105,700
Preferred stock	35,000	$ 35,000	—
Common stock	14,000	14,000	14,000
Retained earnings	351,400	364,700	331,100
Total liabilities	$702,000	$606,200	$765,100

* A new system of inventory record keeping and production scheduling enabled the company to substantially reduce its inventories of raw materials.
** The company acquired new production equipment with book value of $157,000.

candy and tobacco jobber, was the only other broker of that type who carried Mercer's products.

Marketing Strategy

As a result of the apparent lack of opportunity to develop a private label nut business, Mr. Sayre was seeking ways by which Mercer could increase sales and profits from their own brands of nuts. He realized that the largest potential market lay in the supermarket field, but he also knew that he and his brokers had been unsuccessful in getting permanent distribution in this area because the company was presently unable to finance an advertising program which would be large enough to please the supermarket and chain store buyers. He was, therefore, seeking alternative opportunities which would provide short-run gains as well as get the company into a position which would eventually enable it to carry on a more elaborate program and hopefully gain acceptance of Mercer's products by independent and chain supermarkets.

One proposal by which Mr. Sayre thought the company might be able to accomplish this objective had come to him in late May, in the form of an offer from Craig Foley, Sr., the President of Foley's Limited, to give the Mercer nut lines Canada-wide distribution through candy and tobacco brokers to cigar stores, restaurants, corner grocers, etc.

Mr. Foley's offer was initially attractive to Mr. Sayre because, if it succeeded, it would give the Mercer nut lines distribution all across Canada and in a type of outlet which generally did not carry Mercer products even in Southern Ontario and Quebec. Mr. Foley, who was 67 years of age, had been a broker for Mercer for six months, during which time he had given the "Bamby," 'Chieftain," and "Par-tee" nut lines wide distribution in candy and tobacco outlets in metropolitan Toronto. Mr. Sayre stated that Foley was the only broker they had who had done a satisfactory job with these kinds of outlets and that Foley-Mercer relations had always been good.

Foley had never operated outside the Toronto-Windsor area, but Mr. Sayre suspected that he wanted to do so now in order to enlarge his business and be able to "pass on a nice inheritance to his son, Craig, Jr., who is now being groomed to succeed his father." Mr. Sayre had never met Craig, Jr., but the Mercer salesman who dealt with the Foley's had told Mr. Sayre that he was confident in the younger man's ability to take over from his father.

Mr. Foley stated that he could induce many local and regional candy and tobacco jobbers to sell Mercer nuts. His proposal was that he would begin calling on and soliciting the business of some of the people he knew from across Canada while he attended the Food Brokers Association of Canada convention in Banff in early August. Following this he felt he could build on his previous contacts in, and knowledge of, the trade and eventually become what Mr. Sayre called a "master broker" for Mercer. Mr. Sayre expected that if Foley were to be successful with the Mercer line he would want to add others in order to build up even more business. For his services Foley would receive an overriding 2 percent commission on all sales made by the brokers he contacted, while the firms Foley worked with would receive the usual 5 percent commission. Terms to the final buyer would be 2/10, net 30, and Mercer would be able to refuse to accept any order.

As he evaluated Foley's offer, Mr. Sayre recalled that two years before, while Mercer was introducing their "Eldorado" line of gourmet nuts, they had been approached by a gourmet food broker in Ottawa with whom they had not previously done business who offered to build them a national brokerage system for "Eldorado." At the time this broker's business was restricted to the Ottawa-Montreal area, but he felt he could build up a business which would satisfy Mercer's wishes. Mr. Sayre and Mr. Mercer had turned down the proposal, for they felt that the Ottawa firm could not handle the assignment. Instead they went ahead with their previous plan to distribute "Eldorado" on their own and build sales by means of trade advertising and sampling by mail. As a result the "Eldorado" line was handled for Mercer only by brokers who specialized in gourmet foods and, thus, could not be sold by Foley.

Mr. Sayre knew that there were other firms who called themselves national candy and tobacco jobbers, but he expected that they would be much like Mr. Foley or the

Ottawa broker in that they had national aspirations but only local or regional activities. He also had speculated on his own ability to do with "Bamby," "Chieftain," and "Par-tee" nuts what he had been slowly doing with "Eldorado." He wondered if he could use trade advertising and mail samples to build up nut sales to the candy and tobacco trade, thus saving the 2 percent commission Foley wanted and also retaining more control over the distribution of these products. Mr. Sayre further wondered if there might be some other way of compensating Foley. He felt that since Mercer had to assume all the credit risks, and since Foley might some day lose interest in the Mercer line for any number of reasons, the 2 percent commission might not be advisable.

As of late June, while he was thinking about selling nuts to the candy and tobacco trade, Mr. Sayre had no idea what volume of business he could expect to get from Foley, but he said that plant capacity was approximately double the present output.

• Make recommmendations which you think would result in an optimum increase in the profit contribution of the company's packaged nut lines.

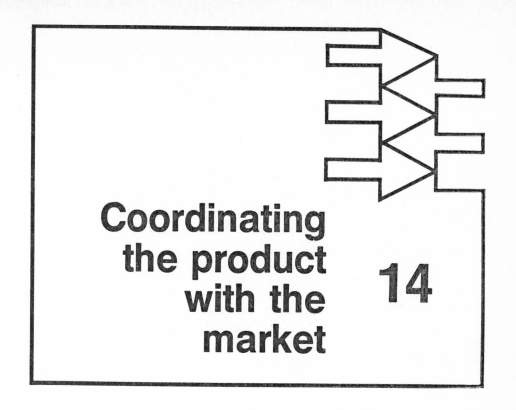

Coordinating the product with the market

14

Where the ultimate success of a product or a service depends upon the voluntary choice of the consumer, management's task is to forecast and to have available the products or services to satisfy these choices. The sales forecast is used to design an administrative program that succeeds in having the right amount of products available at the time needed. To have too great a stock or to have products that are not demanded means that capital and space are dormant when they might otherwise be productive. Having too much stock on hand also means that merchandise may lose its value either by physical deterioration or by obsolescence. When this happens, the products will be completely wasted or sold at a loss. On the other hand, if the forecast underestimates demand and there is not enough merchandise to satisfy requests, sales and resulting profits are lost and customers become disgruntled at the company's mismanagement. This coordinating function designed to assure the availability of the right product at the right time and place is described as *merchandising*.

THE ROLE OF MERCHANDISING

Success in meeting the product availability challenge is at the very heart of marketing and applies at every level of the product flow. This marketing flow consists of a channel with a series of systematized inventory storage points to supply anticipated needs. At each one of these points decisions as to what, how much, and when to make or to buy specific products are vital issues affecting a company's growth and profitability. Examples of success or failure at different levels of the market will be helpful in visualizing the reality of this problem.

Applicability of Merchandising at All Market Levels

At the primary market level the farm surplus problem, over several decades, exemplified a failure to coordinate product availability with market needs. The tremendous costs of these surpluses to the nation's taxpayers provided evidence of the undesirable results of the failure to coordinate product availability with market demands in agriculture.

At the manufacturer's level 80 percent of the new food products that are offered on the market fail. In these instances the problem is not only how much to make or buy but also what to make.

A study by Theodore L. Angelus of 75 new products that failed determined that the major reason for new product failure was a lack of significant difference from existing products that served the purpose.[1] Other reasons for failure were: poor product positioning, bad timing, poor product performance, and wrong product for the company.

Examples were:

Insignificant product differences
1. Hunt's flavored ketchups (pizza, hickory) not sufficiently different from regular ketchup.
2. Easy-Off Household Cleaner. The aerosol foam cleaner was not, to consumers, significantly easier or better than liquids such as Formula 409.

Poor product positioning
Revlon Super Natural Hairspray. To consumers super equals more holding power; natural means less holding power. The consumers did not know what the product represented.

Bad timing
In 1968 seventeen new brands of household cleaners entered the market; Easy-Off, Whistle, Power-On, and others failed.

Poor product performance
General Foods cereals with freeze-dried fruit failed because the cereal became soggy before the fruit became soft enough to eat.

Wrong product for the company
1. Even giant Procter & Gamble failed twice trying to get a large share of the hairspray market (Hidden Magic and Winterset/Summerset).
2. Colgate, after several tries, has not made a success of food products.

At the retail level the basic problem is the same, although the administrative challenge is somewhat different. In the case of the farmer and the manufacturer, the problem is what to produce or what to make; but the retailer must determine

---

[1] Theodore L. Angelus, "Why Do Most New Products Fail?", *Advertising Age* (March 24, 1969), pp. 85-86.

what, when, and how much to buy. Failures in retailing are as common and just as costly. A study conducted by International Business Machines indicates that every dollar's worth of merchandise which the average retail store sells, sales of 98 cents are lost, because the stores do not have the merchandise available that customers want. One continuing study indicates that for medium sized and small distributors and for small sized retailers, about 35 percent of the items accounts for over 90 percent of the profits, while approximately 20 percent of the stock in most stores should not be on the shelves because it is not wanted by customers.[2]

The extent to which a condition of unbalance exists was made evident in a survey of eight typical retail stores that were competitors in dry goods lines (see Exhibit 14-1). Three of them were nationally known chain stores. Surveyors shopped these stores for items that should have been a regular part of their stock. For 43 percent of the requests, the specific item was not in stock. Even the store with the best score was out of stock on 25 percent of the items. One store in the group was out of stock on 63 percent of the requests. The results of the survey were presented to the managers, and each agreed that the items requested from his store should have been a part of the stock.

Marketing activities should impel people to buy. Certainly the coordination, or adjustment process possesses such quality. To have available the exact goods that the customer wants, when and where he wants them, decreases sales

Exhibit 14-1

OUT-OF-STOCK CONDITIONS IN EIGHT RETAIL STORES

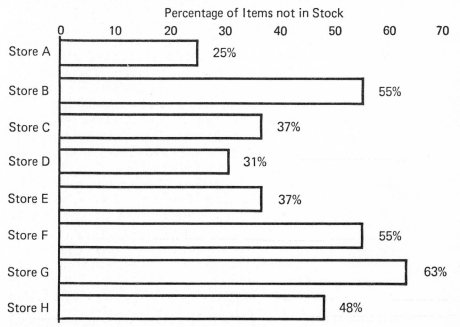

Percentage of Items not in Stock

Store A — 25%
Store B — 55%
Store C — 37%
Store D — 31%
Store E — 37%
Store F — 55%
Store G — 63%
Store H — 48%

[2] Continuing and unpublished study by Lloyd C. Pierce, codirector, University of Utah Small Business Management Development Program.

resistance and encourages the forward movement of goods. On the other hand, failure to have the right goods sets up sales resistance. No merchant, however, expects this coordination process alone to move the goods. He is aware of the fact that price is an equally important factor which influences the consumer to buy or not to buy. Even when the product is attractive and the price is fair, some selling or promotion may be a necessary ingredient in triggering the sale. Thus, we have all the elements of the marketing mix operating together as one. Price, promotion, and place must be integrated into the program with the product offering to achieve maximum sales.

Definitions of Merchandising

The Committee on Definitions of the American Marketing Association defines *merchandising* as "the planning and supervision involved in marketing the particular merchandise or service at the places, times, and prices, and in the quantities which will best serve to realize the marketing objectives of the business."[3] The word "merchandising" has had so many and varied meanings that this one has not been readily accepted, but the concept of coordination of demand and supply is one of the most vital in successful market management. The term merchandising will be used to describe the planning and administration necessary to achieve an optimum coordination of product availability with current demand.

Relationship of Buying to Merchandising

Is buying synonymous with or a subordinate part of merchandising? These two terms are often used together. Occasionally they are used as synonyms. Certainly, as merchandising is described, buying is an essential ingredient. In retailing or wholesaling, the decisions of what and how much to buy are usually made by buyers who frequently decide sources from which merchandise will be purchased. Such execution of the immediate purchases, however, is not all there is to the coordinating process. The buyer in a retail establishment usually operates within the range of maximum and minimum stock allowances. Buyers are also advised of a price range. On the other hand, the merchandising function includes the formulation of policies to guide the buyer. Policy makers set the maximum and minimum stock figures and the price ranges.

Department stores separate the functions of buyer and merchandise manager. The latter coordinates the activities of the buyers. He does no buying. Frequently he is aided by divisional merchandise managers. Thus, we see the buying function as one activity in the execution of the merchandising plan. Behind the act of buying, however, research into product demand, formulation of policies, coordinating and altering policies are all parts of merchandising and serve as guides to the buyer.

Buying and merchandising can be more clearly differentiated in the field of manufacturing. The merchandising responsibility here is in making a product line

---

[3] Committee on Definitions, *Marketing Definitions* (Chicago: American Marketing Association, 1960), p. 17.

that will satisfy and stimulate a demand. This is in contrast to retailing and wholesaling, where the task is to buy the products. In both cases the coordination of demand and supply are essential. It is true that there are buyers in the manufacturing business. Yet the purchases here are composed of raw materials, fabricated parts, or other goods that are not products for resale. Thus, we see buying as a supporting and subordinate function included in the merchandising program. The term is not synonymous with merchandising. Merchandising is broader and includes the buying operation.

Ingredients To Be Coordinated

It may help us to see why merchandising should have a meaning distinct from promotion if each of the fundamental elements of its components is viewed in relief. First, the product itself must be considered. To what degree is it desired by the buying public? How does it compare with new products that competition is offering? What degree of preferences do past responses indicate? Is it holding its own in the race with existing products on the market? Thus, the whole question of product desirability must be considered.

Then, in view of product desirability, what amount should be purchased or made? This decision must be made by manufacturers, such as Remington Rand and International Business Machines, when they contemplate a year's production schedule. It applies to typewriters as well as to electronic data processing machines. The same problem confronts the retailers who sell these products to the public. The intensity of desire for the product and the number or volume required to satisfy the desire are strategic factors. They must be appraised and coordinated to obtain an accurate projection of the number to make or buy.

The third ingredient is time and place. IBM must have an adequate number of typewriters in Los Angeles, or within a few days of Los Angeles, if it is to realize the sales potential which exists in that area. The market for these typewriters in the Los Angeles area cannot be projected perfectly. Time is required if they are to be shipped in. Yet a decision must be made as to how many should be available at specific times in that area; sales may be lost if the wrong decision is made. Thus, the problem of product adjustment involves the following: first, the desirability of the product itself; second, the amount of the product required for the market; third, the time period over which the demand will be expressed; and fourth, the administrative planning and activity to meet the demand at the appointed place. There is ample evidence supporting a need for emphasis of this function in view of the present failures to achieve satisfactory performance.

Coordination of product offerings with current demand, or merchandising, provides a quality of availability which is essential in the movement of the products toward their ultimate market. This function of coordination is nothing more or less than management's market forecasts successfully administered into sales. In accomplishing this administrative task, the buyer's intuition, unaided judgment, or memory are not enough. A method or a system and carefully formulated policy as aids to judgment are essential. By studying the merchandising problems at each of the institutional levels—primary producer, manufacturer, wholesaler, and retailer—the nature of management's challenge in merchandising will be more clearly understood.

THE PRIMARY PRODUCER'S MERCHANDISING PROBLEMS

Product coordination can be a difficult problem for primary producers. Lack of proper balance of output with demand for products of mines, forests, fisheries, and the problem of surpluses from farms are evidences of failures to coordinate supply with demand.

Extractive Industries

Within limits, the rate of production in mines can be controlled by management decisions. Supply of and the demand for the product are such that predictability of both factors with a minimum factor of error is possible. Although producing and consuming firms are comparatively few, they are competitive. They supply as much as the market demands at prevailing prices, and the supply of these products has a tendency to be highly elastic. As demand pushes the price to higher levels, the volume produced increases greatly.

Mine operators do not have the powers of adjustment by innovation possessed by the manufacturer. Kennecott Copper Company, in its smelting processes, may change the form or shape of its product to make it more convenient to industrial uses; but it cannot invent a new item that will give the company a definite advantage over competition and make other products obsolete. Its customers, General Electric and Westinghouse, introduce changes in the models of their appliances almost annually to increase the demand for their product, but such a course is not open to Kennecott. The area of management activity available to this company is confined to determining how much can be sold, finding a buyer, and reducing unit costs.

The adjustment of the supply of timber to demand is a longrun problem. Reforestation and the development of new timberland are activities performed now to meet a demand that will exist years hence. The nature of this business is such that the coordination of supply with demand extends over a period of years. Furthermore, decisions and policies often transcend the interest and the initiative of the firm and become a matter of public policy. The Department of Interior is the administrative body representing the government that manages a program of husbanding much of the supply of timber.

The government is also vitally concerned with this entire area of raw materials supply from the standpoint of national defense. In the event of a war, strategic materials are essential. The government has entered into the control of such resources. Supplies and reserves are recorded and analyzed. Stockpiling and the development of materials are guided by the knowledge of developing demands and calculated supplies. When the supplies are not available to meet known future demands, research for new products is encouraged.

Coordination of Supply and Demand in Agriculture

In agriculture the problem is different. Farms in the United States number approximately 2.8 million. Farms are getting larger. Although they are becoming more like a business in operation, there are still problems of coordinating the immediate supply with the immediate demand. Each farmer is limited to a few crops. The uses to which these crops are applied are also limited. For example, southern farmers cannot drastically change their basic pattern of production from cotton and tobacco. Those in the Midwest have little that can be planted but wheat and corn. General Motors can develop a new model that will make the old models obsolete and thus create a market, but farmers are not in a position to influence either the supply or the demand in this manner. Furthermore, there are so many farmers that the decision of one farmer has little influence on either the supply or the demand.

The area in which the farmer can adjust his product to meet a current demand is very narrow. If we take an overall and practical view of the farm problem, it is very closely related to a merchandising failure. Simply stated, it is evidence of a failure in coordinating the immediate supply with the immediate demand.

THE MANUFACTURER'S MERCHANDISING PROBLEMS

Two principal areas confront manufacturers in their merchandising problems. The first is adjusting the flow of currently used products to meet the demand. The second is in developing new products.

Established Products

Two difficulties are present in merchandising established products. First, there is the danger of losing sales because of not having a sufficient supply in stock or of becoming overstocked in terms of a falling demand and being forced to take markdowns. The second problem, which is closely related to the first, is the danger of a product losing its market position. Before corrective action can be taken, however, management must know how serious the trouble is and the specific reason for the maladjustment. We recall the example of the large pipe company that was overstocked with obsolete pipe valued at $100,000. Until an inventory was taken of the stock, the management was not even aware of this waste. When the inventory was computed, corrective action was taken by cutting down on the production of slow-moving items with which the firm was overstocked and by cutting out those products for which there was no demand.

Inventory Control. Stock-control programs can avoid such costly experiences and frequently reduce capital requirements for a desirable inventory level. The following is an illustration of a simple inventory control method employed by a medium size distributor. Note that this simple system incorporates all the elements required to assure the proper item at the right place, time, price, and quantity.

Step 1: Prepare a card for each item (there were approximately 700 items).

$$\text{Item } \#UC \times \text{Usage} = UV$$

Item #UC × Usage   = UV
(unit cost)   (number of sales   (unit value)
              of the item in
              the past year)

$$UC \times \text{Usage} = UV$$
$$\text{Item } \#1234 \; 2.00 \times 50 = \$100$$
$$\text{Item } \#4321 \; 5.00 \times \; 0 = \;\;\; 0$$

Step 2: File all cards in a box in order according to UV. Highest unit value card first and on down to 0 unit value cards.

Step 3: Total the unit value shown on all cards.

Step 4: Start with the highest unit value card and add unit values shown on cards until 90 percent of total unit value is determined. In this example that was 35 percent of the items carried.

Step 5: Count all 0 unit value items. That was, in this company, 20 percent of all items carried. These items were disposed of.

The distributor now keeps careful watch on his inventory to discern any shifts in demand, examines new items for possible inclusion in inventory, and has a program to dispose of 0 value items.

A firm with several thousand items must have a more elaborate system, very likely computerized, but the basic ideas are the same. A commonly used method is that installed by a large shoe machinery company that had to keep thousands of parts available for both repair and manufacture. In this method an established figure for stock minimums and maximums on each item serves the purpose of control. Each time a withdrawal is made, the number of parts withdrawn is entered on the record, and the balance is recorded. When the minimum is reached, enough stock remains to provide for a production period and a safety factor in case of trouble. A notice of this stock condition is returned to the control office whenever minimum stock conditions are recorded. The return of the record is the signal to replenish the stock to the maximum again. At the end of a period, the total sales figures yield the rate of sale and become the basis for a production schedule. The maximum and the minimum stock figures can be revised if tolerances have been narrow or if stock has been greater or less than needed.

Another example in a different area also reveals the nature of the merchandising problem and how to meet it. It is exemplified by a large food manufacturing company. The problem here was different because the product had an element of perishability as did the products from which it was made.

Therefore, the company had to watch its stock carefully. The unknown factor with which the company had to contend was the amount purchased by the ultimate consumer. The inventory reserve had to be kept at a minimum and never was allowed to become greater than a two-week supply. Sales of the company were approximately $40 million a month, or $500 million annually.

The company went directly to the consumer level to get its coordinating information. The steps used were: District sales managers were required to submit projected budgets of sales three months in advance. One month later each manager reviewed his report, noted changed conditions, and then reviewed it with his division manager. Necessary revisions were made as a result of this final discussion. One month before shipment was due the division manager compiled his reports with last-minute revisions and sent them to the central office. The central office then made a master budget and assigned the production to plants throughout the nation. Raw material orders were placed and production was effected to meet the demand as estimated. Differences could be absorbed by the inventory, which was controlled on a first-in, first-out basis. Naturally, a district manager who was constantly off on his estimates would be given help. However, seldom did such action become necessary.

In other instances the manufacturer's product is not perishable, and a significant portion is sold to retail stores through wholesalers. Since the product is not perishable, it can remain on the shelves and in the warehouses of retail and wholesale firms. Such an arrangement makes it very difficult, however, for the manufacturer to control production so that it coordinates with consumer demand. After subscribing to a store audit service, one manufacturer of drug and cosmetic items discovered that there was a six-month lag between the time when consumer sales at the retail stores began declining and the time his warehouse sales reflected this decrease.[4] For example, warehouse sales increased through the period January to December, but consumer sales fell off sharply in June. Wholesalers and retailers continued to order and fill their shelves throughout the year since the product had experienced a rapid growth during the previous months. After a period, wholesalers and retailers found their shelves full of a product that was not selling. Had the manufacturer been informed of the slow-down in sales six months earlier, he could have corrected the difficulty by changing the product, by price adjustment, or by a selling appeal, whichever the situation required.

Influence of the Computer.[5] The essence of merchandising as related to established products is time. If the manufacturer could know exactly what

---

[4] The best known store audit service is that provided by A. C. Nielsen. In providing this service Nielsen selects a sample of stores and during specific periods makes a record of the stock on hand of the item being studied at the beginning of the period in each of these stores. The merchandise purchased and placed in stock during the period and the amount in stock at the end of the period are then used to compute a specific sales figure.

[5] An excellent description of the impact of the computer on marketing is presented in "Computers Begin to Solve the Marketing Puzzle," Business Week (April 17, 1965), pp. 114-138. Even though ten years old, the article presents the topic well.

product the consumer wanted at a given moment in time and had the capacity to supply it immediately, there would be no merchandising problem. The shorter the time that exists between the decision to produce and buy and the expression of customer choice, the smaller the risk. Such a shortening in time decreases the amount of merchandise that needs to be impounded at storage and reservoir points and reduces the incidence of loss on merchandising failures.

The entrance of the computer into the scene has brought a veritable revolution in reducing the time required to get feedback on sales at different market levels. Fast transmission of sales data broken down by unit sales, margin, location, and time is made possible by the systems being installed in certain retail outlets. The cash register is replaced by a small computer terminal which translates and relays the information to a data processing center as the sales are rung up by the checkout stand operator.

Owens-Illinois is one company among hundreds that have automated the merchandise system into a computer program at the manufacturer and distributor levels. The Owens-Illinois headquarters in Toledo, the processing headquarters, is connected by wire to 100 different sales and manufacturing headquarters. When an order comes in, the computer system determines if the product ordered is in stock (and its location) and sends a release and a shipping order for the plant to ship it. A most significant part of this transaction is being able to supply the merchandise to the customer in 35 hours instead of taking a period of several weeks; in addition, the information is made available at every point in the reservoir or storage system.[6] Printouts from the computer can inform every person responsible for storage or production what stock conditions are at a moment's notice. If management wished to do so and had the production-marketing flow sufficiently routinized, the computerized system could order the production department to order the new materials for a production cycle that would replenish stock by the amount of the sale. A part of this same computer printout can compile the rate of sale. Computers make it possible to improve the quality of the merchandise forecast by enabling management to include many more market influences in the sales forecast.

Corrective Action. The merchandise control system, whether automated or traditional, is for one purpose alone. That purpose is to inform the management of what is happening to the merchandise flow so that proper action may be taken to keep it flowing at an optimum rate. When sales of a well-established product increase or decrease, a coordinate increase or decrease in production may be all that is required. When the decrease is chronic and the product is a significant part of the company line, however, more analysis may be required. The product may need revising or replacing. It may be that a new advertising slant, a new package, or an entirely revised sales program may be required. The additional analysis may require market research that will reveal why the product is slipping or which of the competitors has the market and why. Corrective action is usually possible once the facts are known. Any system of control adopted should enable management to avoid delays and point to the problem areas.

---

[6] Ibid., p. 115.

New Products

One of the first requirements of building a successful new product program is to accept as reality the permanence of the new product trend. The emphasis given this subject by industry during the last decade is consistent with the progressive changes that have characterized every significant field where new knowledge and administrative skills have been factors. There has been as much new knowledge accumulated since World War II as was accumulated throughout all ages preceding this period. Ninety percent of all the scientists that have ever lived are functioning today. The rate of change itself is accelerating.

Organizing for New Products. There is no place where the marketing concept, which implies unity and interaction of all divisions of the business, has more impact on the business organization than in the area of new products. Programs for established products can often be routinized. Their continued sale and delivery may require a minimum of interaction between the different specialized divisions. However, in the instance of new products, there must be constant interaction and free communication between specialized divisions. The divisions which are most important in developing a successful new product are marketing, technical research, and production. It is inconceivable that technical research could turn out a product that meets optimum standards in market desirability and production feasibility without active collaboration and feedback from marketing and production. It is also quite likely that marketing and production could supply information which would reduce significantly the amount of research necessary by making strategic information available. Likewise, marketing must be completely aware of the needs and limitations of technical research and production. In other words, the amount of interaction and interdepartmental communication necessary to bring all relevant data into focus at the time and place of significant action-taking requires these specialized areas to operate almost as a single division.

An organization might take many forms to achieve such a unity of action. First, there may be no formal new product organization at all. Interaction may take place entirely on an informal basis. When a positive and communicating attitude prevails among staff members, communication on this subject may be quite satisfactory. Second, there may be a new product team composed of men from each of the strategic areas who meet to discuss and execute new product strategy. Third, there may be a new product committee which synthesizes data and serves as a helpful informational and motivational catalyst to the operating divisions. Fourth, there may be a new product development department with men specializing in each of the vital areas to serve as liaison with the area of his specialization. Although the incidence of failure in new product ventures is great, it could be decreased significantly by an organization for new product development which is able to bring the many skills required for new product development and marketing into a complete unity of rapport and action.

Stages in the Product Life Cycle. Even before the recent trend to develop new products, marketing men have observed a tendency for new products that enter the market to mature, grow old, and die. This tendency is even more apparent today and has become a center of management concern. Exhibit 14-2 shows how the product life cycle is usually divided into four stages. First is the *development stage*. In this stage management feels its way into the market with concept tests, bench tests, and test market projects. During a part of this process the product itself may be undergoing certain changes in response to research findings. The final period in this stage takes place when the product is offered in the market with a full quota in production and a complete commitment of funds to selling and advertising. Here it is important to note that the great majority of products never get out of the development stage. Those that do enter the second stage or the period of *market growth*.

Exhibit 14-2

STAGES IN THE PRODUCT LIFE CYCLE AND PROFIT CYCLE

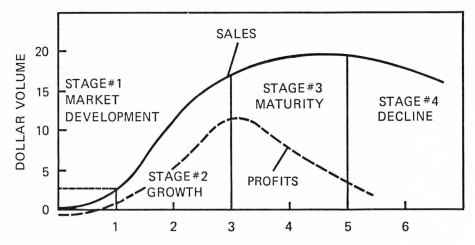

The beginning of the growth is marked by a rapid increase in the sales curve over the development curve; this is often described as the "take off." Success in the introduction of a product means that other producers will endeavor to copy features of the product and win part of the market. Since inventories have to build up with the distributors and dealers, the factory sales are greater than consumer sales. This phenomenon inflates the hopes for projected sales. Price competition enters the picture; and if the company itself does not begin to innovate, the competition will.

At the stage when most of the prospective users have adopted the product and the pipelines are full, the *maturity stage* begins. Sales level off since inventories are well stocked and the number of new users or adopters decreases. Attempts to achieve and hold brand preferences in spite of these developments involve product differentiations, many of which are very minor. Yet in most instances they are sufficient to justify an entirely new promotion campaign. In contrast with the development stage, when the manufacturer depends on the distributor and dealers to push the product, in the maturity stage the manufacturer of the product is forced to use magazine, radio, and television advertising in a campaign to gain the acceptance of the consumer. The distributor and dealer may in the maturity stage handle similar products of several manufacturers since he can no longer profit by giving attention to the brand that came on the market first. Each manufacturer must continue to court the distributors and dealers with discounts, price concessions, and special deals. But even these special efforts are often not enough to hold a company's market when all manufacturers are doing the same thing.

The *decline stage* begins when for one or more of a variety of reasons, none of which are readily obvious, the sales of the product level off or decline. Such an eventuality often means that the sales of some of the competing companies fall off, and they are forced out of the market at great costs. The companies that remain are those that have been the most successful in anticipating the changes in the marketplace. By revitalizing its program with a realistic plan relating to the product, its price, the channels through which it is sold, and its promotion, a company may preserve the market share of the product indefinitely.

Profits in the Product Life Cycle. A common profit curve is that shown by the broken line in Exhibit 14-2. During the development stage profits are less than zero because of the large expenses attendant to entering the market. Profits tend to peak near the end of the growth stage and then fall off during maturity since by definition the maturity stage is one of increasing competition. Companies increase promotional efforts and price competition becomes strong with resultant lower profits.

Anticipating the Decline with a Plan. A knowledge of the nature of the life cycle and the forces that influence it is important to the marketing manager. Such knowledge will prompt him to plan ahead with programs that prevent the losses which the decline brings. The causes of the decline which must be anticipated can be one or a combination of the following developments:

1. The novelty of the product wears off.
2. New developments render the product obsolete.
3. After the development growth campaign, the excitement wears off; and the company marketing personnel lose enthusiasm.

Company management should be aware of all these dangers and plan to offset them. The program to accomplish this objective should be explicitly set forth and given as much support as the new product program itself. Some of the possibilities for offsetting declines are:

1. Discover through product and market research new uses for the product among its present users. Such usage might become new copy themes to preserve the rest of the advertising programs. Du Pont accomplishes this goal by tinting nylon hose so that, rather than owning a few staple colors, a distinct tint becomes necessary for each different costume.
2. Stimulate a more frequent usage of the product by present users with new advertising programs. Dr. Pepper's 10:00 to 2:00 and 5 o'clock programs and Coca-Cola's "Pause That Refreshes" are illustrations.

3. Expand the market to include new users. Different age groups, social classes, or reference groups might be brought within the company's target although they were originally outside the company's original market.
4. If the company sees no prospect for the exploitation of any of the above alternatives and it is committed to a source of new motivations for the product, it might develop new uses for the product. Some differentiation in the product might be desirable to give the new users more helpful promotional materials. (Timing in all these moves is important. The company should always be aware of what is likely to happen in six months so that the plan can be ready to execute before a market decline becomes a deflating and costly experience.)

Company Policy for Development

Another policy decision a company must make is the method which it is going to use to grow or to stay abreast of the market in a changing product era. Most companies view growth as an essential characteristic of any business organization. One president remarked that "business is like riding a bicycle; either you keep moving or you fall down." While it is desirable for a company to grow by developing new products, the risks are great. Booz, Allen and Hamilton report that out of 40 ideas which appear to have promise as a new product, only one succeeds (see Exhibit 14-3).

Some companies have grown by acquiring companies with successful products. Others wait until new products cross the threshold of development and then enter their brand and profit by growth sales. Home freezers provide an example of this tendency. Deepfreeze promoted the idea, but other brands came on the scene and profited even more than the original promoter. If a company chooses this course of action, it should be aware of the necessity to organize quickly and to achieve selling and producing impact equal or superior to the company that was on the scene first. This in itself is a major management challenge that may be as difficult as developing the product from the beginning. However, some companies have the management skill and promotional resources required to imitate profitably other company's products. Also, a company may find it profitable to imitate new products as well as develop its own; for example, National Biscuit Company is a pioneer and has developed the major share of the company's new products, yet Ritz and Waverly Wafers were first offered and developed by competitors.

The implication of this discussion to merchandising is significant, since keeping a product that meets customer needs today presupposes a carefully planned and vigorously administered new product program. Such a program may involve the development of new products, copying others, or acquiring companies with successful products.

Segmenting Markets

A very important policy which a company must formulate relates to its plans for market segmentation. If the company is small, its problem will likely be simple. It can define its market precisely; and once defined, its products,

Exhibit 14-3

DECAY CURVE OF NEW PRODUCT IDEAS BY STAGE OF EVOLUTION (80 COMPANIES)

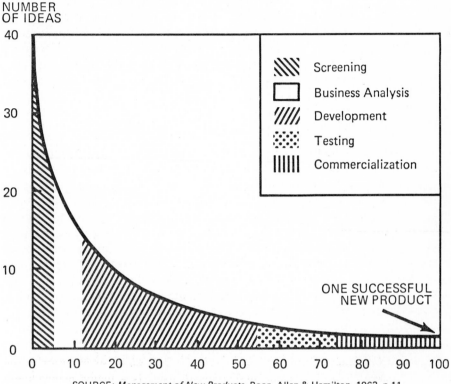

SOURCE: *Management of New Products,* Booz, Allen & Hamilton, 1963, p.11.

innovations, and promotion program can be designed to satisfy this particular market.

For a larger company the problem becomes more complex. The company's line of products may appeal to several class groups, interest groups, or age groups, or it may be a product that will satisfy the mass market. The company must decide the extent to which it is going to tailor a special product and promotion campaign to satisfy specific groups whose tastes are peculiar to their own group.

With greater production capacity and a sharpening of marketing tools, some companies now find it possible to cultivate groups that have specialized demands and tastes. For example, General Foods produced Yuban Coffee for people who may prefer a foreign type of coffee even though it is sold in competition with the company's own Maxwell House. Ford's entrance on the market with Thunderbird was an attempt to single out a group with sporty tastes and high incomes as a segment of the automobile market. The theory of the segmented market is that a company that makes a specific promotion and price appeal with a product designed to serve a certain group can be more effective and profitable than it can if it takes a generalized approach to the market. In some instances the product might not necessarily be unique, but segmentation is achieved by the use of promotion programs on the channels used.

However, it is possible to go too fast and too far with segmentation. For example, even though the Thunderbird started as a high-priced car for people with a high income and a flair for a sporty car, the market has broadened to include a wider range of the population. Also, the Mustang, in spite of its sporty styling and its price appeal to economy and youth, stimulated desire in the entire market with some success. Both cars sold beyond the segment for which they were originally designed.

THE MIDDLEMAN'S MERCHANDISING PROBLEMS

The term merchandising has been more frequently applied to the retailer and the wholesaler than to the manufacturer. There may be two reasons for this. In the first place, the importance of the merchandising challenge in coordinating immediate supply with immediate demand has only recently been recognized because of the emphasis on new products and change. In the second place, a major part of the middleman's task is in making coordinating decisions. The middleman is not occupied with production. He carries many more lines of merchandise than the average manufacturer makes. Each day the middleman makes a multitude of merchandise decisions and decides what product to buy and how much. On the other hand, the manufacturer makes merchandise decisions as they relate to the products of his line. Although the manufacturers' lines are broadening to include more products, so are the retailers'. Most manufacturers produce far less than one hundred separate items; the ordinary supermarket carries over five thousand items. Hence, while the manufacturer's individual merchandise decisions are more significant, the retailer makes many more.

With each product decision, the manufacturer risks greater dangers than the retailer. There are fewer products over which to spread the losses caused by mistakes in judgment. Also, the engineering, tooling, and promotion that are necessary to offer a single product are much greater in the case of the manufacturer than the expense of stocking a product is to the middleman. The success of middlemen is closely tied in with merchandising decisions. Merchants who fail to supply the wanted merchandise or who load up on old stock at the cost of not keeping a supply of products that are in current demand represent the marginal and submarginal operators. Their problem is to select the right product at the right time for the right person rather than to make it.

Wholesaler's Merchandising Problems

The wholesaler stands between the manufacturers of the lines that he carries and the retailers whom he serves. He communicates significant marketing information to each. The wholesaler is closer to the consumer market than is the manufacturer. Both his orders and his forecasts may become important guides to the manufacturer.

It is not uncommon for wholesalers to be trusted with the merchandising or coordinating function in retail stores. While it is not necessarily typical, it is not uncommon for a representative of a food wholesaler to make out his own orders, which the retailer signs with very little examination. Merchants realize that the wholesaler's salesmen have more access to trends and changes than they do. Especially since the growth of the chain stores and larger types of stores has the wholesaler felt a keen responsibility to keep his retailer customers posted on what is selling, how fast it is selling, and at what price. In the case of chain stores, the wholesale and retail functions for many products are combined in one company. The relationship then becomes one in which the retail store deals with the company warehouse, but the adjusting function remains.

The problem for the wholesaler is to select the line of products that he wishes to carry. He must then keep his stock in balance to keep retailers supplied with their needs. He may find himself overstocked and be forced to take markdowns just as the retailer does. His buyers also must be keen in the performance of the selective function. They must meet sales people from thousands of manufacturers and select those products that will move through the retail stores they serve to the consumer. Failing to achieve excellence in this activity, wholesalers may lose patronage and find themselves stocked with goods for which there is little or no market.

The rewards that accrue to those who excel in making the stock available are great. One large wholesaler on the West Coast reported that his company was able to fill 96 percent of the requests that came from customers. The average for his type of business was 80 percent. Some wholesalers fell to 50 percent. It is significant that this company increased its sales during recession months of January, February, and March of 1958 by 18 percent. During this period sales of competing firms were plummeting to low levels. Excellence in merchandising was one of the reasons for this company's successful "bucking" of a downward trend.

In wholesaling, as well as in other fields, we visualize a problem of adequate stock control and a sales analysis system. Management must be kept alert to the coordination of stocks on hand and rates of sales. Programs must be devised to take corrective action before stocks begin to pile up and sales begin to lag. Successful management of this activity is the wholesaler's contribution in adjusting the flow of goods to satisfy a current and effective demand.

Retailer's Merchandising Problems

The retailer is at the point where the merchandising decisions with respect to consumer goods are put to the final test. The fate of the product depends upon whether the ultimate consumer will buy in profitable volume. It behooves the retailer to anticipate the wants of the consumer so that there will be a minimum of product resistance at this point of the flow. Decisions as to what to buy, how much, what quality and price, and from which supplier are the responsibility of the buyer in the retail store. Since these decisions are so vital, the retail buyer is viewed as a person of responsibility. He is usually compensated in proportion to the significance of the department for which he buys to the profit of the store.

The buyer accomplishes the adjustment task with the aid of management tools. One of the important tools consists of records for stock control that reveal slow-selling merchandise and high inventory stocks as well as "shorts" and "outs." Such records may also indicate the extent of sales volume lost because of a failure to have adequate stocks of merchandise.

New York University interviewers conducted a survey in the three largest shopping centers on Long Island that indicates the extent of sales lost because of poor merchandising. The survey revealed that 25 percent of the shoppers who took the trouble to drive to these centers left without having made their planned purchases. When asked why, they gave the following reasons:

Price too high 9%
Poor service 6%
Merchandise stocks inadequate 72%

Methods Used by Retailers to Keep in Touch with Markets. It is the responsibility of the retail buyer to communicate with sources of supply that excel in supplying the most desirable merchandise. Retailers have adopted a number of methods by which they keep alert to the best opportunities for merchandise. Many of them visit the market centers of the nation. They observe arrays of offerings; they meet with other retailers from different parts of the country; they receive advice from advanced sources as to the market trends. Naturally such trips provide these merchants with opportunities to shop for price advantages. They also become acquainted with sales promotion techniques that will assist them in moving the merchandise of their own firms.

Some retail firms belong to buying groups and cooperate with each other in their buying. Such affiliation serves two significant purposes. From the economy or price standpoint, retailers are able to save as a result of pooling their orders and getting volume and quantity discounts. Another great advantage is the fact that they exchange merchandising data and thus assist each other in following trends. Often one store senses a great sales possibility in a product that some of the other stores fail to stock. On the other hand, when a buyer sees evidence of the sales of certain products lagging in stores throughout the country, he can watch his own stocks in that area more carefully. Some of the larger store groups may even conduct fashion counts in selected areas to guide their buyers. Or, they may conduct consumer opinion studies as a means of discerning factors that will please the customer most.

Some firms also establish *resident buyers* at the marketplace in order that they may have contact with the best and the latest products on the market.

Some Typical Methods of Control. One retail institution uses a special form to control seasonal items. The entries show the date the seasonal lines start to sell. The form also requires the recording of ordering dates that will assure the arrival of merchandise. A final reorder date is included to prevent orders from being submitted too late in the season. As in the case of all other forms, this one is but an aid to judgment. Stock-sales records on the floor may be needed to supplement it. Each season is different, and merchandise lines increase and decrease in popularity. No system that is based entirely on past experience is adequate, but such experience is usually a valuable guide.

Another method of stock control that embodies a method of regulating the "flow through" and that supplies a record of rate of sale is exemplified by a stock plan which sets a maximum in terms of a week's supply. Such a stock requirement may be the sum of a reserve in a week's supply, plus the length of time that may be required to get delivery, plus the period of reorder. The formula used in this instance is: Maximum (in week's supply) = Reserve (in week's supply) + Delivery period + Reorder period.

For example, by past experience it is known that an article is selling at the rate of 12 a week. It would be dangerous to wait until the stocks get down to 12 before a reorder is placed, even though there was a normal delivery period of one week. The rate of sale may increase or the delivery may, because of some irregularity, take more than a week. In this case an additional week's stock may be set up as a reserve safety factor to insure against such an emergency. Thus, the proper time to reorder is when the stock reaches 24 items. Then if the stock is a very slow mover, a four-week supply, or 48, might be ordered, thus necessitating reorders only once a month. On the other hand, if the items are considered fast selling or if there is risk entailed in their becoming obsolete, orders may be submitted weekly. If the weekly rate of sale were to change, the amount ordered and the amount kept in stock could be changed accordingly and automatically.

Stockturn. Another aid to keeping stock in line is to watch the rate of stockturn (see Chapter 12, page 241, which discusses computations and other significant characteristics of stockturn). This guide can be used to watch a single item, a stock classification, a department or section, or the whole store. Management should determine the dollar value of the stock on hand that is necessary in any one of these areas under study. It should allow for variety, safety, and delivery period. Then the desirable rate of sale should be determined, and from these figures a stockturn figure can be determined. The stockturn falling below the desired level becomes a signal for corrective action. Much help may be obtained from sources that collect and publish stockturn figures from other stores. For example, the Controllers Congress of the Retail Merchants Association, in its annual publication of merchandise operating ratios, publishes stockturn figures for over 112 divisions of department and specialty series. Some typical stockturn figures are as follows:

Department Stores (small)	2.4
Drugstores	4.0
Grocery Stores	12.6

Jewelry Stores (primarily cash and open credit) 1.1
Men's Clothing Stores 2.5
Cutlery 6.0

The use of stockturn rate can be illustrated by using cutlery, which averages a stockturn rate of 6. This represents a one-half stockturn per month. If the sales of this item were 100 a month, 200 should be in stock on the average. If the stockturn for cutlery should fall to 3 or 4 times per year, the department manager should look for (1) increasing numbers of slow-selling items, (2) overstocking in general, (3) reasons why sales in general were slow, or (4) other specific reasons for the condition. If, for example, he finds that the cause is a slow-selling line, he can mark this line down, clear it out, and use this money for faster moving items.

Effect of the Computer on Retail Merchandising. The fantastic improvements that can be made in retail merchandising with the computer can best be illustrated by some examples already in operation. J. C. Penney's system requires that the small punched tickets taken off merchandise be sent to Los Angeles or New York, whichever is closer, on the same day as the sales transaction. These tickets are placed into machines that transfer the information to punched cards and then to magnetic tape which is fed into digital electronic computers. The computers have been programmed to maintain records of each store's stock by individual product. At intervals that may vary with the kind of stock under consideration, the computer will scan the inventories and send out shipping orders to replenish stock to desired levels.[7] On staple items this system seldom requires human attention. With fashion items and those of a less staple nature, the orders would not be automatic; and the changes incident to fashion trends would have to be adjusted more frequently with the aid of human judgment.

In the food business, where such refinements may appear to come more slowly, the results are equally as tangible. To envision the potential area of control, it will be helpful to visualize the problem of maintaining adequate stock at the point of ultimate purchase. Some of the manufacturers have built warehouses so that they can supply their accounts more readily. In these instances there are five reservoirs or storage points before the food products reach the consumer. There would be one inventory at each of the following points: the plant, the warehouse, the distributor, the retailer's stock room, and the retailer's display. In addition to these inventories, there also may be significant amounts of supply in transit. Each one of these storage points is deemed necessary to assure a supply of the product at the point of purchase when it is needed.

To reduce the amount of stock in each of these inventories, manufacturers are constructing data links with major retail chains. For example, Kellogg's has a data link with the Safeway Stores. By this linkage system Kellogg is informed automatically of the stock of each Kellogg item and the amount that is sold daily. When the stock reaches a certain level, the order is filled automatically. As evidence that such a system works successfully, Pillsbury's director of

---

[7] "Computers Begin to Solve the Marketing Puzzle," *Business Week* (April 17, 1965), p. 115.

information quotes an official of one of the Spartan Stores, which Pillsbury serves with a data system, as saying that Spartan Stores have saved enough in storage costs and lead time to build an entire new store.[8]

With computer service, Stop and Shop, a Boston supermarket chain, has experimental stores with no back-room storage facilities and a replenishment schedule that on some items has been cut from nine days to less than 24 hours. Under such a system it appears that it may be possible to eliminate much of the reserve storage space costs. This system of communicating stocks in retail stores to the manufacturers is spreading rapidly. It may only be a few years until every manufacturer of consequence will be completely aware almost daily of his stocks in storage throughout the nation. Such knowledge would be possible by linking with enough retail stores to provide an accurate sample of daily product sales. To those retail stores that are too small for computer service, automatic control systems can be integrated with the checkout system. By sending the checkout tape to a central computer service, the store can be served by a computer center operating at night. When the business opens in the morning, the proprietor can know what his stock is and order accordingly.[9]

Under a system that is so automated, retailers will be able to synchronize perfectly their stock requirements with sales rates. It will enable the merchants to replace the slower selling items or lines with those that show promise of greater volume. Such decisions will not be completely automatic but will require considerable judgment. Although the computer can be helpful in the decision of what lines to drop and which to add, there will be elements of judgment here that only man can perform, since the number of alternative courses of action will tend to multiply.

QUESTIONS AND ANALYTICAL PROBLEMS

1. Define the term "merchandising" as it is used in this chapter.

2. What are the principal reasons for failure of new products? Cite examples other than those in your text of product failure and identify the principal reason.

3. What is the significance of Exhibit 14-1?

4. What ingredients of a business operation must be coordinated for successful merchandizing of a product?

5. What similarities and what differences can you identify in the merchandizing problems of extractive industries and those of manufacturers of consumer goods?

6. What divisions or activities in a firm must be coordinated for a successful organization for new products?

7. What are the identifying characteristics of each stage in a product's life cycle?

8. What determines the profit curve as related to the sales curve in a chart of product life cycle?

9. What positive actions can a firm take to delay or offset the decline stage of the life cycle of a specific product? Give two examples from personal observation or journal articles.

10. Describe in detail and evaluate one method of stock control you personally observe in one of your local retail establishments.

---

[8] *Ibid.,* p. 125.
[9] *Ibid.,* p. 138.

Case 14 • THE KIMBALL CHEESE COMPANY

The Kimball Cheese Company, which was nestled in a very attractive setting in the Rocky Mountains, specialized in producing a high quality blue cheese. The company had been a family business for 103 years, and it had a secret recipe for a product that was affectionately called "Old Blue." Over the 103-year period, the Kimball family was content to be "comfortably well off."

Relying strictly on reputation, Kimball Cheese sold directly to retailers who used order blanks sent to them through the mail. Free tours offered to tourists attracted approximately 200 people daily. No additional money was spent on advertising since Kimball Cheese felt that the free tours were sufficient.

Sales had remained constant for the past three years at $800,000 yearly. A review of their retail customers revealed that only 12 percent of the stores within a 500 mile radius (their normal range of business) carried "Old Blue." Cheese consumption within the area, however, had increased 4 percent annually during the same period, with the major increase occurring in sliced sandwich cheese.

Since Mr. Kimball IV was due to retire from his position as president in three months, his son was most anxious to implement what he called "a more progressive policy involving greater internal utilization of profits."

• What problems would the son encounter in implementing a more progressive policy? Make a proposal for retaining and increasing sales which includes all the aspects of a marketing program.

Price—the adjusting mechanism 15

Price is the mechanism by which the commodities making up the flow of goods are adjusted to the desires of consumers. Price is also a significant marketing management function because it is a resistance factor to the purchaser, and generally one of the most effective methods of increasing sales is by lowering prices. On the other hand, since price is the source of income for the seller, the higher the price the seller can get for his product, assuming a given cost, the greater are his profits. The course management chooses to follow in establishing prices is a vital factor in a company's success or failure. Although prices are strongly influenced by market forces, management exercises considerable discretion in establishing price policies and in setting prices. Again we emphasize that price policy, even in its adjustment function, is interdependent with product and promotion policy. Yet the successful integration of these policies into a management program depends upon a knowledge of the specific characteristics of each. Therefore, this chapter and the next chapter will be devoted to acquiring a perspective of price. In this chapter price as the principal mechanism that adjusts the commodities in the flow of goods to the desires of the people is discussed.

It has been stated previously that a market is a general area where the forces of supply and demand meet to set a price. The forces of supply and demand as they apply to an economic product are present in nearly every phase of life. Many of the decisions or choices people make daily have some connection with markets and prices. For example, an important reason for the increase in university enrollments is the cultural gain that accrues from a college education. Another factor influencing the decision to attend college is the strong demand for those trained in college. Graduates are able to exact a much higher price for their services. Furthermore, the profession in which one chooses to make his contribution and from which he hopes to gain an adequate income is a most significant market decision. One's choice may be influenced to some extent by the price people will pay for the satisfaction he produces.

When some class members are deciding whether they should go to Europe this next summer or buy a new automobile, they are making a market decision. They weigh the satisfaction on the one hand against the price (cost) on the other. The choice of a home, clothing, food, and entertainment all involve market decisions.

ECONOMIC FOUNDATIONS FOR PRICE DETERMINATION

For two given products having similar characteristics, costs of the products tend to approach a uniform figure. Also, preferences people have for such products have common characteristics. Based on these realities, economists have developed a conceptual scheme which describes the means by which prices of such products are influenced by costs and consumer preferences. Product costs and desire for products operate in a dynamic market to establish limits on the amount that is produced and sold and on the prices that are charged. In order to understand how this price-making process operates, basic economic concepts will be introduced and illustrated in a model: and this model will be examined in relation to realistic marketplace situations.

Costs and Revenues

This discussion is based on money costs and revenues and on the assumption that the firm wishes to maximize its profits. To illustrate the economic process involved, the model used will be a hypothetical shoe manufacturing company seeking an optimum point at which to price its shoes. The product is sold in competition with other similar shoes in a specific market. The shoes are a popular brand, and some prestige accrues to them because of the brand name. It is assumed that the shoes should sell at different prices than competitive shoes and that more units would sell at lower than at higher prices.

Basic to the whole concept of discovering the price that will maximize profit is the determination of the point where total revenue exceeds total costs by the greatest amount. This computation is complicated somewhat by the fact that unit costs tend to vary according to the amount produced, and unit revenues vary according to the amount placed on the market at a given time. To discover the point of optimum balance between total costs and total revenues, marginal costs and marginal revenues must be determined. Knowing how these magnitudes are determined and how they are interrelated is essential to an understanding of the price-determination process.

Marginal Cost. It has already been stated that costs vary according to the volume of units produced. Economic studies show that in most instances where fixed and variable costs are involved a point is reached as volume is increased where the cost per unit increases with each added unit of production. As volume of production and sales increases, the per unit fixed cost diminishes. On the other hand, as the output increases and the production and management coordination processes grow more complex, the variable unit cost decreases at a slower rate or increases. Frequently such costs increase faster than unit fixed costs decrease; therefore, the total costs increase—a phenomenon described by economists as the law of diminishing returns. Strategic to this discussion, though, is the cost element called *marginal cost*—the amount of cost that is added as a result of producing and selling one additional increment of the product. This phenomenon will be understood more clearly when it is introduced in the model illustrating the production and sale of shoes.

Marginal Revenue. The price or the average per unit revenue that is received is influenced by the amount of a product that is offered on the market. When a useful and desired product is offered, there are usually a few buyers that would be willing to pay a comparatively high price for it; but there are more people who would be willing to buy the product at a lower price. Therefore, when only a few products are offered, a high price could be obtained. With each additional unit that is offered, however, theoretically it would have to be sold to one who would pay less than the previous buyers. As a progression of this process continues, the price would continue to decrease. All purchasers of the product would buy the product at the lower price since theoretically it would be impossible to sell to each buyer at the highest price he would be willing to pay. Regardless of the intensity of his desire to buy the product, he would insist on paying the same price as the lowest buyer. The strategic question then is what change would the sale of each succeeding increment of the product make in the total revenue of the firm. This amount would be the *marginal revenue*—the amount by which the total revenue is changed by the addition of one more unit of product to sales. It should be noted that this amount will not be the same as the price received for the additional unit. When the additional unit is offered at a reduced price, the price of all other sales will decrease to the amount of the lowest price at which there was a sale. Therefore, the marginal revenue will usually be less than the price or the average revenue.

Optimum Price for Maximum Profits. This brings us to the hypothetical shoe company which is presented as operating at different production levels of from 1,000 to 9,000 pairs of shoes (see Table 15-1). The company judges that any change in production levels, to be economic, should be at least in increments of 1,000 pairs. For example, note at the production level of 3,000 pairs that the average variable cost (determined by dividing the number of pairs produced into total variable costs) is $7.66 per unit. The average fixed cost (total fixed cost divided by the number of shoes produced) is $4, making the average total cost $11.66 per unit. At this production level the total cost would be $35,000, which is $4,000 more than the total cost of producing 2,000 pairs of shoes. The $4,000, then, is the marginal cost at this level of operation.

The average revenue is equal to the prevailing price for the shoes. We note that, as the amount that is offered on the market is increased, the average revenue (price) decreases from $17 at the 1,000 unit production level to $1 at the 9,000 level. At the 3,000 unit production level, average revenue would be $13 per pair of shoes. At this point in production the total revenue of $39,000 would be $4,000 greater than the total costs, and this figure would represent the company's profits. If the company increased its operation to 4,000 units, the marginal costs would be $2,000; marginal revenue, $5,000; and total profits, $7,000. This $3,000 increase in profits is the result of marginal revenue exceeding marginal costs by this amount. The next step in the progressively increasing production point is strategic in this illustration. At the 5,000 unit production level, the marginal cost increases from $2,000 to $3,000, while the marginal revenue decreases from $5,000 to $1,000. Thus, if the company were to increase its production from 4,000 to 5,000 pairs, its profits would be smaller by $2,000.

Table 15-1
AN ILLUSTRATION OF THE LAWS OF INCREASING AND DIMINISHING RETURNS

Quantity (1,000's)	Average Variable Cost	Average Fixed Cost	Average Total Cost	Total Cost (1,000's)	Marginal Cost (1,000's)	Average Revenue (Price)	Total Revenue (1,000's)	Marginal Revenue (1,000's)	Profit (1,000's)
1	$12.00	$12.00	$24.00	$24	—	$17	$17	—	$– 7
2	9.50	6.00	15.50	31	$ 7	15	30	$13	– 1
3	7.66	4.00	11.66	35	4	13	39	9	4
4	6.25	3.00	9.25	37	2	11	44	5	7
5	5.60	2.40	8.00	40	3	9	45	1	5
6	5.50	2.00	7.50	45	5	7	42	– 3	– 3
7	5.86	1.71	7.57	53	8	5	35	– 7	–18
8	6.63	1.50	8.13	65	12	3	24	–11	–41
9	7.78	1.33	9.11	82	17	1	9	–15	–73

By presenting these relationships graphically, it is theoretically possible to determine the strategic points with even greater precision. In Exhibit 15-1 note that the marginal revenue curve and the marginal cost curve intersect at point *P*, or at approximately $2.5. The average revenue would be slightly under $10, and the number of shoes offered on the market would be between 4 and 5 thousand pairs.

The intersection of the marginal revenue curve with the marginal cost curve is strategic. These magnitudes represent the amount of change in the total revenue and total cost. Therefore, when marginal revenue is greater than the marginal cost, the profit spread between total costs and total revenue is greater. When additional units are added after the point of intersection, the amount added to costs is greater than the amount added to revenue, and the total profits are smaller. Therefore, the optimum price would be that point where the marginal revenue and the marginal cost approach equality.

Practical Value of Marginal Concepts

This pricing explanation has its roots in neoclassical, or Marshallian, economics. It represents a sound view of establishing a price to maximize profits.

Exhibit 15-1

GRAPHIC ILLUSTRATION OF THE LAWS OF INCREASING AND DIMINISHING RETURNS

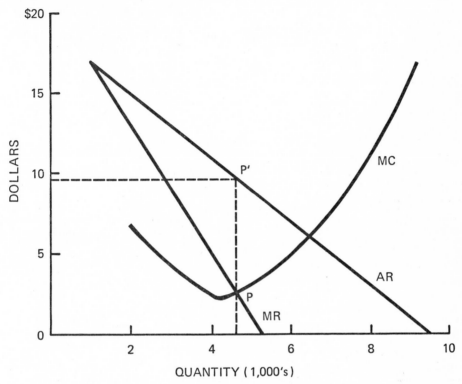

QUANTITY (1,000's)

When this concept was first described by Alfred Marshall, land, labor, and capital were the basic cost factors; and the demand for products was much less complicated. The soundness of the basic theory remains intact, but in its application costs have become much more complex than the simple measure of the classical factors of production. Also, the competition for thousands of new and innovated products has added an infinite number of influences to the revenue curve.

Marshall's theory presumes that costs should be computed on the basis of the entire production cost. On most products sold today, fixed costs should include development costs and the cost of product failures before a successful product is developed. Unit product cost should also include a distribution of selling and administrative costs. Frequently, many of these costs are incurred at points remote from the time and place where the specific cost they add to each product can be determined. To include them in unit cost figures requires much effort and many estimates. Furthermore, a price policy may dictate that a price be established for a period, such as a year, as is the case with automobiles and some packaged goods. In the course of such a period, under a dynamic system of management, a company may change its operations to reduce its costs, which might influence the point where marginal cost curves increased. It is also likely that in the course of a year the firm's advertising and selling program may influence volume and thus have an effect on the marginal revenue curve. It is, therefore, impossible for a company to follow the marginal cost and marginal revenue rule in the absolute sense. Such a course would require a change in price with each change in the position of the cost or the revenue curve.

Impact of New Concepts on Cost

Because of accounting difficulties and frequent changes in demand, the rule of maximizing profit by pricing at the intersection of marginal cost and revenue curves has not been given great attention. However, the entrance of the computer will make accounting data available instantaneously. These data will include comprehensive amounts of information formerly beyond the scope of conventional accounting. Thus, a new emphasis on cost as related to price may be imminent. Another very important feature of modern computer accounting is the fact that when a change takes place in costs, the change can immediately be recorded and become a part of the current computation. The same can be said of the revenue side of the equation. Indeed, with these changes it is possible that in the modern firm the marginal cost and the marginal revenue intersection may be kept in constant focus.

ALLOCATION FUNCTIONS OF PRICE

If improvements in accounting and price adjustments do take place, it will mean that the economic resource allocation function of price will be even more effective. Since price involves people, as well as products and services, let us cite an example to show how the price of products, as well as the price paid for the services of people, enters into the allocation of resources to achieve optimum cost-satisfaction goals.

Suppose a change takes place in customers and social patterns that moves the average revenue curve of a product to a higher level. It is conceivable that the interaction of advertising and selling of the hypothetical firm and the other firms might have hastened such changes. If, in our example (Table 15-1 on page 291), the increase in demand took place after the fourth unit was produced, there would be an increase both in the total cost and the marginal cost. Such an increase would occur because the marginal revenue curve would intersect the marginal cost curve at a higher level. This increase in cost would mean that the company would purchase more resources than it did before and probably pay a higher price. A wise management would seek to add resources to those productive factors which would bring about the greatest increase in production at the smallest cost. Certainly essential raw materials would be needed; and other costs which may be added are labor and capital cost for additional machines or plant space.

Management must, in fact, purchase in the commodity, capital, and labor markets these necessary resources to effect the increase in production. This entire process is complicated and involves the interaction of many forces. In today's industrial complex there are hundreds of alternative courses of action management might elect to expand production capacity. Furthermore, the market for each of these factors of production is greatly complicated by nonprice competition considerations. Yet even at the risk of oversimplification, it will be helpful to see the effect that changing prices have on the allocation of one important productive resource—engineers. Using engineers as an example will illustrate the principles involved in handling other allocation adjustments.

Effect of Price on Engineer Resources

The student who chooses engineering as a major subjectively weighs the costs of engineering versus the satisfactions that will come from such a career. The costs consist of an expensive education of a specialized type which cannot be acquired by working on a job. An engineer will probably not attain as high a salary as a business executive, and his job does not provide as much interacting with people as do many jobs, such as teaching. On the satisfaction side of the equation, engineers have the respect of society, obtain a high beginning salary, have job security, and participate in many creative activities.

One who is considering becoming an engineer and who weighs the costs versus the satisfactions is, in part, influenced by money costs and the prospects of money returns. Thus, when there is a comparative shortage of engineers, salaries rise and succeed in attracting more engineering students. This illustrates the fact that by means of market decisions reflected in price (salary for engineers) society redirects its resources to achieve desired results—a concept which applies at all points in the allocation process and influences in like manner all products and services.

Effect on Costs and Products of Adding Engineer Resources

The costs that make up the total or the marginal costs represent resources such as management skill, technical knowledge, labor, and materials. When output is increased, the need for resources is increased. As we have indicated, each of these resources is priced in terms of cost and satisfaction elements in somewhat the same manner as a product is priced.

When an extra engineer is required, he must be hired from a limited market. Assuming no other engineers have been laid off, this addition will increase the aggregate demand for engineers. The price of such an addition will be determined by market forces. The price and marginal revenue of the product will increase, and the marginal cost will also increase since the firm will have to pay a higher price for the engineer, assuming there are no layoffs from other firms. With the limited supply available, the engineer will be taken from another firm which has a lower marginal cost and marginal revenue balance; and, thus, there will be a shift away from a less desirable to a more desirable product.

The change in the desirability of one product as compared to another is at the very heart of the allocation process. The market and price mechanisms are the means by which such changes take place. It is significant to note that it is consumer preference, as reflected in the average revenue curve, that triggers this all-pervasive change. We have assumed that the engineer was hired away from another business, but this may not be the case. If the man hired is just out of college, price is still an allocating factor; for the company making the preferred product can afford to bid more for his services.

A significant fact in this example is that the demand for final products reflects back into the productive processes and influences the price of all the resources. The manager of the company in our example may have found in analyzing his problem that he could have chosen to employ more labor or to install another machine to increase his output. The price at which labor or capital was available influenced his choice, and the price of labor or capital was also determined by the price of the products in which they are used. In an economy which is based on the market system, the influence of price is all-pervasive in the allocation of the products consumed by the ultimate consumer. The price of these products also influences the prices of the raw materials, labor, capital, technical skills, and managerial skills required to make the product. Thus, price is at the very heart of the process by which the allocation of goods and resources are determined, and this allocation decision is theoretically based on equating marginal cost with marginal revenue. When reasoning in this context, however, one should not overlook the growing complexity of the calculations and the varied influences of the nonprice factors which influence market decisions.

Pricing is frequently not the dominant factor in management decisions that the economics model suggests. Pricing is only one element of the marketing mix and, in many companies, much more attention may be given to product design and quality, promotional activities, or channel decisions, than to pricing.

Price Theory and Profit Maximization

We have already stated that the validity of the theory of price resulting from marginal costs equilibrating with marginal revenue is based on the assumption that all firms attempt to maximize profits. Also, we have already noted that because of accounting limitations this objective could only be approached and not realized in an absolute sense. However, recently there has been much debate as to whether or not the top-priority objective of a business should be to maximize profits, or whether firms actually desire to maximize profits.

Seldom will a business enterprise admit that it attempts to maximize profits by charging the highest price which the market will bear. There appears to be two basic reasons for this. First, unfortunately, the profit motive in some circles has acquired a meaning that is not complimentary to social objectives. Although there is much evidence that at many points the social contribution of business and the profit motive are compatible, acquired prejudices render recognition of this fact difficult for many people. Consequently, there is a tendency to avoid the admission that profit is the basic motive. It is also true that business firms are beginning to see themselves as service institutions with social and community responsibilities. In such instances there is honest debate as to what priority profits should have in relation to objectives of community service and national productivity.

The other factor which may prompt a business firm to depart from a strict profit maximization policy would be the company's market strategy. An outright maximization of profits might invite or stimulate unwanted competition. On other occasions a company may produce beyond the profit maximization level to achieve a market share which appears to be desirable in point of time to the company. It is conceivable that most companies never operate at the exact or approximate level of profit maximization. For purposes of strategy and public acceptability, or the personal objectives of the owners, they have other motives.

As an example, the Drake Hotel in Chicago, with a staff approximately 20 percent larger than most hotels its size, has been consistently profitable, but net income is rarely over three percent of revenue and has been below one percent in several years. "There is something here one can't get elsewhere—only we have the staff to do it. . . . This is one of the choice pieces of real estate in Chicago and (we) regularly get offers to sell, but there is no present intention to sell. . . . We could take the money and build a bigger place, but we couldn't duplicate what we have here, and I don't think we'd like to run one of those efficient glass and steel outfits."[1]

The importance of profits in the perpetuation and continued growth of a company cannot be minimized. No company can continue to operate without either profits or an outside subsidy. Profitable companies can command increasing power over resources. They can maintain positive support from stockholders, banks, and the community of customers and workers. Therefore, wherever firms might rank profits in their hierarchy of values, they cannot be ignored. Whether a firm wishes to operate at maximum profits or not, it should have the facts to know the point of profit maximization and the reasons for not achieving profit maximization, such as the failure of management, the relative priorities of objectives, or the influences of the overall market strategy.

THE PROCESS OF PRICE DETERMINATION

Earlier in the text it was pointed out that man's quest is to satisfy his desires and that the marketing process provides a means of bringing into focus this satisfaction and measuring it against a corresponding obstacle or resistance. These resistances or negative forces we describe as cost.

In the language of business, desire can be looked upon as a magnitude whose satisfaction can be expressed in specific units of money. The process of obtaining satisfaction requires cost or effort which can also be measured in money units. The equilibrium which results from the interaction between cost or resistance and satisfying a desire is closely related to the price-determination process. This interplay can be well illustrated in the primitive economy of Robinson Crusoe. If Robinson Crusoe wished to eat berries, he had to pick them. Picking them was related to cost since it provided resistance and required effort. In return for effort, he satisfied a desire. The psychic counterparts of marginal cost equating with marginal revenue are illustrated when Robinson Crusoe reached the point where the effort or resistance brought about a certain degree of fatigue or an

---

[1] *Wall Street Journal*, February 6, 1974, p. 1.

unpleasantness which relates to costs. On the other hand, as Robinson Crusoe ate more berries, he received a decreasing amount of satisfaction from each berry he ate. This phenomenon illustrates the principles of *diminishing marginal utility*.

With this background we are able to state a concept describing the theoretical framework of price determination. The workable price of a given product is set at the point where the marginal utility or satisfaction is equal to the marginal cost or disutility. In our present competitive society, man is faced with almost infinite alternatives relating to both cost and satisfaction. There are few limits to the methods by which man can supply cost or effort to create satisfaction for others and, thus, earn money to satisfy his own desires. Indeed, in choosing where to apply the effort which makes the supply of goods possible, the individual carefully surveys areas where the satisfactions are desired most. With such a perspective he will be able to choose a point at which to apply himself that will reward his efforts to a maximum.

On the other hand, seldom does the spender of income consider only one product as a means to satisfaction. There are thousands of alternative satisfactions to which income might be applied. Yet these facts do not change the reality of our price-determination explanation. Man attempts to maximize his satisfaction and minimize his costs by choosing the alternative which provides him the most desirable balance in cost and satisfaction. Even in the choice of his work as well as the items which he buys, he measures the positives against the negatives. The money costs and return, however, have a strategic influence on his choice. Insofar as it is possible with the information available, man seeks the optimum in cost adjustment between the resistance forces and the positive satisfaction rewards of his desires. The specific point where action is taken to determine price is at the last point where the marginal satisfaction is greater than the marginal cost. This phenomenon will be illustrated later in an example.

Practical Implications

In our previous discussions we have reasoned in the context of classical or neoclassical economics. The whole concept of marginal analysis thus far has been based on fixed and variable money costs and their relationship to an average revenue curve which normally declines as greater amounts are made available on the market. While these discussions dealing with tangible money magnitudes are valuable to management in determining price, they do not include all the forces which the marketing man might consider in price determination. The price decision, whether rationally determined or the product of an impulse, is a subjective decision of the buyer.

Elements of Demand

The demand curve rests on or is supported by the desire for the product. The number of people, the satisfaction which they judge they can obtain from the purchase of the product, and a number of forces that attend a market situation influence the demand curve. Particular elements of demand are (1) the "buyer's worth" judgment, (2) the "buyer's will" evaluation, (3) the significance of money to the buyer, and (4) the buyer's judgment of the seller's position and attitude.

In the "buyer's worth" judgment, the buyer's intensity of desire for the product is influenced by his own desires, goals, and incentives, as well as by qualities of the product.

The "buyer's will" evaluation arises from the area of unreflective judgments. The buying process is a complex of many subjective forces coming to a focus at the moment of purchase. Often the reasons for purchase cannot be traced to a goal or to conscious reasons. Perceptual bias, of which the buyer is quite unaware, may influence the decision. An optimistic person would respond one way to a certain stimulus, while a pessimistic person would react in just the opposite way. During increasing prices, there is a tendency to feel that the market is improving; and there is a stronger will to buy. On the other hand, when prices are falling, a negative feeling seems to prevail; and there is a tendency to withhold purchases.

The significance of money is an important factor to the buyer in exercising a choice or in making a bid for a product. The value of money to the buyer is a prime factor in determining whether or not the individual chooses to spend it for the goods offered. It is true that many people are more careful in apportioning their funds to their demands than others. Certainly this attitude toward money will have an influence on the price that a person pays for a product. Such an attitude may vary from one period to another and, thus, be a factor on which to base judgments.

The last element of demand is the buyer's judgment of the seller's position and attitude. In making a purchase, the buyer will be influenced in the price that he is willing to pay by the seller's ability to hold out at the price offered.

Interactions of these four elements of demand result in *demand elasticity*. The buyer may view the seller's position as weak. He anticipates an adjustment of the price downward. Such a condition may lead the buyer to bid a lower price in order to influence the seller's offer to a lower price. Such an estimate of the market situation may prompt the buyer to delay his bid in the hope that the seller's position will force him to lower the price, as in the case of a manufacturer overstocked or a retailer going into the fall season with many summer items still in stock.

These four qualities—the buyer's worth concept of the product, his sentimental or subconscious feelings regarding the product and the market, his feelings as applied to money, and his judgment of the strength of the seller's position—all affect the position of the demand curve for a specific product. The demand curve for the product will tend to move to the right if: (1) the worth feelings of an individual for a contemplated purchase are strong and the unreflective or sentimental factors favor this product above other alternatives; (2) the money available to the individual at the moment seems to be plentiful so that the subjective value of money is comparatively low; and (3) the buyer judges the seller's position as strong so that he will probably not reduce the price as a result of bargaining. If the reverse of the above conditions prevails, the demand curve will tend to move to the left.

Elements of Supply

We are primarily concerned here with the obstacles to the gratification of human desires. The supply of goods available to gratify human desires comes only as a result of work and saving. Those who exert efforts to wrest goods from nature provide them in exchange for money and offer them for prices at which they get a favorable return for their efforts. Elements of the supply curve include costs to produce or offer goods or services.

Expense Cost and Disutility Cost. Two types of costs enter into the price at which a seller offers a product. Naturally, he wishes to obtain from the product all money costs he expended in acquiring it plus all the handling costs entailed in storing it and offering it for sale. But, if the sum of all these *expense costs* were all the seller could anticipate, it is doubtful if he would continue in his business of selling. For the product that he offers not only should pay these expenses, but the price should also include the irksomeness of labor and managerial activity which he may have undergone in acquiring the goods for sale. He also might have waited to purchase the goods for resale until he could finance the transaction. Then, too, there is the question of the risk and the hazards that he must undertake. These costs or resistances and others of like nature, even though they are not out-of-pocket expenses, might be called *disutility costs*. Expense costs can be measured. They are considered money costs paid for producing the product or for acquiring it. It would be difficult, however, to subject disutility costs to accurate calculation. Yet consciously or subconsciously they do influence the seller in selecting the price at which he chooses to sell the product.

Unreflective Judgment or Market Sentiment. The will to sell, like the will to buy, may not always be subject to rational calculations based on objective market facts. Rather, decisions to sell at a given price may be the result of an emotional attitude toward the product or the market. The parties to a price war, for example, often let personal feelings enter into their calculations. The feelings of buoyancy that attend the boom and the feelings of pessimism which attend the panic are examples of this tendency. The custom of obtaining certain markup percentages or of allowing discounts even though the conditions that prompted their original computation no longer apply furnish another example of such influences on price judgments.

DEMAND ELASTICITY

Demand elasticity is an important factor for management to consider when it is setting prices. As defined by economists, a demand for a product is elastic if a decrease in the price of the product results in an increase in the total revenue or if an increase in the price results in a decrease in the total revenue. As used in marketing, *demand elasticity* refers to the degree of sensitivity of sales volume to price. A product which responds to price change with large changes in sales volume is said to be very elastic; but if the volume change is minimal as a result of a change in price, the product is described as being slightly elastic. The demand for some products is, of course, more elastic than the demand for others. For example, an increase or decrease in the price of unbranded salt would change the volume sold but slightly. In the first place, the amount of the consumer budget spent on salt is very small. The uses to which salt can be put are limited, and there would be no great increase in the volume sold no matter what the price. In the second place, there are no close substitutes for salt which would be purchased if the price of salt were increased.

On the other hand, the demand for a brand of soda crackers would be very elastic. This would be true first of all because there are many brands of soda crackers which have similar qualities. A price decrease would pull many sales away from competition, and a price increase would encourage consumers to buy other brands which would serve their purpose almost as well. It is also possible that, unlike salt, the actual amount of soda crackers consumed regardless of brands would rise or fall with an increase or decrease in price. The elasticity of demand for any product would depend on the worth feeling of the consumer for the product, the amount of the product that it would take to satisfy the desire for the product, or the volume required to reach the margin of satiation. The substitute uses for the product would tend to decrease the marginal utility for a single brand and increase the demand elasticity. In the majority of cases, the products on today's market are branded products. Substitutes can be adopted if prices are not consistent with cost-satisfaction balances when compared with alternatives. Thus, most products tend to have an elastic demand.

FACTORS INHIBITING PERFECT PRICE ADJUSTMENTS

If price performed its allocation function perfectly, adjustments would occur immediately in response to changes in the elements of demand and supply. The market would be a perfect equilibrator, and the point of the equilibrium of these two composite forces would always be the market price. In actual market conditions, however, prices are seldom that sensitive to such changes for several reasons: first, some prices are administered by an agency; second, some prices are set by a government authority; third, some prices are subject to monopoly influences; and fourth, the perfect competition that should be present to bring about the adjustments is the ideal rather than the reality.[2]

Administered Prices [3]

Administered prices, by definition, are prices set by a seller or group of sellers, and which change infrequently. In oligopolistic industries, even with no

---

[2] It should be noted that, even if the market were accurately sensitive to the demand and supply forces, it would still not serve the economic allocation process to the complete satisfaction of society. For example, society through its legislative processes has decided that there should be a more equal distribution of income than was allocated by the market system. Hence, we have the graduated income tax. There are still other social problems related to economics where adjustments are needed which the market itself may not accomplish. The problem of urban blight, fair employment for minority groups, and possibly still more equitable distribution of income are examples. These are topics, however, that would normally be treated in a course of social economics.

[3] The term "administered prices" has acquired sinister implications as a result of considerable literature dealing with conspirational action. However, there is a positive and sound connotation for administered prices which is discussed by Robert F. Lanzillotti, "Why Corporations Find It Necessary to 'Administer' Prices," *Challenge: The Magazine of Economic Affairs*, Vol. 8, No. 4 (January, 1960), pp. 45-49.

communication between firms to set prices (which would be illegal), the experience of each firm is that if you cut prices, the competitors will match the *cut,* and if your *raise* prices, the competitor will hold their prices in order to pick up some of your business. Hence, there is reluctance to change prices—in other words, prices are administered. Government action to set or restrain prices is also sometimes called administered pricing.[4]

Two aspects of administered prices inhibit the complete flexibility of price movements. In the first place, it is unusual for a firm that sets its price for a period to change it immediately whenever the factors affecting demand and supply change. Rather. the firm will watch these shifting forces and price the product in the following period according to a summation of the experiences up to the time of the decision. The second factor is that the firm may control production rather than allow a free market to exercise the production control in order to achieve a profitable price.

The element of rigidity that results from such a practice has certain virtues. The stability of our economy depends on the soundness and health of business firms.[5] The firm that operates at capacity and sells on a competitive market has characteristics of insecurity. Its risk is great. There is no assurance that the price will remain sufficiently high to support fixed commitments. This is the condition of agriculture today. Indeed, we see some indications on the part of the government to do the same kind of planning for agriculture that many individual business firms do for themselves and to attempt to administer agricultural prices.

Government Influences on Prices

When a government agency controls prices, market forces are, of course, restricted. In portions of our economy, such as in the field of highway construction, the government is a party to market transactions. In addition to influencing prices through participation in markets, the federal government sometimes actually sets or helps to establish price limits through legislation.

It is good economy, in some instances, for resources to be controlled by one firm or a few firms. Electric utilities, telephone, water, and, in some instances, transportation services are examples. These are essential to the welfare of the community. These services have a large proportion of fixed costs and, therefore, require high volume operation. Hence, states or municipalities grant such firms exclusive privileges of operation in the interest of economy and better service. With no competition to affect prices, rates are set by a governing agency.

In the areas of utilities and transportation, competition is not adequate to perform the price-determining function. This is also true of a few other goods and services. For example, the price of milk in some areas is determined by a formula which is derived jointly by the government and producers. In all price-setting functions where the government acts, it is intended that cost factors be given true

---

[4] For theory of oligopoly and price administration see Paul A. Samuelson, *Economics* (9th ed.; New York: McGraw-Hill Book Co., 1973), Chapter 26.

[5] Although it is implied in this discussion that administered prices tend to promote economic stability, it is also possible to administer prices in order to stifle competition and promote monopoly. For five views on this subject, see *Administered Pricing: Economic and Legal Issues* (New York: National Industrial Conference Board, Inc., 1958).

weight and that fair profits be allowed. The main problem in such instances is that cost itself is difficult to determine accurately and that it changes at different volumes. Often rate-setting bodies are accused of being influenced by special interests. Their decisions may not always be a true reflection of the public desires; but even so, in the instances where prices are set by authority, the forces of demand and supply converging at the marketplace are a major influence in establishing prices. Since all facts regarding demand and supply are difficult to discern, administration of the pricing function by a government body is subject to imperfections just as when pricing is done by individual firms. Sometimes there is an attempt to adjust the entire economy by price regulation, as in the Nixon administration Phase I and Phase II regulations of the early 1970's, which set maximum allowable price increases.

Monopoly

Competition between buyers and sellers should result in a fair price to consumers. When one firm can exercise undue influence in either the buying or the selling phase, however, the resulting price may not be what it would be under conditions of free competition. At one time only one firm controlled the material and patents from which aluminum was made.

The monopoly problem from the standpoint of the national economy is not in the area of control of materials and patents alone. Size and power give some companies undue influence on the market. For example, General Motors sells approximately 50 percent of the passenger cars in the United States. Such a condition may not illustrate monopoly in the absolute, but it indicates influence that is certainly greater than perfect competition.

In many fields one company tends to dominate the industry, and in many others a few companies exercise great influence. In this instance we have a condition described as *oligopoly*—a condition in which several companies compete for a given market. Each company watches the other and responds according to its own best interest. Many of the business organizations in the United States would be in this classification.

The question has not be settled to the satisfaction of all as to whether the influence that large companies have in determining price is good or bad for the economic system. There is virtue in the economy of mass production that is inherent in large-scale industry. A company that has power over resources can use such power as a benefit to the economy in many ways. On the other hand, harm results from becoming so large that others are prevented from entering the competitive field. Is it not possible that better management methods might result from the incentives that arise out of competition?

Monopoly power, whatever its source, has a significant influence on price. Hence, it also has an effect on the manner in which our resources are allocated and how goods flow from the producer to the consumer. It is well to note, however, that absolute monopoly is as rare as is perfect competition. In spite of the fact that General Motors has an influence on competitive price setting, a significant degree of competition exists between the auto makers and in other areas of oligopoly.

Imperfect Competition

Another factor that inhibits perfect price adjustments to conditions of supply and demand is imperfect competition. Before we proceed, however, the conditions of perfect competition should be examined. Perfect competition is only hypothetical. The concept is useful only in that it provides a point from which to judge the degree of departure from a concept of perfection. Actually the competitive market might be viewed from two poles—perfect competition and absolute monopoly. The provisions for perfect competition for a given market and a specified product, simply stated, are as follows:

1. The presence of a large number of buyers and sellers is necessary so that the activities of any one of either group will have no appreciable effect on the total demand or supply and, consequently, the price.
2. The products offered on the market must be identical in every respect.
3. There must be a complete and accurate knowledge of the product and of the condition of supply and demand available to all buyers and sellers.

It is also assumed that the terms of sale and services rendered as a part of the sale will be similar and that buyers and sellers in the market will attempt to maximize their gain.

On the other hand, if any one firm reaches the size where its individual transactions influence the market, it enjoys some degree of monopoly. Likewise, if a product is different from other products with which it may compete, the product is not purely competitive. It is obvious that it would be impossible for consumers to be acquainted with the quality and terms of sale of every product class offered on the market. Thus, we see that imperfect competition is the only competition that really exists.

Product Differentiation Precludes Direct Comparison. Our original concept of competition referred exclusively to the area of price, but today firms compete in so many areas and with so many product variations that it is seldom possible to make direct comparisons with prices. The consumer is now confronted with a number of choices with varying components, including services, of which price is only one. For example, the housewife might now ask herself, "Shall I buy my milk from my neighbor's daughter's boy friend, who delivers a little late for breakfast, but whose package attracts the children and whose product is bottled by a nationally advertised firm? Or should I pay a penny less and buy my milk at the store? At the store I receive premium stamps, which I am saving. I admit I am utterly confused by the claims for quality that these two dairies offer. Therefore, they mean little to me."

Or the man of the house may ask, "Shall I buy a Chevrolet or a Plymouth? I will consider design, resale value, distinctiveness, economy of operation, safety, and past prejudices. In view of these considerations, do a few dollars in price make a difference?" With all these differentiating qualities, the price is still a significant factor. If a few dollars made no difference, a few more would probably influence the decision. Yet a whole new world of competition beyond strict price consideration has been introduced by technology and innovation.

If there ever was any validity in the claim to perfect competition, moves to differentiate and innovate have long rendered it obsolete. Today it is seldom that any one firm matches the product of any other firm sufficiently even to make a direct comparison. Furthermore, it is unlikely that one could make a direct price comparison of the same products offered by a particular firm during two or three consecutive years.

Product differentiation may be viewed from two points of view: First, it may be motivated by an attempt to make comparison impossible, while attempting to accentuate the fact that differences make the product superior. Second, it may be considered as an attempt to add some satisfaction to the product that will please the consumer. A short-run view of the tendency may tend to favor the first view. Many of the innovations appear to be inconsequential frills. Yet the mass of these frills as they accumulate may add a considerable sum of satisfaction in our consumption pattern.

There is nothing in increasing innovations that is not in harmony with the price-determining process. All innovations are designed to increase the desire intensity more than the increased cost. The market is the device that measures whether or not the innovation actually does provide satisfaction to make the product increase its market share.

Market Communications Are Imperfect. Our present market is often imperfect in one other important quality that characterizes perfect competition. Complete and accurate knowledge of all products or of the conditions of demand and supply that attend their sale is seldom available. There is evidence that the quality of market communications is improving. It has become a recognized fact in our market studies that it is as important to communicate the qualities of a product to the point of decision as it is to produce the product itself. As this truth becomes increasingly evident, we can expect greater effectiveness in communicating significant information.

QUESTIONS AND ANALYTICAL PROBLEMS

1. Price is an adjusting mechanism. Explain.
2. Define: (a) marginal cost, (b) marginal revenue, (c) average revenue.
3. What factors are involved in determining the optimum price for a product or a service?
4. Prices can be the basis for an allocation process. Explain.
5. Not always do firms place maximization of profits first in a list of company objectives. Why not?
6. Define and explain the so-called buyer's worth concept. Buyer's will or sentiment arises from the area of unreflective judgments. Explain and give an illustrative example.

7. List each of the so-called elements of supply and state a short example of the effect of each upon prices.

8. Define demand elasticity. Find evidence of one product with low demand elasticity and one with high demand elasticity. Explain why the demand elasticity varies between the two products.

9. How much control does a manufacturer have over the price at which he will sell his product?

10. Prices ultimately have their roots in the subjective feelings and choices of people. True or false? Why?

11. Are there any virtues (for the economy at large) that result from administered prices?

12. How can we justify government aided monopolies and consequent "price fixing"?

13. Define: (a) monopoly; (b) oligopoly.

14. Compare prices that are likely to result under conditions of (a) monopoly and (b) so-called imperfect or workable competition.

15. What conditions are necessary to produce pure and perfect competition?

16. Examine the prices of one type of product in your vicinity. Compare the prices, for example, of kitchen appliances, television sets, and automobiles. How much price competition exists? Also, look for any relationships between price, location, type of retail store, and advertising policy.

Case 15 ● SODA BURST

The new products department in the Frozen Foods Division of the National Foods Corporation felt that they had discovered a new product that would be a mild sensation. The name of the product itself, "Soda Burst," was attractive. Also, the product had desirable qualities that would be a positive factor in its sales. Soda Burst was an ice cream soda with all the qualities of the soda-fountain version, yet it could be served quickly in the home. It was prepared by placing a square of ice cream in a parfait glass with a tablet. The ice cream came in a variety of flavors and was packaged together with the tablet. The chemical reaction between the ice cream and the tablet when water was added made the ice cream soften while it swelled and fizzed just as in the ice cream soda. The company tested the concept with a number of samples and obtained a positive response. It then conducted a number of bench tests wherein the product was actually prepared and packaged. Samples were then given to a panel of housewives, and they tried Soda Burst in their homes. These housewives were enthusiastic and reported that their children were excited about the possibility of having ice cream sodas at home.

However, when placed on the market at 20 cents a serving in test market centers, the product did not sell enough to enable the company to break even. The company did enough research to isolate two possibilities for the lack of response. First, the product may have been priced too high. Second, when the ice cream was not placed in the freezer soon enough after it was purchased, the fizzing process was dulled, and the flavors were not as sharp as they were in the original tests. Some members of management favored these actions: (1) package three units of the product together—this package could be sold for 50 cents, or about 17 cents (this price was a minimum which the company could sell the product for and still break even) for each unit; (2) include in an advertising campaign information as to the necessity of placing the ice cream in the freezer soon after it was purchased. Other members of management considered both of these ideas impractical and contended that the product should be dropped from the line.

● What information should the company obtain to assist it in making a price decision, and how should it go about getting such information? What steps would you recommend the company take with respect to the product?

Pricing problems and policies 16

Chapter 15 indicated that price was the principal guide in the allocation of resources to areas of greatest human satisfaction, that price is partially controllable by management, and that the skill with which the firm prices its product is an important factor in the sales of the product and the profits of the company.

PRICING PROBLEMS AND POLICIES OF THE PRIMARY PRODUCER

When a manufacturing firm discovers that its product is not finding favor on the market, several avenues of corrective action may be taken. A change may be made in the package, or a new promotional program may be adopted. Both of these moves may give the product a new and different character in the eyes of the consuming public. However, in the case of the primary producer—both in agriculture and the extractive industries—the character of product is less flexible. Promotion programs similar to those used by manufacturers of branded products are difficult for primary producers to apply. Furthermore, within the limits set by various standards, the products of primary producers are similar, regardless of the different companies that produce them. For this reason greater direct price competition prevails than is the case with manufactured products. The seller has little control over the price of his product—his price is determined by the market forces. The forces of supply and demand are more difficult to influence than is the case with prices set by manufacturers or retailers.

When prices vary as a result of cyclical or other economic changes, the primary industries usually absorb a great portion of the change. Consequently, in such industries price fluctuations are greater than in the manufacturing and trade industries, which plan their prices. The latter buy resources according to their prospects for sale and produce what their observations indicate that the market will absorb. When there is a change in market demand, the manufacturer changes his product, and the merchant changes his purchases to suit the demand.

PRICING PROBLEMS AND POLICIES OF THE MANUFACTURER

Of all the classes of marketing institutions, the manufacturer probably plays the dominant role in adjusting the product to the demand. He has many choices open to him in deciding what will be produced. Within a range of his cost limitations, prices at which he sells can be set as he chooses. Once a manufacturer sets his price on a product, that price influences the price at which the product sells to the final user. Retailers and distributors have some discretion in the establishment of prices at which they offer the goods for sale, but they are strongly influenced by the manufacturer's price.

Methods of Pricing

The economic theory model of price setting in Chapter 15 is actually used by some firms. More frequently, because of the difficulties discussed in Chapter 15 in the section "Practical Value of Marginal Concepts," other methods of price setting are used. The following discussion is an overview of the considerations facing one who must set a price.

Influence of Cost on Price. We have already discussed the relationship of marginal cost in the determination of price. Theoretically, cost as a factor depends on changes in cost and revenue at different anticipated volumes. It also depends on long-term and short-term strategies. Consequently, it is only one factor among many that should influence price. There are several reasons, however, why cost is so popular as a means of setting price. One reason is that it has an ethically sound basis. There is no public clamor about a firm's pricing if it charges a reasonable amount above cost. Furthermore, cost is a concept that can be objectively quantified. Within the limits that have been set by accounting methods, we can approximate costs. Costs make a good starting point for discussion.

Cost-price formulas can be phrased in different manners. One simple method is to include materials, overhead, and selling costs and to add 10 percent of this total for profit. One appliance manufacturer figures his materials at 29 percent, labor at 7 percent, overhead at 8 percent, sales expense at 3 percent, gives his distributors a 40 percent discount, and adds 13 percent for profits. If you assume in this instance a price to consumers of $100, the company's price to the distributor would be $100 minus $40 dealer discount, which would give a gross return of $60 to the company. Of this amount $47 would be cost to the company and $13 would be profit.

All companies using such a pricing method have some formula for basing their computation on cost. Economic justification for such a practice from an old economic view is that in the long run prices tend to equal normal cost. The theory defends the position that if price were above total costs, which included capital and new entrepreneurial costs, enterprise would be attracted. New competitors would force the price down to a cost level. On the other hand, if the price were below cost, submarginal firms would fail, thus decreasing competition enough that the price would rise to a normal price.

Price Setting Not Dominated by Costs. In spite of claims that manufacturers' prices are based on cost, it is difficult to determine the extent to which this practice is generally applied. If a product shows evidence of an unusual appeal even though the cost may be comparatively low, an addition to the price is often made as a result of the strong demand. Building extra satisfaction into a product with minimum costs and reaping the rewards of a higher price are considered a legitimate field of operation of a free-enterprise institution.

In terms of our discussion on price determination, the practice of basing price on costs is not entirely sound. Recall that the adjustment process in an economy depends upon the joint forces of supply and demand finding an equilibrium in the marketplace. This equilibrium is significant since it represents a balance between the forces of desire gratification and the forces that restrict such gratification. To price on cost alone ignores the forces of demand in the price-making process. Such a policy may thus have the ultimate effect of slowing the profits accruing to the firm and also of preventing desirable adjustments in the economy. For example, a company may price a new product at cost ($100) plus 10 percent ($10). The product may sell an adequate volume to yield the company a satisfactory profit. Yet if the company were to study the demand for the product, it might sell equally well at $150. If this were true, the company could afford capital and labor to expand its plant and increase its profits. The company would enjoy higher profits, and more resources would be attracted to a product that the public found desirable.

It is likely that competition would also be motivated to produce the items. This latter condition would reflect the true response of the economy to the product. The cost-plus basis fails to take into consideration the competitor's moves. Pricing strategy that is successful always operates with an eye to what competitors are doing or what they might do as a result of the firm's price action.

Still another weakness in the argument favoring total emphasis on costs is the fact that exact approximation of future costs is not possible. The economic picture is so dynamic that costs are constantly changing, and they vary with the volume of sales. The concept of normal cost in our present economy, like pure competition, is more hypothetical than real. Before the long-run conditions have an opportunity to become effective, products have become obsolete and the firm is making profits out of innovations. The interest of the firm or the economy as a whole will not be best served if too much emphasis is given cost in the pricing program.

Meeting Competition

In pricing any new product, a firm should always consider the impact of its action in terms of the competitors' reaction.[1] To price for a high margin of profit is to invite competitors into the production of the article. A decision to do so would be influenced by the amount of profit that might be realized before competition enters the market. The time required to enter a market depends upon the difficulties of product and package development and the time required to organize a promotion and sales program. A high, immediate margin may be desirable if the life cycle of the product is brief. In such instances the company may reap quick profits and then develop a new product to repeat the cycle. Such a shift may be difficult, but it is typical of our dynamic era of rapid change and innovation. A company may develop a program of research and analysis, enabling it to read market trends accurately. It may then set up a coordinated and effective product development program. If such programs are successful, the company will likely realize its goal of high profits from frequent innovations. Such an undertaking requires great skill in administration and is usually attended with increased risks.

On the other hand, if a company wishes to retain significant volume in product sales over a period of time, it may lead its competitors to low-margin prices and build up its volume and prestige. We are assuming that the products in question have a degree of price elasticity.

A company must also view its product in the light of competition from its substitutes. The price of butter is definitely influenced by the price of oleomargarine. Railroad passenger fares have a relationship to bus and plane fares. It may be that the trading position of substitutes is stronger at some price levels than is the demand for the original product. Hence, the reaction of all types of competitors should be recognized as influences on the firm's pricing policy.

When entering a market with a new product, one has a choice of price strategies. One, he may simply add all manufacturing and promotional expenses plus a profit and hope that the product will find a market at the resultant figure. That would be a simple, full-cost method. The manufacturer may, as a short-run strategy, set a price which covers only variable costs. He may say to himself, "The plant is not running at full capacity and the sales we now have must cover all fixed costs. If I can get that special order at a price just high enough to cover the variable costs of producing the order, and a little bit more to contribute something to the fixed costs, it is worthwhile." That must be only a short range pricing method since very soon other customers will expect the lower prices. It may be used for a somewhat longer period if a manufacturer is introducing a new product and believes that he can get a foothold in the market with a relatively low price and then strive to achieve sufficient economies or reach sufficient volume that the product can bear its share of all

---

[1] Jon G. Udell asks, "What are the key policies and procedures common to successful marketing managements in various manufacturing industries?" In attempting to answer this he examines pricing strategy very carefully in "How Important Is Pricing in Competitive Strategy?" *Journal of Marketing*, Vol. 28 (January, 1964), pp. 44-48.

costs. Two, he may set out to "skim the cream" off the market. That strategy is to enter the market at a relatively high price, on the assumption that there will be some demand for the item regardless of price. That strategy is not often possible but is sometimes attempted if the following conditions are present:

1. Demand is likely to be relatively inelastic. Novelty items—fads or new developments such as television, high fashion items, or 8-track sound—have had low price elasticity at their introduction.

2. The product carries a strong patent or is difficult to copy, hence competition is not likely to develop soon; or conversely, there is high probability of imitative products soon and the firm wishes to recoup development costs rapidly.

3. The firm cannot easily determine how much price elasticity or potential demand exists for the product. Hence, the product is offered at a high price with the expectation that some development costs will be covered even if there is not great demand.

A third strategy is *market penetration* pricing. Marketing penetration is usually a long-term commitment and is an attempt to capture a large mass market quickly and hold it. Conditions favoring a penetration strategy are:

1. High degree of price elasticity for the product.

2. The product has features that make it readily acceptable—felt tip pens and pocket calculators are examples that meet these first two conditions.

3. The company believes it can produce the item at lower costs than can most other producers.

4. Economies of scale in manufacturing and distribution are large.

Sales of ball point pens in the United States illustrate both skimming and penetration strategies.

Reynolds International Pen Co. purchased rights from an Argentine inventor to a new concept in pens and introduced the ball point pen in New York City in November, 1945. At a production rate of 10,000 pens per day, unit costs were 50¢. Reynolds promoted "miracle newness" in a heavy advertising campaign and in the first week sold 30,000 pens at a retail price of $12.50 each. In three months, the company sales volume, at factory prices, was $5,674,000. Profits were calculated to be $1,558,600 after taxes. Initial investment by Reynolds was $26,000. Soon other manufacturers were offering ball point pens for under $1.00. Reynolds cut prices to meet competition a couple of times, then sold out, keeping a fortune.

Mr. Bich had introduced a pen under his name in France. He entered the U. S. market after ball point prices declined with the lowest priced pen. BIC pens now sell, as you know, for 19 cents—a penetration policy.

Price, Promotion, Quality

A manager confronted with a pricing problem must also concern himself with promotion and quality. It is difficult to view these several factors separately. The ideal combination for the manufacturer is an optimum combination of product, promotion, and price. No matter how good a product may be, its virtues may become known only to a comparative few if the seller does not underwrite the proper promotion and advertising program. Likewise, it is possible that a product of ordinary, but dependable, qualities may enjoy prestige sufficient to bring a high price if its promotion program is handled with sufficient skill. Quality today is not necessarily synonymous with durability. Qualities of longevity and durability may be among the factors considered, but the dynamics of the present age causes buyers to put greater emphasis on the ability of the product to yield immediate satisfaction than upon the length of time over which satisfaction accrues.

The promotion program should achieve two objectives. First, it should communicate with real impact the satisfaction-giving qualities of the product. Second, the promotion program should achieve effective coverage in the area of the product's potential market. Once these objectives have been achieved in the planning, the firm can consider the right price.

In this connection price has a dual effect. Price is an index that measures the force of demand for a product. But more significantly, it imparts a quality dimension in its own right. The merchant cannot afford to ignore the platitude that is accepted without question by many consumers: "You get just what you pay for." Such a statement is true in enough cases to give it lasting psychological impact.

It would be a mistake, however, for a company that wishes to build a name for integrity to attempt to burden price with the task of carrying the quality appeal for its product. On the other hand, the reverse emphasis may be equally dangerous. If a company wishing to gain a high volume of sales places its product on the market at a low price, there may be danger of suggesting a low-quality product. The result may be a reduction in sales. The optimum combination of promotion, quality, and price might be described as follows: The promotion program would be right that would build as much quality into the product as it would merit in the test of actual use. The price should be set at a point consistent with competition of similar quality, at the highest level that would harmonize with the price-volume factors we have discussed.

Price Leadership

A company may wish to consider the influences of a dominant seller setting a price. In many product classes one company exercises unusual initiative in its pricing policies. This tendency exists in the steel, cement, and oil industries. For example, steel companies are influenced by United States Steel Company for their steel prices. Even when (as is usually the case) there is no strict follow-the-leader policy, the dominant company's price becomes a benchmark or a guide. Prices of similar products may not be the same as the leader's, but the reason for the difference is logical in the light of the leader's prices. Even products that are differentiated are often closely tied to the leader's price.

The leadership pattern is usually not based on price agreements, which are, of course, illegal. Rather, the decision to follow a leader may result from a high regard for the experienced judgment of the leader's pricing skill. It may be the result of a habitual quicker response of the leader to the changes in market conditions, or from following the initiative of the firm that became dominant because it was first in the market with its product. Usually such a firm is respected by its competitors and sells to a significant share of the market.

Greater influence in pricing is usually exerted by a firm that has the proper combination of skill, dominance, and intiative. Such influence is partly the result of the fact that the setting of price on a product cannot be reduced to absolute formulas. Pricing, as we have stated, is still in large part an art, even though it makes maximum use of science. Thus, it is natural that the opinion and activities of others be given considerable weight for two main reasons. First, it may be wise competitively not to depart from a pattern set by competitors; and second, the price selected may represent a fairly accurate judgment of the equilibrium of the forces of supply and demand. The price resulting from the interplay of these forces may best be determined by joint observation and experiment. Such a practice does not necessarily imply illegal collusion.

Pricing a Full Line of Products

A company selling a number of products faces the problem of pricing the combination in a manner that will best meet the objectives of the company.[2] Here again we find a strong temptation to use cost as a basis for pricing. Such a policy has the weaknesses described. For example, a company could add a certain percentage to the total manufacturing cost of each item. In such an instance we find no influence of the different demands for these products. Neither is competition as a factor given weight. Although such methods may be widely used, they leave much to be desired in terms of achieving the objectives of the most desirable price.

Another method that such a firm may use is to aim certain products at a specific segment of the market. Such products can be priced according to the optimum volume for the market that they are to attract. For example, a firm, even through the same distribution system, may sell products on a luxury market, a medium market, and a mass market. Such a policy may be used by companies selling radios, tires, appliances, and possibly some kinds of food products. For example, if you were to shop for tires, you would find that most tire manufacturers offer several qualities at different prices.

A company may adopt a rather flexible policy of watching each line of products and then adapting the price to the elasticities of that market. Such a policy requires skillful and careful watching. If it is managed properly, it can maximize profits and strengthen the company's competitive position. In such instances the product may be priced most profitably at different levels according to its life cycle. It is also possible that the competitive position of a product within a line may change with the growth of the company or other

---

[2] When a company contemplates a full line of products, how much concern should be given to the complementary effect and the competitive effect these products might have on one another? Pricing in these instances becomes an effective tool in achieving optimum results, reports Alfred R. Oxenfeldt in "Product Line Pricing," *Harvard Business Review* (July-August, 1966), pp. 137-144.

companies with which it is in competition. A policy of adjusting the line favorably to such changes may become a temporizing program of meeting expedients unless it is properly defined, understood, and managed. The policy may be to adjust to a maximum profit for each product according to its demand elasticity, its demand relationships to other products in the line, the competitive situation, and costs.

The price of a product may be sufficient only to cover variable costs and contribute to the fixed costs. For example, a food manufacturing firm prices one competitive high-volume item low enough to meet competition no matter how low the price. Such a policy gives the company volume and a reputation for competitive equality. Profits accruing to such a company result from high margins on items that are differentiated where the price competition is not direct. In these instances fixed costs are partially absorbed by low-margin volume items. In this fashion, then, pricing becomes a game of strategy in which human judgment and art are significant factors. Profit on individual items is subservient to profits on the entire line.

Discount Policies

Discounts are given to buyers by manufacturers to serve different purposes. One very common discount, the *cash discount*, represents a reduction in price as compensation for paying bills before they are due. It actually may represent a collection expense to the company, since accounts that are allowed to lag may become costly to collect. Because no firm that has sound credit will knowingly lose the discount, the tendency to keep accounts current is encouraged by the discount. If this discount privilege is open to everyone on the same basis, no discrimination can be charged.

A *trade discount* represents another type of reduction from list price. This discount is given to a certain class of customers because of their functional contribution in moving the goods. For example, a large retailer buys directly from a manufacturer who sells his line principally through wholesalers. In such an instance the manufacturer may quote a smaller trade discount from list to the retailer than to wholesalers in the same area. Such a policy avoids the charge of discrimination against the wholesalers and the smaller retailers who buy from wholesalers. Furthermore, it recognizes the special function performed by the wholesaler and compensates him for his services.

A company may also give a *quantity discount* and sell at a discounted price if the volume purchased by the buyer justifies such a practice on the basis of cost savings. A policy of giving discounts on a volume basis encourages larger purchases. In some instances firms extend the privilege of a quantity discount to cover all the purchases made during a specific period. The discount rate may be set to increase as the volume of purchases increases. For example, in the course of a year, discounts may be given on the amount purchased each month. The rate would vary in proportion to the amount purchased. If less than $200 is purchased, there may be no discount. From $200 to $600 the discount may be three percent. The rate of discount increases by graduated amounts to a top limit. Such a discount policy may not only reduce handling costs by the firm, but it may also increase sales.

Firms may use discounts for a number of other purposes, such as encouraging purchases during a slow period or as wedges to swing strategic accounts in their favor. Care must be used that such discounts are not discriminatory as defined by the Robinson-Patman Act.

In effect we may view a discount as a significant part of the price-making process. Discount policy is motivated by desire for profit, market position, and stability. With these purposes in mind, the main problem in administering discounts is in conserving and building solid relationships with the trade. Poor management of discounts may cause trouble for the company, in terms of both trade relations and the law.

Geographic Price Differentials

Getting the product to the right place at the right time is as important as producing the product. This problem arises in pricing, since the cost of such a movement must be considered in setting a price. Frequently transportation costs are a major portion of the cost of a product. There are three general categories under which different policies may be described. First, there is the f.o.b. shipping point pricing method; second, the uniform-delivered pricing method; and third, the basing point pricing method.

F.O.B. Shipping Point. The f.o.b. shipping point method in pricing automobiles is the simplest. The price is quoted net at the factory. Additions to net price depend on the distance the purchaser is from the factory, the means of transportation available, and its cost. There are certain disadvantages to this method. Where the transportation is a significant part of the price and where volume sales are important to a firm, it is difficult for a company to operate outside of its own market area. Competitors in the local market areas may sell at lower prices. Yet it is often desirable for a firm to extend its market area in order to obtain a sufficient volume to enable it to make a profit.

Uniform Delivered Price. At the other extreme from the f.o.b. shipping point method is the uniform-delivered pricing plan. Under this plan a company can compete in all areas of the market. All of the transportation costs of the customer are absorbed by the seller. This method is desirable where the freight cost does not constitute a significant part of the cost of the product. It has the advantage of giving all firms equality at the market. If actual costs are recognized as a pricing base, however, this principle violates the cost concept of pricing. It costs more to sell to distant customers than to nearer ones. The uniform delivered price method is sometimes called "postage stamp pricing." This term describes the method aptly. For example, a person living in Columbus, Ohio, can send a letter across the road or to Seattle, Washington, for the same price.

A variation of the uniform-delivered pricing method is used by many firms. It is called *zone pricing*. The company sets up a series of prices for zones at varying distances from the plant. Usually the amount of the transportation charge for each zone is in proportion to the distance of the zone from the shipping point. Thus, the actual cost variation is in proportion to the amount charged. There may be instances in which a company may use a zone plan centered at a point where the firm's greatest competition is located, which may be some distance away from its own plant. In such a case charges are not proportionate. If there is a variation of the zone arrangement away from costs of reaching the shipping point, it is based on competitive strategy.

Basing-Point Method. We have noted that the uniform rate tends to place cost burden on buyers near a shipping point and favors those at a distance. On the other hand, the f.o.b. method tends to limit the market of a concern to the vicinity of its operation. This transportation factor is especially significant when delivery cost is a comparatively large part of the cost of an item. In order to solve this problem, the basing-point method of charging freight has been devised. The basing-point method became well known as a result of the system used by the steel companies known as "Pittsburgh plus." According to this plan, regardless of the point of origin, all transportation charges for the shipment of steel were calculated by adding the freight from Pittsburgh to the destination. The legality of such a plan and similar plans is now suspect, although not outlawed, by the Federal Trade Commission. The basing-point plan, however, does achieve certain goals not possible under the previous two methods. By selecting a point that is agreed upon and strategic, a company may avoid the high costs of freight absorption that might have resulted from shipping points under the uniform-delivered pricing method. At the same time a company can compete equally in all areas of the market and use the same base prices.

The Federal Trade Commission recognizes the problems involved in uniform delivered price. It views the f.o.b. pricing method as a means of creating what might be termed "location monopolies," a situation which does not protect competitive conditions. For this reason the Commission dislikes to take a stand against basing-point agreements as such. The Commission states that it is only against such agreements when they tend to restrain trade. The Commission agrees that on some occasions the basing-point arrangements may even encourage trade and competition. Industry, however, is not satisfied with this explanation. The great difficulty is in knowing when the Commission and the courts will declare agreements as "restraining," and when the agreements will be viewed in a positive light to encourage trade. The twilight zone of the antitrust laws appears to be frustrating in this area. A solution to this problem is needed.

Public Relations and Pricing

Does the company charge all the traffic will bear? This is a statement frequently heard when pricing is discussed. In the present era a company is greatly concerned about its public image. Price officers today are aware of reactions resulting from the adoption of high prices. Business, as we have pointed out, acquired a new sensitivity toward the public in the depression of the 1930's. Since that time firms which sell to the public have become circumspect regarding any activity that will prejudice their case in the eyes of the public. One of the strong reasons for encouraging cost as a factor in pricing is that the public may view with misgivings any price which is known to be greatly in excess of the cost. There still lingers in the public mind the concept that there is a ''just price'' and that just price is related to cost. Such a concept dates back to and beyond the Dark Ages. But it still remains as an influence in the pricing of merchandise even today. The public still has its own idea of ethics, and the progressive business firm is prone to honor it.

PRICING PROBLEMS AND POLICIES OF RETAIL STORES

Retailers, like manufacturers, enjoy an area of discretion in the establishment of prices. Although some prices are set by resale maintenance contracts and others are suggested by the manufacturer, when compared with the primary producer, notably the farmer, the retailer enjoys much freedom. He can establish his prices at a high or a low level. He can buy the merchandise at price levels of his own choosing in a large number of cases. He can price individual items according to his judgment of what will benefit him most.

In retailing, as at the other levels of the market, pricing is the art of discovering a desirable equilibrium that will maximize the satisfaction of desires and minimize the costs of the consumer. In the case of consumer products, the ultimate consumer is the final arbiter. From this standpoint, the retailer's price decision is of great significance in maintaining the flow of goods to the consumer.

Coordinating Price Policy with Other Policies

The price policy of the retail store must be carefully integrated with the other policies of the establishment. If one were to compare the entire operation of Lord and Taylor in New York City with Klein's, many differences would be evident. The stores are located in different sections of the city. The people who habitually travel in those areas belong to different social classes and reference groups and have different levels of income. Merchandise lines carried, personnel employed, services provided, and fixtures in each of these stores are consistent with the individuality of the stores. Lord and Taylor caters to a high-income group, and all policies are selected and administered accordingly. On the other hand, Klein's seeks high volume with a low-price appeal, and its policies are so established. The one goal both types of stores have in common is to maximize profits and to build prestige among a large group of customers.

During recent years there has been a tendency for stores to move into higher priced merchandise. Average incomes have increased—more people have been able to purchase better merchandise. Stores that used to feature price with enthusiasm now feature quality. Some stores have changed their policies to conform to this change. A notable example of this change has been Ohrbach's in New York City. This store changed its location from 14th Street to 34th Street and added higher priced lines to its offering.

Some stores are so large that they can appeal to a wide price range. For example, Macy's famous low-price economy policy is still effective advertising. Yet such a policy does not prevent Macy's from attempting to build prestige with a quality appeal. In some of its advertising the store features quality as well as low prices.

In spite of a retailer's attempt to reach a certain level of customers, stores try to attract as broad a grouping as possible. In seeking to avoid the restrictive influence of being classified within a specific price range, some stores have endeavored to place different classes of merchandise in different sections of the store. Some have even carried this point beyond the bargain-basement idea. They have several shops within the store featuring different qualities of merchandise. Such a policy is an attempt to capitalize both on the quality and the low prices. Under such a policy there is an overlap. Many of Macy's customers shop at Lord and Taylor and vice versa.

Some stores can vary price levels more than others. Food stores have some freedom to price at higher or lower levels even though the line of merchandise is quite standard. Prestige, services, location, and advertising policies may give such stores a character that enables them to vary their prices. The same condition exists for drugstores. In the area of dry goods, hardware, and furniture stores, even greater pricing freedom is possible.

It is likely that one policy may complement another. One store operator in a competitive department store cluster chose a policy that provided volume and low-price appeal. To prevent the impression that low prices meant poor quality, however, the slogan which was used in the advertising for the firm was, "The Store of Dependable Merchandise." On another occasion, the manager of a branch of chain stores in a midwestern city conducted a survey to determine customer response. He found that the people in the city considered his merchandise quality as being very low. In truth the merchandise was of a quality comparable with that of the competitors in the city. The low prices were the result of the operating efficiencies of the chain organization. The manager changed his advertising policy and instructed his clerks to talk about quality merchandise. During the next year the store increased its sales and profits materially.

Whatever the price policy adopted by a retail firm, it should be carefully planned and defined. Such planning makes it possible for policies to harmonize. Only in this manner can the store exert the maximum selling impact on the segment of the population to which it is directing its merchandise appeal.

Meeting Markup Goals

In former years retailers with no training and little accumulated information used custom and convention as guides to pricing. They would price "by ear," so to speak. Concepts of scientific management, however, began to find greater favor among marketing groups. Merchants became more conscious of goals; profit goals, sales goals, and gross-margin goals were established. Merchandise was then purchased and priced in harmony with the profit goals of the store.

For example, a certain chain of furniture stores on the West Coast wished its units to be known as high-class stores. At the same time it wished to enjoy the volume that can come only as a result of moderate prices. The management also wished to price the merchandise at a level that would move the furniture with a minimum of markdowns. In order to achieve this merchandising goal, the company set its gross margin aims at 42 percent of the selling price. The company tried to limit markdowns to 5 percent of the sales. The company then determined its initial price level by means of the following formula:

$$\text{Initial Markup \%} = \frac{\text{Expense} + \text{Profits} + \text{Reduction}^{[3]}}{\text{Sales} + \text{Reduction}}$$

Specifically, this chain of furniture stores might plan a profit of 6 percent, expenses of 36 percent, and a reduction of 5 percent of sales. In this case we would have:

$$\text{Initial Markup \%} = \frac{36\% + 6\% + 5\%}{100 + 5\%} = \frac{47}{105} = 44.7\%$$

This arrangement would give the store a maintained markup of 42 percent (36% + 6%) after markdowns. In the particular store there was little variation from this plan insofar as the initial markup was concerned. Practically all goods were marked at this level. Reductions were not always so easy to control. Many times the markdowns exceeded the level planned. Meeting this predetermined goal posed a real challenge to store buyers and sales people.

In many stores the uniform markup rule is not used in pricing, even though a specific goal is set. These stores mark similar types of merchandise at different levels according to desirability and according to competition. When such a method is used, the buyer or the merchandise manager must keep the established goals in mind. Periodic footings may be made in merchandise ledgers to discover how nearly the goals are being kept. In the event that the average markup being achieved is higher than the plan, the buyer can adjust the markup accordingly by marking some of the merchandise lower. Naturally, merchandise should be selected that can be priced accordingly. On the other hand, if the merchandise markup at a certain date is below goals, some merchandise will be marked to higher levels. There may be a markup goal for every department or classification of merchandise. Pricing strategy might be exercised within each of these areas. The average of all the departments will equal the overall markup for the store.

For example, a small limited-line department store with four divisions may have a markup goal of 39 percent. For reasons of competition and handling costs, the merchandise in each division may normally carry a different markup. The results of merchandise operations for a certain period may be as follows:

---

[3] Retail reductions include markdowns, stock shortages, and discounts to special classes of customers, including employees.

	A	B	C	D	TOTALS
Net Sales	5,000	6,000	4,000	7,000	22,000
Cost of Goods Sold	3,000	3,500	3,000	4,000	13,500
Markup	2,000	2,500	1,000	3,000	8,500
Markup%	40%	41.7%	25%	43%	38.7%

A division manager may be in charge of each of the sections, and the manager of the store may work with each of the men in assisting them to meet markup goals. In the example, the store is falling short of its goal by .3 percent. This amount is not serious, but the management is aware that it is falling below its goal.

Meeting markup goals is more than the mere making of correct computations. It involves selecting the proper merchandise, pricing it with discrimination, displaying it to give it maximum sales impact, and training salespeople to present it properly. Pricing it at a level that will provide the least resistance to merchandise movement and which will still give the retailer the greatest return is a significant function of moving the goods.

Elasticity in Retail Pricing

The retailer does not always know the relationship of price to volume on each item. Even if this relationship were discovered by experiment, it is questionable whether it would remain the same for long periods of time. Yet there is a relationship of price to volume of sales, and the price established should be set in the interest of overall and long-term profits. The wise price maker will attempt to price goods according to their sensitivity to price changes. The merchant pricing for profits will reduce prices when the increase in volume is sufficient to net the same or greater gross margins than the present price brings. This is assuming that increased volume will bring no significant changes in expenses. On the other hand, the price of merchandise that tends to have inelastic demand can be increased without decreasing volume to a point where the increase received maximizes profits. It is possible to determine a volume that will justify a price by a simple formula, although it is quite obviously more difficult to determine whether the volume will be realized.

For example, an article costing 60 cents with a 40 percent markup, thus selling at $1 at retail, may average sales of 10 units a week, providing a margin of $4. If the price were to be reduced to 80 cents, a change in volume would be expected. How much would the increase in volume have to be to bring the same gross margin? The formula is as follows:

$$\text{Ratio of new unit volume to old} = \frac{\text{old dollar markup}}{\text{new dollar markup}}$$

Using the figures given in the above example:

$$\frac{\$0.40}{\$0.20} \times 100 = 200 \text{ as an index}$$

The store would, therefore, have to sell twice as many units to realize the same gross margin as under the former plan.

In the case of the price increase, we may wish to determine the amount that sales might decrease without loss of gross margin if we were to increase the price. The same formula would apply. Let us assume that we wish to sell the item costing 60 cents for $1.20 rather than $1.

$$\frac{\text{(old) } \$0.40}{\text{(new) } \$0.60} \times 100 = 66\tfrac{2}{3}, \text{ or } \tfrac{2}{3} \text{ as many sales as made before would bring about the same gross margin}$$

These simple examples illustrate in a very practical manner the importance of demand elasticity in pricing. Even though exact sales cannot be predicted at different price levels, judgments resulting in the gain or loss may be more nearly approximated if these formulas are kept in mind. Indeed, these examples embody a principle that applies in all price decisions, whatever the market level might be.

Competitive Strategy in Pricing

It is the aim of the management of all retail stores to impress upon the customers the wisdom of purchasing merchandise at its store. Even the stores with quality appeals and high prices attempt to impress their patrons with the fact that they receive more for their money. Each wise seller shops his competitor and develops a strategy which gives him some positive advantages that can be used for promotion purposes. The customer is not usually qualified or disposed to make a scientific price judgment. A store might select a few well-known and carefully chosen items, price them low, dramatize them, and, thus, impress the public with unusually low prices. In this manner the store might build a reputation for value. This strategy prompts stores to price at about the same level those items where prices can be directly compared and then to realize higher margins on items where direct comparisons are not likely to be made.

A well-known technique illustrating this practice is the *loss leader*. A store selects a popular piece of merchandise and prices it well below competitors. This item is advertised vigorously. A store may have a double motive in such a policy. First, it may wish to have many people visit the store and purchase other merchandise on which it realizes a satisfactory margin of profit. Second, the store management may be motivated by the fact that the advertising of a low-price item may impress upon the public the idea that it is the store's policy to offer good values.

This strategy may take many forms. For example, in Table 16-1, 10 of 144 stores are ranked in order of dry grocery prices, of which 51 items were surveyed. Note that Store A was low in general groceries. Yet, this store ranked almost at the high point of the list, or 136th, on fresh produce and 123rd out of 144 on meat. Other stores show similar price patterns. The strategy of Store A is to build low-price prestige and volume on its dry grocery sales. The management realizes that if it can create store traffic with dry groceries, it will sell a larger share of fresh produce and meat, which command higher margins.

Table 16-1
TEN SUPERMARKETS WITH THE LOWEST PRICES FOR 51 GENERAL GROCERY ITEMS WITH RANK IN PRICE FOR EACH CLASSIFICATION OF MERCHANDISE

STORE SYMBOL	LOCATION	TYPE	GENERAL GROCERY ITEMS	MEAT	PRODUCE	FROZEN FOOD	ALL ITEMS
A	New York	LC	1	123	136	51	113
B	Portland	IND	2	9	19	55	20
C	Dallas	NC	3	16	51	23	6
D	Columbus	NC	4	49	56	18	17
E	Chicago	NC	5	24	116	29	15
F	Dallas	LC	6	27	62	99	18
G	Denver	NC	7	32	37	93	16
H	Los Angeles	NC	8	102	4	4	49
I	Los Angeles	NC	9	119	8	6	64
J	Providence	NC	10	51	32	59	25

LC—Local Chain   IND—Independent   NC—National Chain

This survey was conducted by the Marketing Department of Brigham Young University.
The Survey included 144 stores.
The store with the lowest prices in each category was ranked #1, etc.

Odd Prices and Psychological Prices

Odd prices were originally adopted as a means of preventing clerks from pocketing money from a sale. If a book sold for $10.00 and was paid for with a ten dollar bill, it would be easy for a dishonest clerk to pocket the money and not report the sale. If the book cost $9.95, however, the clerk would have to ring up the sale on the register or record the sale with a cashier. In addition, the view has long been held that pricing goods at $4.95 or $4.98 rather than at $5 increases sales greatly. This view assumes that the fact that there is no appreciable difference in the prices escapes the consumer's consciousness. That the psychological sound of 98 cents creates less resistance than $1 sounds plausible, and the fact that such techniques are universally practiced is an indication that this view is widely held. However, empirical evidence is lacking to prove that this concept is true, and there has been no agreement on which odd prices are most effective. In a study which attempted to gather empirical evidence, a large mail-order firm made a catalog, split-run test on an item. The item was priced in one million copies of the catalog at one-cent intervals from $1.99 to $1.98—that is, one million catalogs priced the item at $1.99; a second million copies, at $1.98; and so on. There was no conclusive evidence that any one of the prices in the series was more effective than another. It would be most helpful if we had more evidence to support the theories which influence the setting of prices.

Price Lines

In the field of shopping goods, retailers must decide whether to use price lines or to price at a variety of levels. A *price-line* policy is followed when a store selects a specific price within a certain price range. For example, a specialty store, instead of pricing suits which cost the store $40 and $50 at prices yielding a goal of 40 percent markup, or $66 and $83, prices all the suits at $75. Extreme examples of this policy were the men's wear stores that carried only suits and top coats at a single price. Although most of these stores have changed their policy today, they still adhere to a rigid price-line policy of offering suits at only two or three prices. There are virtues in such a policy. It is simple. The stock control problem is made easy. It resolves itself into keeping an adequate variety of styles, sizes, and colors in each line. The task of making a choice is also simplified for the consumer. Making the price-quality evaluation is often a frustrating experience for him. Setting a price line tends to avoid much of this confusion and makes a decision easier. Smaller stock may be required to satisfy customers. The purchases may be concentrated into popular price lines. Bookkeeping and marketing are routine, and it is easy to compute the retail price on items of stock.

On the other hand, difficulties may be encountered in using price lines. Some customers may prefer a price between price lines. A store may have price lines including $1, $1.40, and $1.80. Such customers may wish to pay $1.25, but not $1.40; or $1.75, but not $1.80 for goods priced in this zone. On the other hand, the store may gain by actually selling merchandise for $1.80 to those who would normally have paid only $1.75.

Another difficulty with price lines is that they are inflexible. The price lines of stores become habits. They may lose their appeal when they are changed. A problem arises when the general price level goes up or down. If the price of merchandise to the store increases, it must choose between three alternatives: it may increase its prices and lose the positive effect of that price habit and simplicity; it may get poorer merchandise and trade down on quality; or it may continue to sell at present levels and take a smaller margin on sales. Of the three, the last may be the most desirable. It may be possible for the store to retain its price structure, accentuate its price appeal, and build enough volume to compensate for the lower margin. In the case of falling prices, the store also may find it necessary to make adjustments. It may lower its prices or adopt a better quality for the same price. In the interest of building goodwill and prestige, it would seem that in this instance the latter alternative may be desirable.

During the last two decades, prices have shifted so much that stores have found it necessary and desirable to change their price lines often. The merchandise itself has changed in character so greatly that price lines no longer have the rigidity they once had. Price lines are still very much in evidence, however, and adjustments are made as changes require them.

CONCLUSION

In summarizing a discussion of pricing, several points should be noted. First, the skill of the merchant depends in great part on his ability to assess properly the subjective forces that lie behind supply and demand. Objective and quantitative research may be necessary to aid this program. The enlightened marketing management must then set up an administrative program which will support the prices it chooses. Such administration not only includes the setting of an optimum price; it also involves coordinating a product policy and a selling program with the pricing function. Selling in this instance refers to advertising, promotion, and the providing of a desirable environment for the selling transaction. Just as in the case of all marketing, the successful performance of these functions requires keen judgment and decisive action in a constantly changing and dynamic marketplace.

QUESTIONS AND ANALYTICAL PROBLEMS

1. What are some of the reasons why supermarket chain groceries strive for a maintained markup of around 18 percent to 20 percent, while department stores average markups of approximately 40 percent?

2. "Cost should not dominate price setting." Explain and evaluate this statement.

3. Is price leadership in an industry evidence of monopolistic practices? Can price leadership practices ever be justified legally? Ethically?

4. What is a loss leader? Evaluate the use of loss leaders by retailers.

5. Define (a) trade discount, (b) quantity discount, (c) f.o.b., (d) uniform-delivered price, (e) basing point.

6. Give an illustration of how pricing should conform with other policies in a retail establishment.

7. Draw a skeleton outline of an income statement. Show which items affect the markup to be achieved by a retailer.

8. In the table on page 320 what are the possible reasons why each of the four departments has a different markup percentage?

9. Evaluate the use of an odd-price policy.

10. Define and illustrate price lines.

11. Evaluate price cutting as a competitive device. Consider probable effects on sales volume and on net operating profit.

12. A manufacturer of fans desired to reduce the suggested retail price which was $79.95. A committee of sales and production men made cost-saving suggestions, of which the following are examples:

> 2" motor stock cut to 1½".
> Simplify coil winding.
> Eliminate back screen's washer.
> Simplify trunnion mount.
> Redesign base and mounting.
> Reduce packing material.

All their suggestions, if put into effect, would allow a saving of $5 in the manufacturing cost. An additional 12 cents per fan would be saved by leaving the blades unpainted. What questions should be considered in determining whether to put the cost-saving suggestions into effect?

Case 16 • THE FAIRVIEW COMPANY

The Fairview Company specializes in manufacturing ladies' hand mirrors and has enjoyed a prominence in the industry for the past decade.

Fairview has two mirrors—one retailing for $5 and another for $8.50. The majority of mirrors (70 percent) are sold through drugstores; the remainder are sold in variety stores. Sales have been maintained at a constant level for the less expensive model, but the market share has decreased from 45 percent to 30 percent during the past three years. Much of the decrease is attributed to the current trend of increased demand for larger and more expensive beauty items. This provided the stimulus for adding the $8.50 "Lovely Lady" model three years ago. Sales of the "Lovely Lady" have increased 10 percent yearly since it was introduced. The following figures are available:

Year	Model	Unit Sales	Profit Margin
1972	$5.00	870,000	5%
	$8.50	150,000	6%
1973	$5.00	870,000	4%
	$8.50	165,000	7%
1974	$5.00	870,000	3%
	$8.50	171,500	7%

Fairview has recently been approached by several large discount house chains who are desirous of carrying Fairview's less expensive model. Before doing so, however, they demand that they be able to retail the mirror for $4.50. Such action is feasible since a relatively high markup is currently being used in the drugstores. The chains claim that a 20 percent increase in unit sales can be achieved if action is taken immediately.

• What pricing policy should Fairview employ? Are there any better courses of action available to Fairview?

Marketing communications 17

The large brass tray that means "barber shop here" in Denmark, the red rag or red flower tied on a pole extending over the doorway of a hut high in the Andes Mountains which indicates that *chicha* (a potent local brew) is on sale, and the man beating a drum crying out his wares in a market are means of communicating to possible customers the availability of a service or product, just as is the newest, full-color, completely orchestrated television commercial.

Promotion of products and services is a necessary component of a free economy and most likely lowers prices because of its effect on reducing the cost and effort of searching out required goods and because of inducing large-scale manufacturing. For our purposes here, we will define *promotion* as that communication which secures understanding between two persons for the purposes of bringing about a favorable buying action and for achieving a permanent, or at least long-lasting, confidence in the company and the product or service it provides.

This chapter will discuss the following topics: first, the role of selling in general in the total marketing process; second, the promotion mix, which includes an examination of the specific role of advertising in identification and demand creation and attention to the principal criticisms leveled at advertising; third, the importance of the use of brands as a selling aid to both the manufacturer and the middleman; and, fourth, the importance of personal selling at the different levels of marketing institutions, with emphasis on the retail selling problem.

THE ROLE OF SELLING

Buyers cannot be manipulated, but some communication can produce an awareness of a latent desire. That kind of persuasion or selling is necessary to keep the economy going.

Communication Necessary to Move Goods

The success of the producer is dependent upon his ability to persuade others to consume his product. Before the other party will purchase the product, he must be made aware of it and motivated to acquire it. To see more clearly what the function of selling really implies, visualize a situation in which all forms of selling are totally absent. Assume that General Motors develops revolutionary changes in an automobile that provides transportation more economically, more safely, and faster, in a more beautiful vehicle. Assume further that neither the company nor any of its agencies undertake any selling activity. The company officers or the workers at the plant may talk about the vehicle. Passersby may view it as the new model comes off the production lines. It might even be that the government would furnish a complete description with specifications for the car in a publication similar to the *Federal Register*. The question then arises, how long would it take for reliable word regarding the qualities of the car to reach Los Angeles, New York, and Miami?

Granted, there would be some communication, and it might gather momentum as it progressed; but the time period necessary to bring about a complete covering of the market would be uncertain and slow. Furthermore, the information passed by word of mouth would probably be much less reliable than the sales and advertising information we now have. A new automobile model probably would stimulate person-to-person communication as much as any item on the market. What would happen if the item had little or no appeal, or at most, an ordinary rather than a spectacular appeal?[1]

Specific Contributions of Selling

There are at least three reasons why goods may fail to move at a satisfactory rate through marketing channels, assuming, of course, that the money and credit machinery of the economy are functioning at a reasonable level. These reasons can be stated briefly in the following manner:

1. The pattern of goods produced and offered on the market may not coincide with the wants or the desires of the consumers. This failure of marketing institutions to merchandise skillfully increases the resistance of consumers to the movement of goods.
2. People may choose to save for security or for gain rather than to convert the returns from their products or services into consumption goods.

---

[1] "When properly defined, selling is identifiable as a force whose origin in society is associated with the highest of human aspiration—the will to be free and the will to create." From an address by George W. Robbins. In this address Mr. Robbins discusses the question of selling ethics in terms of the total society. See George W. Robbins, "Is Selling Good for Society?" *Vital Speeches of the Day* (New York: City News Publishing Co., March 15, 1955), Vol. XXI, p. 1117.

3. There may be a lethargy on the part of the consumer that causes him not to exchange the returns from his production for consumption goods.

A successful sales program should influence all these factors. First, effective selling tends to move goods even though they are not the exact choices of consumers. The retail salesman may sell the customer a substitute or something better than what he originally wanted. Often he creates new wants. Second, effective selling creates desire so strong that goods mean more than the security of savings. We do not wish to cast reflections on the time-honored custom of saving. There is a difference in saving for liquidity or safety and saving for gain. Both are related and have their virtues; but in terms of moving goods and for the economy at large, there are times when they can be overdone and dangerous. Third, regarding lethargy or failure to consume because desires have not been awakened, potential demand can be made dynamic and effective by a successful selling program.

Thus, a demand is created for goods that would not exist without the selling process. There is, in the economy, greater productive capacity than the present distribution machinery can sell. It follows, then, that any program which stimulates demand for a product performs a significant function in bringing the product into being. Without demand stimulation there would be no need for, nor could we support, the enormous production machine of which we boast.

Relationship of Selling to Business Management

Up to this time our discussion has related selling to the economy. Yet nothing has been said that would not be relevant to the individual business. The economy is merely the sum of the individual business firms and the people they serve. The individual business firm does the selling that creates the demand. Each firm tends to prosper in proportion to the prosperity of the entire economy. The firm which does the best job of selling is the firm—other things being equal—that gains the highest profit.

The sales transaction is the strategic focal point in the marketing process. Without it there would be no marketing. There are two fundamental ingredients to the sales transaction: first, a product that will satisfy a desire; and second, a desire seeking satisfaction. In our economy the initiative for supplying the product rests with business management; and, as already indicated, business has also assumed the responsibility for creating the desire. It is business management's responsibility to supply a desirable product, to inform the public of its offering, and to motivate it to buy. Skill in the selling program is one of the important tests of management success.

Business firms engage in various types of selling. It may take the form of advertising in magazines, television, radio, newspapers, or other media. The product may be put in an attractive package and skillfully displayed. Salespeople selling the product may be given special training. Especially in the early stages of a new product's life, the purpose of selling is to stimulate new demand that did not exist before. Much selling is designed to win a sale away from a competitor. This is the function of management.

Interrelationship of Selling, Pricing, and Merchandising

Since marketing is best understood as a flow of goods, the goal for the business firm is to maintain this flow. The factors of the marketing mix are responsible for keeping this flow active, and these factors are interdependent. Thus, merchandise policies adopted by a firm influence the prices it can charge and the promotion program it will use, and vice versa.

For example, several years ago Armour introduced Dial soap. The name was short, easy to remember, and euphonious. It lent itself well to promotional copy, but a name is only a small part of a promotion plan. The selling program of this product was built around the word "hexachlorophene." The name of this chemical product imputed confidence by scientific association, and it was not too difficult to remember and pronounce. The promotion featured a toilet soap that prevents body odor because of the scientific qualities which it possesses, including a distinctive fragrance. In this way, product qualities were ingeniously integrated into promotional resources. Satisfaction qualities were such that they could be effectively dramatized.

Other factors of the marketing mix—pricing and place—were also skillfully blended into the pattern. The company faced the alternative of setting a price at the level of ordinary toilet soap, which at that time sold for 7 to 9 cents a bar, or selling the product as a specialty item and pricing it in excess of the popular price. If the product itself and the type of advertising that was used to sell it could assure the product of a special identity with the consumer, it would be consistent to ask a price that was in harmony with product quality and promotion goals. The soap would not have the same quality appeal if it were sold at a lower or competitive price. The company reasoned in this manner, and the soap was priced to sell as a specialty at retail for 25 cents. With the product, promotion, and price established to give the product prestige, the company accordingly chose to place the product in prestige stores. Department and drugstores were chosen as the outlets through which to introduce the product.

Thus, the entire marketing pattern was designed to give the impression that the soap appealed to a class market. After the soap was introduced in prestige stores and at a high-quality price, the company broadened distribution to include food and variety stores and reduced the price to 18 cents. The results were phenomenally successful. Meat packers had been failing to break into the soap business for years, yet Armour and Company in 1954 realized a $3 million profit on the sale of this soap. This amount was the same as the company's overall earnings on its $2 billion meat business.

The significant fact from the point of view of selling was that the entire promotion campaign was logically integrated with the product, the price, and the place where the product was offered for sale. In other words, moving goods through marketing channels is not just a matter of promotion, pricing, or selling. Successful marketing is a combination of all these activities integrated into a positive plan of strategy wherein all are interdependent.

The Bona Fide Sales Transaction

We might now pose the question, isn't it possible for sellers, by the use of effective selling techniques, to exaggerate the qualities of the product and to consummate a sale without giving the customer the anticipated satisfaction? Undoubtedly such has been the experience of many consumers. Often people are oversold on products. It is difficult to discern whether value is commensurate with cost, since people are reluctant after a purchase to admit that their judgment was not sound. If the business firm is viewed as a growing and enduring organism, however, a high percentage of such sales would weaken the company's competitive position.

With due respect to the great significance of promotion in the movement of goods, the ultimate test of the sales transaction is whether or not the product gives satisfaction commensurate with cost. In the case of a product or a firm, if the sales transactions fail to meet this standard, its future is dim. To give the customer the expected satisfaction is not only a matter of ethics but also a matter of sound business policy. Indeed, one can generalize and say that a sale in which the satisfaction is less than the cost tends to be a depressant on sales and to demoralize the business stature of the seller. This statement is based on the fact that the major segment of our economy consists of a type of business that is planning for the future, rather than the type that depends on quick profits. Sales have been made and will continue to be made of merchandise that is disappointing to the buyer. But these are not the transactions that provide the structure and strength of a growing economy. Firms that participate in such programs are not among those that endure.

THE PROMOTION MIX

Marketing communication may be classified into two types of activity—advertising and personal selling. As noted above, to be effective the promotion program must fit company policies in other parts of the marketing mix. Further, the portion of promotional effort accomplished by each type of communication activity is determined by the nature of the product, the type of customers approached, and possibly, the stage of the life cycle of the product.

One manufacturer of proprietary drug products allocates almost 80 percent of a multimillion dollar promotion budget to television advertising. In contrast, one cosmetic manufacturer spends under 3 percent of sales on advertising, although the industry average is approximately 15 percent of sales, because it chooses to allocate most of its communication budget to a house-to-house sales force.

Broadly speaking, a relatively large portion of the total promotional budget will be allocated to personal selling when products are first introduced, when the product is complex, and when the market is concentrated. Obversely, this means that personal selling is probably too expensive and likely not feasible if the product is generally accepted, low-priced, and has a potential market among tens of thousands, or millions, of families. Hence, a large share of promotion budgets is allocated for advertising by detergent and drug-item manufacturers, and a low percentage of sales and promotional dollars appears in the advertising budgets of technical equipment manufacturers.

Conditions favoring the use of advertising as the principal ingredient of the promotional mix are those identified over two decades ago by Professor Borden in *The Economic Effects of Advertising*:

1. A favorable primary demand trend. When volume in an industry is expanding, the firm can try for a portion of the expanding total.
2. Opportunity for product differentiation. Not only can product differences be explained and exploited in advertising, but usually when there are noticable differentiations, margins can be wider; thus funds are available for promotion.
3. Hidden qualities of importance to consumers are present. Mechanical excellence of mechanical products and the efficacy of drug and cosmetic products are not discernible; hence, consumers rely on brands and advertising messages. When qualities can be judged at the time of purchase, as with textiles or fresh vegetables, advertising of brands is less important.
4. Emotional appeals relevant to the product are present. Cosmetics and travel can be sold through appeals to glamour and romance in contrast to potatoes, for example, about which little emotional excitement can be aroused.[2]

In 1972, 11 drug and cosmetic companies, 4 soap and cleanser companies, and two candy companies were the only firms among the 100 largest advertisers who spent 10 percent of sales or more for advertising. They are all intensely competitive industries where primary demand continues to rise. Product differentiation is usually present, most of the products they sell are priced at less than $1.00, and frequent repeat purchases are the rule.

Advertising

Advertising serves both as a means of identifying products and as a means of stimulating demand. Further, it is used to accomplish these tasks by informing people *en masse*. These tasks consist of attempts to transmit feelings, commitments, and convictions, as well as to transmit them persuasively. In order to describe briefly how such tasks are accomplished, we will not distinguish between advertising and sales promotion but will discuss both together.

Advertisers use the following media and devices to tell their message:

Printed Media	*Outdoor Media*	*Electronic Media*	*Promotional Devices*
Newspapers	Billboards	Radio	Brands
Magazines	Posters	Television	Display materials
Business papers			Trading stamps
Farm publications			Games
			Lucky drawings
			Free samples
			Price reduction
			Coupons

Advertising Expenditures. Table 17-1 shows how approximately $23 billion of advertising expenditures in 1972 were allocated to the various media. A

---

[2] Neil H. Borden, *The Economic Effec's of Advertising* (Homewood, Illinois: Richard D. Irwin, Inc., 1942), pp. 424-432.

discussion of allocation of advertising budgets is not pertinent here, but note the use made of various media for national and local advertising. Newspapers and radio derive most of their advertising income from local advertising, while all the other media draw more heavily from national advertising.

Table 17-1
DISTRIBUTION OF ADVERTISING EXPENDITURES BY MEDIA
—1972

	Percent of Total	Dollar Expenditures (Millions of $)
Newspapers	30.2%	$6,960
Television	17.9	4,110
Direct Mail	14.5	3,350
Magazines	6.4	1,480
Radio	6.6	1,530
Business Papers	3.3	770
Outdoor.................	1.3	290
Miscellaneous *	19.7	4,541
	99.9%	$23,031

* Miscellaneous includes costs of company advertising departments, signs, advertising novelties, motion pictures, art work, and mechanical costs not counted elsewhere.
Source: *Advertising Age* (November 21, 1973), p. 62.

Promotional Strategy. For effective use of marketing communication, (1) the target segment of the population must be identified, (2) the medium or combination of media best suited to reach that segment must be selected, and (3) the proper theme or message must be determined.

In Chapter 3 market segmentation was introduced. Here we will say only that the producer must determine which segment of the population would be interested in, and gain value from, his product. A considerable amount of judgment will be exercised, since for most products it is not obvious which will be the target segments of the population. To whom should one attempt to sell sailboats, for example? Is age a factor? What income is necessary before a family will consider sailing as a hobby? Certain geographical areas far inland would appear to be ruled out, but one must remember that man-made lakes are being developed (Oklahoma, for instance, now claims more acres of fresh water for recreation than most other states). A detailed knowledge of attitudes and activities of the people and topographical characteristics of the area would be minimal information to have. Research methods and sources of information to assist in discovering and defining such areas were introduced in Chapter 13.

Selecting the Medium. While people cannot be conveniently categorized, there are certain media that have particular appeal for persons with special interests. For example, we have outdoor and sports magazines, so-called shelter magazines for home and garden information, intellectual magazines which preview other publications, and well-managed radio and television stations that select certain audiences and arrange programs to attract them.

Each major city has rock and roll stations, "good-music" stations, and TNT (time, news, and temperature) interspersed with pop records. In general, the audience can be predicted from the type of programming employed. However, there are enough exceptions that a careful analysis should be made of the station's claimed audience makeup. For example, a chain-link fence company quadrupled its business after advertising at midnight on a station that claimed the teenage market. Furthermore, if one examines trade journals, one will note that not only do the advertisements feature industrial products but also the advertising copy uses the language of the industry. Thus, to be effective. the medium, the theme, and the language must be congruent with the target segment of the population and the product being sold.

Selecting the Advertising Theme. In Chapter 13 reference was made to research designed to discover consumer motivation. Why is it that (as noted by a critic of business, Thorstein Veblen, at the end of the 19th Century) "a fancy bonnet of this year's model appeals to our sensibilities today much more forcibly than an equally fancy bonnet of the model of last year . . . it would be a matter of utmost difficulty to award the palm for intrinsic beauty to one rather than to the other of these structures"?[3]

Since advertising must appeal to large numbers of persons to be economically feasible, it is requisite that a central theme be selected which will elicit favorable buying action.[4] For some products, price and quality are the prime determinants. For others, demographic and economic measures of the market tell us where to place advertising and whether or not it is sufficient to state that such and such is available at "X" price. For still others, it is necessary to find a theme that appeals to some emotion. Various pretesting devices have been developed for advertisements which help to identify effective appeals. These do not identify the motives of persons, but they do attempt to measure reactions and determine whether the proposed advertisement would result in a favorable response.

Types of Pretests. The simplest pretest in conception, but one that can be difficult to construct and apply, is the checklist technique. The following hypothetical example illustrates how this technique can be used in evaluating three proposed advertisements:

	Advertisements			
Factor	A	B	C	
Attention Value:				
Strikingness	2	4	1	
Clarity	4	4	5	(Scored on a scale of
Intensity of Feeling	1	4	1	1 through 5 with 5 be-
Meaning Value	2	2	1	ing maximum.)
Memory Value	1	4	1	
Action Value	1	3	1	

---

[3] Thorstein Veblen, *The Theory of the Leisure Class* (New York: The Modern Library, 1954), p. 131.

[4] What happens to an advertising or sales message after it has been received by the customer? M. Dale Beckman reviews numerous studies dealing with this subject and among other findings he discusses some roadblocks to communication in "Are Your Messages Getting Through?" *Journal of Marketing,* Vol. 31, No. 3 (July, 1967), pp. 34-38.

The difficulty with such tests is the usual lack of objectivity in judging. Also, even the best of the three in the example may not be an effective advertisement.

Panel Tests. Simply stated, panel or jury tests consist of having several persons—who are considered to be likely users of the product being advertised—examine and judge the advertisements. In some cases panel members are asked to rank the advertisements by selecting the best, the next best, and so on. In another use of panels, the members are asked to make paired comparisons. Here the respondent is handed only two advertisements and is asked to select the better of the two. Sometimes the panel member is promised a gift if he selects from various advertisements the product he would like. This technique supposedly elicits more thoughtful answers.

Whatever variation of panel testing is used, there is provision for discussion which frequently allows the advertiser to catch misunderstandings and wrong impressions before the advertisement is run. Critics of the method state that such tests can often determine whether the advertisement tested creates or enhances a desire for a product, but the tests do not indicate the advertisement's attention value or its power to induce a purchase.

Recognition and Recall Tests. This method involves determining whether persons remember having seen a particular advertisement. One way is to make up a dummy magazine, leave it with the respondent for examination, and then ask him later whether he had recently seen the new Crest advertisement, for example. If he had, the respondent is asked to describe the advertisement. The presumption is that an advertisement that is noticed and remembered is likely to be effective; however, there is no assurance that a remembered advertisement will produce sales.

Market Tests. Perhaps the most common type of market test is the inquiry response. A limited run of the advertisement is made and a count taken of inquiries received. Inquiries may be invited in a coupon offering some inducement or by an offer hidden in the body of the copy. Unfortunately, this may be more of a test of the offer than of the effectiveness of the advertisement.

A full-scale run of the advertisement may be made in a limited geographic area to test effectiveness before the advertisement or even a campaign is run nationally. The principal advantage of this kind of test is that it really measures sales effectiveness. The disadvantages are that it is expensive and takes considerable time. Also, the variables in the market may not be truly representative of other markets.

Evaluation of Advertisements. For the electronic media the principal evaluations consist of counting the number of persons listening or viewing. Hence, this is more an evaluation of the media than of the advertising message.

Basic approaches used to measure broadcast audiences include personal interviews (often by telephone) at the time a certain program is on the air; mechanical systems that involve connecting an electronic device which records the station or channel turned on; and diaries in which the panel members are asked to record the programs watched, number of persons watching, and their sex and age. These approaches have been criticized recently because of the methods used in selecting respondents. Basically the statistical methods employed are sound, however. The information obtained is the share of the audience by programs and stations. This is determined by the percentage of sets in use which are tuned to a particular program. The program rating, on the other hand, includes all sets in the area, not just those turned on. Also, the composition of the audience is measured and reported by age, sex, and other features, such as income and residential area, that may be of interest to the client.

Printed media are measured principally by recognition and recall tests. The oldest and best known rating service is that provided by Daniel Starch and Staff. Their procedure is to measure degrees of reading. Interviewers go to a sample of households and ask the respondent to go through the publication with them. Each item is rated as: *noted*–the respondent remembers seeing the item; *seen-associated*—the person read the name of the product or service being advertised; and *read-most*–the respondent read half or more of the copy. If the percentage who *noted* is substantially greater than the percentage of *seen-associated,* it means that whatever caught the readers' attention was not relevant to the product or that reference to the product was too inconspicuous.

From such studies one can determine the value of (1) size of the advertisement, (2) frequency of insertion, (3) color as compared to black and white, and (4) one campaign in comparison with another. Many organizations use variations of the recognition and recall method.

Evaluation of Advertising Campaign Effectiveness. Ideally one attempts to determine the effectiveness of advertising on sales independently of other factors. This is an almost impossible task, but some methods are used to make measurements of advertising effectiveness in terms of sales.

The measurements of effectiveness discussed above are based on the premise that favorable attitudes are equal to or related to buying action. That concept is open to question. Hence, there are now attempts to measure each element of a buying decision and relate it to action response. One method being tested is the so-called DAGMAR (Defining Advertising Goals for Measured Advertising Results) procedure. Usually advertising goals are set and measured in terms of message registration, product image, and preference level achieved.

A refinement of panel testing is the competitive preference pretest developed and used by Schwerin Research Corporation. Panel members are invited to participate in a drawing for a merchandise prize. Each respondent selects from a large number of brands the item he wants to win. After the drawing, panel members view television commercials. They then receive another list of the same brands to check for preference, and another drawing is held. Relative effectiveness of the commercials is thereby measured by the changes in preference before and after viewing the commercial. Even though a lottery is not the same as a purchase, this technique comes closer to a buying response than other panel-opinion methods. Other attempts, made possible by computers, involve operations research procedures that are designed to identify and measure the intensity of each variable affecting the sales of a particular product.

The retail audit is a means used to measure sales and, thereby, advertising campaign effectiveness. Since shipments from the factory may not correspond to purchases of the product at the retail level, periodic audits are made of movements through retail outlets, most commonly every 60 days. One of the companies that contracts to make retail audits provides clients with information on total consumer purchases, dealer purchases, inventory levels, stock outs, and market share. These data are obtained by major market areas, total city size, type of stores handling, and percent of sales accomplished by chains and independents. By examining general economic conditions and other factors, such as weather or competitor's activities, it is possible to estimate fairly closely the effectiveness of advertising.

Arguments Against Promotional Activities

In view of all the positive claims made for advertising, why do so many sincere people object to advertising? Probably one of the reasons is a basic problem of communication. Many persons who have cultivated sensitivities to the good and the beautiful are offended at the language of advertising. Furthermore, they feel insulted at being classed with the mentality to which advertising appeals. When we view the matter in a practical light, however, many advertisers would not be able to pay the cost of advertising if it did not appeal to the masses. It is through the savings of mass production that a company can afford to pay $50,000 for a double-page spread in a popular magazine. The advertiser must communicate effectively with the greatest number of people. One authority expressed it in this manner: "Since common experience is essential to communication, the greater the number to be reached, the simpler the communication must be."[5]

In some fields, of course, advertising appeals and copy are directed to certain segments of the market. Advertising to professional men uses professional language, and advertising to trade groups uses the language of the trade.

Exaggerated Claims. One of the common complaints about advertising is the fact that advertisers make exaggerated claims regarding their products, such as the statement that "no other . . . can make this claim." Superlative statements are made with seeming abandon. In addition, claims are made for many products that do not ring true. Two comments are pertinent in this connection.

First, although in the light of some standards these claims may be indefensible, they are not much different from ordinary conversation in many circles. A Dodger fan talking about his favorite pitcher or a political candidate speaking during a national campaign often indulges in exaggerations of a comparable nature. According to the judgment of the advertisers, such strong appeals are necessary to get action; and since the advertiser seeks sales and profits, he certainly is going to use every means at his command to achieve his

---

[5] Donald Desinger, "The Film and Public Opinion in a Symposium," *Print, Radio, and Film in a Democracy* (Chicago: University of Chicago Press, 1942), p. 78.

goal. Careful advertisers are beginning to realize, however, that such overstatements may be to their long-time disadvantage.

Second, an exaggerated claim may be based on an actual utility that the advertiser has difficulty in communicating to the public. The present significance of the utility may not bear any proportion at all to the emphasis given the subject by the advertising campaign, but the overemphasis is used to get attention and action. This practice of overemphasizing the importance of the utility possesses elements of dishonesty by its implications. Even so, it may have long-run benefits, and it is difficult to prevent without inhabiting freedom of expression.

The recent cases before the Federal Trade Commission regarding excessive claims in advertisments for aspirin are addressed to this point. What is being asked is that only true claims be made. The manufacturers of Crest toothpaste had difficulty in presenting the proven virtues of the new product. Finally, they decided to introduce Crest only with black and white advertisements with factual statements, no pictures, and no large headlines. This was to avoid any appearance of flamboyance and overstatement.

Lack of Social Responsibility. Probably one of the most frequent charges against advertising is that it is motivated by profit and not by the welfare of the individual or society. Satisfaction claims made by the advertising may not be genuine. The product may not be as represented, as we have indicated, although time usually will reveal such irregularities. Advertising may attempt to stimulate habits that a majority of the people may feel are bad for society.

On the other hand, society has certain checks on excessive abuses. In some instances laws may serve as a check on advertisements, as in the case of pornographic information. Some media which carry advertising may sift it to avoid attempts to instill habits and to establish customs that are generally felt to be degrading. For example, the national radio and television networks refuse whisky ads. The public conscience itself stands on guard against flagrant abuses. Businessmen should encourage the community to criticize advertising that is socially undesirable. Certainly such criticism is one of the safeguards of the democratic process.

Advertising must be viewed as part of the whole business process. Seen in this perspective, advertising is recognized as a force that awakens latent desires. It provides information that enables customers to make discriminating choices. Because advertising is the expression of individuals who are impelled by motivation of profit and self-preservation, it is sometimes unduly aggressive. Overaggressiveness or dishonest advertising, however, contains the seeds of its own destruction in a free and communicative economy.

Industry Action Against Abuses

There are misuses and abuses of marketing communications. No one is more concerned about this than responsible marketing executives. For many years there have been positive programs to assure that the consumer is better served. The national truth-in-advertising law, consumer action movements, and ethical advertising committees in Better Business Bureaus have been established to regulate unethical and misleading advertisers. Trade papers and general business magazines are carrying frequent criticisms and positive suggestions for the improvement of ethical practices by marketing organizations. Many advertising agencies and media refuse to handle advertising of questionable taste or to accept certain products.

One can, of course, argue that despite these activities there is much to criticize. True, but the fact remains that there are large numbers of responsible persons in business who willingly accept the responsibility of working to decrease the abuses.

BRAND AS A SELLING AID

A brand permits a company to crystallize positive goodwill associations around a name. The brand name becomes a symbol of quality that influences the person to choose the company's product. The more favorable and the more powerful such associations are, the greater the selling power of the product. Such positive associations may be the result of many factors. The product itself may yield a high degree of satisfaction that recalls favorable association when the name is spoken. The package may be attractive. The company that sells the product may have achieved a good name because of its public relations policy or reputation for selling a line of products which has gained prominence.

One may enjoy drinking Coca-Cola; but if there were no name with which to associate this experience, the consumer would find it difficult to repeat the experience. The information and motivation that were a part of this experience would not have been preserved. They cannot be recalled or transferred with a product unless the product has a name. In a sense, then, a brand name might be considered a receptacle wherein the goodwill associations of the product may be stored. Putting it in still another manner, a brand may be considered a reservoir of crystallized salesmanship or goodwill.

Brand names are becoming more important on the marketing scene. With the increase in sales there has been a corresponding increase in advertising. In national advertising, newspaper advertising has held its own, magazine national advertising has increased significantly, and radio advertising also has increased. In addition, the television advertising cost has been superimposed upon the other costs. This increasing volume and increasingly effective advertising have given advertising a much greater selling impact. As a result even furniture is beginning to feature brand names. If we add to this tendency the increasing use of self-service, where there is no sales clerk to influence a choice, the use of partly presold brands by advertising becomes even more important.

Influence of Brand on Selling Methods

The discussion of brand is significant to promotion and selling because the power of a brand influences the process by which the product reaches the market. We have noted that the product must have the aid of some positive force pushing or pulling it through the marketing channel. This aid may be in the form of a wide margin of profit to the middleman. Or it may be a brand preference created at the consumer level. Such preference makes it possible for the middleman to sell the product with a minimum of effort and at a small cost. Naturally the firm that can include both a margin and a positive brand appeal assures itself of a satisfactory volume of sales.

Procter and Gamble establishes strong demand with the public through advertising its brands. This company also allows conventional margins of profit to middlemen and also sends sales representatives to the distributors and retailers. Naturally the use of all these means to sell the product is expensive. Because of the huge volume of its sales, the per unit cost of selling the product is so low that this company can employ all the promotional methods described and still realize a satisfactory profit. The example illustrates an organizational unity wherein the various methods of selling are combined to achieve the objectives of the seller.

In some instances a brand name becomes so widely accepted that its goodwill can be applied to other products. For example, Gillette, for many years, sold only razors and blades. The name was then applied to shaving cream and men's toiletries. The company's best selling item is now the Gillette Cricket butane lighter.[6]

Kinds of Brands

Brands may be classed as manufacturer's brands and middleman's brands. As the name implies, a manufacturer's brand carries the name the manufacturer gives it. It is not necessarily the name of the company; Lincoln and Mercury, for example, are products of Ford Motor Company. In some cases, however, the product does carry the name of the company, as in the case of the Ford car. Usually, although not always, the manufacturer's brand is marketed on a national scale and is therefore called a national brand. A middleman may also adopt a brand name to identify his product. In most instances the middleman operates in a restricted region of the nation. For this reason his brand is sometimes called a local brand.

Manufacturer's Brand. The manufacturer's brand usually carries a stronger selling impact than the distributor's or middleman's brand. The national brand has the advantage of advertising on national radio and television networks. It is advertised in widely and frequently read magazines. It is sold in greater volume and can support a much larger advertising budget. It may carry the selling impact of Coca-Cola in soft drinks or Del Monte in canned vegetables.

For this reason, nationally branded items can command a higher price for comparable quality. Since the nationally branded product has usually won a preference, it maintains a stable price more easily during periods of price declines than does a local brand or nonbranded item. The goodwill attached to a national brand makes it a desirable product for the distributor to stock. Such preference gives the distributor easier access to the market.

---

[6] "Global Report," *Wall Street Journal,* May 20, 1974, p. 6.

As in the case of the good name of an individual, the branding of a product carries with it some responsibility. If the product quality does not meet desirable standards, ill will can accrue and discourage the use of the product just as easily as goodwill can support it positively. Some distributors may avoid the use of national brands because of their higher price and narrower profit margin. Some retailers and distributors stage large campaigns to place their own private brands ahead of national brands.[7] Such a policy can boomerang, however, when the national advertiser has established a strong preference with the ultimate consumer.

Middleman's Brands. The shortages of World War II had a negative impact on the middleman's brands. These brands have never made a strong comeback since that time. Middleman's brands are found mostly in food items. During World War II shortages of food and material made it difficult for the local distributors to maintain their brands. Manufacturers found it possible to sell all they could manufacture under their own label, and it was to their advantage to do so. The careful price-comparison shopping that characterized the 1930's, when the consumer movement was in full swing, did not exist during the war period; subsequently, such a condition favored the nationally branded item.

There are advantages, however, that the distributor enjoys if he can be successful in establishing and maintaining brand prestige in his product. Owing to the conventionally higher price of the national brand, the distributor may put a better quality of product on the market at a low price and win goodwill and prestige. Also, a certain amount of independence results when a distributor has brands of his own. He is not at the mercy of price, margin, or promotion changes of the national brands that may be to his disadvantage.

Nevertheless, few distributors can be completely independent of national brands. The distributor must play his cards wisely or he may lose the privilege of handling some of the popular brands. If a distributor directs too much attention to selling his own brands, the manufacturer may find other wholesalers or sell his product directly to the retailer.

It appears that there may be an increase in the number of distributors' brands in the future. The goodwill that is attached to a brand name is a property right. Attached to it is a certain amount of strength and security. As distributors become larger and stronger, they will want to strengthen their position by acquiring the goodwill themselves. For example, we have the A & P with Eight-O-Clock brand coffee. Also, Macy's store has 20,000 items manufactured especially for its own business with a private brand label.

Some have questioned the economy of multiple brands offered on the market. Special promotion and advertising are required to popularize and sell brands. It is an expensive undertaking. On the other hand, competition is desirable, and brands are a means of making competition effective. The more

---

[7] Harper W. Boyd, Jr. and Ronald E. Frank explain that private food labels are becoming more popular each year and discuss some of the implications in the article, "The Importance of Private Labels in Food Retailing," *Business Horizons* (Summer, 1966), pp. 81-90.

brands that seek the patronage of the consumer, the greater will be the concentration of skills competing to give the consumer the best product.

How Many Products Under A Brand Name?

Over how many products may the influence of a brand name be spread and still be effective? The answer varies for different products and different situations. It is probably easier and less confusing to popularize one brand name with one product. When a company wins goodwill and acclaim for one product, however, it is a temptation to apply the same goodwill association to others. Thus, we have Heinz 57 Varieties, which now number in the hundreds. The company uses the technique of spreading institutional goodwill over all its products, probably to advantage. Some companies attempt to achieve both goals. They popularize the brand name of the individual product and also build general goodwill for the trade name of the company. As an example, the National Biscuit Company promotes over 200 branded products. In all of its advertising and promotion, the company features its company trademark, "Nabisco."

Ingredients and Stability of Brand Names

As a result of modern studies, it has become increasingly evident that the sources of human action are difficult to discern accurately. Frequently, people themselves are not completely aware of why they do what they do. For the marketing man this field of study is significant for two reasons: first, in planning the product it is a distinct advantage for the firm to understand the deep-seated desires of the customer and to know how to satisfy them; second, in appealing to the customer in its promotion, a company can be more skillful in communicating the qualities that its product possesses if it is aware of the real desires of the people. Much emphasis in motivational research is placed on determination of real reasons for choice.

In discussing brands in this vein, Burleigh B. Gardner and Sidney J. Levy make some pertinent observations.[8] They point out that the reasons often given by the customer for buying are not the real reasons. They indicate that many of the claims made by companies for their products are stereotyped and repetitive. If these claims do influence people's choices, the manner and setting in which they are expressed are often as important as the claims themselves. In other words, it is the whole experience of the customers with the product that influences choices. The product, the package, the advertising, the company, its past record, the quality, and the type of prestige it has with other people influence the individual. All these ingredients enter the picture to help influence a brand loyalty. These broad areas of possible appeal increase the scope of management responsibility if it is to maintain a strong preference for its brand.

What we know about brands leads us to believe that brand loyalty is of a tenuous and unstable quality. In most instances it must be maintained by

---

[8] Burleigh B. Gardner and Sidney J. Levy, "The Product and the Brand," *Harvard Business Review*, Vol. XXXIII (March-April, 1955), pp. 33-39.

constant vigilance. When any one of the factors essential to the establishment of goodwill loses its effectiveness, the reservoir may soon be dissipated. On the other hand, the long-standing good name of many products retains a capacity to convey a positive influence on choice after many years of use, without too much effort on the part of management. These cases, however, are so few as to be exceptions. Each product and situation must be considered in terms of its own history, environment, and peculiar characteristics.

PERSONAL SELLING

For some time personal selling was in a dark corner as far as academic and sometimes even corporate interest went. Now there is a resurgence of study and interest in this most personal of the functions of a discipline that is involved with people. It is becoming increasingly evident that persuasive person-to-person communication is essential to the intelligent use of many new products and processes.

Role of Personal Selling

A major advantage of personal selling in a promotional mix is that it provides the opportunity for explanation of complex products or ideas in the context of one person's problems; information can be made specifically applicable to one customer's needs. The salesman's principal role is to aid in decision making. The following list suggests some of the elements of a professional salesman's task.

1. Distribution advice—He will know his territory and developments in it. He will see how his present outlets are developing and alert his management of any changes in products or methods of distribution that will affect their business.
2. Counseling customers—He will understand the problems of his customer. In the case of industrial customers, he will understand their manufacturing processes and help them solve problems. He will know the inventory level requirements of his customers. He will help distributor customers keep abreast of product development, control procedures, and aids for their customers.
3. Advertising assistance—He will interpret company advertising to customers and in turn provide ideas to his company for advertising purposes based on customer needs. He will show his customers how to use his company's advertising to increase the customer sales.
4. Responsibility—Above all he will maintain interest in customer problems and in his company's policies and relate the two. A professional salesman is not only motivated by financial gain but also derives satisfaction from providing the best possible service. He carries with him the responsibility of helping his customers buy what is in their best interest.

Personal selling expenditures are approximately three times total advertising expenditures in the United States. Yet there is little formal research designed to improve the effectiveness of personal selling. Most of the articles written and research done on evaluation of sales personnel is inconsistent with the basic task of selling. Evaluation of salesmen is usually based on number of calls made, new accounts obtained, degree of product and customer problem knowledge, and relationship of expenses to sales volume. The job of a salesman is to create interests, identify needs, and achieve preference for his company's product line. Clearly there is room and need for new directions in research and measuring techniques in this area.

Personal selling can be divided logically into two main divisions: the first involves the manufacturer and the second, the retailer. Although the wholesaler or distributor may also have a selling problem, this problem includes somewhat the same characteristics as the two main types.

Sales to Industrial Users

The importance of the industrial salesman as a communicator of new products and processes is increasing. The rapid growth of research and technology has accelerated the tempo of change. New developments make old methods and processes obsolete. It is the job of the industrial salesperson to keep his customers aware of changes in products and to introduce the new products available. Also, the salesman must attempt to increase the number of customers. Competition with other industrial firms makes it necessary that salespeople with technical or engineering background explain and demonstrate the technical qualities of the products as they compare with others.

The efficiency of our industrial machine would be greater if all the known new methods of production were being used by industry. For example, many dairies have not yet adopted trucks and pallets for loading and storing purposes. Many warehouses have not adapted floor plans to permit the extensive use of labor- and time-saving devices. Objective data indicates that costs can be reduced drastically if such equipment is used. One large firm recently adopted a conveyer system to load delivery trucks from a branch warehouse. Under the most conservative computation, the adoption of the system reduced the cost for operating this branch by 25 percent. Accounting experts claim that the efficiency of the accounting system could be increased by the use of machines. Benefits would accrue both from a reduction in costs and an increase in useful information.

Naturally, in some instances a variety of circumstances may make such savings difficult. In many cases, however, methods and machines could be replaced with profit. The failure to discuss and help eliminate these inefficiencies is in a sense an indictment of the salesman. A great social loss results from savings that are technically possible but which have not been adopted. Just as in the field of consumer products, the selling process in the industrial area is charged with the responsibility of conveying information to customers and of motivating them to buy. As in the case of consumer goods, the sale of the product is as important to its use as is the making of the product.

Sales to Wholesalers and Retailers

Sales by manufacturers to wholesalers and retailers, in the majority of cases, consist of consumer goods. The problem is one of informing and motivating to increase sales. It is important for our purpose that we view this problem objectively as a sales operation. There are, however, other aspects of the problem. It would not be wise for a firm to sell to a company that did not have the facilities and the skill to continue the product's movement toward the ultimate sale. The manufacturer is dependent upon the wholesaler and the retailer to move the product to the consumer. If they are inefficient in this process—their costs high, and their service poor—the manufacturer's product suffers. The manufacturer may elect many different channels for putting his product on the market. His success depends on selecting the combination that best complements his own skills. The manufacturer not only must sell to wholesalers and retailers, but he also has the task of doing what he can to see that his product reaches the consumer. His message should carry the greatest impact at the consumer level at the least cost. However, whether the manufacturer chooses to deliver the product completely through the market channel to the ultimate consumer or whether he decides to delegate some of the task by selling to wholesalers and retailers, it is important that all parties who handle the product be willing to carry on the selling and be capable of doing so.

If the manufacturer can make his product sufficiently popular with the buying public, he may not need an elaborate sales force to visit wholesalers and retailers. Retailers are likely to stock his product if there is a consumer demand. The manufacturer, therefore, must choose the most effective method of promotion. Should he aim his message at middlemen for their promotional efforts, or should his advertising attempt to create a suction force at the consumer level? Both methods are frequently the answer, but they require effective strategy that every business firm must work out according to the circumstances peculiar to that particular business and its products.

If a company is attempting to sell a new vacuum cleaner that must be demonstrated in the home, the problem is more difficult. Under these circumstances it may be necessary for the manufacturer to take the product directly to the housewife for a demonstration. Personal selling will have to carry a greater share of the selling burden. The plan is influenced by the qualifications of the available institutions to do the job. In any event, the selling operation must include getting the sales information to all parties involved. The information must reach them in such a manner that they will desire the product either for their own use or for resale at a profit. The combination of methods and institutions available to achieve this end is infinite in variety. Thus, the creative salesman and the creative advertising copy writer are in great demand.

In the area of industrial sales whether such sales are made directly to other industries, to wholesalers, or to retailers, the personal salesman is essential. In the present era of change especially, advertising cannot tell the story in sufficient detail and with great enough accuracy to close the sale. Advertising alone is not adequate to cope successfully with competitive strategy.

The Retail Selling Problem

The vending machine that made and sold hot dogs was invented early in the decade of the 1920's. It was voted the oustanding development of the year.

The experts who so rated it were of the opinion that it was the first step toward a system in which a large proportion of the retail buying would be made by a vending machine. Now, out of retail sales totaling over $400 billion, vending-machine sales comprise less than one percent. This example points again to the fact that the desires of the consumer are in large measure unpredictable. We cannot predict the exact product the consumer will choose; neither can we describe the method by which the consumer will choose to buy the product. In a competitive system it is imperative that, whatever the method used, it must be the one which a significant number of consumers prefer. Otherwise, the product will go unpurchased and the seller will lose his patronage.

Self-service. In the field of food, drugs, and hardware, the idea of self-service has been readily accepted by the public. It is a matter of controversy today as to whether personal selling at retail is necessary. We see low-paid and poorly informed salesclerks giving inadequate service to customers. Frequently, the customer does not receive the information that is necessary or he is forced to wait for a clerk for service. Proponents of extending self-service to other lines also point to the great cost of maintaining a staff of salespeople. In a store having sales of $10 million, this cost would amount on the average to $800,000 for selling personnel. It is argued that for a great deal less money, descriptive tags could be put on the merchandise that would be more informative than salesclerks, and the customers could help themselves. This method has much in its favor. Self-service is spreading to more and more stores.

It is doubtful, nevertheless, if the time will come soon when all products are sold in this manner. This is partly because of habit and partly because of the reassurance that comes from a transaction that takes place with the aid of another person. As merchandise gets more costly and innovation more frequent, it may be more difficult for the written description to answer all the questions that may come to the mind of the consumer.

The best use of self-service in stores other than food and drug appears to be in combination with salesman-customer service. Stores set up several self-service checkout stations for routine purchases, but salespeople are available for items that require explanation. In several organizations this works well—customers can pick up single items with little delay, and salespeople earn more because they are free to sell the expensive items.

Another factor would make a merchant wary about depending entirely on merchandise display to do the selling. The retail salesman who is trained to sell and is strongly motivated can make a great difference to the sales volume. If two stores selling merchandise that may be marketed both ways were placed side by side, the store with a well-trained and eager sales staff would likely receive a greater share of the business.

One more factor may have some influence on this trend. Increasing productivity accruing as a result of improved management and technology is increasing the productivity of workers. As productivity increases, the wage rate also increases. If such conditions continue to develop, they will influence the pay rate necessary to obtain retail clerks. The wise management will make the adjustment by hiring only the productive clerks. It will place them in the departments where they can sell merchandise of a type that requires selling. Such merchandise will be selected on the basis of whether or not volume and margins can be increased by sales efforts. In the case of other merchandise, it is likely that there will be a continuation of the trend toward self-service.

Door-to-Door Selling. In terms of the total volume of sales to the ultimate consumer, the subject of door-to-door selling does not merit great emphasis. It comprises slightly more than one 1.3 percent of sales. There is a good reason, however, that we should consider it in our treatment of selling. It is the simplest form by which the manufacturer can reach the ultimate consumer with his product.

Advantages. In taking the product directly to the consumer, the producer has several advantages. First, by personal contact with the customer, he can achieve a greater impact with the information he may wish to impart. Personal contact can also convey a stronger motivation. Especially is this true when it is accompanied by a carefully planned demonstration and a well-illustrated sales brochure. Personal contact and demonstration are particularly helpful when a product is first being introduced to the market. The door-to-door salesperson can focus his entire attention on the single product or the single line of products, and the customer's attention is not distracted by competitors' offerings.

Second, the manufacturer selling directly to the consumer avoids the problem of building and maintaining relations with such institutions as wholesalers and distributors. Innovations by wholesale institutions may make a change of routes to market more desirable. When a company entrusts the sale of its product to others, it must be constantly alert to see that the product gets the proper promotional attention from these middlemen.

A third factor which favors the door-to-door type of distribution is that it provides strength during depression times. There are three reasons why this is true. First, the company that brings the product to the customer's door can bolster lagging sales. No sales organization has ever been in a position where it could not increase its sales by expanding its sales operation. Thus, it appears possible that when sales are difficult to obtain, the direct sales method is the surest method of maintaining sales. In the second place, salespeople are easier to recruit in depression times. Many qualified men are out of work during this period and are eager to maintain themselves by door-to-door selling. A third reason why door-to-door selling enjoys an advantage in a depression is that a great share of costs are selling costs which vary directly with the rate of sales. When the sales fall, therefore, fixed costs to be paid out of a decreasing income are less.

Disadvantages. On the other hand, the door-to-door sales manager has many problems. The greatest challenge, which we have mentioned, is the maintenance of a trained and adequate sales staff. Door-to-door selling is not considered pleasant work. High earnings are possible, but the average earnings of door-to-door salesmen are low. The practice has been abused by many salesmen who have used high-pressure methods and have made exaggerated claims for their products. This practice has conditioned many consumers to resist door-to-door efforts. Men who succeed in door-to-door selling are in demand by other firms because of the excellent training it affords. Therefore, the good men tend to leave the profession, and the poor become discouraged.

Another major disadvantage of the door-to-door selling method is the fact that it is costly. It is estimated that one company, which is typical of door-to-door operators, paid 40 percent of sales for commissions, 7 percent for field supervision, and 13 percent for general overhead and administrative costs. This amount totaled 60 percent of the price of the product. This percentage is greatly in excess of the selling margins of the manufacturer, the wholesaler, and the retailer when the conventional method of distribution is used. The reason for this high cost can be traced to the volume of merchandise sold. While wholesale and retail establishments have a high fixed overhead expense, they complete a much greater number of transactions in a single day. Selling costs of personal salesmen account for an average of 8 percent of the retail store price, compared with the 40 percent of the door-to-door salesman. It must be remembered, however, that out of the 40 percent the salesman must pay for his transportation costs and, also, any merchandise storage costs that may be involved. In the retail store there are no travel expenses for salesmen, and storage costs are considered a part of maintaining the institution.

Local ordinances prohibiting door-to-door selling are also making it increasingly difficult for door-to-door operators. The number of cities that have adopted ordinances that make it a misdemeanor to call at a home uninvited to solicit business are increasing throughout most of the nation. The problems that constitute the real challenge are the maintenance of an adequate sales force, the high cost of door-to-door selling, and new legal barriers to door-to-door selling.

Qualities That Make for Success. Certain companies have met these problems of door-to-door selling successfully and have realized adequate earnings on sales and on invested capital. Examples of such companies are Avon Products, Fuller Brush Company, Electrolux (vacuum cleaners), and Real Silk Hosiery. These companies, which show earnings up to 15 percent of the sales, have advantages in either or both of two important areas. For one thing, the production cost of the products they sell is a small percentage of the selling cost. Second, a special quality makes direct price comparison difficult. Avon Products, a cosmetic, exemplifies the first type, and Fuller Brush is an example of the second. These qualities permit the seller to build special and distinctive psychological values into the product. Such values cannot be compared directly with those offered at retail stores.

QUESTIONS AND ANALYTICAL PROBLEMS

1. Why are salespeople necessary? Why not perform the sales function with informative advertising alone? Answer in two parts: (a) applying to retail selling and (b) applying to industrial goods sales.

2. How are the price of a product and the promotional campaign used to sell the product interrelated?

3. What are the elements of a successful transaction; that is, what sort of selling is necessary if the firm is to move its goods and prosper over a long period of years?

4. In *Advertising Age* each year, in August issues, is a compilation of data on the largest 100 advertising budgets in the United States. Find the 10 companies who had the largest dollar allocation for advertising. (a) What kinds of products do they sell? (b) What percentage to net sales does the dollar expenditure on advertising represent for each of the companies? Explain the wide variation.

5. Under what conditions will a company most likely spend the largest portion of its total promotional budget on personal selling? Under what conditions will advertising be the principal ingredient in the marketing mix?

6. What are the trends in total expenditures for advertising by each medium in the United States?

7. What is the basic factor considered in selecting an advertising medium for a particular product? The basic factor underlying selection of an advertising theme?

8. How can testing improve advertising effectiveness?

9. Why has increased emphasis on brands been reflected in increased magazine and television advertising?

10. Why might retailers favor middleman brands (also called private brands) over manufacturer's brands in some instances?

11. What is brand loyalty? How is it achieved?

12. What are the major marketing problems confronting the manufacturer who produces consumer goods for sale through wholesalers and retailers?

13. What conditions favor self-service?

14. What are the advantages and the disadvantages of door-to-door selling from the point of view of (a) the salesman, (b) the manufacturer, and (c) the customer?

Case 17 • GENERAL DESSERTS

Late in February, 1972, the research and development team of General Desserts discovered what they considered to be "a fantastic innovation." The team had spent two years developing a nonfattening substitute for whipped cream. The new product was in a powdered form which could easily be marketed either in an extremely small package or could be put in a package which the consumer could also use as a mixing bowl at home. The only ingredient that the consumer needed to add was water.

The new product compared favorably with actual whipped cream in price, and General Desserts estimated that they could market their new product at 14 cents per pint below the price of whipped cream. No other product compared in price or content.

The product was distributed among company employees for testing purposes. Most of the employees reported favorably in regard to texture and ease of mixing. However, there were some unfavorable comments concerning flavor so that the company was seriously planning to add a variety of colors and fruit flavors to the product. Such additions would cost approximately 4 cents per pint. Since all technical development had been completed and testing was favorable, General Desserts had decided to turn the product over to the advertising department.

• In outline form prepare a general advertising campaign for General Desserts. Be sure to include such items as a product name, a slogan, a statement of strategy, media to be used, general tone of copy, and any other items that you feel are important.

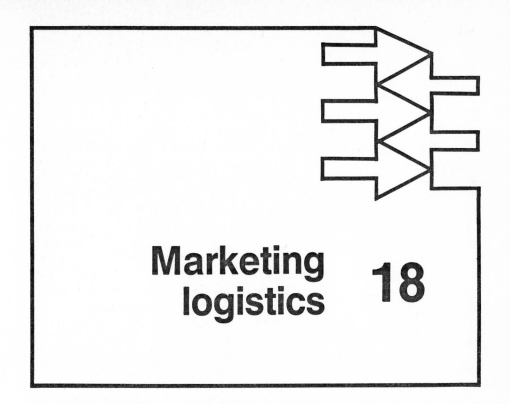

Marketing logistics 18

There is no question about the importance of transportation, handling, and storage in providing a wide range of products to markets throughout the world. It is quite common to find as much as 25 to 35 percent of the total costs of a manufactured product accountable to physical distribution of the goods. [1]

Consequently, there is now developing much effort to make physical handling and distribution more efficient. It has been noted that in most modern factories everything is well organized, with little waste in time and materials. When products reach the shipping dock, however,

> . . . chaos begins. In many cases the product moves by inappropriate means of transportation and often in undesired quantities. It may well be protected by the wrong kind of package. It is almost sure to be picked up and put down needlessly. It is stored in warehouses that may be badly located for today's shifting markets or not needed at all, and it is likely to be controlled by the wrong kind of paper work. [2]

A systems approach to physical distribution, which we can call marketing logistics, is gaining attention. *Marketing logistics* can be defined as the conception and management of a physical distribution system that will assure optimum inventory levels at all stages of the distribution process to enhance overall marketing efficiency.

---

[1] John F. Magee, *Industrial Logistics* (New York: McGraw-Hill Book Company, 1968), p. 20.
[2] "New Strategies to Move Goods," *Business Week* (September 24, 1966), p. 120.

LOGISTICS CONCEPT

The importance of the logistics concept arises from the way goods are manufactured and distributed. Take, for example, a food manufacturing company that produces many items under one brand. This company has several plants; however, not one of these plants manufactures all the company's products. Some customers want to place one order for a mixture of items which are produced at various locations. At this point the company's problem is how to ship in a single truck or a railroad car the full range of items ordered by one customer. This, in essence, is a marketing logistics problem for the company.

Let us further say that this company maintains 128 warehouse facilities to which each manufacturing plant sends its products. These warehouses are used to receive, mix, and ship the products. Although the company is aware that it is adopting a costly procedure, it believes that the better service provided by having full-line stocks near each market center is worth the extra cost. Moreover, the company exercises care in assuring that each shipment from a plant goes by the lowest cost means; it also attempts to keep the inventory at each of the 128 warehouses at a minimum level consistent with minimizing out-of-stock conditions.

For maximum effectiveness two things are still missing in the control exercised by this hypothetical company. First, the company has failed to realize that maximum efficiency in one activity frequently may not support the total effectiveness of a marketing organization in view of conflicting objectives in a typical manufacturing company. The marketing department, for instance, would like large inventories; whereas, the finance and accounting departments would like to see minimal stock levels. In another instance, the marketing department would like to be assured of frequent short runs on production lines; whereas, the production department would like long production runs. Or the marketing department would push for fast order processing; whereas, the finance department would settle for a slower, inexpensive system for order processing. Again, the marketing department would like to have warehousing facilities near all customers; whereas, the finance department would be content with less warehousing and the production department would prefer in-plant warehousing. As each functional executive strives to achieve maximum efficiency in his area, it is likely that overall effectiveness will be reduced, or at least there is good reason to believe that it will not be maximized.

The other factor overlooked by the hypothetical company is that it is difficult to measure all costs when accounting is done for each separate function. In the above example the company neglected to consider the cost of the extra inventory investment. Although inventory level at each of the 128 warehouses was relatively small, when added together it proved to be startlingly large. The effort to meet the demand for slow-moving goods required transporting goods from one warehouse to another, a cost which the company did not consider.

Logistics Concept as a State of Mind

In the logistics approach the first concern should be the total value as seen by the customer. *Total value* includes the properties, desirability, and availability of the goods. It must be noted that customers do not buy a group of well-managed activities but rather an end product that meets needs when and where they are desired. This may require a regrouping of activities and a coordination not possible under traditional organizational structure. Even where there is no reorganization of duties, there can be an understanding by all executives that changes may be required in product design, methods of shipment, warehousing policies, and costing of activities at various stages of distribution. It is necessary to be always aware that, to the customer, worth is the quality provided by manufacturing, the attraction generated by selling, and the service provided by distribution.

Logistics View of Inventory Levels

A more effective inventory management will result if there is complete understanding of the reasons for inventories and of the functions they perform. Inventories exist because (1) customer demand is not uniform nor is it completely predictable, (2) it takes time to make or to move a product, (3) it is usually inordinately expensive to manufacture and distribute items unit by unit in response to individual orders, and (4) some products require seasoning until they reach a certain quality level—products such as ice cream, wine, and lumber.

Logistically, four functions are performed by inventory, and a certain stock level must be maintained for each. These functions are:

1. For efficiency in manufacturing, *process stocks* or certain items must be on hand because of the time required for some manufacturing processes and because of the time required to move raw materials, goods in process, or finished goods from one place to another.
2. *Lot sizes* required because one produces, ships, or buys in larger lots than are immediately required. A consumer may buy several cans of fruit at one time while the grocer finds it convenient to buy 50 cases at a time and to stock his shelves a case at a time.
3. *Safety stocks* required to assure proper levels of inventories in the face of variations in demand or delivery.
4. *Seasonal stocks* arising from uniform production and seasonal demand, such as garden tools or Christmas items, or those developing because of seasonal production and near-uniform demand, such as canned fruits and vegetables.

Ideally, each inventory should be at absolute minimum for maximum efficiency of the distribution process. This goal is clearly impossible of perfect achievement because of unforeseen delays due to weather, production breakdown, and the like. As the explanation of the logistics concept becomes clearer, hopefully it will be feasible to aspire to approach the ideal goal by the effective use of all factors in the distribution system.

IMPORTANCE OF PHYSICAL DISTRIBUTION— DOMESTIC AND INTERNATIONAL

In manufacturing it is rapidly coming to be true that to stay alive and prosper a manufacturing concern must be prepared to meet competition coming to its prospective customers from any place within the one big market which is the U.S.A. No part of the big market can be ignored, and new technical developments have this very thing in mind—to enable a producer economically to reach further and further into the national market. Take such a traditionally localized product as milk. When I lived in Valparaiso, Indiana, as a boy, milk deliveries were not even town wide, but a matter of capacity of your neighbor's cow. Milk has become regionalized by rapid transport. . . .

This statement by David E. Lilienthal [3] describes the decline of distance as a barrier to competition and broad markets.

In an article on the function of advertising in expanding markets, one advertisement pictured a healthy child eating a melonlike fruit with great glee. The caption read, "Delicious Durian for Dessert." The durian was described as a fruit so mellow and delicious that it tasted like "ambrosia bathed in May moonlight." Even the husk made "chestnuts shed their shells in shame." Why were we not eating durian in the United States? There were three obstacles: first, durian has a very unpleasant odor; second, it is extremely perishable; and third, it is grown only in certain parts of the Far East. If history repeats itself, we shall yet eat durian. By means of plant breeding, the fruit may be developed with a pleasing odor. The other two obstacles may be overcome by improvements in transportation. These obstacles are being removed with great speed, and we are now in a market larger than the United States—it is a world market.

Contribution of Transportation and Storage

Goods in their trek from raw materials to finished products are either in transit or in storage. Frequently, storage is necessary at both ends of a transportation link to achieve maximum economies. The wholesaler of canned goods may have to store his products for a period if he buys them in carload lots, but his savings in freight costs would be greater than his storage costs. Also, a canner may store and defer transportation until he can achieve the economies of carload rates. Transportation and storage are interdependent and become a single problem of costs in achieving the goal set forth in our discussion of logistics.

Transportation and storage are important marketing functions. They (1) increase the variety of goods available, (2) broaden the area of competition, (3) make specialization possible to a greater degree, and (4) increase satisfactions and reduce costs for the buyer and the seller.

Increase Variety of Available Goods. As we gain more skill in providing economical transportation and storage, the area of the firm's market broadens. A greater array of goods is available for our convenience. It may be South American caronoba wax, Australian wool, Indian spices, or Lybian rubber. Domestically, the Seattle housewife can buy Tide detergent at the same price that is paid by a consumer in Cincinnati, where Tide is manufactured. The San

---

Diego factory worker can buy Arch Preserver shoes for the same price that he might pay for these shoes in the city of their manufacture—Beverly, Massachusetts. Economical movement greatly increases the variety of goods available to the American consumer and enhances his standard of living. By the use of improved methods of transportation, the business manager broadens markets, reduces costs, and increases his volume and profits.

Broaden the Area of Competition. Were it not for low-cost transportation and storage, we could have no competitive national market. Continental Can would not be in competition with American Can; Colgate would not be concerned with the share of the market gained by Crest; nor would National Biscuit Company in New York City be anxious about Purity Biscuit selling as a competitor in the West. Yet because of transportation and storage, competition is effective throughout the nation. Every company operating a plant within the borders of the nation must be keenly alert to the activities of its competitors. The fact that they are miles apart geographically does not insulate them from the necessity of providing equal or better values at comparable costs. Indeed, innovations in transportation and storage facilities have improved competition by making location monopolies more difficult to accomplish.

Make a Greater Degree of Specialization Possible. Transportation and storage are necessary for specialization—specialization is necessary for mass production—mass production is necessary for low prices. If Eastman Kodak were forced to sell its entire output in Rochester, the volume would not be large enough to justify the degree of specialization necessary to maintain the efficiency of the production line. A decrease in specialization could result only in increased costs. Furthermore, transportation and storage make it possible for the entire nation to enjoy the benefits of California and Florida citrus fruits, Washington apples, Minnesota Valley corn, Maine and Idaho potatoes, and Seattle salmon and tuna. If each locality were to train its own people to manufacture the goods they used and to grow the products they consumed, their supply would be diminished and their variety would be restricted. Transportation and storage make specialization by task and locality possible. Specialization in both of these areas is fundamental to low prices, maximum variety, and high volume.

Immediate Availability of Goods. Storage is essential because the buyer does not wish to wait for merchandise to be shipped from its point of production when he chooses to buy. He wants the goods now. Consumer wants cannot be anticipated daily or weekly or even monthly with perfect accuracy. Retail stores find it necessary, therefore, to store goods in order to have them available when they are wanted. A typical food store carries enough food in storage, measured in terms of dollars, to carry it for about 22 days of sales. The drugstore carries a 60-day supply. Department stores carry about a 90-day supply of goods. The aim of the management of each of these institutions is to decrease the stock necessary to meet its demands or to increase the demands and in this manner shorten the period of time stock is kept in storage.

There are three dangers in avoiding storage costs by decreasing the size of the inventory. The first is that the store will not carry the specific goods desired by customers. The second danger is that even though the store might carry the goods as a part of its line, it may run short of desired goods temporarily. Both of these situations result in lost sales, and the store is not able to satisfy its customers. A third reason is that such a policy requires more frequent delivery of a smaller volume of goods. This, in turn, results in an increase in transportation rates and extra administrative costs. Thus, at the retail level, storage is necessary to give the customers the satisfaction they desire and to achieve economies of transportation.

At the wholesale level the same factors apply. A wholesale establishment is an assembly point and a storehouse. Thousands of manufacturers send their goods to hundreds of wholesalers to be re-sorted and stored until ordered by the retailer or other wholesalers, or possibly by manufacturers.

If the wholesaler does not have goods available for the retailer in a short period of time, the retailer must carry heavier stocks at a point where rent and storage costs are higher. The wholesaler can also buy in carload lots more frequently than the retailer can and realize savings in transportation costs. As is the case of the retailer, wholesale management attempts to reduce its stock to as low a point as possible, thus reducing storage cost and danger of obsolescence. At the same time, wholesale firms wish to carry a line that will enable them to compete successfully and to have enough of the right goods on hand when they are required.

Likewise, the manufacturers must coordinate production with the anticipated orders of the wholesaler and others. These firms give the product its final form. Once Selby Shoe Company, in Portsmouth, Ohio, makes a piece of calf hide into a ladies' shoe, it cannot be recast. If fashion changes before the supply is sold, some sellers will have a loss. On the other hand, if the shoe style persists in popularity, the company must have the shoe in stock or lose sales. As has been pointed out, the coordination of goods produced with the current demand is the function of merchandising. In examining the flow of goods from manufacturing through retailing, it is evident that storage is important to the proper function of merchandising.

Each of the stopping places in the channel of any material requires a certain amount of storage. Indeed, while marketing has been described as a vast system of tributaries, the flows must, in nearly all instances, emanate from reservoirs of stored goods. In but few instances is there a daily movement of goods in and out of the reservoir in uniform amounts. Rather, the purchases on the consumer markets trigger the movement back through every channel. Goods move into the retail store when its stocks dwindle, as purchases take place. Reservoirs of goods at all levels must be adequate to meet the immediate needs of the consumer market, which cannot be perfectly predicted.

Using Elements of the Physical Distribution Process for Competitive Advantage

Most retailers and wholesalers do not want to carry any larger inventories than they have to. The manufacturer who finds a way to make fast, dependable deliveries can thus gain a big competitive edge. Many manufacturers are gaining that edge by a total overhaul of their distribution system. Sometimes the way to greater profits is to increase warehousing costs. As an example, let us consider the Hammond Valve Corporation, a company in Chicago that makes bronze valves. They formerly distributed their products through jobbers. In the mid-1960's they decided they could boost their profits by improving service to their customers. They opened six regional warehouses. Now it takes them two days to service a customer's order instead of six weeks. Sales have more than doubled in the past five years, and the greatly increased volume and lower unit production costs have far outweighed the added costs of operating warehouses. For other companies the analysis of physical distribution can mean fewer warehouses. It can mean, for example, going to air freight, as Raytheon and American Optical Company have done.

When Gillette introduced a new blade, they used air freight to rush the blades to market, but this added cost. Finally, a management study group, by the use of a computer model of a distribution system, found that by revamping the paper work they could cut down the number of days it took to process an order. The company then could return to low-cost surface freight for routine shipments and still keep up delivery schedules.

What is best for one company is not necessarily best for another, as illustrated in the following two examples. Johnson and Johnson, the surgical supply manufacturers, used to ship to every part of the country every day. They now hold back shipments to take advantage of full truckload rates and find the service just as fast. By proper order-handling procedures they can ship whole truckloads at a time and avoid repeated intermediate handlings that cause delay, soiling, or loss. They ship on a scheduled basis. Now when they have a true emergency, they can handle it efficiently. On the other hand, Singer Sewing Machine Company used to ship machines once a month, but now it ships four times a month. The company now pays less-than-truckload rate which is almost double the carload rate, but this is more than offset by lower inventories in stores. Most of Singer's 1,600 Sewing Centers are in high-rent districts, making inventory costs relatively expensive; hence, the somewhat higher freight rates are offset.

H. J. Heinz Company has recognized warehousing as one of the company's biggest problems. A vice-president asked himself these questions concerning the distribution system: [4]

1. How many warehouses should we have?
2. Where should the warehouses be located?
3. What customers should each warehouse service?
4. What volume should each warehouse handle?
5. How can we best organize our entire distribution function?

H. J. Heinz has several factories with many mixing points where products from several factories are assembled for large shipments. They have dozens of

---

[4] Harvey N. Shycon and Richard B. Maffei, "Simulation—Tool for Better Distribution," *Harvard Business Review,* Vol. 38, No. 6 (November-December, 1960), pp. 65-75.

warehouses and thousands of customers. Heinz Company is typical of many manufacturing companies, particularly those in the food processing field, that have a number of manufacturing plants spread across the country, many of which were located years ago as sources of supply. They have customers who almost always like to get a mixed shipment, including the products of various plants. To add to the problems, the population centers and principal markets have shifted, brand identification has become important, and large retail operations make possible increasing customer selectivity. There is increasing demand to shorten the length of distribution time. The particular problem at Heinz came from changes in the market. Originally Heinz had 68 warehouses placed geographically to handle a great many low-volume customers. With shifting populations and the growth of large-volume retailers, some of the warehouses were not in the proper places to serve this kind of a market and were no longer needed. Hence, the question arose as to which warehouses to retain and how best to allocate customer volume among warehouses, mixing points, and factories.

The Heinz problem was solved by a simulation model. The proper use of computers allowed them to do a cost analysis for each of a number of possible distribution systems using various assumptions as to sales patterns. The evaluation of a great number of "what-if" questions narrows the range of alternatives from which management can make a proper selection. It does not remove the necessity nor responsibility for someone in management to make a decision, but it does provide a range within which someone in management can make a decision based on his experience and knowledge of local conditions.

Time—A Critical Element

Time must be considered in two ways: (1) the time needed to complete a process, to make something, or to move an item from one place to another and (2) the time that must be allowed because an activity or process may not start immediately.[5] For example, information may be sent periodically in batches rather than as each bit of information develops. Also, there may need to be an allowance for time spent between issuance of an order and getting the process started, due to backlogs of work.

Costs can be assessed to both kinds of time. A recent example of the costs of time involved in completing a process was the added expense incurred in moving oil from Middle-Eastern production to points in Europe. From Libya to West Germany, a normal schedule is 26 days through the Suez Canal to the South European pipeline terminal in Marseilles at a cost of $.95 per ton. When the canal was closed, as a result of the 1967 war, oil from Persian Gulf ports was shipped around the Cape of Good Hope to Marseilles in 57 days at a cost of over $20.00 per ton.

The important element is the cost of capital tied up while time passes. The marketing manager of a motor freight line tells of a publishing company that has

---

[5] Recent time analyses have failed to consider order service time as a variable. R.P. Willett and P.R. Stephenson in "Determinants of Buyer Response," *Journal of Marketing Research* (August, 1969), p. 279, indicate how buyers are influenced by time differentials.

much of its printing done in the Far East. Most of the publisher's customers are in states east of the Mississippi River. The company had shipped the books by water from the printing plant through the Panama Canal to a port on the East Coast. The motor freight salesman suggested that the books be unloaded at a West Coast port then be shipped by truck to customer locations. That did not appear attractive to the publisher, since freight costs would be increased by almost 56 cents per hundred pounds. The salesman showed them that they would save, on the average, 18 days on each shipment. Savings on the value of the inventory during that time would not only offset the extra freight charges, but would be worth almost 10 cents per hundred pounds in addition. Hence, it is total time costs that must be calculated, including costs of capital, storage, risks, and chances of lost sales.

Time costs are difficult to measure accurately; but it is well to attempt some close estimate of the value of convenience of use, reliability of maintenance, and product availability, which are all functions of time. In some markets, such as for automobiles, one can observe how customers will pay more to obtain the desired product immediately, even when it is not urgently needed. There are also completely rational desires for immediate and reliable deliveries. A manufacturer may well pay a higher price to suppliers who can guarantee fast and reliable service, because this will reduce his materials inventory requirements and lower the threat of disruption in his manufacturing operations.

At the dealer level, as pointed out in our earlier discussion of merchandising, the cost of lost sales may be great. It is hard to assess the effects on future business of present sales lost due to out-of-stock conditions. Consequently, considerable attention must be paid to having a proper product mix for customers at the desired time.

The ability of the physical distribution system to offer services and, thereby, enhance the competitive position can be measured by:

1. The speed with which an item can be provided to a customer.
2. The reliability with which the average speed of service is achieved.
3. The degree of immediate availability of the item.

Service always costs money. Increased speed can be achieved by higher speed of transportation and order communications or by moving stocks closer to customers. These changes must be made with care since arbitrary service policies may impose waste on the distribution system.

COMPONENTS OF PHYSICAL DISTRIBUTION SYSTEMS

Patterns of market activity directly control the design of an effective physical distribution system. A study of market activity is required to learn where customers, or potential customers, are located; what they buy; and in what volumes they buy. From this information customary patterns of purchase are derived. This will apply any place in the world. The answers will differ because of local desires, beliefs, and facilities; but the method of determination of the distribution system best suited to any market will apply.

Principal components of a physical distribution system that must be designed and integrated for maximum effectiveness are:

1. Information system. An information system is needed to assure that proper inventory levels are maintained at all stages of the system. This includes a communications and order-processing system to facilitate integration of all components and provide facilities for controlling the entire distribution system.
2. Materials handling and packaging. These components involve considerable capital and also directly affect all other elements of the system.
3. Storage facilities. Particular attention should be paid to the design of storage facilities (both internal and external) in order to assure proper handling and to reduce the cost of moving goods into and out of the inventory holding points.
4. Transportation. Principal considerations for judgment in relation to this component are speed, reliability of performance, and cost.

Information System

Marketing executives have for a long time had an awareness that marketing effectiveness is limited by information gathering and processing capability. Wholesalers were among the first to use electronic data processing equipment to provide information for the establishment of reorder points. Alcoa and others have communication networks which tie together regional sales offices and manufacturing plants in order to facilitate control of inventory. A goal of some manufacturers and retailers is a system that includes a device attached to every cash register in the country that could transmit information on sales simultaneously to each supplier and transporter of the store's merchandise.

One of the most elaborate existing systems is the Pittsburgh Tele-Computer Center of Westinghouse Corporation. All 53 industrial products warehouses of Westinghouse are connected with each company sales office. Each order obtained by a sales office is teletyped to the Pittsburgh Center computer. The order is processed, and shipping orders are prepared and sent over the wire to the warehouse closest to the sales office. Total time for the entire process is under two minutes. In the computer memory are stored the levels of each item in inventory in each warehouse. The computer is also programmed to signal each reorder point. The company reports that shelf stock has been lowered from inventory valued at $33 million to $18 million. Savings are worthwhile since the cost of carrying industrial electrical products at Westinghouse is about 20 percent of sales.

A few other companies have similar systems for processing orders for consumer goods. Sears Roebuck and Co. maintains a fashion goods warehouse in New Jersey where, in addition to order processing, the computer is connected to an automatic warehouse so that goods ordered are selected and moved to the shipping dock without being handled manually. The merchandise controller for Sears reports savings from the system but stresses the fact that it is not possible to compute judgment. Buyers must exercise human judgment to assure that proper goods are in stock.

Important to the logistics concept of physical distribution is the linking of a physical-distribution information system with other information systems of the business. Several of the available business data systems are designed to allow for integration of operational control systems so that production, shipping, stock ordering, and cost accounting information can all be served from a single input. Information can then be fed out to whatever operating function requires it.

Handling and Packaging Materials

In the discussion below, with respect to the various transport carriers, are examples of new developments in materials handling. Hence, this brief discussion is here simply to emphasize the importance of considering materials handling methods as they affect the physical distribution process.

One purchasing agent for a large concern that buys many millions of dollars worth of goods each year states that almost 100 percent of the materials received from the many suppliers are improperly packaged. Common packaging faults are: excessive weight per unit; improper protection, difficulty of handling, loading, and transporting with available facilities; and waste of time in packing and unpacking the product due to excessive packaging. One supplier was advised that it was not necessary to use a package which included an outside wooden crate, a heavy cardboard box, and an inner wrap of grease-resistant, water-proof paper. Elimination of the cardboard box reduced the weight by 30 percent and the cost of packaging by nearly 50 percent with no consequent danger of damage to the product. It also increased the ease of packing and unpacking.

A large portion of the nation's goods are packed by packaging contractors. It is not surprising, then, that many manufacturers pay little attention to this component of the distribution process. They should, however, contact competent packaging specialists who have access to strong, lightweight materials that can provide nearly perfect protection while also providing a package that can be handled by common methods.

Storage

For proper integration into the physical distribution system, storage facilities must be properly located and must function efficiently in the processing activities of warehousing.

Location of Storage Facilities. Any supplier has one of two choices to make regarding warehouse location. A centralized storage policy can be adopted. This would mean that all shipments to customers will be made from one location. For some basic materials and products such a policy is feasible. If a steady flow of the product is required, provision can be made to ship in such quantities and on such schedules that the customer will always have the product when it is required. For example, an iron mine in Peru owns its fleet of ore carriers and makes regular shipments to Japan. This requires loading facilities and stocks in Peru sufficient to meet shipping requirements at all times. It also requires large storage facilities in Japan to receive the large quantities of ore carried in each vessel. As long as the shipments are made regularly, the time required to cross the Pacific Ocean is of concern only as regards cost of the vessel and crew and the investment in ore during the time of shipment. Many manufacturing plants operate with supplies coming from one distant point, and this is possible so long as the supply comes in a steady flow.

When, however, requirements of customers fluctuate in volume and in particular items needed, it is necessary to provide supplies close enough to the customers so that undue delay is not encountered. The growth of steel and copper wholesale operations in or near developing manufacturing centers exemplifies this kind of requirement. Manufacturers of many types find it impossible to make continuous and uniform production runs and must, therefore, depend on having needed raw materials and components readily available. At the same time it is uneconomical for them to build up large inventories of such goods. Hence, the other choice for a supplier is to establish warehousing facilities close to manufacturing centers.

Location Studies. Application of mathematical methods made possible to computers are now common in studies to determine optimum numbers and locations of storage points. Typical computations that must be made would include the following:

1. Costs incurred from lost sales because of the distance from storage points.
2. Costs of operating storage facilities.
3. Transportation costs from manufacturing facility to branch warehouses.
4. Transportation costs from branch warehouses to customers.
5. Costs of maintaining inventories at branch warehouses.

To determine these costs, it is necessary to know the quantities required in storage and in transit, usual order quantities, speed of supply desired, and product mixes required at each location. From these requirements it is easy to see why simulation models have been of interest to large suppliers. For those to whom simulation does not seem applicable, linear and a few nonlinear studies as well as heuristic approaches have been used. Some practical applications of these kinds of studies have resulted in relocation of storage points.

Several major appliance manufacturers have established storage for complete inventories at a freeport center [6] near Ogden, Utah, from which to service the Intermountain and West Coast areas. Their decisions followed studies made by the armed forces during World War II and during the Korean War (1950-1953). Linear programming computations showed the armed forces that supply centers near Ogden constituted a more efficient location for all West Coast points than any other single location. Ogden is roughly equidistant from each large West Coast city. With one large stock there, it is possible to provide rapid delivery to each West Coast market. It is considerably less expensive than having stocks of goods in each of the several major markets.

Processing Functions of Warehousing. Warehouse design obviously depends on the job to be done. Consequently, it is worthwhile to decide in detail just exactly what is to be accomplished. The following list looks simple, but unless provision is made to assure that each activity fits well in the system of physical

---

[6] A freeport center is an enclosed area where goods may be received, processed, and shipped free of various state taxes.

distribution, it can be a hindrance to overall effectiveness. Such functions are: to receive goods; to identify and sort; to dispatch goods to storage, hold, and recall; to select and pick goods; to marshal shipments; and to dispatch shipments. It is presumed that proper material handling equipment for palletized as well as loose items will be provided.

Means of Transportation

The means and relative importance of transportation in the United States are shown in Table 18-1.

Railroads. Note that railroads still are the most important means of moving cargo. This is because there is no more efficient use of power in transport over land.

Recently railroads have been introducing innovations to provide better service and gain back some of the business they have lost as well as to share in the increasing tonnages hauled. One of the profitable railroads in the country is the D&RG which has a rigorous road through the Rocky Mountains. It is now making a comeback for a number of reasons, but the primary reason is that, in contrast to other lines, they have reduced the number of cars in each train. By increasing the speed and decreasing the handling required for making up and distributing the trains, they are gaining back business that had been lost to other handlers.

A number of lines have built larger cars which have brought savings to shippers. Railroad costs do not go up proportionately with the volumes they carry; hence, rates are often less per ton when big volumes are shipped in the new large cars. In the meat-packing business savings have been made by using the larger cars. The vice-president for distribution and transportation of Armour and Co. says:

> For many years, meat moved in refrigerator cars kept cool by ice and salt. The normal weight of the load on which rates were based was 21,000 lbs. Now, meat moves in far larger cars cooled either by mechanical or chemical means with much better insulation and is moved at the rate of 100,000 lbs. per car. The difference in rates is about 1¢ a lb. or $1,000 a car.

To Armour, who ships about 8,000 tons of pork a week, 1¢ a lb. is a substantial amount. It has meant that to take full advantage of these savings, Armour and other meat packers have moved their stockyards and slaughter houses away from consuming areas and closer to growing areas. Hence, they not only can ship more meat for less money and have it arrive in better condition, but also they need not ship the unusable parts of the animals as far.

The rack cars on the railroad which handle automobiles (12 per car for a standard size automobile, and 15 per car for a compact size) have recovered automobile shipping business for the railroads by reducing shipping costs per automobile.

Trailer-on-flat car innovations, commonly called piggy-back, have brought some business back to railroads. Joint motor-rail rates are now established to most parts of the United States. There are only rough estimates of the volume of

Table 18-1

VOLUME OF FREIGHT SHIPMENTS BY TYPE OF CARRIER (BILLIONS OF TON-MILES)

Year	Total Volume	Railroads Volume	Railroads % of Total	Motor Vehicles Volume	Motor Vehicles % of Total	Inland Waterways Volume	Inland Waterways % of Total	Oil Pipelines Volume	Oil Pipelines % of Total	Airways Volume	Airways % of Total
1950	1,094	628	57.44	173	15.80	163	14.93	129	11.81	.3	0.029
1955	1,298	655	50.43	223	17.20	217	16.68	203	15.66	.6	0.037
1960	1,330	595	44.73	285	21.46	220	16.56	229	17.19	.8	0.058
1965	1,651	721	43.67	359	21.76	262	15.89	306	18.56	1.9	0.116
1966	1,759	762	43.33	381	21.66	281	15.95	333	18.93	2.3	0.128
1967	1,776	742	41.79	389	21.88	281	15.85	361	20.33	2.6	0.145
1968	1,839	757	41.16	396	21.55	291	15.85	391	21.28	2.9	0.157
1969	1,895	774	40.84	404	21.32	303	15.98	411	21.69	3.2	0.168
1970	1,936	771	39.83	412	21.28	319	16.46	431	22.26	3.3	0.170
1971	1,930	746	38.64	430	22.28	307	15.90	444	23.00	3.4	0.176

Source: U.S. Department of Commerce, Bureau of the Census, *Statistical Abstract of the United States: 1973* (94th ed.; Washington: U.S. Government Printing Office, 1973), p. 538, #884.

cargo handled by the method of hauling motor trailers on railroad cars, but it is worthwhile business for some lines.

For some of the bulk commodities, such as coal and grain, there are so-called "unit trains" which are semipermanently coupled trains that shuttle back and forth between one shipper and one consignee. They avoid intermediate freight yards, improve dependability, and cut costs. Savings are sizable over ordinary freight since a loaded car on the average spends 20 hours of each 24 on a siding or a freight yard.

By promoting a long-existing rate device, railroads have made the use of inland freeports even more attractive. This rate is the so-called intransit rate. Inventories can be reduced through intransit storage and transloading. To make use of *intransit storage* a shipper will forward carload lots directly to a centralized storage facility from his several manufacturing plants. Goods are then stored until orders are received from customer outlets. In some cases the goods may be repackaged or even assembled. The carload of mixed goods then can be forwarded to the final destination. The manufacturer thus provides maximum flexibility and still pays only the standard transcontinental through rate, with a small added charge for intransit storage.

In the second method of inventory reduction called *transloading,* a car of merchandise starts out from a manufacturing plant destined for either a shipper transloader or a railroad transloader, not a centralized facility. If the shipper transloads, the car can be shipped to a central location where the goods can be unloaded and stored. At some later date a portion of the car can be mixed with other goods and sent to any location. The shipper is charged only a small additional intransit fee for the service. If the railroad transloads, full cars are sent to a central location where they are separated into three or four car groups, each of which is then shipped to a different customer. In effect, through transloading either by the shipper or by the railroad, a shipper can receive less than carload service and still pay the cheaper carload rate.

Motor Carriers. The motor truck brought a new mobility to goods. It brought productivity to areas that had been unproductive and greater productivity to areas which had been productive. Two examples serve to illustrate the point.

The towns in southwestern Colorado and southeastern Utah were farther away from a railroad than any cities in the United States. Like the upstate dwellers in New York in 1820 before the Erie Canal, they were merely self-sustaining. With the coming of the truck they were able to specialize in the production of wheat, beans, sheep, and cattle and to accommodate tourists. Many grew wealthy. But most significant was the discovery of uranium. This area became the center of the nation's uranium boom. It would have been a costly and slow process to build railroads to all points where productive mines were established. Trucks, however, served the purpose well. Even with makeshift roads, it was possible to get ore out. The industry grew with facility and without handicap.

Now let us view the west side of Manhattan Island, either early in the morning or in the evening. This at the time when trucks are either beginning or terminating their day's travel. Some of this traffic is within the city, but much of it is awaiting the turn to go through the tunnels. Thousands of trucks pass through these tunnels daily carrying millions of pounds of goods. Without trucks to make the deliveries and pickups on this island, it is possible that trade would be restricted by at least one third.

Thus, both in areas having a sparse population and in heavily populated sections, trucks provide place utility that increases market areas, intensifies competition, and increases the volume of marketing activity. Not only have motor trucks increased the amount of traffic they have hauled, but also their share of the transportation business has increased from 15.8 percent in 1950 to 22.3 percent in 1971 (see Table 18-1 on page 362). There are several reasons for such an increase.

On most short hauls trucks can save the shipper time, and time is a significant factor in merchandising since it is closely related to cost. Even on long hauls trucks frequently can save a shipper some time. Railroads move faster than trucks, but the switching, unloading, and picking up of cars enroute slows up the freight train considerably.

Truck schedules are so flexible that they can meet unusual time requirements of a shipper. They can go out of their way for a pickup or a delivery. They might vary a time schedule for the convenience of an order. The shipper also can ship a smaller load than a railway carload and get a full-truck rate. Furthermore, the packing expense is less than with the railroad.

In certain transactions the number of intermediaries in the market channel is reduced because of truck service. The use of a truck makes the channel sufficiently flexible for the producer to sell directly to the consumer or retailer. On occasion, the trucker himself may be a merchant middleman. When a railroad is used, a shipper with transportation facilities on both ends of the route is usually necessary to handle the transactions. When the merchant trucks his own merchandise from a supplier, the use of the truck reduces one step in the buying-and-selling process.

Regarding rates, for a specific shipment a comparison may favor trucks slightly or truck rates may be higher than rail rates, depending on the product and the haul. In terms of overall cost of moving goods from factory dock to destination, the truck usually is cheaper for short hauls because the truck rate includes pickup and delivery, and there is usually little or no packing cost.

The new interstate highways allow larger and heavier trailers to be pulled on bigger and faster tractors by a team of drivers who alternate driving and sleeping. The average over-the-road truck in the United States will be able to double the distance of its travels. This means manufacturers can double the marketing areas or cut storage space and inventories.

Trucking companies are concerned, as are the railways, in the conflicting views regarding the use of highways. They point to increasing taxes that they pay, and they object to increasingly stringent regulations. More study is necessary to discover data relevant to a mature policy in this area.

At this time, it is impossible to predict what effect the energy crisis will have on motor transportation. Reduced speed limits and the possibility of fuel rationing certainly could shift a significant amount of the goods trucks haul to railroads. The policies set by the President's Energy Council could accelerate the decline of some agricultural truck farming operations that are dependent upon trucking for their survival.

Water Transportation. Water transportation has grown significantly in volume even though its share of the total freight handled has declined. Note in Table 18-1 that its percent of total shipments has been increased from 14.9 percent in 1950 to 15.9 percent in 1971 but that total ton-miles has increased from 163 billion to 307 billion.

The principal items of shipment on waterways are raw materials—iron ore, grains, coal, chemicals, sugar, coffee, cotton, and rice. The areas where inland shipping via water is most extensively practiced are the Great Lakes, the Mississippi River and its tributaries, the coastal rivers, and the canals. The principal canal is the New York Barge Canal, formerly the Erie Canal.

Developments in water transportation continue to be made. The St. Lawrence Seaways plan, which opened the entire Great Lakes area to seagoing vessels, and navigation projects by the army engineers are examples. It appears that this method of transportation will become more important as such developments continue.

There is increasing interest in facilitating movement of goods between intercontinental and intracontinental carriers. A substantial part of all surface transport cost is accumulated in terminals. This is particularly true of water transport. Costs are incurred in loading and unloading, transfer to ground transportation, and serious losses due to pilferage and damage. Much work is now being done on containers that are interchangeable between carriers which are expected to reduce these terminal costs.

Waterway travel is not as rapid as the railways or the trucks. In some instances, depending on the arteries, it is seasonal, since there must be sufficient water depth to carry the vessels. Floods are also a factor that may interfere with, or even destory the movement of goods. These factors must be balanced against economies of the waterways.

Pipelines. Pipelines are not often recognized as a significant part of our transportation system, but they carry almost one fifth of the tonnage that moves through the transportation arteries of the United States. They are exceeded in volume only by railroads. Presently they enjoy over 23 percent of total freight shipments in the United States.

The versatility of pipelines that makes it possible to transport at different intervals crude oil, gasoline, kerosene, fuel oil, and gas has increased the usefulness of the lines. This diversity of uses has also increased the volume. Thus, it is possible for pipelines to charge much lower rates. In fact, the crude oil cost per ton-mile shipped via pipeline was estimated by the Interstate Commerce Commission as 1.98 cents as compared to 10.62 cents by the railroads. For refined products, such as gasoline, kerosene, and fuel oil, the rate was 4.39 cents per ton-mile by the pipelines and 11.19 cents by the rails. Pipelines would be much more widely used if they were more numerous and were accessible to all the areas where petroleum products are used and produced. The great differential in cost is encouraging such extensions.

The greatest building project of oil pipelines was prompted not by economy, but rather by safety. Submarines during World War II sank so many tankers off the Atlantic coast that the government moved to protect this central supply line by installing two of the longest pipelines constructed at that time. The "Big Inch" runs from Longview, Texas, to New York and cost nearly $80 million. The "Little Big Inch" stretches from the Texas Gulf coast to New York and cost approximately $67 million. Both of these lines carry natural gas at the present time. Another project that surpasses either of these in its scope is the Trans-Canada pipelines running from the western boundary of Alberta, Canada, to Winnipeg, then to Toronto, and thence into the United States. At present the pipeline is 2,250 miles long and was built at a cost of $350 million. The gas supply that it transports is adequate also to extend the line further into the United States.

Because of the economy, the flexibility, and the increasing use of pipelines, there will probably be an extension both of trunk lines and of feeder lines to carry an increasing share of petroleum, gas, and other products in pipelines.

Air Transportation. In 1971 air traffic accounted for only 0.18 percent of the freight tonnage of the United States. If the dollar value of the goods transported were considered, the portion would be different. Only goods that have a comparatively high intrinsic value can be carried by air freight. The rates average approximately 22 cents per ton-mile as compared to 1.3 cents for railroads and 6.5 cents for trucks. Several factors are important in setting rates on air freight. On the cost side of the analysis are the bulk and weight of the product. On the demand side, the desirability of the product ascribed to it by the buyer or consumer must be considered, as is the case in all other price-determining calculations. Further, there is the dimension of time that often makes a product a prospect for air transport. Some products are shipped by air because of a quality of perishability. Fashion goods, flowers, and some vegetables and fruits are in this category. Time also is strategic in the case of repair products that may be vital to the operation of a plant; or it may be an important competitive factor, as in the case of a merchandising establishment that wishes to offer a new product first to its clientele.

It is also possible that quick deliveries by air transportation may make it unnecessary for businesses to carry large stocks. It is costly to manufacturing and merchandising establishments to maintain inventories to meet contingencies. A manufacturer may be required to stock a supply of spare parts to guarantee the continued operations of its own machines or those of its customers. In a merchandising establishment extra investment may be required for items within unpredictable rates of sale. If supplies run short, air freight can supplement them without impairing the efficiency of the operations.

An instance of this kind was reported when an airline flew a 20,000-pound steel rod from Philadelphia to Los Angeles. The shipment could have required two weeks by rail. Furthermore, no elaborate and expensive packing was necessary. Certainly this plant would have found it expensive to have been idle during the period required for the product to come by rail. Plant operators never know when a repair part is going to be needed; thus, a large store of various products would otherwise have to be available.

In the case of the merchandising establishment, one line of skirts of a certain style and color may sell more rapidly than others. This item may have been purchased in the same quantities as other lines that proved to be less popular. With air freight, a new order of skirts might be obtained overnight. If it were not for air traffic, these merchants would need to order a larger stock of all skirts in order to avoid the embarrassment and ill will of being short of the popular numbers. Such a course would require markdowns and possible losses in the other lines of skirts. In making such adjustments possible in less time, the merchandising function is simplified. Storage costs, markdowns, and merchandise investments can be reduced, sometimes by substantial amounts.

Proponents of air freight agree that the cost factors are such that it is unlikely that a high percentage of freight tonnage will be directed to air travel in the near future. They suggest, however, that in the areas which we have described there are still many savings possible that business firms are not exploiting to their profitable potential.

Products that are transported now are machinery (much of which is made up of automobile and airplane parts), women's wearing apparel, drugs, printed matter, sea food, cut flowers, and perishable food products. With improved technology and the continuation of the educational program, air transport probably will become even more widely and intensely used.

Airline executives are aggressively pursuing innovations. One example is the quick conversion (QC) aircraft. It is designed with seats and kitchen compartments mounted on pallets which ride on rollers in the floor of the airplane. During night hours when passenger traffic is light, the seats and kitchens can be pulled out and stored in less than 30 minutes, leaving a clean platform for cargo. This is expected to drive down air freight rates. Several airlines are encouraging use of air cargo pallets that the interchangeable between medium-sized aircraft and long-range cargo jets. Hence, it is possible to prepare a load for a feeder line that will transport the cargo to the major airport for transfer to the largest cargo planes which transport across the country or intercontinentally.

TRENDS IN TRANSPORTATION

It is worthy to note a recently completed study by the U. S. Department of Transportation that forecasts a boom in certain types of transportation. Table 18-2 indicates that policy makers project a slightly increased usage of aviation freight and pipelines. At the same time, both trucking and railroads are forecast to decline over the period of 20 years from 1970.

Table 18-2
TRENDS AND PROJECTIONS OF TRANSPORTATION INDUSTRY
ACTIVITY IN MILLIONS OF DOLLARS[1]/IN BILLIONS OF TON MILES

	1970	1980	1990
Aviation			
Freight	860.0/3.858	3,182.8/13,989	7,701.1/33.266
Railroad			
Freight	11,034.2/740.027	14,510.0/966.575	18,167.0/1,223.056
Truck			
Intercity	12,643.7/195.643	21,657.4/325.248	30,752.0/458.713
Domestic Water			
Freight	1.417.3/586.333	2,026.6/810.515	2,687.4/041.719
Pipeline			
Intercity	1,197.1/403.080	1,795.5/613.953	2,491.1/851.819

[1] 1969 dollars

Source: U.S. Department of Transportation, Office of the Secretary, *National Transportation Report: 1972.*

TRANSPORTATION RATES

The reduction of transportation costs had almost an explosive influence on market areas. The growth of competitive areas is still in process as further economies are devised. Barriers similar to those that separated buyers from sellers in 1830, when the first railroad was operating, still exist. The barriers, time and distance, must be overcome by the expenditure of funds. The story of transportation is the story of reducing these costs.

Why Rates Are Set in Interstate Commerce

The rate is the price charged for the services of the carrier. The price, however, cannot find its equilibrium in a comparatively free market. This decision was made when the federal government was given the power to set rates in interstate commerce. There were three main reasons why a free competitive price was considered unwise.

First, the inability of railroad services to move from one market opportunity to another and the great amount of invested capital preventing easy entry into the field would make it possible for railroads to discriminate against one community and favor another. For example, a railroad might be competing with another line in a certain area. Such competition might cause such a railroad to reduce its rates below cost. This course would then encourage the road to seek higher rates where there was no competition. This policy would discriminate against the buyers in the latter market area since the extra transportation cost would have to be added to the costs of goods shipped in and out of the community.

Second, it was discovered that railroad operators often profited by favoring some customers over others. Rail operators were often tempted to give concessions to big shippers in order to gain volume. Volume to pay fixed costs is more necessary for profits in railroad operation than is the case of retail stores. Their fixed charges are such a high proportion of costs that break-even points are high. Such discrimination favoring the established large shipper against the small is a violation of democratic principles. In order to protect the right of free competition, the government was forced to step in and set rates for shipments.

The third reason why free competition failed is corollary to the second. The competitive struggle to achieve volume would force the railroads into bankruptcy. A railroad might continue to operate by paying out-of-pocket expenses, often neglecting repairs and failing to set up reserves to replace worn plant and equipment. Such a policy would cause it to give the public inadequate service and not satisfy its obligations to financial backers, which in turn would make it difficult to raise funds for extension of services. The very nature of this competition might force two roads into ruinous practices even though their respective managements were perfectly aware of the consequences.

Market forces failed to meet the need in allocating resources justly and adequately in the field of railroad transportation. The same conditions do not apply in the case of motor trucks for the following reasons: (1) Investments are small enough in motor equipment that many operators compete for business. Should one operator raise rates to a locality or to an individual, there would be others to take the business at a competitive price, if it were profitable. (2) Cutthroat competition would not be serious insofar as the public is concerned. The failure of one or two trucks or truck lines would not seriously impair the transportation facilities of a whole community. Such failures would serve as a corrective warning to other operators. Since, however, the bulk of the transportation is carried by railroads, and since trucks compete with railroads, regulation of rates must apply to both types of travel.

General Philosophy of Rate Setting

In approving rates, the government must face the problem of allocating costs between distances and products in order to get the goods moved and at the same time maximize the national satisfaction. To supply transportation requires tremendous capital commitments as well as large operating costs. The cost of giving the service should be considered, but it is impossible to apportion specific costs to each different class of product. For this reason the cost, as far as the product characteristics are concerned, has less importance than has the value of the product. In other words, demand has a strong influence on the price charged. Such a philosophy gave rise to the expression, ''Railroad rates are based on what the traffic will bear.''

The government is guided by two major objectives in approving rates. First, the rates established must be fair to the agencies providing transportation and the areas that they serve. The other basic objective is corollary to the first: to broaden the area of competition by diminishing the cost of overcoming the distance barrier. The best example of how this goal is achieved is evident in the method of making transportation costs less than proportional to distance. According to one rate schedule, even a doubling of the distance from 5 to 10 miles, or 100 percent, increases the cost from 66 cents to 68 cents, only 2 cents, or about 1½ percent. If the distance is increased by ten times to 50 miles, the charge is increased by only 29 cents. In other words, the cost of a 900 percent increase in distance is matched by only a 44 percent increase in cost. This type of rate structure explains why Quaker Oats can be sold at the same price in Miami as it can in Cedar Rapids where it is manufacturered. Railroads are the dominant traffic carriers; ttey set the pattern for all rates although there may be some variations.

Government's Changing Function

Basic reasons for the need of the federal government to regulate certain aspects of transportation have been discussed. Developments have been away from regulation and in the direction of freedom of competition. Few products or geographic areas today are completely dependent on railroads. Each transportation agency is competing with the members of its own type, and different types are competing with one another. Such competition stimulates research and innovation in the direction of recapturing the incentives and motivations that arise out of free competition. This change is in harmony with the American system of industrial growth. It is commendablethat the federal government sponsors a policy that encourages this competition with its attendant efficiency and innovation.

PHYSICAL DISTRIBUTION MANAGEMENT

An effective system of physical distribution can never be built if concern begins only at the shipping dock. Norge Division of Borge-Warner Corporation exemplifies organizations that utilize the concept of marketing logistics. For that company all distribution functions (starting with forecasting, production scheduling, and continuing through warehousing, order processing, and shipping) have been consolidated into one department under a director of physical distribution. The following changes have been effected as a result.

Until 1964 the price of Norge's home appliances practically doubled from the end of the production line to the hands of the consumer. There were six departments at Norge (in addition to distributors at the Norge plants and to distributors at the wholesale and retail levels), all of which had a hand in distribution but without common direction or common policies. The traffic department shipped the best available way so that shipping was a matter of expediency of the moment. According to the president of the company, sometimes warehouses were underutilized and sometimes it was necessary to rent outside space to take overflow. An excess of one product sometimes forced Norge into what the industry called a "loading program," which is pushing surplus products off onto dealers with special concessions that boost accounts receivable and cut profits. Now, under the director of physical distribution, the company has ceased loading distributors. The company has substantially reduced plant inventories, distributor's inventories, and accounts receivable. This has resulted in the reduction of overall investment and, at the same time, in an increase in profitability. A specific step was the establishment of a regional warehouse at Utah's freeport for Norge's West Coast distributors. Norge plants around the United States ship and complete line of appliances, mostly in carload lots to the freeport center. From there Norge can make deliveries to West Coast dealers in four or five days instead of twenty, which was the average before, and has achieved a 50 percent reduction in dealer inventories and accounts receivable.[7]

Other companies may not wish completely to regroup management activities, but they should be aware of the controls which are necessary to assure that customers' needs are met in a manner and at a cost which is competitive with firms that may be giving more attention to changes in physical distribution systems.

A McKinsey Company Survey on physical distribution reported that firms who rated high on their scale of excellence in logistics developed the following information:

1. Transportation costs.
   a. Total costs for the company and each operating division by rail, common-carrier truck, and company-operated truck.
   b. A comparison of those costs to sales this year versus last.
   c. Total transportation from plant to warehouse and total transportation costs from warehouse to customer. Inbound freight figures and penalty cost figures for partial shipments.
2. Warehousing costs.
   a. Total.
   b. Public warehouse costs per square foot per dollar of product handled.
   c. Company operated total costs (in the plant and in the field) per square foot per product per dollar of product handled.
3. Inventory performance, actual versus planned.
   a. By location.
   b. Low-volume items.
   c. Cost of carrying inventories.
4. Quality of service on time-order performance.
   a. Percent of orders shipped on time.
   b. Severity of late orders and customer problems.
   c. Comparison with competitive service on liability, speed, time, and delivery.[8]

In summary, it can be said that the logistics approach calls for intellectual rather than mechanical changes. A real systems approach to physical distribution will almost certainly require some shifting of duties and responsibilities. This is due primarily to some of the conflicts noted earlier among a marketing executive, a finance executive, and a production executive, who try to achieve maximum efficiency in their respective tasks, but at a cost to the overall effectiveness of the firm.

---

[7] "Overhaul at Norge Speeds Deliveries—and Profits," *Business Week* (September 24, 1966), p. 126.

[8] John F. Stolle, "How to Manage Physical Distribution," *Harvard Business Review* (July-August, 1967), p. 43.

QUESTIONS AND ANALYTICAL PROBLEMS

1. Define marketing logistics.
2. What four basic kinds of inventory appear to be requirements of all industries? What logistics problems are posed by these requirements?
3. What elements of the physical distribution process may be used in marketing strategy for a competitive advantage?
4. (a) What are the basic components of any physical distribution system? (b) Will each assume the same importance for any two companies? For your answer to (b), compare any two companies that manufacture similar widely used consumer products. Then compare the results with the physical distribution requirements of a manufacturer of a different kind of consumer product.
5. Explain intransit storage. What advantages can use of intransit storage provide for a manufacturer whose materials for production are located at great distances from his markets? Cite three industries that should be able to benefit from proper use of intransit privileges?
6. What organizational changes will most likely occur for any company that adopts a logistics concept of marketing?

Case 18 • THE PHILO FILE COMPANY

Organized in 1947, the Philo File Company presently produces 14 different types of filing cabinets ranging from small cardboard files to large office files. The company is in good financial standing with its creditors, and Philo's future looks bright.

Originally all cabinets were shipped directly to customers on an individual basis from the plant in Los Angeles. Since that time, however, business has expanded to the point where most sales are made through retail office supply stores. During this period a distribution system gradually evolved which many company officers are beginning to question. All cabinets are still made at the original plant. During the years of growth, five warehouses were built and maintained by Philo throughout the entire state of California. Since all five warehouses are situated next to railroad tracks, Philo has found it convenient to ship all cabinets to the warehouses by rail. Then orders are delivered from the warehouse to the retailer by trucks owned and operated by Philo.

The number of cabinets sent to the individual warehouse is dependent upon forecasts made by the warehouse foreman. Thus, inventory size varies substantially from warehouse to warehouse. However, as a general rule, each warehouse tries to maintain full storage capacity. If inventory levels exceed capacity, then excess inventory is sent by truck to the neighboring warehouse.

• What basic rules of marketing logistics is the Philo Company violating? Should corrective action be taken? If so, what should the company do?

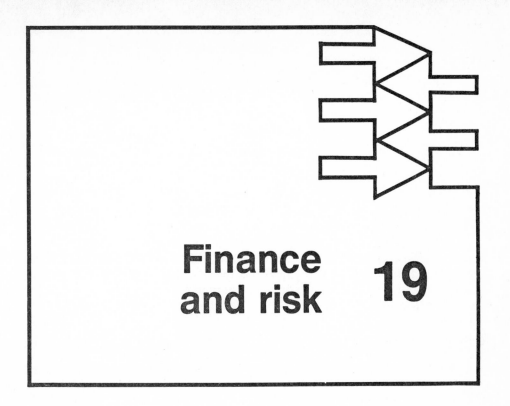

Finance and risk 19

A merchandising firm is established primarily to facilitate the movement of goods from producers to consumers. Consequently, marketing executives do not have as a major responsibility any one of the functional areas of marketing. Their task is the smooth blending of all functions into one operation that will create a successful merchandising venture. Even so, if there is to be the required efficiency of each functional area, there must be sufficient understanding of it to enable its proper integration into the whole. On that basis we approach the study of finance. The following discussion will highlight the areas of finance, credit, and risk with which most marketing managers should be conversant.

FINANCE

The marketing mix, as described in Chapter 1, did not identify finance as one of the major ingredient categories. It must be emphasized, however, that credit, for example, is one of the variables that can be managed to achieve a competitive advantage. Also, there is an almost complete integration of the financing function with marketing operations. Banking, insurance, credit, and investment firms deal in large measure with buying and selling organizations. It is, indeed, even more difficult to separate marketing from finance than it is to separate finance from production. The money management aspect of business operations is so completely entwined with marketing that it is safe to say that skill in dealing with financial problems is essential to successful marketing.

Competence in Finance Necessary in Marketing

Three examples will illustrate this interrelationship. The first example is concerned with the problems of starting a new business; the second illustrates how problems in the area of finance arise from normal changes in economic conditions; and the third example deals with the effect of credit-policy decisions on the rate of sales and growth of a major national chain.

In the first instance two graduates from a school of business who were trained in marketing were confident that they could make a success as merchandisers. They envisioned the development of a chain of men's and women's ready-to-wear stores. They had only one asset, however—a line of credit that the suppliers of their father's store were willing to grant them because of confidence in the father. It required some time for them to convince the owner of property at a desirable location of their ability to establish a profitable operation, but they did so by selling him on their own ability and the soundness of their marketing plan. Once he committed himself to constructing a building for them, it was easier for them to raise additional money for equipment and inventory. For the first several years the most challenging problem of these young men was that of meeting their fixed financial commitments. Today they are in the process of expanding the number of stores they operate as rapidly as they can acquire desirable sites and personnel. But their first and greatest challenge was that of raising the necessary funds and meeting heavy fixed financial obligations during the early period of their business.

The second example involves a department store with an annual sales volume of $30 million. During World War II this store had an annual stockturn rate of six. Forty percent of its sales were for credit, and the average credit customer paid his account in 30 days. Since the company paid 90 percent of its wartime earnings as taxes and dividends, it did not have cash reserves on hand in 1945. When the war ended and merchandise was more plentiful, the store increased its inventory from $5 million to $7.5 million, requiring an increase of $2.5 million in merchandise investment. After the war its credit sales incresed from 40 percent to 60 percent, or from $12 million $18 million per annum. Had the average credit account outstanding remained on a 30-day basis, this change would have cost this store only $500,000, with the money turning over 12 times in a year. Since, however, the average outstanding account reached the age of 60 days, or a credit investment turnover of only 6 times, the extra capital needed increased by $1 million a year. Added to this $3.5 million demand for capital were the increases necessary for renovating and remodeling the store and the higher prices that were required for both merchandise costs and construction. The officers of the company recommended that the building which they occupied be sold to raise the necessary funds for these purposes. Their recommendation was denied, and they were forced to apply to several New York banks for loans.

Incidentally, the practice of selling the store building to insurance or real estate companies is common among large merchandising establishments, as has been previously discussed. Such a practice enables the firm to invest its funds in merchandise that turns over rapidly rather than having it tied up in real estate which yields only a nominal return.

The third example involves one of the largest chain store organizations. This firm was well known for economy, for selling for cash only, and for low prices. During the decade of the fifties, when incomes were increasing and credit sales were popular, the firm was concerned about the wisdom of its cash policy. As an experiment it adopted a credit policy for a group of its stores. The results were surprising, even to those who had advocated credit sales. In every instance sales increased. In one large city the increase was as great as 30 percent, and there were subsequent reports of much larger sales gains. Needless to say, the chain established credit in its stores as fast as the proper credit machinery could be installed. Here, again, is an example where the problem of finance is completely entwined with the promotion program and influences the sales made by the firm.

It is impossible to separate marketing, production, and finance problems and to deal with them separately. They are so completely interdependent that they must be viewed as a unity.

Role of Finance in Marketing [1]

Certain aspects of financing a merchandising operation are different from problems of financing other establishments, and some discussion of these aspects is desirable.[2] Particular emphasis is given here to "circulating," or "working," capital, since it is especially important for a merchant to estimate the amount of it required for effective operation of merchandising activities.

Financing is required for the distribution of goods not only to provide the physical plant, equipment, and organization for distribution but also, and often more important, the financing of finished goods inventories. Although a manufacturing firm can achieve maximum economy only if it can schedule operations to provide regular full employment of men and machinery, sales almost never follow a straight line through a year. There is the further complication that manufacturers and large distributors are often expected to pay cash for the goods they process or resell, but their customers expect credit for some period of time.[3]

The case of a medium-sized appliance manufacturer who sells his products to several distributing companies further illustrates the role that

---

[1] Explanations of financial institutions and uses of credit for marketing organizations can be found in the following: Robert H. Cole and Robert S. Hancock, *Consumer and Commercial Credit Management* (4th ed.; Homewood, Illinois: Richard D. Irwin, Inc., 1972); Carl A. Dauten and Merle Welshans, *Principles of Finance* (3d ed.; Cincinnati: South-Western Publishing Co., 1970), Part 2; Robert A. Johnson, *Financial Management* (3d ed.; Boston: Allyn and Bacon, 1966), Parts 1 through 4, which are especially pertinent for marketing establishments; and Harold A. Wolf and Lee Richardson, *Readings in Finance* (New York: Appleton-Century-Crofts, 1966), especially Parts III and IV.

[2] Among the excellent treatments of financial institutions and credit are Herbert V. Prochnow (ed.), *American Financial Institutions* (Englewood Cliffs, New Jersey: Prentice-Hall, 1951), and T.N. Beckman and Ronald S. Foster, *Credits and Collections* (8th ed.; New York: McGraw-Hill Book Company, 1969).

[3] Robert M. Kaplan states, "It is surprising how many credit managers say with pride that their companies are renowned in their industries, by customers and competitors alike, for having a very stringent credit policy. These companies, however, are not maximizing profits (unless they are operating at capacity), are creating an umbrella under which competition is invited, and are probably causing considerable frustration in the sales force." See "Credit Risks and Opportunities," *Harvard Business Review* (March-April, 1967), pp. 83-88.

financing—particularly credit—plays in our economy. Annual sales of these appliances had been forecast with a fairly high degree of accuracy in recent years. On the basis of sales estimates, the manufacturer scheduled production on an almost straight-line basis throughout the year. The sales pattern of his product to ultimate consumers, however, fluctuated widely. Suppose that he could sell finished goods only as the dealers could in turn make sales to customers. How would he level his production to achieve economy and efficiency? It is obvious that he would need extremely large inventories in both finished goods and raw materials. How would he finance such inventories? It is possible, of course, to start business with an equity sufficient to furnish the huge amounts of working capital required to provide storage space and to supply inventories of such size that all sales demands can be met regardless of how unequal the shipments are during a year. This is not, however, efficient because of the large amount of capital tied up in inventories over long periods.

Sales volume in the nation's automobile business was of relatively minor importance until arrangements were completed that allowed dealers to receive and store automobiles without providing cash for the purchases. This is true also with the appliance manufacturer. His dealers find it impractical, even in cases where it is possible, to tie up all of their capital in inventories of appliances during seasons of low sales.[4]

Sources of Working Capital

Providing one's own financial resources is not the only means of keeping goods flowing through marketing channels. Various credit and finance facilities are available to marketing institutions.

Mercantile Credit. Mercantile credit remains the most widely used method of short-term financing of retail and wholesale firms. *Mercantile credit,* or trade credit as it is sometimes termed, is extended by one business firm to another in ordinary business operations. A large proportion—about 85 percent of all sales of manufacturers and wholesalers—are made on credit.

Commercial Banks. Commercial banks are second only to suppliers of mercantile credit as sources of working capital for merchandising. If we accept the premise suggested earlier in the chapter that the merchant should furnish his own working capital for basic operations and borrow to provide funds for peak seasons, it follows that he should establish bank credit connections. Funds borrowed from commercial banks cost the merchant less than those from other sources, including mercantile credit, if he does not take cash discounts; and good credit standing with commercial banks will place larger amounts of money at his disposal. Of course, there may be disadvantages in relying heavily upon banks. Notably, money may not be available in time of stress; and further, bank funds

---

   [4] The editors of the *Harvard Business Review* report that in cooperation with the National Association of Credit Management, they sponsored a survey which showed that more and more companies were liberalizing credit practices and treating their credit departments as credit centers. The data on this survey was analyzed and reported by Merle T. Welshans in "Using Credit for Profit Making," *Harvard Business Review* (January-February, 1967), pp. 141-156.

may not be available for his use over long periods. The latter disadvantage has been offset since 1935 by the widespread use of term bank loans.

Sales Finance Companies. Sales finance companies have as their business the purchase of installment paper from dealers. One will often notice in automobile salesrooms, appliance outlets, and furniture stores that the contract sales forms and rate charts are furnished by a particular finance company. When a credit sale is made, the dealer supplies the pertinent information and then offers the paper to the sales finance company.

The organizers of sales finance companies, in almost every case, have been businessmen who were confronted with the problem of selling on time and paying cash for the goods they sell. In 1905 the two men who were selling Encyclopedia Americana on an installment plan were such successful salesmen that their working capital was all tied up in notes receivable. They organized a finance company to sell the paper to investors in order that they could continue selling. Other merchandising lines followed their lead, and in 1919 General Motors Acceptance Corporation was organized to finance sales of automobiles. That was the beginning of large-scale financing of consumer goods.

Factoring Companies. The producer of goods may finance current operations by outright sale of his accounts receivable to factors. Under this arrangement the factor usually agrees to pay from 90 to 95 percent of the face value of all accounts receivable immediately on receipt of his copy of invoices. After he collects the accounts, he submits the balance less his commission. The factor makes two charges: (1) a discount on the accounts, usually around 1 or 2 percent per annum higher than the prime rate and (2) a commission which is commonly 1 to 2 percent of the face amount of any receivable he accepts. While this may sound like a fairly high cost for funds, it must be remembered that the borrower escapes most of the cost of a separate credit and collection department as well as the cost of having large amounts of capital outstanding and not available for his business.

Factoring companies first became important in this country in the textile trade. That line of business was early characterized by a large number of small mills which needed to get their money back to purchase raw material inventories. Since it was common for the mills to sell through agents located in the textile markets, the agents gradually assumed the function of credit investigation and risk-bearing. At the present time, this financing function has been divorced from selling; and although there are factoring companies who still deal mainly in the textile trade, others are now quite common in lumber, paper, shoe, clothing, fur, electrical appliances, fuel, oil, furniture, glassware, and china.

Floor-Plan Financing. With the widespread distribution of highpriced consumer goods, such as automobiles and appliances, floor-plan financing has developed. It is quite common now for a manufacturer to ship goods to a dealer but for title to the goods to pass to a third party, which will be a bank or other financial institution. The goods are on the floor of the dealer's showroom for display and sale, but the dealer actually holds the goods only as a trustee of the financing company. At the time of sale, the dealer turns over the proceeds of the sale, less his share, in payment of the note held by the lender.

Floor-plan financing can be advantageous to the manufacturers and the dealers. The manufacturer can ship goods as they are manufactured and thus avoid a costly inventory problem. At the same time dealers are benefited. Since their sales may not always coincide with the manufacturer's production schedule, the dealer could readily tie up all his available capital in inventories during certain periods.

Warehouse Receipts. Within regularly established sources of funds, it is usual for special conditions to result in modifications of practices to facilitate commerce. The development of financing arrangements built around warehouse receipts is a good example of such an adaptation. For example, a young man who started a small woolen glove business produced gloves during all months of the year, but sales were confined almost entirely to two or three fall and winter months. It was impossible for him to finance the purchase of raw materials, meet a steady payroll, and do any sales promotion until he learned of warehouse receipts. Now he stores the gloves as they are completed, obtains warehouse receipts, and uses those documents as security.

Warehouse receipts are documents provided under the Uniform Warehouse Receipts Act and the federal Warehouse Act. When such receipts are rendered by a bona fide warehouseman (legally defined as "a person lawfully engaged in the business of storing goods for profit") and meet the standards provided in the Warehouse Act, they constitute very acceptable security. Since such receipts show the quantity of goods stored along with identifying descriptions, a banker can be assured of the existence of the security offered.

A further use of warehouse receipts for financing has resulted from *field warehousing*. For purposes of convenience and to reduce the cost of storage, the concept of field warehousing has been developed. Under such an arrangement goods intended as security for loan purposes are stored on the premises of the borrower but under conditions that permit their supervision and control by a regular warehouseman. These arrangements are common in a number of industries.

Consumer Credit—Effect on Sales

A study at one university relates to beliefs of retail executives that sales would fall off significantly if credit facilities were removed.[5] Without exception, all store managers in the study believed that credit had a positive effect on sales even though it was not possible to determine the extent of such effect with any precision. Also, as mentioned earlier, it is very clear that chain store organizations which formerly sold only for cash and have begun to grant credit have increased sales.

The following advantages of offering credit were quite uninformly stated by the executives who responded:

Advantages
1. Convenience and service for customers.
2. For repeat business—building up customer loyalty.

---

[5] An unpublished report prepared for the College of Business, University of Utah, by Dr. D.T. Verma in 1965. Respondents were retail executives of western states.

3. Increasing buying ability and level of living of customers.
4. Increasing sales volume.
5. Promotion device to increase sales.
6. Meeting competitive pressures.

Disadvantages
1. Overextension of credit privileges—credit too prominent and common.
2. Expense of handling accounts.
3. Tying up funds in accounts receivable.

Consumer use of credit for purchases of both durable and nondurable goods is increasing. In Table 19-1 one can see that in the relatively prosperous year of 1950, consumer credit was 10 percent of disposable personal income and was just under 19 percent in 1973. Increases in consumer credit amounts displayed in the table reflect changing attitudes towards indebtedness. Fringe benefits for workers, including retirement pay and medical insurance, remove important future worries. Going in debt no longer carries the moral stigma once attached in certain cultures. Most persons taking on increased indebtedness believe they can handle the payments. There is some belief, however, that increasing rates of personal bankruptcies illustrate that not all families should be so optimistic.

Table 19-1

USE OF CONSUMER CREDIT IN THE UNITED STATES (BILLIONS OF DOLLARS)

Year	Total	Installment Credit	Installment a % of Total	Disposable Personal Income	Total Consumer Credit as Percent of Disposable Income
1950	$ 21.5	$ 14.7	68%	$206.9	10.3%
1960	56.1	43.0	77%	350.2	12.2%
1970	127.2	102.1	80%	689.5	18.4%

   * As of end of June, 1973.
  ** Preliminary estimate of annual rate as of end of first quarter, 1973.
    Sources: *Federal Reserve Bulletin*, June issues 1971 and 1973; "Consumer Credit" and "National Income" tables.

Regulation of Consumer Credit

In Chapter 11, "The Government in the Marketplace," reference was made to the Consumer Credit Protection Act (Public Law 90-321). That act resulted in the Uniform Consumer Credit Code (UCCC) which was to be incorporated into the Uniform Commercial Code of the various states. Of particular interest to buyers and sellers are those portions dealing with sales on credit.[6] They are:

---

   [6] For the specific provisions and full explanation of this legislation see the Annotated Code for the state in which you are interested. Ask for the Uniform Commercial Code including the Uniform Consumer Credit Code.

(1) simplification and clarification of laws governing retail installment sales, consumer credit, small loans, and usury.

(2) rate ceilings on allowable interest charges on credit sales. Quite commonly the state laws provide maximum charges that may not exceed the greater of either of the following: (a) 36 percent per year on unpaid balances of less than $300; 21 percent per year on unpaid balances of more than $300 but less than $1,000; 15 percent per year on unpaid balances over $1,000; or (b) 18 percent per year on the unpaid balances of the amount financed.

(3) provision for cancellation by consumers of any conditional sales contract resulting from solicitation of sales at a consumer's residence. A common provision is that the buyer has the right to cancel the contract until midnight of the third business day after the day on which the buyer signs an agreement or offer to purchase. The seller may retain a cancellation fee—often five percent of the cash price but not exceeding the amount of any cash down payment.

These parts of the UCCC are made part of the Uniform Commercial Code adopted by the various states, and they particularly relate to Article 2—Credit Sales, and Article 9—Secured Transactions of that Uniform Commercial Code.

Nature of Consumer Credit

Data on consumer credit covers borrowing for household, family, and other personal expenditures except real estate mortgage loans. Some indication of relative amounts loaned for the various kinds of expenditures will assist in understanding consumer credit. In Table 19-2 the types and sources of loans are listed. The table covers only installment credit. In 1972 there was an additional $30.5 billion in noninstallment credit outstanding; that includes $12.7 billion in single payment loans, $8.0 billion in charge accounts, and $9.7 billion in service credit (credit owed to institutional sellers of services, the largest portion of which is that owed to hospitals and physicians).

The data in Table 19-2 reflects the increasing practice of borrowing from a bank, sales finance company, or credit union to pay for consumer goods. Note that over 86 percent of all installment financing is done through financial institutions, even though the merchant may arrange the credit.

Open-Account Credit. In general, the volume of business done on open-account or charge-account credit varies according to the type of retailer. Usually it is found that the higher-price department stores and specialty shops sell a considerable portion of their goods on 30-day credit terms. It is not unusual, in fact, to find specialty stores doing as much as 80 to 90 percent of their total sales volume on open account. Throughout the United States, 30-day credit accounts for almost half of the total sales volume of specialty stores and department stores.

Installment-Account Credit. The growth of installment-sales credit has largely paralleled the growth of the automobile industry and its financing in the United States. There were, however, earlier examples of installment selling. In 1850, for example, a sewing machine company used this method of promoting

Table 19-2
PURPOSES AND SOURCES OF CONSUMER INSTALLMENT CREDIT—1972
(BILLIONS OF DOLLARS)

	Amount	Percent of Total Installment Credit
Purpose		
Automobile	$ 46.5	35.5%
Other consumer goods	40.4	30.8
Repair and modernization	6.4	4.9
Personal loans	37.7	28.8
Total Installment Credit	$131.0	100.0%
		Percent of Total Installment Loans
Source (Financial Institutions)		
Commercial banks	$ 62.5	47.7%
Finance companies *	33.1	25.3
Credit unions	17.5	13.4
Other misc. lenders *	2.7	2.1
Retail outlets	15.3	11.7
Total Installment Loans	$131.1	100.2% (because of rounding)

* "Finance companies" consist of sales finance, consumer finance, and other finance companies. "Miscellaneous lenders" include savings and loan associations and mutual savings banks.
Source: Computed from data in *Federal Reserve Bulletin* (June, 1973), p. A-54.

sales, and the Encyclopedia Americana was sold on "long-payment terms" around the beginning of the present century.

Installment credit differs from open-account credit in three respects: (1) a down payment is required; (2) periodic payments, usually uniform monthly payments, are required; and (3) interest or carrying charges are levied.

The cost to the consumer for installment credit varies widely. On examining the advertisements in a newspaper for goods available "on time," one will note that some firms state clearly how much a consumer pays for credit. A television set, for example, may be advertised at $250 for cash or for $50 down and $25 a month for "x" months.

There are, however, firms who hide credit charges in such statements as "no down payment required, no monthly payments, no interest or carrying charges"; but one will notice that the prices they charge are very high for the quality of merchandise, and that the customer is actually paying a high rate for credit.

Legislation commonly called the Truth-in-Lending Bill which passed in 1968 has the following provisions:

1. All finance charges must be disclosed in writing.

2. Information about cost of credit shall be itemized both in dollars and cents and in approximate true annual interest rates.
3. Annual interest charges shall be carried in advertisements.
4. Statements of finance charges shall include such extras as credit insurance and other fees.

It is presumed that disclosure of the actual amount being paid for credit will assist families to buy more wisely.

Universal Credit Cards. Credit-card financing is not new, but there has been a marked increase in the use of so-called universal (or bank) credit cards which is worth noting. At the end of 1972, 1,588 banks offered credit-card service. While bank credit cards are spreading, they are mainly concentrated in three geographic regions. The largest amount of credit-card financing is in the San Francisco Federal Reserve District, with the Chicago and New York districts following. Bank credit-cards plans are almost equal in credit outstanding to oil company credit cards.[7] One should be alert to the possibilities of developing a cashless and checkless economy, with resultant shifts in competitive positions of retailers.

At present many retailers have joined universal credit-card plans, but no specific, wide-scale information is available about general shifts in competition resulting from the adoptions. One study has been made of appliance dealers in Illinois, and the only conclusion is that most are neutral to the use of such credit plans. There is dissatisfaction among small dealers over the charge (maximum of 3 percent of retail sales price which is normal for in-store credit department operations). Those few who strongly favor the plans generally allow the use of credit cards for service call charges and for sales of small appliances. Some credit cards limit purchases to $50.

It does seem that, inasmuch as the banks are now responsible for billing and collections, small merchants now have available credit facilities that were previously too expensive.[8]

Sources for Consumer Cash Loans

It is sometimes said that it is cheaper to borrow money with which to pay for an automobile, furniture, or a major appliance in one lump sum than it is to finance purchases through the dealer by means of installment payments. That is certainly true if one can borrow money at a lower rate than the installment charges and interest. This brings us to the subject of the cost for obtaining cash by borrowing from various sources. Institutions from which consumers may obtain loans are commercial banks, credit unions, industrial banks, sales finance companies, small loan companies, and pawnshops. These are listed roughly in the order of ascending costs to the consumer.

Commercial Banks. Commercial banks have shown increasing interest in consumer loans since the 1930's. They are necessarily selective in their lending,

---

[7] "Consumer Installment Credit," *Federal Reserve Bulletin* (June, 1968), p. 469.

[8] "Bank Credit Card System: What Illinois Retailers Think," *Merchandising Week* (August 7, 1967), p. 11.

but persons with good credit reputations will find it worthwhile to establish credit connections with a commercial bank. While the consumer will pay a higher rate on a small loan than the rate charged for larger loans to business firms, commercial banks still remain the cheapest source of loans for most consumers who can qualify.

Credit Unions. Credit unions originated in Europe and were later adopted in the United States, beginning in New England in the early 1900's. The credit unions are usually organized by and for the employees of a particular company or institution. Members of a credit union buy one or more shares of stock, usually at a nominal cost of $10 to $25 per share. They are urged to deposit savings also. From those funds loans are made to members. Interest rates on loans are usually about one percent per month on the unpaid balance. Credit unions frequently have lower net rates than any other source of consumer loans.

Industrial Banks. Industrial banks grew from the needs of industrial workers. Typically, factory workers had no collateral to aid them in getting loans, and their only assets in the early days of this century were the skills they possessed. Some persons were dismayed at the rates and practices of loan sharks, who were the only apparent sources of emergency funds for such people; and they developed the industrial banks of which the Morris Plan Banks are an outstanding example. From such banks an industrial worker who has a cosigner for the note can obtain funds on his reputation and record of employment. Since the loans are usually not large and the risk is somewhat greater than in the case of loans made by regular commercial banks, and since there is no collateral, the rates charged are higher than commercial bank loan rates; but they are far less than the usurious rates paid to loan sharks.

Small Loan Companies. Almost every person is at some time in need of emergency funds. Illness, accidents, fires, and other mishaps occur; and the typical family, regardless of its thrift and diligence, will at one time or another find the burden of such tragedy too much for its finances. Because there has always been this need for emergency funds, there have always been sources of such funds. For many centuries lending was hidden or underground, which meant that such people as loan sharks could operate. Beginning quite early in this century, many states passed laws designed to bring the small loan business out in the open where it could be regulated to the extent that legitimate operators would be attracted to the business with consequent benefits to borrower-consumers.

Most states have consumer finance loan regulations based on a model statute drafted by the Russel Sage Foundation (1916-42). Since 1969 the model has frequently been the Uniform Consumer Credit Code. In general, the statutes allow licensed lenders to charge between 2 and 3 percent per month for $300 or less with reduced rates for additional amounts up to a limit of $2500.

Some states still attempt to regulate the small loan business by usury laws which permit a maximum rate of 10 percent or less per annum. A legitimate small loan company cannot operate under that restriction. Where legitimate small loan companies do not operate, undercover lenders are still present, and consumers pay higher rates. Commonly an interest rate equal to the usury rate is advertised, but then the borrower is forced (1) to pay a service charge for putting his loan on the books; (2) to purchase life insurance as well as health and accident insurance at a very high cost to assure repayment of the loan; (3) to pay an appraisal charge ostensibly to repay the lender for expenses incurred in examining the collateral offered; and (4) to pay other charges made to cover the cost of operating a credit loan business. It is not uncommon to find that the minimum charge for installment purchases in such states tends to be 50 to 60 percent per annum or even higher. Unfortunately, many people gullibly believe that they are protected by a 10 percent usury law.

This brief treatment is intended only to show how the function of financing is integrated into the marketing process. In common with other marketing functions, finance must be considered and understood if the marketing flow is to be made effective and efficient.

RISK

It has long been recognized that the entrepreneur is entitled to compensation for the risk he bears. Indeed, risk-taking is generally assumed to be a primary function of an enterpriser. It need not, however, be blind risk-taking for which the market manager is compensated. He may reduce uncertainty either by shifting risks through insurance or by reducing risks through better management. To the extent that he is successful in this phase of management, he reduces costs and increases the probability of having his business prosper.

There are many so-called visible risks, such as loss or destruction of property; but they do not particularly concern us in this discussion, since a prudent manager will either shift those risks to insurance companies whose business it is to assume such risks or, as in some companies, establish a self-insurance fund. Here we are more concerned with business risks that result from changes in prices and in the demand for products, which cannot be precisely anticipated. Even this type of risk varies. For example, a manufacturer who produces only made-to-order goods is subject to less risk of loss than one who manufactures highly perishable products, such as bakery goods or ice cream, for a wide market in a competitive field. Further, the ice cream manufacturer's business is affected not only by economic conditions but also by the vagaries of the weather.

Hence, we can see that market risks vary with the time element, the distance between producer and consumer, and the type of goods. Superior handling of market risks will not by itself, of course, assure the success of the business. Certainly, however, improper estimation and handling of the risks involved may well mean the difference between failure and success. Consequently, a brief résumé of the variety of risks facing a marketing venture and of the methods for handling them is proper at this point.

Kinds of Risk

Insurers sometimes classify risks very broadly as controllable and uncontrollable. Among the *controllable risks* are visible risks, such as damage or loss of property through fire, theft, or flood. Inside the business itself, we have the possibility of loss from theft or fraud. When we insure a property, we pay a specific premium and thereby handle the risk for a regular cost. In case of loss, we are compensated; hence, it is said that we handle the risk on a budgetary basis and know exactly how much the risk is costing us. By far the most important risks to a marketing concern, however, are the *uncontrollable risks* that arise largely from condititions external to the firm, such as changes in general economic conditions. It is impossible to buy insurance to protect a firm from loss suffered from this type of risk.

Let us use as an example a high-fashion item that is quite expensive. Let us further assume that it is well proved that in this business, when general economic activity declines by 1 percent, the sale of this product generally falls off approximately 15 percent. Now, how will the seller price such a product? Since he desires a profit from his operations, he will of course recognize this risk element and consider it as a cost of doing business. Such a cost will be reflected in his selling price; and the very fact that he is attempting to protect himself may place him in a precarious position since the price of his product, including the "risk cost," may be high relative to other similar products. This is not an unusual case, for with various modifications the problem of uncontrollable risks exists in almost every marketing concern.

Methods of Reducing Noninsurable Risks

Managerial attention is directed toward risk reduction because of the effect of risk on cost. There are several ways in which a firm can reduce such risks. One is to attempt to gain some trading advantage. An example is the firm with a highly advertised brand name that has gained much consumer loyalty or the firm that has a completely unique product feature protected for some years by a patent, such as the Ronson lighter or the Gillette razor blade.

Another method is to develop trading techniques that enable the seller to enjoy a fairly well-protected market. The guarantee against price declines used by some firms is an example. Other methods include (1) producing only made-to-order, unique products; (2) effecting exclusive agreements with leading retailers because of some element of rarity about the product; and (3) selecting and carefully training a sales force that can outsell competitors.

Finally, and most important perhaps, is the increasing attempt to improve all phases of marketing management. A firm that, through marketing research, gains information of sufficient quality to improve its predictions and planning for sales has reduced risk of loss.

A FINAL WORD

Decisions concerning financial problems illustrate a major theme of this book. Successful marketing of a product is dependent upon a well-integrated application of the best principles of business operation in all its phases. The probable effects of action in areas of initial financing, inventory evaluation and financing, credit policy, and methods of handling risk must be carefully considered. Policies and methods of execution in all these areas must be adequate and effective if the firm is to maximize the satisfaction in the products and services it provides at costs that will attract customers.

QUESTIONS AND ANALYTICAL PROBLEMS

1. For a medium-sized men's clothing store, what finance-related problems can you cite? Be specific and identify as many as possible.

2. Define working capital.

3. What is the best source of working capital for retailers? What factors may change your choice of the best source?

4. Define: (a) sales finance company, (b) factoring company, (c) floor-plan financing.

5. What is field warehousing?

6. How did consumer credit develop in the United States?

7. What is the relative importance of installment financing to noninstallment financing by consumers? For what kinds of products is each of these two types of financing likely to be used? Do you observe any changes?

8. Check the going interest rates and actual cost of borrowing in your community on consumer loans to be used in the purchase of household appliances at: (a) commercial bank, (b) credit union, (c) industrial bank or Morris Plan bank if your community has one, (d) sales finance company, (e) small loan company. Why do differences as well as similarities in the charges exist? Does each credit source quote the full cost of borrowing in its stated interest rate?

9. Interview two merchants who promote credit sales. What changes in customer reaction to credit have they observed since the Truth-in-Lending Bill was passed?

10. What is a so-called universal credit card? Interview a retailer who accepts such cards to determine (a) what costs, if any, are assessed to him for the use of the service and (b) the effect of the cards on his sales volume.

11. Why is the cost of credit from a small loan company usually greater than cost of credit from (a) a commercial bank and (b) a credit union?

12. "By far the most important risks to a marketing concern, however, are the uncontrollable risks that arise largely from conditions external to the firm. . . . It is impossible to protect a firm from loss suffered from this type of risk." (a) Are there actually any "uncontrollable" risks? Cannot some protective devices be instituted to control, in some measure, every risk? (b) How can a firm reduce noninsurable risks?

Case 19-1 • THE CLARK COMPANY

Mr. Clark, president of the Clark Company, heads a corporation which produces ski bindings. Clark bindings are sold throughout seven Western states, and they have the reputation of being well-built and expensive. Many professional skiers in the West use the bindings and recommend them to serious beginners.

Because of the seasonal nature of the product, the Clark Company found it necessary to obtain financial help which would carry them through the summer months. They had recently received especially large orders for the coming season, and it would be necessary to add another crew during the coming summer. Approximately $50,000 was needed to cover the additional expenses, and Mr. Clark was uncertain as to how the funds would be raised. He was considering the following suggestions made to him by his financial advisor:

1. The current accounts receivable balance (worth $30,000) could be factored at normal rates (in the summer of 1974 that was a prime rate of 11% plus 3%). The remaining funds needed could be obtained from a small business loan company at an advertised rate of 3 percent monthly.
2. Clark could obtain a term bank loan for the full amount and pay a rate of 12 percent per annum.
3. Approximately 40 percent of Clark's suppliers offer credit. Clark could switch completely to suppliers which do offer credit and, thus, have approximately $25,000 available immediately. The remaining funds could then be borrowed from the bank at 12 percent a year. However, switching suppliers would also mean using materials inferior to those presently used.

What plan would you recommend to Mr. Clark? Are there any other alternatives available?

Case 19-2 • PLASTICO COMPANY[9]

A purchase order inquiry was received by the Floor Covering Division of the Plastico Company. A leading passenger plane manufacturer requested a proposal for a rubber substitute for the conventional cloth rugs used as flooring in commercial planes.

The purchasing agent for the plane manufacturer expressed discontentment with the short service life of the cloth rugs now being used. He emphasized that the substitute should not only be attractive but, most important, must be able to withstand spillage of food and beverages, vomiting, and normal wear experienced by a flooring material without permanent staining or other damage. In addition, the cost of the substitute rug must be competitive in price. Only by possessing features warranting their consideration could the substitute induce the customer to pay a higher price.

A New Product Evolves

After considering the customer requirements, the technical department of the Floor Covering Division designed the "AirO Rug." The new product consists of a vinyl-coated fiberglass cemented to a sponge rubber backing material. Extended tests indicated that this new idea was the answer to the customer's needs. The surface material is highly abrasion resistant, soil proof, and requires very little effort to clean and maintain. The sponge backing imparts a cushion effect to the foot much as the conventional cloth rugs. A variety of colors rivals any offering of the conventional rugs, and the estimated service life of the product is five years.

The Floor Covering Division is able to use a top material and sponge that are production items currently being manufactured by the Industrial Products Division of the Plastico Company. As per company policy, material costs transfer at the standard cost rate only; that is, no profit is included between interdivisional finished goods transfers. The Industrial Products Division must also maintain quality standards, replacing any material deemed unacceptable and rejected by the Floor Covering Division.

---

[9] This case was prepared by Professor George M. McManmon of the University of Akron as a basis for class discussion. Cases are not designed to present illustration of either correct or incorrect handling of administration situations.

This source of supply results in the receipt of high quality materials at a minimum cost. Then too the raw materials do not necessitate outlays for facilities to produce them. Because the raw materials are produced in an adjacent building, incoming transportation costs are nonexistent; and lead time on materials is to be a maximum of two weeks.

Elements of Cost

Answers to inquiries reveal the coated fiberglass costs $3.82 per yard in a 36-inch width; the sponge, $1.07 per yard in the same width. From the test samples, the product engineer calculates 100 square feet of AirO Rug needs 1.7 gallons of cement, which costs $3.65 per gallon. Using similar products and manufacturing operations as a basis for their computations, the Time Study Department estimates 1.72 direct labor hours at the rate of $2.20 per hour to construct 100 square feet of rug.

The Production Department submits anticipated manufacturing operation costs. These monthly prorates include: supervision, $560; inspection, $70; miscellaneous indirect labor, $42; floor space expense, $320; and small tools and expense materials, $30. Three building tables costing $660 with a service life of five years and a material-cutting machine with a service life of ten years costing $240 must be purchased as a prerequisite to beginning the production. Selling and administrative expense will be $2,150 per month, which includes an outlay of $750 semimonthly for advertising AirO Rugs in *Aviation Age*, a trade magazine.

Production Procedure and Capacity

The production procedure for AirO Rugs is as follows:

1. Roll out sponge on table, and cut to desired length.
2. With paint roller, cement the entire top area of the sponge.
3. Allow cement to tackify (dry slightly) for approximately 15 minutes.
4. Apply top material on sponge and roll with hand roller to insure adhesion.
5. Trim edges and clean top area with cleaning solvent.
6. Pack for shipment.

Assembling the rugs is performed on three 20-foot-long building tables. As one table is being used for cementing, the other two may be used for laying the top material for final finishing. In short, three building tables are required to keep the assemblers busy and the production process flowing smoothly.

The requirements of the market prevent AirO Rugs from being an off-the-shelf item. The color selection offered the customers must equal or surpass that of the competition, the cloth rug. To meet the changing demands of the industry, the Plastico Company specially tints the vinyl of the top material according to each customer's specification. Because the color requirements change from time to time for each customer, top material cannot be prepared in advance.

The complete production cycle to build three 20-yard lengths of rug requires an average of 3 hours and 20 minutes. Based on a 173-hour work month, the optimum capacity figures to be 3,114 square yards per month. Experience proves, however, that actual capacity in assembly production such as this generally turns out to be at about 77 percent of optimum capacity. With this past history as a guide, actual production capacity is deemed to be 2,659 square yards per month.

Customer Potential

The home office of the Floor Covering Division Sales Department telegraphs the particulars of the AirO Rug to branch sales offices with a request that they obtain other potential customers' reactions to the new product. Technical tests revealing a useful life of five years for the rug are relayed in detail along with small samples to branch salesmen.

From the accumulation of responses, the home office determines that a conservative estimate indicates a potential of 600 square yards per month. Cloth rugs have an average life of one year and sell for $4.80 per square yard. Installation costs are not included in the selling price of either rug, but they are estimated at 50 cents a square foot for the cloth and 60 cents for the AirO Rug.

• What do you recommend as a base selling price? What would be the break-even point at this price? What considerations other than cost were influential in helping you arrive at this decision?

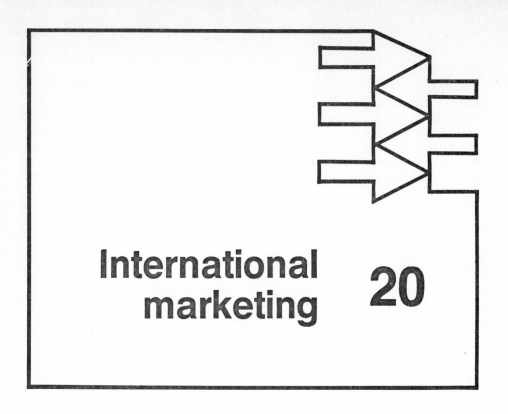

International marketing 20

The quest to satisfy desires at minimum costs does not stop at national boundaries. American Coca-Cola provides "the pause that refreshes" from Saigon to San Salvador, and the German Volkswagen competes with American compacts in their own dooryard at Detroit. Human satisfactions are significantly enhanced by the international exchange of goods. The ancients increased their satisfactions by trading salt and bronze across thousands of miles. The modern consumer can call on the services of an infinite variety of skills and resources from the far reaches of the Arctic to the heart of equatorial Africa. He can enjoy as floor covering oriental rugs from the Far East or polar bearskin from the extreme Northwest. A world market is not just in the making; it is a fast-growing reality. Its growth is powered by the forces that we have discussed—the insatiable desires of man. New desires have been created and satisfied by extending market boundaries to include world markets.

Following a brief discussion of the importance of international trade to our national economy and to the firm, this chapter provides an overview of the developing trends in international marketing, the forms of overseas business, some of the peculiar problems and rules for success in international marketing, the sources of information and assistance for export markets, and finally, the implications for social and economic change in the world that are directly related to international marketing.

IMPORTANCE OF INTERNATIONAL TRADE

The importance of international trade to any country depends upon its resources, internal requirements and abilities to consume, and political considerations. In the United States exports and imports account for approximately 7½ percent of the gross national product. It is estimated that each $1 billion of exports by U.S. firms results in an additional 100,000 jobs in this country. In agriculture, forestry, fisheries, and mining, a little over 11 percent of total employment in the United States is attributable to export; for manufacturing, nearly 7 percent of total employment results from exports.[1]

Table 20-1 contains data which indicates what international trade means to some other nations. The data is not strictly comparable in every instance to that for the United States, but it does display general relationships. Note that the nations shown in Table 20-1 had a larger portion of their gross national product accruing through international trade than did the United States. Even so, of total world trade in 1971, consisting of $362.8 billion in imports and $348.0 billion in exports, the United States accounted for a larger share of that trade than any other single country. In 1971 the United States' share of total world imports was 13 percent, and its share of exports was 12½ percent. By comparison, the six nations in the European Economic Community (Common Market) accounted for 27 percent of total world imports and 29 percent of total world exports.[2]

Increasing populations, improvement in the economies of many countries, and increasing ease of communication and transportation point to growing opportunities in marketing outside traditional domestic areas. Hence, companies are increasingly interested in investing anywhere in the world that they can get the best return, in purchasing raw materials or fabricated parts wherever it can be done at the lowest cost, in manufacturing products wherever it can be done most productively, in selling the output where it is most profitable to do so, in recruiting personnel wherever it is best to secure them, and in conducting research and development where it can be done most effectively. Certainly many small and some large business firms will continue to operate on the local scene. But the promise of profits by adopting any or a combination of the above activities cannot be overlooked. The world market is a reality, and the alternative opportunities that exist for investment of funds, sale of products, or purchase of raw materials are resources which must be looked upon as opportunities, regardless of their location.[3]

TRENDS IN INTERNATIONAL TRADE

For the most part, trade between nations consists of market transactions between individual business firms. During the last decade it has become common to see advertisements of foreign goods in North American magazines. Also, the advertising budgets of United States shippers abroad have been increasing.

There is nothing to indicate that in the long run an industrialized market of one country grows at the expense of other countries' markets for manufactured

[1] Bureau of Labor Statistics, *Monthly Labor Review* (December, each year).
[2] *United Nations Statistical Yearbook: 1973*, "World Trade by Regions and Countries," Table 146. This data was compiled before the United Kingdom, Ireland, and Denmark joined the EEC.
[3] One of the classical industrial stories on the international scene is that of the Japanese Mitsubishi group. Their history is colorfully told by Robert Lubar in "The Japanese Giant That Wouldn't Stay Dead," *Fortune* (November, 1964), pp. 141-148, 272.

Table 20-1
PORTION OF GROSS NATIONAL PRODUCT OF IMPORTS AND
EXPORTS FOR SELECTED COUNTRIES—1965

COUNTRY	Percent of GNP Imports	GNP Exports
Western Europe		
Germany (Federal Republic)	18%	17%
Netherlands	32%	33%
Belgium	31%	30%
Norway	29%	29%
Switzerland (1969)	26%	25%
Latin America		
Peru (1969)	17%	15%
Venezuela (1965)	22%	32%

Source: Derived from "Individual Country Data," *Yearbook of National Accounts Statistics for 1971* (New York: Statistical Office United Nations, 1973), Vols. I and II.

goods, or vice versa. Indeed, the contrary may be true. Industrial activity adds qualities to the goods that provide satisfaction. If the resources and skills of one nation can add values that are unique when compared to other nations, such satisfactions can be marketed. There is little reason why such a process cannot add to the sum of total world satisfactions. A nation that becomes industrialized can, by selling its manufactured products to a second nation, enhance the level of living of the nation with which it trades, as well as its own. The greatest volume of trade takes place between industrialized nations.

We cannot expect such an evolution to take place without some unpleasant economic adjustments. For example, it is reported that in 1960 the automobile manufacturers in Germany had financial difficulty because they counted too heavily on the American market. Evidently the American compacts were more successful than was anticipated. On the other hand, some of the earlier difficulties of American models were traceable to foreign competition. We view such adjustments on the domestic scene as evidence of wholesome competition. Higher satisfaction levels occur when parties involved in foreign competition make adjustments to manufacture and sell products that create new demands and satisfy new wants.

Conditions Favorable to International Trade

The amount of international trade probably will continue to increase in volume. Two conditions will influence this trend: (1) the lowering of the distance barrier due to improved transportation and communication facilities and (2) the development of a political climate conducive to favorable relations between trading nations and an accompanying willingness to facilitate the exchange of different national currencies.[4]

[4] Bertil Ohlin, *Interregional and International Trade* (Rev. ed.; Cambridge, Massachusetts: Harvard University Press, 1967), especially Chapter VI, "Some Fundamentals of International Trade," and Part Four, "International Trade and Factor Movements," which discuss these fundamentals of world trade.

There can be no doubt that improvements in communication and transportation will continue. Air travel is decreasing the distance between world points at a sensational rate. By means of modern communications, every community today is sensitive to what is taking place in other communities of the world. An increasing proportion of space on the front page of today's newspaper is devoted to the foreign scene. Telephone, telegraph, and radio also have increased the ease of making contacts abroad. From the standpoint of technical developments in communication and transportation, there is every reason to believe that the amount of foreign trade will increase. Increased travel makes people aware of foreign products. When they are alert to the existence of foreign products, novelty itself, aside from other desirable qualities, increases the intensity of the desire for such products.

Trade between nations is somewhat more complex because of political barriers that do not exist in the case of domestic trade. The level of international economic activity within a nation is in some degree dependent upon the attitudes and the policies of the governments involved. Hence, trade agreements are often made between nations, and loans are arranged to facilitate trade. Such arrangements may or may not serve to increase the amount of trade, but they often affect the kind of trade and influence the customer with whom it is conducted. For example, several groups of nations have attempted to organize themselves into trading blocs.

Common Markets

As it became apparent that markets tended to follow the larger-scale, and often quite complex, manufacturing and trade methods, comprehensive efforts to remove many trade barriers ensued. The various common markets, each with different characteristics and often different objectives, are movements to secure larger markets and to obtain the economies of large-scale production.

The European Economic Community (EEC)—commonly called the European Common Market—resulted from a major effort to build a large market among several countries. It was established by the Treaty of Rome which provided for the following: elimination of tariffs within EEC; one external tariff between EEC countries and the rest of the world; a common antitrust law; tax unifications; and removal of restrictions on movements of manpower and capital within the community. Charter members of the European Economic Community were Belgium, Netherlands, Luxembourg, Germany (Federal Republic), France, and Italy. The United Kingdom, Ireland, and Denmark have recently become members.

Other existing international trade blocs are the European Free Trade Association, consisting of Austria, Switzerland, Norway, Portugal, and Sweden; the Central American Common Market, made up of Costa Rica, Guatemala, Nicaragua, Honduras, El Salvador, and Panama; and the Latin American countries and Mexico. There are also negotiations between several African nations for trade arrangements designed to result in a future common market agreement.

Other Government Actions to Influence Trade

Government actions that influence trade include international agreements that facilitate the flow of goods and also those policies adopted by one country to increase its own exports.

International Agreements. Provisions for multilateral actions on tariffs and for facilitation of monetary supports are important aids to increasing world trade.

In 1948 most nations outside the communist bloc approved and signed the General Agreement for Tariffs and Trade (GATT). This agreement replaced the former practice of negotiating only bilateral trade treaties. Signers of GATT meet about every two years to bargain for tariff reductions that will apply to all. On June 30, 1967, 53 countries signed agreements specifying tariff cuts of 50 percent on a wide range of industrial goods and reductions of 30 to 50 percent on many more. That meeting, commonly called the Kennedy Round, also specified that nontariff barriers would be reduced or eliminated to enhance trade between the signers and the less developed nations.[5]

The International Monetary Fund (IMF) was established in 1944 to relieve money exchange shortages, to provide some stability to the values of exchange, and to reduce variations in those values. Members, upon request, may be supplied with the currency of another nation in exchange for gold or for the currency of the purchaser. Support of the Fund allows a purchaser to pay dollars or pound sterling, for example, even though his country has a temporary shortage of the required currency.[6]

Along with tariff and currency exchange agreements to facilitate trade, multicountry formulas have been set up to stabilize price fluctuations within industries, such as mining, that typically have frequent market shifts and consequent wide swings in prices. Also, patterns of negotiations have developed to stop unilateral restrictions when a product from a developing economy threatens existing markets for that product, as in the case of the large supply of textiles from Japan in the 1950's. Agreements were made gave a degree of protection to the United States' and the United Kingdom's textile mills and yet allowed a sizable quota of Japanese materials to enter those countries.

There is a trend toward multination solutions to trade problems; and it is reasonable to expect a reduction, albeit slow and gradual, in barriers to world commerce.

Single Country Policies to Increase Exports. Most nations provide some aid to their exporters. It may be only an advisory service, or it may be more direct assistance, such as exempting export firms from some taxes or providing insurance against loss on credit transactions.

Consistent with tradition in the United States, government assistance has been for the most part advisory only (see pages 404-406). In 1962, however, a limited form of credit insurance on export sales was instituted. There is also a 14

---

[5] "GATT-Kennedy Round Attacked Trade Barriers," *International Commerce* (July 10, 1967), p. 2.

[6] Roland L. Kramer, *International Marketing* (3d ed.; Cincinnati: South-Western Publishing Company, 1970), Chapter 20, "Foreign Exchange Control," succinctly presents methods, problems, and international agreements pertaining to payments for goods in international commerce.

percent income tax reduction on sales in the American hemisphere under the Western Hemisphere Trade Corporation Act. Also, there were established in early 1972 Domestic International Sales Corporations (Commonly called DISC). A company that establishes a DISC for foreign sales receives substantial tax benefits. These are attempts to encourage export business by United States firms.

European countries commonly, and for many years, have allowed excise tax exemption on exports. Also common among European nations is comprehensive government sponsored insurance against credit losses arising in foreign trade.[7]

Exchange rate manipulations, including devaluation of a nation's currency, have been used to increase exports. For example, in the autumn of 1967 when the British pound was devalued from $2.80 per pound sterling to the present (summer, 1974) price of $2.31 per pound sterling, there was the short-term effect of making British-made products a good buy for dollar-holding customers. Behind devaluation is the idea that if a country can sell X number of products at $2.80, it will sell X + Y number of products at $2.40. Effects of devaluation are too complex to cover briefly, but there is a real question as to whether or not devaluation achieves long-term trade advantages for a country. The two United States dollar devaluations (1972 and 1973) have been credited by government fiscal specialists with the improvements in the nation's balance of trade.

Government activities may alleviate temporary tensions, increase opportunities for desirable trade, make funds available for productive investment, and perform other service functions. But governments, as such, unless they own and operate productive resources, can only influence the long-run increases in trade by performing some of the above services to improve the environment in which productive enterprise operates. In the long run, a country must produce marketable goods and services to exchange for goods and services when its foreign currency gets tight. Increased productivity or decreased consumption is the only answer.

THE DECISION TO ENTER INTERNATIONAL MARKETS [8]

As in an important business decision, prime motivation for entry into international markets will depend upon how each individual firm views its challenges and opportunities. Among the principal reasons for the decision to "go international" are (1) opportunity for increased profits, (2) protection of present operations, and (3) a desire by management to make the company international in scope.

Opportunity for Increased Profits

The firm may identify a need for its present products in some other country and decide that it is easier to increase volume by meeting that need than to penetrate further into the domestic market.

---

[7] John Fayerweather. *International Marketing* (Englewood Cliffs, New Jersey: Prentice-Hall, 1965), Chapter 2.

[8] David B. Zenoff, *International Business Management* (New York: Macmillan Company, 1971), Chapter 2.

A manufacturer of specialized mining equipment in the Rocky Mountain states found sufficient opportunities in other countries that his domestic market sales now account for less than half the total earnings of the company.

European automobile manufacturers found markets in other countries for this reason; United States pharmaceutical producers found that relatively little expense was required to sell certain products in other countries. After expending large sums for product development, the extra business is welcome.

Sometimes a firm takes a long view and enters a market that appears to be developing in the belief that when the country provides large and profitable opportunities, it will be those firms with early entry who benefit. Hence, we saw five automobile manufacturers establish assembly plants in Peru. Any one of the firms could easily meet the total demand, but each wanted a foothold on what appeared to be a profitable market several years in the future.

Protect Present Operations

You will note advertisements and news stories about Chase Manhattan Bank, Bank of America, J. Walter Thomson, Marsteller (advertising), Booz Allen Hamilton (accounting and counseling), as well as other service businesses stating their ability to serve clients in international trade. Many of those firms had to follow important clients to other countries or lose them to competitors in those countries.

If you examine the data on international trade, you will note that marketing and processing of raw materials account for approximately 50 percent of the total each year. Hence, companies requiring those materials have long been in international markets.

Desire to be International in Scope

Singer, Eastman Kodak, IBM, and many smaller companies have had since their inception an objective to achieve world wide operations. In part that objective derives from a careful evaluation of production and market opportunities and in part from a desire for the prestige that such operations carry.

FORMS OF OVERSEAS BUSINESS

International marketing takes a large variety of forms. A firm may keep its manufacturing plant in North America and sell its products to a foreign distributor or to retailers abroad. It may, however, move its manufacturing facilities to the scene of the market. Another common move is to effect a joint enterprise venture with ownership of facilities shared by nationals of two or more countries. Licensing of processes and provisions for technical advice are becoming widely used. The firm's concept of international marketing will depend on its level of involvement in foreign markets, which can be generally categorized into levels or stages.

Strictly export business is all that may be involved at the first level. This usually arises from a surplus of goods produced for the home market. By the same token, it can be strictly import business, where something from abroad is needed to complete the home-market line. There is a minimum of change in company outlook or organization. Usually the product for export is not changed, or it may be modified only slightly in superficial characteristics, such as color, flavor, package, or the like to find more ready acceptance in the foreign market. At this stage a firm will likely make an arrangement with a *combination export manager* (CEM). CEM's are agencies who conduct business in the name of the manufacturer, the principal. In general, the advantages and disadvantages of using a CEM are the same as those for using a domestic agent middleman.

A second level is that of involving some of the company's personnel abroad for foreign licensing and export of technical knowledge. At this stage market opportunity is discovered, and the best way to reach the market is determined to be an arragement with a local company in the market whereby the product can be manufactured to meet local needs. The owner of the product provides design and engineering assistance but does not become too involved in financing and marketing.

Leads for companies desiring to export or to license operations overseas (1st and 2nd levels) can be obtained from the World Trade Opportunities section at the back of each weekly issue of *International Commerce*. Most states in the United States now have export councils or export committees who, working with the U. S. Department of Commerce, will furnish leads for international trade as well as assistance in making initial arrangements for export or licensing.

A third stage is reached when the company decides to establish operations overseas with substantial investment of funds and managerial time. It follows that more executives in the company will be required to develop international skills and interests.

Fourth-level involvement is that experienced by the truly multinational or global enterprise. Most frequently, at this stage foreign marketing is not separated from the domestic operation. By this we mean that each functional head, such as vice-president of production, vice-president of finance, and vice-president of marketing, is responsible for that function wherever located—whether in the home country or abroad. The reasoning here is that in a global business the influences in any one market must be considered as they affect every other area of operation. Among companies that are truly multinational are Norelco (Holland), Shell (Holland), Lever (England), Singer (U.S.A.), and National Biscuit Company (U.S.A.). They are examples of firms that become involved in the countries where they do business, select executives from various countries, and have a global outlook.

PECULIARITIES OF INTERNATIONAL MARKETING

When one enters a new area in the domestic market, he undertakes to understand the possible reception of his product based on consumer needs and desires. While it is not easy for one to identify and understand basic motivations, it is relatively much less difficult to do so in one's own country than in another because perhaps 80 to 90 percent of the cultural patterns in his own area are known to him simply because he has grown up with them.

It is a mistake to believe that responses to a particular appeal will be the same in different countries. Personal values do differ between cultures. A marketer approaches his home market value systems almost intuitively because they are at least somewhat familiar. In another culture he must be aware that responses will probably differ because the interactions between persons and their environment are influenced by the fundamental social institutions. Hence, it is imperative that he learn enough about social systems to avoid gross errors.

As a minimum, one contemplating entry into a foreign market must consider the following: cultural differences that will affect acceptance of his offering; his promotional methods and overall management operations; legal constraints and requirements; currency risks and restrictions; and technological considerations.

Cultural Differences and the Marketing Concept

As a guide one may use a model of the four basic societal systems of his target market—namely, the family system, the religious system, the society system, and the educational system. Values which affect decision making, sources of satisfactions, and consequent buying methods can more readily be identified if such a model is followed.

It is true that numerous anthropological studies have suggested that differences among people in any one culture are greater than the differences between one culture and another. It is not wise, however, to assume from that conclusion that response to a product or an appeal will be identical with that found in the home market. No marketing decision should be based on self-evaluation analysis; that is, one should never presume that acceptance or rejection of an idea or a product by another people will be for the same reasons that he would accept or reject the idea or product. Evaluation of the product must be made from the point of view of the people in the target market.

At export meetings it is common to find a manufacturer who decides to go into a market because the products available in the market are technically inferior to those he produces. The washing machines for sale in that market, for example, may all have wringers; or the few water heaters he saw are small with long recovery rates; or food products are packaged in bulk. If he presumes that because his product meets needs in the home market it will sell itself in the target market, he may well be in error because of differences in income levels, buying habits, and value systems.

The importance of understanding other markets is treated by Edward T. Hall, formerly with the Government Affairs Institute:

> With few exceptions, Americans are relative newcomers on the international business scene. Today as in Mark Twain's time we are all too often "innocents abroad" in an era when naiveté and blundering in foreign business dealings may have serious political reprecussions.
>
> He should understand that the various peoples around the world have worked out and integrated into their subconscious literally thousands of behavior patterns that they take for granted in each other. Then, when the stranger enters, he behaves differently from the local norm, he often quite

unintentionally insults, annoys, or amuses the native with whom he is attempting to do business.[9]

It is dangerous to become a "cultural expert" after reading a travel brochure or even after making a brief visit to a country. One should, at least, follow the advice in the section on "Assistance in Understanding the Country" on page 405.

Agreements

Methods of arriving at a meeting of minds to consummate a valid contract vary in different trades even within nations. Among foreign countries the differences are greater. Is a business transaction consummated only when written contracts are signed? Or are there customs based on moral principles on which one can count as being valid? If the latter is true, what is their nature in different cultures? The written contract violates the Moslem's sense of honor. He is insulted if he is asked to sign a contract. Improper timing in a price agreement may lead to problems. In certain parts of the Middle East, if one takes a taxi, for example, he must set the price by a haggling process before the ride; otherwise, the taxi driver will be able to charge any price he chooses. The patterns of different agreements between different nations are infinite in number. American businessmen must realize that people in each country think that their own code is the basic one and that all departures are dishonest. The seller and buyer in a foreign nation should become acquainted with the practices in the respective areas where he buys and sells if he expects successful dealings.

Dimensions of time, place, material possessions, friendship, and agreements are all areas that influence the attitude of foreign buyers and sellers. They differ as between different nations. No writer has collected information so that it can be handed in capsule form to the enterpriser who is engaged in foreign trade. The patterns must be acquired by research and by each firm being alert to the form the patterns take in each world community. Failure to recognize their existence can result in resistance to the flow of goods, to low profits, and to business failure.

Legal requirements and currency exchange limitations and methods can be determined from information prepared by the United States Department of Commerce. Quite commonly there are *tariffs*, duties levied on quantities or physical characteristics of products; *quotas* on quantity or types of goods that may be traded; and restrictions on money movements, such as amounts of allowable capital net flow, deposits required for imports, or currency exchange rates that vary according to types of transactions.

---

[9] Edward T. Hall, "The Silent Language in Overseas Business," *Harvard Business Review*, Vol. 38, No. 3 (May-June, 1960), p. 87. Hall discusses the psychological point of view in dealing with people of different nations. It is from his discussion that we obtain many of our ideas in dealing with the differences in business customs.

The editors of the *Journal of Marketing* have responded to the growing interest in the international marketing scene by including a number of contributions dealing with the subject.

Technological considerations include such simple things as whether products are made for 220 or 110 electrical current, metric measurements and the like, or more important differences, such as inability of certain machinery to operate because of natural phenomena.

Encompassing all of these are considerations of what are the most critical elements in gaining a competitive advantage. When Volkswagen entered the United States market, the company understood that customers would be reluctant to purchase the car because of fear of poor service. Consequently, dealers were required to provide more service space, spare parts, and training of mechanics than was usual.

A study of the sale of United States aerospace products in Western Europe shows that an extremely important aspect for the selection of suppliers is the ability to support their products effectively.

> U.S. companies with product support facilities in Europe are in a much better position to compete with local manufacturers than those U.S. companies that have no European facilities. This is a critical element as the logistics must be secure in the event of temporary interruptions of supply lines. This can only be achieved by either the availability of spare equipment from local suppliers or stocks. Since it is very expensive to keep large stocks, the emphasis is placed on the availability of spares from local sources. This is a further reason that a U.S. manufacturer must have at least a licensing arrangement with a local manufacturer if he expects to compete successfully for new military applications.
>
> The availability of a local representative also eliminates to a large degree problems of communication between the supplier and the end user. The communications gap is considerably larger with aircraft manufacturers than with airlines as there are fewer opportunities, particularly for buyers of aircraft manufacturing companies to gain some experience in the U.S.[10]

Some Rules for Success of Multinational Firms

Enterprises that have moved beyond strict exportation and have established manufacturing facilities in another country have learned some rules for long-range success. Interviews with executives of such firms have revealed several suggestions.[11]

Staff the Firm with Overseas Nationals. There are two good reasons why a company should staff its overseas operations with the nationals of the country concerned. First, this is an excellent method of instilling confidence in the people that the company is sincere in wanting to be accepted. It is a means of bridging the psychological gap that exists between foreign people. The closing of this gap is absolutely necessary in making sales. Second, they are already acquainted with the difference in the patterns that we have previously discussed. Aside from the great advantage of winning the cooperation from local people because their

---

[10] From an unpublished study by Manfred O. Rothmaier, product manager of American Aviation Corp., export distributor for Lear-Siegler Corp., Munich, Germany, December, 1973.

[11] Based on interviews by the authors with executives in the United States, Egypt, South America, Republic of the Philippines, and Western Europe over the past ten years.

compatriots are employed, it may in many cases be less expensive to train nationals in the policies of the company than it is to acquaint company employees with the psychological patterns of the nationals. Mr. Stanley C. Allyn, Chairman of the Board, National Cash Register Company, states that his company has 22,000 employees abroad, only six of whom are Americans. He believes this policy pays and states:

> This policy has a most important by-product. When my associates and I visit an overseas operation, we are not insulated from the nationals by layers of Americans who might or might not have adjusted themselves to an understanding of the local scene.
>
> We are able to talk directly with the nationals because there is no one else to talk to. It is almost that simple and we propose to keep it that way.
>
> In these complicated times, this policy of avoiding insulation is even more important than it used to be. While the United States has been growing more internationally minded, many other countries are growing more nationalistic.
>
> It has been our experience that nationals acquire the necessary knowledge of our business with the same facility as Americans. More importantly, they know their own people . . . and the problems of their own country . . . far better than outsiders.
>
> By having so few Americans in our overseas organization, I do not want anyone to think we do not furnish our skills and techniques. An American who knows how to increase production can often be a more valuable ambassador than a lecturer on the fine points of democratic philosophy.[12]

Invest Profits in Countries Where Earned. The profits of a business are not solely its own. Local employees and the economy of the country must also benefit from the operations of the business. Thus, part of the profits from operations in a foreign country must be invested in that country.

In the United States in the fight against the development of chain stores, local merchants and their supporters complained about the profits leaving the scene and going to the large financial centers. If such hostility develops among regions within the United States, how much more likely it is to develop between distant nations. The investment of profits builds confidence in a company's commitment to become a permanent part of the nation in which it operates. Often, currency restrictions prevent a company from transferring its funds out of a country. In any event, however, investing within a country is an excellent technique in gaining support of the nationals that may pay off in greater sales volume, less persecution in the event of hostile demonstration against foreigners, and the obtaining of talented and loyal nationals for employees.

Provide the Product the People Want. Customers abroad must be given what they need and want—not what a business thinks will sell because it is successful at home. It is a gross error to think of foreign markets as mere dumping grounds for excess products. Obtaining a global view of the international marketing concept necessitates studying foreign markets even more carefully than the home market in order to determine specific needs. Such study may result in a

---

[12] Roland L. Kramer, *International Marketing* (3d ed.; Cincinnati: South-Western Publishing Company, 1970), pp. 382-383.

product or an idea that will benefit the entire country. Sometimes, of course, a slightly changed product will succeed in different markets, but for a variety of reasons. National Biscuit Company, for example, has learned that in Puerto Rico, soda crackers are a desired bread substitute; in England, they are eaten only with cheese at snack times; while in the United States, the principal use of crackers is still with soup.

Promotion of products must be based on local desires and characteristics. Sometimes the basic theme developed in the home market can be adapted by local advertising agencies. At other times an entirely new theme must be created. "Put a Tiger in Your Tank" has been translated and used in almost every market in the world with great success. Food products, by contrast, almost always require different promotional messages from those in the home market, perhaps because there are many taboos and social customs surrounding food in every nation.[13]

Contribute to the Country's Economy with Worthwhile Projects. Another way to achieve the goodwill of the people in a country where one engages in foreign trade is to participate in activities that promote that country's economy. An example of such a contribution is the Quaker Oats Company's involvement in the production and distribution of *incaparina* in Colombia. *Incaparina* is a food supplement made of various cereals, soybean, and cottonseed. It is roughly similar to milk in the nourishment that it provides. Although its adoption and use involve a changing of habits, several governments in Latin America are interested in it because of severe protein and essential mineral shortages in the normal diets. Its cost is about one tenth the price of a glass of milk. Quaker Oats is promoting its use because "it seems like a worthwhile, socially desirable thing to do." Interestingly, this product has become successful enough that it will probably break even during its fourth year of promotion. The results of research and promotion on *incaparina* are being made available to manufacturers in other countries.

Carefully Select and Train Marketing Executives.[14] Home-market executives who are sent abroad must be selected and trained with great care, and this applies to their wives, also. It is difficult to reveal feelings and attitudes that suggest equality unless they are really felt. In many foreign nations, the wealth of the Americans prompts them to set themselves apart from the nationals whom they mistakenly consider inferior. Not only does such behavior indicate poor breeding, but it is a violation of the basic concept of selling and human relations. Such a program must be more than a company policy. It must almost be a religion. The men chosen to work in a foreign land must be selected with this characteristic in mind. If relationships of equality can be achieved and be

---

[13] Stephen Schleffer and S. Watson Dunn, "Relative Effectiveness of Advertisements of Foreign and Domestic Origin," *Journal of Marketing Research*, Vol. V (August, 1968), p. 296.

[14] Y. Hugh Furuhashi and Harry F. Evarts indicate that international marketing to be performed professionally, requires special training. They discuss what should be included in "Educating Men for International Marketing," *Journal of Marketing*, Vol. 31, No. 1 (January, 1967), pp. 51-55.

genuine, they not only will lay the foundation for profitable overseas operations but also better understanding between nations as well.

It is also important that overseas employees not be considered as stepchildren. Both home office employees sent abroad and local national employees must be considered and treated in the same manner as are their counterparts at home. Corn Products Company, among others, has adopted a policy that requires compensation, monetary and other, to be equalized. National Biscuit Company executives have adopted policies that assure equal treatment of local executives, of people in companies that are acquired abroad, and of persons sent from the United States to a foreign operation.

General Electric works to select men who above all are competent in their jobs and who can train local managers to replace them. They will not send a man abroad until he has been successful in a domestic job. They insist that any man going abroad be adaptable. As a final check before a man takes an overseas assignment, he and his wife must spend a minimum of one week, and preferably two weeks, in the area where he will work. On assignment both the man and wife go to language school.

Respect the Traditions, Religious, and Sensitivities of Foreign People. A company must be certain that all its executives who work or travel in the country respect the customs, traditions, religions, and sensitivities of the people. Building a bridge of common understanding and goals among people is a significant by-product. Such attitudes and understandings not only build positive relations between the home office and the foreign operation but also develop a tie with people of different nations.

Other Factors. In order to further guarantee dealings which will in the long run be profitable to a company and also build relationships that are amiable between nations, there are some other factors that a company must recognize. A company must not attempt to control or to intervene in the political life of the country in which it operates. Such control or intervention is psychologically unsound. It will not be accepted. Any company that attempts such control will be criticized and accused. Criticism and accusations are injurious to goodwill relationships on which sales volume is built.

On the other hand, in the interest of building goodwill, a company should judicially lend its support to the positive development and growth of the host country. Without showing partiality to minorities or specific pressure groups, a company, to enjoy the goodwill desirable to support its market objectives, should participate in the economic and social life of the host country. Especially should a company avoid the ill will and negative results that might accrue from not honoring its contracts and keeping its commitments. Such contracts should be based on the customs and laws of the foreign nations in which the operations are taking place.

The above suggestions and generalizations go deeper than ethics and international relations; they are part of the enlightened view that pervades all marketing, whether domestic or foreign. In a competitive era, there are many alternative choices available to a customer. Influences that give the product or the company a personality of its own, or an image, tend to affect the transaction positively or negatively. The image of a company operating abroad can very easily be built or injured by the discreetness or indescreetness of its behavior. A native people are more sensitive to the activities of a foreigner than they are to their own people. A foreign person or firm is conspicuous and must learn to operate in a glass house for business reasons.

SOURCES OF INFORMATION AND ASSISTANCE FOR EXPORT MARKETS

In this section the emphasis is on information sources that are of most value to smaller businesses interested in entering the export market. Firms that have reached the level of global or multinational business usually will have developed their own sources.

The principal difficulties encountered by a small firm desiring to enter the export market are (1) obtaining market information that will enable it to assess the level of demand for its product, (2) selecting the best channel for distribution of its product, and (3) determining cultural differences that affect business and social practices that will in turn affect its relationships with the country and its customers.

In the United States the first step in obtaining market information should be a visit to the nearest field office of the United States Department of Commerce. At that office one can obtain materials and assistance that will be of significant help, as described in the following paragraphs.

Trade Lists

Each trade list costs $1 and gives the names and addresses of firms that make, buy, or sell specific commodities or services in one country. It also contains a summary of the market potential for the commodity in question, government regulations affecting trade, basic information about each firm listed, and some general information on the country concerned.

Bureau of International Commerce (BIC) Trade Contact Surveys

The Field Office will help one prepare the request for a trade contact survey that is tailored to specific requirements of a firm. The survey is done by the staff of the commercial attaché of the embassy in the country in which the company is interested. It is designed to help one find several qualified firms in that country who are interested in selling one's product. A trade contact survey usually requires about 60 days to accomplish and costs $50.

Exposure of the Product in a Country

The manager of a firm may also request the Field Office for aid in getting his product introduced into a country by any of the following methods.

Trade Missions. Trade missions may be organized by the government or by industry; in any case, the functions of these missions are similar. Four to six businessmen from the United States visit a country to introduce business proposals from the United States to that country. They meet with local businessmen who wish to examine each proposal and who, if interested, are put in touch with the United States firm concerned. Trade missions also carry back to the United States business proposals made by foreign companies. These proposals and trade mission reports are published in *International Commerce,* a publication available at the Field Office or by subscription.

Trade Fairs and Trade Centers. With the aid of the Field Office, a product can be put on display in one or more of the 400 international trade fairs held each year at the six permanent trade centers in London, Frankfurt, Milan, Tokyo, Stockholm, and Bangkok, or at the Sample Display Centers located in Beirut, Manila, Nairobi, and Bangkok. There are also smaller versions of the trade centers, such as the Business Information Centers, which are distribution centers of business proposals by firms who do not wish to display their products. Such centers are established at international trade fairs where officers from the United States Department of Commerce are available to discuss the proposals with interested local businessmen and to help make commercial arrangements between interested companies.

From the above mentioned services a firm should be able to get the initial information he needs to overcome the first two difficulties encountered when making its entry into the export market, i.e., obtaining market information and selecting trade channels. It should be noted that the office of the commercial attaché in an embassy is primarily a service office designed to help in the initial stages of entry into a market. According to one experienced commercial officer, a company that has its own office in the country abroad will usually be better prepared to solve specific problems than will the United States Department of Commerce.

Assistance in Understanding the Country

In overcoming the difficulty of understanding cultural differences and local business practices, some assistance can be provided by the office of the commercial attaché of an embassy. A number of commercial officers have made the following suggestions for gaining understanding about a country and its business practices:

1. Obtain from a Field Office, local library, or marketing departments of firms already doing business in the country a reading list that will acquaint one with the particular country.
2. On a personal visit to evaluate the market, if the country is not known or if one is an infrequent visitor, the embassy can hopefully provide an unbiased view of the economy. Also, the embassy will usually be able to arrange interviews with people one should know, such as managers of other United States companies doing business with one's potential customers.
3. Do sufficient homework before visiting the country. Allow enough time for the trip, considering holidays, working hours, and customs of negotiations. A

most common fault is to plan an itinerary that does not allow for delays due to closed offices on holidays, long lunch hours, long negotiations, and the like. An understanding of the language aids in interpreting polite acceptance or polite rejection and in making an overall evaluation of one's acceptance. Hence, one should start at home to arrange interviews with persons who can help one make such interpretations and evaluations.

4. Be careful of decisions based on one or two visits with United States citizens in the country. Some will have "gone native" and not understand one's dilemma, and others with only short exposure will be full of misinformation. Local executives of United States firms already doing business in one's sector will probably be good sources of information.

5. Do not be too ready to assess all differences in trade practices as inferior to one's own. It is trite but essential to be flexible and understanding. Enough sensitivity and perception should be developed to allow one to make an objective appraisal of the capabilities of the representative who will carry one's business in that country.

SOCIAL AND POLITICAL IMPLICATIONS OF INTERNATIONAL MARKETING

We have indicated that marketing processes might have an effect on the national stability, so also might we view the impact of marketing on relations between nations. The satisfactions that people enjoy from consuming goods are real. Desires for such satisfactions will motivate them to enter into transactions wherein they will become familiar with peoples and ideas unique in their background. We quote again from Allyn:

> I have asked myself more than once on a trip abroad: "Why is it that business finds a way to survive and grow in the face of the same obstacles that seem to stifle understanding among nations?"
>
> In my opinion, the basic reason is that business is *forced* to acquire an understanding of the customs of a country and the traditions and preferences of its people and to conduct itself accordingly.
>
> You either establish a common meeting ground, or you do not do business. . . .[15]

Such activity leads them to an understanding of foreign people and their motives. There are common characteristics in all peoples that the market brings to the surface. When the natives of one nation wish to trade with another, it is necessary for men to recognize these common qualities and to do business on the basis of them.

The concept of the free market itself has qualities that recommend it to all people. It makes possible a way of life that permits freedom of choice. Other things being equal, all individuals would prefer to have this freedom. It is a basic quality of a healthy individual, although many people have never had the opportunity of learning to enjoy it due to poverty or politics. Furthermore, the free market tends to reward every man according to the significance of his

---

[15] Roland L. Kramer, *International Marketing* (3d ed.; Cincinnati: South-Western Publishing Company, 1970), p. 387.

contribution. The value or the significance of this contribution is not the decision of any one individual or group. The value is determined by the choices of people who select freely among the alternatives offered at the marketplace.

Such a process tends to maximize satisfactions of not only the consumer but also the producer who makes his choice of what to produce by considering his own likes, dislikes, and capacities and by taking his cue from the desires of consumers. These characteristics are common to all people, though dormant in some. They furnish a basic frame of reference where men become closer and more understanding by communicating in market activity that overcomes communication barriers.

Example from *The Ugly American*

An excellent example of the process of building a bridge between people of different nationalities was furnished by the engineer in the novel *The Ugly American* by Lederer and Burdick.[16] This example depicted the success of an engineer who had devised a method of pumping irrigation water up to farm terraces with a reconstructed jeep engine. The process would save the people many hours of burdensome toil in carrying water. The engineer skillfully appraised the barriers that he would have to overcome to gain acceptance of his device. His problem was to avoid appearing as a wise and potential benefactor to a proud people who would be repelled and insulted at his stooping to assist them. Sensing their disposition, he humbly sought their advice and help in the development program. By enlisting one of their trained associates and permitting him to acquire a genuine sense of participation, he completed the bridge of understanding. With the assistance of this man and other local associates, the pumps were produced and marketed throughout the country.

We mention this example since it includes many of the ingredients of a successful foreign market transaction. It illustrates a method whereby different nationalities can be brought together by a common goal. Communicating skills are developed that are common to them both and which grow into friendships. These relationships, if correctly consummated, are sound because of the basic truth which we have mentioned as characteristic of all market transactions—that both parties to a transaction gain. Such activities, if carried on in the proper attitude and consistent with the philosophy we have described above, can become a power for democracy throughout the world.

World Order and the Market

Men engaged in international trade have an opportunity and an obligation to increase an appreciation for and an understanding of the problems and aspirations of all people. Unfortunately, there has been exploitation of people and resources, and there will probably continue to be some short-sighted exploitation. Nevertheless, many business executives recognize that international trade is a link among segments of the world which increasingly

---

[16] William J. Lederer and Eugene L. Burdick, *The Ugly American* (New York: W. W. Norton & Company, 1958).

serves to make people in one nation sensitive to the needs and goals of people in other nations.

Peace Corps volunteers and other young people who work as part of a foreign community make friends and come to believe that the community in which they are working is a fine place. Businessmen who approach their assignment in other countries with a long-term outlook and a desire to provide gains in satisfaction to their workers and customers also develop an appreciation for the culture and people of those countries. The cliché "enlightened self-interest" has meaning of great importance in foreign operations; for long-range investments require order, and civil order can be accelerated through actions and policies which allow all parties to business transactions to benefit.

It should be realized, although it may seem to be in the realm of the unattainable ideal, that because of the freedom and abundance that can result from market transactions, they can be a major force in bringing civil order and a chance for peace. Physically, "one world" is now a fact; economically, it may soon become a fact—a fact which can contribute to peace in our world.

QUESTIONS AND ANALYTICAL PROBLEMS

1. What is the portion of the United States' gross national product which is accounted for by export trade?

2. Select any two nations who receive a higher portion of gross national product from international trade than does the United States. Explain the factors that make the differences in portion of income attributable to international trade.

3. What general types of products does the United States export? Import?

4. Which countries are the principal customers for United States' products? From which countries does the United States gain the bulk of its imports?

5. How many products from other countries are advertised in the most recent copy of one of the mass circulation magazines?

6. Look in a nearby retail store for foreign goods. How many different items are there? What type are they? In what types of retail stores are they most numerous?

7. How many "common markets" now exist? Examine the most recent volume of the United Nations Statistical Yearbook and determine United States' sales to and purchases from members of three common markets. What conclusions can you draw? Are the member nations purchasing less from the United States than they did before the organization of the common market? Explain.

8. (a) Make a comprehensive list of factors that presently encourage international trade. (b) Make a list of factors that presently inhibit international trade.

9. What actions can a government undertake to enhance the international trade of its country's firms? Select any country and find that country's policies and actions regarding foreign trade.

10. What multinational agreements or facilities presently exist to enhance international trade?

11. Draw a simple chart to illustrate the various levels of company involvement in foreign trade. Try to find a local example of a company at each level.

12. What should a company executive know, as an absolute minimum, about a country he is considering as a market?

13. Review the rules for success of multinational firms in this chapter. Write, in one sentence, the essence or underlying philosophy of all the rules.

14. What government assistance is available to a United States firm that wants to assess the potential for its product in another country?

Case 20 • THE VERICOLD COMPANY

In August of 1966, the Vericold Company decided to expand internationally. Although its reputation as a producer of refrigerators was not outstanding, Vericold usually captured about 12 percent of the American market. As a result of a trip to England, Mr. Gates, Vice-President of Marketing, became aware of a possible new market for their product. Most refrigerators on the English market were substantially smaller than American models, and many even lacked a freezing unit. In addition, Mr. Gates noticed that approximately 50 percent of the families did not own a refrigerator even though they purchased fresh milk and vegetables daily.

Plans were made to begin exporting Vericold's low-priced model which was to sell in England at $155 (comparable to a $185 American model). Since such action would provide a very low profit margin, Vericold planned on a large sales volume. Fortunately parts were interchangeable, and the variance in voltage did not require a major production change. Vericold was able to distribute the refrigerator through a large appliance chain of over 300 stores. The company planned on manufacturing in England if sales warranted such action and thus avoid high transportation and tax expense.

A large advertising campaign was begun which was directed towards the middle class (approximately 55 percent of the people). The slogan, "The Best Council, A Vericold," was used as a play on words directed towards people living in council homes (large housing estates built by the government and rented to the people). Approximately 45 percent of the population lived in such housing developments.

The sales figure for the first year proved to be extremely discouraging. If the additional expense incurred in exporting the product were considered, the company did not break even. Mr. Gates sadly prepared his proposal for action which was to be given at the next meeting of the Board of Directors.

• What information should Mr. Gates obtain before making a recommendation? What factors would be different in marketing the product in England as contrasted to marketing it in the United States? Would the play on words appeal to the English?

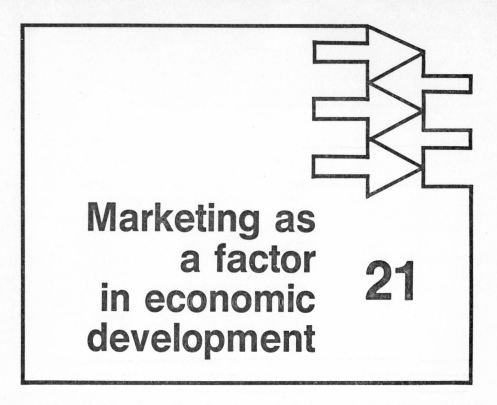

Marketing as a factor in economic development

21

There has been a prevailing view that marketing programs and skills are only necessary for those countries whose production programs have matured to the point where surplus products are created. In examining this premise in this chapter, consideration is given to the process of economic development and the role of marketing in this development. In discussing the problems incident to economic development, marketing functions are singled out and examined in a different setting than when viewed in the context of a nation that is economically mature. By seeing marketing in this different perspective, it is possible to perceive additional dimensions of the forces which marketing performance exerts in the growth and functioning of an industrial economy.

INGREDIENTS OF THE DEVELOPMENT PROCESS

At progressive periods in history, different ingredients have been emphasized as the strategic factor in the economic or industrial development of nations. From 1914 to 1929 national resources were considered to be the strategic factor. Those nations which were endowed with fertile land, adequate water, and a desirable climate were expected to develop rapidly. More study, however, revealed that something additional was needed. It is much more obvious today than it was in 1929 that there is not a perfect correlation between natural wealth and the kind of economic abundance that characterizes a modern, developed nation. Many nations that are richly endowed with natural resources have been unable to get an industrial development program under way. On the other hand, some nations seem to have possessed qualities that have made deserts blossom.

After it was determined that something in addition to natural resources was needed, capital was given strategic emphasis. Other factors essential to development have been listed, such as minimum standards of public order, law enforcement, and achievement motivation.

Recently more emphasis has been given to the entrepreneurial ability that was lacking in developing nations. Yet of late it has been pointed out that failure to take a long-term view of the requirements of the industrial process, as well as insufficient knowledge and experience, often deflects entrepreneurial skill away from the promotion of industry in a developing nation. The more recent indications are that failure to achieve satisfactory growth cannot be explained solely on the basis of the scarcity of the factors of production. Rather, development depends on calling forth and enlisting those resources that are hidden, scattered, or badly used.

The Binding Agent

The force which pulls these hidden, badly used, and scattered resources together into a production pattern has been described as a *binding agent*.[1] The success of this force depends upon the discovery of the productive factors, collecting them, and organizing them into an enterprise. The will or initiative to discover these resources and convert them into a productive unit develops from a *growth perspective*—an awareness of the possibilities of the unit as a part of a growing economic or industrial organism. An essential part of this perspective is the energy and drive to take positive action in the face of risks. Such energy and drive is the result of the overall vision of the industrial process and a knowledge of where the productive unit will fit into the evolving industrial complex. The will to organize and produce also comes from a faith in the future of the evolving industrial complex within the country. Such faith arises in part from observing the growth which other similar countries have achieved. It is possible that this will to action or initiative might arise within a government which will assign men to the various tasks; or, in an economy where individual freedom is emphasized, the initiative will grow out of the faith and understanding of individuals or groups of individuals. In either case, the perspective must be clear enough for one to see where the new industrial units will fit into and supplement the evolving industrial economy.

The Industry Linking Process

Once the above qualities are successfully organized into a unit in an economy, the unit triggers a multiplying effect on trade beyond the confines of the business itself. The unit creates markets for those from whom it buys (backward linkage)—for example, a cement factory creates a market for paper bags and other supplies and equipment. The unit also supplies goods heretofore not purchased to those to whom it sells (forward linkage)—a steel company would not only supply wire, pipe, nails, and construction equipment but also charcoal and fertilizer.

---

[1] Albert O. Hirschman, *The Strategy of Economic Development* (New Haven: Yale University Press, 1958), pp. 4-6.

The ability of a company to establish these linking relationships is vital to its success. The quality and the cost of those goods acquired from the backward linkage are prime factors in the company's total cost and the quality of its end products. Likewise, the relations established by sales in the forward linkage supply the money with which the company pays its costs and rewards its owners. The difference between the costs paid to the backward links and the income from the forward links is the strategic factor in determining the efficiency or the desirability of the firm. In a free market economy this difference is described as profits.

These relationships backward and forward are so significant that they cannot merely be assumed to exist nor can they be given only passing attention by management. They must be thoroughly studied before heavy and strategic investment commitments are made. Furthermore, linkage must be carefully managed so as to minimize costs and maximize returns.

Marketing and the Linking Process

No economy today can reach heights which satisfy present populations whose anticipations are high and growing on the basis of agriculture and barter alone. The production of a wide array of goods desired by such a population depends upon a significant number of productive units and also upon organizations responsible for the transfer of products between organizations and to consumers. This transfer of products from one firm or individual to another is a basic function. It is as vital to the economy's prosperity as the production process itself. Indeed, it is the linking process that binds the firms together into a complementary industrial and commercial program.[2] No firm can exist in isolation. The linkage process then is an expression of the binding process which brings the factors of production together into a national productive unit. The relationships backward that are developed and maintained consist of buying goods and services; the forward linkage is made up of selling relationships. These two functions are the core of marketing. In a specialized economy, such as an industrially developing economy must be, they have to be given even more attention than in an economy that is mature for two basic reasons: first, the resources which are hidden, scattered, or badly used are strategic to the country's development and should not be wasted in failure; second, there are fewer previous examples of channels already established by other successful firms which supply prototypes to follow.

One of the reasons why this need for giving attention to the linkage has not been sensed in the past has been the prevalence of scarcity in a developing economy. There has been a general presumption that, when goods are scarce,

---

[2] The concept of linkage corresponds closely with the term channels in traditional marketing. However, the term in the context of developing nations has additional meaning. In a traditional marketing system, channels already exist in most instances and the decision is between alternatives. In a developing country, either the linkage or channel has to be created, altered, or at least investigated more carefully. The development and availability of a channel or linkage can be more vital in a developing country for these reasons as well as for the importance of avoiding the waste of strategic or scarce resources. For this reason we will use the term linkage in this treatment. For a thorough and comprehensive treatment of this topic, see Hirschman, *op. cit.*, pp. 98-119.

people will seek them out; the goods will not need selling. This condition may exist in a primitive economy where products are well known and market patterns do not change over a period of time. In a developing industrial economy, however, goods are undergoing a process of rapid change; and if they are not publicized, many people will not know about the products. It is, therefore, essential that some organized means be provided for communicating the qualities of and availability of products and for motivating people to buy them. This is the function of marketing.

CASE HISTORIES

Marketing transactions are intangible. Their impact on a process cannot be noticed clearly unless the whole process is observed and the cumulative impact is recognized. In order to visualize the impact of marketing, it will therefore be helpful to illustrate by way of case histories. These histories will describe strategic segments of economic processes found in developing countries and will pinpoint specific areas where frustrations develop due to lack of marketing knowledge and skills. The first history will deal with the Egyptian economy; the second, with Russia.

The Case of Egypt

Before becoming overinvolved in international intrigue and conflict, Egypt provided an excellent example of a country with a positive commitment to economic development in the years 1956 to 1965. In 1956 President Nasser set a goal to double the country's income in ten years. Significant progress was made in increased per capita income, reclamation of resources, improved education, and the achievement of other progressive goals. Attempts were made to provide a maximum of private initiative by organizing individual businesses under the leadership of a board of directors and a chairman. The businesses were organized to compete with one another and with international firms. Some of their costs and prices were set, however, to meet national minimum wage and price goals. Profits were expected, and to a limited extent management efficiency was judged on the basis of profits. However, the government representatives made allowances when prices and costs set by the government rendered it impossible to make profits. The government owned the majority of the stock in these companies and used the profits for further industrial development.

The Egyptian Iron and Steel Company. Egypt, with its limited arable land, has been unable to produce enough food to satisfy the domestic demand. Although a significant amount of high-quality, long-staple cotton is exported, it is hardly enough to pay for other agricultural products that must be imported. It is, therefore, imperative that Egypt convert labor into goods if she succeeds in a growth program. Basic to this industrialization program was the construction of the steel mill. The mill consisted of two blast furnaces and steel processing equipment to complement the iron ore capacity. This development appeared especially desirable since there were large deposits of iron ore in the Aswan area of Egypt. (It is also notable that the iron and steel industry required and stimulated a greater proportion of linkage, both forward and backward, than any other type of industry.)

Soon after the Egyptian Iron and Steel Company mill was established, however, it experienced severe financial problems. The United States Agency for International Development consultants were called in to provide assistance. Here are excerpts from the consultants' report:

The Egyptian Iron and Steel Company needs very high grade operational and administrative consulting skills in specific areas as follows:

a. Marketing.
b. Quality control.
c. Manufacturing.
d. Mine and mill maintenance.
e. Finance and cost control.
f. Organization and procedural planning.

Although each of these areas is of importance, we would emphasize the overriding significance of marketing and quality control as administrative areas requiring the most urgent consideration.

Fundamental to the possibility of developing a successful steel company in Egypt is the issue of evaluating the market potential for tonnage by product grades and size range. In its present state, rolling mill sizes have resulted from limited market exploration resulting essentially from deductive evaluation of customs data covering a period of years which, we were advised, provided no segregation of steel imports or consumption classified in a manner suitable for use as a basis for determining what rolling facilities would be provided to meet the needs of a predetermined market.

That the Company is not prepared to merchandise its output may be best illustrated by observing that its finished and semifinished inventory on the ground has grown during the last 12 months from 13,700 tons to nearly 45,000 tons, of which about 40 percent is in ingots.

Based on October 1959 inventory and sales as reported to us, current inventory by products exists as follows:

Product Class	Tons of Inventory	Months of Inventory on Ground
Ingots	21,651	Infinite (No Sales)
Slabs	1,476	Infinite (No Sales)
Billets	8,652	2.5
Rails	1,443	11.4
Bars	1,500	3.5
Shapes	4,834	8.1
Plates	3,361	5.6
Sheets	1,671	4.5

Bearing in mind a reasonable standard of carrying no more than 30 days of product in inventory, these data show a serious inventory problem which illustrates the importance of integrating production with prevailing sales opportunities. The Managing Director of the Egyptian Iron and Steel Company is aware of this serious problem, but he is beset with difficulties in attempting to overcome it.

Immediate recognition must be accorded to importance of marketing activities as a major factor bearing on the eventual success of the steel company. This requires identifying and securing the technical skills needed to obtain measured answers on a continuing basis to questions such as the following:

a. Is the company offering for sale the sizes and specifications of products which are best adapted to the prevailing market?

b. Is the company seeking to sell the types and numbers of customers which it should qualify itself to serve properly and profitably?

c. Is the company using the most economic method of reaching the customers which the company should seek to sell, as determined by questions enumerated above?

d. Is the company offering to sell its product at prices which are as satisfactory to securing a sufficient volume of the type of business needed from the customers it seeks to sell?

e. What consideration should the company give to the developing of technical aids which the company could use to advantage in the development of customer relations?

f. What form of organization is most suitable for developing the administrative ability and capacity of the sales division?

g. How should sales activities be related to mill operations so as to enable both most effective scheduling of shipments to customers as well as most efficient operation of the mill from a production control standpoint?

From the standpoint of developing the Egyptian Iron and Steel Company as a going concern able to carry its weight in an economic sense, the development of a marketing organization under a Director capable of approaching these questions is an urgent necessity.[3]

Obviously the country neglected to study the forward linkage relationships for its products. It depended on import statistics to determine the pattern of production. This procedure was unsatisfactory for two basic reasons: first, considerable time had lapsed since the import pattern had been used; second, the Egyptian economy was undergoing a complete change as a result of the revolution.

In addition to the problem of business organization for the market which the consultants discussed, we note two purely marketing problems. One was the basic failure to merchandise. The company certainly did not coordinate its products with its market, for it was making a large number of products for which there was little or no demand. The second basic failure was corollary to the first; there was no organized sales effort.

It is conceivable that some, though not all, of the products placed in inventory might have been sold if information about such products along with the motivation to buy had been properly conveyed. In this instance a sales department in the field would also have provided a feedback to the mill regarding

---

[3] From *Consultant's Report Covering Limited Survey of Operations of the Egyptian Iron and Steel Company,* December, 1959, pp. 9-10.

the character of the existing demand. Such information was needed as a guide to corrective action.

Other Examples. During the winter of 1963 and 1964, there were serious shortages of consumer goods available on the consumer market in Cairo. The Ministerial Committee on Organizational Affairs held a meeting to investigate these shortages and issued the following report:

> . . . in most cases the shortages on the market of consumer goods resulted from lack of coordination between the organizations in various sectors. It has become clear . . . that most consumer goods are available in abundance, but the distribution is unsound.[4]

On another occasion a bicycle factory purchased expensive equipment to assemble bicycles automatically. Once this equipment was purchased and installed, the company learned that the dealers who purchased the bicycles did not want them assembled. Apparently they had the time to assemble them and wanted to continue to do so. In this instance it is possible that the merchandising mistake of providing a product that was not wanted might have been overcome by an effective selling program to convince the dealers that in the long run the bicycles might have been assembled with less cost by mechanical means. In either case the correct application of merchandising or selling would have been required.[5]

It is clear to those who have had experience in developing countries that these failures, due to the lack of understanding of marketing, are general and are not confined to the history of one country. It is to the credit of the people of Egypt that deficiencies such as those noted above were brought to light and published so that the weaknesses could become the basis for corrective action.

The Case of Russia

The history of the Russian economic experiment is well known. It will best serve our purpose if we examine one of the linkage systems which the Russians themselves have analyzed. Such examination will enable us to see where marketing knowledge or experience might have saved considerable time, frustration, and expense in the process of development.

The Distribution of Drugs. The production and sale of drugs provide an apt illustration of circumstances that are characteristic of marketing in a period of innovation. Drugs serve a vital purpose in protecting and restoring the health of people and, if their usefulness is understood, they will be desired and purchased readily. Yet there are new developments constantly. Changes have to be communicated, and a certain degree of education is needed for their proper introduction and adoption. Such a linkage system is similar to the system needed for the majority of products that are being sold in developing countries. In order

---

[4] *The Egyptian Gazette*, January 21, 1964.

[5] A. A. Sherbini, "Marketing in the Industrialization of Underdeveloped Countries," *Journal of Marketing,* Vol. XXXIX (January, 1965), p. 28.

to see the similarity of the problems that arise in a marketing context, we will discuss the linkage in terms of the elements of the marketing concept discussed in Chapter 2. These elements are (1) the product, (2) its availability, (3) advertising and selling, and (4) pricing the product. We will measure the results with a marketing process operating in an environment of freedom which permits a spontaneous response to change and circumstance.

The Drug Product.[6] In Russia new drugs are developed by government-sponsored institutes, but new products are not given a brand name. Such a designation is unnecessary since there is only one of each kind of product available, although it may be manufactured in several plants. A Pharmacological Committee in the Ministry of Health serves as an advisory committee on drug development. This committee prepares literature describing the drugs and their use and also recommends the adoption of new drugs as well as the dropping of others. Such a practice is in marked contrast to a free market system where these decisions are made by the producer and the doctor.

Still another committee, not in the health division but in a department of pharmaceuticals and medical technology, works directly with the drug manufacturers and sales divisions. This committee serves two functions. First, it insures the standardization of the drugs produced. This function is closely related to quality control. Second, it edits or makes necessary additions to governmental literature on pharmaceuticals.

The success of this system in meeting the needs of the people is described in the Russian publications as follows:

> Our industry does not always produce medicaments of good quality. And so it happened, for instance, that from the overall number of pharmaceuticals which were sent this year for evaluation to the Central Pharmacological Institute, more than half were rejected, mainly ampules. The rejects were found especially often in the products of the Khabarovsk and the Novosibirsk factories, in the Kharkov factory called *Zdorovie Trudiaschikhsia,* and in the Moscow factory named *Semaskho.* . . .The above examples show that the workers of the chemico-pharmacological industry do not always work conscientiously.
>
> Every year there is an increase in the production of various drugs in our country. Many of them are sent for evaluational testing to the Central Pharmacological Research Institute. In the last year, for example, 112 various drugs were sent to us—ampules, tablets, and others. And, it is deplorable that 75 percent of them did not meet the requirements of the official governmental pharmacopoeia and the technical standards. In the first three months of the current year, the Institute received some dozens more of the pharmaceuticals and this time again, for the 74 tested 58 did not meet the requirements.[7]

---

[6] In discerning the case of the Russian marketing system as it applies to drugs, it should be pointed out that the United States has its problems, too. The Kefauver investigation, among other problem areas, revealed some margins between costs and prices where corrective action was needed.

[7] Raymond A. Bauer and Mark G. Field, "Ironic Contrast: U. S. and U. S. S. R. Drug Industries," *Harvard Business Review* (September-October, 1962), pp. 89-97.

In summing up the problem, after four decades of attempting to make this system work the following conditions were admitted to exist:

1. The quality remains substandard.
2. Minimum standards become maximum.
3. The system of inspection was cumbersome, expensive, and to a large extent ineffective.

As a result of such observations, the companies who manufacture these drugs are required to place the name of the factory on the box. This practice enables the committee to take corrective action when poor quality is discovered by inspection. This change is one step in the direction of a brand name, but it leaves undone one very important function which a competitive market would achieve. The competitive market gives the medical doctor a choice between one or more products and, in making such a choice, the consumer becomes an active agent in assisting to achieve quality control.

Product Availability. Another concept of marketing which we have given emphasis is merchandising or coordinating the product with its demand. This area involves the concept of time in getting a product where it is wanted when it is needed. In Russia, during the first nine months of the year 1961, this subject of linking research and development with the market production and distribution to the consumer received special mention on five different occasions. The following quotations are typical:

> We have too few scientific research institutes concerned with the search for new pharmaceuticals. . . .It is a secret from no one that in our country the period from birth of a new preparation in the laboratory to its introduction into practice is on the average from three to four years. In some cases it is seven years. . . .
> . . . Already four years have elapsed since *bilann* was produced. This interval is sufficient to study the drug from all sides, to test it clinically and, having established its useful action, to legalize it and place it into the practice of medicine. But this has not yet been done. The Pharmacological Committee until now has not delivered the drug its "right of life" and this is why it is not being produced anywhere.[8]

It appears in this instance that one or two or both qualities normal in a healthy marketing operation are absent. Either the essential communication between the laboratories and the manufacturers is not provided for, or those who man the posts to make such communication effective fail to do so. Steps are being taken by the Russian government to reduce this time. It must be noted that, even in a free market economy, care must be taken to protect the public from a too hasty adoption of new drugs. But once cleared by the authorized agencies, certainly the marketing institutions should have the drug in the hands of consumers in less than four years.

Selling and Advertising. In order to avoid the excessive waste which characterizes their advertising and selling program, the Russian planners

---

[8] *Ibid.*, p. 94.

attempted a more economical means of marketing communication. Instead of sending salesmen or detail men out to sell the drugs, they compiled the information into a one-page flier. The material describing the drug was carefully edited and sent to the physicians who would normally prescribe it. Again the health authorities expressed anxious concern about how the system was working. Eight complaints appeared in the semiweekly house organ of the drug trade during the first seven months of 1961. Extracts from those complaints follow:

> Information about new drugs is given irregularly so that practicing physicians do not know about them and are deprived of the possibility of using them. The process of replacing old-fashioned drugs by new and more efficient ones is too slow. . . .
> . . . Too much time is wasted in pharmacies on compounding prescriptions and this is only because the physicians do not know about the pre-compounded drugs . . . obviously, only very few general practitioners follow the literature in which the new drugs are described. . . .On the other hand, pharmacy employees do not inform physicians about existing drugs. They do not come to the polyclinic and do not promote the new pharmaceuticals.[9]

The other official organ of the drug trade, *Pharmaceutical Affairs,* also published articles complaining of the "lack of well-established information about medical novelties."[10] As a result of this agitation, representatives are now being sent from pharmaceutical warehouses, pharmacies, and subdepots to the clinics to inform the clinics about new products. These representatives also get feedback from the clinics about their reaction to products and discover new needs which the clinics have. The Soviet government supports this program and criticizes those pharmacies that do not cooperate with it.

Again, we see a step taken in recognition of the fact that communication processes that are so essential to the distribution of goods do not take place automatically. It takes motivation and emphasis, which are characteristics of the marketing system, to make these communication processes effective.

Pricing. Much of the dynamics and flexibility of marketing phenomena in adjusting to technological and consumer-oriented change results from the allocating function of price. Previous to 1930 the price of drugs in Russia had no relationship to their cost. Since that time, however, the planners, in the interest of capturing motivation and assigning responsibilities, have given price greater emphasis. Realistic cost-related prices are assigned to each product. Each firm is given a quota of drugs to sell and is expected to make a profit. In these instances profit has become a criterion for the soundness of management. Still, under the Soviet system there are problems that arise which normally should be easily solved in an effective, traditional marketing system.

For example, under the Soviet system of assigning cost-related prices and using profit as a means of assessing management effectiveness, firms stock only the most profitable items. Consequently, the Soviet press regularly reports

---

[9] *Ibid.*, pp. 91-92.
[10] *Ibid.*

shortages of glucose, talcum powder, tincture of iodine, and bicarbonate of soda, which are all low-price and low-profit items. In a traditional marketing system, on the other hand, a drugstore which is constantly out of low-price but frequently used items would lose its patronage to a competitor who carries such products with regularity. The marketing firms in a traditional marketing system seek an overall profit based on high volume rather than a profit only on high-margin items. Indeed, they stock low-price items not only to complete their lines but also to use for promotional purposes.

Other Developments. In each of the above instances, after considerable trial and error, steps have been taken to adopt a procedure which would have been obvious to one schooled in marketing. Furthermore, it appears that the Russian government is recognizing that even more marketing of the spontaneous and free type would be desirable. As early as May, 1947, Radio Moscow began accepting advertising "to disseminate market information" and, according to the report, "Soviet citizens listened happily and demanded more." Professor Istvan Varga at the Karl Marx University in Budapest states: "Socialist advertising is not competitive in character but helps fill an economic plan by exerting an active influence on demand."[11] What Professor Varga is in effect describing is the demand creation function.

Since late in the 1950's advertising volume in Russia of both the printed and broadcast variety has enjoyed a steady increase. Despite such increase, however, there is evidence in the Russian press that many attractive products including both manufactured goods and foods are rotting or becoming obsolete while people are queueing for things that people of other nations find less attractive. This is primarily because the public has not been made aware of the more attractive items by selling and advertising. Artichokes and asparagus, for example, are spoiling in marketing stalls "while hundreds queue daily for the more familiar cabbages, carrots, and tomatoes."[12] As in the case of the Egyptian steel, in Russia they neglect to put the right product at the right place with proper advertising and selling in order to educate people on its availability and desirable qualities.

Reports from Russia, nevertheless, indicate that the dramatic interest aroused by competition aids motivation to the movement of goods. Hence, competition is beginning to find favor. The Russian system could have reduced its period of growth by many years if these lessons, which it has learned and is still learning, could have been adopted without half a century of trial and error experimentation. The principal contribution of Liberman, the Russian economist, lies in his defense of marketing as a means of harnessing the productive resources in an economy. He is making the Russian people aware of the positive influence created by the interaction of people who are left free to buy and sell as they choose.

---

[11] James W. Markham, "Is Advertising Important in the Soviet Economy?" *Journal of Marketing,* Vol. XXXVIII (April, 1964), pp. 31-37.

[12] Berend H. Feddersen, "Markets Behind the Iron Curtain," *Journal of Marketing,* Vol. 31, No. 3 (July, 1967), pp. 1-5.

HOW MARKETING CONTRIBUTES TO ECONOMIC GROWTH

The examples taken from the Egyptian and Russian scenes illustrate the frustrating effect on economic development that results from failure to apply marketing practices. Our next concern is to examine the discipline of marketing as a factor which contributes to more rapid economic growth.

The Marketing Discipline

The developments which frustrated both the Egyptian steel and the Russian drugs were to be found in the failure of the linkage process between the points where the product was produced and where it was consumed. In each instance management lacked an awareness of what the developments would be until they were learned by trial and error. This learning process was expensive in time and money and exerted a negative influence.

The entire process could have been in large part avoided if management had enjoyed a degree of maturity in the meaning of the marketing concept which has been defined as:

> An awareness which enables one to assess the relationships of the interdependent forces—direct and indirect—and their influence on each step in the administrative path of a product through the various phases of idea conception, production, and distribution, with the focus always on maximizing the consumer's satisfaction and his purchase of the product at a price which is profitable to him and to the company.[13]

It is evident that the men charged with the responsibilities of distribution clearly lacked this awareness. The basic characteristics of the marketing process as it might exist in any country have been studied both intensively and extensively during the last decades. The development of the concept idea has thus made it possible to understand marketing and see its needs in every economy and in every language. The flow of goods in an economy is the result of the interplay of many forces. It requires the mechanical communicating devices as well as patterns of information flows by which a knowledge of the goods and the satisfaction they will provide can be conveyed. A knowledge of the basic drives and motives of people must be understood in order that communication can be effective.

In the developing countries especially, the achievement of these goals requires even greater study. A successfully administered marketing program requires this communication and coordination to be of a high order. This process cannot be routinized, for each situation requires a different solution. The pattern of action may be similar to others, but there is something distinctly individual which characterizes each transaction. There are processes, functions, goals, and subgoals, however, that have much in common and can be understood and

---

[13] Ray A. Goldberg makes an excellent case for the application of business knowhow including the total market concept to agriculture and the food industry in foreign countries in "Agribusiness for Developing Countries," *Harvard Business Review* (September-October, 1966), pp. 81-93.

adapted to fit individual circumstances by a management that is either trained or thoroughly schooled in marketing. Peter Drucker made this point clear when he stated that ". . . marketing is critical in economic development because marketing has become so largely systematized, so largely both learnable and teachable. It is the discipline among all our business disciplines that has advanced the furthest."[14]

In brief, the marketing discipline has accumulated and described a collection of conceptual schemes that are strategic in the performance of the business process. In the context of our discussion of science, these conceptual schemes are useful. They make it less necessary to depend on trial and error to reach economic goals. They could have been most profitably applied to the Egyptian steel and Russian drug cases. Their application would have saved much time, money, and human frustration.

Marketing as the Prime Mover to Development

In our previous discussion we emphasized the binding agent that husbanded the hidden, scarce, or badly used resources into a unit that fits logically into a forward and backward linkage system. Such a unit depends on four factors:

1. The ability to make or secure the basic product through production, import, or purchase.
2. The ability to become aware of the need or desire for the product and to assess the magnitude of such a need.
3. The ability to develop a forward and backward linkage system which supports the firm's program.
4. The ability to move into a market situation with action.

As has been pointed out before, an effective unit can be established by a government in a planned economy or by the entrepreneur in a free market economy. But it is important to recognize that motivation or enterprise is in itself not enough to make a business successful—all the factors mentioned above are equally essential. The degree to which business success depends on marketing skills should also be noted. Certainly genuine marketing insight is needed for assessing the potential of the need and desire for the product, for stimulating this potential, and for appraising the means for reaching backward and forward to buy and sell products.

In commenting upon the importance of marketing in developing economies, Peter Drucker states:

> Marketing occupies a critical role in respect to the development of (underdeveloped) "growth" areas. Indeed, marketing is the most important "multiplier" of such development. . . .Its development, above all others, makes possible economic integration and the fullest utilization of whatever assets and productive capacity an economy already possesses. It mobilizes latent economic energy.[15]

---

[14] Peter F. Drucker, "Marketing and Economic Development," *Marketing Management Viewpoints: Commentary and Readings,* edited by S. George Walters, Morris L. Sweet, and Max D. Snider (2d ed; Cincinnati: South-Western Publishing Company, 1970), p. 54.

[15] *Ibid.,* pp. 47-48.

Corollary to the above statement are the views of political scientist Hans B. Thorelli who states:

> No vehicle is more powerful than contemporary marketing philosophy in changing attitudes in a manner conducive to improving standards of living in a democratic society. Existing distribution structures in the transitional nations constitute a roadblock to, not a channel for, economic development.[16]

According to these two respected authorities, marketing has been developed as a discipline to the point where it can be used effectively to bring unused resources, including managerial skill, into effective utilization.

Point of Inducement

We have already indicated that in an industrial economy a functioning system of interdependent firms must comprise a linkage which coordinates their efforts in the interest of production. We have also indicated that there must be an initiative or a will to risk in starting a business enterprise which in turn creates needs and markets for additional growth units. The questions might be posed: Is there a pattern for such development? Where should such a unit begin? Two cases can be cited as a basis for an answer.

In Colombia and Peru, Sears stores were responsible for literally hundreds of manufacturers getting started. Sears, partly because of exchange restrictions, could not import the volume of goods it needed to sell; as a result, it became a very powerful unit from which links extended back to stimulate the foundation of manufacturing businesses.[17]

Another example is cited by A. Coskin Samuli who describes the emergence of a group of wholesalers in Turkey. These wholesalers were so skillful and enterprising that they actually brought into being manufacturers through backward linkage and retailers through forward linkage. The wholesalers sensed a potential demand among the Turkish people. They were also aware of the resources to produce and distribute that could be developed by manufacturers and retailers. They, therefore, stimulated both groups into activity by convincing the manufacturers to go into business and make goods which they convinced the retailers to set up shop and sell. These manufacturers and retailers developed as successful and prosperous units.[18] There are many other examples where manufacturers with marketing skills were the prime agents in development undertakings.

It therefore appears obvious that the linkage comprising a marketing system can begin where the right marketing ingredients are present. In free market

---

[16] Hans B. Thorelli, "Political Science and Marketing," *Theory in Marketing*, edited by Reavis Cox et al (Homewood, Illinois: Richard D. Irwin, Inc., 1964), pp. 131-132.

[17] Sears executives report that "U. S. firms have a very good selfish reason to see countries such as Peru develop rapidly. If Sears Roebuck del Peru were not making a significant contribution to the economic betterment of Peru, it would not be acting in its own self-interest. Economic progress . . . means more customers for Sears." See William R. Fitsch, *Progress and Profits* (Action Committee for International Development, Inc.), 1962.

[18] Coskin Samuli, "Wholesaling in an Economy of Scarcity: Turkey," *Journal of Marketing*, XXVIII (July, 1964), pp. 55-58.

economies, business firms arise spontaneously to complement businesses already established. In a socialist economy where planning is dominant, the planners would be wise to recognize the latent skills of their people and encourage them in their major interests. Such a course would be more likely to capture a commitment for getting a complete linkage system under way.

QUESTIONS AND ANALYTICAL PROBLEMS

1. What is meant by "binding agent" as used in this chapter? By "linking process"?

2. Explain, with examples, the relationship between marketing activities and binding and industry linkages.

3. What marketing management lesson can be learned from the example of the Egyptian Iron and Steel Company narrated in this chapter? From the Russian pharmacy example?

4. What specific contributions to economic development can elements of the marketing discipline make?

5. Define again the phrase "marketing concept." Relate elements of the marketing concept to economic development.

6. Several of the developing nations are establishing schools of business. Assume that you are a citizen of a nation in which nearly all industrial goods and many consumer goods were in short supply with a consequent sellers' market. A proposal is made to establish a marketing curriculum in the newly established school of business in your country. Argue against the proposal. Argue for the proposal.

7. "Marketing is the prime mover to development." What restrictions or difficulties can you find to make you not accept this statement? On balance, do you accept the statement? Why?

Case 21-1 ● THE REALCOLD ICE COMPANY

Hamad Kamal was seeking a solution to a problem of conflict between business ethics and custom. Kamal was the general manager of the Realcold Ice Manufacturing Company that employed approximately 50 deliverymen-salesmen in the area of a large city in a developing country. Since there were few electric refrigerators in some of the sections of the city, there was a large market for ice. In June, July, and August the demand for ice was more than double what it was during the regular season. With the incomes of the lower and middle class increasing, Realcold Company found it did not have the capacity to meet this summer demand. In the face of this scarcity, the salesmen were instructed to favor their steady, oldest, and largest customers. Rather than follow instructions, however, the salesmen would deliver the ice to the highest bidder and pocket the difference between what they collected and the regular price. Spot checks on this operation indicated that the practice enabled a significant number of men to triple their monthly income. The pay scale of the salesmen was on the basis of a fixed minimum plus a commission. Compared with other workers in the same class, it was considered adequate.

Mr. Kamal had spent considerable time going to school and working in England and the United States. As a result of this experience, he was convinced that productivity and efficiency in business were closely related to the honesty and integrity of the workers. He also recognized that extra tipping or "baksheesh" as it is termed in the Middle and Far East is a long-established custom which is not considered dishonest by a large portion of the population.

● What steps should Hamad Kamal take, and how should he proceed to make them effective? Is there a relationship between productivity and efficiency and business integrity?

Case 21-2 • WORLD WIDE PUBLISHERS[19]

World Wide Publishers, a long-time leader in the greeting card industry in the United States, began its international operation in the 1930's when a salesman began selling its line of products in Canada. Realizing the potential greeting card market in Canada, the firm soon established a subsidiary to handle the Canadian operation.

Shortly following the success in Canada, another subsidiary was established in Leeds, England. The English operation was very successful and the World Wide name was considered to have an excellent reputation in the English greeting card industry.

In the late 1950's World Wide investigated the feasibility of entering the continental market and engaged a Swedish marketing consultant firm to do research on the question. As a result of its favorable finding, World Wide formed three separate subsidiaries in France, Germany, and Italy.

In the United States everyday cards and seasonal cards each account for 50 percent of the total greeting card volume. Note paper, party goods, and various sundry items were also handled by World Wide because of the similarity in the channels of distribution used both for these products and their well received card line.

The German subsidiary began with a limited line of studio (contemporary) cards and gift-wrap paper. Such a limited line of products, of course, involved a smaller capital investment by the parent company and a smaller staff to operate the firm.

The procedure used by the German subsidiary to produce cards was to copy successful cards marketed by the parent firm in the United States. The designs were a replica of the United States cards with a German translation of the American text printed on the card. Many times a text would lose something in the translation. For example a card that was humorous in English would not always be humorous in German. Also, because of cultural differences between the two nations, a text appealing to Americans would not necessarily appeal to prospective German customers. The net result was that greeting card sales in Germany were significantly less than originally anticipated.

There were also marked differences in product design and quality. Traditionally the German greeting card was either of the single fold or postcard variety (see Exhibit 1). A great deal of workmanship went into the design of these cards but seldom was any text or message required since it was customary in Germany for buyers to write their own message on the inside or back of the card.

World Wide introduced "sentiment"[20] to the German greeting-card market. A prepared verse on the inside of the card was something new and different in this market. World Wide also introduced the Frenchfold type of card (see Exhibit 1). In addition to product innovations, they established an entirely new approach to greeting card merchandising in Germany with the introduction of the American type floor-stand rack, which held 120 cards.

Prior to the innovation of this floor-stand rack, merchandising of greeting cards had been carried on in a haphazard manner. A counter 4½' to 6' in length usually held all the cards in the store. The lower-priced cards were piled in a bin in the center of the counter. All the cards were individually wrapped in cellophane, and the more expensive cards were laid out flat at the ends of the counter, often under glass, and had to be asked for specifically.

---

[19] This material has been prepared under the direction of Professor Charles H. Dufton, Northeastern University, for use in educational purposes. It is not designed to present either a correct or incorrect illustration of the handling of administrative problems. Copyright © 1966 by Northeastern University.

[20] Sentiment: A technical word used by the industry to connote written verse. Not to be taken literally, the word "sentiment" in the greeting card industry relates to the *message* conveyed by the card.

Exhibit 1

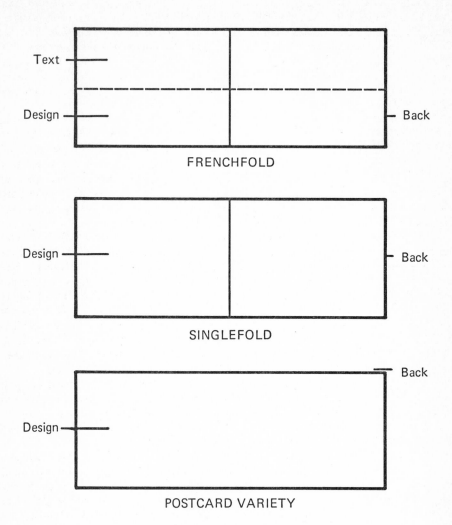

The management of World Wide considered the innovation and implementation of their merchandising program in Germany to be very successful. They had found it possible to employ in their German subsidiary many of the techniques proven successful in the United States, where they were considered outstanding in quality of product ("sentiment") and in merchandising innovations, particularly at the retail level.

The main retail outlets that sold greeting cards in Germany were the chain stores and the department stores. To these retail outlets the firm introduced its highly successful stock control program. This program was, in effect, an automatic stock rotation and reordering system that freed the retailer from concern about inventory control and selection of merchandise when reordering.

The only advertising carried on by World Wide was through trade journals. The company placed its main emphasis and reliance on personal selling. The sales force was made up of 12 native German employees trained and supervised by the sales manager. The territories were geographically divided according to the distribution of population. The sales manager was formerly a salesman with the parent company. He had a strong German background as his parents had lived in the country. He spoke fluent German.

The American military market in Germany was completely divorced from the German subsidiary. This market was handled by the parent company with products shipped from the United States directly to a sales representative based in Germany. Management felt the subsidiary unable to handle this market because its line was not extensive enough nor did it have the facilities to print in English.

The company thought its pricing policy to be competitive despite the fact that its prices were slightly higher than those of German manufacturers. Most of World Wide's line was priced at one mark (25¢) or less. It was discovered that the one mark, 40 pfennigs, and two mark cards (35¢ and 50¢) did not sell well in the German market. Management attributed its slightly higher price line to the fact that the cards offered by local German competitors were smaller and had little or no verse. The retailers' markup in both Germany and the United States was 100 percent. For example, a card selling for 50¢ cost the retailer 25¢.

When approaching retailers with their line, World Wide was faced with two obstacles. The first one was that German manufacturers always supplied with each card a tissue envelope with a colored lining. World Wide, however, supplied a regular white envelope without colored lining or tissue. The second obstacle that World Wide ran into was the long-established practice of the German firms to wrap their cards individually in cellophane. This was done because traditionally greeting cards had always been a low-turnover item at the retail level, and the cellophane protected the inventory while it was in stock. World Wide packaged its cards in individual, white envelopes in lots of 6, 12, or 24, depending on the card, and wrapped the lots in a brown envelope. The retailer then removed the cards from the brown envelope and displayed them on the rack.

To overcome the German traditions, World Wide told greeting card retailers that it was introducing sentiment into the market; and, therefore, the cards had to be read and could not be wrapped in cellophane. World Wide felt the envelope not to be as important as the card and stressed the idea that it was putting more quality into the card rather than the envelope, which was thrown away after opening.

By 1964 the line was expanded to incorporate a variety of everyday (birthday, anniversary, etc.) cards and seasonal (Christmas, Easter, etc.) cards. The line was not as extensive as the United States line but was considered adequate by management for the German market. Sentimental design and text was never a big seller, and long flowery verses did not sell in Germany. Verses had to be kept to a minimum of one or two lines to be at all successful.

The firm continued to employ native, German-speaking translators to translate the texts of cards selected for presentation to the German market. Since it was important, however, that the cards be adequately adapted to the German language and cultural sensitivities after translation (particularly in an industry where, in the words of one World Wide executive, "sentiment in our most important product"), a more selective means of choosing which American cards to use was a constant challenge and a constant opportunity.

By 1964, however, and despite the high levels of prosperity characterizing the market areas serviced by the German subsidiary, its sales had not achieved the desired volume nor even the desired rate of growth. The high administrative and initial startup costs incurred to launch the German subsidiary and required to continue the product and merchandising innovations that had been introduced by it were of increasing concern.

Company executives believed that the introduction of sentiment and of effective merchandising practices and controls at the retail level to the German greeting card industry had been steps in the right direction. They also believed, however, that factors other than product design and retail merchandising methods were operating in the German greeting card market to limit prospects of any immediate increase in the rate of sales growth.

Germans, for one thing, do not send each other as many cards as Americans do because they are by custom and tradition a very formal people. As a result card sending is more of an occasion, a fact which might relate to the preference and frequent insistence upon individually wrapped cards. Current analyses of the German market were suggesting, however, that there had been a gradual shift to the informal, partly due to contacts the German people have had with the many Americans living in their country.

In late 1964 the company was reexamining the many factors present in the German greeting card market and the opportunities for further progress and contribution in it. A number of possibilities were under consideration. Among these was the possibility of negotiating sale of part of the German subsidiary to a German publishing company. Under the proposed terms of sale, the company would recoup a significant proportion of its unamortized administrative and initial costs. World Wide executives felt the German firm had a good reputation, was familiar with the market and temperament of the German greeting card purchaser, and could easily carry on the operations of the firm. The German firm would continue to use the American cards, for which World Wide would receive a royalty, and there would be a sharing of profits and expenses at a ratio not yet worked out. While no decision had been reached, serious consideration was being given to the possibilities inherent in such a negotiated sale.

• Prepare a report for the World Wide executives outlining what you consider to be the important factors which are responsible for limiting the sales growth of the German subsidiary and making recommendations with respect to the proposed sale of the subsidiary.

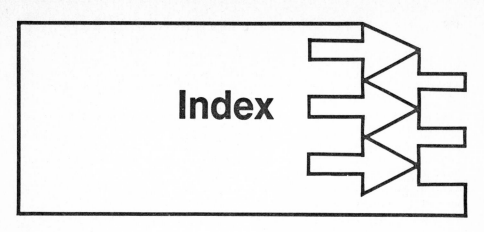

Index